# The Irish Brigade 1670–1745

# The Irish Brigade 1670–1745

## The Wild Geese in French Service

D. P. Graham

Pen & Sword

**MILITARY**

AN IMPRINT OF PEN & SWORD BOOKS LTD.
YORKSHIRE – PHILADELPHIA

First published in Great Britain in 2019 by
Pen & Sword Military
An imprint of
Pen & Sword Books Ltd
47 Church Street
Barnsley
South Yorkshire
S70 2AS

HB ISBN 978 1 52672 773 2
PB ISBN 978 1 52676 624 3

A CIP catalogue entry for this book is available from the British Library.

Typeset in India by Vman Infotech Private Limited

Printed and bound in the UK by TJ International Ltd, Padstow, Cornwall

Pen & Sword Books Ltd includes the Imprints of Pen & Sword Aviation,
Pen & Sword Family History, Pen & Sword Maritime, Pen & Sword Military,
Wharncliffe Local History, Pen & Sword Select, Pen & Sword Military Classics,
Leo Cooper, The Praetorian Press, Remember When, Seaforth Publishing and
Frontline Publishing.

For a complete list of Pen & Sword titles please contact
PEN & SWORD BOOKS LIMITED
47 Church Street, Barnsley, South Yorkshire, S70 2AS, England
E-mail: enquiries@pen-and-sword.co.uk
Website: www.pen-and-sword.co.uk

# Contents

# Siúil a Rún

I wish I was on yonder hill
'Tis there I'd sit and cry my fill
'til every tear would turn a mill
Is go dté tú mo mhúirnín slán*

Chorus (after each verse):
Siúil, siúil, siúil a rún
Siúil go sochair agus siúil go ciúin
Siúil go doras agus éalaigh liom
Is go dté tú mo mhúirnín slán

I'll sell my rock, I'll sell my reel
I'll sell my only spinning wheel
To buy my love a sword of steel
Is go dté tú mo mhúirnín slán

I'll dye my petticoats, I'll dye them red
And 'round the world I'll beg my bread
Until my parents shall wish me dead
Is go dté tú mo mhúirnín slán

I wish, I wish, I wish in vain
I wish I had my heart again
And vainly think I'd not complain
Is go dté tú mo mhúirnín slán

But now my love has gone to France
To try his fortune to advance
If he e'er comes back, 'tis but a chance
*Is go dté tú mo mhúirnín slán*

*\* Go, go, go, my love*
*Go quietly and go peacefully*
*Go to the door and fly with me*
*And may you go safely, my darling*

*(Siúil a Rún (pronounced 'Shule Aroon' meaning 'Go, my Love') is a traditional Irish song which is sung from the point of view of a woman lamenting her lover, who has gone to France to pursue a military career. It has been suggested that the song refers specifically to the Irish Wild Geese (at the very least through the reference to 'France' in the final verse) although it is possible that it was composed later with the intention of highlighting historical events. 'Johnny Has Gone for a Soldier' is a well-known American variant. It is arguable that the lament is a metaphor representing the mother country, the relative plight of Irish exiles, and the vain hope of return to an Ireland which, as the years pass, becomes increasingly unrecognisable.)*

# Acknowledgements

I would like to thank, in no particular order, Harman Murtagh, Padraig Lenihan, and John Childs, for stirring an interest in a fascinating period, which not not die...

# Foreword

My interest in the Irish Brigade started with Justin McCarthy, Lord Mountcashel; indeed he is the topic of the first book in this series detailing the, perhaps, forgotten conflicts and personalities of seventeenth-century Europe. Where did this interest stem from? To answer that, we have to travel back to 2000, and a series of research documents. The little known Battle of Newtownbutler, fought in Ireland during the war between Jacobite and Williamite, is considered by some a large skirmish, by others a stark turning point in the war. But, perhaps more so than any other period, it is the personalities present at that battle who garner interest, and who represent a generational slice of military history in the British Isles, whose echoes are still felt: Mountcashel, Anthony Hamilton, whose brother besieged Derry, William Wolseley, who would fight at the Boyne, the Enniskilleners (Inniskillingers) and their officers, who can be found throughout the following campaign. The story and characters are the stuff of legend. Indeed, it is in this vein that we see the story emerge, for it is not simply a retelling of history that we are engaged in; there is a European context and, moreover, the genesis of the fate of a nation that underpins the events.

Step back, and refocus, and we see MacCarthy, Patrick Sarsfield, the wily Tyrconnel, James II, Berwick, his illegitimate son, and a thread that at least partially seeds the history of Europe, just as the exiled Irish brigades thread their way through the doubts and ignorance of a foreign military establishment, and gain eventual admiration from their French masters.

It is more than simply a series of 'facts' and accepted beliefs that we deal with here, it is the story of Irishmen who are pawns in a grander scheme of the sometimes tragic, sometimes fatally flawed, story of Ireland, struggle against the odds to fight for a sometimes ungrateful king and land in foreign parts which remain foreign to most of them and, yet, their legacy remains, embellished upon the vast tapestry of European history like some vital stitch or keystone that it is impossible to ignore.

Such is the narrative of the Irish brigades; a story of exile, battle, dashed hopes and dreams of returning to their native land. Triumph and tragedy aplenty, and far from the stuffy old history of a time, and a century, which cannot be ignored. Ironically, their very presence makes the thought of repealing the penal laws that are enforced upon Ireland anathema to the British establishment, lest the long and vengeful fingers of Jacobitism, through James II's descendants, threaten to rock the very foundations of the British Empire.

The story of the Irish Brigades and the Wild Geese has been told before. In fact, such is the popularity of the desperate band of soldiers, exiled from Ireland, searching in vain for a king deserving of their bravery and thus, ultimately, a way home and a means of escape from the yoke that bedevils their idealistic view of their homeland, has become the stuff of legends. Many stories have been told, and tales spun of those brave soldiers of the Irish Brigade. One wonders if the timing had been different, if the right leaders had made decisions at the right time, if the French had only done this or that in support of them, would the history of the British Isles have been radically different.

The Wild Geese themselves, whose very souls were thought to return to Ireland, after having fled their homeland, were destined never to return. They were recorded as 'wild geese' in shipping records, lest their real identities be found out. Hence the adoption of the term over a period of years, as men yearned to return to an Ireland which had been romanticised and made legendary, and of course, which no longer existed.

Indeed, we could argue that this is the tragedy of Irish history, in that there existed a fabled land of legend, a land where Gael and Old-English would live in peace and defeat the New English, their lands intact and unsullied. But old Ireland had gone forever.

As stated, that self-same story has been told many times and yet I can't help but feel that much of the story remains *untold*. We hear of the bravery of Patrick Sarsfield, yet precious little of the high regard in which Justin MacCarthy, whom James made Lord Mountcashel at the 1689 Irish Parliament, Sarsfield's predecessor in French service before the second siege of Limerick, was held. We hear that the Wild Geese set sail for France, leaving Ireland in its time of greatest need, as if such an act, in defence of their religion were something new and untested, and yet few know the story of the Irishmen who fought for France in the 1670s under the great French generals of the time, such as Turenne. To tell the story of the Irish Brigade, therefore, it has always struck me that we must reset that band of time wherein the story is set, and give a deeper and wider context, rather than focus on the band of soldiers who left Ireland after the depredations of the

Jacobite war. It is too narrow an overview and gives little context to readers, denying the very stuff of the legend of Irish troops in French service.

I make no apologies, therefore, when I start this story in the earlier part of the seventeenth century, then develop our context and setting forward into the latter part, when Patrick Sarsfield, Justin MacCarthy, and the Hamilton brothers and other Irish notables fought for the French in English service, their religion precluding them from martial service elsewhere. We see their struggles and understand the nature of their experience, well before they return to Ireland and the events that lead to the first despatch of Irish brigades to France in 1689, before the familiar story of the Wild Geese which we normally understand after the second siege of Limerick in 1691. Thence to the continent, although, rather than focus on the familiar stories of the Irish proving themselves, we'll look at the campaigns and their design, sometimes to further define the nature of French *Glory* or *Gloire*, and proving little else in a strategic or tactical sense, and how the Brigade developed until it became a recognised facet of the French army.

The crux of the story occurs during the reign of Louis XIV. Historians have argued over the nature, source and direction of Louis's foreign policy; whether it was as a direct result of waning Spanish imperialism, the economic threat of a growing Dutch trade empire, natural barriers and the presumed threat of France's neighbours, or indeed or the very nature of *la Gloire* itself, which dictated the younger Louis's views and actions. Others argue that the very crude and brusque nature of monarchy and government of the time was such that actions were purely reactionary, and Louis was assuredly a king with little patience for the long game and therefore simply a man of his time.

What is certain is that English, French and Dutch contrasting efforts at political gain on the European stage, and the ensuing drama, would have its victims, Ireland, and the fledgling army that it had fostered, becoming one. Louis's motives were never quite clear, albeit that the propagation of delay, threat of a Catholic Army on William III's flank and thousands of enemy troops who could ultimately be utilised on the continent, were of course a card that he could play in the endless political game of European dominion. From their origins in French service under Charles II, through the development of an Irish Catholic Army which would see its rise and fall under James II, to a fighting force which would rarely be allowed to fight together, despite the banding of units for particular battles, the Irish troops, the bands of Wild Geese, left their mark on Europe in a time where the early modern period was not only forged, but through whose activities, we see much of the Europe that we can identify with today finally defined.

*Chapter 1*

# The Irish Diaspora

Historical precedents of troops serving foreign masters are present throughout history. Whether Greek mercenaries or Apache scouts, Swiss mercenaries or Hessians in America, the stories of those troops who were sold, hired, enslaved or simply sought gainful employment in times of war are numerous, their deeds heroic to nefarious, and their activities noble or desperate. Tales of those serving foreign masters regale history sometimes as a boon, sometimes as some relic of hidden guilt to the host country. In the case of the Irish, however, the story is not only a tragedy of sorts, but long in its spinning – a true Irish drinking tale perhaps, resplendent with heroes, villains, tragic final acts and last words.

Who better than Irish exiles, indeed tragic figures forever longing to return home with a winning army under a triumphant king, even a Jacobite king, in a righteous act of taking back their homeland in support of his stolen crown? It is the stuff of fantasy stories, the theme of which seems like some northern European legend; a tale that Joseph Campbell might see as part of the 'monomyth'. Yet, as we shall see, romantic visions of a united people are far from the truth, in this or any other diaspora wherein troops of many flags fought for foreign causes, and even against each other.

By the late 1600s, even the very definition of the Irish warrior class had been rewritten. Justin McCarthy was descended from the native Gaelic Irish, while Patrick Sarsfield was an 'old-English' settler, who ultimately married Honora de Burgh, herself part of an old Norman family. Yet they were allies against an English Protestant ascendancy who, in common with so many other European courts, saw Ireland as a route for first Spanish, then French invasion. In Cromwellian eyes, those self-same Irish lands were a means of payment for loyal troops during the first Civil War. The Irish, of whatever Gaelic, Norman or overtly English lineage they were, simply could not win. This perhaps was their tragedy, rather than an inability for the Wild Geese to return to a homeland which had never really existed or, at the very least, existed only as a stylised memory. In the expanding span of time wherein the Irish diaspora persisted, they romanticised that home still further.

To be Irish now is even less clearly delineated than was even possible in earlier centuries. Amongst Americans it is seen as a status symbol, thus leading to the creation of not insignificant political power amongst the voting population. In contrast, much of the Irish identity of the Scots-Irish, or Ulster-Scots, many of whom would colloquially become known as 'Hillbillies' in later years – a nod to King William III, and most of whom were Protestant, would be forgotten, or at the very least subsumed into their American identity.

In fact, almost every European nation identified the Irish as Scots, which bears witness to their complex lineage. The Romans named the peoples who lived on the island and raided the British coast as *Scotti*, from which Scotland later took its name after raiders settled there, naming the land *Dal Riada*. In the fifth and sixth centuries, the Irish would establish abbeys and universities across the European continent.

In the early part of the sixteenth century, Spain had been the first country to benefit from Irish soldiers' service, mainly for the Eighty Years' War, where the Dutch would fight for their freedom in the Spanish Netherlands, an area which would become the crucible for Europe's wars in the century that followed. Still more Irish would then fight in French service, and French and Spanish Irish would soon face each other across the battlefield dominated by early matchlock and pike. The Spanish would allow their fighting Irish to become integrated not just into the army, but into Spanish society too.

France had also welcomed Irish soldiers from the earlier part of the century, although it would be the Jacobite War in Ireland that would form the mainstay of the troops who would be most famously known as the Wild Geese, so called, perhaps, so that the cargo could be given a name that would not create concerns with port authorities about the movements of Irishmen who joined the armies of France and Spain. The term itself is used to refer more broadly to the large groups of Irish soldiers who left to fight on the continent in the sixteenth, seventeenth and eighteenth centuries.

Irish had also served in Danish and Swedish armies during the Thirty Years' War in the first half of the century. They had served the Holy Roman Empire and the Austrians, their descendants fighting even into the twentieth century. Others fought with distinction in Italy and even Prussia.

The first Irish troops to serve under a continental power formed a regiment in the Spanish Army of Flanders in the Eighty Years' War in the 1580s. The regiment had been raised by an English Catholic, William Stanley, from native Irish soldiers and mercenaries, whom the English authorities wanted to extricate from the country in the wake of rebellion and insurrection. He was commissioned by Elizabeth I to lead his regiment in support of the Dutch United Provinces. However, in 1585, motivated by religious factors and Spanish gold, Stanley defected to the Spanish side with the entire regiment.

Following the defeat of the Gaelic armies of the Nine Years' War (1594–1603, not to be confused with our later terminology when referring to the war across Europe of 1688-1697), Ireland was shaken by the 'Flight of the Earls' in 1607. Hugh O'Neill, Earl of Tyrone, Rory O'Donnell, Earl of Tyrconnel and their followers in Ulster, amongst other lords and Gaelic chiefs, fled Ireland, hoping for Spanish help in aid of their insurrection, but King Philip III of Spain refused the request, seeking no further war with England.

However, their arrival led to the formation of a new Irish regiment in Flanders led by Hugh O'Neill's son John and including notable officers such as Owen Roe O'Neill and Hugh Dubh O'Neill, perhaps predictably, more political than its former cousin in Spanish service and hostile to English rule in Ireland. Roman Catholics were banned from military and political office in Ireland in the early seventeenth century; meaning that, the Irish units in the Spanish service began attracting Catholic Old-English officers such as Thomas Preston. These men had more pro-English views than their Gaelic cousins and therefore there was considerable resistance to plans to use the Irish to invade Ireland in 1627. Many of the troops in Spanish service returned to Ireland to fight after the beginning of the Irish Rebellion of 1641. When the Confederates were defeated and Ireland occupied after the Cromwellian conquest, over 30,000 Irish troops would flee the country to seek service in Spain. Some later deserted or defected to French service, where the conditions were seen as significantly better.

In the eighteenth century, Spain's Irish regiments served in Europe and the Americas. The Irlanda Regiment was stationed in Havana from 1770 to 1771, the Ultonia Regiment in Mexico from 1768 to 1771. Even by the time of the Napoleonic Wars, three Irish infantry regiments still formed part of the Spanish army. Heavy losses and recruiting difficulties diluted the Irish element in these units, although the officers remained of Irish ancestry. The Hibernia Regiment had to be reconstituted with Galician recruits in 1811 and ended the war as an entirely Spanish corps. All three regiments were finally disbanded in 1818 on the grounds that insufficient recruits, whether Irish or other foreigners, were available.

From the mid-seventeenth century, France was in the ascendant, rapidly expanding its armed forces, whereas Spain was a power in decline. France then supplanted Spain as the main goal of Catholic Irishmen seeking a career in the military. Foreign troops would account for some 12 per cent of all French soldiers in peacetime and 20 per-cent of the army during wartime. In common with the other foreign troops, the Irish regiments were paid more than their French counterparts.

The turning point came with the Jacobite War in Ireland, when a response to Louis's financial and, somewhat limited, military aid was expected after the war began in 1689. Mountcashel would lead 6,000 men to France in 1690, while Sarsfield would follow a year later with 15,000, the party including 6,000 women and children in what has since become known as the Flight of the Wild Geese. The fully-armed and equipped Irish Army would never return, despite multiple attempts at a renewed 'Descent upon England'[1].

The Catholic Irish gentry were permitted to recruit soldiers for French service, albeit discreetly until 1745, the authorities seeing it as preferable to orchestrate large numbers of young men leaving the country rather than have them determine to find ways around the Penal Laws that were in force or have large numbers available that could foment rebellion at the slightest provocative whim on the part of Gaelic lords. After a composite Irish detachment appeared and supported the Jacobite rising in Scotland in the same year, recruitment was banned. After this point, the rank and file of the Irish Brigade was increasingly non-Irish, although the officers continued to find their way from Ireland.

By the time of the complex and defining, at least for Britain and Prussia, Seven Years' War (1756-63), recruitment was limited considerably. There were a few volunteers and the sons of former Irish officers, but again rank and file were made up from foreign volunteers. By this time, there were still seven regiments active in the Brigade: Bulkeley, Dillon, Clare, Rooth, Berwick and Lally's, and the cavalry regiment of Fitzjames. By that stage the regiments were French in all but name, as the Franco-Irish families that spawned their leadership had lived for so long in their adopted country that their perceptions of the Ireland to which they felt destined to return were far from reality.

With the French revolution, and suspicion surrounding many of the Irish 'foreigners', the brigade ceased to exist as a separate entity and became integrated into the French Army. They still wore their distinctive red coats, something which they insisted upon whenever the matter came into question, and at least be known informally by their former titles, but the blow meant that many Franco-Irish officers left the service, their oaths having been made to King Louis rather than the nation of France, a common theme, even in the early years of the Brigade.

In the years after the defeat of the Jacobite army in Ireland, ending with the siege of Limerick in 1691, Patrick Sarsfield would take the 'Wild Geese' to France. Before him Justin MacCarthy had done the same, although it is Sarsfield who is more vividly remembered, perhaps due to the ending of the war which heralded his leaving with 15,000 Irish troops who refused to change allegiance and follow William. Anti-Catholic penal laws, subsequent to the war, promoted conversion of Catholic to Protestantism amongst the eldest sons as the only legal manner in which they might inherit their fathers' estates. Ironically, such actions would entail that younger sons would venture to Europe to serve with the brigade in large part.

With the Peace of Ryswick in 1697 Louis XIV, at least for a time, disavowed the lineage of James II, technically disbanding his Irish army, although times were not so straightforward and ,with the start of the War of the Spanish Succession and the emergence of Marlborough as a new style of military commander, defeating the myth of French invincibility, the brigade fought on with the French army, becoming one of its more elite forces. The troops would not be formally disbanded until the French Revolution a hundred years later, although by that stage, and in the wake of the futile attempts by the Stuarts to win back their throne, their identity and purpose had been removed, their fate sealed.

*Chapter 2*

# The Plantation of Ulster

It seems somewhat marked, and perhaps even illogical, that we might begin our story of the Irish Brigades with Ulster, stranger still, perhaps, that we begin said story with James I's Ulster plantation. Key to this action, however, are the stories of George Hamilton and Donough MacCarthy, Lord Muskerry, in whose hands lay the future of the Jacobite cause in Ireland, the flight of the Wild Geese, and support for James's heirs in their vain attempts to regain their father's and grandfather's lost thrones. Both were married to sisters of the Duke of Ormonde, whose axis in the power play that follows also plays an important part in our story, albeit on the fringes of the debate.

The story of the Hamiltons, in common with most famous Irish and Scots-Irish families of the day, is linked closely to the important events that occurred in the British Isles throughout the seventeenth century. The history of the family's connection with Ireland runs through the collective reigns of the more notable English kings. The family saw the rise of James I and the plantation of Ulster, the subsequent Civil War of Charles I, the English Commonwealth and the ensuing restoration of the monarchy of Charles II, ending only with the rise of Irish Jacobitism under the short reign of James II, and its inevitable decline under William III. Even then, the remaining Hamiltons were instrumental in furthering the ambition of James II's son, the 'Old Pretender', whose son in turn later led the final resurgence of Jacobitism as 'Bonny Prince Charlie', and saw the wholesale destruction of his cause in the British Isles, at Culloden. The lives of the Hamiltons, therefore, stand testament to an important segment of history within the context of the region and, to some extent, that of Western Europe.

The story begins with the plantation of Ulster. The 'Irish adventure' of James I and the movement of Scottish and English settlers to Ireland is a tale in itself. The Hamiltons were to play a decisive role both in its inception and its relative success. Of course, matters are rarely so simple, as is evident in so much of Irish history. Although the plantation is well covered in primary sources, an examination of its beginnings in Scotland, and the resultant links with Ireland, is entirely relevant in this instance.

Plantation in Ulster and Ireland as a whole was not a new idea. The reasons for the scheme were similar across a number of reigns. Ireland was seen as lawless, as a backdoor to Spanish, and later French, invasion, and after the Reformation, a 'godless' land. Scots had migrated, or re-migrated if we stretch the timeline back far enough, to Ireland as far back as the thirteenth century. Until the sixteenth century, in fact, Lowlanders and men from the Scottish Isles served as mercenary soldiers or *gallowglasses* (a term originating from the Gaelic *Galloglaigh*), hired by the Irish chiefs and warlords in their endless feuding. Land was granted as payment in many cases. Over the next few hundred years, and in a similar manner to the assimilation of the Norman Old-English into Irish society, the Scottish mercenaries became integrated.

Migrations continued but, as the sixteenth century progressed, the island Scots tended to stay in the north and their visits 'home' were distinctly shorter. Prominent amongst the 'New Scots' were the MacDonnells, Lords of the Isles, who began to dominate the north-east coast line of Ulster, and whose name became synonymous with alternating bouts of feuding and alliance with the Irish O'Neills. This occurred amidst English attempts to solve the confusing Irish problem with force, tempered, in turn, with periods of misconstrued alliances.

Intermarriage with the Anglo-Norman heritage of Ireland, most notably Margery Bisset, heir to two-thirds of the Glens of Antrim, meant that by the mid-sixteenth century, the MacDonnells were in Ulster to stay. As the Tudor monarchs in England stretched their authority towards the potentially dangerous situation emerging in Ulster, conflict was inevitable. The Scottish 'settlers' did not recognise the English monarch. By the 1550s Queen Elizabeth I had seen enough and the Earl of Sussex was ordered to stop Scottish expansion, and thus establishment, in the north. English response to the Scots was divided between bouts of violence on one hand, in some cases using the Irish lords as allies, through to an acceptance of the Scots' position in Ulster on the other, an early indication of the extent to which the Irish situation could become confused and thus difficult to impose a solution upon. The native Irish made the situation worse. Shane O'Neill, for instance, rebelled against English rule in the early 1560s and then, after submitting to Elizabeth, attacked the Scots, and promptly changed sides again to raid in the south. The Scots, not known for their forgiveness, killed him in 1567.

Elizabeth was forced to recognise the MacDonnell presence in Ulster by the 1560s. Until the end of her reign the situation in Ireland as a whole developed into a complex political quagmire of alliance and rebuttal where it seemed that no party would, or indeed could, win. Power plays between English and Scottish crowns, the MacDonnells, the O'Neills, the McQuillins and the O'Donnells, threatened to destabilise the situation at every turn. By the end of the decade, the threat of intermarriage between the 'clans', thus consolidating the Irish position at the expense of the English one, was enough to convince England that colonisation could be a viable option.

The colonies would fail, perhaps inevitably, but the concept would not be forgotten. The end of the century heralded further discord in the shape of another O'Neill rebellion, this time with MacDonnell backing. James MacDonnell controlled the Glens of Antrim and the entire Route, essentially the eastern half of Ulster, by 1596. Although a small part of Ireland as a whole, the fact that MacDonnell controlled such large areas and had backed recent rebellions, created significant difficulties for the crown. Not only did the presence of the Scots reduce English ability to assert dominance in the area, but it was also recognised that MacDonnell was a Catholic. In the eyes of the English monarch, Ireland represented a backdoor to invasion, a route through which the Catholic Spanish or even the rising power of the French, could invade England. This single strategic factor would underlie much of the policy that dictated events in Ireland for the next hundred years.[1]

The seventeenth century began in Ireland with the 'Nine Years' War'. Between 1594 and 1603, Hugh O'Neill, Earl of Tyrone, led the Gaelic lords of Ulster in successful forays against English troops. At the Battle of Yellow Ford in 1598 the English army suffered over 2,000 casualties.[2] Hit-and-run skirmishes typified the conduct of the war. Elizabeth's senior military men could do little. However, the crown would have long memories regarding the dangerous potential of Irish insurrection.

In 1601, during the war's last throes, a Spanish intervention at Kinsale on behalf of the Irish proved ill founded. Tyrone's failure to link up with his newly-arrived allies proved the death knell for the campaign and the Irish army was routed. The war and its resultant famine destroyed much of the country and killed a significant proportion of the populace, yet Tyrone's desperate position was still strong enough to earn him generous terms from the English. In the end he lost 'only' 300 acres of land. The terms, however, were related to the imminent death of Elizabeth; her successor, James I, would have offered Tyrone more generous terms, it being thought in England at least that he had clandestinely aided the Irish during the war. By March 1603 the Elizabethan era had ended. Even after the queen's death, political spin was at work as Lord Mountjoy attempted to negotiate the capitulation of the rebellious Tyrone without letting him know that the queen had recently expired, a fact that might have allowed O'Neill to hold out for better terms. The Anglo-Irish political game had to be played in a most delicate manner after all.[3]

The Nine Years' War was over, but its effects had been far-reaching, at least for the English government. The whole affair had, at best, sown discontent and, at worst, terrified the authorities in England, a fact that had allowed Tyrone to retain much of his power and influence whilst handicapping English authority in Ireland. Despite warnings from the Dublin administration, little was done to stop the slow erosion of English forces in Ireland to the extent that they soon numbered less than 1,000 men. Tyrone, perhaps predictably, had not been dissuaded from his original aims. By 1605 he was considering further revolt and still retained close ties with the Spanish. He also chose to ally himself with those 'old-English' whom he thought he could trust. Traditionally the enemies of the native Irish, impending administration changes in Ireland meant that the old-English/ Anglo-Norman faction were juggling their affiliation to Rome with their loyalty to the crown. That same affiliation would last well into the Jacobite period, with notables such as Tyrconnel and Sarsfield tracing ancestry to old-English settlers.

It was hoped that the accession of James I would mark an era of religious toleration. However, James would have little room for Counter-Reformation sympathies. Chichester, the Lord Deputy, saw the implicit security concerns connected with a continued English presence in Ireland and the implications for ultimate mastery of the isle. He had witnessed enough to convince him that Ireland should be 'Protestantised', even moving to the extent of reinstating some of Elizabeth's anti-Catholic measures.

A new era was to come with a new king, at least in terms of expansion into Ireland. The colonisation that James I would promote was not new in concept; both Mary and Elizabeth had attempted similar schemes. James's design, however, unlike its predecessors, would become firmly rooted in Irish society; conditions had changed dramatically. James VI of Scotland was now also James I of England. Two kingdoms, previously at odds, were now united. In addition, James could readily see both the disadvantages with continued confusion over Ireland's sovereignty and the clear advances that could be made with a successful colonial, and thus Protestant, expansion. The expected plantation of somewhat under-populated lands, given the degree of royal support, was tempting to many English settlers, and especially so for many of the Scots. Even prior to the plantation, James Hamilton, Viscount Clandeboye – not to be confused with James Hamilton, Earl of Abercorn, with whom the story of the Hamilton family begins – was familiar with the situation. So useful was this early settler, and his influence so great, that James made him the resident Irish agent at the English court. He would later own much of the land in County Down in Ulster. For many of those enterprising Scots who followed, the experience would prove just as fruitful.

James had changed the entire spectrum of relations in the British Isles, both Anglo-Scottish and, now, Anglo-Irish. The plantation would change the scope of what in Elizabeth's time had effectively been a national security concern - the invasion route for foreign armies, no less. In addition, religion had its role to play. The Reformation, firmly rooted in English society and, at least partly, in Scotland, showed little sign of progress in Ireland. The Ulster plantation then was primarily concerned with extending English influence and promoting security in the more rebellious areas of the land. James had no wish to suffer the rebellions that had beset Elizabeth's reign. He saw his plantation as a method of sowing the seeds of security and, ultimately, English prosperity. The design of the English monarchy had remained relatively fixed regarding Ireland; the furthering of that design had now been brought into sharper focus.

Despite setting events in motion that would ultimately create a clash of cultures in Ulster, the plantation proved to be one of the most significant migrations in seventeenth-century Western Europe. The immediate aim of the settlement was to secure English interests, both in terms of influence and security. There were obvious similarities with the American adventure, but only in terms of subsequent commercial interests, Virginia being less of an obvious door to invasion, whose security could remain a problem solely for the colonists.

The Anglo-Normans and the Gallowglass mercenaries had become assimilated or 'Hibernicised'. Since Henry VIII the Protestant reformation had been seen in Ireland as the ultimate symbol of English power and, to some extent English will, an attempt to affirm sovereignty in Ireland, and not a new religious movement. Matters were still far from peaceful on Irish soil; the Earls of Tyrone and Tyrconnel, amongst others, could still rebel. Early in James's reign, however, the Irish position would be rapidly undermined.

Between 1605 and 1607 the scene was set for rebellion once more. Would a pact between old-English and native Irish see an end to English power in Ireland? In 1607 an unprecedented event took place that not only made land available for plantation, but also dealt with immediate English concerns over stability. The 'Flight of the Earls', brought about partly through political machination, would have important ramifications for Ireland and the success, or otherwise, of the plantation.

As the Nine Years' War with Elizabeth had ended, the English monarchy had  played the Gaelic lords off against each other through the promise of land 're-grants' under English law. James's post-war re-grant to O'Neill and O'Donnell had angered many of those crown servants – servitors – in Ireland at that time, most of whom had fought against the previous rebellion, after all. To see land re-granted to their former enemies did little to pacify the more influential English gentry. Amongst them was Sir Arthur Chichester, in charge of the Carrickfergus garrison, and the most successful servitor in Ulster. He had defeated the Clandeboye O'Neills and would later become Lord Deputy of Ireland. Sir John Davies, another key servitor, would later become Attorney General. They were convinced that a plantation should occur and that it must succeed, and both were keen to see the status of the Gaelic lords reduced, perceiving them as an obvious threat to the crown.

Davies was insistent that the native Irish should be subjects of the crown, rather than of their Gaelic lords. The land re-grants, which increased the Irish leaders' power and influence, were therefore a problem, in terms of his aims at least. Through his political intrigues and dealings with the Irish, he had gained something of a reputation amongst them. For the most part the Gaelic leaders feared his influence and, by 1607, many were convinced that he was conniving against them. The earls of Tyrone and Tyrconnel had been persuaded that Davies was gathering evidence of a potential rebellion. And so, in 1607, a large band of Irish chiefs and their retinue, around one hundred people, fled to Europe. Included were the Earls of Tyrconnel and Tyrone and Cuconnaught Maguire of Fermanagh. Their departure marked the disintegration of Gaelic Ulster and opened the way for the plantation. The earls would not return.

The flight was quickly followed in the spring of 1608 with O'Doherty's rebellion. Although the situation was quickly defused, English fears had apparently been confirmed. The Irish situation, in the eyes of the English parliament at least, had once more been allowed to fester and get out of control. A combination of the chance to obtain Irish lands from the now departed earls, and a re-affirmation of English fears of rebellion, was enough to herald unprecedented Anglo-Irish strategic planning, which would have far-reaching consequences for the Hamiltons.

Influenced strongly by Chichester, James initially planned a limited plantation of Ulster and the lands of the Irish earls.[4] These he would fill with loyal servitors and English and Scottish settlers. Recent events in Ireland, mixed with new rumours of Tyrone's imminent return, kept the situation there fluid enough to make planning for the scheme a priority. Motivated by events, this unique attempt to solve the Irish, and Ulster, problem, and thus undermine future insurrection, was radical enough to have serious implications for the future.

The confiscated, or 'escheated', lands left included those of Tyrconnel and Tyrone, and around half of County Fermanagh. Shortly afterwards, additional areas were both surrendered and further confiscated, making land available in Fermanagh, together with substantial tracts of Armagh, Donegal, Cavan and Coleraine, all in the northern 'quarter' of Ireland. Only land belonging to the church was exempt. Some was re-granted to remaining Gaelic chiefs, some was given to Protestant bishops; the majority, however, would be available for James's plantation.[5]

And so to the Hamiltons and their part in James's plan. For many noted Scottish families, the plantation would create an opportunity for migration and commercial success. The Scots were, of course, assured of at least some of James's favour in the impending scheme; with the end of the Tudor line and the advent of the Scottish Stuarts this was only to be expected. This would not be accomplished without hard work, however. Despite James's clear motives about the plantation, based on both commercial and strategic concerns, he would leave plenty of room for his kinsmen and countrymen within the auspices of the scheme. The Scots would also retain a sense of duty to God and king, and those who had loyally served James in the past would find clear benefits should they be persuaded to follow through on his plans for Ulster. In the end James would have plenty of volunteers. Both English and Scots would be given the responsibility of transforming what many saw as an economic and strategic burden into an ultimately strong and viable asset for the crown.[6]

However, the plantation would be a very Protestant concern, at least initially. Religion had been the weak link between Ireland and England during Elizabeth's reign. English clergy rarely preached the gospel in Irish whilst Rome filled Ireland with well-trained Catholic clergy. The natural disinclination of the native Irish to adopt the new religion was therefore exacerbated by the political failings of the English in Ireland. Roman Catholicism was ostensibly the religion of the mainstream of the native Irish population. Its roots were not deep though, at least when compared with Spain or France. The turmoil of the previous century had meant that religious knowledge was not as entrenched as it could have been. Elizabeth and the state church, however, had not taken full advantage of this.[7]

Both Scots and English were involved in the original application for the new lands. Unlike the English applicants, many of the Scots were of the 'middle classes' or were petty gentry, less aristocratic than their English counterparts but perhaps more enthusiastic and keen to see financial gain. Most of those who did apply did not see the true costs and nature of the myriad problems that they would face in Ulster. Indeed, Scots had made applications for over 75,000 acres of land in Ireland and, in the end, had applied for more land than was actually available. Nonetheless, the king, eager to make a success of his new venture, took a personal interest in those persons who would be responsible ultimately for the success or failure of the entire affair; he intervened on behalf of many of the Scottish 'undertakers' who would take land in Ulster. There were to be nine chief Scottish undertakers, each of whom in turn would be responsible for the division and allocation of land amongst the settlers.[8]

Amongst these men was one James Hamilton, Earl of Abercorn, from Renfrew in Scotland. The eldest son of Sir Claud Hamilton, and a grandson of the second Earl of Arran, James had been made earl in 1603 at the age of twenty-eight and had served on the commission that had proposed the union between England and Scotland.[9] The earl was therefore a natural ally and supporter of the king. He had served James loyally even before his accession to the English throne, and had been a justice of the peace and a member of the Scottish council. He would be rewarded for his efforts. In fact, the earl had been convinced by the king himself to embark upon the dangerous expedition. In so doing, he would provide strength and support for the other undertakers and those who retained some influence with the new English monarchy. Abercorn also had the distinct advantage of being one of the wealthier Scottish nobles, a factor that would weigh heavily in his favour when the plantation had to be supported financially.[10]

The planters began their work in earnest in 1610 when they crossed the Irish Sea to stake their claims in the escheated lands of Ulster. Through his influence in James I's court, Abercorn was initially able to increase the scope of his original share of land. His influence, however, could be curbed. Despite his preference for particular nominees to be granted land in Strabane in County Tyrone, some planters were foisted upon him. In the main, however, Abercorn was successful in obtaining land grants for his immediate relatives, a step that would have important ramifications for the future of the Hamiltons.[11]

County Tyrone had represented one of the largest O'Neill areas of control in Ulster, forming as it did one of the family's most ancient seats of power. With thousands of arable acres of land, it was also an area that would prove difficult for the plantation commissioners to ignore. The Earl of Tyrone's flight and subsequent attainder was enough to make much of the land forfeit to the crown, including those portions that still ostensibly belonged to Irish septs, clansmen, and tenants of the earl. The Flight of the Earls had changed the rules. Although English undertakers moved into the county initially, the area around Strabane was being kept for some of James's favoured Scots. Strabane had been previously occupied by the descendants of Arthur O'Neill whose Clann-Arte O'Neill had held sway at the start of the fifteenth century. The current family head, Neal Connelagh O'Neill had become powerful in the area, having helped English officials unite two rival clans and keep the peace. The region also contained two strong castles in the shape of Newtown and Strabane. The usefulness of such native 'peacekeepers', however, was ended after O'Doherty's rebellion. The plantation commissioners were resolved to make grants of land to O'Neill (3,000 acres in Dungannon) under the conditions of James's plan, but most of the old Clann-Arte lands in the area, now forfeit, were divided and distributed amongst the Scots. Around 13,500 acres would be devoted to the Scottish planters.[12]

By the early part of 1610, sixty-one Scots had been granted areas of the escheated territories.[13] Despite the presence of some of the king's favourites in Ulster, Abercorn had secured land for four of his relatives. His brothers, Sir Claud of Schawfield and Sir George of Greenlaw, obtained 3,500 acres between them.[14] Another George Hamilton, possibly a cousin, received 1,000 acres in Strabane while Abercorn's brother-in-law, Sir Thomas Boyd, received 1,500 acres.[15] In a manner similar to the earl's preferential treatment, many of his relatives had been rewarded for their previous service to King James I.[16] However, the questions now were more closely related to successful settling and planting of the Strabane area. The disparity between the success or otherwise of both English and Scottish planters is striking. Success was on no account guaranteed and, in many cases, land was either sold on to the more entrepreneurial planters, or abandoned completely. Even Abercorn would remark on the initial difficulties of the task at hand.[17]

The earl was well aware of his responsibilities as an undertaker within the escheated lands of the Irish. His land in Dunalong and Strabane, 3,000 acres in all, formed a small part of the total plantation that included other areas of

Counties Tyrone, Armagh, Donegal, Cavan and Fermanagh. Although there were sixty-one Scottish undertakers in the province, not all of them would lead successful settlements. The undertaker was responsible for fortifying the area, building housing and ultimately promoting the success of farming, general prosperity and expansion. Abercorn's lands were situated due east of the river Foyle. The area was rugged and hilly, yet there were large expanses of arable land, most of which lay near the river. With a degree of commitment and money, settlement could be relatively successful.

Abercorn had a distinct advantage over many of the other undertakers and planters; he retained a considerable amount of influence with James I. For instance, he was permitted to draw twenty-five men from the Irish army to aid him in the construction of his settlement, a service unavailable to other planters.[18] Other favours would follow; he alone amongst the Scots would be given rights to use any shipping on the Scottish west coast to further his Irish development programme. In return, Abercorn arbitrated in disputes on behalf of the crown and remained for the most part a loyal and influential servant.[19]

Of course, he would use the king's favour to his own advantage. When dispute arose with the Audleys, his English planter neighbours, perhaps over the king's Scottish leanings, Abercorn was able to report on their anti-Scottish sentiments. Although this caused James to take offence, the matter was eventually settled. The earl would not remain idle about Irish politics or the business of Irish land either.[20] By 1614 he was administering the estate of his deceased brother and had already purchased Sir Thomas Boyd's lands in Strabane. Where an undertaker had capital it was advisable to buy what amounted to cheap land in the early stages of the scheme. Abercorn would also make political manoeuvres, although not altogether successfully. He had attempted in 1613 to have his daughter Lucy married to the son of Randall McDonnell.[21] The matchmaking was ultimately unsuccessful. Abercorn's influence in Irish affairs may well have been significantly enhanced had the plan succeeded. His timing, use of royal influence and a certain degree of luck, had meant that his lands and those of his relatives would become amongst the most successful areas of all those settled. The earl and his younger brother, George Hamilton, would see significant success on the eastern banks of the river Foyle. Carew's survey of 1611 had much to report:

> The earl of Abercorn, chief undertaker, has taken possession, resident, with lady and family; and has built for the present near the town of Strabane some large timber houses, with a court 116

feet in length and 87 in breadth, the groundshells of oaken timber, and the rest of aller [alder] and birch, which is well thatched with hearth and finished; has built a great brew house outside his court forty-six feet long and twenty-five feet wide. His followers and tenants have since May last built twenty-eight houses of fair copies; and before May, his tenants, who are all Scottishmen, built thirty-two houses of like goodness. He is preparing materials for building a fair castle and bawne which he means to put in hand for the next spring. There are 120 cows in stock for his own use.[22]

With large timber houses, defensive walls, together with around sixty well-housed tenants and their families within the Strabane area, the earl had prospered. Whether the planters had been supplemented by existing Scots, or perhaps by Scots serving in the army, there was no question that Abercorn clearly had seen success in the initial stages of the scheme. By the time of Bodley's report in 1613, and the absorption of Boyd's lands, there were almost one hundred tenants on Abercorn's estates.[23] In nearby mountainous regions of Tyrone, there had been little settlement. In some cases, a single family still existed. Wealth, luck, influence and location had all contributed to the earl's success and made a considerable difference to his fortunes. Those far from communication routes, or those who were ill prepared or restricted by lack of wealth or resource, had suffered badly during the entire affair. George Hamilton would also have benefited from the influence of his older brother, with regard to both the king and the development of lands in Ireland. His lands had also prospered, although not to the same extent as those of Abercorn.

Sir George Hamilton, Knight, has a proportion of land, and resident, with his wife and family. He has built a good home of timber for the present, sixty-two feet long and thirty feet wide. He has brought over some families of Scots, who have built themselves a bawne and good timber houses, eighty cows and sixteen garrons among them.[24]

George would benefit still further, however. Bodley's survey in 1613 had established that many of the original undertakers had expanded and those who had not seen success had for the most part moved on, to be bought out by the more successful planters. Of the Scots, the Earl of Abercorn and his brother George were the most successful. By 1614 Abercorn's lands had doubled when compared with his initial allocation.[25]

Irish feelings about the planters were usually hostile. The influx of settlers, although by no means large, was enough to put pressure on the Irish in terms of changes in local customs, instances of uprooting due to expansion and the creation of potentially dangerous religious differences. In many instances, the Irish deeply resented the interference of James and the intrusion of the settlers. Despite the Flight of the Earls and earlier Elizabethan attempts to remove the Irish 'swordsmen' from the political scene, enough troubled native Irish remained to threaten the plantation. For many in the north, a deep resentment of the Scots would grow and even overtake the existing hatred of the English.

This was a crucial consideration for two reasons. Firstly, despite the initial successes, the plantation remained a relatively small affair, even by the 1620s. Pynar's survey of 1619 noted that, in some areas of George Hamilton's estates, the Irish outnumbered the settlers by four to one.[26] In the end, the plantation was relatively successful in its own right, but not in supplanting the native Irish to the extent that James had hoped. By the end of his reign the flow of settlers would decline significantly, providing a foothold only. Even in Strabane the expansion programme had stagnated to a large extent by 1622. Secondly, the influence of Scottish Presbyterianism was becoming prevalent in Ulster, a focus for many of the settlers, and seen by the Catholic Irish as another symbol of intrusion. It was obvious to all that the plantation was designed to capture large tracts of Ireland for Protestantism. In Ireland, questions of religion and religious conflict were never far away.

These points are brought into sharper focus as we return to George Hamilton, younger brother of the earl. In 1617 the Earl of Abercorn's young son was made baron of Strabane, mainly due to the earl's success in 'planting a colony of brave men, professing the true religion, in Strabane barony, and many well fortified castles for the defence of Ulster'.[27] However, Abercorn died in November 1618, leaving his son James as his sole heir. He was about sixteen at the time. He had three other sons, the youngest of whom, another George, was around eleven or twelve years old.[28] As the young James was still a minor, Abercorn's brother, George Hamilton, became his guardian. George then became responsible for Abercorn's lands, in addition to his own estates and those of Sir Claud Hamilton. He was now the most successful man in Tyrone and one of the most influential in western Ulster.

Of course the king would have recognised his influence and authority and hoped to develop his role in Ulster still further, were it not for the fact that George Hamilton was a devout Roman Catholic. Abercorn's influence with the king and a distinct lack of evidence to the contrary marks Abercorn as a Protestant. The brothers' father, however, Lord Claud Hamilton of Paisley, had been a Catholic, as were Abercorn's brothers, George and Claud. Abercorn's sister, Marion, who had married Thomas Boyd, thus explaining his inclusion in the initial settlement, had also been criticised by the Privy Council of Scotland for her passionate Catholic viewpoint and would ultimately be excommunicated in 1628.[29] Events had made George Hamilton one of the most powerful men in Ulster, controlling five important proportions in Strabane and thus an influential Catholic player on the stage of James's previously very Protestant plantation.

Although circumstance had caused the situation, Abercorn's death had set in motion a chain of events that would lead to Sir George's elevated position; it was not altogether unexpected. If his father had also been a Catholic, that one of his sons should follow his father's religious beliefs is not entirely surprising. What is surprising, however, is that Abercorn and his siblings were given such clear support by the monarchy, an indication perhaps both of Abercorn's influence and James's belief that he was the right man for the job, whatever the risks. James and the English court knew about George's religious beliefs. As early as 1614 instructions were issued about the action that should be taken; Sir George should either be persuaded to convert or be removed from Ireland. The order, however, was never carried out and Sir George Hamilton had remained in Ulster.

Stranger still were the events that followed. Now the guardian of both Abercorn's and Sir Claud Hamilton of Schawfield's offspring, Sir George set about converting them to Catholicism. The young Hamiltons would be instrumental in changing everything, ensuring that what James had considered an area of great success within the plantation would be governed by Scottish Catholics.[30] By 1622 Sir George was actively surrounding himself with his supporters. By 1630 Catholic immigrants from Scotland, and even Jesuit priests, were being attracted to Strabane, to the extent that the Bishop of Derry warned of 'imminent rebellion'.[31] In contrast to other areas of Ulster, where pious Protestant ministers were taking the lead in creating the roots of Ulster-Scots Calvinism, the Hamiltons of Tyrone would be accused of harbouring 'Papists' who had been expelled from Scotland and attracting priests and Jesuits to Strabane. The area was noted by some as becoming the 'sink' into which the worst aspects of 'Scottish corruption' ran![32]

Due to economic conditions in Scotland, the number of natives seeking their fortune in Ulster again increased. By virtue of circumstance, therefore, George Hamilton had been able to introduce a Roman Catholic enclave into the very heart of plantation Ulster, an effort that would have far-reaching consequences. Hamilton's settlement, however, would sit alongside the other main power blocks now emerging in Ulster and Ireland as a whole. On the one hand were the 'old-English' settlers, descended from their medieval brethren who had settled in Ireland in the twelfth century. On the other were the native Irish. These two were now faced by the Ulster Scots, who were mainly Presbyterian. Although no one side could have predicted the future circumstances of the relations between the groups, the seeds of alternating political alliances and divisions were being sown. With the death of James I in 1625, and the accession of his son as Charles I, events would occur that would hurtle Ireland and the rest of the British Isles toward bloody warfare on an unprecedented scale.

It is to the fourth son of the successful Earl of Abercorn, another George Hamilton, where our attention now turns. George had been eleven or twelve when his father had died in 1618. Records are scant regarding his life in the early 1620s. By 1627, however, as with many of his contemporaries, he had decided upon a life in the military and obtained the command of Sir Roger Hope's company of foot.[33] 1629 would see a further twist in the young Hamilton's fortunes when he married Mary Butler, third daughter of Thomas Viscount Thurles. Her brother, Lord Thurles, would later become the powerful Duke of Ormonde, an influential Protestant who would be pivotal in matters pertaining to Irish affairs in the years to follow. Another of his sisters had married Lord Muskerry, representative of the powerful MacCarthy family in Munster. Ormonde would feature heavily in the lives of both families in the years to come, as we see the emergence of the Ormonde 'axis' in terms of Ormonde's policies toward those who had married his sisters.

This George Hamilton is referred to as 'Sir' George in many sources, and there is even discussion related to his being created a baronet of Nova Scotia in 1634. Prior to the bloody events of the 1640s, however, there is evidence to suggest that his continued adherence to his Catholic faith not only cost him his commission but that he was imprisoned on various occasions. The same sources describe him as being both loyal and gallant.[34] He would find favour with his new brother-in-law, Ormonde, who, despite the objections of a number of influential parties, was keen to see Hamilton's career develop, for the sake of his sister, if nothing else.[35] It would prove to be an influential act of support.

The Hamiltons had followed the route of the medieval old-English in terms of their Catholic identity. They had not followed the Scots Calvinism of their lowland brethren and, in fact, had now more in common with the native Irish. To a large extent, they were becoming embedded in the land, displaying the same flair for accommodation that had allowed their Gallowglass ancestors to settle relatively peacefully in Ireland. The test of loyalty for the parties now present there, however, was still to come.

A contemporary map of Ulster, showing inset of Enniskillen Castle. (*British Library*)

*Chapter 3*

# Rebellion 1641–1651

A n exhaustive analysis of the significant and far-reaching events in Ireland during the 1640s would demand many volumes. However, it is pertinent in this instance to outline the key events and thus set a context for the unfolding drama. The English Civil War, and its links to events in Scotland and Ireland, provided the crucible for the destabilisation of a monarchy and the death of a king.

The early years of the seventeenth century had seen upheaval and displacement amongst the Irish in Ulster, through the combination of plantation and the new political and socio-economic environment. After the Flight of the Earls and the transplanting of settlers to the lands of the erstwhile Gaelic lords, most Irish tenants were, in turn, transplanted to more mountainous or less fertile areas. In the end the move to 'plant' had been a political one, an attempt to exorcise the threat of rebellion and invasion and to seize the initiative after the departure of so many of the Irish ruling classes. The new planters and settlers had become established.

The plantation had, however, still fallen short of one of James's ultimate aims. The Reformation and Protestantism had shown little hope of taking root in Ireland, at least not in the way that he had hoped for. Indeed, Scots Presbyterianism was having the opposite effect to a large extent, creating stronger divisions rather than promoting a fundamental change of religious bias.

The 1630s saw a series of national incidents which created tension and growing discontent. Native Irish indebtedness to the settlers, centralised government, failed harvests and an increasingly poor economy had their inevitable negative effect on the bulk of the native populace.[1] The decade not only witnessed growing frustration in Ireland, but across the three Stuart kingdoms, a series of events that would unleash an unprecedented war across the British Isles. The events, although perhaps peripheral to the carnage that occurred on the continent in the shape of the Thirty Years' War, are nevertheless connected to the 'general crisis' occurring in Europe at the time.[2]

James's limited intervention in the wider European conflict had had little success and Charles I remained isolated from the affair for the most part. That gave him time and resource to concentrate on England. His attention to uniformity of religion offended both Puritan and orthodoxy alike; indeed in the 1630s it was even suggested that Charles's deviation from orthodox Protestantism, his close ties to William Laud, the radical archbishop of Canterbury, and the influence exerted by his mother, Henrietta Maria, and her Catholic associates at court, implied 'popish' ties – an anathema to both Puritans and Parliamentarians alike. Charles and Laud's own self-confidence would prove unpopular, as would the established monarchy. England, however, would not be Charles's sole concern.

In Scotland Charles had followed the lead of his father, becoming involved with the thorny issue of land titles. However, it would be religion that would confound even his most loyal supporters. James, in his attempt to create a royal stranglehold on the Presbyterian Church or 'Kirk', had left a legacy that Charles not only upheld but expanded upon. Visiting Scotland in 1633 Charles had much wider ranging and, as far as the Scots were concerned, divisive plans in mind. His subsequent attempts to introduce the English *Book of Common Prayer* in Scotland in 1637 were met with riots and instability. It was the beginning of a movement that would see a very British revolution. Scottish clergy, nobility and gentry alike backed the movement against what they saw as religious tyranny. It focused attention, creating a Scottish cause worth fighting for. Charles had unwittingly opened a door to violent reform that would be difficult to close. By 1638 a National Covenant had been drawn up against the prayer book, in many respects, despite its restrained language, a direct challenge to Charles's rule in Scotland. Alexander Leslie, an experienced Scottish officer serving in the Swedish army, returned home and many soldiers serving on the continent followed; James had, after all, deported thousands of Irish and Scottish mercenaries and swordsmen to the continent where they learnt, to his son's infinite regret, how to make war. The Scots began to recruit.

By 1638, despite the lack of an English standing army, Charles was determined to fight, preferring not to give in to the Scots' 'damnable demands'. With the English militias being of poor quality and, in some cases, unreliable, Charles called upon his Irish allies. Randal MacDonnell, Earl of Antrim, was ordered to supply 5,000 men from Ireland. When Antrim suggested that experienced Irish officers should be 'brought home' from mainland Europe, men such as Owen Rowe O'Neill and Maurice MacDonnell, he incurred the wrath of the Lord Deputy of Ireland, one Thomas Wentworth, Earl of Strafford.

Wentworth had been lord deputy since 1633. His aims were centred on the interests of the crown and, to that end, he had highlighted religious conformity, control through plantation and an improved economy and a more 'civilised' society in Ireland. Needless to say, he proved somewhat unpopular with the Irish. His interference with their land titles also meant, in stark contrast to previous years, that he actually fostered an uneasy alliance of Catholic and Protestant against his schemes. The further alliance of Scots Covenanters and Parliamentarians was enough to see Wentworth's downfall. His meddling in Antrim's affairs, combined with abortive attempts at gathering the force together, was enough to undo Charles's request for Irish reinforcements in 1639. In Scotland, however, the request had further destabilised relations with the monarchy, forcing more and more supporters to join with the Covenanters.

War was inevitable. The first and second Bishops' Wars heralded the start of the conflict in Scotland and England. Irish reinforcements, still hoped for, remained elusive, despite further promises from Strafford, and plans were fraught with delay. By spring 1640, with money running out, and despite appeals in the short Parliament, the Covenanters once more seized the initiative in Scotland. By August English forces had been defeated on their home soil at Newcastle. Charles was forced to enter into negotiations.

The Long Parliament that would herald the start of the English Civil War began in November 1640. Few dreamt that it would sit until 1653. Foremost in the members' minds was the 'buying off' of the Scots, reform of the English church and the removal of Charles's more radical advisors, such as Strafford. Parliamentary efforts to forbid its own dissolution without members' consent unashamedly eroded the royal prerogative. Strafford, accused of coercion with the Spanish and blamed for Charles's reluctance to disband the army, was executed in May 1641, an act which distanced the king from his parliament still further. Meanwhile, the army argued that its back pay had been used to pay off the Scots, religious concerns had not been addressed and economic depression created rioting in the streets of London. Consensus and peace seemed further away than ever. The monarchy was weakened and disliked. Charles, it seemed, had little support and, worse, had now backed himself into a corner. There was still hope, provided that matters remained peaceful in the three kingdoms. Matters in Ireland, as always, were difficult to predict.

1641 would prove a pivotal year for Ireland, too. The Irish had been quick to condemn Strafford despite Charles's hopes that he could escape the accusations with his life. The Irish Parliament had provided a considerable body of condemning evidence at his trial with regard to his governance. Only when all hope was lost for Strafford in May did Charles disband those troops in Ireland who had been mustered for his defence. By August, however, he once more attempted to re-establish the force for use against Parliament, should it be so needed. Yet events in England and Scotland were peaceful, and it appeared that the troops would not be required.

The original order had granted credence of sorts to the muster of Irish troops that had been taking place, however. Since the start of 1641 various Irish plans had been developed with a view to overthrowing the plantation in Ulster through the seizure of key towns. Taking advantage of national confusion, and of what appeared to be a weak monarchy, and bolstered by the calamitous events of the 1630s, Phelim O'Neill, Lord Maguire, Colonel Hugh MacMahon and others can only have regarded Charles's orders to raise troops as the perfect veil of legitimacy to draw over their actual intent.

The rebellion and its timing plunged the British Isles into war once more. In what to all intents and purposes was a surprise attack in October 1641, in one fell stroke, an attempt was made to destroy James's plantation, eliminate Irish feelings of alienation and alleviate the economic depredations and cycle of Irish debt that had accrued through the 1630s. If English authority could not be overcome through fiscal means, then the Irish would strike at the heart of its kingdoms, when it was at its weakest and the country was beset with internal strife and the threat of bloody civil war. For an example of a weak monarchy and the potential success of insurrection, the Irish had only to look to Scotland and the covenanting armies and at what they had achieved. It was the Irish rebellion that would see the turning point for the whole affair and mark the point of no return for Charles's monarchy. Had matters been different in England, an Irish insurrection would surely have been crushed, but events across the kingdoms were in a state of constant flux, a fact which O'Neill counted on for success.

The rising erupted in Ulster on 22 October (o.s.) and, although attempts to take Dublin Castle were unsuccessful, O'Neill's men captured Newry, Armagh, Charlemont, Mountjoy Castle and Tandragee, but some strongholds such as Enniskillen, Coleraine, Londonderry and Carrickfergus remained uncaptured. By November the rising had spread to Leinster and Drogheda was besieged. Events quickly got out of control as the native Irish saw an opportunity to right perceived wrongs and reclaim lost estates. By December much of the country was involved. O'Neill claimed royal commission for the rebellion, fuelling rumour of Charles's and even his mother's complicity in the affair and Parliamentary fears of yet another Catholic conspiracy.

Historians are frustrated by the lack of clear evidence with regard to the number of Protestants murdered during the insurrection. It was certainly much less than the propaganda of the time would indicate, of over 150,000. There were, after all, only around 60,000 settlers in Ireland at the time. There is enough evidence to suggest, however, that at least 4–5,000 were killed as the rebellion took hold. Other Protestants were evicted from their holdings as the former owners or, in some cases, insurgents took charge. Atrocities occurred, indeed it is difficult to think of any Irish conflict at this time taking place without some element of massacre amongst civilians, especially in an era when thousands of them were dying in the Thirty Years' War in Europe. Inevitable reprisals meant that thousands more died, on both sides. More would suffer from famine and disease in the ensuing Irish war. In the opening months thousands of refugees descended on the remaining Protestant strongholds. The massacre fostered a legacy of paranoia and fear amongst the remaining settlers in the years to follow and, as with so many contemporary Irish stories, repeated tellings of the events would increase the resultant impact on the population as the years passed.

From the outset George Hamilton made himself useful to the Royalists. Most of his work involved carrying out clandestine missions for Ormonde. Both Hamilton and Muskerry formed close relationships with their influential brother-in-law. Hamilton was also directly affected by the rebellion, despite his religious affiliations. At Doonally, where he employed English families to work in his silver mines, sixteen people were murdered in cold blood.[3]

Phelim O'Neill and his Ulstermen burnt Strabane Castle, still the home of Claud Hamilton's widow, to the ground. The insurgents allegedly took the lady with them. Depositions at the end of the war, however, would point to Lady Hamilton's involvement in a scheme to hand Strabane over to O'Neill.[4] Despite some initial success, the Irish forces had not achieved their goals by 1642 and both the standing army, over 2,000 infantry and almost 1,000 horse, and Protestant settlers alike rallied to fend off further attacks. In Ulster leading Protestants were able to raise around 10,000 men by 1643. In Dublin Ormonde began to rally Leinster forces loyal to the king and was able to make his own attacks.

Although division in Britain had helped cause the Irish revolt, both English and Scottish governments had common purpose in seeking to hinder and defeat rebellion in Ireland. Despite the initial surprise and gains of the Irish forces, Ormonde had distinct strategic advantages by the start of 1642. Men from the standing army held important ports in Munster and Leinster

– Cork, Dublin and Drogheda. Settlers in Ulster garrisoned Enniskillen, Belfast and Londonderry. In the short term, these towns could be held and, by March, 3,000 English reinforcements had arrived and Tichbourne was able to win back some strongholds in Louth. The offensive slowed, however, as supplies dwindled and Irish raiding parties became more daring around Dublin.

The Scottish made their move in Ireland in April 1642 as a Scots force that would ultimately number 11,000 began to arrive, under the command of Major General Sir Robert Monro, another experienced officer and veteran of the Thirty Years' War. In a direct effort to uphold Scottish holdings in the north, they were able to clear much of east Ulster of insurgents by the summer. The safety of Ulster settlers was their primary concern, however, as their tactics involved strategic sweeps of the countryside in force, sometimes skirmishing with O'Neill's troops but with few actual engagements. They would massacre any *creaghts*, Irish herders, seize their cattle and grain, and thus effectively deny the Irish any form of sanctuary or supplies through a primitive scorched earth policy. While the tactic did not defeat his enemy, it at least fulfilled Monro's aim of protecting the settlers.

However, both Ormonde's and Monro's victories relied on O'Neill's inability to effectively sustain his men on extended forays. The Irish *creaghts* could not supply the necessary resources for field armies and O'Neill was forced to adopt hit-and-run ambush tactics to compensate, a ploy that had ultimately failed before, and would be unlikely to succeed against a well supplied force now. By the summer over 35,000 Protestant troops were available in Ireland; more would have followed had it not been for the outbreak of the English Civil War in August. Three Protestant commanders were the principal leaders of these men: Ormonde in Dublin, Monro in Ulster and Morrough O'Brien, the Lord Inchiquin, in Munster.

The onset of the expected conflict between Parliamentarian and Royalist had its effect on Ireland, limiting offensive forays to destroying crops and livestock, since supplies for a protracted campaign were simply not available and it was difficult to draw the Irish into battle. The Irish, however, saw a further change in their own fortunes. By the summer of 1642 Owen Roe O'Neill and Thomas Preston returned to their native land. Both seasoned professional soldiers, they had learned their bloody trade on the fields of Flanders. With them came 1,000 Irish veterans, and an opportunity for The O'Neill to re-ignite the conflict. In addition to military aid, 1642 saw the formation of the confederation of Kilkenny, a supreme Catholic governing council that co-ordinated operations throughout Ireland. Together, the new confederacy and O'Neill's experience would breathe new life into the fledgling Irish army.

Ormonde's relatives remained close to him, as did his brothers-in-law, George Hamilton and Donough MacCarthy, Viscount Muskerry. Hamilton remained a reliable and loyal ally, carrying out several important military and political tasks for the duke.[5] He clearly had involvement in matters at a purely military level. His order for several thousand muskets and powder in March 1643 indicated his involvement in logistic and strategic concerns at the outset of the conflict.[6]

The changes in Irish fortune had given new impetus to Phelim O'Neill's war effort. With Owen Roe O'Neill in command of the Ulster forces and Preston in charge of the Leinster army, rapid attempts were made to instil discipline and increase the standard of military training in the erstwhile raiding force; it seemed that Phelim's leadership had lacked consistency and the military experience that was so essential. The attempts at training worked, since by mid-1643 Preston was driving Ormonde's troops back upon Dublin, and in Ulster the Irish saw victory at Armagh. In England, the civil war was reaching deadlock, a state of affairs that required foreign aid on one side or the other.

By the height of the summer, the Irish Confederates held most of Ireland, except for Dublin and its vicinity, County Louth, parts of County Cork and scattered pockets of resistance in Ulster including County Antrim and towns such as Londonderry and Enniskillen. The impasse in England, however, meant that both sides there would approach Protestant forces in Ireland for aid. There were four strong armies there: the Irish in Ulster, Munster and Leinster, the Scottish force in Ulster, British Parliamentary forces in Ulster and Munster, and troops loyal to King Charles, under Ormonde, mainly around Dublin. One can imagine how confused the situation must have been, even prior to the requests that were to follow.

In spring 1643 Parliament approached the Scots and Charles approached Ormonde. Indeed, matters in England had come to a head, and Irish intervention seemed the only way forward. Charles, perhaps desperate, urged Ormonde to negotiate a truce with the Irish Confederates. Of course it was inevitable that the Irish, in their now strong position, insisted that a truce be based on religious freedoms and recognition of a Catholic 'pecking order' in Ireland, a concept that horrified the Ulster Scots who believed that such negotiations would allow the Irish to increase their strength. They were also concerned at the idea of removing their own troops to England, thus weakening their position in Ireland. In the end, however, negotiations did bear fruit. The Irish and old-English were ultimately convinced that loyalty to Charles would win them the recognition that they so desperately craved. The Confederacy after all, in terms of their constitution and religious aims, still remained loyal to the English king; the alternative could prove considerably worse. A one-year cessation was therefore agreed in September. This missed opportunity to make gains upon their temporary military advantage, however, proved disastrous for the Irish Confederacy. Had the strategic position in 1643 been built upon, instead of dissolving into complex and ultimately fruitless negotiations with the king, matters at the end of the decade might have been very different. However, the die had been cast.

In the short term there were still some benefits for the Irish. Matters favoured the Confederates as the temporary alliance between Scots Protestants in the north and Ormonde's Protestants in the south was disrupted. Ormonde and Lord Inchiquin were left to defend Leinster and Munster; Confederate attentions were turned on the Scots. In 1644 Randall MacDonnell, Earl of Antrim, in accordance with Confederation wishes, sent reinforcements to Montrose's army in Scotland, where they helped engage a Scots Covenanter army, thus preventing a worsening of affairs in England. Although this in turn drew a few thousand men from Monro's force in Ulster back to Scotland, it was not enough to make a difference in the north. Indeed matters in the Irish army of Ulster seemed confused and lacked clear planning, especially so with the appointment of the inexperienced Earl of Castlehaven as supreme commander of the large Ulster force, much to the annoyance of the vexed O'Neill and Preston. The result was a lack of co-ordination and action. A timely campaign against a substantially diminished Protestant force, no more than 20,000 in 1645 and 25,000 in 1646, may have paid dividends, but the Confederation, formed to organise and synchronise military events, was instead proving a military liability. A consistent strategy was not evident within the body that even now showed signs of factional splits. Too many opportunities had been missed and, despite their loyalty to the king, the Irish army could not help Charles as he was successively defeated on the mainland. Scots and Parliamentarians, bolstered by the lack of attacks upon their positions in Ireland, were becoming stronger.

Lord Inchiquin had also re-examined his allegiance, switching to the Parliamentarians in 1644 through frustration at both Ormonde and Charles's apparent disregard for him. This gave the English Parliament important gains in southern Ireland, and once more exacerbated the deadlock that was developing. The arrival in late 1645 of Giovanni Battista Rinuccini, the papal nuncio, far from uniting the Irish Confederate factions, instead split them wide open. He showed nothing but disdain for possible treaties that had been close to success, and took personal charge of politics within the Confederacy. Although overtly dangerous to the united front, he did, however, finance O'Neill to the extent that he was able to carry the day at Benburb in March 1646, defeating a large Scottish force. However, his support for the war effort turned out to be inconsistent. A clear strategy was still not evident and when there was a plan it appeared to be reactive in nature. By the end of 1646, despite failed attempts to capture Dublin, O'Neill could not prevent its surrender to Parliamentary forces by Ormonde.

During Ormonde's leadership George Hamilton had sat as governor of Nenagh Castle. His uncle had also held Roscrea Castle in Munster for a time; it was inherited at the time of George the elder's death. In September 1646 the Irish forces attacked Roscrea. Lady Hamilton and a few other women were allowed to live. The other residents of the castle were not so fortunate and 'man, woman and child were put to the sword'.[7] Ormonde, so careful to take pains to ensure his sisters' wellbeing, was fortunate indeed. He may, however, have taken steps to ensure the safety of Hamilton's children. Despite the war and the obvious proximity of events at Roscrea, the children remained safe; it is possible that they remained at Nenagh. The youngest of the family at that time, Anthony Hamilton, was born around 1645.[8] He had, by then, two older brothers, James and yet another George, although in subsequent years the family would grow to nine, with six sons and three daughters.

Despite the best efforts of the Irish it was too late for proactive measures, as Michael Jones and a Parliamentary force of 3,000 men landed near Dublin by June of 1647. Charles had been defeated and the first English Civil War was over. Ormonde, by now having little choice but to co-operate, had handed over the capital. Parliamentary forces had a significant foothold in Ireland despite opportunities and continual fighting against the inevitable. In August Jones made his first moves outside Dublin with over 4,000 men; these in turn were joined by Protestant forces from Ulster and the north, swelling the army to over 5,000 infantry, 1,500 cavalry and nine cannon. Jones did not have long to wait and met Preston's Irish force at Dungan's Hill where a young Richard Talbot, future Earl of Tyrconnel, would also fight.

The Irish were subsequently broken, six regiments fleeing the field and Jones captured both officers and intelligence, enabling him to go on to clear east Leinster and undo the military stalemate that had existed for so long. Despite O'Neill's attempts to take action in Connaught, he was ultimately stymied by a mutiny within his army over pay. Jones had no such concerns as he took the field once more in October; on this occasion his attention was focused on Irish forces remaining in north Leinster. Reversing the gains recently made by O'Neill and Preston, his strategy was based on securing Dublin, not only to preserve his lines of supply, but also to allow for additional reinforcement.

Lord Inchiquin had also seen his share of success with the aid of English reinforcements and supplies, having sacked or taken key towns in Munster. November saw him face an army of over 8,000 Irish under Taaffe with a force of 5,000. Using a cavalry flanking move, Inchiquin routed the Irish, in one fell stroke destroying the integrity of the Munster force. This permitted him to go on and capture most of the key towns in Munster.

O'Neill, always enterprising, and now once more in control of his army, also attacked towards Dublin in November, ultimately to within seven miles of the city. His lines of supply were weak, however, and the onset of poor weather prevented further movement. Jones's foray from Dublin was almost a formality and the Irish army retreated, in no condition to fight. Logistical contrasts, made worse by the number of Parliamentary victories, were starting to make a difference on the battlefield. The ending of the fighting in Britain signalled the end of support for the Irish. The war, however, was not yet over.

In spring 1648 civil war broke out again in England, successively putting continued success for Jones in doubt and giving a reprieve to the Irish forces. The war in Ireland quickly dissolved into a resource-grabbing situation. In the Irish case, their strategy was based on preventing the enemy living off the land. In some respects, this worked. Gravely concerned with the Irish stranglehold around Munster, Inchiquin changed sides once more in April 1648, signing a ceasefire with the Confederates. Although this would ultimately help carve a Royalist alliance against Jones and Parliament, Owen Roe O'Neill would not agree with the truce. It seemed that the factions were as lively and divisive as ever. In fact, his refusal to join the confederation, and his persistent threats, meant that confederate resources were actually being used to defend Leinster and Connaught against him. In late 1648 he would even draw up a temporary ceasefire with Jones, and trade meat for powder; the divisions can only have helped convince Jones that the factions in Ireland lacked a co-ordinating command structure and could be destroyed piecemeal in the field. Although he was effectively outnumbered three to two, his enemy remained ineffectual, allowing him to hang on to his gains. In Ulster Parliament seized the key ports of Carrickfergus, Belfast and Coleraine from the Scots.

Amidst the confusion Ormonde returned in September 1648 with orders from Charles to gain a settlement with the Confederates. He set to work and, by January 1649, had brokered a pact wherein the Irish would be promised religious toleration in return for loyalty. Perhaps a focus for the Irish war effort together with dedicated leadership could make a difference. Royalist naval manoeuvres quickly blockaded Parliament-controlled ports and, by July, the victorious Ormonde took Drogheda and manoeuvred to lay siege to Dublin with the allied armies of Preston, Inchiquin and Taaffe. However, the close links between the three kingdoms in the British Isles would once more be brought into focus. Jones was reinforced at this critical juncture as Parliamentary victories in Britain permitted the removal of regiments to Ireland.

Continued Parliamentary victories heralded the end of the second Civil War. The execution of Charles I in January 1649 ended the political power struggle that had shaken the three kingdoms to their core for ten years. For England it was a significant turning point but, with all eyes now turned on Ireland and with little real hope of support, the outlook was dire for the Irish and those remaining loyal to the crown. Indeed, Parliament's swift action to raise money for the venture through both tax and the funding of 'adventurers', who would be rewarded with land in Ireland, ensured that by March 1649 a force would be sent to resolve the issue once and for all. Oliver Cromwell himself would command the troops.

Ormonde once more looked to the welfare of his relations and his own defence. He commissioned Muskerry to take charge of maritime affairs, of some consequence if matters had proved different in terms of foreign aid but ultimately futile with English control of the sea.[9] Hamilton also had a change in role, one that would see some difficulties in terms of its execution. At the start of 1649 he had been appointed Receiver-General for the Revenues of Ireland, no easy task with a war on; severe financial difficulties and the multiplicity of hindrances complicated matters considerably. Removing weekly allocations of grain and money from the counties did little to endear either Ormonde or Hamilton to the Royalist-Irish cause. He wrote to Ormonde:

> I now employ with myself to bring in the corn of the counties of Tipperary, Limerick and Clare, and other weekly applotments

thereof, and of the county of Waterford, which cannot be done without horse, though I employ the most part of my own company of foot in that work, which is the reason none of them can be spared to be sent to the field to wait on your Excellency. And believe me the horse and foot are now of greater necessity than ever for bringing in of money, which without considerable parties can never be got in, as the case now stands.[10]

Lord Dillon later wrote to Ormonde suggesting alternative methods of gathering and allocating resources.[11] Hamilton's thankless task was being made no easier it seemed.[12] Others were more damning with their complaints of his methods:

What small quantity of corn lay in Lower Ormonde and the County of Tipperary, and by me intended to be brought to the Shannon side to secure it, is seized up by Sir George Hamilton (as he saith) by his Excellency's [Ormonde's] orders, which I never see.[13]

On the strategic scale Ormonde had not moved fast enough. His cautious nature would ultimately be his undoing. In addition, he was losing favour with the Royalists. In August he marched against Dublin but English reinforcements had already arrived, increasing the size of Jones's force in the capital and enabling him to make forays against the Irish–Royalist coalition. In a surprise attack he routed Royalist troops at Rathmines. Inchiquin withdrew due to rumoured fears of seaborne invasion of Munster and 12,000 seasoned English troops were able to land at Dublin by mid-August. If Ormonde hoped once more for a resurgence of war in England or a supply crisis, he would be mistaken on this occasion. The Cromwellians were in Ireland to stay. Fed on a diet of stories of Irish atrocity against Protestant settlers and unrighteous rebellion against English law, Cromwell had arrived to right what he saw as the final wrong of the three kingdoms conflict – that of Ireland. As his attacks at Wexford and Drogheda illustrated, he was in no mood to discuss religious freedoms with the Irish. His motives were plain, simple and motivated by Parliamentarian hopes that rebellion in Ireland would become a thing of the past. That is not to say that deals were not forged. The Earl of Antrim escaped mostly unscathed in return for his co-operation, and Protestant Royalist garrisons were allowed to switch sides. However, native Irish resistance was dealt with savagely.

Despite Ormonde's spirited determination in attempting to defend walled towns and his reconciliation with O'Neill, who would die in November 1649, his foe was too strong and too well supported to alter the outcome. Sir George Hamilton's absence from Roscrea, in pursuance of his delegated tasks, would have its effect on the suffering Lady Hamilton. In December 1649 the Irish army visited Roscrea once more in the form of a regiment of horse. On this occasion, and facing apparently little resistance, they decided to stay for two days. Lady Hamilton complained of their riotous behaviour. With their taking an 'excess of meat and drink', they used the town's barns and houses to quarter their horses and troops. In addition, they would not leave until paid to do so and subsequently threatened to burn the town to the ground, until placated with further offers of money from Lady Hamilton. Leaving eventually, they carried with them 'liveries, saddles, bridles, horselocks, pots, pans, gridirons, brandirons, plough irons, spades, bedding, carpets, women's gowns and petticoats'. These items could only be 'bought' back. However, it would be the last raiding opportunity for the Irish at Roscrea.[14]

By mid-1650 the Irish-Royalist alliance had resorted to guerrilla warfare once more and the end was in sight. Factional infighting, inept leadership and circumstance had destroyed Irish hopes. The English Parliament would make the decisions that affected Ireland's future.[15] The arrival of Cromwell heralded the end of the fragile Irish dream and meant the deaths in many cases of those accused of having had involvement in the 1641 rebellion. Cromwell was determined to have an end to the matter, even if this meant additional bloodshed, as required to extirpate the phantom of Irish rebellion from the English psyche. By the spring Cromwell's troops had made significant advances into Ormonde's territory. All three field armies had been defeated and Ormonde, after making the Marquis of Clanricarde his second-in-command, left the country for France in December. The Irish fought on, after a fashion, although bickering and argument even at this stage characterised their relations.

Some remained positive despite the apparent futility. Muskerry wrote in 1651, 'the enemy has been master of the field wheresoever he came, and have sat with two armies before Limerick and Galway', and of the Irish troops, 'they have renounced all kind of condition and quarter and are resolved to die upon the place rather than expose themselves to the mercy of a cruel and perfidious enemy.'[16]

Despite Muskerry's hopes, it would take more than limp rhetoric to stop the Cromwellians.

Clanricarde, also hopeful despite the odds, was similarly vocal:

> I conceive it almost impossible to prevent the nation's sudden falling into enemy's hands, and on the other side it appears as impossible to me for them to gain the kingdom if aids come not out of England, for though they are powerful, vigilant, active and united, yet they are not so numerous, though assisted by very many of the Irish, as to grasp or secure half the kingdom to themselves.

His views on Irish infighting, however, remained scathing:

> Then to our credit be it spoken, though numerous and indifferently well armed, we are so stupid and backward to use in our own defence, so wedded to a little private profit and present ease, though ruined in future, so factious and inclined to emulations, jealousies and distinctions of families and provinces, and the soldiers so given to liberty and rapine for want of certain pay and seasonal provision, that each week produces such unexpected changes as renders it impossible for me to contrive or design any settled course of safety or preservation for them. Yet if some money, arms and ammunition should arrive, none can tell what wonders may be wrought. However, I shall strive to the last to keep up the diversion here, that neither the rebels themselves nor others by their conquest of them may be a disturbance to His Majesty in his other dominions, and if I could more powerfully serve him, I am confident I should not continue in so sickly a condition, and I shall presume upon your favour at all times when occasion is offered to give that testimony. [17]

Despite the relative unpopularity of Hamilton's role, he retained his reputation as a clandestine-style 'operator' within the political scene, acting as an agent for the powerful Royalist lobby. His instructions from Ormonde for his 'Journey into Ireland' in August 1651 typified his continuing close relationship with his brother-in-law and the Royalist cause.

1. You are with all possible expedition to repair to some part of our kingdom of Ireland remaining under our obedience, where being arrived you are to use all diligence in getting where the lord of Clanricarde, our Lord-Deputy, shall then be and in delivering him our letters herewith delivered you.

2. You shall give him and such others as by him you shall be directed an account of the many hazards and difficulties of our escape, and of the kindness and civility wherewith we are now received in this kingdom.

3. You are to let him and them know that we omit no industry or solicitation to procure supplies for that our kingdom, and that we doubt not to be able before the next summer to send them very considerable assistances for the relief of our good subjects in that our kingdom.

4. You are to let them know that we repose great confidence in their fidelity and the continuance of their good affections to us, notwithstanding the great discouragements that our late misfortunes and the prevalence of the enemy in that kingdom may have given them, and that we desire them to be assured of our constant and affectionate care of that our kingdom, and our just sense of their incessant endeavours for and suffering in our service, and that we remain steadfast to those graces and conditions derived to our good subjects by the articles of the late peace, whereunto we shall with great cheerfulness make such further additions as their constancy in these times of trial shall merit.

5. You are to return as speedily as possibly you can with a present account of the condition of that our kingdom, of the number of the forces there, and the preparations and resolutions for our future service, as also of all things most necessary for the enabling them to prosecute the war.

6. You are to make particular application to the Lord Viscount Muskery and having communicated to him these instructions, and all things committed to your trust to bring us his sense and advice upon all the matters relating to our subjects and service in that our kingdom.

7. You are to propose unto them the securing of some harbour or port where such supplies may be safely discharged, and that may be most useful at present, and on your return to bring us notice of the harbours or ports that shall be secured.

8. You are in the communication and management of these instructions to govern yourself entirely by the directions of the Lord of Clanricarde for the general, and by the Lord Muskery for those parts where he commands.

9. In case you shall be necessitated to land in Munster, where my Lord Muskery is, you are to be advised by him concerning the means of conveying your despatch to the Lord of Clanricarde, and in all things for our service in the performance of these our commands.[18]

Hamilton it seemed, was given a task that centred on morale-boosting efforts, communication with Ormonde's allies but, most of all, Ormonde was concerned with acquainting himself with the developing situation. He, of course, would have been looking for opportunities to return to Ireland but the chances of victory against Cromwell were becoming more remote. Ormonde benefited from the close relations with his relatives – both Hamilton and Muskerry played pivotal roles within the war effort, fostering close relations that would endure for years to come.[19] Ormonde also used his influence, it appears, to secure a future for Hamilton's eldest sons, James and George. Hamilton wrote to the Duke in September 1651:

> I give your Excellency many thanks for your care to place my son George in a condition that I hope may enable him to acknowledge it with better service than I have ever been in condition to do you. James begins early as your Excellence is pleased to advertise me, of which I will be at care to prevent as I may, though I know nothing so like to prevail in that case as good counsel and some way of employing his time to divert idleness which is the greatest curse of that gentlemanly vice. God convert him and forgive those that were before him ....[20]

Hamilton was obviously concerned that his sons should have a future of sorts, in the military or otherwise, and sought Ormonde's influence in France. This plea would pay real dividends for the family. Indeed, Hamilton's words would indicate that George at least had already secured a position in France. Despite all he could do for his relatives, however, Ormonde's hopes of a last great Irish resurgence were in vain.

Charles II, who had been 'unofficially' crowned in Scotland in 1651 and to whom the remaining royalists looked for the English succession, also sought knowledge about Ireland. His unsuccessful attempts to take back his father's throne were perhaps expected in the face of the well-organised Parliamentarians. In his communication with Clanricarde, however, it was Hamilton once more who was used as a trusted agent.

> I should give you assurance of the great sense I have of your merit and present danger, both which have as great a part in the inducements of my sending Sir George Hamilton to you as any other advantage I can expect from his employment.[21]

Seventeenth-century Ireland.

Limerick was captured in October 1651 and Galway in April 1652. Although fighting on a smaller scale would go on for another year, including Muskerry's all but futile defence of Ross Castle in June,[22] the war was, to all intents and purposes, over. In contrast to the Irish Confederacy, Cromwell's forces had been well led and motivated, and lacked the deep-rooted divisions that still existed within the Irish camp. Ormonde had escaped the wrath of Cromwell and thus evaded the series of trials and executions that followed the war, a Parliamentary solution for those who had fomented rebellion and been involved in any manner with the murder of settlers.

Sir George and his family had remained in Ireland at the time of Ormonde's departure. By 1651 the family consisted of seven children, five sons – James the eldest, George, Anthony, Thomas and Richard – and two daughters – Elizabeth and Lucia. Securing the welfare of his eldest sons was not Sir George Hamilton's only difficulty, however. Always a speculator, a trait perhaps inherited from his father, he had spent considerably during the Irish war. Of course, he had spent much of his own cash in securing ammunition and arms for Irish troops, at a cost of £3,000.[23] In addition, he had several interests in the king's mines in Ireland prior to the war, investing a significant amount of money and work in creating an economically viable concern. The loss of both labour and mining interests had cost him around £20,000.[24] We can also speculate that, in his time as Receiver General, George may have used his own funds on occasion. He had gambled the balance of his money on a ship that he had speculatively despatched to trade on the continent. However, it was seized in France and, despite all his efforts and appeals to Ormonde, there seemed little that anyone could do to release the vessel.[25] In Hamilton's own words, 'I am totally ruined, having no other stock of substance than what was there adventured in setting forth that frigate …'.

More trouble was to follow. After failed attempts to get further aid from France while still in Ireland,[26] Hamilton had little choice but to follow Ormonde; he had, however, made more than a few enemies at home in his time as Receiver General. Amongst these were the Irish clergy, who accused him of dishonesty in the course of his dealings. Whether or not there had been any truth in the allegations, Hamilton stayed in Ireland to clear his name. Having done this successfully, there perhaps being little foundation in the accusation to begin with, he left for France in spring 1651. Some of his children would ultimately return to Ireland, although many years would pass, and the circumstances would be entirely different.

*Chapter 4*

# The Gendarmes Anglais

Despite the last minute accusations of the Irish clergy, Sir George Hamilton had escaped the persecution that followed the Irish war relatively unscathed. Donough MacCarthy, Lord Muskerry, had not been so lucky. Despite being allowed to leave with some troops for Spain after the siege of Ross Castle, he received an unfriendly welcome. Returning to Ireland in 1653, he was immediately arrested and imprisoned in Dublin, accused of involvement in the murder of English settlers early in the war. He became one of the many Irish awaiting trial. A lack of clear evidence and a spirited defence meant that Muskerry was eventually released in 1654 when he, too, left for France with his family.[1]

Hamilton and Ormonde had no such trouble from the Parliamentarians. Indeed, Cromwell had allegedly professed his great regard for the Duke and Lady Ormonde.[2] The Hamilton family's time in France would have a decisive impact upon their outlook. The Scottish plantationists, who had tried to settle in Ireland and been uprooted once more, found in France an education for the next generation of Hamiltons, and perhaps a cultural pedigree of sorts.

There is little evidence to suggest exactly where the Hamiltons settled initially. Previous communication with Ormonde would indicate that the family resided in or around Caen in the northern part of the country.[3] Certainly Ormonde's family appears to have gone there in 1648. French references also note Caen as the birthplace of at least one of the Hamiltons. It is likely that the two youngest children, John and Margaret, were born in France.[4] The family later moved to Paris, where the children were educated, where they would have grown up in Louis XIV's enlightened capital, very different to the war-torn Ireland that so many of them had known.

Sir George Hamilton still had concerns over his own finances, despite the fact that he had escaped English wrath. In this respect, he was not alone. Most, if not all of the Royalist exiles, although not destitute, were in a position where funds that had existed for landowners and the 'gentry' classes were simply no longer available. Land had been seized and, as in Hamilton's case, much of the money available had been spent on either defence of estates, raising troops or toward the war effort in general. Indeed, even the royal court in exile would suffer similar privations. Hamilton's attempts to appeal to the French court for relief were also in vain. Ormonde, once more perhaps mindful of his sister's welfare, and aware of the maturity of Hamilton's two eldest sons, did take steps to ensure their futures and that of the other children as far as he could.

He wrote to Lord Henry Jermyn in 1652:

> Sir George Hamilton goes towards you with all the recommendations from this to that Court that can be thought necessary to entitle your Lordship to a mediation for his concernments upon which he principally hopes for success. He has made many expensive and dangerous voyages for the late and this King and entirely lost his fortune by his faithfulness to them against the rebels of all their kingdoms ....[5]

Using his considerable influence in the exiled court of Charles II, Ormonde found positions for James, the eldest brother, and his younger brother George. James is to be found with Prince Rupert, of English Civil War fame, in Heidelberg in 1655 and had a place within Charles II's court[6] while George junior was made a page of the king.[7]

By 1654, with the arrival of Muskerry in France, to be once more united with his family, Ormonde had a considerable number of 'dependants', all related in one way or another and sharing the poverty and privations of the exiled court. Muskerry, in a similar predicament to Hamilton, had three sons and one daughter.

Of his sons, Cormac MacCarthy was the eldest. He would make his way in life as a soldier fighting for the Irish regiments in French service, part of Charles's retinue allied to the French army. Callaghan would study for the priesthood. The youngest brother, Justin MacCarthy, who was of a similar age to Anthony Hamilton, would no doubt have been educated alongside and grown up with the younger Hamiltons. The destiny of these two at least would be entwined.

Lord Muskerry had one daughter that we know of, Helen.[8] She studied with her cousin, George Hamilton's daughter Elizabeth, at the Port Royal convent near Paris, where Callaghan MacCarthy would also reside for a time in his pursuit of the priesthood.[9] There Elizabeth learned not only the finer points of French culture and etiquette, but would also gain a fine education and, of course, the skills that would enable her to become the very model of courtly life in later years. Indeed, all of the younger members of the two families would receive excellent French educations, an experience that would prove useful in the years to follow, not only in their inevitable dealings with the French, but in their respective involvement in the game that was English political life.

One could imagine that, for the fathers, George Hamilton and Lord Muskerry, matters had settled to the extent that they could relish the peace that they had so long hoped for, albeit in a foreign land. It was not to be, however.

There was, for instance, the small matter of Charles's loyal Irish subjects' continued involvement in the wars of France. Muskerry's son Cormac, for example, like so many of his Munster colleagues, served within one of a number of Irish regiments then fighting in French service. Disenchanted with the futile conflict against Cromwell, many Irish had fled to France even before the end of hostilities in Ireland. Charles II also encouraged the formation of such forces; in this way the loyal Irish could fight for the English crown against the Parliamentarians, at least in some manner. By 1652 a regiment of Irish horse and a regiment of foot fought under Turenne and the Duke of Lorraine. Most of these troops were later placed under the command of Charles's brother James, the Duke of York, a man for whom the Irish would hold a particular attraction, yet the relationship would become a poisoned chalice, for both sides.[10]

The war with Spain had continued after the French civil war of 1648-1653, the *Fronde*. Confirming the position of the young Louis XIV, the civil war had also created a bitter contest between two of the greatest French generals, the Vicomte de Turenne and Prince Condé of the Bourbons, both of whom were experienced officers. However, the *Fronde* had set them at odds, with Condé fighting on the Spanish side against his bitter rival. Irish troops, who had also been loyal to the Spanish in years past, fought both in French and Spanish service and inevitably would fight each other on the battlefields of Europe. The 'French' Irish, now within the Duke of York's Regiment, whose apprenticeship to Turenne had gained him tremendous experience as an officer, although not as a general of armies, had fought bravely in the continued conflict with their Spanish enemy.[11]

Still embroiled in politics, George Hamilton became involved in a number of dangerous tasks for the king. Much of this was also hidden to some extent from Lady Hamilton, who presumably had had more than enough of her husband's adventuring and felt perhaps that the family deserved a break from the rigours of the dissolute English politics of exile. Ever loyal to the king, however, Sir George took part in a number of secret missions. He would, in the event, concoct myriad excuses ranging from royal requests through to family errands for their sons, in order to allay the suspicions of his wife, no easy task in itself we can guess.

Writing to Ormonde in 1654, Hamilton recorded:

> I told her I was inclinable to her opinion, but it was fit to know more from you of that matter before I undertook a journey of that charge and trouble. This I only tell you that you may thereby understand I may haply upon this pretence get more freely from her when my other business here is in a readiness of which as yet she knows nothing, nor of my intention for any other journey, till I make a collection of all that may most ease her from the womanish apprehensions I doubt will appear in her on knowledge thereof.

Indeed it seems that Hamilton would suggest a solution to the problem, not only perhaps to preserve the secrecy of his communication with Ormonde, but also to further allay the fears of his suffering wife:

> Percie Church told me the other day that if a way were laid of sending your letters to Liege to some merchant there and sending us your address how to address ours to that merchant for you, we might by that way have a more certain and more speedy intercourse and twice a week, for by such a way some letters have been already received from Spa.[12]

Hamilton had already been involved in various assignments back to the British Isles. In 1654 he had been employed as an envoy to the Hamiltons remaining in Scotland, in the wake of Middleton's invasions, arriving too late, however, as Middleton had already been defeated.[13] Returning to Europe, he had travelled on errands for the king between the various locations of Charles's roving court. There were repeated efforts to re-enter the British Isles with Hamilton being used as the king's agent in the affairs.[14] Lack of success in Scotland did little to dampen Charles's efforts to snatch back his father's throne. Desperate to raise an army, he could do little without his dedicated Irish and English troops. In the case of the Irish he was especially keen that those who had remained loyal should be sent back to Ireland to aid him in his efforts. This plan, however, with the Irish being scattered between the warring French and Spanish factions, would prove problematic with regard to securing the troops' release for such an adventure. To this end, Charles needed significant representation to go to Spain to plead his case. It was perhaps inevitable that two noted Irishmen would represent the king in Madrid. Sir George Hamilton and Lord Muskerry left for Spain on an errand that, if successful, could affect the future of the English succession.

Hamilton, predictably, had already created sizeable debts in Belgium whilst with Charles's wandering court. He borrowed still further to make the journey to Spain. In May 1657 he made contact with Muskerry in Madrid. There they met with Sir Henry Bennet, the king's 'man' in Spain, who put a roof over their heads for the duration of the adventure; indeed without his intervention the two Irish nobles would either have starved or quickly changed their minds regarding the plausible success of the expedition. As matters stood, despite a warmhearted welcome and gracious reception from the Spanish court, the men waited five months for an inconclusive and thus unenthusiastic answer. Ultimately, they had been close to poverty for the entire period, relying on Bennet's charity. The two returned to Charles's court by summer 1658, for the most part penniless. Charles himself fared little better, as the terms of foreign exile in a monarchy without a crown began to bite.[15]

Any attempts at securing the elusive English throne, however, would prove unsuccessful in the short term; the European strategic situation remained as fluid as had the civil wars in the British Isles. By 1656 a number of English and Irish regiments remained in French service. Indeed, Muskerry's son, Cormac MacCarthy, had carved a fine reputation in French service, having been made Colonel of his Irish regiment of Munstermen. Despite its very European side, the Franco–Spanish conflict had also been dominated by the question of which side Cromwell and the English army would take. In the end, Cromwell's hatred of Spanish Catholicism and attraction to Spain's riches in the new world meant that a pact with the French would be drawn up by 1657. Inevitably, perhaps, Spain then courted Cromwell's enemy, Charles II. Despite the Duke of York's reticence to comply with Spanish wishes, the monarchy in exile would ultimately ally itself with Spain to the detriment of the duke's relationship with the French General Turenne. In addition, Irish troops across the contested regions allied themselves to first one and then the other side, with conflicting loyalties to king or their Catholicism or both, the result of which meant that French 'Irish' and Spanish 'Irish' would still face each other on the battlefield. Indeed, questions were raised as to the apparent ease with which some troops, including Cormac MacCarthy's, had switched sides, ultimately staining the reputation of the Irish troops to some degree.[16]

Cromwell's pact with the French was made good by 1658 when 6,000 troops bolstered the French army in Spanish Flanders. The year's campaign centred on the English Channel towns of Dunkirk, Mardyk and Gravelines. Turenne's siege of Dunkirk triggered a response from Spanish troops under Don Juan, although Turenne, the meticulous planner, won a critical victory. A shrewd Condé, still in Spanish service, changed sides after the battle. Dunkirk fell and the nineteen-year-old Louis XIV, who promptly handed the town to the English as had earlier been agreed, watched as the besieged Spanish garrison emerged. Other French victories followed and, by 1659, Turenne's war-winning strategy had convinced the Spanish to sue for peace. France would keep most of the conquered territory but, of greater import to the future of a fractious Europe, she had now succeeded Spain as the dominant military power.[17]

Dramatic change was also underway in England where Cromwell died in 1658. His son Richard was unable to prevent radical military figures and politicians from overthrowing him and re-instating a purged parliament. Ultimately, the decision was made to recall an exiled king, a decision that would restore Charles II to the throne that he had sought for so many years.

During the fractious period of history with which we are concerned, there was a constant demand in times of war for experienced troops and, to a larger extent, competent troops. In the Irish a king or noble could expect to see both, and this, even before those same troops had been exiled from their former country in an attempt to curb their usefulness, and perhaps even their willingness to fight for a broken cause. The irony is that the Jacobites and Irish were becoming inextricably linked to each other's fate. To use a distasteful metaphor, theirs was a marriage of convenience, an abusive relationship, and a marriage sealed by fate, with all the possibilities of a tragic end in store for both parties.

The Hamilton brothers share their beginnings in exile with Charles II with the Muskerry family, the MacCarthys. Both fathers had been involved with Ormonde during the war in Ireland after the 1641 rebellion. Both had worked together on quasi-secret missions for the king. It is inevitable that they would find favour with the new king, perhaps even more inevitable that their offspring might also be given some impetus in terms of joining the favoured circle of Charles II.

A young Sarsfield, McCarthy, Tyrconnel, and, in turn, English notables such as John Churchill, better known by his later title of Duke of Marlborough, who would later feature in the war in Ireland, and the young Monmouth, illegitimate son of Charles, all would serve with English and Irish troops in French service, fulfilling Charles's new obligation to Louis XIV, and in the French war against the Holy Roman Empire. More importantly, they all had unique and important destinies.

Despite the travels of the Irish abroad, it would be remiss of us to forget the early 'work' of Irish military personalities. This is pertinent for several reasons. We see immediately the early military careers of the MacCarthy and Hamilton families, who are relevant throughout the Confederate War in Ireland during the English Civil War and, indeed, whose members, such as Justin MacCarthy and Anthony and Richard Hamilton, became vitally important in the war that followed. It is MacCarthy, for instance, who, after the Battle of Newtownbutler, became the first Irish general to lead troops to France.

The story starts, however, after the events of the Restoration, and stems partially from the relative popularity of the *Famile* d'Hamilton.

The Hamilton family had survived the rigours of the civil war and the subsequent bouts of poverty, bordering on abject at times, that accompanied the roving court of the young Charles II. Conversely, the sons and daughters of that particular family appeared to be carving out rather successful careers, if not reputations, amongst the new English court.

In a triumphant return to England Charles took the throne in 1660, the end of puritanical regimes on one hand, and the beginning of decadence and court intrigue on a world stage on the other. For George Hamilton and his young family, the return did not occur straightaway; it would be 1661 before a move to England was even possible. A subsequent return to Ireland would then be possible. Charles was, at the very least, a king careful to cultivate important and, ultimately, influential friendships. Hamilton and his family were therefore important, and it was imperative to reward those who had been kind to him during the interregnum. He would be especially kind to those who had suffered exile and relative poverty with him; much of the financial benefits that Hamilton had lost during the war would be returned. He would, for instance, be granted back his lands and have new lands awarded; his grant with regard to mining interests in Ireland was also returned. Muskerry, too, had his lands returned.[18] A rightful king, restored to glory, could be benevolent to his friends, it seemed. The restoration of land, finances and royal favour were not enough to prevent continued financial difficulties, however.

George Hamilton senior, father to six sons whose fate was tied to the future relationships between Ireland and France, still found himself in arrears, most likely in tune with debts that he had failed to settle during his time in France with the king in waiting. Indeed, we can speculate that lands and property returned post-conflict, after the devastation of an Irish war, may have fallen short of that expected. He found himself under arrest in 1665 due to his indebtedness, and released only by order of the Lord Chamberlain. The lesson was not learned, however, as he would spend the subsequent months squandering what little the family had retained.[19] Little remains known, at least in terms of specifics, about this period in the Hamilton family's life; there is evidence, however, to suggest that Hamilton senior had been more than simply an advocate of the king in exile. He retained the full confidence of the new monarchy and was still being selected for those special missions in whose concoction the king appeared to excel.[20]

Indeed, it is arguable that, despite his carelessness with his own finances, his reputation with the king helped seal the trust and position that would be left to his sons and daughters. There were six sons and three daughters. Upon their return to England in 1661 the family lived in a large residence in Whitehall, despite the return of lands in Ireland. The oldest of the boys, James and George, took full advantage of the flagrant reversals that had emerged with the demise of puritanical England. Indeed, bearing their lineage and relative importance in mind, it would have been surprising if the two men had not become embroiled in London's intrigues, courtly affairs and notoriety, as young men are wont to do.

The third son, Anthony, who would see almost all of our story unfold, whilst also being directly involved, would later write of their escapades during the period. These two would partake in the reform of Puritan England with gusto. Their affairs with maids of honour and other men's wives were only bested by their connection to the intrigues of Lady Castlemaine and other notables. They flirted with the most beautiful women, wore the finest clothes, and were noted as some of the finest dancers in the English court, gambling, duelling and womanising their way through the Restoration period in a manner that was echoed by many of their Irish contemporaries. Indeed, it is arguable that it was expected in this new royal establishment.

Of the two brothers, James was perhaps the more significant. From the start he seemed to fall into the role of a courtier:

> The elder of the Hamiltons ... was the man who of all the court
> dressed best: he was well made in his person, and possessed those

happy talents which lead to fortune and procure success in love; he was a most assiduous courtier, had the most lively wit, the most polished manners, and the most punctual attention to his master imaginable: no person danced better, nor was anyone a more general lover: a merit of some account in a court entirely devoted to love and gallantry.[21]

Not only did James display talents that would gain him much favour in early Restoration society, King Charles had also noticed him. It would have been surprising if he did not, thanks again to the position that his father's reputation had helped place him in, and the skills that his movements in the highest echelons of courtly society had earned him. Charles, chief among the intriguers, would later, albeit temporarily, help obtain the hand of a maid of honour of the Princess Royal for the young Hamilton and also offer him one of his discarded mistresses.[22] By the late 1660s honours were being heaped upon James Hamilton as he sat within Charles's inner circle of stylish rakes. Apart from favours, land grants and pensions, he was also appointed groom of the bedchamber.[23] He was made 'Ranger of Hyde Park'[24] and also Provost-Marshal General of Barbados.[25] Membership of Charles's inner circle meant more than mere honours, however. James, in a manner much like his father, was employed on missions related to affairs of state. These were mainly concerned with playing the role of envoy for the king when visiting the French court, and passing messages to Charles's sister Henriette, now married to Louis XIV's younger brother, and known as the Duchess d'Orléans. James was recruited as an envoy to other courts, but it is to Charles's sister that he was especially entrusted.[26]

Of course, such fame comes with its own form of contemporary bad press. Samuel Pepys described James Hamilton as one of those who led the king astray, deflecting him from the advice of his more noble servants.[27] James's travels to the French court also landed him in trouble. Arlington, who had at one time helped George Hamilton senior in Spain, and Ralph Montague, the new ambassador to the French, were both concerned about the influence that James had with Henriette.[28] This is to be expected to some extent since, for a sister in a foreign court separated by the English Channel, relying upon James Hamilton for communication with her brother, a close relationship was inevitable. Both had been close, and it is likely that this particular Hamilton would have tried both French and English patience. Indeed, the French too were somewhat exasperated with his 'meddling'. Cominges, the French ambassador in England, called him a young man 'without experience' who conspired against France, a predictable reaction from the suspicious French authorities aware of the apparent importance with which Charles had graced his journeys.[29] He had come from nowhere, something that the French authorities could not abide. Although there is no clear evidence to suggest that James Hamilton may have been a spy in addition to his role as English envoy to Henriette, it is almost inevitable when we consider the nature of his father's dutiful service to Charles in the earlier decade.

James was also disliked because of his close association with, and continued loyalty to, his uncle, the Protestant Duke of Ormonde. He had little choice in this instance; the two families were still very closely connected and the Ormonde relationship would have a continuous and considerable influence on all the Hamilton boys' prospects in the years to follow. James at least was grateful for his uncle's benevolence and his loyalty did not seem in doubt.[30] Whether Ormonde played any part in the arrangement of the marriage that followed is not clear, but he did break the news of the event to James's mother. At some stage in the 1660s James had married Elizabeth, the daughter of Sir John Culpepper.[31] In itself, such a marriage would be expected of a loyal courtier and cavalier. What was not expected was that James would change his religion, since Elizabeth Culpepper was a Protestant. His mother, a devout Catholic, and ever watchful of her boys' spiritual welfare was devastated, the news being delivered to her in a 'kindly' manner by her Protestant brother Ormonde. She replied:

> I was never more afflicted or surprised then when I found in your letter the unworthiness of James, who I know too well to believe from him that he had any other dislike to the religion he has left then that he could not profess it living so great a libertin as he did; and the assurance he had that it would be an obstacle to his marriage with Mrs Culpeper, for whom he had this unhappy affection about four years ago; and at that time did he resolve to become an apostat, rather than not have her. He has a dear bargain of her, if she be so unfortunate as to be engaged to him, and I am confident that she would never have much satisfaction in one that has forsaken God for her. I am most certain that it was no apprehension of being out of the way of salvation made him thus base. He has no such tender conscience as you will find in a little time.[32]

Not all the news of the time would be disappointing to Lady Hamilton, however. Around the same time, her daughter Elizabeth Hamilton was also married. The circumstances of this attachment were entirely different, and at this point another character of note enters our story. The match on this occasion would be made with a Frenchman, a man who had a profound effect on the destiny of the Hamiltons and their continued connection to France, and French service – le Chevalier de Gramont.

The chevalier's biography would later be written by Anthony Hamilton and become a literary classic. For now, it is pertinent to outline some of the more notable events in his life, as recorded by Hamilton. A possible descendant of the French King Henri IV, Gramont was born in 1621. Intended for the priesthood by his parents, he decided for himself that a life in the French military would hold better prospects. After all, there was a war on; French involvement in the Thirty Years' War was late but influential. He had been an aide-de-camp for both Condé and the Duc d'Enghien. Present at several of the major battles of the war, he was by 1648 a senior officer under Condé, remaining with him through his time in Spanish service until 1654 when he returned to the French fold. Despised by Mazarin as an insolent timewaster, Louis, however, liked him. It is perhaps indicative of the confused moral re-assessment of the time that he was welcomed in England.[33]

A gambler and womaniser, Gramont had chosen to upset a member of the French court, an act that resulted in his exile, albeit temporarily, from France. It appears, however, that he had already met several influential members of the English court, even featuring in a court ballet with the Duke of Buckingham and James, Duke of York, brother to the king. He travelled to England in search of the flamboyant and excessive lifestyle with which he had made his name, but from which he was denied in France. He appears to have been present in England during Cromwell's era, ending up in London later in 1663, where Cominges reported to Louis that the English were quite agreeable to the arrangement.[34]

Strange indeed that the xenophobic Restoration court should warm to a vainglorious French lackey. Gramont, however, was different. Far from displaying characteristic Gallic arrogance, his was a refined and conducive air. He was friendly, accepting of English tradition without parading his own, and impressed most of the English people that he met with his uncharacteristically 'non-French' manner.[35] Apparently still having some means, most of which was gained from gambling and cards, and still a lover of women, something which must have been quite agreeable to the rest of the court, he would procure the finest gifts from Paris for the noblest of London's ladies. Looking glasses and perfumed gloves were mere trifles compared to the superb coach that he presented to the king, or the splendid parties and banquets that he threw, with musical accompaniment and the finest food and wine, usually delivered from Paris.

Gramont was the toast of the English court. The attention that he paid to the ladies remained unfaltering, in particular for one Miss Elizabeth Hamilton. It is unclear whether Gramont had known Elizabeth during her time in France. She had even then 'turned heads', inspiring at least one member of the exiled court to consider marrying her.[36] Other admirers included the Duke of York and Cominges would record Mademoiselle d'Hamilton dancing with King Louis.[37] Indeed there were many unsuccessful suitors including the Dukes of Richmond and Norfolk, Lord Falmouth and even Richard Talbot, a man whose destiny lay in Ireland.[38] Such notables held no attraction for Elizabeth Hamilton, however. Only one man appears to have found favour in her eyes, le Chevalier de Gramont, a man with little means save what he had won through cards, a man who was at least twenty years older than she, and a man who yet lived by his wits and charm. It is this charm, perhaps, that attracted the young lady to the French nobleman and yet, by the same token, Gramont was very much taken with the Lady Hamilton.

The relationship appeared to blossom to the extent that by the end of 1663 both English and French courts were talking about the pair. Charles, writing to his sister in September, described how he was looking for a rich wife for the *Chevalier*.[39] Cominges also wrote to Louis relating the beauty and grace of the young Mademoiselle d'Hamilton, and Gramont's attentions, tempering the news a little with a statement of Miss Hamilton's apparent lack of wealth. There also appears to have been some *helpful* intervention by members of the Hamilton family:

> I think that at first the chevalier did not mean to go so far in this business, but, be it that conversation has completed what beauty began, or that the noise made by two rather troublesome brothers may have had something to do with it, certain it is that he has now declared himself publicly.[40]

The intervention of the Hamilton brothers, most likely James and George, may have been simple coaxing or a natural instinct to protect the welfare of their sister. Another anecdote from the period, however, relates a quite different state of affairs. Around the same time, Gramont was notified by his sister, the Marquise de Saint-Chaumont, that his return to France would no longer be hindered. Gramont, conscious of his developing relationship with Elizabeth Hamilton, was somewhat reticent to leave, at such a critical juncture perhaps? Only Elizabeth persuaded him that he should in fact make the journey, although it is not clear what promises, if any, were made. Upon reaching France, Gramont quickly discovered that his sister was in fact incorrect in her assumption, and he gladly returned to England. This version is repeated by Anthony Hamilton in his *Gramont* memoirs and accentuates the fact that Miss Hamilton had given her permission for the journey.

Another version of this story is more closely linked to Cominges's 'troublesome brothers' idea. Gramont, on his way to Dover, was overtaken by the two Hamilton brothers on horseback and asked if he had *forgotten* something. Upon being pressed, the reluctant chevalier immediately returned to London and married Miss Hamilton. It is likely that both stories contain some elements of truth and there are other versions of the famous French anecdote.[41] Whether Gramont had got last minute 'cold feet' or had in fact desired to return to France, the 'troublesome' Hamiltons, it appeared, were having none of it. The marriage, by now inevitable, took place in December 1663.[42] The King of England presented a substantial wedding gift, a jewel purchased from the Earl of St Albans for £1,260.[43]

The couple continued to live in England for much of the following year. Their first child, a son, was born in September 1664.[44] The family left for France two months later, Gramont's exile apparently at an end.[45] Charles, in communication with his sister in France, recommended the Lady Hamilton as 'as good a creature as ever lived'. As for Gramont, who had made such an impression on the English court, he would always be welcome in England.[46]

Although Gramont's exile was at an end, it was inevitable that he must still have had visible enemies in the French court. The new object of French interest, the Lady Gramont, must have offset much of this anger and resentment, however. Charles's sister Henriette would soon become a close friend of Elizabeth, ensuring that the Gramonts were warmly welcomed into France.[47] Accepted into French society by the 1670s, and echoing the larger-scale links between French and English courts, the Gramonts attracted the attentions of visiting English notables. These included Lady Castlemaine's daughter and Lady Sunderland who dined with Madame de Gramont.[48] In addition, Gramont would present one John Churchill, the future Duke of Marlborough, to Louis XIV; Churchill was then serving with the English battalions in French service.[49]

Gramont, although safely returned from exile in England, continued to espouse the English cause in the French court. Indeed, at times he promoted that cause to the extent that he risked once more being condemned to exile in England. In the end, however, the marriage and continued relationship with Charles's sister Henriette would closely echo the developing relationship and form of alliance that began to exist between the two countries.

Although James Hamilton's change of religion through his marriage had caused consternation within the family, he was still an influential and highly respected member of Charles's court. George Hamilton, the younger, would see his share of success in France, while younger brother Anthony, who would have been around nineteen by 1665, would join him on his French expedition. Of the other brothers, Thomas would enter the Royal Navy around the mid-1660s, while Richard and John, still too young to forge their own futures, would have important parts to play later. Of the Hamilton ladies, the noted Elizabeth's influence in the French court alongside her husband, le Chevalier de Gramont would grow. Her two younger sisters would still have been too young for marriage.

As an example of this point, consider the following: while Richard besieged Derry under Jacobite command in 1689, his brother Thomas was involved in the fleet action that sought its relief for the new English king. John, too, played his part for the Jacobite cause. In 1691 he had senior command over much of the foot at Bloody Aughrim, a battle that doomed the Jacobite cause in Ireland and saw Sarsfield's leaving by October of the same year. Of the Hamilton ladies, Elizabeth, 'la Belle 'Amilton', would see future influence, not only in the French court, but with Louis himself. Such matters were still in the future, however. For now, it was George Hamilton who would be the leading light of the family.

The younger George Hamilton, who had enjoyed the pleasures of Charles's court after the Restoration, had not had the courtly success of his brother. That is not to say that he was not successful in his own right, but his influence with Charles and the English court seems less important than that of his older brother. For George, however, this would matter little, since it would be his reputation with the French court that would determine his success. He had started as a page to the king. After the Restoration he had intrigued and tasted the pleasures of English courtly society. His younger brother Anthony later related his intrigues with the women of the court in his biography of *Gramont*. George finally married, in 1665, one of Anne Hyde's, wife to the Duke of York, maids of honour. This was Frances

Jennings, a sister of Sarah Jennings, the future Duchess of Marlborough. Frances would also have her part to play as the Irish question emerged.[50]

Once more a change of religion was involved. Rather than another Hamilton becoming a Protestant, undoubtedly much to the relief of Lady Hamilton, in this instance the bride became a Catholic. It is this decision perhaps that is indicative of the direction that George Hamilton's career would follow. His refusal to follow the path taken by his older brother would have repercussions in terms of his chosen calling, that of the military.

George had entered the King's Life Guards in 1667, firstly as a cornet (a lieutenant) but later rising to the rank of major with a view to spending a large part of his life in the army – a busy profession for the times, if an inherently dangerous one.[51] For a Catholic, even in Restoration England, a life in the English army was by no means guaranteed. Catholic officers wishing to pursue a career had little real choice but to serve abroad. Even in the early 1660s, English officers, and indeed Parliament, would not accept Catholics in the army establishment. Various oaths and acts would eventually preclude Catholics from holding public office in England. These matters would remain an underlying theme of Charles's entire reign. During the 1660s, however, even cautious attempts to show toleration toward Catholicism were met with suspicion. Worse was to follow in the 1670s; for now, when Charles attempted to dispense with the requirements of one act, Parliament would respond by issuing another. In 1663, for instance, the introduction of the Conventicle Act required Charles to attempt to banish all Jesuits and Catholic priests. Ultimately difficult and to a large degree ignored in some parts of England, the call for such action would be repeated in the years to follow.

Fear of Catholicism had much to do with a deep-rooted fear of absolutist rule in the French mould. This in turn was fuelled by the implications of religious disorder, possibly leading to another civil war in the minds of many, something the entire country feared. In addition there were general concerns over French intentions and power. Parliamentary fears were also fuelled by circumstance. The great fire of London in 1666 was blamed in many quarters on rebellious Catholics. The Dutch naval war fought in the late 1660s had Catholic conspiracy cast as its source; indeed it was during a naval battle in that conflict that Cormac MacCarthy, son of Donough, was killed by cannon shot while standing beside the Duke of York.[52] As Dutch ships sailed to the mouth of the Thames in 1667, the blame was squarely placed on the shoulders of Vice Admiral Sir Edward Spragge for reason of his being an 'Irish Papist'. Many in Parliament felt that important and influential positions had been taken 'out of faithful men's hands into Papists'.[53]

To this end, Parliamentary proclamations against Catholics were reinforced and those who refused the Oath of Allegiance, which denied the Pope's right to depose kings, and the Oath of Supremacy, which acknowledged the king as the head of the Church of England, were to be disarmed. In effect, such proclamations meant that devout Catholics could not serve in the English military, and even the Irish military held little hope for service since it was still dominated by Cromwellians.[54]

In September 1667 Charles's Royal Guards regiments were purged of Catholics, their dismissal being based on the fact that they had refused to take the Oath of Supremacy. English and Irish Catholic officers had then little choice by the 1660s but to serve abroad. Indeed, Charles encouraged this to a large extent by declaring that they could leave England as they pleased, to countries where they could 'earn their bread by their swords' until such times as English service could be re-established.[55] For George Hamilton, however, the matter was far from complete. Already assumed to be a leader of the cashiered men, probably through his lineage since his experience at this time must have been lacking, he was secretly approached and persuaded that dismissed men would be welcomed in French service – though as an English or Irish force.[56]

The need for troops in French service had less to do with political allegiance with England than it did with the urgent requirement for men to fight Louis's latest campaign. Louis's wars of the 1660s and 1670s, unlike his protracted later conflicts, were fought with the French concept of *gloire* or personal glory foremost in his mind.[57] These wars formed part of the early years of the French king's reign, his youthful impetuous nature tending to add credence to his relentless pursuit of his war aims. There was more than glory at stake, however; the long war with Spain had ended in 1659 after the Treaty of the Pyrenees had been signed. The result was that Louis had a Spanish wife, the Infanta Marie Thérèse, daughter of the Spanish King Philip IV from his first marriage, and thus heir to the riches and lands of Spain. The treaty had, in fact, catered for this somewhat dangerous oversight; Marie's claims to her Spanish inheritance would be removed upon the payment of half-a-million *escudos* to France; but this sum was never paid. For Louis, this meant that he could somewhat shrewdly state that his royal wife still had a claim with regard to her Spanish inheritance; and the Spanish Netherlands that the Dutch had earned in their own war of independence with the Spanish were certainly a prize worth having.

By 1665, however, Philip IV had died, leaving the infant five-year-old Carlos II on the throne, a son from his second marriage. Louis could not openly argue with the succession but he did maintain that his wife had continued inheritance rights over Carlos in terms of Spanish property. Such intrigues are of course typical of seventeenth-century treaty negotiations and their aftermath, and in any event it is unlikely that Louis would ever have agreed to a covenant wherein the divine right of royal inheritance was even remotely questioned. In many respects, this was the opportunity that Louis had been waiting for. According to the law of the Spanish Netherlands, the daughter from a first marriage, in this case Marie, had inheritance rights over Carlos in terms of Spanish property; in other words large tracts of land in the Spanish Netherlands could become the property of France. Louis would use this claim as a prelude to war. In 1667 he began to build an 80,000 strong army in preparation for renewed war with Spain.

As Louis's plans developed, he anticipated aid from the Dutch. The French naturally expected Dutch help. Had Louis not supported them in the Spanish war? Had he not stood by them against the English and helped defend their borders? Indeed, it had been French support of the Dutch during their war with the English that had precipitated a recall of English troops then serving in France, although this request was rebutted by Parliament for fear of the return of armed Catholic regiments to England.[58] At the outset, Louis little expected a Dutch refutation of his plans. The first moves took place in 1667 when the ageing Marshal Turenne once more led French troops against their traditional enemy, the Spanish. The young King Louis XIV watched from his carriage as events unfolded before him, together with his wife *and* his mistress. Louis basked in his conquering glory, as the ruthless French war machine flattened the Spanish defences. There were few battles, principally small skirmishes, the war being mainly composed of sieges. These were relatively short endeavours and, by the end of 1667, the result of the campaign did not seem in doubt.

The Dutch, however, had become concerned with regard to recent events and were not as reliable as Louis had anticipated. With growing realisation, they began to fear that a weak Spanish neighbour was infinitely preferable to a strong French one, led by an aggressive king with dreams of conquest and glory and apparently with the intention of controlling Europe. The Dutch debated their reaction to the war, fearing French ambition.

They had been fighting the English at sea, but French aggression created the need for a treaty with England by mid-1667. By the start of 1668 the Dutch, English and Swedish formed the Triple Alliance, threatening the French with a war that would re-establish the borders initially set by the Treaty of the Pyrenees if Louis continued his aggressive moves. Incensed by apparent Dutch betrayal, Louis concluded a treaty with Spain. He would not easily forget the matter, however.

***

In the midst of his Spanish campaign Louis's urgent requirement for men had borne fruit. In the late 1660s two regiments left England for French service, one under the command of Colonel Henry Staniers and the other, a Scottish regiment, under Lord George Douglas, which had in one form or another been founded for French service in 1633.[59]

Returning to George Hamilton, who had been offered command of a similar regiment of Irish Catholics that would fight in French service, there was now a chance to gain the military and command experience that was not otherwise available in England. The imminent appointment would create consternation in the Spanish court and, perhaps, resentment in England. Parliament did not want closer ties with France; both the Dutch and Spanish were at the time considering treaties with England and, indeed, the Spanish complained to both Charles and his brother James, Duke of York, that the French seemed to be financing the plans and gaining English troops to whom they themselves should have been entitled.[60] Charles, who, it seemed, had been playing a dangerous political game, insisted that the endeavours of what he considered to be Irish 'mercenary soldiers' were none of his affair. He remained unconcerned over the events, while unofficially reassuring the French that Dutch efforts to obtain the men would remain unsuccessful, even communicating his thanks to Louis for his aid and for the naming of the regiment. The *Gendarmes Anglais* was born. Charles and Louis, outwardly strange bedfellows, were becoming closer than ever in political terms.[61]

Ruvigny and Louvois, son of le Tellier, and the new French Minister for War, both still mindful of the understandable resentment of the English Parliament, advised speed in terms of the preparations required to secure the troops; in fact, the Spanish were doing everything that their political will could muster to stir Parliament, which would meet in October 1667, into action. Rumours were already spreading and parliamentary officials had met Arlington, stating their intent to take their grievances to Charles and re-direct the troops to Spanish Flanders.[62]

Certainly, when Parliament did eventually meet, these matters were paramount, but their only direct action in the matter was to argue successfully that no additional men or horses, outside of those already mustered, should be allowed to leave the country.[63] This action in retrospect seems almost timid and, although the original intent may have been watered down somewhat through Charles's direct influence, there is also an indication that getting rid of many of the troublesome Catholic officers might actually have been seen as an advantage in England, so long as they could be retrieved if matters took a turn for the worse with the French.

George Hamilton, however, reported to Louvois that parliamentary measures, although stopping short of disbandment, had in fact had a serious effect on his attaining the number of men required. Even lack of horses remained a problem. Louvois, despite Ruvigny's advice to let matters settle for a while, encouraged Hamilton to send men across in small parties, at the very least to keep matters in motion; the longer Hamilton stayed in England, the more difficult it would become for troops to reach France. Louvois also advised him that French horses would be just as good as English.[64]

Hamilton agreed in principle, but still delayed. But by the beginning of February 1668, with monetary aid from Louis, George Hamilton reached Ostend with 100 men and even some horses.[65] A company at least had reached France; these numbers, however, would not be adequate in terms of forming a battalion for French service. An indication of Charles's wholehearted and consistent approval of the scheme is given through Hamilton's gaining of a knighthood prior to his departure.[66] He would henceforth be known as Sir George Hamilton, a title which his father had so nobly borne in the service of both Charles II and Charles I; indeed, John Evelyn the famous diarist would later describe the younger Hamilton as 'a valiant and worthy gentleman'.[67]

There is evidence to suggest that Anthony Hamilton also accompanied his older brother at this time; in his early twenties, he, too, would attempt to forge a military career, and also, being a devout Catholic, his prospects whilst remaining in England would have been somewhat limited.[68] Indeed, he must have welcomed a return to France which, although not the country of his birth, was where he had been educated and reached manhood. To some extent, the journey must have seemed like a homecoming and an acceptable escape from the growing anti-Catholic sentiment, fires and plagues that marked this part of Charles's reign. He could thus rejoin French society.

For the French the prospect of foreign and indeed Irish troops was nothing new. Irish troops had fought in French service even before the 1650s. With the arrival of Hamilton on French soil, those present of Scottish descent were incorporated into the *Gendarmes Ecossais*, a regiment that had been in French service for so long that it was 'Scottish' in name only and by the fact that its commander was traditionally a noble-born Scot. This had changed in 1667 when Louis himself became the nominal captain of the regiment, which formed part of his bodyguard.[69] For the balance of the troops, honours awaited. However, the group remained small in number; indeed, with the filtering of those Scots present into the *Gendarmes Ecossais*, Hamilton was at less than company strength. Nevertheless, a company was ostensibly formed and named the *Compagnie des Gendarmes Anglais*, the next English regiment in French service and one that would earn itself significant honours in the years to follow in a manner similar to many of the foreign regiments serving in French service.[70] Louis himself would once more be the stylised 'Capitaine' of the company, with Hamilton serving more pragmatically as captain-lieutenant.[71] The flag was more ostentatious than those of the French regiments, showing a symbolic sun toward which eight eagles soared.[72] For Louis, the 'Sun King', there can have been no finer form of flattery.

For Sir George Hamilton, it seemed that the immediate future at least was secure. This fact and the familial connection to all things French may help explain his next action; he asked that he might become a French citizen.[73] The request was wholeheartedly granted. For Hamilton, whose reasoning perhaps had more to do with reducing the degree of embarrassment to Charles, the appeal was an important one. He could not now be used as a direct extension of English politique. Parliament could not touch him. He would remain loyal to Charles, but would not provide an embarrassment, should the matter of English troops in French service be at issue. His actions are perhaps unsurprising. Although he had spent part of his life at the French court during the years of exile, he could now also practise his religion freely. He spoke fluent French and could embark on the career of his choosing. For Anthony Hamilton, too, the less complicated aspects of French service must have been attractive.

One year later, Louis would compliment the services of his Gendarmes Anglais. In the presence of Louis and his queen and most of the notables of the French court at the Bois de Boulogne, the company was reviewed, along with Louis's other guards regiments and companies. The Gendarmes Anglais were commended, and Hamilton was given a pension of 2,000 crowns per year in addition to his pay.[74] The only complaints that seem to have been levelled against the company were few and slight; the great Condé had disagreed with their hunting in the grounds of Chantilly, and others had complained of the Irish hunting habits, a minor infraction perhaps, and not serious enough to annoy Louis.[75] The helpful presence of Hamilton's sister Elizabeth and her husband of course aided matters at court. Had George needed any help with the Sun King and the court, their authority would certainly have paid dividends. As it was, it seemed that he had become quite successful in his own right. Financial matters, in true Hamilton style, would become difficult to manage, however.

Louis's pension to Hamilton in addition to his military pay appears to have been insufficient. The perennial familial financial problems dogged Sir George as it had done his father. He returned briefly to England in 1670 in an attempt to secure the pension that Charles had promised at the time of his marriage. Louis, hearing of his difficulties, sent him money to assist in his journey, in addition sending him a message in the hope that Charles and he could assist in his making a living.[76]

On the European stage, Louis now fed his political ambition rather than conquer Spanish lands. Europe had enjoyed a relatively quiet period since the Treaty of Aix-la-Chapelle in 1668 and the forming of the Triple Alliance against him. By 1670, however, he would break the pact, first by paying off the Swedes and then by agreeing to the secret Treaty of Dover with Charles II. This to some extent was very much in Charles's interest. It allowed for payments to be made to the almost empty English coffers on the basis that Charles would help Louis with his impending war with the Dutch. Due to the nature of its second condition, the continued secrecy of the treaty became more critical. When the time was right in England, Charles would announce his conversion to the Catholic faith. Whether Charles was serious or not about his potential conversion, its discussion could ensure the presence of a French army to support him if he converted and, of course, Louis would secure a British ally. For Charles's part, he would not allow himself to suffer the fate of his father whatever the cost, and if this meant playing a political entertainment with the French and the English Parliament then so be it. The Dutch, who had also been in supposedly secret talks with Louis, would be completely outwitted and war would become inevitable. To a large extent the influence of Charles's sister Henriette helped broker the agreement, despite the political machination of both parties. Present with her party at Dover were the Count and Countess de Gramont; Gramont it seemed still remained a very potent symbol in Anglo-French relations.[77]

Matters of greater significance would overshadow the negotiations, however. On returning to France, Henriette would die under certainly suspicious, if not mysterious, circumstances, although some modern historians consider that she had a significant illness rather than poison or similar means being involved. The tale of murder in this regard, and the fractious nature of the relationships with her husband, Louis's younger brother, and her alleged affair with Louis form a story in themselves. In the end, James Hamilton, who had so faithfully carried out his duties for both Charles and his sister, was present at the post mortem, foul play having been suspected.[78] One source would indicate that James was present at Madame's funeral although others state that he would have been in Italy at this time.[79]

Henriette's death caused consternation in England. Rioters surrounded the French embassy and murder was the cry on the lips of the mob. Gramont attempted to pacify the vengeful feelings of the influential members of the court, such as the Duke of Buckingham, who appeared to be most perturbed with the entire affair. In the end Gramont would not only claim credit for calming Buckingham, but would accompany him to France in an attempt to talk of peace and a military alliance. Had the Treaty of Dover been widely known at this time, then matters might have been entirely different. Had Buckingham known, for instance, that he was negotiating a treaty that meant little to the already satisfied French, who had in effect obtained agreement with England on all the conditions that they required, the repercussions in England would have been devastating.[80] Gramont continued in his position as French envoy to the court of Charles II. Both he and the Hamiltons were now intrinsically connected to the politics and military aspects of the war that would follow.

*Chapter 5*

# The Irish at War 1671–1685

By 1672 Louis's preparations for the Dutch war were complete. A French army of over 100,000 men lay in wait. True to the word of his alliance, Charles's forces fired the opening shots with a naval attack in March. By May French troops were on the move. The terms of Louis's treaty meant that, by the early 1670s, he could recruit English and Irish troops for French service in a manner similar to that carried out in the 1650s. The agreement was not, however, entirely based on political goodwill; Parliament's insistence on the removal of Catholics from the military forced Charles to relocate many officers from the British army, as had been done with George Hamilton.

In April 1671 Hamilton had been appointed Colonel of the Gendarmes Anglais. He requested and obtained permission to raise a regiment of Irish troops. These men had been similarly cashiered or prevented from pursuing a military career in England due to fears over Catholicism. It was men such as this, perhaps inexperienced, yet enthusiastic for French service, whom Sir George Hamilton hoped to attract. The *Regiment d'infanterie Irlandais* was to be comprised of fifteen companies each of one hundred men.

The Treaty of Dover required that Charles supply and effectively sustain up to 6,000 men in French service, should a war begin with the Dutch. An exemption, however, existed within the treaty that permitted a reduction to 4,000 should conditions dictate that Charles was unable to supply the requisite amount of troops, either through Parliamentary activity or due to the relative cost to the English crown. Buckingham's treaty, despite the bluster of the recent debate with Gramont, actually alluded to a similar agreement. For now, the secrecy of the Treaty of Dover inadvertently remained intact through the activities of Buckingham.[1]

Charles was indeed in financial trouble, despite French aid; he requested that the funds to be directed toward the troops destined for Louis should instead be invested in his navy, the arm that would in fact directly support French efforts in the initial period of the coming war. As recompense Louis was invited to raise a force of 8-10,000 men in the British Isles, though these would of course have to be maintained by the French. Louis immediately

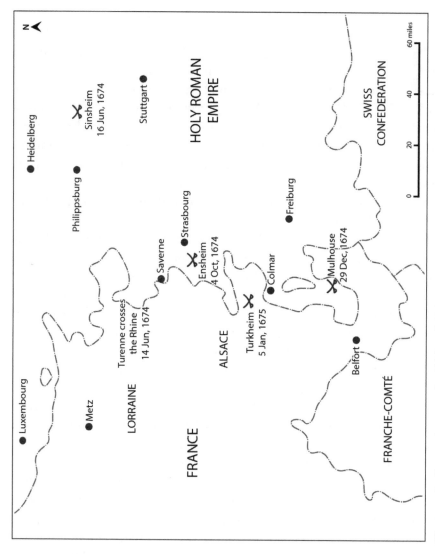

Turenne's Campaign on the Rhine 1674–75.

agreed, taking up the offer and bringing 2,000 English troops initially, along with nobles such as the Duke of Monmouth, to France. Louis now had an English regiment at his disposal and was keen, in the spirit of his agreement with Charles, to supplement those meagre Irish and Scots forces that he already had. Another secret treaty signed in February 1672 outlined that Charles was in fact no longer bound by the previous agreement with the French, but would have to allow for the provision of recruits in the years to follow. Charles agreed, though could not have foreseen the issues that lay ahead.[2]

The result of Charles's decision would have repercussions for the Irish. By mid-1671 he gave orders to the Lords Justices of Ireland that they should allow the raising of a regiment of Irish foot to the tune of 1,500 men for the service of the King of France. The intermediary and chief recruiting 'agent' would be Sir George Hamilton, Colonel of the Gendarmes Anglais. Still fearing the wrath of Parliament, Charles further ordered that it would not be prudent to have the matter made public and recruitment and transportation of the regiment were to be carried out with the utmost secrecy.[3] Under the circumstances, this request seemed difficult to implement, and it is likely that both Spanish and Dutch agents or indeed their sympathisers in Ireland would eventually become aware of the scheme. Nevertheless, Hamilton continued with the vital task ahead. He recruited the 1,500 men required.

The conditions set out by Charles were not exacting but were in line with English as well as French requirements. The men were all to be of the required age and sturdy, clothed and armed with a sword and belt; all other arms and munitions would be of French supply. By September the Irish regiment was ready to disembark. George Hamilton's dealings in the entire affair were noted by at least one source as 'diligent', 'discreet' and respectful with all parties involved.[4]

Upon arrival in France, the men were to swear their service to Louis in all things save acting against King Charles. Should there be conflicting loyalties due to future treaty or disagreement, Louis promised that the troops would be released, free to march to any port and sail home.[5] In reality, abandonment by one's patron country or monarch usually meant a surplus of poverty-stricken and hungry soldiers roaming the countryside with wild abandon, but the promise of the French king was enough to convince most of the troops at the time.

Both George and Anthony Hamilton had been present in Ireland for purposes of recruiting during the spring and summer of 1671. We know this because in May, a curious incident occurred at Dublin Castle. Early on the morning of the 19th a fire had broken out in a storehouse. By the time it was discovered it was evident that the storehouse itself would be lost, and that it contained gunpowder. In order to save the castle, however, it was clear that a number of adjoining buildings would have to be destroyed – by the use of the powder barrels, these of course being stored in the burning building. Anthony Hamilton and his cousin Lord John Butler entered the burning storehouse, undoubtedly at great personal risk, obtained enough powder to do the job, and subsequently set about destroying the adjoining buildings. This act, which although perhaps uncharacteristic of the more modest Anthony, had saved Dublin Castle, the seat of the Irish Parliament.[6]

By September 1671 the Irish recruits were ready to leave. George Hamilton would be praised for his conduct and carriage with all parties concerned with the affair. Indeed it seemed that this Irishman alone, lacking the overzealous nature of his older brother and the quiet reserve of Anthony Hamilton, left an excellent impression with all with whom he came into contact, be they Catholic or Protestant, French or English; even with those diametrically opposed to Hamilton's point of view, it seemed that his manner appealed to all.[7] There were, however, still problems despite the apparent secrecy regarding the Irish regiment's recruitment; as in 1667, the Spanish had not only become aware of the scheme, but were once more disturbed by its potential. Unlike the previous occasion, however, the troops did not just form a company, around 100 men; instead an entire regiment was involved and Spanish fears centred on the availability of such troops to the French who could reinforce their substantial army, a force which had already proved its aggressive intent in the Netherlands. The Condé de Molina, the Spanish ambassador in London, once more expressed his disapproval and concern on behalf of the Spanish empire. Charles, in feigned ignorance with regard to the activities of George Hamilton for purposes of assuaging the anger of the Spanish, assured Molina that Hamilton had no express permission to carry out such activities. Arlington would further assure Molina that matters relating to Roman Catholics who may once have been in the employ of the king and his friends in Ireland, but who were now in the service of the French court, could not be counted as matters which were the responsibility of the English crown, and indeed no articles had been breached in the entire affair. Political spin thrived within the English court of the seventeenth century.[8]

There are conflicting reports with regard to Louis's satisfaction with the Irish or lack thereof. One source describes the regiment as being very good, with excellent officers who were of 'fine stature' and 'good birth'.[9]

Another English report cited the Irish troops in French service as being so ill received that they were left in garrison.[10] In reality, the former seems more likely, as events would prove. Indeed the use of foreign troops, or even French troops, in garrison duty was commonplace; the reference is probably misunderstood and, bearing in mind the nature of Parliament's interest in foreign troops serving abroad, perhaps intentionally so. Hamilton would, however, have some concerns with the French authorities.

In mainland Europe, Louis prepared to unleash the French army on the Dutch, the ultimate victims of his political ambition. Three massive armies headed for the United Dutch Provinces; Turenne would lead 50,000 men north along the left bank of the Meuse while Condé would lead a large force along the right bank and Luxembourg would lead an army of French allies in Westphalia; 100,000 French troops would face a small Dutch force of 40,000 men. These were, however, mostly dispersed in garrisons, and were certainly not prepared for the French onslaught. Caught in the midst of the war to follow, the young William, Prince of Orange, led around 14,000 Dutch troops. In July, he would be named Dutch Stadtholder with executive authority, replacing the slaughtered De Witt brothers as bloody rioting shook Amsterdam. Civil unrest would become commonplace as the French advanced, taking more and more territory with apparently little to stand in their way.

In June the Irish regiment under Hamilton joined the French army, after Turenne's successful passage of the Rhine.[11] Hamilton and his men therefore had not been present during the taking of the many fortresses along the river, although they were present with Louis at Utrecht, which was taken by the end of June. Sidney Godolphin, an Englishman serving with the foreign troops wrote concisely of the competitive situation in which many of the officers found themselves, together with an interesting perspective on Louis himself:

1. From the Camp within two days of Utrecht June 28 1672
    Instead of talking to you of the conquests of the army which in themselves are vast (yet little if you saw the pitiful defence that was made by the Dutch) I will entertain you with the greatness of the court here which in my opinion is at least as considerable. For, my Lord, 'tis not to be imagined the infinite number of brave and knowing officers that are about the King nor what a world of young gentlemen of quality there are in the army perpetually ready to seek all occasions where 'tis possible to get any reputation or learn any

experience; besides that the King himself does really distinguish very well of men's merits and seldom fails to reward those that deserve it before they expect it; he is very careful to provide for the convenience and for the subsistence of the soldiers and very painful in his own person, always marching on horseback in the heat and in the rain, all this that I say is really due to him and more of this kind, yet I am of opinion that if the Prince of Condé had not been hurt, the Army had been yet farther advanced than it is, the Army when the King commands in person seeming most commonly but to receive these places which before had yielded upon the summons of the Prince of Condé or M. de Turenne.[12]

By July Turenne had reached Nijmegen. The Dutch, however, had not given up, as the French threatened Amsterdam itself. Louis's revenge was almost complete, though William's forces had one card left to play. The sluices and dams that held back the floodwaters from the Dutch countryside were opened; the resulting deluge bogged down French progress, just as the Dutch had hoped. The delay was well planned. Winter was about to set in, limiting strategic moves just as William's political manoeuvres had also come to fruition; troops from the Holy Roman Empire and neighbouring German states were about to come to the aid of the Dutch. In addition, Louis's alliance with England was by no means secure; Parliament, now realising the full import of an alliance with the French, was beginning to ask significant questions. Louis's European plan, as with his ground offensive, had become bogged down.

Turenne's forces were moved to Germany in an attempt to hold back Imperialist and Brandenburg troops who posed a considerable threat along the Rhine. The French invasion had lost momentum, although the war was far from over. Turenne, still active, and a real threat despite the presence of Dutch allies, entered the lands of the Elector of Brandenburg. The French troops' plunder of the towns and local countryside would eventually force the Elector to sue for peace.[13] Both Irish and English troops had been present during the Brandenburg operations. The Irish troops would spend the winter in Zutphen on the River Yssel.

Apparent success and popularity prior to arriving in France would, however, be shortlived. In winter quarters, the French war minister Louvois plagued Hamilton; indeed it seemed that the conduct of the Irish troops under their Irish commander was questionable at best. Louvois would complain with regard to the murder of a local burgher by one of Hamilton's men, although the Irishmen would plead their case, stating that that had been accidental.[14] In addition, Louvois would point to disorderly conduct amongst the Irish; they had allegedly stolen 'everything that came near them'. The value of such 'booty' would have to come out of Hamilton's pay.[15] Other men became involved in brawling with French troops.[16] The Irish, too, did little to help themselves, refusing to allow French counsel in their courts martial. The French described the officers involved as 'difficult to deal with'.[17]

Quarrels were widespread even inside the regiment. Gustavus Hamilton, brother of the Earl of Limerick (not to be confused with the later governor of Enniskillen) and Thomas Dongan, of the English regiment, would argue. Hamilton would temporarily suspend Dongan for his conduct in the affair, although many Irish officers would side with him, creating factions and a degree of internal strife.[18]

Problems of this nature would not have been isolated to Irish regiments in contrast with French troops. If the Irish quarrelled and in some cases seemed less professional in the eyes of the French there were many reasons, not least of which was the degree of intolerance on the part of members of the French court. The main reason for the restless nature of the Irish, we must assume, was that since the regiment had been recruited they had been involved in few actions during the war. Such inactivity would not last long. Winter quarters usually involved the raising of recruits to cater for desertion, death in battle and disease. For Hamilton in 1672 this task was made relatively simple, not only since the regiment had been newly raised but also since he was given the choice of around 400 men from the regiment of Roscommon. Once more, Louis would comment on the good order and quality of the foreign regiment in apparent contradiction of Louvois's concerns.[19]

In January 1673 Charles had also directed Essex, then Lord Lieutenant of Ireland, to give George Hamilton grace to recruit around 600 men for his regiment. The extent of the treaty with France was, of course, to be kept secret. By February George and Anthony Hamilton once more found themselves in Ireland; the secrecy of their mission, however, was debatable. French ships had been ordered to pick up the Irish troops in a remote corner of the County Kerry coast line. Their appearance instead at Kinsale gave the game away completely, and plans were set back for a time. Indeed, from this point on, matters in Ireland would prove more difficult, and the relative simplicity with which troops had so far had been raised would not last.

Eventually though, the troops were mustered; among the recruits was the thirty-year-old Justin MacCarthy, youngest son of Lord Muskerry, a young officer forced to seek his fortune in the Irish military serving in France, a man whose destiny in Ireland was entirely entwined with that of his cousins, the Hamiltons.[20]

By spring 1673 Hamilton's regiment received the orders that they had been waiting for. They were to join Turenne's forces on the Rhine, facing the troops of the Holy Roman Empire and the Elector of Brandenburg. There would be little time for internal disputes in the regiment now. Louis, in expectation of a glorious and ultimately victorious offensive, divided the French army into three elements for the campaign. He would personally lead one army along the Meuse with 40,000, whilst Condé would maintain pressure on the Dutch at Utrecht and Turenne's troops would cover the upper part of the River Rhine. Amongst the successes would be Louis's capture of Maastricht; the Dutch objective, however, was still inundated with floodwaters and relatively impassable to an attacking army. Turenne's thankless task consisted of a large-scale delaying action that would attempt to prevent the Imperial army linking up with its new Dutch allies.

Hamilton reached the army of Turenne by May. His new commander remarked that the foreign troops appeared 'very good' and well prepared for the service to follow.[21] Hamilton wrote to Secretary of State Williamson in England in June, relating his contentment with the situation. His only concern was the degree of inactivity that his troops were still forced to bear, perhaps illustrating the difficulties that had led both to Louvois's complaints and strife within the regiment. Hamilton displayed little concern that Turenne's force numbered just over 20,000 men; indeed he would remark on the degree of confidence that both he and his troops had in the general, believing him to be 'invincible'.[22]

Henri de la Tour d'Auvergne, vicomte de Turenne, was over sixty years old when the Dutch war began. He had been a soldier for most of his life, starting his career alongside his renowned uncle Maurice of Nassau at the age of fourteen. He had for most of his youth been a Protestant, although he converted to Catholicism in 1668, and had actually started his military career with the Dutch before quickly entering French service. He had first shown his capabilities during the Thirty Years' War, and by the end of that conflict was one of the dominant generals in the field.

Now, having fought across Europe in every major war involving the French, he was still at his peak; Napoleon himself would later remark that his genius grew more dominant as he aged. By this stage of his life he had become expert at the war of manoeuvre or 'strategic evasion'. To some extent this meant *war without battle*. The inefficient nature of firearms and, to some extent, drill, somewhat defines the nature of battle in this period, as we shall examine later. Memories of the Thirty Years' War remained fresh in many minds and the costly results of battle both in terms of casualties and desertion proved prohibitive for many armies and their ability to engage in protracted campaigns. Had one general even wanted a fight, there was never any guarantee that his opposite number would comply, as battle was a last resort for most. Many armies would simply walk away until a more advantageous position could be found, until an edge could be achieved, and even then many generals would fight only reluctantly. A more contemporary and in some ways admirable manner of engaging the enemy was to cut lines of communication or to outmanoeuvre the opponent into an area where he could neither sustain nor stabilise his troops, thus forcing a retreat. Feints and decoys could also be used to pull the enemy from advantageous positions. The general employing such strategies, however, needed to be aware of logistical support and have a clear perception of the potential speed of his own men and the relative position of the enemy, thus preventing his own force being outmanoeuvred by a more methodical opponent. Repeated strategic advantage could thus create the climate for final victory in a campaign without a shot having been fired.

Noted generals of the time were respected for their ability to wage war, although many had fought in few battles. Those that did occur were usually decisive, since months of manoeuvre and strategy had been used to strike a single devastating blow. That being said, many wars that resulted in stalemate were due to the matched wits of the opponents, constantly manoeuvring around each other. Indeed it seemed that shoe leather in many campaigns would become a more prized commodity than gunpowder. For Turenne's part he had become an expert in this type of warfare, as had a few of his contemporaries. He had obtained a superior grasp of battle through his Thirty Years' War experience and, unlike many accomplished generals of the time, was prepared to engage in it where necessary. If a gap existed that defined the balance between the manoeuvre warfare expert and the accomplished battle tactician, Turenne would fill the role admirably for many. His fame and expertise appealed to those seeking experience. Two young soldiers serving with him, John Churchill, the future Duke of Marlborough, then with the Gendarmes Anglais, and Claude Hector, later Duke of Villars, would clash on opposing sides during the War of the Spanish Succession thirty years later. Both would learn significant lessons and masterstrokes from the veteran campaigner and master strategist.[23]

Although commanders wanted to avoid battle until one or other had gained the upper hand, when it became inevitable, tactical considerations became important. The latter part of the seventeenth century would see a period of transition in terms of military thinking. The era that marked the rise of the nation's standing army would also see the demise of matchlock and pike and the advent of technological and military improvements with the introduction of flintlock musket and bayonet. However, the changeover would be a slow and expensive one and, during the 1670s, changes were for the most part limited. On a tactical rather than operational or strategic level, warfare was entering a significant new stage, limited only by the specific nature of weaponry and its uses. Despite being described as part of a military revolution of sorts, the period would be more evolutionary, at least in terms of tactical innovation and technology. In Louis's French army, where change through the course of the late seventeenth century would be slower than that of England or the Dutch states, there would be a steady reaction to the advantages of infantry firepower. The infantry pike would be replaced by socket bayonet, reliable flintlock would replace archaic matchlock and even methods of firing the muskets of the infantry battalion would undergo significant change as platoon firing began to be considered over firing by ranks.

Infantry formed the largest part of most European armies, around 80 per cent in the French army. Although cavalry could invest a fortress and, indeed, inflict a devastating blow upon poorly motivated infantry, the foot soldier formed the building block of the army, assaulting breaches, garrisoning fortresses and forming basic elements of manoeuvre. Many of the infantry methods used were dictated by the technology and nature of the weaponry in use. By the late seventeenth century, a mixture of matchlock musket and pike still dominated the battalion. Both had a chequered history. The pike had seen action since the Middle Ages when it dominated the battlefield, but its use in the late 1600s was being relegated slowly to that of defence against attacking cavalry. With the reduction in use of cavalry lances and the advent of the pistol, the pike began to reduce in length to around eleven to fourteen feet, with a reinforced iron tip. Many French experts, including Vauban, opposed the continued use of the weapon as firearms became more critical on the battlefield and extended 'firefights' became more frequent when armies eventually did meet.[24]

The musket of the time was a smoothbore muzzle-loader that had been present in one form or another for some time. The matchlock musket, certainly the most common in the 1670s but whose numbers would start to dwindle towards the end of the century, suffered from a number of distinct disadvantages. A lit match-cord, usually smouldering hemp or similar material soaked in nitrate solution to permit a slow burn, would be clamped in the firing mechanism. Pulling the trigger then snapped the match into the powder pan, setting off the powder charge in the smoothbore barrel and firing the musket ball. The weapon required a very complex reloading procedure and suffered from a number of problems related to the match, not least of which was the fact that rain could place a significant restraint on a battalion's aggressive intent.

The matchlock musketeers also carried measured charges of powder in a bandolier, known to the English as the 'twelve apostles', which turned the infantryman with a lit match in his hand into a potential firebomb. There was, in addition, a total of thirty-three separate reloading actions to carry out before the musket was ready to fire again, all while balancing match, powder – and nerves – in the face of enemy fire or attack. The importance of training and drill is obvious, if the battalion was expected to fire more than once in a battle. Maximum range could be 200 yards or more, although effective range was more like eighty yards. The psychology of battle, therefore, meant that firefights were close and personal affairs, at least if either side wanted to do any sort of damage via volley fire. In addition, two discrete schools of thought were in place. The French traditionally favoured the charge, and melee, while the Dutch and, eventually, the English would begin to consider other experimental methods in terms of firing by platoons, such that a constant fire could be maintained through sections of the line shooting in sequence; the pressure from continuous fire being more advantageous than single, infrequent firings in terms of upsetting the opposing formation's integrity.

These relative disadvantages were addressed to a large extent through the development of the flintlock musket, which would gradually supplant its less efficient cousin. The change would take time, however; much of the problem for the French at least would centre on economics and the capital outlay required from regimental colonels to make the change. The flintlock design relied on a piece of flint in the mechanism rather than matchcord. When triggered this would strike an iron plate and ignite the powder in the pan. The approach was more easily handled as there was no live match-cord and thus less danger of accidents with loose powder; indeed, the new musket could be slung or otherwise manhandled much more easily, and only required around twenty individual movements to reload, allowing an increased rate of fire with trained troops of two to three shots per minute. The introduction of paper cartridges also removed the dangerous loose powder practices. Pre-packaged before battle, the ball would be wrapped with a charge of powder, the soldier would bite the end off, prime the pan with powder and ram the ball into the barrel, together with remaining powder and paper wadding.[25]

The pike, too, was changing. Plug bayonets appeared in the 1670s. These were inserted into the barrel of the musket, a fine idea in terms of arming the entire battalion with short 'pikes' for defending against cavalry, although the position of the weapon completely removed the ability of the musketeer to fire. Socket bayonet designs that locked in place *around* the muzzle, enabling the musketeer to continue to load and fire, would appear by the late 1680s, although the pikeman would not entirely disappear yet. With the dwindling numbers of pikemen in the infantry battalions as the century wore on, and little universal adoption of the bayonet, the problem of how to defend the musket-carrying troops against cavalry remained. By the 1660s the French army battalion typically had one pikeman for every three musketeers; by the 1680s and 1690s the ratio had shrunk still further to one pike per four muskets, making it increasingly difficult to defend the entire battalion against enemy horse. The French had experimented with lining the ranks with a single row of pikes, *fraising* the battalion, although the more common method by the 1670s was to place elements of pikemen on the flanks of the battalion as well as in the centre. The options were not perfect, however.[26]

To understand this it is necessary to grasp the layout of the infantry unit. At this time, the infantry battalion itself was normally made up of four to five 'ranks' deep and around 120 'files' wide, giving a rough average of 600 men, although this varied greatly. Two battalions normally made up a regiment, although this was not always possible in wartime, and distinction between battalion and regiment is not always clear-cut in period sources. Generally officers would stand at the battalion's rear but sometimes in front when attacking. The files were separated for practical reasons. Loose powder and lit match was a lethal enough combination without keeping men packed tightly together. This meant that matchlock-armed troops had to maintain safe distances between ranks and files, typically six paces for ranks and one to three for files, one pace being roughly equal to two and a half feet (the standard measurement of an infantry drill sergeant's pace-stick remains at 30 inches today). The nature of fire combat, and the unwieldy matchlock, meant that the battalion could only fire when halted. Protracted exchanges took place at thirty to eighty yards until one side broke.

The battalion would normally have twelve or thirteen companies of fifty to sixty men each. From the beginning of the century the practice of the infantry counter-march had been popular. In this method, five or six ranks of musketeers, running from end to end, would form up. With matchlocks, gaps would be required due to loose match, but these would also allow men to move back and forward through the files, running from front to back. After firing, the front rank would move to the back of the file and commence reloading; as the second rank fired they would then move to the rear and so on, until the original rank was back at the front, and ready to fire. The method required training and discipline and only permitted one rank to fire at a time. The battalion could retreat or move forward depending on whether musketeers moved from front to rear to reload or rear to front to fire. Slower reloading meant that battalions needed to remain 'thick' in terms of ranks, to keep up a steady fire.

By the 1680s these methods were becoming outdated. The French adopted the 'fire by ranks' method where the first four ranks would kneel as the fifth fired over their head. Then the fourth rank would fire as the fifth reloaded, then third, then second and so on. A volley could be made more devastating by firing two ranks at once with one stooping as the other stood, the French having no intervals 'between' files for muskets to fire through; even this method, however, was being superseded rapidly by the Dutch and English who, by the end of the century, were adopting methods such as platoon firing. With this, the infantry battalion was divided into eighteen platoons, in turn grouped into three *firings*, with close intervals and only three ranks. Each *firing* included platoons along the length of the battalion. One *firing* would shoot simultaneously with three ranks, the third shooting through intervals in the second, and the first kneeling. In real terms this meant that more muskets were brought to bear at any given time.[27]

The French, however, were slow to grasp the developments, unlike other European countries. They would not adopt paper cartridges fully until the 1700s and flintlocks, although seeing limited introduction in the 1670s, would not be universally adopted until 1699, due to financial constraints and the political ramifications of poor French designs in the early days of development. French troops were still using methods such as firing by ranks in the eighteenth century.[28] The French were also firm believers in the infantry charge, a facet of the battlefield which, until the more complex developments of the latter part of the century, usually succeeded if troops were well trained and disciplined. The charge was something French troops excelled at, and thus their preferences may have hindered development of alternative tactics, at least until the advent of more effective and consistent firing systems and regimens meant that charging a well-trained and organised line became very expensive in casualties.[29]

This type of combat was close, deadly, and strained the nerves of the troops to breaking point. It is easy to see why so much lay in the hands of the officer who had to encourage the men, preserve good morale and, most of all, keep steady and controlled volleys of fire going for as long as possible, all this while attempting to avoid being shot from the saddle himself. The focus in the French and English armies was on training, both to increase the efficiency of troops and improve their morale in battle. In France the requirement for regular drill within individual regiments was seen as critical. It highlighted the importance of order, training and command within the battalion. Drill was also used to instil rules of movement into the troops so that they could manoeuvre, deploy and retire when necessary. The French ethos was more concerned with maintaining discipline, efficiency and order, since this could physically win battles before bloody close-range combat ever took place. Indeed, the French felt that it took five or six years to create a good infantry regiment in comparison with one year for cavalry.[30]

Cavalry's primary function on the late seventeenth-century battlefield was to defeat enemy horse, and then concentrate on infantry and guns. Although it could never replace infantry, its ability to charge home before heavy casualties could be inflicted was seen as a distinct advantage. Although, by the latter part of the century, the cavalry sword was invariably used in the charge, some remnant of harassing fire from cavalry pistols may have been included, again showing the transitional nature of tactics at this time. Dragoons were also a major feature of the battlefield: being part light cavalrymen and part musketeers, they could serve as highly mobile infantry or be used to skirmish against exposed flanks, usually using flintlocks. Troops or companies of mounted troops were formed from thirty-five to sixty men. The main projectile fired by the artillery of the period was solid shot, although grapeshot and canister were also used. The late seventeenth-century artillery piece was invariably cumbersome and difficult to move once battle had commenced. The French system, as in other areas of its military establishment, suffered from a lack of standardisation and many different calibres were in use. Artillery was still in its infancy, however, as an active arm of the military and was frequently organised by authorities outside the army. The men handling the guns could be a mixture of hired civilians, officers and infantrymen.

In terms of tactics, rigid rules were difficult to find for planning a battle, although choice of terrain and superiority in numbers were obviously critical considerations. Line of battle usually consisted of two main lines with 300 paces between each, with cavalry taking the flanks. Dragoons normally made up the second line or reserve if infantry was lacking. A further reserve was sometimes kept as a third line. For artillery, the commander in the field preferred high ground, giving the guns as wide a field of fire as possible. In the attack, it was rare for one side not to break before contact was made. The officers had their work cut out to maintain order in conditions where marching in cadence was not used and the battalion could be under fire. The nature of those conditions and mode of attack can be traced directly back to the firearms in use; this changed as firearms became more effective. The defender could open fire at twenty to sixty paces, hoping to cause enough casualties to destroy the impetus of the charge, and allow a counter-charge. Even if the attacker pushed on, he could easily become disordered as the battalion crowded in on itself. The defender, if he held his position, could maintain good order for a counter-attack or stand. Such actions required good morale, well-trained and well-led troops. It should also be recognised that such tactics were still very much in development right through the latter part of the seventeenth century.[31]

Returning to the Irish on campaign, Turenne's task was to prevent a link-up between a large 25,000 strong German–Imperial force and their Dutch allies, while simultaneously protecting the Alsace region and preventing nearby German states from joining the fight.[32] The task would clearly be a difficult one; indeed it seemed hopeless in light of a combination of Imperial moves along the Rhine together with the presence of a most able enemy commander, Raimondo Montecuccoli. Throughout the remainder of the campaign year, August until November, the two generals would play a game of manoeuvre and counter-manoeuvre, in an attempt to gain the upper hand.

In the end, the advantage fell to Montecuccoli who was better supplied. Imperial reinforcements were thus able to aid Dutch troops as they laid siege to Bonn, which the French surrendered in November. Once more Turenne placed his troops in winter quarters in Alsace and Germany. Matters on a wider European scale were not proceeding as Louis had planned either; in late August, Spain, the Dutch United Provinces and Emperor Leopold signed the Hague Alliance. Louis was forced to restrain his demands on the Dutch, and his enemies' alliance placed the initiative solely with them. Towards the end of the year, Brandenburg re-entered the war, along with some German states and the Spanish. Louis now had a significant proportion of Europe ranged against his ambition. It would no longer be an easy war to fight.[33]

For the Hamiltons, there were also important matters occurring at home. England had been fighting the Dutch at sea since their declaration of war in 1672. By 1673 the Dutch had defeated an Anglo–French fleet. Thomas Hamilton, born fourth amongst the six brothers, served with the Royal Navy. Also present at sea by this time was James Hamilton, eldest of the brothers and favourite of Charles II. Amongst the many titles granted by Charles, James also carried that of Lord Commissioner for Prizes and had become the colonel of his own regiment of foot, a regiment that was being carried in cramped conditions aboard HMS *Royal Charles*. The ship had a chequered history, being the same vessel that had carried Cormac McCarthy, son of Donough and cousin to the Hamiltons, during the sea fight with the Dutch off Lowestoft in 1665. Then the young Irishman, who had also been a favourite of James the Duke of York, had been blown to bits, his 'blood and brains' flying in the duke's face.[34]

The irony that such a similar event should occur on the *Royal Charles* is striking. James Hamilton had complained of the 'intolerable crowd' aboard the ship and his difficulties with recruitment since the regiment appeared to be at sea for most of the time.[35] In May, in a sea battle at Schonvelt, he was wounded severely. Whether through cannon fire or the violent explosion of the ship's timbers, his leg was blown off and he fell. He was so close to Prince Rupert, of civil war fame, that many who witnessed the event thought that it had actually been the prince who had fallen. James remained on board ship for two to three days until he could be returned to land, but died at the start of June. Like Cormac MacCarthy before him, he was buried in Westminster Abbey, the first of the Hamilton sons to fall in battle. Other reports would indicate that James had died due to lack of medical attention; one witness reported that the regimental surgeon had refused to board the *Royal Charles* and Hamilton had died due to lack of appropriate treatment.[36]

His aunt, the Duchess of Ormonde, had been with him near the end, perhaps the closest relative to his location. She recorded:

1673 June 7th
I doubt not that you have heard of my nephew James Hamilton's

having lost a leg in the last fight at sea, who died of that wound yesterday at 4 of the clock in the morning, and is to be buried at ten this night. He was a great loss unto his own family and ours, by whom he is very much regretted, and by many more who will find the loss of so generous a friend (for so he was) to all that he could serve that needed his kindness. I could not prevail with myself to write unto my brother Hamilton or my sister upon a subject that I well know will be greatly affecting to them. I cannot say that he died in his reason, for his fever and the gangrene of his wounds made him rave soon after he was brought on shore, until a few hours before he died that he lay quiet, and, as those that were about him thought, was in a sleep and breathing sweet, and so ended without speech or appearance of pain. He showed the greatest patience in the pain that he endured that was possible for man to do, and said nothing that was ill in his ravings but of the business of the sea, and would be silent when he was desired, and knew people, but was not capable of anything that was serious, the disease having so far seized his spirits.[37]

The death was a tragedy for the entire family. Both George Hamilton and Elizabeth, Madame de Gramont, wrote to Arlington requesting that he do all he could for James's widow and children.[38] Ultimately a good pension was awarded to James's wife Elizabeth and her three sons.[39]

The continuing war with the Dutch was becoming unpopular in England. Indeed, it seemed that many in the English Parliament were insistent that France was the real enemy. It was a sign of things to come.

Is it not highly scandalous to the Protestant religion that the King of England, king of a Protestant religion, should stand obliged to make war with a Protestant state till they would grant a free toleration of the Popish religion, restore the Church lands to the Popish clergy, erect public churches for Popish idolatrous worship and admit Papists to an equal share in the government?[40]

Meanwhile the 1673 campaign had been a poor one for the French. Montecuccoli had reinforced William of Orange despite Turenne's attempts to stop him. Would 1674 be any different in a war where the odds were becoming stacked against Louis? At least the English, Scottish and Irish regiments appear to have been appreciated by Turenne, despite their initial lack of involvement.[41] The soldiers of the regiments also appear to have been content with their lot, and their treatment under the general.[42]

Various oaths and acts still precluded Catholics from public office in England; however, Catholics would sometimes take the Oath of Supremacy and Oath of Allegiance in one form or another. Despite Charles's Declaration of Indulgence, matters had become more serious by 1673. With the Anglo-French attack on the Dutch, Parliament was in argumentative mood and forced Charles to enforce rigidly the penal laws and thus withdraw the Declaration of Indulgence. It was also insisted that a Test Act be passed, wherein both officeholders and military commanders should declare their disbelief in transubstantiation, prove that they had taken Anglican Communion and take the required oaths in court with witnesses present. When the act was instituted in 1673 there were several resignations. The most important of these, however, was that of the Lord High Admiral, James, Duke of York, brother to the king and heir to the throne. Rumours had spread in English society for years regarding James's religion. They had now been proven true as James revealed his Catholicism. That summer, after the death of his wife Anne Hyde, he married Mary of Modena, an Italian Catholic princess rumoured to be influenced by the French. The wheels of James's ultimate undoing had been set in motion, and the event did little to instil calm in Parliament.

Under pressure to act, Charles was obliged in February 1674 to make peace with the Dutch Republic. Louis had lost his English ally. He had seen the birth of a dangerous coalition in mainland Europe in 1673 and had made little progress in a Dutch war that he had hoped would be over quickly. This was a serious matter, especially so for those English, Irish and Scots engaged in French service. Despite the fine detail of the subsequent Anglo-Dutch treaty, and the insistence that England and the Dutch Republic not aid their respective enemies, Charles would *not* withdraw the Gendarmes from French service. William, Prince of Orange insisted that he do so but Charles would not be moved, assuring the French that the troops would stay despite the insistence of the Dutch, Spanish or even English Parliament.[43] For now, he got his way; the troops on the continent would remain there.

The wholesale rejection of the French alliance, and the Treaty of Westminster with the Dutch, had surprisingly left the Irish troops unaffected. With the recruitment of fresh men, and the relative inactivity of the Irish so far, we can estimate that there must have been at least 2,000 of them in French service. Some may have been spread across other regiments.

Whatever the case, it is clear that those ostensibly foreign troops played a major role in Turenne's force that numbered just over 20,000 men during 1673. The Gendarmes were made up of one Irish and one English regiment; these in turn may have been broken down into two battalions; indeed the number of recruits at this stage would indicate this division.

The war in mainland Europe had entered its second, more bloody stage. With the entry of Spain and other allies into the war, holding areas of the Dutch provinces became a wasteful aside to Louis's real target, the Spanish Netherlands. The French would once more have to defend the Alsace region, deflect German and Imperialist attacks, and prevent the enemy from intruding into Franche-Comté, a strategic French target for 1674. Louis would also steadily move French troops from the Dutch provinces to Spanish-held territory and the new Mediterranean front. Despite the reverses and stalemates, many of which would continue on other fronts, the next year would see some of the finest generalship and fierce fighting from Turenne, the old master. It would also illustrate, perhaps in common with his Thirty Years' War experience, how Turenne exhibited both the best and worst aspects of that conflict. Despite paying close attention to the welfare of his men, he gave scant consideration to the plight of the surrounding civilian population. More than any other campaign, perhaps, Turenne's actions in 1674 would demonstrate the limitations of manoeuvre warfare in terms of definitively deciding the outcome of campaigns, but would also show the potential for the strategy's use of active defence, a factor that Louis would need to consider more seriously in but a few short years.

Turenne's troops had wintered in both Alsace and in the region of the Elector Palatine, the Palatinate, whose lands were defiled through the foraging, rapine and general plunder that accompanied seventeenth-century armies in the field. It could be argued that Turenne had thus driven the elector into the arms of the emperor. The army exploited the region on the far side of the Rhine throughout the summer. This early form of 'scorched earth' policy was symptomatic of the terrible reality of warfare in this area and exploitation of enemy resources was routinely carried out, most expertly by Turenne's troops. The Irishmen in this case appear to have been particularly adept at plunder and the ill-disciplined behaviour associated with it. The peasants, perhaps understandably, struck out in the form of bloody reprisals against the troops feeding off the populace. Small pockets of soldiers would be ambushed and killed by bands of peasants. When the Irish recognised some of their troops amongst the dead, they indulged in bloody reprisals of their own, burning towns and murdering the locals.

The elector, in desperation, wrote to Turenne in an attempt to stop the slaughter, even challenging the general to a duel. Turenne, despite stating that such acts were commonplace in war, and the natural consequence of his king's orders, had some of the Irish punished. Presumably some of the worst offenders were hanged, which appears to have put an end to the worst of the excesses. It is not clear what part the officers played in this plunder, and how extensively they attempted to stop it. It is clear, however, that for the young Irish troops, such sights were alien, and many of the officers would not easily forget the experience. That is not to say that burning homes, rape and pillage were isolated to the Irish troops. As late as September Louvois considered that villages and towns in the area that did not pay sufficient contributions were showing the French considerable disdain. Within a two-week period, thirteen towns and villages were burnt to the ground and the inhabitants killed or scattered. Symptomatic of the nature of seventeenth-century warfare, perhaps, although, despite the devastation, the acts would be repeated in the same area during the war in 1689.[44]

The year's campaign had started in June for Turenne. He made moves with part of his force toward Phillipsburg, crossing the Rhine to make a pre-emptive strike against General Enea Caprara and the Duke of Lorraine. In a primarily cavalry engagement with 2,000 infantry and 6,000 horsemen, the French met the enemy formed on a hill, in a strong position along the line of advance outside the small town of Sinzheim. While the infantry took and held the town, Turenne's cavalry attacked uphill, led by the general with sword in hand.

The French horse, however, was forced to advance up a thin defile, where they would inevitably be attacked upon reaching the plateau by well-formed Imperial cavalry. Conscious of the potential disaster and reading the battle correctly, Turenne pushed infantry and dismounted dragoons to the flanks to line hedges and vineyards, preventing Imperialist attack. Mixing musketeers with his horsemen, he advanced, steadily pushing the enemy back until they withdrew. Both sides lost around 2,000 men. After this victory Turenne had achieved little more than local gains; his troops were too few in number to attempt pursuit or exploitation of the victory. French troops would for some time be able to convince Imperial and German troops to retreat, simply by crossing the Rhine. Louis quickly reinforced Turenne due to his apparent success.[45]

The battle had also included a particularly notable incident involving Hamilton's English and Irish troops. After the town had been captured, and the fight taken to the plateau, the French forces stood in readiness for the

Imperial counter-attack. Turenne, on his way to inspect a gorge where he had posted some French dragoons, passed close to Hamilton's men. Upon seeing their general, the Irish and English troops displayed their respect by giving cheers, throwing their hats in the air and even discharging muskets, an act that, according to French sources, actually brought on the expected counter-attack. However, Turenne is recorded as being very pleased with his foreign troops, and praised the valiant efforts of Hamilton and Douglas.[46]

For a time, therefore, Turenne had the upper hand, his local masterstroke having made apparent gains. By late August, however, 30,000 Imperial troops under Bournonville threatened the Alsace region. The devastation of the Palatinate had not been without benefit to the French; through manoeuvre, Turenne blocked the Imperial advance and forced his enemy to subsist for a time in the by now devastated region. The advance faltered and was abandoned by September. But Bournonville was not yet defeated and moved his army south to seize Strasbourg. Despite one-time neutrality, the city quickly fell, allowing Imperial troops to threaten Alsace once more. Turenne, fully aware of the imminent arrival of Imperial reinforcements, decided to attack. Moving north to Strasbourg, he effectively split the enemy. By October he had arrived at Molsheim, threatening Imperial lines of communication, supply lines with Strasbourg, and the main body of the Imperial force at Ensheim.[47]

On the morning of 4 October 1674 Turenne moved against the enemy, heralding the start of the Battle of Ensheim. The French deployed into two lines, with cavalry reserves in the rear, the troops also holding a small village called Holzheim. The Imperial forces had deployed around Ensheim and anchored their left flank on a wooded area between the two villages, in apparent adherence to the tactics of the time. Turenne, however, quickly recognised the wood as his enemy's weakness; he would concentrate his infantry assault at this point, in a battle that would bloody the nose of his English and Irish favourites. French dragoons, supported by infantry, led the first assault. Recognising Turenne's intent, Bournonville ordered much of his own reserve infantry into the woods to stop the French attack. As Bournonville threw more and more German infantry into the fray, Turenne bolstered his own position with the English and Irish battalions, the Gendarmes Anglais and Irlandais, including Monmouth's Regiment, Churchill's Regiment and the regiment of Irish troops. Conditions can only have been terrible, as constant rain meant that matchlocks became useless and the battle for the woods must have rapidly been reduced to vicious hand-to-hand fighting where morale, determination and a degree of esprit de corps would dictate the victor. It should also be considered that the French troops were tired from a forty-mile march over mud-soaked fields in the rain. The fight was far from over despite appalling conditions and the desperate fighting of the foreign regiments; Turenne was forced to commit three more infantry battalions from his centre, together with cavalry from his right flank. The desperate clash continued and both Anthony and George Hamilton were wounded, George in three places, with his horse shot from under him, most likely whilst leading his men into the melee.[48]

A French observer remarked that Hamilton and his men 'performed great acts of valour, having with a battalion of his regiment cut to pieces a hostile battalion and dispersed the dragoons who supported it'.[49] Possibly at the moment of their commander being wounded, the Irish and English regiments gave way under Imperial pressure in the melee, falling back on the Régiment d'Anjou, although the Marquis de Vaubrun rallied them and led them on once more. The wood was taken from the French three times and was recaptured on each occasion.[50] After desperate fighting, the French troops carried the day, forcing the Imperials from the woods. Under normal conditions, such a manoeuvre would have resulted in a 'turning' of the enemy flank and thus, for the most part, victory; in this instance French troops were hindered by the presence of significant fieldworks and could advance no further.

Turenne's use of his reserves and main body had weakened his centre, a potential battle-winning factor not missed by Bournonville. In apparent belief that the victorious manoeuvre was imminent, he unleashed the Imperial cavalry at the French centre and the weakened left, this time hoping for a chance to rout the enemy. The seven well-drilled French battalions in the centre retained their composure, however, following their rigorous training and forming battalion squares, leaving little gap to exploit amongst their number. Despite some success against the first line of French horse, second-line and reserve cavalry turned back the Imperial horse with effective counter-charges. By now, with exhausted troops on both sides, the respective commanders knew that the battle was over; the Imperials withdrew in the night, with Turenne's troops too worn out to pursue. Casualties had been high, 3,500 Imperialists and around 3,000 French killed and wounded.[51]

The battle, ostensibly a French tactical victory, had, according to Bournonville, been one of the 'longest' and 'most obstinate'. It had also seen significant use of artillery for the period, the French having fired around 2,500 cannon-balls.[52] The Battle of Ensheim had also been important for George Hamilton and his troops. In the rain, with inefficient and inaccurate matchlocks, the fight would have been decided through deadly melee, rather than more conventional trading of musket volleys. The hand-to-hand brawl would have meant many casualties, and underlined the inherent abilities of the toughest troops and ablest fighters. For Hamilton and his men it had been their first true baptism of fire. Turenne later remarked that Hamilton had done 'all that could be expected', also commenting that, had he not been wounded, victory would have been secured at an earlier stage.[53]

If the fight had been a proving ground for France's foreign troops, on a strategic scale it had been a stalemate. Turenne, for instance, despite his limited gains, had been unable to prevent a link-up between Bournonville and the Brandenburg reinforcements comprised of 20,000 men and thirty-three artillery-pieces. The Imperial-Allied force now numbered 50,000, an army that could reverse many of the gains that Turenne had striven to make. Outnumbered, he had little choice but to fall back to Deittweiler between fortifications at Hagenau and Saverne until he could be reinforced with twenty battalions of infantry and twenty-four squadrons of cavalry, which Louis had ordered Condé to despatch to Turenne's aid, thus increasing his manpower to 33,000.[54]

The French were not exhausted, but neither did they have a strategic disadvantage. As Imperial and allied troops went into winter quarters, the calculating Turenne planned his next move. Believing that the French, too, as dictated by the military convention of the time, had settled into winter quarters, Bournonville and the Elector of Brandenburg quartered their troops between the Rhine and the River Ill.

Turenne was no conventional commander. He planned an unprecedented winter campaign that would remain the single most decisive move in the theatre. Winter offensives were difficult and rare due to their limited chances of success; they relied heavily on well-co-ordinated logistics and supply since foraging was so limited. Indeed, poorly co-ordinated winter manoeuvres could prove disastrous for field armies. However, such moves in the past had been organised without the logistical genius of Louvois, who intervened on Turenne's behalf, bringing his organisational skills to the problems associated with the radical French plan. George and Anthony Hamilton did not take part in the winter campaign although their troops did. It is likely that George at least was still badly affected by his wounds and recovering. By December they were returning to England in the hope of then sailing to Ireland once more to recruit men.[55] It is pertinent, nonetheless, to record the winter campaign of Hamilton's troops, if only to outline their remarkable conduct in this theatre of the war that seemed to fly in the face of the restless stalemate that existed on many of the other fronts.

November passed quietly, Imperial troops still in apparent ignorance of the impending French move. In December Turenne left nine battalions to cover the rear and keep up the pretence of winter quartering and moved with his ablest and hardiest troops, including the Irish, through the frozen Vosges mountains in an attempt to mask his movements. Surviving the cold and what must have been terrible conditions for a march, he linked up with reinforcements from Condé's army in Lorraine. Not prepared to take chances at this stage, and fully aware of the importance of preserving the quality and morale of his troops in what would be a most arduous campaign, Turenne used a rigorous selection process to determine those elite soldiers who would be required both to match the conditions and the desperate battles to follow; amongst these were the Gendarmes of the now absent George Hamilton. Moving these men by mid-December and using the terrain to cover their movement, they crossed the mountains in small groups to re-assemble at Belfort by the end of the month.

The enemy had been taken completely by surprise. The Imperial troops were scattered in garrisons and encampments as Turenne emerged onto the plains east of the Rhine. The French defeated a large delaying force of cavalry near Mulhouse, the only squadrons immediately available to the surprised Bournonville, before advancing towards Colmar where the Elector of Brandenburg scrambled to muster his scattered forces. The elector, despite managing to gather over 30,000 men near Turkheim, had been given insufficient time to organise the force, of course in keeping with the French general's master strategy.

Turenne himself, with 30,000 men, arrived at Turkheim by 4 January 1675. The Elector of Brandenburg, now joined by Bournonville, had assembled a similar number between Colmar and Turkheim. They had, however, left only a small garrison in the latter town while the battle lines of their remaining troops remained thin, overstretched and disorganised. Taking advantage of the chaos, Turenne attacked, launching a feint toward the Imperial centre and left, the main endeavour being directed toward Turkheim on the defenders' right flank. After some difficult fighting, the French secured the town, fending off later counter-attacks. The fighting there had eased some of the pressure on the Imperial centre and flank and, having lost the town, the elector's troops were able to withdraw first to Strasbourg and later cross the Rhine, with little serious French pursuit.[56] For Turenne, the campaign had been a significant achievement. He had forced his enemy from the Alsace region, and now put his troops into well-earned winter quarters.

George and Anthony Hamilton had returned to the British Isles at the end of 1674 in search of new recruits, this time accompanied by their brother-in-law, the politically astute Gramont. For Gramont the trip would be quite pleasant. French ambassador Ruvigny would remark on his penchant for 'winning money' and that he would bring King Louis back 'a portrait of Madame de Portsmouth, which she wishes the King to have'.[57] Ruvigny would also remark that for Gramont this *jolie voyage* would be most lucrative; having left with one hundred *pistoles*, Gramont would return to France with over 5,000.[58] Clearly he was less interested in recruiting than his brother-in-law, English gambling tables having a distinct draw for him.

Matters on this occasion would not be as straightforward as in previous years for the brothers Hamilton. The English Parliament, in obvious discontent with the state of affairs regarding the troops in French service, had issued a proclamation in April 1674 prohibiting English subjects from enlisting in the service of a foreign power without a warrant. The proclamation was then extended via letter to the lord lieutenants of coastal counties, ordering the arrest of those persons who tried to enlist or recruit and thus set sail for foreign powers.[59] If the proclamation was rigidly adhered to, George Hamilton could do little and, in effect, had wasted his time returning to England; it seemed a recruitment drive in Ireland would be impossible. Charles had, however, prorogued Parliament in the interim, a fact that Hamilton could perhaps use to his advantage, as there would be no further sitting until April 1675. With this in mind, he approached Charles who, with an obvious soft spot for his Irish friend, relented, provided that any dealings were conducted with the utmost secrecy and the troops embarked from a location which had no obvious garrison or similar concentration of government troops.

With all that had gone before, it is intriguing that Charles could even believe that such operations could be conducted in secret, especially so in Ireland where it seemed that clandestine methods had little chance of success. Nevertheless, with anticipation that the Dutch ambassador at least would remain ignorant of the plan, the scheme went ahead.

Would the lack of secrecy that had plagued earlier expeditions be apparent on this occasion? What is clear is that earlier attempts at such recruitment had been fairly public affairs, at least as far as Parliament and the rest of Europe's ambassadors were concerned. What likelihood there was of the scheme succeeding at all remained questionable, when officers in foreign service were for the most part 'expected' to recruit, and the political climate remained rich with anti-Catholic sentiment. To make matters worse, George Hamilton would not be involved. His responsibilities in France necessitated an early return to mainland Europe. Instead, Anthony Hamilton was put in charge of the expedition. To help him, Richard Hamilton, his younger brother, remained in Ireland. At some stage prior to 1674 he too had enlisted with the Gendarmes, although it is not entirely clear how long he had been present in France before this.

Prior to returning to France, George Hamilton had arranged with Louvois for French ships to arrive clandestinely at Waterford in March. At Waterford, however, there stood a castle, and a landing there would have flown in the face of Charles's instructions. James, Duke of York, now publicly a follower of the Catholic faith, and it seemed fully involved in the affair, suggested secretly that the port at Dingle should be used, and recommended to Louvois that ships be sent there by March due to its remoteness and the lack of troops. Anthony Hamilton was to be at the assigned meeting place with the Irish recruits. Essex, the Lord Lieutenant of Ireland, met with the brothers, receiving thanks in writing from George for his efforts and being assured that the entire design, by now a very dangerous consideration for all parties involved, had been fully sanctioned by the king. Essex would not intervene unless the matter became 'official' in which case he would have no choice but to make arrests and prevent any assembly.[60] Predictably, Anthony Hamilton wrote to Ruvigny in April: 'It is impossible to be more unfortunate than we have been in what we have undertaken for the service of His Majesty ....'[61]

Matters had indeed become complex; over 900 men had assembled at Dingle, a large gathering that would account for the numbers needed in France with a hard year of campaigning expected. The scheme had, however implausibly, been kept secret and no official word of the recruitment had been made public, or reached the ears of Essex via external sources. Anthony had expected the ships by 8 March (o.s.), slightly earlier than George Hamilton's arrangement (15 March). It is unclear why the dates had been changed, perhaps some later dealings with Louvois. What is clear is that the ships were late. The assembled men had waited for two weeks in March, Hamilton even having to borrow 1,000 crowns to support them. By the 27th he disbanded them. It seemed that the French had let them down, and no ships had been spotted. By the first week of April, however, French ships did appear, but not at Dingle as planned. Instead the French navy appeared at Kinsale in Cork, certainly not the most innocuous of locations along the

Irish coast line. In a panic, Hamilton sent word to the officers in an attempt to re-assemble the recruits but it was too late. The appearance of French vessels at Kinsale had tipped the balance and, as in previous years, the word was out.

Essex, fully aware that matters had got out of hand, was true to his word. He arrested Hamilton's officers, being obliged to abide by the law with the matter now very much in the public domain. Upon hearing of the fiasco, Anthony Hamilton rode to Dublin to have his officers released. He succeeded, but only upon giving his word that he would be responsible for their actions, and borrowing yet more money from Ruvigny. During April Hamilton attempted once more to assemble the recruits, despite tight security amongst the now watchful ports. However, it was Essex who, although perhaps appearing duplicitous, was responsible for the success of the operation; through his own means, and perhaps to save further embarrassment, he ensured that the men did sail with the French ships. Essex later stated that the ships had been twenty days late.[62]

As to who was to blame, it mattered little, since the disaster would help Parliamentary attempts to bring the entire matter to a close; of course late ships and disbanded men were no way in keeping with the secrecy required with the Irish recruitment drive. Essex would find it difficult to give aid in the future without becoming compromised. Indeed, the matter could only exacerbate anti-Catholic and anti-French feeling in Parliament. The entire embarrassment would prevent such attempts being repeated easily.

The 1675 campaign in mainland Europe had started well for the French with Turenne's winter victory. The year also started well for the Hamiltons on their return to France; in March, George was promoted to the rank of brigadier in recognition of his efforts in the previous year.[63] By then the war was being fought mainly in the Spanish Netherlands and the Rhineland, although Louis also had troops in Catalonia under Schomberg and an army in Sicily. Turenne once more faced Montecuccoli, recalled by Emperor Leopold to fight along the Rhine. The Imperial troops had not forgotten Turenne's aggressive winter campaign in Alsace and sought to retake the lost territory. Montecuccoli, now recognised as the only general capable of defeating Turenne, was responsible once more for the safety of the Holy Roman Empire and its Dutch allies.

The old adversaries again played a sophisticated military version of cat and mouse in a narrow strip of land between the Black Forest and the Rhine near Strasbourg, as Montecuccoli attempted to cross the river in force and Turenne countered his moves. Months of marches and counter-marches followed. Montecuccoli moved towards Phillipsburg, to draw out Turenne, who responded with a move towards Strasbourg and the Imperial rear. Armies were split and rejoined, each seeking the single advantage that would deliver victory. By late July Turenne had almost hemmed in the Imperial troops against the banks of the Rhine and wished to finish them before they could make any further attempt to cross into the Alsace region.

As Montecuccoli attempted to retreat east, Turenne intercepted and forced a confrontation at Salzbach on 27 July where a small river separated the two armies. By morning the French left and centre had been positioned, with the right beginning to move. Turenne rarely led from the rear; it was not in his nature. This attitude also applied when, as the armies prepared for battle, he scouted the battlefield to analyse the dispositions of the enemy and thus exploit weaknesses later, at minimal cost to his men. At Salzbach, with the enemy troops seemingly unwilling to engage, a close watch was being kept on Imperial moves. By noon of the 27th Turenne was beginning to believe that Montecuccoli would once more avoid a confrontation and was beginning to retreat. By two o'clock, the Comte de Roye spotted the advance of a column of German infantry and despatched Saint Hilaire, the French artillery commander to Turenne to make him aware of the changing situation. A subsequent messenger requested additional infantry and the presence of Turenne himself at de Roye's position. Two battalions were despatched but Turenne remained where he was; a third request for the general then came from George Hamilton himself, who rode with him to de Roye's position.[64]

Montecuccoli had no intention of retreating; he was manoeuvring for battle and exploiting all the natural advantages on the Salzbach battlefield. He had moved around 600 infantry together with artillery into a churchyard, covered in front by a small stream. Turenne took it upon himself to scout the lines, since this movement would have an important bearing on the positioning of French guns; seventeenth-century field pieces, unlike their more manoeuvrable descendants, were rarely re-located once emplaced. Therefore their tactical positioning was significant due to their restricted battle manoeuvrability and in light of events at Ensheim where artillery had played an important role. Turenne's attention to detail meant that he would go and inspect the position himself, taking Saint Hilaire, the artillery specialist, with him. It is thought that at the last minute George Hamilton warned the general of the dangers of moving too close to the enemy position, especially so as guns were present. Turenne, however, was unperturbed. Whether the enemy gunners were aware of the identity of the officer who approached the position is not clear; indeed had they known that it was Turenne, military honour may have stopped them from firing on the general. As it was, the troops did not hesitate to fire on Frenchmen. The ball tore off Saint Hilaire's arm and struck Turenne squarely on the torso, killing him instantly.[65] The French legend had been killed in, arguably, the most unjust of circumstances.

Hamilton and other French officers raced to the scene, quickly removing the dead Turenne and the wounded Saint Hilaire from further harm. Hamilton then covered the body of his commander in an attempt to staunch rumour of his death getting out amongst the troops prior to the battle and instigating a rout.[66] Despite this, and additional French attempts to hide the truth, word of Turenne's death soon spread. The loss of the French general slowed the momentum of the attack and, ultimately, the campaign.

By the end of July, and with the advantage of poor weather that concealed their movement, the French troops were falling back, pursued with zest by Montecuccoli, who now pressed his advantage and chased the demoralised French army back through the Alsace region. A confounded Louis sent Condé to stem the flood and prevent a disaster, but it was almost too late. Montecuccoli sent his cavalry across the Rhine to Altenheim on a flanking manoeuvre to cut off the French army. The French troops, although brave and determined for the most part to avenge Turenne's death, were poorly led, resulting in some disorder. They managed to march as far as the town of Wilstet before the pursuing Imperial troops caught up with them. A rearguard action was required and the rearguard of the now disorganised French army was made up of two regiments, the dragoons of the Chevalier de Bouflers and the English and Irish infantry of Sir George Hamilton.

Most of the French baggage and cavalry and the majority of the infantry had passed over the nearby river. Their safe passage and further retreat would require a hasty defence against the forward elements of the pursuing Imperial troops, in this case 4,000 infantry and 2,000 dragoons. Forming up in line of battle, Hamilton's men repelled repeated charges from the Imperial troops until it was judged safe to follow the main body. Montecuccoli would not be distracted and the pursuit continued in the hope that, by the time the French had reached Altenheim, the Imperial commander's cavalry flanking force would be set to strike. At the passage of the Schutter river another rearguard action was needed. On this occasion, however, the Irish were not required to carry out the defence. Instead the Champagne Regiment and a force of cavalry were engaged. The French troops were surprised by Imperial infantry and cut to pieces, most of the officers and their commander being killed. The situation was becoming desperate. Despite this success,

Montecuccoli was cautious, to the benefit of the retreating French troops, giving them time to re-form.

Rather than take advantage of the rapidly decaying rearguard action, the Imperial commander pursued his cavalry advantage, pushing more troops along the mountainous route that would permit a surprise attack at Altenheim. However, the Imperial troops had taken too long to move and the Irish and French infantry were waiting for them as they crossed the river. Volley after volley was poured upon the attacking cavalry, French training and well-drilled fire discipline making the difference against numerical superiority. Late in the battle the Imperial cavalry appeared in the French rear. The Irish and French troops fought surrounded by the enemy and Hamilton and his men must have thought that the battle was over. In characteristic style, however, the French cavalry from the main body returned to the fray and rescued their brave infantry. Throughout the day the battle raged but the desperate bravery of the French and their allies began to tell as the Imperials swayed, then broke. The French and their Irish and English troops remained victorious and retreated successfully across the Rhine.[67]

Hamilton had made a major difference to the rearguard actions and may very well have helped save a major part of the French army. Uncharacter-istically for a foreign officer, he was admired by the French for his valiant efforts and made a major general in February 1676.[68] The French also spoke of him as having shown 'the greatest proofs of valour' and the Irish having performed marvellously throughout the campaign, having accomplished 'wonders'.[69] The French celebrated *gloire* wherever they saw it and Hamilton's troops were rapidly gaining an excellent reputation. There can have been little better military experience for them at the time. They had tasted both great victory and the rigours of a demoralising retreat. The troops had remained loyal and stood against the enemy ranged against them. They had bathed in *gloire* and found a taste for it on the bloody crucible of Louis's European battlefields. Louis himself was especially satisfied.[70]

Although it seemed that everything had changed for Hamilton and his men. Turenne was dead and the entire focus of the war seemed distant and unattainable. There would be further disappointment. As winter set in Louvois once more requested that George Hamilton begin recruiting to replace those troops who had fallen through battle or disease.[71] However, Ireland would not prove a lucrative recruiting ground. As the English Parliament had met in April 1675, after being prorogued for more than a year, the French had not expected a favourable outcome for their English troops in French service.

Despite the best efforts of Ruvigny and other foreign ambassadors, Parliament, it seemed, had had more than enough of this particular French outrage. The House proposed that all troops of the crown in French service should be recalled immediately and that the experience should not be repeated. Ruvigny, ever the diplomat, went so far as to urge Charles to be firm with his own Parliament in these dealings, since otherwise a dangerous precedent would be set, an obvious piece of advice from the French ambassador, since it furthered the aims of France.[72]

Charles must have realised that it was too late, although he would suggest a form of conciliation. By May the king was asked to issue a proclamation related to a recall of the troops from France.[73] Charles's answer suggested settlement. He commanded the immediate return of those troops who had passed into France since the last treaty with the Dutch, and forbade future recruitment of subjects into French service. Those troops who had been in French service prior to the treaty, however, would not be recalled.[74] There was understandable disagreement in Parliament, although a subsequent resolution to recall all the troops was defeated by one vote. Despite the issue of the Royal Proclamation related to foreign recruits, men continued to travel to France. Parliamentary objections were all but ignored as Charles once more prorogued his Parliament until October, then subsequently until February 1677. He also remained close to Ruvigny, assuring him that he would not issue another proclamation. To some extent, these matters meant another 'secret' treaty with France as Charles claimed French subsidy for his actions.[75] He still played a dangerous game with many sides on the European stage, with himself as arbitrator.

For George Hamilton, the prospect of raising additional troops in England and, more especially, Ireland had not been removed entirely. He travelled to England once more with Gramont, in December 1675, his brothers remaining with the regiment in France.[76] From there he continued to Ireland alone; there is no record of how successful Gramont was in London on this occasion. With distinctly more tact involved than on previous occasions, the expedition was successful, and Hamilton had returned to France by April.[77] Additional volunteers would continue to migrate to France throughout the year despite Parliamentary protests.

The 1676 campaign would see a great many changes in the fortune of Hamilton and his troops. In common with many of Louis's wars, there had been both great victories and disappointing reversals of fortune. Although none of the defeats had been crushing, the lack of movement in the strategic picture meant that, like so many wars of the period, there had been few real signs of French progress. Louis was by now on the defensive, with most of the powerful nations of Europe ranged against him. In the Alsace region where Hamilton served, Luxembourg replaced Condé. Charles of Lorraine would once more command the Imperial troops. The campaign would see no major battles and would mainly be conducted through sieges, Phillipsburg being the main objective of the Imperial army.

Some movement across the Rhine, limited in scope in comparison with previous years, did take place. George Hamilton had by this time been awarded the rank of *Maréchal du Camp* or major general earlier in the year.[78] By May the French were once more on the move to meet their reinforcements before the Duke of Lorraine could cut them off with his own forces. Once more, in keeping with the bravery and reputation of the foreign troops, and in an apparently exposed position, George Hamilton commanded the rearguard of the French column. Lorraine attacked near Saverne at the start of June, forcing Hamilton to deploy his troops and fight a fierce battle. The rearguard won a victory, holding back a potentially successful attack on what was for the most part a French army on the march rather than deployed in battle formation. The limited gain was achieved at a terrible cost, however. George Hamilton was killed in the moment of victory.[79]

Hamilton, against the odds, had led a mostly Catholic force of Irish and a large battalion of English troops in France, had carved his reputation from nothing, and earned the respect of Turenne, Louis and many other French notables, a feat which many of his contemporaries could never hope to emulate. The troops had been involved in almost every major action in the Rhine campaign and had distinguished themselves tremendously. For the Hamilton family, George's death was another tragic blow, following only three short years after the death of his elder brother James, also in battle.

The French, not normally known for their praise of foreign troops in French service, would express their deep regret at Hamilton's death, praising his merit, modesty, courage and great daring.[80] In England, too, the untimely death of one of Charles's favourites was mourned. Hamilton had been intending to sell his command of the Gendarmes Anglais and thus fully lead his own Regiment d'Hamilton.[81] To this end, in a move made to create a pension for his widow, the regiment was sold, the new commander being ordered to pay 10,000 crowns with a further 2,000 crown pension.[82]

This was small recompense to the distraught Lady Hamilton, now left not altogether destitute, but with six young children and little fortune to speak of. Prior to her husband's death, John Evelyn had described her as a 'sprightly' young woman.[83] After George's death, however, she had greater matters to contend with.[84] Her husband had left significant debts, probably raised through regimental expenses, and the pension granted through the sale of the Gendarmes would not be enough to pay them.[85]

Hamilton, using the foresight that any senior military man of the time had, had attempted to secure his wife's future in the event of his untimely death by making her a maid of honour, a *Dame du Palais*, in the French court, as his sister had become upon her marriage to Gramont. However, his wish had not been granted. Despite the pleas of Charles and the Duke of York to the French, Louis had responded that such a position was not available at the time.[86] Charles, in turn procrastinating about making the lady an English noblewoman, complained to Louis of the expense of such a move, although he did confer the titles of Baroness of Ross and Countess of Bantry and Berehaven on Lady Hamilton.[87] Those titles, however, would have little practical measure in terms of curing her indebtedness and relationship with her creditors. It would not be until 1679 in Paris, where her lover of previous years, one Richard Talbot, would marry her. Talbot was a close friend of the Duke of York, an enviable position that would pay dividends for him in Ireland in the years to follow. He, too, had been in French service, even in the 1650s, having then fought a duel with Cormac MacCarthy over the rights to command a regiment.[88] The marriage stopped the harassment of the 'thousand creditors' that had become such a problem[89] and entered George Hamilton's widow into the game of Franco-Dutch politics that would in the not-too-distant future be played out in a bloody fashion in Ireland.

The Gendarmes Anglais had been a small part of Hamilton's command. As for the Regiment d'Hamilton, the matter was left open. Many quarters, including the family Hamilton and to some extent the French, had expected that the command would be given to one of the remaining brothers in French service, Anthony or Richard.[90] Charles and his brother the Duke of York had other ideas. In an unprecedented move, James asked that Louis should give the command of the regiment to Lieutenant Colonel Thomas Dongan,[91] whose ambition had fallen foul of George Hamilton in the past. Understandably, both Anthony and Richard and, more especially, their sister the Countess of Gramont were distraught by the news that their brother's regiment had been given away.[92] It is likely at this stage that Anthony Hamilton parted company with the regiment and his French service, as he is not referred to in subsequent expeditions to Ireland, and next appears in Dublin in 1681. Whether his leaving the regiment around this time, or the subsequent machinations of Lady Gramont had a part to play, Anthony would remain unpopular with both the French military and, more especially, the influential Louvois in the years to come.

Richard Hamilton remained with the regiment, as did many of the notable Irish and English whose names would become prevalent in British wartime politics in the years that followed. The Duke of Monmouth was a lieutenant general in French service and a Protestant, the illegitimate son of Charles II. He would become the puppet of the Whig conspiracy and the arch-rebel by 1685. John Churchill, whose future as the leading general of his time as Duke of Marlborough would be set in motion by Louis's wars of *gloire*, served in the English regiment. Captain Justin MacCarthy, cousin to the Hamiltons, and a young Patrick Sarsfield both served in the Irish regiments. Their most important battles were still to be fought in Ireland.[93]

Though Dongan was ostensibly in charge of this 'Brigade' of foreign regiments, Monmouth had been 'colonel-proprietor' of Hamilton's troops. By November 1676 he appointed Justin MacCarthy as colonel of one of the regiments and insisted that Louvois allow one battalion to remain in garrison while another two served in the field, thus relieving some of the pressure on the constant need for new recruits.[94] There is no clear record of Anthony and Richard's movements at this time, although it can be assumed that Anthony had left in disgust. Richard probably remained with the regiment, as events will show.

Dongan showed great enthusiasm for his new charge, at least initially, returning to England by October to recruit with a view to making a subsequent expedition to Ireland as George and Anthony Hamilton had done so many times in the past. Parliament would once again meet the next year, so that attempts to raise men could then be curtailed. Dongan would have to act quickly. French attempts to get permission from Charles initially appeared to have been successful, although time was running out and Charles no longer had any intention of becoming embroiled in a pro-French scandal.[95] He did, however, give written orders to Dongan to pass on to Essex and, for this year at least, it appears that recruits were successfully raised, although in the public domain men shipped from Ireland were 'officially' going to Virginia.[96] Louis's foreign troops wintered at Vitry and St Dizier. One of the Hamiltons, most likely Richard, was once more criticised by Louvois for the disorderly conduct of the troops in winter quarters, proving at the very least that he still held a form of command within the regiment, although Louvois's barely concealed contempt for the Hamiltons was very evident.[97] The war was not over but its nature had changed. Although Louis's strategy had essentially been defensive, there had been some remarkable manoeuvres along the Rhine. Turenne had gone and the loss had affected Louis's strategic decision-making. The war would now reach its climax where significant gains would be minimised and each side would strive to finish the conflict in positions as powerful as possible. The nature of the coalition and the odds stacked against Louis meant not only that he would have to settle for a resolution, but that he would have to increase the size of his army to 250,000 men to perpetuate the stalemate. Créqui would defend the Alsace region as Luxembourg had been moved to the north. The ebb and flow that had characterised the war of manoeuvre under Turenne had ended, and most engagements in the campaign were sieges, with only one major French victory over William at Cassel. By 1678 peace negotiations were well underway, although the year would still see ferocious fighting as each side competed to gain as much territory as was practicable in the death throes of the conflict.

Parliament met in February 1677 with increasing concern about the relative progress and potential threat of Louis, his large French army and his ultimate war aims. Yet another bill for the enforced return of the king's subjects in France failed, much to the consternation of Spanish and Dutch ambassadors.[98] It was clear that such activities could not proceed indefinitely. Louis took the Dutch city of Ghent by March, in an attempt to secure peace before Charles II was forced to take the Dutch side in the war through the inevitable anti-French sentiment of his Parliament. Although the peace treaty was signed by 10 August, fighting did not cease until the 15th by which time William had attacked French forces at St Denis, west of Mons. Fighting continued along the Rhine until October when the two shattered armies went into winter quarters. Louis's taking of Ghent had the desired effect of increasing the pressure on all parties to sue for peace although he would inevitably have to return it to its Spanish masters.

The French, too, were under pressure to gain an understanding before English troops entered the war on the allies' side. Despite the arrival of an English force in May, Louis reached agreement with Charles on their neutrality, but the bargain would not hold for long. The Treaty of Nijmegen, signed with the Dutch, was soon followed by agreement with the Spanish and Imperialists. Louis made a great many gains from the deal and obtained many valuable cities, only having to give up a number of fortresses and his dominion over Phillipsburg and Lorraine. The French retained Freiburg and a bridge over the Rhine. The Dutch regained all land captured by the French. The Spanish were the real losers, since the devastated Spanish Netherlands had been broken up amongst the main protagonists. Although Louis's initial aims had been reduced, he had made significant gains in the Netherlands and was still perceived as a significant threat throughout Europe.[99]

For Dongan's men, too, change was in the air. Large-scale anti-French events were occurring simultaneously. Dongan's recruitment expedition was recalled by December 1677 due to deterioration in Anglo-French relations. In November Charles had arranged for the marriage of William of Orange to his brother James's eldest, and Protestant, daughter Mary. By January the following year, England and Holland had signed a peace agreement, Parliament met and it seemed that France and England would be at loggerheads, if not at war. Louis, conscious that the slightest pretext could anger an aggressive English Parliament over which he no longer had any influence, ordered that recruiting for his foreign regiments be curtailed immediately. Indeed, all officers in French service were to have departed for England prior to Parliament's meeting; further resources spent on these troops would, in Louis's view, be wasted.[100]

The order that had been expected for so long was announced in January, and the troops were recalled, despite Charles's expressions of benevolence to the French.[101] Louis, intent on keeping to the terms of the Anglo-French agreement, would not send any troops home until after open war between France and England had been declared. In real terms this meant that the troops were closely watched with growing suspicion in France.[102] With Irish, English and Scottish troops, both Catholic and Protestant, even the French remained unsure as to where loyalties would truly lie.

Louis would not allow the troops to leave until officially cashiered. There was no grateful thanks for having done their duty for France, despite the protestations of the Dukes of York and Monmouth. A spate of accusations of insulting behaviour and general disorder amongst the troops followed, whether real or imagined; the effect of French alienation of the men who had fought so hard under their flag was to drive England deeper into the arms of the Dutch, an alliance which seemed to make more sense in the light of attempts to cashier and 'sack' the loyal English, Scots and Irish.[103] Had there been any attempt to show goodwill to the Irish due to their Catholicism, this was quickly scuppered through Dongan's claims that he had been poorly treated and remained unpaid.[104] Everything, it seemed, was falling apart.

For Richard Hamilton events were completely different. By April 1678, with matters for many of the foreign troops revolving around their decommissioning, he complained to Louvois of Dongan's mismanagement of regimental finances.[105] The Hamilton-Dongan feud was far from over. Louvois, in an uncharacteristic display of accord with the Hamiltons, agreed. Dongan was cashiered and Hamilton made a lieutenant colonel. However, matters with Louvois were far from over, despite his insistence that Louis was aware of Hamilton's 'merit'.[106] In the interim period between attempts to cashier the regiment and procrastination on the part of the French, Hamilton and the remaining troops were stationed at Aix. In this period the qualities of this new Monsieur d'Hamilton were expressed by the French garrison commanders, in terms of his attention to duty, before the regiment was moved to Roussillon.[107] By August peace negotiations had been completed and France and the Dutch Republic were no longer at war. By the end of 1678 the foreign troops had been disbanded. Some were drafted into another foreign regiment in French service, the German regiment of von Furstenburg. For other soldiers poverty-stricken abandonment in France was to follow until an opportunity to return to England presented itself. Hamilton would be one of the lucky ones, obtaining command of the French Régiment de Navailles.[108]

The reasons for Hamilton's rapid advancement are not altogether clear, but one incident may shed some light on the events. Richard's sister had at some stage in 1678 publicly humiliated Louvois at court for his apparent reluctance to promote her brother. Whether the matter had a direct bearing on Hamilton's new-found popularity or not, the incident was something that the scheming Louvois would neither easily forget nor forgive.[109]

Anthony Hamilton.

Elizabeth Hamilton, later *la comtesse de Gramont.*

The promotion had been to Richard's liking as a new Régiment d'Hamilton, wholly a part of the French army, served in the Roussillon region of France. An army without a war to fight made for neither rapid promotion nor historical record, although Richard seems to have served in the regiment until 1685 without further significant incident. He would have learnt much in terms of command and the rigid French drill systems with which Louis's armies had fought their way around Europe. This experience would be vital to his future martial pursuits in Ireland. A year after Hamilton's promotion, however, in 1679, the family would receive more bad news; George Hamilton senior, their father, had died, a man who had been through so much under two English kings, and lost his two eldest sons to war. By the following year Lady Hamilton had also died. It was the end of an era for a family that had suffered much during civil wars, exile and a financially difficult return to England and Ireland. Anthony Hamilton, now the head of the remaining family members, had already returned to Ireland. Richard would eventually follow, as would John, while Thomas continued to serve in the navy. A return to Ireland, for most of the family, held the next, if not the greatest, challenge.

# Chapter 6

# A Return to Ireland

1 678 had been a pivotal year in English politics with regard to the rest of Europe. Support for a Dutch alliance had increased significantly and Louis began to be seen as England's enemy. Much of this sentiment could be traced back to the royal marriage in 1677 between William, Stadtholder of the Dutch provinces and Mary, the eldest daughter of James, Duke of York. Not only did this ensure that the two countries moved closer together both politically and militarily but it gave William a significant interest in British affairs, now that he was part of the succession and could gain the crown. William, by virtue of the latest Dutch war, could not trust the French monarch and since it seemed that Louis's lust for conquest could not easily be satisfied, the need for allies was crucial.[1]

Having returned to England, there was little hope for the Irish officers who wished to use their military experience in English regiments. An Irish Catholic regiment was too much of a political taboo to serve in England as part of the army. Paranoia in England had been simmering during the war. Anti-Catholic hysteria had reached new heights and matters would get significantly worse with the advent of the 'Popish Plot'. The plot would become one of the strangest, yet markedly far-reaching, events in British history. The degree of tolerance that had been shown toward Catholics would be stretched to its limits as events took hold.

It is pertinent to outline the particular form of paranoia that gripped the populace and led to the plot's credibility in the eyes of English society. Louis XIV dominated a large portion of a mostly Catholic Europe, a form of Christianity that Englishmen associated with absolute monarchy, an anathema to the ideals of the English Parliament. To many Protestants, the aim of the Catholic Church was to impose such governing ideology on the world. With the civil war of the 1640s fresh in the minds of many, the parallel events that had then occurred in Ireland, a Catholic uprising in the British Isles, gave credence to the concerns of many Englishmen.

Hysteria verging on general panic at the prospect of Catholic rebels usurping the throne was all too evident. When events conspired to light the fuse of anti-Catholic paranoia, fear of rebellion became increasingly common. Astonishingly, the Catholic community in England had managed to survive the onslaught, although it was significantly reduced in size and influence due to the penal laws enforced throughout the sixteenth and seventeenth centuries. There were, of course, exceptions, and some Catholics did take the oaths in contravention of Papal directives; others, as in the case of the Hamiltons, who sought military service, had simply transferred abroad. However, the laws had fallen out of favour. There had been scares and minor bouts of hysteria of course, Charles's marriage to the Catholic Catherine of Braganza, the second Anglo-Dutch war and the alliance with the French. Even the Great Fire of London had allegedly been an arsonist's plot propagated by dissenting Catholics, or the French, or any other convenient scapegoat. Many Catholics obviously wished for French support and Papal recognition of England. In reality, however, they were too few and lacked influence.

The public face of Charles's Catholic leanings after the 1670 Treaty of Dover would provide further concern. In March 1672 he suspended the penal laws to the horror of magistrates and high court judges alike. Louis's war on the continent had been a distant threat, yet now it seemed to many members of the English parliament that the French monarch was at the back door. The Anglo-French naval attack on the Dutch drove Parliament to force Charles to remove his Declaration of Indulgence, and rigidly enforce the penal laws. The Test Act soon followed. By 1677 Parliament sought to ensure against future 'mishaps' through the introduction of a bill barring any member of the royal family marrying a Catholic bride without the consent of Parliament. Questions were raised over the succession. William and Mary's marriage in November 1677 was shortly followed by the birth of a son to the Duke of York. Although the infant died within a few weeks, the perceived threat of a Catholic successor had become all too clear to Parliament, thereby threatening to displace Mary and Anne, James's Protestant daughters, from the crown.

Such were the conditions under which the Popish Plot was unleashed, an atmosphere of fear and doubt, ripe for the use of propaganda, anti-Catholic rabble-rousing and royal intrigue. Titus Oates and co-conspirator Israel Tongue claimed that there existed a Jesuit plan for the assassination of Charles II, which would leave the throne empty for James, a Catholic king. Fate and coincidence conspired to give credence to the whole affair. Subsequent events would bring James close to ruin. As if this was not enough to rouse suspicion, the unexplained murder of Sir Edmund Godfrey, a judge whom Tongue and Oates had first approached with details of the plot, only made matters worse. Frenzied anti-Catholic hatred swept through the country; treason trials led to the conviction and execution of twenty-four Catholics, while many died in prison.[2] Troops destined to serve in Ireland after their return from France were no longer trusted. Many were arrested and imprisoned, although many finally made it back to Ireland, including Justin MacCarthy and Patrick Sarsfield.

The force of public and parliamentary opinion in light of the plot, however implausible, was very strong. Many officers returning from France took this as their signal to flee the country, many of the Irish troops returning to Ireland. Some who did not escape were executed at the end of the plot, as news spread that Irishmen had apparently been involved in Godfrey's murder. The witch-hunt in England continued and the wave of anti-Catholic and anti–monarchist feeling enabled the pro-parliamentarian 'Whigs' to gain significant ground in the commons over the 'Tories', whose allegiance was to Church and King.

Opposition to James would not end simply with the plot's intrigues. In 1679 the Earl of Shaftsbury, leader of the Whig opposition to Charles II, put forward the Exclusion Bill, designed to keep James off the throne. His exploits came to naught as fears of a new civil war meant that opinion swayed towards the Royalists. Parliament was once more dissolved in 1681. James would survive all these attempts to circumvent his right to succession, although the frenzy stirred up by Oates's depositions would last for years.

Anthony Hamilton, who had left French service and his officer's rank around 1677, had ultimately returned to Ireland. By 1681 he was established in Dublin, in all likelihood there to look after what interests his father had in Ireland after his death, or as a means of escaping the anti-Catholic hysteria that beset England. However, he would be haunted by the Hamilton family curse – indebtedness! Having taken a lease of his uncle's property in Nenagh, his subsequent investments or attempts to make money on the property were unsuccessful. In the midst of these activities, both Anthony and Justin MacCarthy, who had escaped prosecution in England and returned to Ireland as the effective leader of the returning officer cadre, were implicated in their own 'Popish Plot'. A rogue witness implicated a footman who had served both Hamilton and MacCarthy abroad in another twisted element of the overall scheme.[3] Although he was given little credence, this was something that Hamilton clearly did not need and he appears to have left Ireland for a time at least. His cousin, the Earl of Arran, remarked to his father Ormonde:

Since the new plot informer is watching for a proper conjuncture to gain belief, or some persons in power that may seem to give credit to him. I will examine some persons here concerning him for I am told that he has been Justin Macarthy's footman and also Anthony Hamilton's; but Justin is now in the country, and Anthony is absconded, there being many writs out against him, and the best fund he has to pay his numerous creditors is the lease he has from your Grace of Nenagh, and that I think very proper for your Grace to purchase, and to that purpose I have writ to my Uncle Matthew having heard that you had formerly a mind to have that lease up. I am told my cousin Hamilton's intention is to go for England.[4]

The plot in Ireland proved to be little more than hysteria. The very real problem for Anthony Hamilton, however, was that of his debts. It is likely that Ormonde became involved, and Anthony did return to Ireland. In 1684, after the evacuation of Tangiers and the imminent return of many Irish troops, Ormonde considered Hamilton as a potential commander of a dragoon regiment.[5] The appointment would never be made, although Anthony remained in Ireland.

In February 1685 Charles II died from a stroke. Despite his faults and his apparent opposition to James's religion and his Catholic succession, he could not deny his brother his right. However, he had been prudent enough to ensure that his nieces, James's daughters, had been brought up as Protestants. This ensured Mary's marriage to William and a Protestant succession if all else failed. James's second wife, the Italian Mary of Modena, had borne no male children, at least by 1685. Charles had also been farsighted enough to declare Monmouth, his son and erstwhile commander of the English troops in France, officially illegitimate, thereby denying his right to the throne. The subtle Charles had also remarked to William that he expected James to last no more than four years on the English throne. William would not forget his uncle's statement. During Charles's last week, as his stroke took hold, James took measures to ensure that, should his accession be threatened, the militia and the army would uphold order. Sunderland issued directives that those entering England via her ports were to be searched and arrested if necessary. There were to be no immediate grabs for the throne, however, not just yet.

Richard Hamilton remained in France in command of his regiment. He served with some distinction although the wars of Louis XIV were temporarily halted.[6] These years marked a barren period for further promotion, despite the earlier attempts of Charles to gain recognition for the young Hamilton.

Promotion aside, he was reasonably successful in France. He was one of the few 'foreigners' who commanded a French infantry regiment, was for the most part liked and respected, and had become quite the French courtier. However, he would fall foul of Louvois once more. Passing comment on the state of his men, Louvois criticised the regiment. Hamilton disagreed, blaming too rigorous an inspection and offering, now that James was on the throne, that he could return to England and have his services more fully appreciated. Louvois in turn responded that Louis would hold no man against his will. An enraged Louis then informed Hamilton that he could leave for England as and when he wished, adding that, were it not for his sister la Comtesse de Gramont, he would have been thrown in the Bastille over the affair; Elizabeth's influence was still powerful, it seemed.

Hamilton sold his regiment. Indeed it seemed that he, too, had incurred debts during his service. These he paid. The French court then reported that he had been disgraced over a relationship with Louis's daughter, the Princess de Conti, although James's accession to the throne may have more clearly motivated the young Hamilton to move on. Shortly before leaving Paris, he once more courted notoriety. Walking in the gardens of the Royal Palace with the Marquis d'Alincourt, the pair became involved with a number of swordsmen. As insults were traded and swords were drawn, the two faced twice their number and had to call for help to avoid being killed. Louis was incensed that such behaviour could occur in his Palais Royal gardens, but took no action knowing that this would only delay the departure of the 'mad Irishman'. The court had a different version of events, believing that the two had fought a duel over the same lady, and the fight with armed men had been a cover-up. Whatever the truth, there were still many who were sorry to see Hamilton leave. He had been described as courageous, handsome and kind, but he was returning home.[7]

Hamilton had been encouraged by events in England and the possibilities that surrounded the new king. Despite the opposition manifest in the Popish Plot and the Exclusion Crisis, James II succeeded his brother peacefully. He was not a subtle man and his determination to improve the lot of his Catholic subjects would heighten the ever-present fears amongst the Whigs, that the new king's religion and 'Francophilia' would encourage absolute government. Although some degree of antipathy was predictable, England as a whole remained essentially Royalist, at least initially. Within months, however, James had a more pressing concern than the simmering fears of a Protestant Parliament, that of protecting his throne. Monmouth had been in Holland when Charles died and remained confident that the revulsion from the English population against a Catholic king would create support for his attempt to take the throne.

His landing at Lyme Regis in June did not create the support that he had predicted, and despite his claims that Charles had been secretly married to his mother, and that James had both started the Great Fire of London and poisoned Charles, his rebellion was limited to the West Country. James's reaction was swift. By July troops under Lord Feversham had routed the rebel force at Sedgemoor. Monmouth, the Protestant Pretender, was executed in June.

The defence of the throne had not been simply a matter of defeating the rebels on land; there had been a number of naval victories. Thomas Hamilton, who had joined the navy in the mid-1660s, had risen to the rank of captain and had for a time served in the Mediterranean where he had captured a large Algerian man o'war and overseen the return of many of the troops from Tangiers. His command had extended across eight naval ships and he was chosen, aboard his latest vessel, the *Kingfisher*, to head an expedition against Monmouth's ally, the Earl of Argyle, off the west coast of Scotland.[8]

Argyle had returned from Holland with Monmouth and had taken control of Ellengreg Castle on the Scottish west coast. His task had been to create a magazine of powder and stores and defend it so that it could take on the role of Monmouth's last bastion should matters go badly in England. Thomas Hamilton's squadron was tasked with capturing the position. The imminent arrival of the English squadron was enough to convince Argyle's men to flee, and they abandoned the castle. However, they had set a trap for the sailors, placing lit match in the store that held over 500 barrels of powder. Hamilton, having landed and been warned of the imminent trap, somehow managed to prevent the explosion and save his own life and those of his men. In addition, he had captured enough powder to arm the rebellion, firearms 'enough to arm thirty thousand men', and colours, undoubtedly held pending the result of action on land.

James had gained confidence from the whole affair, both on land and at sea; his enlarged standing army had grown to almost 16,000 men and had remained loyal and thus convinced him that he could attempt to make the changes in English society that he had envisioned. Whigs saw the situation quite differently. A standing army would be a symbol of enforcement. In reality James lacked the finances for a very large army, certainly not akin to that of Louis XIV. Sedgemoor, however, had re-spawned some of the latent fears that had remained hidden beneath the surface of English society.

James did not immediately disband the troops after the threat to his throne was removed, leading to Parliamentary accusations that it would become a Catholic army. He protested that with such threats to English security he could hardly disband her army. He could have ridden the storm, and bided his time. Instead, he played into Parliament's hands in Ireland.

Calculated political activity had once more become fashionable during Charles's reign and had been used to great effect by James's Irish 'advisor' and friend, Richard Talbot. Talbot had used the system to further his own ends, but to a larger extent than most could ever have dreamed of. He had married George Hamilton's widow, Frances Jennings, sister to Sarah Jennings, wife of John Churchill, the future Duke of Marlborough, and had entered James's inner circle. James's proclivity for Irish adventurers had meant that Talbot had found noteworthy success and possessed some influence with the then heir to the throne. Descended from an old-English family, he had been brought up during the 1641 conflict. He had fought for Thomas Preston and the war had had a great influence on him, developing his political opinions and motivations. His old-English loyalties meant that he possessed a degree of kinship to the church but was also keen to pursue what he saw as the Irish rights. He was, however, looked upon with some suspicion, especially so amongst the native Irish.

The twenty-six-year-old Talbot had met the then twenty-three-year-old Duke of York in 1656 in the exiled court. Talbot would form the principal influence on James's decision to become involved in Irish politics in later years, a decision that would seal his fate. Even then, James had helped secure Talbot's military and, ultimately, political position. By the time of the Restoration and the monarchy's return to England, Talbot was a Gentleman of the Bedchamber. Such position and relative importance in the court allowed him to focus on the representation of the Irish questions that were important to him. By then he had little real interest in the Catholic Church, his main focus being the Irish land question. He assumed correctly that the balance of power in Ireland would lie with those who owned and controlled the land. He had had his way to a large extent during the Restoration settlement, supported mainly by the 'old-English' Royalists, many of whom regained their estates. Talbot had been heavily involved in the Acts of Settlement and Explanation, but these affairs earned him as many enemies as friends. The Irish had needed a powerful representative, a champion even, and Talbot had filled the role for many. Talbot as Irish champion highlighted the cause of those Royalist Irish and many benefitted from Charles's and James's reigns. He disagreed with Ormonde on many matters, but his unwavering loyalty to James and relative importance in Irish eyes ensured that his position remained relatively strong. Talbot's power and influence would reach its zenith during the mid-1680s.[9]

1685 would become a pivotal year for Ireland, the Hamilton brothers, and those Catholic officers who had remained loyal to the crown. Richard Talbot would take centre stage. In June James made him the new Earl of Tyrconnel, fully aware that giving Talbot more influence at this time would cause suspicion. James would try to take the steps that would make the English army more accessible to Catholics; he dispensed with the requirements of the Test Acts for many officers, creating his own troop of Life Guards, all Catholic. In reality, the English Catholic officer population would remain at only 10 to 15 per cent of the army by 1688. In Ireland, however, the situation would change both rapidly and dramatically.

The Irish army had been almost exclusively Protestant at the start of 1685. Officers were composed of members of the Protestant aristocracy but the army was not a wholly professional organisation. Despite numbering over 7,000 men, the quality of the troops was below average and even poor in comparison with their European and English cousins. Most soldiers had some training and were familiar with drill and at least a degree of military discipline, but many saw their military role as a 'part-time' affair and would pursue other work as the need dictated. Morale and the quality of equipment in Ireland were also suspect. Matchlocks, pikes and swords were badly in need of repair. This essentially Protestant Irish army would have been useless at Sedgemoor, for instance, but had the potential at least to be turned into a reliable fighting force. James was determined to 're-model' it.

For such a task, the king, who had never been to Ireland, needed advice. He turned to his friend Richard Talbot, now Earl of Tyrconnel, in an act that would have far-reaching consequences for both England and Ireland. James would come to believe, perhaps naively, that Ireland was a restless Catholic nation that he could govern justly. He would never have this opportunity in England, that of dispensing his own form of religious justice and supporting the Catholic population, with the promise of their loyalty and support in return, support that would be lacking in England.

Tyrconnel, to James's ultimate detriment, saw the situation quite differently. James's subsequent policy towards Ireland was a direct result of Tyrconnel's persuasion, although he had radically different aims. His main goal was to overthrow the land settlement, the cause for which this old-English Catholic had fought for so long. That clearly meant a replacement of the Protestant hegemony, a task that could only be accomplished through careful manipulation of the new king's wishes.

The *interpretation* of James's wish to help the Catholic population of Ireland was key to Tyrconnel's plan. Matters would hinge on disarming the militia and hamstringing the existing Irish Army. Ultimately the military Protestant force would have to be replaced with a Catholic one, in terms of both officers and men. The unseen danger for James was Parliament's interpretation of such efforts, and their subsequent perceived intent. If Protestant troops and officers were replaced with Catholics, was this a model for a re-structuring of the English army? Would reform be carried out in Ireland to create a Catholic standing army that could then be used to enforce James's policies across the Irish Sea in England? For James, these questions created a political quagmire.

Tyrconnel's plans began in summer 1685. Having persuaded James to recall the Duke of Ormonde to England, and thus to some extent free to make revolutionary changes, he needed to introduce some well-chosen Catholics into the Irish Army. Ormonde, very much in keeping with the tide of Irish events, had discovered his replacement as Lord Lieutenant by Clarendon, by reading a news-sheet on his way to London. A contemporary wrote:

> the Duke of Ormonde, Lord Lieutenant of Ireland, is removed from that government ....
> ... his regiment given to Colonel Talbot; the privy council is dissolved and a new one appointed, and some talk as if there were a design for the papists regaining their estates in that kingdom.[10]

Tyrconnel also had to convince James that the existing Protestant officer corps in Ireland could form the basis of parliamentary-derived resistance. He was given what can only be described as free rein over the re-organisation of the king's Irish forces. In July he instructed that officers in the militia were to ensure that their troops' arms were kept in their own houses. This ensured that such weapons, belonging to the Protestant troops, could be collected easily at a later date. Within a few short weeks, with James's backing, Tyrconnel assumed full control of the Irish military. What occurred next can be construed as a reform or, more distinctly, a purge. Tyrconnel's broad aim was to replace Protestant officers with old-English Catholics whilst sacking the rank-and-file Protestant troops and replacing them with native Irish; such efforts were drastic and if carried out too quickly could have serious repercussions for the army, but Tyrconnel would not be stopped.

This endeavour was, at least initially, his own private interpretation of James's Irish and definitively pro-Catholic 'policy'. He did not have royal sanction for any reform or purge of the existing troops, although it is clear that James must also have turned a blind eye to the proceedings to some extent. Of course Tyrconnel had his own agenda, that of freeing Ireland from Protestantism and the essentially divisive problem of the land question. He could not publicly reveal his intentions at this stage, although his standing with James and the king's apparent ignorance of the affair allowed him to approach his goal. Despite protests from Clarendon, the new Lord Lieutenant, public denial was the norm, although it was clear to many of the gentry what the ultimate aim was.[11]

The Hamiltons, being ostensibly loyal, French trained, and Catholic military officers, would benefit from the new regime. New Catholic regiments were being created; of these a regiment of dragoons was formed. Almost immediately upon his return from France, James appointed Richard Hamilton as colonel of a regiment that he would be charged with raising.[12] Anthony and John Hamilton would not be viewed as so important as the more experienced Richard, whose French experience allowed him to find his true calling in Tyrconnel's eyes at least, although they would receive commissions in the new Irish army.

Anthony became a lieutenant colonel in the notorious Sir Thomas Newcomen's foot regiment, while the younger John became a lieutenant in Lord Mountjoy's Regiment.[13] By the start of 1686 the next phase had begun. Lord Clarendon arrived in Dublin as the new Lord Lieutenant. He later said of Newcomen:

> Sir Thomas Newcomen has desired my leave to go for England, and he will embark within a day or two: you know his dependence, and upon that account I did not think fit to refuse him. He hopes to get his commission of Major General under the great seal renewed, which he says, he first obtained by the favour of this King, when Duke. If he does not gain his desire, I shall not be sorry, nor will anybody else here; for I never knew a man more hated.[14]

Clarendon, it seemed, had more trust in Anthony than in the commander of the regiment, even asking him to investigate personally a murder charge against one of the regiment's captains.[15] In the case of Anthony Hamilton, Clarendon's trust would not founder on the rocks of Irish political ambition;

he would clearly gain respect for him. His powers over the army, however, were somewhat limited.

Clarendon's position was relatively untenable, in light of the military 'revolution' that was underway. He was instructed by James to direct Tyrconnel, by now a lieutenant general, to increase the pace of reform in the Irish army; this would ultimately lend credence to the activities. Tyrconnel was in turn instructed to review the army periodically and replace those 'unfit persons' with others more qualified for the posts. The meaning of such direction was left open to interpretation – ultimately Tyrconnell's reading of the situation.[16] Despite Clarendon's protests, there was little that he could do against the powerful Tyrconnel who was apparently backed by the king.

By the end of 1685, and with gathering impetus, the purge had reached new heights. Over 1,000 men had been replaced in the army. 1686 would see more 're-modelling'. James had not been so naïve as to give Tyrconnel the lord lieutenancy of Ireland but pressure was mounting. He was well aware of the importance of the Protestants in Ireland; they formed the basis of revenue, family connections and, more importantly, guaranteed the support of Parliament so long as Ireland remained subservient. James, despite the fact that he had issued no clear instruction for Tyrconnel's activities, was slowly losing control of this most important of political aces. By 1686 the situation was wholly in the hands of Tyrconnel. Review and muster of existing troops became bywords for replacement and disbandment. In July over 300 men were removed from the Irish Guards in one day. By September over 5,000 men had been replaced. Excuses for these activities such as removal of 'old' and 'unfit' soldiers abounded, but there was by then little subtle masquerade left with regard to the purging.[17]

The Muster-Master-General wrote in September 1686 regarding Tyrconnel:

> The abstract of the Army as it now stands contains an estimate of Roman Catholics entertained to June muster, but since that there has been a general disbanding of the old Army, so that he is apt to believe that already two-thirds of the Army at least are Roman Catholics. He has marked the commissioned officers that are generally reputed to be Roman Catholics. The Lieutenant-General of the Army having power to make what changes he pleases in the Army under commissioned officers has lately appointed Romish chaplains to the regiment of guards, the Earl of Ardglass's regiment and Col. Russell's regiment, and several others are expected. The writer may count some for Roman Catholics which are not such,

yet on the other hand he is confident many more are omitted which might have been added.[18]

Replacing two-thirds of the Protestant Irish Army with Catholics was by no means an easy task, even with the changes in the political climate. For Tyrconnel to have moved so far and so fast was indeed a major coup. So rapid was the purge that some contemporaries, notably the Marshal of the Irish Army, Lord Granard, were convinced that he commanded royal authority in the entire affair.[19]

Tyrconnel's subterfuge was almost complete, and even if some guessed at his lack of royal prerogative it mattered little now, as they were relatively powerless in the situation that was developing. In September 1685 he dismissed all the officers of his own regiment who had received their commissions from Ormonde. His pretence at surprise when asked about the affair was symptomatic of his ability to get away with it.[20] The purge would reach its height in the year to come, as he grew even more confident.

Justin MacCarthy, in circumstances similar to the Hamiltons, had also clearly benefited from the new Irish political scene, being made major general in the army. He, too, benefited from the trust of Clarendon early in his tenure, although MacCarthy's Irish loyalties would ultimately prevail.[21]

Anthony Hamilton would not be such an active member in Tyrconnel's scheme, unlike both his brother Richard and his cousin Justin. His remarkable lack of enthusiasm, probably indicating his less relevant position in the Irish army, was based on his belief that the remodelling was not sound. Clarendon related of Hamilton's plight in the affair in June 1686:

> If Lieutenant-colonel Anthony Hamilton may be believed (and I take him to be the best of that sort,) he is in great trouble for these changes; especially for those in his own regiment. He says, the men who are put out of that regiment are as good men as are in the world; and he does not think so of those who are in their rooms. He says, every one of those officers whom he particularly recommended both to my Lord Tyrconnell and Sir Thomas Newcomen, are put out; and that those who are put in, are men who will bring no honour to the service.

In some apparent vindication, Clarendon ended the letter: 'You will believe, I am not displeased to see them have dissatisfactions amongst themselves.'[22]

Whether this incident created a bond between the two, the new Lord Lieutenant was keen to advance Anthony's career. Perhaps Hamilton's discomfort with the strategic direction, and ultimate repercussions, were based on wider concerns. In any event, he trusted Hamilton's judgement with regard to Newcomen's Regiment more than that of its colonel.[23] By July Clarendon was recommending Hamilton to be promoted to full colonel and as a potential member of the new Irish Privy Council.[24] When Anthony sought to go to England for a time, Clarendon's recommendation was striking:

> he is a very worthy man, and of great honour, and will retain a just sense of any kindness you shall do him; he has been in very good employments and esteem when he served abroad; and men of honour cannot always brook the having little men put over their heads, who in the judgement of all the world are not equal to their stations. This gentleman has lived as he ought to do towards me, which I cannot say of everybody here;

Clarendon would sum up, 'He will give you a different account of many things here, from those of his own religion.'[25]

The Protestant Clarendon saw Anthony Hamilton, and his opinions, as a way out of his desperate situation. He trusted the king, realised the reality of the situation in Ireland, and yet remained relatively powerless, perhaps believing that James could not possibly sanction such activities. If Hamilton had similar opinions then he could help voice Clarendon's concerns. By October he was a colonel, and was given control of his own regiment.[26] He would, however, like the Lord Lieutenant, remain relatively powerless and, as an expression of Clarendon's unease in the situation, would have little influence in either Ireland or England.

Clarendon held Richard Hamilton in far less regard; indeed Richard's efforts to pass into England for a time were met with less enthusiasm.[27] Richard Hamilton's views about the purges and the Lord Lieutenant would prove to be the antithesis of his brother Anthony's; he would be responsible for discharging many of the Protestant troops. Justin MacCarthy, too, would follow Tyrconnel's example with relish, making radical changes within his own Irish regiment, and remained widely popular amongst the remaining troops.[28]

Richard's regiment of dragoons had contained such notables as Patrick Sarsfield, freshly returned from French service. Amongst the cornets in the early days of the regiment was one Thomas Lloyd, a man who, being a

Protestant, would probably have lost his commission, and is undoubtedly the same cavalry leader who helped reinforce resistance at Enniskillen a few years later.[29] Further changes in the Irish establishment were afoot whether Clarendon liked the situation or not. James, determined to improve the standing and position of his ostensibly loyal Roman Catholic subjects, restructured the Privy Council in Ireland. The Irish civil administration was being rebuilt in the absence of the oaths so beloved by Parliament and the Whigs. Through Tyrconnel the last bastions of the former Protestant hierarchy were removed by the Privy Council and the Judiciary. Positions were allocated in May 1686 to Richard Hamilton, Tyrconnel and Justin MacCarthy, amongst others; Anthony Hamilton would also join the ranks of the council by the end of 1686.[30]

Clarendon's temerity was such that he could not fail to comment on the grumblings within the army. Protestant officers and troops could do little, as Tyrconnel continued to avail himself of the Lord Lieutenant's apparent warrant:

> Lord Tyrconnell told me though the troops in the gross appeared well, yet he had marked several men, who upon account of their age, and for other reasons, were not fit for the King's service. I answered, that he well knew the King's pleasure therein, and that in obedience thereunto I had given him full power to put out and put in such common men, and non-commissioned officers, as he thought fit; and therefore I would not meddle in that matter: but I did desire, that whatever men he thought fit to put out, it might be done regularly, and due certificates made thereof to the Muster-master-general, whereby I might grant warrants for the pay of those men so put out; which had not been observed in several places in the countries, where the new officers had dismissed great numbers of men, some even whole companies, without giving them any certificates of what  was due to them.[31]

Clarendon had little influence over the continuing policy. By mid-1686 it was made clearer that matters were out of his hands, yet his frustration at his lack of authority and inability to act became apparent; such frustration appeared to fall upon Tyrconnel and Richard Hamilton:

> But sure I am, I will be content to be condemned for any ill step I have made here, and any Catholic shall be my judge. Why then

must I have this ignominious disgrace put upon me? Might not I have been employed to do what has to be done in the army; and if I had not done it, or not well done it, had there not been a better reason to be angry with me than there is yet? Lord Tyrconnell himself, after all his infallible skill, cannot draw up a regiment, which is visible here; and when a troop or company is drawn up, he sends an order to the Captain to put out such men as Colonel Richard Hamilton shall mark: could not I have done that as well?[32]

Clarendon's early experiences with Richard Hamilton, as with MacCarthy, are positive, yet the relationship would not last. He had even agreed that MacCarthy should be promoted to major general. However, James went further, making Tyrconnel a lieutenant general and Richard a 'Brigadier of the Army in Ireland'. Clarendon complimented them to some degree in the early days, although there was evidently some inexperience within Hamilton's Regiment. In September 1686, he wrote:

At Cork the Major-general's [MacCarthy's] regiment is quartered for the present, for the conveniency of seeing them all together: I saw them all drawn out, and exercise; which they perform as well as can be expected from men who have no longer in the service. Next week five companies of them are to march to Waterford, where they are to winter. Last night I came to this place, where Colonel Hamilton is at present, and his whole regiment of Dragoons. I have also seen them exercise, at which they are as adroit as is possible for new men to be: it is, indeed, a very fine regiment and need not be ashamed to appear before the king, if there were occasion. The men are raw, are apt to commit too many disorders, and some of their officers being young and unexperienced did not keep them in so good discipline as they ought to have done; but the Colonel's having been a little time with them has done them (I hope) all good, for he will have order observed.[33]

Richard further exacerbated the discipline and experience concerns within the Irish army by becoming closely involved with the cashiering of troops under his command. The new Irish army was untrained and unaccustomed to military drill, discipline and weaponry. The majority of the old-English and Irish officers were inexperienced and unable to maintain discipline; the repercussions of the actions would prove far-reaching. Both Hamilton and

MacCarthy supported Tyrconnel's attempts to undermine the Protestant militia, requesting the further removal and storage of weapons. Richard Hamilton played a major role. For instance, his brother's former regiment (Thomas Newcomen's) of 850 men would grow from having around 100 Catholic officers and men in September 1685 to over 700 one year later.[34]

Clarendon's time in Ireland, as he himself had predicted, was rapidly coming to an end. He had been, to some degree, a scapegoat for James's and Tyrconnel's schemes. Neither could move too quickly there within the framework of parliamentary England; Clarendon had been a convenient stopgap. The unassuming Lord Lieutenant, relatively powerless, could do little as his trust in his Irish 'friends' was slowly eroded in the sweeping tide of the new Irish ascendancy. If Clarendon did not altogether trust Richard Hamilton, at least he had had hopes on coming to some arrangement with MacCarthy.[35] Both MacCarthy and Hamilton, however, would conspire against him over deductions made from the Irish army's pay, stating that the army was 'in such want of subsistence' that 'they should all be ruined'.[36] Clarendon would soon realise how naïve he had been; he had few friends amongst the Irish and his time as the puppet Lord Lieutenant was fast coming to an end.

By February 1687 he had been recalled and Tyrconnel was promoted only to Lord Deputy, a title bestowed by James, who was still not naïve enough to grant full title to an Irishman with the increasingly suspicious eyes of English Protestantism looking on. However, Tyrconnel, in the absence of a new lord lieutenant, was effectively in charge. For the native Irish, it was a time for rejoicing; for the Whigs, despite James's attempts to reduce the impact of the change, it was justification of their suspicions. Clarendon's inability to influence the continued purge of the army meant that little could be done to stop it. By the summer of 1687 there was little need to further disguise or otherwise hide the reverses that were occurring. They were all too apparent. Tyrconnel not only had control of the army, but the country. Leaving London with his new commission, he was accompanied by both Anthony and Richard Hamilton, and by his wife.[37]

James met with Tyrconnel over a two-day period in Chester during August. There is little accurate record of what was discussed, although the future of Ireland and the Irish army were most likely prominent issues. Despite the changes that had already taken place in the Irish military and society in general, James could not afford to give Tyrconnel a complete free rein over the still very English dominion. Parliament would not stand for radical revolutionary change. However, he was eager to secure his throne.

Speculation was rife that Tyrconnel had been summoned to England to be reprimanded over his policy in Ireland. This would not be the case. Although there is no definite evidence of what was discussed, French reports indicated that James not only backed Tyrconnel's actions but also agreed to his plan to put Ireland under French protection in the event of his death. The Act of Settlement was also supposedly discussed, but James stopped short of repealing it altogether.

Tyrconnel reviewed the army in the summer to establish how many Protestants were left rather than to remove any remaining 'unfit' personnel. By autumn 1687 the purge of officers was all but complete; only two Protestant colonels remained, a matter that created its own problems. When reviewing the army, Tyrconnel paid little heed to the real problems that were being fostered. Rather than focusing on the decaying administration, reduction in financial support, and the advancement of relatively poor Irish gentry, who were unable to support their regiments, he focused on removing the last Protestants, who had some experience of running the Irish army. Their removal would undermine the already sub-standard force.

Tyrconnel's preference for old-English Catholics over the Protestant gentry in the officer corps also had an influence on discipline, level of training, and thus readiness that had existed. This situation could only be exacerbated by the replacement of the rank and file. Ill-supported by untrained officers, lack of discipline and training would bedevil the fledgling Catholic Jacobite force and the cause of both Tyrconnel and James. Clarendon's reports related to MacCarthy and Hamilton's superior troops were not representative of the balance of the new army. Although the Hamiltons, MacCarthy and a few others had experience in France and were, to a large extent, professional soldiers, their numbers were too few to have real impact on the Irish army. Around thirty-six officers from the French service would re-surface in the newly modelled Irish force, less than ten per cent of the officer corps. Matters were made worse by their wide dispersal across the different regiments, in turn diluting their overall effectiveness. Had they been concentrated in two or three 'crack' units then matters might have been very different.

Throughout 1686 and 1687 civil disorder between displaced Protestants and Irish troops bedevilled Dublin. There was little alternative employment for the cashiered men and, despite Clarendon's requests for compensation, little had been done. Despite some deaths and the general disorder, many displaced troops travelled to England, the Anglo-Dutch Brigade or the Imperial army in Hungary. Some officers returned to their estates. Many turned to brigandage since, in most cases, the officers had put considerable amounts of their own funds into their regiments and thus were destitute.

At the same time ill-disciplined Catholic troops were abroad throughout the country and, in many cases, plundered rich Protestants and trading ships. Such acts were viewed as a form of retribution against the Protestant hierarchy that had for so long formed the ruling class. The actions also gave a clear indication of the poor potential for any serious use of the raw troops for protracted offensive or defensive activities. Social distinctions that had previously existed in the Irish army, between officers and rank-and-file were now not so distinct. Officers no longer inspired the fear and respect required to effectively run a seventeenth-century army, but in many cases encouraged and aided the unruly behaviour. Whether class distinction had been right or wrong, its existence had kept the army disciplined. It was clear that the purge had moved too far and too fast.

The Irish army in 1685 had lacked training but its officer corps was relatively experienced, at least in terms of running the organisation, a social elite of sorts in terms of administration and funding, sitting as part of the recognised establishment. Tyrconnel, with the intention of furthering his aims on the land question, overturned the establishment and created an army that could do little to further his or James's aims. Experienced officers such as Hamilton, MacCarthy and Sarsfield were all too rare, and too thinly spread to make a real difference. Despite the attempts at drill and exercise that were made, most notably at the Curragh camp in the summer of 1686, their effects were diluted through the rapidity of the purge.[38]

Much of this must have been obvious to both Tyrconnel and James. To this end, there can have been little intention to use the Irish army as any more than a vehicle to further the political pursuits of Irish Catholics by 1686. It could not be used effectively in England, nor could it be used to exercise James's will; indeed it is questionable how much it could have been used in active defence of Ireland. For the English Whigs, however, the events in Ireland were interpreted very differently. There had been rumours of James' intention to 're-model' the English army to favour Catholics. He had, perhaps inadvertently, shown the Whigs that he could do this in Ireland; added to this was the threat of a Catholic army being made ready across the Irish Sea, and the stories from displaced Protestant soldiers who had ended up in England. The scene was set for yet another change in English politics and, ultimately, the monarchy. There was no evidence to suggest that James had any absolutist intent, but the Popish plot had shown that a

Protestant Parliament did not need a substantial degree of evidence to foster anti-Catholic sentiment and, ultimately, a very English revolution.

The events of the 'Glorious Revolution' of 1688 had a measured effect on the events that followed in Ireland. There were many key questions in England related to James' future but, for William, there was only one key concern, that of the English succession. Until autumn 1687 Mary of Orange, William's wife and James's daughter, was viewed as the obvious successor, since James's young wife, Mary of Modena, had no surviving children. In 1687, however, she was pregnant again. A boy would secure a Catholic succession and mean that William's preference for an English alliance against the still aggressive Louis XIV would become impossible. The relationship between William and his father-in-law immediately became estranged, setting in motion a chain of events that would see Charles II's prediction of his brother's brief tenure on the English throne proven correct.

*Chapter 7*

# A Revolution and a King

At the beginning of 1688 James wrote to his son-in-law insisting that the English regiments then serving in Holland be recalled, a plan apparently initiated by Tyrconnel. Suspicion of William's use of these troops was forefront in James's mind. William would not accept James's alternative suggestion of an Irish Catholic commander for the men, and the Dutch States General eventually agreed that the officers could return to England. Many of the rank-and-file would be allowed to leave at a later stage. Most of the Protestant officers and soldiers stayed. These, and some of the disbanded Irish Protestant troops, may have had some influence on William's decision to take action in England, although that seems less likely when taken in context with the other more important deciding factors. In any event, Tyrconnel warned James in August 1688 that a coup d'etat with designs on the English throne was being developed in Holland.

English opinion may have been swayed to a larger extent by the policies of the king. Late in 1688 James was urged by the French ambassador to bring Irish regiments to England to strengthen his position. The use of Catholic troops to protect England in a climate of impending 're-modelling' of the army, whether real or imagined, could only harm James's position. At the end of September Tyrconnel was ordered to despatch three infantry regiments and a dragoon regiment to England. Amongst the infantry was Forbes's Regiment, one of the few Irish units that had kept a large proportion of its Protestant troops, proving that Tyrconnel was no fool perhaps, although, in the event, it would be a proviso that would have little effect.

Anthony Hamilton's regiment also landed.[1] The dragoon regiment, which had been that formerly commanded by Anthony's brother Richard, was also included in the force, although now commanded by Colonel John Butler, a cousin to the Hamiltons. Richard had instead received a regiment of horse.[2] For the most part, Tyrconnel had been careful to select regiments that would, in theory, create fewest problems in England. There were many Protestants and he must have believed that the inclusion of Anthony Hamilton at least, with his well-known reserve over the recent purges, would help smooth matters. All of this apparent goodwill, however, was destroyed, almost overnight, by the behaviour of MacElligott's Regiment.

MacElligott's men became known as the 'Terror of Portsmouth', drinking, robbing and assaulting the inhabitants of the town. An Irish soldier fired a shot into a Protestant church, playing into the hands of the Whigs. The Duke of Berwick, James's illegitimate son, later attempted to recruit some of MacElligott's troops into his own regiment whilst he was governor of Portsmouth. Five Protestant captains were dismissed because of their refusal to accept the troops. James's image suffered as William used the event to provide him with useful propaganda. Incidents such as this helped to alienate many of the Protestant officers against James's policy and one cannot avoid the obvious comparison with earlier events in Ireland and the fear of 're-modelling' in the English army. The entire episode had backfired.

A strong Tory parliament had allowed James various freedoms and he was able to create a standing army which carried the day at Sedgemoor and defeated Monmouth in 1685, giving him the confidence to make changes in legislation that would improve, to a certain extent, the situation of the Catholic population who had been denied public office by various acts of Parliament. James's 1687 Act of Indulgence, which repealed various laws against non-Anglican worship, combined with his interference in parliamentary issues and the work of Tyrconnel in Ireland, highlighted the Whigs' fears; concerns centred on a Popish king and a Catholic army allied with France did little to encourage belief in James's unbiased intent. Events would conspire to undermine his reign. William had been disturbed at James's conduct and the subsequent birth of a male heir in June 1688. Despite Whig attempts to discredit its authenticity, there was enough evidence to convince William to listen to those who prompted him to take action; any potential loss of English support in the inevitable war against Louis would prove problematic, especially so if an Anglo-French alliance brought English troops into conflict against him. A combination of this threat and the fear that his wife Mary could be cut out of the succession meant that William could not afford to remain idle.

When James's son, the new Prince of Wales, was born, Louis XIV also rapidly understood the potentially dangerous situation. He despatched the ever-faithful Gramont to England. On this occasion, unlike so many others, Gramont would not have time for drinking and the gambling tables; his secret orders from the French king were centred on determining those measures that James was taking against the increasingly likely attack from William. He would be required to determine the strength of the English Army and the Royal Navy, conditions for protracted defence and, more importantly, the likely loyalties of English officers in the event of invasion. This last concern would be a most difficult matter to pinpoint, yet such intelligence would dictate the manner in which the invasion of England would be fought; a bloodless coup would be something Louis could ill afford, and certainly he could not easily act against it with French troops. If this were not enough, Gramont was also commanded to find the leaders of the parties opposed to James, to converse with them, and using his 'insinuating manners' to gain intelligence regarding the means and timing of any plot designed to undermine or indeed overthrow James.[3]

James seemed less concerned about the entire affair, the prospect of losing his kingdom apparently the furthest thing from his mind. Dalrymple recorded that 'While tempests were on all hands gathering round King James, he interested himself only in reconciling the King of France with the holy see and in the fate of the war against the infidels'.[4] In this atmosphere Gramont could find no evidence of a plot and would return to Louis in September 1688 with a present of 1,000 guineas, but little else in terms of intelligence. All was apparently quiet in England, despite rumours of action from the Dutch, and Gramont had turned up little.[5]

Action from William, however, would prove to be a very real prospect. The decision to move in a well-supported English coup had already been taken. William's fleet landed at Torbay on 5 November 1688, prepared to embark on a task fraught with risk. He could not admit openly to his European allies that he sought to depose James, nor could he be sure of English support despite the propaganda and the best efforts of some Englishmen. But he was sure that England would be a vital ally in the war with Louis that would surely come. In return, he would offer a free Parliament and an end to Whig fears of absolutist monarchy.

The move was a pre-emptive strike against a new Anglo-French alliance, an alliance that would inevitably see new attacks on the Dutch if created. Although there had been peace between Holland and France since the Treaty of Nijmegen in 1678, Louis and William had become locked in a personal battle of wills: another war became inevitable. Louis had made efforts against Dutch trade, persecuted French Huguenot Protestants after the revocation of the Edict of Nantes, and made calculated political alliances throughout Europe with a view to renewed attacks in the Spanish Netherlands; England was one ally that William was determined should not fall within the French purview.

James initially resolved to fight. With the approach of the Dutch ships in early November, four regiments of horse under Sir John Lanier, another officer with experience in French service, the Earl of Arran, Ormonde's son and the Hamiltons' cousin, Colonel Conner and Richard Hamilton were sent towards Ipswich. Another three regiments were sent towards Colchester. William's decision to land at Torbay had meant that the regiments sent to intercept were not required and would be moved. Lanier, however, would later declare for William. He also would have declared for the Prince of Orange had he landed at Ipswich and, in conjunction with his officers, had resolved to secure the colonels of the other three regiments, including Hamilton, had the landing taken place there.[6]

James then surprisingly lost his nerve, perhaps fearing widespread desertion in the wake of John Churchill and Sunderland's early defection to William's cause. In the main, however, military disloyalty was not as widespread as he feared. In the event, most of James's soldiers remained faithful, despite the presence of Irish troops in England and the purges that had occurred in Ireland. Their allegiance never seemed seriously in doubt. However, sufficient concern had been raised amongst a small officer corps to encourage William and, indirectly, defeat James. The common soldier remained loyal to his king. The fact that a conspiracy existed and that senior officers in the army had created it seems to have unnerved James at the critical moment and allowed the 'bloodless' revolution to continue. Churchill's defection had not been a spur of the moment decision. James had known that William had agents in his army, but the scale of the problem and the conspiracies founded by secret quasi-military societies such as the 'Treason Club', the 'Tangerines', composed of ex-Tangiers officers, and the members of the Anglo-Dutch Brigade seem to have been underestimated. Unlike their counterparts of a later era, the officer in the seventeenth century was an opportunist, if not altogether a mercenary. Many officers served throughout Europe, making contacts at many levels. The fact that a military conspiracy could be hatched with influential English politicians then seems less surprising, especially since standing armies were such a new concept, and their loyalty not always guaranteed.

With the defection of many influential officers, and James's inability to know whom he could trust, Richard Hamilton was appointed major general over the remaining troops in mid-November, but there was little left to command.[7] On 9 December the Queen and the infant Prince of Wales were sent to France; James's attempt to join them was upset when he was captured and returned to London, then to Rochester. Accompanying the King along the Thames on what would be his final journey in his native land were Lord Arran, Lord Lichfield, Lord Dumbarton, Lord Aylesbury and Richard Hamilton, five loyal subjects, whom James must have felt were the last friends that he had in the world.[8] He made his escape from Rochester by 23 December (o.s.), escaping to France and his wife and child.

Misinformation characterised James's intelligence at the time of the invasion, although he had had little choice about the disposition of his forces. Despite foul weather, William's landing was unopposed, and the advantages of James's striking early against an amphibious landing were lost. The country was now certain of one thing: it would join in the Grand Alliance's impending war against France, at the very least to ensure against James's return to the throne. William had let his father-in-law's escape attempt succeed, mainly to ease the suffering of his wife, whose father's throne he had taken. Despite fears over the number of Irish troops then in England, most of them would return to Ireland.[9]

What of the Hamiltons in England, however? Would their loyalty to a Catholic king become their undoing? Anthony Hamilton's regiment was quickly disbanded in the rapid re-organisation that followed William's accession to the throne, Anthony probably making his way back to Ireland with many of the other Irish troops. For Richard there would be a period of imprisonment on the Isle of Wight with many Irish soldiers until such times as the new authority could work out exactly what to do with them. Ultimately, some would be re-integrated into the army, but for Hamilton circumstances would change significantly.

In Ireland, the 'Glorious Revolution' had created a crisis. Tyrconnel's immediate fear was that both he and Ireland would be William's next target. Irish Protestants rallied immediately both to the revolution and King William; the events in England did to some extent provoke a reaction against Tyrconnel. Now that James was no longer king, Protestant rebellion against the changes that the Lord Lieutenant had wrought became a reality. Plans were made to seize Dublin Castle and kill Tyrconnel, but these came to naught. Ulster Protestants appealed directly to William; at Londonderry the gates were famously shut against Lord Antrim's regiment; the threat of early action was quickly galvanised by rumours of impending massacres of Protestants to an extent not seen since the 1641 rebellion. Many people panicked and there was a rapid flight of families to Great Britain; Tyrconnel issued a public statement with reference to such rumours in an attempt to avoid panic and thus prevent the possible threat of Protestant action amongst those who chose to stay. By the same token, news of James's flight caused concern amongst the Catholic population, who became more fearful of a rapid Williamite descent on Ireland.

In the north, many Protestants, who could form *en masse* in Ulster more so than any other region, created armed associations for their defence. Events at Bandon in Cork would see the immediate involvement of Justin MacCarthy. In County Down in Ulster the objective was to preserve 'the public peace of the nation … in these distracted times wherein no lawful government is established in the kingdom of Ireland'. In Sligo, Protestants were determined to 'unite with England and hold to the lawful government thereof and a free parliament'. At Londonderry the gates had been closed, but Tyrconnel, ever the skilful diplomat and politician reached agreement of sorts with the garrison, and discussion was re-vitalised by the admittance of the Protestant troops of Lord Mountjoy's Regiment, one of the few regiments aside from Forbes's that still contained Protestants despite the purges.[10]

Speculation became rife about William and Tyrconnel, no longer concerning invasion, but in terms of negotiation over Ireland and its future. Was Tyrconnel willing to submit? Many Protestants believed so, as did some Catholics in Dublin, at least initially, since the odds stacked against Irish resistance seemed too high. At this point Richard Hamilton once more entered the Irish debate. Through the Protestant Judge Keating and Sir John Temple, the Irish solicitor-general and brother to the ex-English ambassador to The Hague, word travelled to William of Tyrconnel's apparent intent to disband the troops he had mustered and to remove the levels of government he had created. His wish was only that Catholics could return to the positions that they had occupied at Charles II's death.[11] Despite the apparent incredulity of the communication taken in the context of more recent events, it was taken seriously by William, who had little faith either in the likelihood success of an immediate attack or in the Royal Navy. To this end, and as recommended by Sir William Temple's son, the previously captured Richard Hamilton was sent to Ireland to negotiate in January 1689.[12]

Many English politicians disagreed with the plan, believing that an invasion army or fleet would be more effective 'negotiating' tools. William disagreed, at least initially, and there seems to have been a belief in the potential for ending the problem without a fight. This was in William's best interest. Ireland could be used as a staging post for James's attempted return to England, or worse, a French attack, if it remained in a viable position. Either way, a protracted fight in Ireland would become a thorn in William's side and would use up valuable military and associated resources that could be more effectively used on the continent. A diplomatic answer would have benefitted William, possibly more than any other party. However, such solutions were not to be. Hamilton's arrival in Dublin was greeted with bonfires and celebration: 'the papists lit bonfires when Dick Hamilton came over; they said he was worth 10,000 men'.[13]

Richard Hamilton's defection was unexpected, at least by William. For the Irish it appeared that it was almost inevitable. Hamilton, despite his being regarded as a 'papist', had been seen as a 'man of honour' who had 'great credit with Tyrconnel'.[14] Indeed, upon being given the mission, Hamilton had given his word that he would return to England if an agreement could not be negotiated. For a time at least, his return was expected.[15] However, Hamilton had little regard for the honour of the situation. Indeed, he may have been swayed by the same public opinion that had affected Tyrconnel in Ireland, or felt little honour toward William whom he regarded perhaps as a usurper. In either event, if Hamilton ever returned to England, it would not be as a free man. The subsequent investigation into Hamilton's actions carried out in August 1688 displays some measure of both the theatrical and perhaps the nature of propaganda and its influence used at the time.

Major Done recorded that he had been in Dublin in January 1689 and had been informed that a vessel had arrived from England. Amongst the passengers he counted seventy red-coated soldiers and eleven military officers, including Colonel Richard Hamilton, whom he recognised. The officers proceeded to a local tavern, where Done overheard them. After toasts, Hamilton is credited with laughing and boasting at the nature and success of his 'shamming' of the Prince of Orange with the belief that he had an interest in persuading Tyrconnel to 'lay down his sword' and submit. Upon being asked how it was that William could believe him, Hamilton boasted that he also gained a pass for himself and troops, ending with 'Had King James been so well advised as he might, he need not have come out of England for want of friends to support him.'

After further bragging, Sir Richard Nagle and Secretary Ellis arrived by coach – Hamilton jokingly states 'How, Brother Sham, are you there? The kingdom of Ireland is beholden to you and I, for averting this storm off from them; else you had had ere this an enemy in the bowels of the kingdom'.[16]

It is with this statement for the first time that the discourse reminds us of the serious nature of the activity. Hamilton's involvement had indeed delayed a rapid invasion of Ireland, and Tyrconnel's activities may have been cleverly designed to gain precious time; the Irish saw the retrieval of Richard Hamilton as a bonus. Additional witnesses at the investigation remarked on Tyrconnel's clear intention to submit, having even removed the hangings from Dublin Castle and sent many of his goods away in fear of imminent invasion. The arrival of Hamilton, however, had changed everything. Tyrconnel's attitude toward Protestants and his former diplomacy changed, commissions for raising troops were issued and thoughts turned once more to war rather than peace.

There are probably elements of truth in all of the accounts but it is likely that there was no clear conspiracy to bide for time or regain Hamilton. Circumstance would have invariably played its part. It is likely that Tyrconnel did consider negotiating with William since James had fled, and in early 1689 it was not altogether clear what role William would fill in England or what his attitude to Ireland would be. It is also equally likely that Irish public opinion, swayed by the changes in the army and society, could also have persuaded Tyrconnel that there was a greater threat to his own life if he didn't carry on. It is possible that pressure from the Irish majority could have also persuaded Hamilton as it had persuaded Tyrconnel or it may indeed be true that he held little stock in William's request; in any event the dice had been cast. For John Temple, who had instigated the entire affair, responsibility lay heavily. Judging the amount of blood that would inevitably have to be spilt to take Ireland, and taking the blame for the entire effort, he drowned himself in the Thames in April 1689, leaving a hastily scribbled suicide note.

> My folly in undertaking what I could not execute hath done the
> King great prejudice which cannot be stopped.
>   No easier way for me than this.
>   May his undertakings prosper.
>   May he have a blessing.[17]

One nineteenth-century historian's comments regarding the affair seem almost pertinent enough to repeat:

It is not impossible that Hamilton may have really meant to perform his promise. But when he arrived at Dublin he found that he had undertaken a task which was beyond his power. The hesitation of Tyrconnel, whether genuine or feigned, was at an end. He had found that he had no longer a choice. He had with little difficulty stimulated the ignorant and susceptible Irish to fury. To calm them was beyond his skill. Rumours were abroad that the Viceroy was corresponding with the English; and these rumours had set the nation on fire.[18]

Whether Tyrconnel had been wholly serious or not, he had adapted to the circumstances of the political situation. The mainstay of the population seemed resolved to fight the matter out, and the French ambassador d'Avaux recounted that, had Tyrconnel given in to William, he would have been 'burnt out of his home', and the Irish would have sided immediately with France.[19] Irish public opinion was at the very least a great leveller in terms of diplomatic solutions. However, William's hesitancy over military action in Ireland had been based on his faith in just such a solution. Had he realised that this would never have worked, he would most certainly have tried to take action quickly, decisively and before the arrival of James in Ireland, despite the problems with the English army, funding and Parliament's political wrangling. The Irish Jacobite view was very clear with hindsight; that Tyrconnel had made 'a prudent show of wavering' and that he 'strove to amuse' William's agents.[20] If William had acted quickly he would have 'easily effected what afterwards cost him so much blood and treasure'.[21] There would most certainly be blood.

Tyrconnel had ultimately sided with James. Ireland was in the position where he and his most competent generals, including Richard Hamilton and Justin MacCarthy, had the opportunity to prepare the army and the country for war. French aid was essential, and James's arrival could also be effectively designed to both preserve Louis's support and give the army a figurehead. If all went well, Ireland could sue for terms through its position as the 'thorn' in William's side. Tyrconnel acted swiftly and decisively, at least at the start. Through his own scheming he disposed of Mountjoy, the potential Protestant leader, by sending him to James in France on a fool's errand.

The French ship that brought the Marquis de Pointis to assess the potential of the Irish army returned to France with Lord Mountjoy and Sir Stephen Rice. Mountjoy had in mind a recommendation to James that he should urge Tyrconnel to submit to William; Rice would conversely assure James of Ireland's loyalty and urge him to prevent Mountjoy's return to Ireland.[22] Mountjoy was quickly imprisoned in the Bastille, where he would remain until 1692.

The condition of Ireland at the time is most aptly described in Tyrconnel's letter to James in January:

> By our letters from England, Sir, which constantly come hither as formerly, I have had from time to time the particulars of your Majesty's deliverance out of the hands of your Enemyes, to the unspeakable Joy of all good men and this your Kingdom. I have been ever since in great disquiet not to have heard one from your Majesty until the arrival of Monsieur Pontys, which at first gave me great expectations of considerable sums from thence, but your Majesty's and My Lord Melford's Letters did much surprise me, for I find his great business here was to know the State and Condition of this Kingdome, of which I thought your Majesty very well informed, by my continual applications and care to inform you of every particular relating to It, ever since your accession to the Crown; However since I see It out of your Majesty's Memory, I have in answer to your Majesty's Instructions sent my Lord Melford an answer to every Article of them which comprehends the condition of this Kingdom.
>
> I find by what I can gather by Monsieur Pontys Discourse that the King his Master is well enough dispos'd to succour us with arms and ammunition, but I find him very indifferent upon that Article which most concerns us, and of which we stand in greatest need, which is money, and without which this Kingdom must be infallibly lost. True it is that with arms and ammunition I may assemble a considerable Body of naked men together without clothes, but having no money to subsist, all the order and care I can take will not hinder the ruin of the Country, nor a famine before midsummer.
>
> Your Majesty cannot be ignorant how the City of London hath already furnished the Prince of Orange with 300,000 livres. Sterling for the reduction of this Kingdom, with promise of as much more Money as he shall need for that service. His troops are now marching towards Chester, Liverpool, and Bristol, and they will certainly be supplied with all those necessaries which we want. I

do avow, Sir, I have been as much deceived in the hopes with which hitherto I have flattered myself; that the King of France would spare nothing to preserve a Catholique Country, by which he, as well as your Majesty, might very well count upon great advantage in some reasonable time.

If, Sir, your Majesty will in person come hither and bring with you those succours necessary to support this country, which may not exceed the present allowance given you there (which, as I hear, is 200,000 livres a month) with arms, ammunition and some officers (a particular whereof is here enclosed as well as to My Lord Melford), I will be responsible to you that you shall entirely be the master of this Kingdom and of everything in It; and, Sir, I beg of you to consider whither you can with honour continue where you are when you may possess a Kingdom of your own plentiful of all things for human life. And because there are a multitude of reasons which are too tedious on that subject to write, I have desir'd Monsieur Pontys to explain them to your Majesty, having acquainted him with the whole state of this Kingdom, and whom I find so much in your interests as I am absolutely persuaded he will use his utmost skill and Industry to serve you.

I shall very soon make a bold stroke for your service, which will prove of the last good or ill consequence, of which he will fully inform your Majesty.

I will conclude this letter, Sir, by conjuring your Majesty to consider the condition of this kingdom, and by seriously reflecting upon what I have humbly offer'd to determine the fate of this poor loyal People, if we cannot be supplied to order such course for their preservation as your Goodness and Mercy will move you for their security in these dismal circumstances.

In obedience to your Majesty's commands I humbly represent to you the state of your Kingdom of Ireland in the following Answers, given to the several Articles of your Majesty's instructions.

Your Majesty's Kingdom of Ireland is divided into 4 Provinces, viz. Leinster, Munster, Connaught, and Ulster. The Catholiques of the City of Dublin in Leinster may be guessed to equal in number all other Religions there (not including the soldiers, who are all Catholique). The Catholiques in the rest of that Province are 40 to one of the people of all other Persuasions. The Catholique inhabitants of the Province of Munster are thought to be 40 to one of all other Persuasions. In the Province of Connaught the Catholiques are 200 to one of all other Persuasions. The Catholiques of Ulster are not so considerable, by reason of the greater number of Scotch Presbyterians there, yet may be thought to be as many as all the rest. The said 4 Provinces contain 32 Counties or Shires well planted and inhabited by a numerous people not easily reckon'd; all the Catholiques are unanimous and most zealously affected to your Majesty's service, but amongst the Protestants, generally tainted with the Principles of England, there are not in the whole Kingdom one hundred that may by relied on to serve your Majesty.

As to the Army there are 4 Regiments of Old Troops, and one Battalion of the Regiment of Guards and 3 Regiments of Horse with one Troop of Grenadiers on Horseback.

I have lately given out Commissions for near 40 Regiments of Foot, 4 Regiments of Dragoons, and two of horse, all which amount to near 40,000 men, who are all unclothed and the greatest part unarmed, and are to be subsisted by their several officers until the last of February next out of their own purses, to the ruin of most of them; but after that day I see no possibility for arming them, clothing them or subsisting them for the future but abandoning the Country to them: but after all if I may be supplied by the last of March with those succours that are necessary which I press in my letters, I doubt not but I shall preserve this Kingdom entirely for your Majesty.

As to your protestant subjects here, the most considerable of them, as well as Peers as Commons, are now in England, soliciting the Prince of Orange to invade this Kingdom, many of them having taken commissions from him, and have sent his commissions to several Protestants here. That the Lord Kingston, Lord Mount Alexander, Lord Blany with several other their Protestants adherents are now in actual rebellion in the County of Sligo, and in several other parts of Ulster. That knowing your Majesty's pious care of your Protestant subjects and have been very tender of them, and have of late by Proclamation assur'd those in rebellion of your Majesty's free pardon if they forthwith return to their allegiance, to which I fear at this juncture they will be hardly persuaded.

...I have rais'd 35 or 36,000 men but without arms to defend them, cloths to clothe them, or money to subsist them, or any visible way to maintain them, unless by letting them live on the spoils of the People, which in six months time will destroy both nation and army.

Tyrconnell

(Addition)

To advance before the middle of March at farthest 500,000 crowns in cash, which with our own Industry shall serve for a year.

To send me besides the 8,000 fire arms already sent 6,000 Matchlocks more and 6,000 firelocks.

To send me at least 1,200 swords.

To send me 2,000 Carbines and as many cases of pistols and holsters.

To send me a good number of officers to train.[23]

The end of the letter at least demonstrated the nature of military shortages in Ireland, despite the number of troops available.

Promises of French aid encouraged Tyrconnel and by the end of January he had given commissions for almost forty regiments of foot, with four of dragoons and two cavalry, a total of almost 40,000 men.[24] Wasn't this the Catholic army that James could lead? The French envoy, the Marquis de Pointis, who had arrived in January, noted that men were of poor quality and that most were very poorly armed, although their enthusiasm was noted.[25] Enthusiasm did not win wars, however. Tyrconnel agreed that, rather than French arms, French money was the priority. He asked James to pass on the plight of the troops to Louis, promising Irish land as security, an indication perhaps that the situation was becoming desperate. The men were not paid, and despite Tyrconnel's best efforts, the Irish troops began to fend for themselves making the Protestant 'associations for defence' appear all the more necessary, the lack of discipline suggesting that old scores were in fact being settled.

John, the youngest of the Hamilton brothers, was by now an active officer in the Irish army. In February he travelled to Paris, perhaps with communication from Tyrconnel, and by the 17th he was moving toward Brest with other English and Scottish officers in anticipation of James's leaving for Ireland.[26] He would sail with over eighty other officers accompanying the former king.

For Tyrconnel, the situation by March of 1689 was far from perfect. He had quashed rebellion for the most part but still faced difficulties in Ulster. Despite his skilful manipulation, there were still many concerns to be addressed. He had successfully disarmed the Protestants in Dublin. The massive Irish army of 40,000–50,000 men would remain on paper only. Those assembled were unruly, poorly trained and were causing more harm than good. A rebellion in Bandon in Munster, although quickly stopped by MacCarthy, was indicative of what could happen should the Protestant 'associations' gain an opportunity to band together. Such activity could quickly get out of control, especially where Protestant numbers were high. In Ulster, this is exactly what was occurring. Derry and Enniskillen had become centres of Protestant resistance. The sporadic breakdown of law and order and the perceived need for the Protestants to protect themselves against rogue Jacobites made the situation worse for Tyrconnel's administration. Despite this, he was particularly concerned to show that he was striving to be impartial and objective to both sides.[27] However, he would be forced to take action in Ulster.

Ormonde had returned to Ireland. His diary entries for 27 February and 8 March 1689 (o.s.) noted:

> This morning some sugar plums were given after the portion, for the letters of the packets were given out, though searched and opened before, but no Gazettes delivered, and the Lord Deputy had, as it was reported, three letters from the King to be kind to his Protestant subjects that were loyal. This evening the sham of the King's landing and the French was laughed at, it being a mere device to amuse the Protestants while they were disarmed; but the thing being done, out comes a declaration, a mere ridiculous thing, and a detachment was sent to Ballinderry in the county of Wicklow, in which many Protestants were got, but it was given up and many of them made prisoners, John Price, etc., and this evening bonfires were made for joy of an express to the Deputy that the King would be here on Saturday or Sunday, but this was quashed, the business being over, and the soldiers punished that began the thing, but the party was found still for the King's coming, the Lord Mayor ordering all the streets of the city to be mended and gravelled, which made Protestants to believe that there was some farther design on foot, so that had there been shipping and free passage many thousands would have left the kingdom, their discontents

being heightened by some reports of raising a contribution for the army and plundering the city. This great work of disarming the Protestants gave thousands of arms to the Papists, and made them not fear doing what they pleased, for now they quartered upon private houses and prepared for an expedition into the North.

The forces began to march to the North, and next day the train of artillery, consisting of seven brass pieces [and] two iron ones with empty carriage. More of the forces went daily. An express brought a declaration from King William and Queen Mary, commanding all to lay down arms, and come under their standards, else to be prosecuted as robbers and traitors ; on the 7th out comes a proclamation against several Lords and gentlemen of Sligo and Ulster, as Lords Massareene, Mount-Alexander, Kingston, etc.[28]

Ulster, the seat of James I's plantation, was where Tyrconnel's problems lay. In the western portion, Protestants from outlying regions flocked to Londonderry and Enniskillen. In the east, the centre of resistance lay at Hillsborough in County Down. Ulster had not undergone the ravages of the Jacobite army amongst the populace, as had the southern areas. News of those events, however, gave rise once more to fears of a repeat of the events of 1641. Armed groups were raised and by the start of 1689, only Carrickfergus and Armagh were held securely by Tyrconnel's men. A 'supreme council' led by the Earl of Mount-Alexander and comprised of the northern aristocracy was set up to co-ordinate resistance. The council made appeals to William, although early action in Ulster was ineffective and schemes to disarm Catholics at Belfast and Carrickfergus came to naught. By February a second attempt was made against Carrickfergus. Despite its failure a form of truce was agreed in the town, wherein one of the Jacobite regiments there was disbanded and the residents were permitted to organise their own defence; all this occurred on the basis that Tyrconnell was kept informed of the developing situation.[29]

The spectacle was set for a surge of resistance against the burgeoning efforts of the Jacobite regime. Richard Hamilton would play a crucial role in the first battle of the war. With both feet now firmly in James's camp, Tyrconnel was determined that the Ulster problem should be quickly remedied and Hamilton would be his instrument. Initial attempts with regard to the Ulster Protestants' surrender had come to naught. To this end, on 7 March, Tyrconnel proclaimed that a free pardon would be granted to those who laid down their arms. Those who persisted in their 'wicked designs' and 'treasonable practices' would be treated as 'Rebels and Traitors' and would feel the full force of the Jacobite army. In the same proclamation he forbade his troops to use force on the innocent. Mount-Alexander and nine co-conspirators were given no hope of pardon for their actions.

With James's imminent arrival, together with an influential French contingent, Tyrconnel wanted to offer good news, hoping to provoke enthusiasm with reports of the defeat of Ulster resistance. With the exception of Ulster, Ireland had been mobilised in support of the Jacobite army, the population being ordered to supply foodstuffs, clothing, money, arms and horses. Where these were in short supply they were confiscated from Protestant houses and the aristocracy. Tyrconnel's means, ruthless and effective, helped equip a 2,000 strong Jacobite fighting force for a northern raid which Richard Hamilton, now a lieutenant general, would lead.

In common with those groups who would later resist at Derry and Enniskillen, the Protestants of eastern Ulster had appealed directly to William for aid. His response assured them that he would indeed take early steps against the 'oppressions and terrors you lie under' although no military aid would reach them yet.[30] With William's encouragement in mind, however, the council responded vehemently to Tyrconnel's proclamation; they would only have dealings with the Lord Deputy dependent on the safety of their religion, lives and liberty. Mount-Alexander could do little to prevent divisions in the supreme council that he led. Tyrconnel, eager to move against any further opposition in Ulster before it could get significantly organised, sent Richard Hamilton and his troops north.

By 14 March Hamilton's troops had reached Dromore in County Down, where he was met by Mount-Alexander's Protestant force. The short action that subsequently occurred can barely be described as a skirmish but it had taken matters in Ireland to a new level. Fighting and dying had started in earnest. The mainly cavalry action, small by European standards, was probably fought in the Dromore townland of Ballymacormack, immediately adjacent to the town. The battlefield lay south of a ridge known as Gallows Hill, and the area, as with so much of the Irish countryside, was surrounded by bogland. Such terrain protected Hamilton's right flank and the town secured his left flank. It seems that he could secure the nearby streets with just a few dragoons. Mount-Alexander's force similarly had their left secured by the bogland, although their right flank lay open, since their battle lines lay beyond the town. Two hundred yards or so to their rear lay some woodland known locally as Crows-Wood. Hamilton had little hesitation in launching a cavalry attack and it must have taken him little effort to exploit the weak right flank of Mount-Alexander. The Protestant force, in common with the divisions in the Supreme Council, appears to have been disorganised and wanting. The necessary cavalry did not arrive when required, and the infantry rapidly broke and fled as it became obvious that the Jacobite flanking move would quickly prevent their retreat. The troops fled through Crows-Wood in complete rout.

Hamilton's victory had been rapid although it appears that he did not pursue. Most of Mount-Alexander's troops escaped, some fleeing through the bog to the east and others over Cannon Hill. Local tradition suggests that most of the troops were not local, since there are no graves at Dromore to indicate those troops killed in the skirmish, numbering around 100. Although the troops were for the most part from Ulster, many chose to leave for Scotland soon after the battle. A popular song of the time traditionally records:

> *The run of Loughbrickland, the break of Dromore,*
> *Made Sandy and Willy take both to the shore.*

So bad had the situation become that Stranraer on the Scottish coast rapidly became filled with Ulster refugees huddled together on the shore, taking refuge from the elements in upturned boats.

Other tradition suggests that the 'Break of Dromore' had undeniably been a short action, recording that a local woman who had gone to 'spectate' had forgotten that she had left bread to bake by the fire; on her return she found that it had not burned.[31]

The Break of Dromore had an understandable effect on both morale and the cohesion of the Protestants in eastern Ulster; matters would prove more difficult at Enniskillen and Londonderry. Mount-Alexander eventually escaped to the Isle of Man while, without a focus or organisation for protracted opposition, other Protestant garrisons in Counties Down and Antrim fell quickly as Hamilton's cavalry force advanced north. There were still around 3,000 armed Protestant troops in the region. Some fled east towards Londonderry and Enniskillen but Arthur Rawdon and John Hawkins, who had also found themselves on Tyrconnel's 'blacklist', rallied what troops were left and headed for Coleraine to the north, with an ever increasing number of civilian refugees in their wake.

Coleraine on the northern coast, which had also been a Protestant stronghold during the 1641 conflict, would once more harbour the remnants of the army. The defences were poor, and would not stand against a determined foe. Major Gustavus Hamilton, this being Viscount Boyne and not to be confused with the later governor of Enniskillen, had attempted to strengthen the town's defences prior to Rawdon's arrival, although he had had little success. By the river Bann, the town's three exposed sides were protected by a mud bank and ditches. Acting in the garrison's favour was the fact that Hamilton's troops had taken their time, looting the towns of Lisburn and Antrim and the surrounding areas. They did not arrive until 27 March.

The following day, having deployed his artillery, Hamilton opened fire on the town as the Jacobite infantry, in skirmish fashion, attempted to negotiate their way inside. Musket duels between opposing regiments and groups came to naught, although Jacobite casualties began to mount and by the evening, in a hail of snow, Hamilton's men withdrew. His rapid advance had been checked. He also had only enough provisions for a further two days, little anticipating a siege of sorts, yet was consoled by the fact that six regiments of infantry, which had awaited him at Charlemont, could be brought up to threaten Coleraine. Hamilton also had another card to play. Perhaps reasoning that by leaving Coleraine and pressing towards Derry he could convince the garrison to move rather than become hopelessly cut off, he abandoned his position. The strategy caught the garrison completely off-guard. As Irish troops looked for a crossing point on the Bann, the Coleraine garrison destroyed what bridges they could and sent troops to occupy strategic points along the river, such as Kilrea and Toome. Other units were sent to the far bank of the river to intercept the crossing attempts of Jacobite troops.

Richard Hamilton's probes were bound to find a weak point since the men required to occupy such a large area in a defensive posture were simply not available. By 7 April, having found boats at Portglenone, Hamilton's dragoons were starting to cross the Bann, threatening the rear of the defenders. Convinced that it would be cut off, and in no condition for a protracted siege, the Coleraine garrison cut its losses and withdrew, as Hamilton had hoped. The troops and a long line of civilian refugees began to walk to the walled city of Londonderry. They were not alone, as the terrified inhabitants of Counties Down, Antrim, Armagh, indeed most of Ulster, began to converge on the small city on the Foyle. However, Hamilton did not move quickly enough to gain an advantage, scattered as his troops were. Although perhaps understandable, he would later be criticised for the lack of action.[32] In strategic terms, Hamilton's move had been highly successful; Tyrconnel can only have been pleased with his progress. For the French, many of who would land in Ireland with James, Hamilton's progress would not be so pleasing. Within a few days, he began to converge on Londonderry and the next chapter of his Irish experience.

For James, the 'Glorious Revolution' in England had confounded his resolve and all but crushed his will to resist. The courageous commander from the 1650s, who had served with the English forces in exile, now seemed incapable of reacting fast enough. Ireland was his last chance. Both Tyrconnel and Louis wanted James to go to Ireland. Tyrconnel knew that he would rally the Irish cause and help channel the vital French aid. Louis may have had some feeling toward a deposed Catholic monarch, but William's seizure of the English throne was a more important matter, and a severe blow to his plans in Europe. If James could be restored to power, he could be a staunch ally, although would a king who had done so little to defend his throne be actively enthusiastic about getting it back? The effort required for such a task would be enormous for the French. The threat of James in Ireland, a pawn in Louis's grand European strategy, could slow William's plans in Europe, however.

Louis's ministers were divided over French attempts to help James and the Irish. Louvois looked gravely upon any attempt at aid, preferring to concentrate on the continental aspects of the war. Seignelay, the Minister of Marine, in contrast maintained that French naval power could make a real difference in Ireland. However, Louvois had been held responsible for many of the reverses and defeats in the previous European war and was out of favour. William's lack of action to date against Ireland also prompted a decision in favour of an expeditionary force. Seignelay had sent the Marquis de Pointis, a naval gunnery officer, to report. Pointis brought word to Tyrconnel from James in January; he hoped that Tyrconnel could defend Ireland until the summer, but there was little hope so far that James himself would come.

Playing to the monarch's pride, Tyrconnel's attempts at persuasion are worth repeating:

> ..if, sir, your majesty will in person come hither and bring with you those succours necessary to support the country... . I will be responsible to you that you shall be entirely the master of the kingdom and of everything in it; and, sir, I beg of you to consider whether you can with honour continue where you are when you may possess a kingdom of your own.

... if your majesty would take a step here to arrange our affairs, you could again return afterwards if you found it necessary.[33]

Pointis's report indicated that Ireland would not hold out for long against William unless French military aid was forthcoming. Later reports focused on the importance of James's presence in Ireland. Not only would it act as a catalyst for Irish resistance against William, but a Catholic monarch would also be an important figurehead. English Jacobites would also support James in Ireland, where they would never condone French intervention in isolation. The additional value to France was the prospect of dividing William's military resources, with the resultant delaying effects on the important European war. After some discussion, French plans were drawn up for Ireland, and for James. Louvois eventually proposed that a small expeditionary force be sent under Major General Maumont, with arms and money together with those Irish and British troops who had rallied under James in France. The expedition would return immediately should there be any news of a 'deal' between Tyrconnel and William, but there was little chance of that now. Otherwise, it was to determine the nature of Irish defensive policy, if any. Preferring rapid defensive preparations, the French wanted to urge Tyrconnel to pay for the army and administration through the seizure of Protestant property. For the French such decisions were easily made, as Louis's persecution of French Huguenots had shown. Matters in Ireland were somewhat different, and the French could never hope to understand the difficult nature of relationships and agendas in Ireland.

Promises of French reinforcements were made. If the Irish could resist until the end of the year, French troops, the seasoned professionals that Tyrconnel needed, would come and ultimately help James invade Scotland and then England, an ambitious plan indeed. The immediate requirement, however, called for the preservation of Ireland to William's detriment, additional arms and the promise of money.[34]

James had also now resolved to go, perhaps having regained his nerve in the face of Irish and French persuasion. Vauban wrote poignantly to Louvois:

I have an idea that when a man plays his last stake he ought to play it himself or to be on the spot. The king of England seems to be in this condition. His last stake is Ireland; it appears to me that he ought to go there, where with the help that the king can give him he can get on his legs again and be supported by those of his subjects who remain loyal to him.[35]

In the end Maumont would not lead the expedition. De Rosen would command. Of Latvian descent, brusque and direct, he would lack the subtlety and refinement that such a mission demanded. Disliked by French and Irish alike, he had seen French service with experience from the Thirty Years' War.[36] Accompanying him would be le Comte d'Avaux, as French ambassador, whose letters give such an insight into the early part of the Irish affair. D'Avaux had a difficult, if not impossible, task allocated to him by Louis. He was to help arbitrate between James's supporters, even though all had different aims and ambitions, Irish, English and French. In addition he was ordered to make attempts to resolve differences between Irish Protestants and Catholics while simultaneously highlighting James's impartiality to both populations. Also he was to make contacts where possible amongst potential English and Scottish allies. D'Avaux was under no illusions that the mission would be a difficult one.[37]

James left Saint Germain on 15 February 1689, in preparation for his journey to Brest and thence to Ireland. Despite poor weather conditions, which held up progress, James and his attendants arrived at Kinsale on 12 March. The first English king, albeit without a kingdom, to set foot in Ireland in almost 300 years. His entourage, together with vital French supplies, sailed with him in a fleet of twenty-two ships. Thousands of muskets, together with ammunition and 500,000 gold crowns were substantial supplies, and would be badly needed. The small fleet had remained unmolested throughout its journey, an indication of how little the opposing fleets were able to interfere with each other's strategic movements at the time. There were few sea battles and many potentially exploitable situations were missed.[38]

A large group of notables travelled with him from France, including relatives, loyal retainers and Jacobite supporters, amongst them, his two illegitimate sons, the elder, the nineteen-year-old James Fitzjames, Duke of Berwick, and his younger brother Henry Fitzjames, the Grand Prior. Berwick was loyal and would soon prove himself as an able soldier and officer, while d'Avaux would describe his brother as a drunkard. Also present was John Drummond, Earl of Melfort, a Protestant Scot who held great sway with James and would be appointed Secretary of State for Ireland, but would prove most unpopular with French, Irish and English, being described by d'Avaux as never having 'inspired confidence'.[39]

Amongst the Irish officers who accompanied James, the aforementioned John Hamilton, Patrick Sarsfield, now a colonel, and Roger MacElligot were present; the French military were also represented. Despite the number of adherents, James had brought urgently required arms, ammunition and military stores from France. The goods were secured in a fort at Kinsale, where James ensured that a full record was given to de Pointis. He could not afford to make French enemies at this stage, although d'Avaux's report of the situation was not favourable.[40]

James called a council of war at Kinsale with d'Avaux, Melfort, Lord Chief Justice Sir Thomas Nugent and Lieutenant General Justin MacCarthy. New troops were raised and James was given assurances about Irish security. English officers who had landed with him gathered up the best horses in the surrounding area and left for Dublin, before the crowds that would inevitably inundate the king and his retinue gathered and made travelling difficult. French officers remained at Kinsale with the arms, ammunition and stores.[41]

D'Avaux's comments on the Kinsale landing indicate how fully aware he was of the problems with the fledgling Franco-Jacobite alliance. His initial report to Louis XIV centred on the key aspects of the Irish difficulties of the time. He reported on the assurances made by Justin MacCarthy and others, about the 'sound disposition' of Irish affairs. Despite such claims, d'Avaux was still concerned not only with the fact that resistance existed in the north, but of how such resistance might strengthen. From his point of view, external issues with Protestant rebels were only part of the problem. He cited James's frequent indecision and his particular concentration on the minutiae of Irish affairs whilst ignoring the more pressing and critical issues. The king's eagerness to set off for Cork, before arms and ammunition had been fully unloaded, or matters with local troops taken care of, boded ill for the future in d'Avaux's view. Although James may have been more interested in quickly rallying his Irish support, he had made a bad start with the influential French ambassador. As were his orders, he would strive to keep matters in check.[42]

James proceeded to Cork where the Irish greeted him with great celebration. He finally met with his old colleague, the Earl of Tyrconnel, the two conferring on conditions in Ireland. Tyrconnel was rewarded for his continued service with a dukedom. He would later bring news of Hamilton's victory in the north, at Dromore. Despite continued resistance at Derry and Enniskillen, the news may have given a lift to spirits, but there was much work still to do.

Richard Hamilton was not as popular with d'Avaux and the French as he appeared to be with James and Tyrconnel. Was there a degree of bitterness left after his behaviour in Louis's gardens? Had he fallen from favour, or did his ostensibly dishonourable actions in his dealings with William earn even the enmity of the French? It is not altogether clear why d'Avaux seemed bitter, although he would record several doubts related to Hamilton in the coming months. Despite urging reinforcement of his position upon hearing of his success at Dromore, he later recalled to Louvois that the defeat at Coleraine was due entirely to poorly-judged conduct of the siege by Hamilton and his men; he had shown poor judgement when attacking, hoping that his arrival would 'scare' the inhabitants into surrendering, and lacked supplies for a protracted campaign or siege. D'Avaux at least believed that a single French battalion could have settled the problem and gone on to take Derry and Enniskillen.[43]

To some extent, Hamilton's actions had been necessary, although reckless and relying heavily on the momentum of his advance. He had gained impetus after the Dromore victory and his approach had driven much of the Protestant resistance back. If Coleraine had been hastily attacked, Hamilton had hoped to benefit from the rapidity of his advance so far. If he had moved too fast and thus outran his supplies, then it was due to his eagerness to make rapid gains, although such a miscalculation could have a serious effect. Had similar measures been taken elsewhere, James's troops would have been in a better position than they were. Whether d'Avaux's contempt is borne out of strategic concerns or arrogance is therefore arguable.

James left Cork on 20 March en route to Dublin, which he reached by the 24th. The entire journey was accompanied by cheering crowds and the king got his first glimpse of the Irish army. The condition and quality of these troops was exemplified by their appearance, many seeming like bandits, and armed only with the ubiquitous Irish *skeine*, a half-pike.[44] This would be of little use on the contemporary battlefield facing the well-drilled formations and numerous firearms of the Williamite forces.

James arrived in Dublin on horseback amidst great celebration and ceremony. A flag flew over Dublin Castle inscribed with the legend 'Now or Never, Now and Forever'. Ormonde recorded in his diary:

> March 24 – The King came to town with far less splendour than the Lord Deputy used to do. He rode on horseback, and Tyrconnell carried the sword, his two base sons riding on each hand of him. He was very courteous to all as he passed by. It is said that he wept as he rode into the Castle.[45]

Such spectacle and hope for the future were far from d'Avaux's thoughts. James's neglect of important issues had done little so far to impress the

French diplomat. There was much work still to be done, with bands of irregular troops and bandits roaming the countryside, apparently out of control. Troops near Dublin had still not been armed or even formed into regiments. Despite the number of untrained levies, and key to the future of Irish troops that would serve once again in France, d'Avaux, in concert with his master Louvois, had noted enough potential amongst the Irish to contribute significant numbers of troops for French service abroad, a fact that would have serious repercussions for at least one of the Jacobite generals.[46] James, too, rather than showing the toleration with which he would later attempt to underline his activities in Ireland, had dismissed Keating, the Protestant Chief Justice, from the Privy Council. He was also reported as showing little mercy to Protestants who had resisted Jacobite troops and *Rapparees*, refusing to grant pardon at the assizes. At least two men were executed for treason, in James's eyes perhaps, now his only means of restoring order in the north. As the rumours of such events spread they would help fuel the fires of Protestant resistance.

In the midst of turmoil in Ulster and approaching warfare with William's more seasoned troops, the calling of a new Irish Parliament in Dublin may seem a ridiculously extravagant notion. There were nevertheless many matters to discuss, although hurried legislation as an apparent counter to years of English dominance in Ireland would do little to breach the walls of Derry or resolve the Enniskillen problem. With the summoning of an Irish Parliament in May, the Irish envisaged resolution of the problems that they had railed against for so long, a repeal of the land settlement and a return of their estates. Decisions against existing legislation, if backed by James, would champion the Irish cause, but would also destroy any last hope of support that he could have hoped for in England. A delicate balancing act was being played by all factions, since if James were ultimately to regain his throne, his interest in the Irish would clearly become diminished.

James was fully aware of the dangers of outright support for Irish matters; d'Avaux, too, had a separate agenda, becoming steadily more concerned with the prospect of French dominance in Ireland and the opportunity to use the best Irish troops and their commanders in the war in mainland Europe. Ireland would prove to be all but a convenient distraction used by the French to irritate William's plans. With such divisive underpinning of the Irish situation, it is understandable that the Irish Parliament, as with so many strategies in the past, was riddled with factional infighting to the detriment of any hope for progress on the issues.

The discussions should also be taken in context with events developing in Ulster. Resistance at Londonderry and Enniskillen was increasing dramatically and Jacobite attempts to control the north were failing. While in some quarters the Parliament was seen as essential, since there seemed no better moment, others felt that obvious questions were being ignored. John Stevens, an English Jacobite who had sailed from Brest, noted that the summer months were wasted in unproductive discussion. If resources and time had been devoted to the siege in the north under Richard Hamilton, events might have been quite different.

> To satisfy the humours of the people a parliament was called, which having sat many days granted the king a subsidy that never turned to any account, but the chief thing they did was repeal the Act of Settlement. Nothing could be more pernicious, or a greater obstruction to the King's service than was this parliament.[47]

The Irish Parliament, the event that would see the zenith of James's and Irish power on the isle went ahead on 7 May. English opinion would frown on James's tampering with the former colony, but he had little choice; he needed Irish backing, both militarily and financially. Had it not been for disagreement between the parties, the meeting might have been more successful. As it was, James's appeals to the Irish that he would relieve suffering 'as far forth as may be consistent with reason, justice, and the public good of my people' would be ill-founded. There would be little room for compromise since, if James did not fight for the people, they would not fight for him.

What the Irish really wanted to hear was James's solution to the land question, a concept that even his English supporters felt unassailable since it underpinned the concept of English control in Ireland. The Irish could show little compromise in terms of a question so close to their hearts. After considerable disagreement and argument, the act was passed, and the Acts of Settlement and Explanation were effectively repealed, despite the complications surrounding those who had owned land prior to 1641. In fact, the old-English-Irish benefited most from the arrangement. Already, the native Irish felt that the years of persecution they had suffered had only been given partial redress. Of course, the nature of the entire bill would depend on the positive outcome of the war, something that seemed far from certain. Stevens once more summed up the Parliament:

First it drew to and kept in Dublin all that time the nobility and principil gentry who before were dispersed at their posts, raising or encouraging and exercising their men or upon actual service.

Secondly, the Act of Repeal being passed, private interest outweighing the public good, every one quitted his command to enter upon his estate, to settle his house, and improve his fortune. And the estated men not content to forsake the service themselves kept with them for their own use all the better sort of country people, so that none but the most rude and useless sort of mountaineers took to the army. Thirdly, the Protestants, who before might have perhaps stood neuter or hoped for some reconciliation, their estates being taken away, were in a manner necessitated to espouse the rebellion, which alone could restore them to their, although unjustly yet long enjoyed, fortunes.

.... Thus it appears by the sitting of this parliament, the army was much damaged and weakened, the king lost the assistance of many of his friends and gained a vast number of irreconcilable enemies.[48]

The Protestants would receive further news that would bolster their resistance; the 'Act of Attainder' listed over 2,000 names of those who had taken part in rebellion against James, armed or otherwise. Ormonde headed the list, which implied that those concerned were traitors. They had to surrender to a judge by August when, after due trial, they could be acquitted. The English Parliament later influenced William in a similar manner, and with dire consequences.

Matters did not all go the Irish way however. Williamites had criticised the Irish Parliament since it sat outside the requirements of 'Poynings' Law', wherein all legislation had to be certified in England. James opposed the bill introduced to repeal the law; he still attached at least some significance to English opinion, while the Irish saw it as another example of English dominion. James would only go as far as declaring that the English Parliament had no right to pass Irish laws. French interest was mostly economic and they sought to achieve a commercial position over Ireland that had been the monopoly of England, although James fought against French bids, if the result would mean the removal of English interest. Similarly, he resisted French suggestions to naturalise all Louis's subjects in Ireland. In terms of religious freedom, James removed the requirement for the 'oaths' but would not go so far as to remove Elizabeth's

Catholic penal laws, and restore the authority of the Pope. He was still at heart a very English king.

The entire affair had done much to dampen the enthusiasm of the Irish. It was clear to many that James had little real concern for Ireland other than as a stepping-stone. If Poynings' Law remained intact, then England could still exert control over the Irish Parliament. While the land question had been settled to some extent, self-government remained questionable. One reason for assembling the parliament in the first place had been to get money for the war and £20,000 per month was agreed. This proved not only inadequate but also difficult to gather.

The event had done more harm than good, and not simply due to the growing Irish realisation of James's real interest. They had hoped to regain their land and hold out against William with French aid, but the French were becoming more concerned with Ireland's role as 'pawn' in William and Louis's European chess game. Had James, the French and the Irish been more focused on a single goal, they might have succeeded, at least temporarily. Protestants and Williamites who had felt that the Irish Parliament had shown them little mercy, despite James's initial clams, would show even less when they gained the upper hand. The Irish Parliament was prorogued on 18 July. It would never meet again. Twelve days afterwards, Derry was relieved. Two weeks after that and Schomberg had landed. The dream in the north had ended.[49]

The factions that would decide the Irish question had for the most part been disappointed by the events in the Parliament. What effect this would have on the defence of the country and any subsequent attempt to reclaim the throne remained to be seen. Even with the imminent arrival of Williamite forces, strategies for defence were ineptly handled and poorly directed. The French had many strong views on Ireland and, more succinctly, its untested army. In contrast with the Irish army of the time, the French forces at the end of the seventeenth century were a living example of how effective a well-disciplined and efficiently drilled military machine could be. It was justifiably feared and respected throughout Europe, the threat of its action helping to create the counter to Louis's aims, a Grand Alliance of European allies required to curb French aggression. The rank and file composing the Irish force then did little to impress the pompous and proud French officer cadre. De Rosen was especially contemptuous:

> Nearly all are without arms and quite naked: the greater part of the
> officers are miserable fellows without courage or honour, a single

cannon shot passing at the elevation of a clock tower throws a whole battalion to the ground and the only way to get them to their feet is to send horses over their bellies.[50]

D'Avaux, however, with a keen eye for exploiting the situation to the benefit of the French, saw things quite differently. In contrast to de Rosen, he saw the great potential of some of the military 'raw material' within the rough regiments of the re-modelled army.

Many of the Irish began to understand what could occur. Justin MacCarthy, now Lord Mountcashel since his raising to the peerage during the Irish Parliament, was unpopular with Tyrconnel, James and their followers, due to his representation of the native Irish faction, and the fact that he told the truth of the situation that he perceived – that James would leave Ireland and the old-English would return to their lands if they could. Such a standpoint made him popular with the French. He wrote poignantly: 'If we are not restored by the King of France or Divine Providence, there is a significant risk, since it is a terrible thing to see the efforts with which we seek our own ruin!'[51]

Different parties had different aims, James even considering the native Irish somewhat inferior in many respects, including Mountcashel, for whom the French had great admiration. D'Avaux was quick to point out the apparent gulf slowly developing between the English and Irish, describing them as 'irreconcilable enemies'.[52] Many of the Irish military were by then more deeply concerned with the prospects for resistance against William than with continued loyalty to a deposed king. Many other matters had been discussed at the Parliament, including plans for Derry and Enniskillen. Despite the lack of focus, the disagreement and the time wasted in pertinent, although poorly-timed debate, the Jacobites resolved to take action. For Richard Hamilton, this would mean continued action at Derry. For Anthony Hamilton and Justin MacCarthy, the short Enniskillen campaign would see a significant turning point in the war.

# Chapter 8

# Justin MacCarthy, Lord Mountcashel

Since Justin MacCarthy, ennobled as Lord Mountcashel, will play an important role in the next part of our story, it is pertinent to outline some of the detail about who he was, and to determine something of the reputation that he had carved out with the French. His father was Donough MacCarthy, the man who had done much for the Royalists during the Irish war in 1641, and who had been the confidant of George Hamilton Senior. Justin was born in Munster in the early 1640s, when his father was embroiled in the complex struggle over the land question, religious freedoms and the English crown.

The MacCarthy family bore a noble lineage and had been part of one of the most powerful ancient clans in Ireland. Munster had been split between the royal houses of Desmond, the MacCarthys, in the southern part of the province, and that of Thomond, the O'Briens, in the north, from the third century until the coming of the Normans in the twelfth. This split, and the inevitable feuding that followed, can be traced back to the second century. The direct ancestor of the MacCarthy family was Eoghan More, son of Olioll Olum, King of Munster in the second century. Olioll divided Munster between his two sons Eoghan, whose clan became the MacCarthys, princes of Desmond, and Cormac, whose clan of Dalcassian princes of Thomond became the O'Briens. In theory, the kingship of Munster alternated between each clan through the years, although this proved to be a futile romantic notion at best. The name MacCarthy was derived from one of the Desmond kings, Carthach, who ruled just prior to the arrival of the Normans in 1169. The MacCarthys lost substantial amounts of their territory to the English during the twelfth century. By the fifteenth century, the Muskerry branch of the family dwelt in Blarney Castle and controlled a large part of County Cork, their ancestral home.

During the sixteenth century, the family adhered to the traditional Irish clan's way of life at the time, cycles of violence conducted with both their neighbours and the English. Dermot MacCarthy, the seventh Lord, played the political game and defeated enemies of the crown, earning the official title of knight of the realm from the Earl of Essex in 1558.

By the time of the succession of the eighth Lord of Muskerry, Queen Elizabeth I held power in England and had little time for petty Irish squabbles, seeing the country as a land of savages. She demanded that all Irish chiefs, be they declared lords or knights, should agree to own their lands under legal tenancy from her. Cormac Teige MacCarthy, the new lord in Blarney Castle, would not submit to the Queen's demand but had no intention of admitting this. Cormac, evidently more of a politician and diplomat than his predecessors, answered the Queen's demands with flattery and obsequious compliments, or 'blarney'. Cormac's power was considerable in Munster, and he could call on over 3,000 men. Ever adept at political manoeuvring, he stayed on the right side of the English and fought for them when Spanish troops landed at Kinsale in 1601 in their vain attempt to aid Hugh O'Neill and Hugh O'Donnell. It was a delicate political balancing act and, despite later being accused of consorting with the Spanish and thrown into prison, Cormac was pardoned. He was knighted by the Lords Justices of Ireland and, before his death in 1616, had also earned the title of Baron of Blarney, a nobleman of the finest Irish lineage, who had led the clan for thirty-three years. He left two sons, Cormac, who became the ninth lord, and his younger brother. Cormac died in 1640 and was succeeded by his son Donough MacCarthy, Justin MacCarthy's father.[1]

Donough would play a major, if not decisive, role in the 1640s during the civil wars that engulfed Ireland. From the Norman invasion until the time of the Tudors English colonists had been absorbed into the Irish population, and had thus developed an Irish identity rather than a distinctly English one. This had not been planned. In fact, the English crown had tried to impose its customs and society on the Irish, not to mention its language. The Irish in turn showed such implicit resistance to these changes over the years that force would be necessary if change were to be implemented. Despite the later moves of Queen Elizabeth I in Ulster, and the imposition of English law, many clans remained loyal to their Irish chieftains. Only fear of Elizabeth's continued colonisation policy forced many of the chiefs to swear allegiance to the crown by 1585, and the native Irish were pushed farther and farther to the west. It took the later decades of the century and a number of costly campaigns to complete the conquest. The fruitful lands of choice were given to the new colonists. Despite rebellion, notably the Nine Years' War of 1594-1603 (not to be confused with the war in the latter part of the seventeenth century), by 1603, and the accession of the Stuarts in England, Ireland was essentially an English province. Disarmed and effectively hamstrung, the

Irish could only look abroad for aid if they sought to further demonstrate their consternation at English dominance.

The colonial situation had left its mark on the country in the form of the 'old-English', many of whom were original settlers but who, in the absence of strict English control, had become a form of Irish elite. By the beginning of the seventeenth century, the mass of the Irish population were committed Catholics, as were most of the old-English. The Irish were still frustrated by the eternal debate with England over their religious and political aims. Loyalty to the crown contrasted with religious loyalties on a scale that could not be compared easily with the rest of the British Isles, where there had been no conflict over land or colonial plantation.

In Munster the most important Irish Catholic nobles of the time were Viscount Fermoy and Donough MacCarthy, Viscount Muskerry. Gaelic and old-English Protestants also held much of the power in the south, namely the Earl of Thomond and Murrough O'Brien, Earl of Inchiquin. Wentworth's abortive attempts at a new phase of Anglo-Irish politics had come to naught by 1640. With the rebellion in 1641, Lord Muskerry, who would later influence the fledgling Irish parliament, initially disbelieved the reports from Ulster, laughing at such preposterous notions. The rumours that reached Cork were true, however, and he had little hesitation in leading the MacCarthy clan against the settlers, driving them as far as Kilkenny, the same garrison town that would become the seat of the Irish parliament, where Donough would have considerable influence. Although fully supporting the Ormonde royalist faction through marriage into the family, Muskerry, already highly supportive of that faction, expressed his concern at the presence and influence of the Papal Nuncio in 1645. His belief was that it would prove disastrous for the country. He would be proven right. By 1648 Ormonde returned to Ireland. Rinuccini was forced to leave, to ensure that Ormonde could succeed. He knew that the inevitable split would force most of the Irish to the Royalist side. Amongst these was Muskerry who, with other Irish lords, would assist Ormonde both in government and war.

Muskerry was still actively resisting in Munster until the end of the war but, by May 1652, the outcome must have been obvious even to the most ardent confederate. Lieutenant General Edmund Ludlow was tasked with removing the problem in the south of the country. Muskerry's forces, although several thousand strong, presented little threat to Ludlow in the field, being ill-supplied and poorly motivated. Their presence in Munster, however, meant that Ludlow had to take action. Muskerry's troops were centred on Ross Castle, a well-positioned fort on a peninsula on the lower lake of Killarney. Ludlow was aware that he had to force Muskerry's surrender if he was to remove the problem of southern resistance. He surrendered in June with around 1,000 men. Another 3,000 in the surrounding area also surrendered. Muskerry, in parley with Ludlow, obtained agreement that he could leave Ireland to fight abroad with 3,000 foot and 600 horse, a wise decision since the English troops held many captured officers whom they judged liable for the killing of colonists during 1641.

Ludlow's letters from the siege also gave some indication as to why ultimate surrender was so forthcoming;

> From the Campe before Rosse,
>    The 24th of June, 1652,
>    The Lord of Muskerry's sonne and Lieut. Col. Knocher O'Callaghan are hostages with mee for the performance of those Articles. God willing I shall hasten northwards with all the force that can bee spared hence, least they should stand in need of them.[2]

This hostage would undoubtedly have been Cormac, Muskerry's oldest son, who had fought with him and would later lead his own battalion of Munstermen in France.

Small pockets of resistance remained. Those Tories who were captured were executed and thousands of Irish were deported to the Americas. Muskerry, however, in common with around 40,000 other surrendering Irish troops, was allowed to leave and fight in Europe under France, Spain or other European states.[3]

Muskerry left for Spain in 1652 after the surrender at Ross castle. However, he found it difficult to be accepted. His very public disagreement with the arrival and intent of Rinuccini had earned him few friends in Spain amongst the exiled Irish or the clergy. By March 1653 he had returned to Ireland and declared himself to the English.

He was received by Colonel John Jones, who wrote:

> The Lord Muskerry is lately landed at Cork, and says he will cast himself upon the Parliament's mercy, pretending the clergy in Spain had determined to murder him, and that Portugal would not entertain him, of all of which I believe but my share.[4]

By the following February, Muskerry was being held in Marshalsea prison, one of many Irishmen awaiting trial for their activities in 1641 and 1642.

Over one-hundred people had already been officially tried, convicted and executed, and he would quite literally be fighting for his life.

The rest of the family had fled to France with the collapse of the Confederate-Royalist pact in Ireland. Muskerry's support of Ormonde's cause during the war is not surprising considering his earlier comments regarding the Papal Nuncio. However, he was also married to Eleanor Butler, Ormonde's sister and had three sons, Cormac, Callaghan and Justin. The youngest, Justin, had been born in the midst of the war. As a young boy he had to live in France with the exiled remnants of the English monarchy. His oldest brother, Cormac, had sought a military career and might well have fought alongside his father. He was a competent officer and gained an excellent reputation with his regiment of Munstermen in exile in the 1650s. The second brother, Callaghan, began studying for a life in the priesthood in France. There is every indication that the young Justin, impressed by the exploits of his eldest brother Cormac, saw the military as a possible future. The family still had to wait in anticipation for a decision from Ireland and the outcome of Donough's trial.

Muskerry had been influential in his time on the Supreme Council of the Confederate government. He had made powerful friends and was not looked upon by the English with the same contempt as O'Neill. This may help to explain why, unlike many of his fellow prisoners, he was given an indication of how the prosecution would unfold, and an opportunity to prepare a defence, while many others were locked up with little idea of what they were accused of until the day of their trial.

In December 1654 Muskerry was charged as an accessory to three separate murders. The first of these involved a group of English colonists, all of whom had been on Muskerry's estate in August 1642 and had asked to be conveyed to Cork in light of their delicate position. To this end, a convoy or bodyguard was provided. However, this did not accompany the group for the entire course of the journey and the English were murdered in cold blood by the road. The second charge related to the previous month when Muskerry reputedly authorised the execution of three men and one woman at the siege of Kilfinny in County Limerick. In the final instance, he was accused as an accessory to the murder of Roger Skinner at Inniskerry, County Cork, in August 1642.

Sir Edmund Ludlow, who had been a commissioner at the trial, made clear in his memoirs the importance of Muskerry being given the opportunity to prepare his own defence in the matter. Ludlow commented on the length of the trial:

The trial of the Lord Muskerry was long, by reason of a clause which he urged in his defence from a printed copy of the articles made with him; which tho it had been unjust of me to grant in the terms there mentioned, yet would have cleared him, and thrown the guilt and blame upon me, for articles given ought to be made good. But this clause, upon search into the original, which I kept, appeared to have been inserted by themselves in the print which they produced for evidence, under pretence of having lost the original articles signed by me. Notwithstanding which, it appearing that tho divers of the English were murdered by the convoy appointed to conduct them safe to Cork; the Lord Muskerry had taken what care he could for their security, and had done what in him lay to bring the person who was guilty of that blood to justice, the court acquitted him and he was permitted, according to his articles to pass into Spain.

Ludlow cast a very different light on many areas surrounding the trial, including Muskerry's role in the events and the entire question of his preparations and integrity. However, if there is foundation in Ludlow's comments it should be remembered that Muskerry was fighting for his life.

He was discharged with a warning from the court about his conduct in the rebellion, and to 'expiate' his conduct 'through repentance'. Muskerry's speech after his acquittal was interesting:

I have not much to say, although I cannot say all I feel in the way of thanks to this Honourable Court, I must say that I have in these whole proceedings met with justice, without any leaning to my prejudice, but that if any leaning hath been it hath been to my favour rather. It is one of the greatest providences that ever I met with this. I met with many crosses in Spain and Portugal. I could get no rest till I came hither, and the crosses I met here are much affliction to me, but when I consider that in this Court I come clear out of that blackness of blood by being so sifted, it is more to me than my estate. I can live without my estate, but not without my credit.

By May 1654, having being cleared of another charge, again of murder rather than simply complicity, he was free. In addition to Ludlow's comments there is a suggestion that Ormonde had a hand in Muskerry's freedom. Lack of damning evidence had never been an obstacle to the Cromwellian courts to date, so the Ormonde angle has some credence given his relationship with his sister Eleanor, and his eagerness on other occasions to return her husband to her.[5] Despite his newfound freedom, and, in common with many of the Irish who had fought in the rebellion, he had lost his estates in the upheaval of the Cromwellian invasion and its aftermath. At least his family were safe in France, but his estates were gone and he had little hope of aid from the Cromwellians. His return to Spain proved fruitless as Ludlow continued:

> I have heard that upon his arrival in that kingdom a faction appeared against him upon account of his former opposition to the Pope's Nuncio in Ireland; so that he finding but cold entertainment there, entered into a treaty to put himself and his men into the service of the Venetians.[6]

Spanish memories of the Irish war and Rinuccini's treatment were still fresh and Muskerry had little option but to leave. Despite rumours of his murder in Dublin, the next few years would see him attempt a number of enterprising recruitment drives.[7]

In 1655 he attempted to procure a commission in France and in the same year, obtained a licence from Cromwell to raise and ship 5,000 men to Poland. He also attempted to raise troops for Venice. All would come to naught, despite the apparent attempts of the Cromwellians to be rid of him from Ireland.[8] His patience and past resistance to Cromwell's forces would be rewarded, at least in part. The monarchy in exile, led by Charles II, made Lord Muskerry the Earl of Clancarty in 1658. Cromwell's death in the same year would signal the restoration of the English monarchy by 1660 when the exhausted English people turned in desperation back to their king.

Exiled with the monarchy in France were the others of the MacCarthy family. Now secure in the knowledge that her husband had survived the Cromwellian examination, Lady Muskerry could perhaps be assured that there would be some future for her family. Her brother Ormonde would not leave her isolated and would do all in his power to secure what estates were available to her husband, should the monarchy be returned to England.

Charles II, in exile in France, also cultivated the creation of Irish regiments for the French. In this way many Irish could still fight for the Crown against the parliamentarians, albeit indirectly. By 1652 a regiment of horse and a regiment of foot fought under Turenne and the Duke of Lorraine. Many of these troops would later be placed under the command of Charles's brother James, Duke of York, when they were incorporated into his own regiment.

By 1656, however, the alliance between the English Commonwealth and France obliged Charles II to seek refuge with the Spanish court at Cologne while the Duke of York moved to Spanish Flanders. Cormac MacCarthy had carved a fine reputation in French service during the 1650s. We can be reasonably certain that he led a battalion or regiment of Munstermen during the wars in Ireland in the 1640s and that he was the mysterious 'hostage' about whom Ludlow talked prior to the siege of Ross Castle in 1652. It is also reasonable to assume that Cormac left with his regiment for the continent at the same time as his father left for Spain. In either event, he had become colonel of his Irish regiment in French service. His men were mostly from Munster, a collection of loyal Muskerry fighters, tenants and dependants.

In 1656 Cormac found himself under siege. Condé, a small though well-defended fortress on the Meuse river, lay besieged by the Spanish. The defenders were mainly Irish under Muskerry, and had held out against Don Juan of Austria, the Spanish commander, for many weeks. With Charles II then securely in the Spanish camp, Don Juan appealed to him about ending the siege through his own intrigues. To that end Charles immediately despatched Cormac's uncle, the Duke of Ormonde, to the town. We can never know the true nature of what occurred, suffice to say that many troops in the garrison surrendered, either due to their loyalty to Ormonde or to the dilemma caused by conflicting loyalties amongst the Irish in the presence of the nobles. Ormonde also tried to convince Cormac to bring his regiment over to the Spanish side. The young MacCarthy replied that:

> It was not consistent with his honour that either he or his men should quit their colours, until, according to his articles, he should march into France; he would then leave his regiment in their quarters, demand his pass, which, by contract, he was entitled to whenever his own king should demand his services, and his regiment should be permitted to march with him.

Cormac saw his only choice in the delicate situation as that of showing loyalty to his king. However, he did not know the decision of his comrade the Duke of York until later. Cormac returned to France. Cardinal Mazarin, the chief minister, who had caused much of the fiasco through his agreement with the English Republic, pointed out that this entire scheme was but a pretext for engaging French troops in Spanish service. Mazarin, although pointing to the reality of the situation, could not dissuade the young colonel, despite promises regarding the benefits that would be available for the regiment. Having obtained his 'pass', thereby ending his military contract with the French, Muskerry passed into Spanish service. He had made the decision alone and had only obtained permission for himself to leave. His men and officers, showing a surprising degree of loyalty, deserted and joined him over the next few days, quitting their French quarters in small groups. A regiment of 800 men was available under MacCarthy for Spanish service by the end of the desertion.

At St Gerlain the Irish garrison became Spanish troops overnight and turned the fortress over to their new allies. The hand of Ormonde had again been involved as his secretary, Sir George Lane, had been present with the garrison. Despite arresting several Irish officers it was too late, and the governor, the Duke of Schomberg, was forced to surrender. In all, the Spanish had gained four Irish regiments who would fight in the sieges and battles of 1656 and 1657 but they were alarmed at the apparent ease with which the Irish troops had come over. Their treachery at St Gerlain, and after the siege of Condé, drove them to insist that the Irish troops swear an oath of fealty to the Spanish government. In their view the Irish loss of honour in the affair could only be repaid through a religious oath, their Catholicism being a little more trustworthy. This stain on the Irish troops' reputation could not easily be glossed over, but the confused situation had meant that desperate decisions had been taken.[9]

A curious episode also occurred upon Cormac's transfer to Spanish service. Despite his good relations with the Duke of York, the young Richard Talbot had also been a rising star in the young James's favour. As already stated, most of Cormac's men were from Munster, his tenants and dependants. A vacancy for a lieutenant colonel had arisen in the regiment, and Cormac, quite understandably, had wished to appoint one of his own men for the position. Talbot also applied for the position. When MacCarthy rejected Talbot, the two chose a manner with which to settle their argument, which was all too common in the exiled court of Charles II. They fought a duel. Although the end result is not clear, both survived but for Talbot the matter was clearly not closed: he appealed directly to James who, in the end, supported him. MacCarthy, in turn, appealed to his uncle, Ormonde, in the hope of putting enough pressure on the Duke of York to make him see sense. A Leinster officer in a Munster regiment holding a position not approved by the regimental colonel would seem uncomfortable for all parties involved. Despite protestations to Charles himself, who would not interfere, the decision to promote Talbot was upheld. It seems that the enmity between

Talbot and Ormonde was fostered at this stage. There may also have been some antagonism generated towards the MacCarthys.[10]

Their reputation somewhat damaged, in 1657 and 1658 the Irish troops appeared to fare less courageously than had been suggested in earlier conflicts. The young Cormac MacCarthy was still involved heavily in the actions that did take place. At the siege of Ardres, in August 1657, he led one of the Duke of York's Irish battalions in the assault. The Spanish army was forced to raise the siege by the appearance of Turenne and the French Army. Cormac directed his Irish troops in giving covering fire so that the Spanish engineers and miners could escape the French attacks.

By 1658 6,000 English troops from Cromwell's New Model Army bolstered the French Army in Spanish Flanders. That year's campaign concentrated on the channel towns of Dunkirk, Mardyk and Gravelines. Dunkirk and Mardyk would become English possessions if secured in return for Cromwell's assistance. Turenne laid siege to Dunkirk in May, triggering Don Juan's march to relieve it with around 14,000 men including his Irish regiments comprising 2,000 men. Critically, the Spanish commander ignored his general Condé's advice and left his artillery behind. Condé, perhaps unimpressed, changed sides after the battle. Don Juan had arrived by June to face Turenne. In a final twist of irony, the French Army still had some Irish regiments, Dillon's for instance, who would fight alongside Cromwell's New Model Army at the Battle of the Dunes.

Turenne, the meticulous planner, manoeuvred his army into position three miles east of the besieged town. Don Juan reacted slowly, despite James's warnings of imminent attack. A sandhill on the Spanish right was quickly reinforced with four Spanish regiments with James's troops to the left of this hill. The sandhill would undo the Spanish, however. In battle a flank secured by a hill would be of major tactical importance but this flank was on a beach, and the tide was going out. Turenne, although a master tactician, would not have taken long to realise that, given time, he could easily outflank the Spanish position. The English fleet was also within artillery range of the hill from their positions anchored offshore.

The English infantry assaulted the hill, pikemen attacking in force. The Spanish infantry broke despite a courageous cavalry charge led by James in an attempt to secure the flank. With the ebbing tide French cavalry surged along the strand, enveloping the flank and causing the Spanish line to disintegrate slowly. The French fought off Spanish attacks in the centre and counter-attacked. The Irish troops, outflanked and with little support, could not sustain the position and broke. Cormac MacCarthy's regiment suffered heavy casualties, caught as it was, outflanked and assaulted from the right flank and front. Most of the Irish troops broke and were captured except Cormac, who escaped the French. Within four hours the battle was over.

The French had won a dramatic victory. Dunkirk fell, and the nineteen-year-old Louis XIV, who promptly handed the town to the English, watched as the Spanish garrison emerged. Other French objectives would fall quickly in the months to come. By 1659 Turenne's victories had convinced the Spanish to sue for peace. France kept most of her conquered territory but, more importantly, had succeeded Spain as the dominant military power in Europe. Dramatic change was also afoot in England where the death of Cromwell would see the return of the monarchy and the coronation of Charles II.[11]

We know little of the events surrounding the lives of the MacCarthy family during the early period of the restoration in 1660, although some points are clear. Donough had regained most of his estates through Charles's Act of Settlement; of course, Ormonde had conveniently arranged most of this. Donough returned to Ireland and his estates with his wife. Cormac undoubtedly returned to England with the Duke of York's Regiment while Callaghan remained in France continuing his studies. Of Justin there is no record, but it is likely that he returned to Ireland with his mother and father. It is also quite likely that, in admiration of his brother, he was keen to pursue a military career.

The Dutch had not been idle in the interim and heavily-armed warships had been constructed to combat the English fleet by the time of the outbreak of the 1665 Dutch War. The restoration of Charles II had given hope to the Orange faction in the Dutch republic; Charles's sister Mary had hoped that her son William would benefit from the king's support in his claim to be stadtholder amongst the Dutch. All was for naught when Mary died of smallpox in 1660 and Charles's hatred of republicanism instilled in him a deep concern for the emerging and, potentially, damaging Dutch commercial influence. The Navigation Act of 1651 was reinforced in 1660 with a more rigid and, for the Dutch, more harmful version. Mary had nominated Charles as her son's guardian, a relationship that would give the English significant influence in Dutch politics in the years to come. It was the republican element of Dutch politics rather than the Orangeism that concerned the English. The unrivalled commercial power of the Dutch also worried the English and, perhaps, made them a little jealous.

Unrest had been fermenting in English circles in the first four years of Charles's reign. Much of this surrounded James, Duke of York, who, as

Lord High Admiral of the fleet would command in any sea battle against the Dutch. His charisma and influence had meant that he was surrounded by a group of angry young Englishmen, eager for war and keen to show him their mettle. Cormac MacCarthy would also have moved in these circles. Incidents in West Africa and America between English and Dutch shipping exacerbated an already delicate situation. However, both countries heavily miscalculated their respective eagerness for war. On the Dutch side, de Witt, the Grand Pensionary of Holland, believed that Charles would never be voted the funds he needed. Charles, on the other hand, believed that the Dutch would never fight another war, since it must have been obvious to them that they would lose significantly against his superior fleet. Both were to be proved wrong.

Pressure from the threat of trade in Africa and the Americas persuaded Parliament to vote Charles over £2,000,000 in order to provide a fleet to protect English trade. The English were spoiling for war. When news of Dutch reprisals along the Guinea coast reached England, ships were given a free rein to prey on Dutch interests in the channel and North Sea. Attacks on Dutch convoys provoked reaction and the Dutch declared war in February 1665. Despite problems with manpower and provisioning, Charles had a powerful navy. He was also determined to use it. By April the English fleet had set sail for the Dutch coast to sit in position to intercept Dutch convoys returning via the North Sea, but the Dutch managed to slip through the English net. The fleet returned home. The Dutch, too, had a large fleet, thanks to the lessons learned between the wars. Their tactics differed, however; they did not fight in line but in small groups, using their smaller size and weight to their advantage, and, perhaps, also due to differences between Dutch provincial groups. If an English ship became crippled, the groups could seize and board her, although English 'line' tactics helped prevent this to some degree. The Dutch also used 'chain-shot', where a short length of chain linked two iron balls: this was normally fired high to shred the rigging of the opposing ships, thus crippling them. Such firing techniques could also be deadly for those standing on deck.

The two fleets, which had been hunting each other, met about forty miles south-east of Lowestoft on the English east coast at first light on 3 June 1665. The English fleet was composed of three squadrons, each of twenty to thirty ships. The vanguard was led by James's cousin Prince Rupert, followed by James aboard the *Royal Charles*, with Lord Sandwich in the rear. The fleets passed each other heading south-easterly, giving broadsides, but most shots fell short, still being too far apart to do much damage.

By 6.00 a.m. the fleets were parallel and in range of each other. Vicious broadsides erupted from both fleets, tearing gouges in timber and men, with the thunder of guns even being heard in London. By midday, with hundreds already killed, and ships full of wounded and dead sinking slowly, the main action was still taking place at the rear of the English line. There, Lord Sandwich in the *Prince* was supported by only one ship and fighting with the Dutch commander Obdam in the *Eendracht* with several other ships. The Duke of York ordered that the *Royal Charles* move in to give aid. Sandwich pressed hard against the smaller Dutch vessels, forcing open a gap in their line. Four Dutch ships became tangled together in the confusion and James unleashed a fireship to end the debacle. One Dutch ship exploded when its powder store was hit, taking the mast of another with it. The vessels began to disperse as the momentum of the Dutch defence was broken.

It was probably at this time, as the Duke of York urged the *Royal Charles* to aid Lord Sandwich, that the fire against the royal ship was at its fiercest. The Dutch would have thrown everything against the timely reinforcements. As the range reduced they would have aimed chain-shot against the rigging of the enemy vessels, or even at those English officers standing on deck urging the sailors on and eager for glory. As James stood on the deck of the *Royal Charles*, however, alongside his loyal aide Cormac MacCarthy and two English nobles, the Dutch fired. The chain-shot that flew towards the group killed all save James himself, 'Their blood and brains flying in the Duke's face – and the head of Mr Boyle striking down the Duke, as some say'.

The shot might have changed the history of the British Isles; instead Cormac MacCarthy had been killed. James retired to bed, quite possibly in a state of shock. Although chase was given to the remnants of the Dutch, the impetus of the attack had gone. It emerged later that this was partly due to the warning given to the duke's servants by his wife, Anne Hyde, that he should not get too close to the battle. James had obviously ignored this advice until too tired or too shocked by the death of his friends to continue, or, perhaps, it was an indication of his limits under the strain of combat. Over 800 English sailors and noblemen had been killed or wounded, but the English had won a victory of sorts. The war would drag on until the signing of a peace treaty in 1667.[12]

After the battle, James's popularity in England soared as he became a national hero. Cormac was buried in Westminster Abbey after a very public funeral. He was thirty-one-years old. Having been a gentleman of the bedchamber to the Duke of York, Cormac was buried with full military honours. Ormonde wrote to his sister conveying his grief at the loss of her son, Lord Muskerry.[13]

Dear Sister,

It is not the length or words of a preamble that can abate the bitterness of the matter. I shall therefore without the affliction of circumstances, tell you it falls to my shame to inform you, that your son Muskery was killed in the late conflict betwixt the king's fleet and that of the Dutch. He was close by the duke his master's side; and with him were killed the Earl of Falmouth and Mr Richard Boyle, the earl of Cork's son. That your son is generally lamented and well spoken of, may aggravate your sense of such a loss; yet it must come to your knowledge, and I that partake in the loss, and am thought fittest to let you know it, cannot forbear to say it.

It must be the work of some time, but principally of pious reflection upon the submission and resignation due from us to the good pleasure of God, to give consolation proportionable to such an affliction. That God, who gives and takes, and always for the best, (if it be not our own faults,) send you all the comfort you need, and make us all ready for that hour which we must all come to, and which your son has past with honour in this world, and (I doubt not) with happiness in the other.

I am,

My dearest sister, your most afflicted
but most affectionate brother.

Ormonde

Donough's grief would be shortlived, for, by August 1665, he also died. Cormac and Donough's tragic deaths left the family bereft of the titular heads of the family. Cormac's twelve-year-old son, also Cormac, laid claim to the Earldom of Clancarty. The child was a ward of Ormonde and lived in England. Tragically, however, in September 1666, a year after Donough's death, the boy also died.

By 1666 Callaghan was still in France studying for the priesthood. He would have been the next Earl of Clancarty but for his studies. Justin would then become the next earl but for the unexpected chain of events that followed. In an unprecedented move, and in apparent anticipation of the wealth that the Muskerry estates would yield, Callaghan, on the verge of taking holy orders, changed his mind, and upon taking the title and estates of Clancarty, then changed his religion, becoming a Protestant.

We can only imagine how embittered the young Justin must have been, although his father had made provision for his youngest son in his will, charging his wife with the duty of providing land for Justin to the value of £1,000 per year. Despite the dowager countess's attempts to further this request for Justin, Callaghan was unwilling to honour it. Ormonde's intervention was required to settle the argument, although he found in Callaghan's favour, insisting that the estate could not afford such an outlay. Land should instead be given to Justin for his own maintenance and that of his family, should he have one. Callaghan, displaying a degree of contempt for the entire affair, had to be persuaded to agree to any form of settlement.[14]

Justin seems to have been particularly close to his mother at this point, which is hardly surprising bearing in mind the recent turn of events. Callaghan's lack of 'brotherly love' and even respect for Justin is more difficult to understand. For now, it was clear at least that Justin would have to make a living for himself. He had looked on his oldest brother with admiration and had probably based his decision on Cormac's very successful military career. Any claim on his father's estate had disappeared and he would, therefore, shape his own future as a soldier.

Having spent time in France and with little potential for advancement in the English army of the 1670s, French service seemed the logical starting point for Justin's military career. An Irish regiment still fought with the French army. As we have seen, Irish Catholic officers wishing to pursue a military career had little choice but to serve abroad. With the French attack on the Dutch, the English parliament, in argumentative mood, forced Charles to enforce rigidly the penal laws and withdraw the Declaration of Indulgence. Officers had little hope of pursuing their trade in Ireland either, even though the Test Act did not apply. The Irish officer corps was still dominated by Cromwellians and Catholic officers seeking experience had little option but to seek it abroad. Charles was forced to offer his Irish troops to the French.

The MacCarthys would have been well known to their cousins, the Hamiltons, and it was inevitable that the choice of military service would only go one way for Justin. In April 1671 Hamilton obtained permission to raise a company of Irish, *un Régiment d'Infanterie Irlandais*, comprising fifteen companies of one-hundred men each, most of these recruited from exiles. Despite the difficulties with landing, eventually the troops were raised.

Among them was the thirty-one-year-old Justin MacCarthy, a young officer forced to seek his fortune in the Irish military serving in France.[15] He would get his first experience of war relatively quickly, serving under Turenne on the Rhine from 1673 to 1675, his first action most likely at Sinzheim in 1674. He would witness the devastation of the Palatinate, and the reality of pillage and the disdain of French military methods of obtaining contributions from the surrounding villages. He would fight at Ensheim in October and witness the terrible battle for the woods, where George Hamilton was wounded, then see the grand winter offensive of 1675 and the taking of Turkheim, and finally take part at Salzbach in July, where Turenne's untimely death ended the French campaign.

The following year would see his service continue at Saverne in October, where Hamilton was killed. For Justin, the death of his cousin and commander must have not only been upsetting, but must have seemed as if a chapter of his life had ended, his first taste of service in Louis's army.[16]

By November 1676 Justin's loyalty and apparent sound service in the regiment would pay dividends. The Duke of Monmouth was a lieutenant general in the French army and had led a regiment similar to Hamilton's. For now, however he was temporarily the colonel-proprietor of the regiment that had belonged to George Hamilton and had previously commanded the Irish regiment within which Justin served. Patrick Sarsfield, who would later gain fame in the Irish war, served under MacCarthy at this time as a lieutenant. Justin was a captain, in charge of a company of Irishmen.[17]

Monmouth had placed Lieutenant Colonel Scott in charge of the troops, although the continual ill health of this officer was a matter of concern. Charles II was also concerned. His troops in French service were apparently being ill-led to the extent that discipline and order were beginning to slip. With anti-French sentiment becoming an increasingly worrying trend for the English king, he sought a solution through Monmouth. Monmouth wrote to Louvois:

> The King, having reflected on Mr Scott's continual ill health, which is the cause that he cannot take the care necessary for governing the regiment well, the consequences whereof are many disorders and the relaxation of discipline, has decided to recall him to give him something else here, and has ordered me to appoint to his charge of colonel-lieutenant Mr Macartie, who will present you with this, and who is a person of quality and merit. He has already served in France, and his brother has commanded a regiment there, and I

hope he will acquit himself so well as to deserve the King's good opinion of him. I beg you to give him a share of your favour and to obtain the King's approval of him. I refer myself to him to inform you as to the affairs of the regiment, begging you to listen to him favourably and to give him such orders as you may deem for his Majesty's service.[18]

Justin soon received his orders from the Duke of Monmouth. He was to go to Paris and meet with Louvois, with the duke's letter of recommendation. Other orders related to the settling of accounts. Scott, it seems, had been lax with the paying out of French money to new recruits. In addition, Monmouth ordered Justin to investigate further irregularities with Scott, with regard to the payment of £30,000 to the regiment in 1675. There was probably more to Monmouth's remarks of Scott's 'ill health' than was immediately apparent. It seemed that the regiment had fallen into some disarray in the interim in its readiness for duty, and Monmouth was taking immediate steps to rectify the situation. Stories of ill-disciplined Irish regiments acting in the king's name in a foreign land would provide too rich an opportunity for the anti-French lobby in England. Justin's last order from Monmouth seemed to echo this sentiment: 'You are to take particular care that the discipline of the regiment be preserved, that both officers and soldiers behave as becomes them in their respective stations.'

It is interesting to note that the young John Churchill was also considered for the post, although turned down by Louvois, the future Duke of Marlborough being 'too addicted to pleasure'. It is not clear what this meant, although, taking it in context, perhaps the French were already developing a liking for the Irish officer. It was clear that a no-nonsense professional soldier was required, and Monmouth was keen to see that the regiment did not disintegrate, urging Justin to push Louvois to permit one battalion to remain in garrison whilst two battalions served in the field. Louvois's meeting with Justin is not recorded, although it seems that his brother's reputation, as well as his own, spoke volumes. MacCarthy's military career and future seemed secure.[19]

The European war was not over, however. The majority of the two battalions fielded would be Irish troops but the nature of the war had changed. Although Louis's strategy had been defensive, there had been some remarkable manoeuvres along the Rhine. Turenne, the master strategist, had gone, however, and the loss had affected Louis's strategic decision-making. The war would now reach its conclusion, where significant gains would be minimised and each side would strive to finish the conflict in as powerful a position as possible. The scope of such a victory was limited significantly by this stage. The nature of the coalition and the odds stacked against Louis meant not only that he would have to settle for a resolution, but that he would have to increase the size of his army to over 200,000 men. Créqui would defend the Alsace region as Luxembourg had been moved to the north. MacCarthy, however, would lead his troops in the Spanish Netherlands for this campaign.

The ebb and flow of battle that had characterised the war of manoeuvre under Turenne was over and most engagements in the campaign were sieges, with only one major battle at Cassel. By 1678 peace negotiations were well underway. Louis took the Dutch city of Ghent by March in an attempt to secure peace before Charles II was forced to take the Dutch side in the war through the inevitable anti-French sentiment of his parliament. Although the peace treaty was signed in August, fighting continued along the Rhine until October when the two shattered armies went into winter quarters.

For Justin the campaign had turned him from a raw officer recruit into an experienced regimental commander. News from England regarding the turning tide of English support meant that the regiment that had fought and died for so long in French service would be disbanded quickly. Unsure of how matters would develop, but certain that disbandment of the French regiment could be problematic, he wrote from Paris to his uncle Ormonde:

> I have once since my coming hither given your Grace the trouble of a letter, but I know not whether it came to your hands. And now, my Lord, I must importune you again, for I am so alarmed at the bill I hear that has passed the House of Commons for the recalling of us out of the French service that I know not what to do unless your Grace can by your interest get me particularly excepted, which is the only hope I have that can prevent my ruin, having been at vast expense to equip myself for the field, besides a certain disappointment of making my fortune, which I am in a good way of doing if I were permitted to continue here. I beseech your Grace, if nothing can be done in this business, at the least that I may have your advice how I shall carry myself, for without it I shall not stir.[20]

Monmouth had decreed that MacCarthy would deduct one *sol* per *livre* paid to his troops for himself. As long the troops remained in French service

MacCarthy would be paid. Monmouth also commented on MacCarthy's 'good service' as colonel of the regiment.[21]

Justin's concerns did have some basis, not only with the ending of the Dutch war, but with events in England. The English were beginning to see the Dutch as more powerful and benevolent allies than the French and the Dutch war heightened the desire to protect England against a dominant France and the fear of French *absolutism*. The political climate that would quickly develop would see a change in Justin's fortune once more.

With the signing of the treaty, and the end of the Dutch war, the English and Irish troops of MacCarthy's regiment returned home to England. The regiments of Gendarmes had been disbanded. Justin's newfound career had been ended abruptly unless he could persuade the king to back an Irish regiment. Tragedy had once more struck the MacCarthy family in Ireland in 1677 with Callaghan's death. His widow had written to Charles expressing her concerns regarding her son Donogh, then eight-years-old and the new Earl of Clancarty. The countess expressed her wish to have the boy's Protestant religion guaranteed by Charles due to his lineage and she was concerned at bringing the boy up in an Ireland where the Catholic Church still held a significant degree of power. Charles wrote to Ormonde, the Lord Lieutenant of Ireland:

> Having received a petition from Elizabeth, Countess of Clancarty, Dowager of Callaghan, Earl of Clancarty, lately deceased, setting forth that the guardianship of her only son Donnogh, now Earl of Clancarty, being about 8 years old is devolved on her as being his mother and a Protestant, and that she desires and designs to breed him up in the true Protestant religion, but has reason to fear her endeavours will meet with much opposition from the titular clergy and others of the Church of Rome, because his father and grandfather were both of that religion and praying our assistance and authority, we therefore require you at all times, as there shall be occasion, to use our power and authority to assist and countenance her in the education of her said son in the Protestant religion, and, if any persons whatever attempt to inveigle or take him away from her or to pervert him in the principles of the Protestant religion to cause such persons to be prosecuted with the utmost severity of the law.[22]

As events would show, the countess need not have worried about the Catholic Church but instead those other forces that would determine the future of her son. The young earl would later write to Ormonde requesting that he be his guardian.[23] It is unclear whether Justin was aware of the turn of events or not, and it is by no means clear about exactly what, or who, the countess was concerned. The events to follow would show just how perceptive she had been.

Having returned to England, there was little hope for the Irish officers using their military experience in English regiments. Their chosen religion meant that they would not be accepted for commissions in England. Charles, however, had no intention of wasting the experience that the men had gained in France. Instead he formed a regiment of Irish troops, led by Sir Thomas Dongan. When relations with the French were restored, plans were put into effect so that the regiment would once more be sent to serve under Louis. An Irish Catholic regiment had too much potential for trouble if serving in England as part of the army, no matter what the king's personal feelings on the matter might have been.

However, anti-Catholic hysteria had reached new heights and matters were about to worsen significantly with the advent of the 'Popish Plot'. It would prove almost impossible for a Catholic officer in England to remain untouched by the chaotic events. In October 1678, even in the midst of the plot, Justin was promoted once more. Colonel Thomas Dongan was commissioned as Lieutenant Governor of Tangier, leaving command of the regiment open. Justin was subsequently commissioned as colonel of the troops, destined now to serve in Ireland.[24]

A proclamation was issued on 30 October, reminding all 'popish recusants' that they should leave London forthwith. In November 1678, as the plot and hysteria had taken hold, Justin was walking outside the House of Commons. Unsurprisingly, he was arrested and questioned, then subsequently told to leave the capital. In effect he could only be accused of ignoring the proclamation, in that he was a Catholic and had not left the city. In a bold move, however, he attempted to exempt himself from the terms of the declaration, being informed that he would have to do so at the Bar of the House of Commons. Within, Ormonde was later told that MacCarthy had:

> Behaved himself so discreetly as to appease the House: yet for example's sake they ordered him to give obedience to the proclamation that night so that all the warriors despairing to come off so well are by his example withdrawn.[25]

Justin had the temerity to oppose the order but could do little against the forces ranged against him and his fellow Irish and Catholic officers. The force of public and parliamentary opinion in light of the plot, however implausible, was too strong. The House also had the wisdom to appeal to MacCarthy's common sense. If he withdrew from London, many of his fellow officers would do the same, an elegant if somewhat unsatisfactory solution for all parties. Many of the officers took this as their signal to flee the country. Not all had been successful. Patrick Sarsfield, now one of MacCarthy's captains, was held under lock and key in Chester with several other Irishmen. Even Justin could not leave as easily as he had thought initially. As he made his way out of the capital and thence to Ireland, he was arrested once more at Barnet and imprisoned. He was eventually released via the Privy Council's decision and an immediate order from Whitehall, stating that Barnet was outside the ten-mile radius that had been outlawed for Catholics. Sarsfield was subsequently released and he, too, sailed for home.

With increased tension in England, many Catholic officers, effectively out of a job since their return from French service, fled to Ireland. Justin's regiment was fast becoming a haven for disaffected Irish military men seeking some sort of protection from the still potent levels of persecution that were to be expected in an England still rocked by the plot. In Ireland so many Irish officers attempted to gather beneath MacCarthy's flag that several were detained. In reality, they had little choice but to seek the apparent refuge of the regiment. Ormonde had been given his own orders regarding Catholics and the Oath of Supremacy had to be rigidly enforced with the troops. Accused by his enemies of permitting Papist elements within his army, he knew that he would be ruined should any soldiers take matters into their own hands or rebel. He wrote at the end of 1678:

> If any ill accident should happen either by the keeping on foot or disbanding MacCarty's regiment, the inconvenience and the blame too will fall on me; the inconvenience by the disorder that must follow the disbanding of so many men that know how to live upon their neighbours when they want bread, and the blame will be imputed to me; for people here are not so reasonable as to consider whether I have or have not orders; the smart will direct them to murmur at those nearest them, who they think might have prevented it.[26]

Much to his relief, plans were finally drawn up to disband the regiment in January 1679. Both Ormonde and Monmouth sought to ensure that some form of compensation was given to the officers, although it is unclear how much of this was paid in the end. While Charles had preferred to keep his Irish officers, in political terms they were becoming a problem, if not an embarrassment. Charles's final note to Ormonde in his letter of January 1679 closed the door on his Irish regiment:

> The arms being delivered up and all accounts adjusted, the Commissioners shall forthwith disband the respective companies and then the officers and soldiers are immediately to disperse to their own abodes and behave in all things as becomes dutiful subjects.[27]

Justin was once more out of work and out of favour as a professional soldier. However, the Europe of the late seventeenth century had more than its fair share of conflict and the market for mercenary officers was lucrative, and for many the only way of pursuing their chosen career. To this end Justin travelled to Denmark in 1679 to pursue service with the Danish Army. The Danes had been allied to the Dutch throughout the war, but also saw the opportunity to regain much of their territory lost during the earlier part of the century to their old rival Sweden. The Swedes had allied themselves with Louis throughout the Dutch conflict, and so the complex alliances in this case played into the hands of the Danes. There is little record of Justin's experiences during this part of the war, although the clash between the Swedes and the Danes was dominated by Swedish success, at least on land.[28]

By 1682 Justin had returned to England. In May he returned to Ireland, having received word that his mother had died. There are few details of the funeral, bar that she was interred in Dublin. Her brother Ormonde left for England shortly afterwards.[29]

Justin's name then appears in a reported conspiracy outlined in letters written by Viscount Preston to the secretary of state. Preston outlined that a number of traitors in league with France would undertake the propagation of an English revolution of sorts with French arms and naval support and, most significantly, the heavy presence of Irish troops. Preston's mysterious informant related that the Irish would be led by 'Colonel Maccarty' amongst others. The plans, reputedly laid down meticulously and with French aid, would dictate the seizing of Cork, Limerick and Galway. Ireland, for so long feared as a stepping-stone for subsequent English invasion, would be used as a French base. The supposed plot was kept secret, and there was little evidence and, in terms of the required logistics and preparation involved, had word got out, similar scenes of panic to those that had accompanied the Popish Plot would have been repeated and the threat of another Irish revolution would have brought severe repercussions. By March 1683 Justin had returned to Ireland.[30]

Justin's chances of successful establishment in the English or Irish military were reduced significantly in the prevailing climate. And so, at the end of 1682, he returned to what was left of his family. He approached Callaghan's widow, Lady Clancarty, who had remarried in June 1682 to Sir William Davis, Chief Justice of the King's Bench. With little hope for the future, he asked if he could become the tenant of Blarney Castle and the surrounding area, having decided to return to Ireland. Justin was informed that the sitting tenant, an English clergyman, could not be 'put out'. Ormonde was in London at the time. The Earl of Arran, Ormonde's son and Justin's cousin, acting as Lord Lieutenant in his absence, was apparently aggravated and disturbed by the entire affair. He wrote to his father that Justin had made it clear that he 'would deal with' the tenant. Initially unsure of how to proceed with MacCarthy, his father having given him no warning of the events that would occur, he was determined not to see Lady Clancarty 'exploited'.

> If M. will not be persuaded to desist, for I find my Lady Clancarty is unwilling to give him an absolute denial, I am resolved to interpose by telling him privately of the imprudence of the thing, and if I cannot prevail that way I will tell him plainly I will appear publicly against it.[31]

Whether Justin had attempted to bully Lady Clancarty or not, it was clear that the Ormondes were set against him. Ormonde wrote back to his son by January 1683 explaining that the greatest inconvenience of the whole affair would be Justin's religion, and he hoped that the whole thing would blow over. It was also clear that Lady Clancarty could ill afford to create friction since, should her only son Donagh die, she would have to provide for her own future to a large extent. Ormonde guessed that Justin had persuaded the young Donagh to write to him asking for guardianship, in the hope of gaining estates or at the very least responsibility for the boy. Despite Ormonde's belief that Justin in all likelihood would improve the estate, his religion would preclude any further progress in the matter. Ormonde's fears over the Irish regiment were still prevalent, especially over its erstwhile commander. Although Ormonde had some feelings for his nephew, Arran had little respect for Justin, considering him the 'improperest man in the world' to be employed in any fashion by his father.

In conference with Chief Justice Davis, matters were 'contrived' by Arran to the extent that the tenant in Blarney would not be removed. It is not clear exactly what transpired. What is clear is that Justin had lost all hope of regaining his father's estates in any form. His religion and the scheming of the Ormondes had seemingly removed all hope of a future in Ireland and, by January 1683, he abandoned his attempts to retrieve the estates. His efforts at arranging the guardianship of the young Donagh, then being educated as a Protestant in Oxford, also came to naught. We can never empathise fully with historical characters in such instances, since we have only second-hand knowledge of life in the seventeenth century. Nonetheless, we can appreciate that a degree of bitterness over the whole affair, so soon after the death of his mother, and with such clear prejudice and intolerance from the Ormondes, must have embittered Justin not only to them, but to the religious and political systems in place in Ireland. Such feelings would inevitably lead to sympathies with the revolutionary change that was to follow.[32]

Lady Clancarty's fears over the young Donagh's upbringing in Ireland had meant that he now resided in Oxford, carefully tutored by the Bishop of Oxford, the dean of Christchurch. By 1684 Justin had returned to England which, although still markedly anti-Catholic, was not so consumed by the hatred that had prevailed during the Popish Plot. James had returned and was in the ascendancy, and many of his Irish friends had also relocated to the court in London. Justin persuaded King Charles to write to Oxford asking if his nephew might visit so that they might see the sights of the capital. The bishop agreed and the sixteen-year-old Donagh promptly travelled to London. The Secretary of State at the time was Lord Sunderland. It is not clear whether Justin's contact with him was by accident or design, although he would have a distinctive influence on his prospects. Sunderland had served on various diplomatic missions for the king, and had been made secretary of state in 1679. His support of the Exclusion Bill had resulted in his dismissal from the post, although he quickly regained it through the influence of the Duchess of Portsmouth, one of the king's mistresses.

He was an important player in James's inner circle and in later years would declare himself a Catholic, before renouncing his beliefs as political expediency demanded. Donagh's arrival in London prompted the plan that Justin and Sunderland must have been discussing for some time. How much of the capital the young man saw is not clear, although he would not leave as he had arrived. In an apparent act of revenge and in an attempt to further his own ends Justin saw the young man quickly married to Lord Sunderland's youngest daughter, herself merely fifteen years old.[33]

There is no clear evidence of who conceived the scheme although it is easy to imagine that Sunderland would have designs on the Clancarty estates. It is also plausible that Justin saw both the secretary of state's influence on his position and a chance for revenge against the Ormondes and Lady Clancarty. In any event the marriage and the scheme were to have far-reaching effects. Donagh would return to Ireland, and later become a Catholic. Had Justin's aim been a subtle form of revenge, then it was complete.

It seemed that the ill luck that had bedevilled Justin had been spent. He was married during this time in England to Arabella Wentworth, the second and younger daughter of the earl of Strafford, Thomas Wentworth, whose involvement in Ireland in 1633 as Lord Lieutenant had resulted in the loss of his head. Arabella was an Englishwoman and details of the relationship and subsequent marriage, whether arranged or not, are sketchy.[34]

The couple would remain childless though Arabella, it appeared, supported her husband fully in the events that followed. By January 1685 the arrangement with Sunderland was paying real dividends for Justin. Two colonels were to receive commissions to command two new regiments in Ireland. Both were Catholics who had served on the continent. More seriously, both were employed in apparent disregard of the Test Act and the legislation that Parliament had so carefully put in place to prevent such experienced Catholic soldiers gaining commands. Colonels Justin MacCarthy and Richard Talbot, in receipt of their new commissions, would not be disputing their appointments, no matter what the reservations of Parliament.[35]

English Protestants viewed the actions at best as a clear flouting of legislation and at worst as the beginning of a pro-Catholic stance on Ireland and the Irish army. Would the fact that a Catholic successor waited in the wings see a resurgence of anti-Catholic feeling in a similar vein to that which bedevilled England during the Popish Plot? Quite possibly, although Charles would hear little complaint about the situation. The Earl of Halifax, the Lord Privy Seal, wrote to the king reminding him of the threat to the Protestant interest in Ireland if such appointments were the sign of things to come. Charles would not be moved, insisting that MacCarthy had been removed from his previous post on his account and had similarly been removed from French service. He had compensated the Irish officer for his loss. Justin's time at court and his relationship with Sunderland had not been wasted effort.[36]

The implication is one of scheming and double-dealing within the king's court. Although popular history has highlighted this aspect of Charles's reign, such political manoeuvring was the norm in courts across Europe. That Justin used it to further his own ends is no surprise. It seems that calculated political activity was fashionable, and also used to great effect by Justin's fellow appointee to an Irish command, Richard Talbot.

Talbot had used the system to further his own ends at every opportunity, but to a larger extent than MacCarthy could ever have dreamed of. The same man had fought a duel so many years before with Justin's brother Cormac over the command of a regiment in France, and by now had entered the inner circle of James, Duke of York. Kenyon outlines that, during the Popish Plot, James's close-knit circle of Irish comrades included a number of 'unscrupulous Catholic swordsmen and professional soldiers', among them Richard Talbot, Henry Jermyn and one Justin MacCarthy.[37]

With the start of Tyrconnel's purges in Ireland, Justin MacCarthy followed Tyrconnel's example with relish. He made radical changes within his own Irish regiment. He removed Captain Thomas Bingham, reportedly absent without leave, and replaced him with Thomas Nugent, who had been one of his officers in France. In addition, he forced the Protestant chaplain in the regiment to share his wage with that of a Catholic priest whom MacCarthy had appointed. The chaplain was given the choice of dismissal should he disagree.[38]

Stationed in his native Munster, near Cork, Justin proved popular amongst his troops. This is not surprising since he was a well-qualified officer and experienced commander of men. His experience would have earned him significant respect amongst his men, especially those Catholics who were new to the military. In reality, the lack of experience amongst the rank and file would cause problems for the bulk of the army as matters progressed. There were, however, clear differences between Justin's reputation regarding treatment of the populace and that of Tyrconnel, as evidenced by the Earl of Longford, a Protestant, who wrote to Ormonde in September 1685:

> I was willing to take this opportunity of acquainting your Grace that from him your Grace may authentically have your account of my Lord Tyrconnel's proceedings with the Mayor and

Corporation of Drogheda, and how insolently he treated Dean Pullein there on Sunday morning before he went to church. He will also tell your Grace what havoc he has made in Sir William's troop, and indeed in most of the troops of his regiment. His lordship was endeavouring to have several of his friends and relations made Sheriffs for the ensuing year, and proceeded so far as to give them promises of it; but I suppose the declaring of my Lord Clarendon Lord Lieutenant has stopped him in his career, and indeed it was but necessary and seasonable, his haughty carriage having so disanimated the Protestants and elated the Papists that the former, or many of them whose effects are only in money, were not only withdrawing from trade but also out of the kingdom, but since the confirmation of the Lord Lieutenant they seem now to assume more courage, and I hope will be so far satisfied as to fall to their trade again.

Col McCarthy's carriage has been so differing from the others that he has by his great civility recommended himself highly to the affections of the people of Cork, though they are notoriously fanatic, and he is as well beloved by the officers of his regiment as it is possible for a man upon so short an acquaintance to be, for he is easy to every one of them and yet keeps them strictly to their duty.[39]

It seemed that, in some respects, MacCarthy's approach was quite different to that of Tyrconnel. Despite the common conclusion that 'might was right' in the delicate situation, Justin was well aware that the circumstances could get out of control at any moment and parliamentary cries of 'rebellion' could quickly fall on Ireland, despite the relative power of the monarchy. He was unique amongst the new Irish officer cadre, which, in turn, created a new problem. The developing Irish army was untrained and unaccustomed to military drill, discipline and weaponry. The majority of the old-English and Irish officers were inexperienced and unable to maintain discipline. The repercussions of the mistake would prove far-reaching. Despite Justin's relative popularity, he still supported Tyrconnel's attempts to undermine the militia, requesting the removal and storage of weapons.

In spite of Clarendon's frequent protestations at the methods used, there was little he could really do. Tyrconnel's browbeating personality seems to have dominated the softer Clarendon at every stage. Indeed, with James's policy appearing to back Tyrconnel, the Lord Lieutenant was relatively powerless.

Clarendon attempted to moderate the situation as best he could, but it was too late, and the army was not under his control. Despite his objections to Sunderland and James, he had to hold back from a clear attack on the policy since it was still unclear how much of the monarch's intent was being enforced. Throughout the summer of 1686 there was still an air of deception and subtlety, although this could not last for long.

Despite the obvious difficulties in the relationship between Clarendon and Tyrconnel, the Lord Lieutenant was on good terms with Justin MacCarthy, at least initially. Clarendon's letters of the time show many facets of the Lord Lieutenant's personality, a man whose relationship with Justin initially seemed close, yet whose weakness through being outmanoeuvred by Tyrconnel and James would undermine and ultimately destroy his authority. It would be unkind to criticise him for this since those prepared to 'take on' Tyrconnel with a view to amending policy would have been rapidly dismissed by James. Clarendon's contact with Colonel MacCarthy related to his request to alleviate the problem of bandits or 'Tories' in the countryside around Cork. From this initial contact Justin appears to have attempted to befriend the Lord Lieutenant.

In the early part of 1686 Justin spent some time at Dublin Castle. This was not wasted, as evidenced by Clarendon's communication to his brother, the Earl of Rochester, during February. Justin, knowing that Clarendon had no regiment of his own, placed his Cork regiment at the Lord Lieutenant's disposal. Of course, this was no accident. Justin sought permission to go to England. He had been made acutely aware that change in the hierarchy of the Irish Army was imminent and it was time to seek further promotion, and Justin still had powerful friends in England. The post of major general would be available and Clarendon recommended Justin over Sir Thomas Newcomen, Tyrconnel's brother-in-law, described by Clarendon as no soldier but 'wretchedly sordid and a brute'.

Clarendon described Justin as:

> a man of quality; for his being a soldier, according to his experience, I think, is not doubted; and he has behaved himself extremely well wherever he has been quartered, with great easiness and moderation, which every body has not done.

His experience as a soldier and a clever politician had stood him in good stead.[40]

Justin reported that muskets and pikes could be made much more cheaply in Ireland than in England, encouraging Clarendon to make this clear to the king in the hope that progress could be made. It is not clear why MacCarthy wanted to force such a matter, although we can make an educated guess. Irish arms manufacture backed by English money could help secure the Irish Army, which would, for the first time, be able to arm itself fully. Was this an attempt to strengthen the Irish position should James be deposed? There may have been more practical reasons for the request. The army's stock of arms was in a very poor state. With the purges very much in evidence, and the relative lack of experience in the army, MacCarthy may have been attempting to give the remodelled army a head start. However, James showed no interest in the request.[41]

Clarendon's recommendation of MacCarthy for promotion to major general was sent firstly to the king:

> This bearer, Colonel Macarty, is so well known to your Majesty, that there is no need of my saying any thing in his behalf, but what he will not give himself leave to say; which is, to give your Majesty an account how infinitely he is esteemed in all places where he has been in this kingdom, his obliging carriage having gained upon every body; which the bishop of the diocese, and several others have told me, and desired I would thank him for the favours they have received from him.

And then to Sunderland:

> Colonel Macarty must not go hence without carrying my most humble service to your Lordship in a particular manner. I need not say any thing to your Lordship on his behalf: his own merit, as well as person, is sufficiently known to you; but yet I must not omit telling your Lordship (in justice to him) how extremely he has gained upon all people, among whom he has lived. The Bishop of Cork and several others have desired me to give him thanks for the civilities they have received from him. I am sure I need not move your Lordship to support his pretensions with the king; but I may assure you his Majesty can employ nobody, in his way, who will be more acceptable to people here.

With such recommendations, it would be unlikely that the position could go to anyone else. Although there is a degree of the extravagant character of the period in Clarendon's praise, it seems that Justin had made an impression. Clarendon's description also gives grace to the notion that MacCarthy was popular amongst the native Irish. He was not one of the old-English and the combination of experience and leadership qualities appears to have increased his popularity amongst troops and the general populace. It seemed that Clarendon could not turn a blind eye to the purges, although he must have known that his complaint would not be heard:

> Colonel Macarty has spoken to me concerning the checks which are out upon officers and soldiers at their musters: that method has always been practised in the army here; but it is an imposition not laid upon the army in England. It does not become me to meddle with any thing I find, which is pretended to be for the King's service, without first representing it to his Majesty; but, I confess, I know no reason why it should be otherwise here than in England.[42]

Early in the year Justin complained at the distance that soldiers had to travel to receive their pay.[43] In fact he seems to have had a general problem with the entire structure and administration of army pay, although this is hardly surprising with the rapidity of the purge in the army. Clarendon was very supportive of his new ally. If MacCarthy could find ways of improving the Irish Army, he would back him. He had, after all, little faith in or influence on Tyrconnel, and Justin must have seemed genuine in his loyalty to the Lord Lieutenant. By April the promotions so long discussed were made. Justin was promoted to major general of the Irish forces. Tyrconnel was promoted again, this time to lieutenant general, whilst Colonel Richard Hamilton, George and Anthony's brother, was made Brigadier of the Army.[44]

It seemed that, in Ireland at least, James was determined to have his way. Irish Catholics had been put in full control of the now Catholic force without the oath. James, perhaps unwittingly, was sowing the seeds of his own destruction. Clarendon, at least, was happy with Justin's appointment as the Irish major general.[45] Matters would be taken much further as James, determined to improve the lot and also the standing of his Roman Catholic subjects, restructured the Privy Council in Ireland. Positions were allocated in May 1686 to Richard Hamilton, Tyrconnel and Justin MacCarthy, amongst others.[46]

The Irish civil administration was being re-structured, again without the oath. James's reforms were far-reaching and significant, but he was proceeding very quickly. MacCarthy's good relationship with the Lord

Lieutenant continued: despite the purges and the slow erosion of discipline and experience in the army, Clarendon carried out a review of troops at Kilkenny in the presence of at least two of its most experienced officers. Previously the Duke of Ormonde's Regiment, they were 'as adroit at their exercise as any men could be and that generally they were better mounted than the light horse in England'.

MacCarthy's new-found popularity and authority increased his ability to criticise and attempt to adjust policy in the king's name. Clarendon records his criticism of the Lord Chancellor, who was reticent to employ Catholics as justices of the peace. Invoking the king's instructions, and Clarendon's apparent confirmation of same, MacCarthy attempted to bully him into submission. His efforts were in vain since many of the Catholics in line for the positions were seen as 'rogues'. He then referred to a bribe that, it had been rumoured, the chancellor had received from the Whigs, which was vociferously denied as a rumour put about by Tyrconnel.[47]

During September 1686 Clarendon reviewed Justin's own regiment at Cork, after visiting Bandon and Kinsale. Of the regiment he remarked, 'I saw them exercise, which they performed as well as is possible for such new men' and 'as well as can be expected from men who have no longer been in service'. In conversation, Justin asked of Clarendon if he would take representations from the Bishop of Cork and from a number of Catholic merchants. His influence with the people of Cork must have seemed like a link with native Ireland to the Lord Lieutenant. Clarendon innocently hoped that all peoples would unite under the king, casting aside ancient fears and enmities. Instead he found that 'the natives will scarce hold any communication with the English, and will hardly treat them with common civility.'[48]

By October Clarendon was able to report on another meeting about forfeited Irish estates. At this point the relationship between Justin and Clarendon started to become strained. Justin left before the meeting ended, prompting Clarendon to write, 'Major-general-Macarty, though he was there, went away at least half an hour before we broke up: how then could he sign a paper of what everybody agreed to, when he was not there at the result, is worth considering.' As the purges in the army continued, Clarendon's comment on the lack of quality in the army is significant: 'This morning I saw the regiment of Guards drawn out and exercise; which they performed as well as could be expected from raw men, for much the greater part of them are raw.'[49]

Clarendon's power and what little respect he had were rapidly being undermined by Tyrconnel, and the decline of his friendly relationship with MacCarthy is evidenced by his change in attitude towards his claim that Irish arms could be made more cheaply than their English counterparts. Earlier in the year he had considered the idea. By October he was prepared to 'forbid him going on in it' if necessary. Tyrconnel and Mr Justice Nugent now interfered with the nomination of Irish sheriffs. Clarendon wrote to the king in protest that he should be assured of his Lord Lieutenant's obedience, but that such interference, obviously designed for Tyrconnel's own reforms was not in keeping with the conventional way of doing things.[50]

Perhaps Justin no longer needed Clarendon, whether their friendship had been genuine or not. James was about to make him the governor of Limerick and it seemed he could now complain freely to the Lord Lieutenant instead of displaying some glib form of reverence to the Protestant lord. In November he was concerned that he had not been informed about murder charges levelled at one of his officers. Despite Clarendon's defence that matters were done this way on England, Justin's mocking reply was that 'it is not so in France'. Clarendon wrote to his brother, obviously worried that he would be 'complained of upon that score'. The rot had set in and, later in November, Clarendon wrote once more regarding Major General MacCarthy, in a different light:

> And now, as to my stay here, for entertainment I will only tell you, that the reports the last letters of the 18th brought, are very various, even among the Irish themselves; some saying, I may stay as long as I please; others that Lord Tyrconnel is to succeed me, and will be here by Christmas: and I am assured, the Major-general offers to lay five hundred to one, that he will be here before March.

By December 1686 Clarendon was alone. That he and Justin had ever worked together with common purpose was but a distant memory. He now became embroiled in an argument over money that began at a meeting with Sir Thomas Newcomen, at which Justin was present, over deductions that had been made from the regiment's companies. Clarendon's aim, as he remarked to Sunderland, was to ensure that the king should have 'as many men as he pays, and that those men should have as much of the money the king allows them as possible'. Clarendon delved swiftly into the matter, also investigating MacCarthy and his regiment. He was aware that his time would be cut short in his position, but he would make the most of exposing any 'slights' carried out by the new Irish ascendancy against the king. It does not appear that he intended to ruin any of those involved, but it was clear that he would not go quietly. However, MacCarthy had written to Colonel Hamilton, then in England, about the small amount of subsistence money for clothing available to the Irish Army, implicating, but not blaming directly, the Lord Lieutenant. Clarendon then had to defend himself to Sunderland, insisting that MacCarthy had portrayed the situation inaccurately.[51]

Subtle accusation and counter-accusation followed, but Clarendon's days in Ireland were numbered. His poignant final communication on MacCarthy is telling, both to his friendship with Justin and his hopes for development of the army.

> As to what you say of the Major-general, I do assure you he has not wanted courtship from me. I will venture to say, if he had been my most intimate acquaintance, and the man in the world upon whom I had most desired to build, I could not have applied more to him: which I did upon the principle of honest sincerity, in memory of his father, and his excellent brother; both of whom loved me very well, and of whose kindness and esteem I can give some instances. I thank God, I was never ungrateful: and I think it is known I love an old friend, and all that belonged to him. Upon this score I entered into this gentleman as if he had been a brother; which ought to have gained the friendship of a generous man. Whether ever I have had a reserve towards him; if I ever had a complaint of any of his officers, I presently referred it to himself and left it entirely to his own determination. In a word, if ever I have failed in any title of friendship, kindness, or civility towards him, I leave it to himself to give the instance.
>
> But I confess it has been apparent for some time, and observed by others, that he has withdrawn himself from me, for what reason I will not imagine at this time; of which I have never taken the least notice, but continued my frank open way to him. ...
>
> As to what you say of the heavings against you and me, God's will be done. Let them heave: we shall still be found honest men, and to have discharged our duties as such. God Almighty bless the King: he will quickly see who serves him best; and he is sure by experience what you and I shall always be.

The falling out of the two former friends was further exacerbated by the unwanted attention that MacCarthy was paying to Clarendon's sister.

> My sister told me, the Major-general had lately written to her: she gave me the letter. I directed her not to admit him to visit her; and if she met him anywhere, to tell him that she had no occasion to trouble him. I was very positive to her; telling her, if she would not be ruled by me, I would have nothing to do with her. She faithfully promised me to be guided by me.[52]

By February 1687 Tyrconnel had succeeded Clarendon as Lord Lieutenant of Ireland. Clarendon's reports related to MacCarthy and Hamilton's troops were not representative of the balance of the new army.

Ormonde recorded that, in October 1688, a vision was reported in the Dublin skyline. Two armies appeared in the clouds, firing at each other. The sound of cannon-fire was reputedly heard by sailors at sea. All of this conjecture seems almost laughable, were it not for the fact that Ormonde reported that MacCarthy also saw the vision, reporting it to the Lord Deputy.[53] If detractors had required proof of the validity of such omens, the ferocity of the Irish war to follow would surely shake the convictions of even the most sceptical.

Although the mainstay of Protestant association and resistance was in Ulster in the northern part of the country, the province of Munster had its own share of armed Protestants, centred on the small town of Bandon, about fifteen miles south-west of Cork on the southern tip of Ireland. It had also been known as Bandon Bridge as it spanned a river. It was a walled town, tracing its history back through the 1641 rebellion. The charter that had been granted to the town by King James I had been superseded by his grandson, James II. Many of Cromwell's soldiers had settled in Bandon and the surrounding area, and had regarded the local Irish population with some hostility. James's accession had meant that many of the Irish now felt that it was time to return the favour, and accusations of treason against the Protestants increased significantly.

Tyrconnel's new Catholic authority, now immersed in making the changes in government that would ensure a very Irish future, had created new charters for towns such as Bandon. Events there were to exhibit in microcosm much of the activity that exemplified the clash then occurring between the two religions and cultures, a clash that would ultimately lead to war.

Few towns in Ireland had remained so devoted to the English crown as Bandon. A mainstay of Protestant power in Munster, the town had a reputation as both loyal and English. Richard Boyle, first Earl of Cork, had left his mark there, founding a deep-seated religious and political heritage. Clarendon had visited in 1686, remarking, 'it is a very pretty town, and well seated upon a fine river; it is an English plantation, made and settled by the old earl of Cork.'[54]

The changes in Ireland as a whole would see a complete reversal of the basis of authority in the town. Under the new charter conferred upon Bandon, Teige MacCarthy from Aglish in Muskerry would become the new provost in 1688 and twenty-four local burgesses would sit with him, appointments which would fire up confrontational Protestant feelings in the town. Catholic authorities were permitted to function under Daniel MacCarthy Reagh, while Captain Daniel O'Neill would command Jacobite troops. News of MacCarthy Reagh's imminent arrival, carrying the new charter for Bandon, had reached the ears of those Protestants who could be easily stirred into action.

Rumours that he also intended raising money from the townspeople, and enlisting soldiers to serve in the Irish army, provided additional encouragement for the Bandonians. If any further persuasion were required, it was also made clear that a Catholic priest would be travelling with MacCarthy Reagh. The Bandonian 'adventurous spirits', supported by locals from Kilpatrick, awaited the approach of the party near the Brinny river, pretending to fish whilst planning an ambush, intending to burn the charter and make the men prisoners. However, MacCarthy Reagh, either through local knowledge or a warning, was made aware of the planned ambush and thus avoided it, taking a different route to the town. Although in many cases Tyrconnel's selection of those who now took their place in civic office was questionable, in terms of their means and reputation, in the case of Bandon this was not so. Those appointed held both social position and had a degree of experience. The provost was a member of one of the oldest and most respected noble houses in Ireland. Colonel Charles MacCarthy, one of the burgesses, was one of the few officers with experience and would later sit in the Irish parliament. Tyrconnel's methods and his delegation of Catholic authority, however, were still brusque. MacCarthy removed the Protestant provost, Mr John Nash, on 20 March 1688. New constables were appointed to preserve the peace. On 23 March the populace was offered the freedom of the town if they would recognise James as their king. Only forty-two people signed the agreement, taking the oath of allegiance to James. The authorities took the further step of publishing a proclamation in June 1688:

> Whereas several summonses have of late been given to the inhabitants of this corporation to appear, and take the oath accustomed for freemen, and for as much as they refuse and condemn the said summonses, now we, the said provost and majority of the burgesses, having taken into consideration the wrong and injury that happen unto the corporation thereby, do and, by our mutual assents and consents, have ordered, that every person of what trade soever shall pay six shillings and eightpence sterling per diem for using every such trade or occupation, either private or public, after the fifteenth day of June next, after the date hereof; and the same to be levied on their goods and chattels, and to be disposed of according to law, or their bodies to be imprisoned, through the choice lying in the provost.

James's reforms had been implemented quickly. The new authorities in Bandon were determined to stamp out the potential for resistance one way or another. Six names only were added when the new proclamation was issued. The Protestants would remain defiant and, by 1689, with events in England having been made clear to the populace, their underlying feeling to resist was strengthened, their feeling that William's next martial step would be to Ireland helping reinforce their convictions.[55]

By early March the rebellion of sorts in the northern part of the country was echoed on a smaller scale in other parts of Ireland, most especially in MacCarthy's home county of Cork. In Bandon matters were slowly getting out of hand. In Munster as a whole, unlike their counterparts in Ulster, the Protestants were in a distinct minority. Despite rumours of elaborate plans and conspiracy, intent upon the seizure of Cork, all schemes were betrayed and thus fell short of open rebellion. At Bandon, however, continued harassment from the ill-disciplined Jacobites together with a number of robberies committed against the townspeople did little to promote good relations.

Matters at Bandon had been in development for some time. The Jacobite garrison under Captain Daniel O'Neill had little reason to feel safe. The town's corporation had been reformed and Protestant remonstrations against the fact that members had not taken the oath were not taken seriously. O'Neill asked that all arms be given up, a request which was for the most part ignored. It is not clear whether O'Neill then called for aid, or if he was forced to accept reinforcements. His garrison consisted only of two companies of foot and a single troop of horse.[56] However, the news of what lay in store for the residents travelled quickly. A few days after O'Neill's statement, word reached Bandon that Jacobite reinforcements threatened the population with force if O'Neill's request was not obeyed. At first glance the news appeared serious, although hardly enough to instil open rebellion. The factor that tipped the balance was the commander of the reinforcements, Lord Clancarty.

Donagh MacCarthy, the young Clancarty, had been married to Sunderland's daughter, Lady Elizabeth Spencer, in 1684, through the machinations of his uncle Justin MacCarthy. He had become a devout Catholic when James ascended the throne. Since then, and in light of the revolutionary events, the young earl had obtained a somewhat violent reputation in Munster. Stories abounded of his and his horse troopers' brutality. He had attempted to take a butcher's horses in Mallow. When the man refused, the horses were seized, only to be returned when the butcher complained to the authorities. The troopers later returned, tossing the butcher inside a blanket where they 'suffered him to fall upon the pavement, till he was so bruised, that he was left quite dead on the spot'. Clancarty himself had also had a Clonmel man strung up by his hair for offending him. Whether or not such stories were true, when it is considered that a substantive amount of rumour and supposition must also have been added to these stories, the Bandonians' reaction to the young Clancarty's approach was predictable. At the end of February 1689 Clancarty marched with his cavalry troopers and six companies of foot toward Bandon. [57]

The remaining Protestants in the town wasted no time, fearing the approach of the earl. Buoyed up by the proclamation that William had taken the English throne, the Bandonians resolved not only to prevent the arrival of Clancarty's reinforcements but on removing those Jacobite troops already in the town. Further impetus seems to have been given to the Protestant scheme with O'Neill's announcement that the Sunday after Clancarty's arrival would witness the celebration of mass in Bandon's Kilbrogan church. An assembly was held in the home of Katty Holt, a Protestant widow and reputedly the local gossip, who lived near the church. Hardinge, a Presbyterian minister, was elected chairman and the disarming of the garrison was unanimously agreed to. On the following Monday morning at dawn it was agreed that the church bell at Kilbrogan would ring, signalling the insurrection. The leaders left the meeting and within a few hours most of the male inhabitants had been enrolled in the scheme.

The following morning, despite the rising of the sun, the bell did not ring. A local story records that Jack Sullivan, the sexton, had apparently lost his nerve. His wife Nancy, however, had not and, after some arguing, she rang the bell herself. The 'Black Monday Insurrection', as it came to be known, could hardly be called bloodless, but it was effective, for the most part because the garrison was surprised completely. The job was made all the easier since the Jacobite troops were not quartered in barracks. Instead they lived amongst the local populace, in ones and twos, making the seizing of arms, ammunition and soldiers all the easier.

By night, O'Neill's garrison was overpowered and their arms and horses taken. Matters did not go smoothly, however, and there is some disagreement in the sources on how many Jacobite troops were killed. One indicates that a sergeant and two troopers lost their lives. Another suggests that eight troopers were killed. Of these, Sergeant John Barry and two horse troopers were actually Protestants who remained in the army – perhaps in Bandon in an attempt to keep the peace. In any event, the fact that soldiers had been killed changed the level of the insurrection from rioting to rebellion, making the action treasonous. O'Neill and his troops were forcibly ejected from Bandon and the gates of the walled town were shut. The Protestants quickly manned the walls, looking to their own defence against Clancarty. They had little with which to defend a town against any military force. Apart from matchlocks, they had six rusty artillery-pieces, which the Earl of Cork had supplied fifty years previously, but they were in such disrepair that they were likely to do more harm to those who fired them than to any attacker.

Bandon was not alone. Captain Henry Boyle, father of the Earl of Shannon, began setting up defences around his house at Castle-Martyr, also in County Cork, with 140 men. William O'Brien, second Earl of Inchiquin, was also inspired to take action, rounding up a number of Protestants and arming them. O'Brien had been brought up as a Protestant in England. He was an experienced soldier who had lost an eye in a sea fight, had fought in Spain and once headed the Tangier Regiment of Foot; he had also been governor of Tangier. He was not simply a disgruntled colonist, and could be a real threat in Munster. Another rising began at Kenmare where the population near the local ironworks felt that a repetition of the 1641 rebellion was inevitable. Bandon was not therefore an isolated incident and, if Protestants were also to rise in Cork, Justin MacCarthy would have a real problem in Munster. A large party of Irish horse and foot entered Cork at midnight in early March and disarmed all Protestants in the town. There is no evidence that Justin gave orders for such actions, but it is likely that he instigated the move. So much could be altered by an armed insurrection at this stage. In the event, the ill-disciplined troops broke into the houses of prominent Protestants and pillaged the nearby villages, taking money and goods. Despite the fact that these events could not have endeared the Protestant population to MacCarthy's, and thus James's, cause, the action had prevented a co-ordinated rising, at least initially.

MacCarthy, using much of the horse that had been taken in Cork, created a fast moving mounted force which could move quickly around Munster preventing the spread of the resistance. With two small field-pieces they proved highly effective without firing a shot. MacCarthy moved towards Castle-Martyr and Henry Boyle. The events that followed could have proven decisive for matters in Ireland. As it was, no serious event had occurred which would further harm James's cause. Had Castle-Martyr and later Bandon seen massacres of Protestants, it would have doomed the Jacobite cause in its infancy. Justin MacCarthy was a good deal subtler than this. Rather than further propagate a Protestant revolution in Ireland, he convinced the defenders of Castle-Martyr that neither 'their persons [n]or estates should be molested' if they submitted. In the face of MacCarthy's guns, Boyle surrendered. He and his followers were transported temporarily to Cork, although his house was plundered. It seemed that MacCarthy could not keep all of his promises, but matters could have been much worse.

He then moved quickly toward Bandon with his artillery pieces in tow. With the capitulation of Henry Boyle, and the fact that MacCarthy's reaction had been so rapid and co-ordinated, Inchiquin could see little option but to give up the action, before it had started in earnest. He advised the residents of Bandon to seek terms with MacCarthy upon his arrival. This was not an easy prospect since MacCarthy's somewhat delicate handling at Castle-Martyr was not to be repeated so quickly. The guns again decided the matter and the Bandonians sought terms.

However, Justin was no longer in such congenial mood. He demanded that the leaders should be given up to him, Jacobite soldiers having been killed. The besieged, although having no objection in the face of MacCarthy's force to discussing the delivery of the town with honourable terms, would not give up their leaders. He took the town easily, nonetheless. As there is no record of further loss of life, it can be assumed that this was done without a fight. Although he would not provoke a massacre, restitution for the matter had to be sought. He immediately informed the populace that ten of the town's principal men would be hanged, after which Bandon would be burned to the ground. This situation would surely have instigated further violence had it not been for the intervention of Dr Nicholas Brady, a local minister, and a follower of James's policies. Whether this was instrumental in his persuasion of Justin or not is not clear. Upon discussion of the matter with Brady, MacCarthy backed down, to an extent.

Having perhaps appealed to his merciful side, Justin's initial anger and frustration at his potential loss of control in Munster had abated and he agreed to an indemnity of 1,500 pounds paid by the residents of Bandon. In addition, the town's walls would have to be destroyed, lest further insurrection should be planned and all arms and equipment removed from Jacobite troops would be compensated for or returned. Most of the Bandonians involved borrowed money from Protestant friends in Cork, including William Chartres, an alderman of the city. Many other residents of Cork became personally liable for the debt. Articles of peace were signed on 2 March between the inhabitants and Justin MacCarthy on behalf of 'His Most Gracious Majesty King James'. The matter, however, was far from over, as far as Tyrconnel at least was concerned. James, too, would become involved upon landing in Ireland

At Kenmare, the remaining outlet for Protestant frustration, Irish Tories (bandits known locally as *rapparees*) had been attacking and robbing mercilessly. Despite appeals to MacCarthy prior to the rising, little was done, although Justin did have Sir Valentine Brown, governor of Kerry, issue warrants to the townspeople so that they could pursue the robbers themselves, a rash action in hindsight. Since there were forty miles of rough hills between them and Bandon, the townspeople similarly prepared to defend themselves. Led by Richard Orpen, some of the miscreants were captured and goods returned, but the matter was not yet over. On hearing that the Cork Protestants were disarmed, Castle-Martyr had fallen and Bandon would also fall, and that no word of help from England had yet come, Orpen had little option. He agreed to terms, stating that his garrison would not be 'plundered or molested', and to 'leave the country or stay in it, as they thought fit'. In the event, the town was plundered and the residents had little choice but to leave the country. No mean feat, in that they were given two small boats with which to accomplish the task. Orpen was also ordered to pay a bond of 5,000 Pounds, but sailed without paying, his thought being that he would be back in Ireland with William's army. Indeed, many of the escaped Protestants who fled to England enlisted with William's forces, resentment begetting the need for revenge.[58]

Justin's rapid intervention had saved the Jacobite cause in Munster and Cork. His muster of a rapid moving mounted force complete with artillery had prevented the insurrection becoming co-ordinated and effective. The matter became more critical when word of the imminent arrival of King James from France reached Munster. However, Tyrconnel was not at all happy with Justin's handling of the situation. He wrote on 10 March, concerned

> that a treaty was entered into with the people of Bandon, until the authors of the disturbance were brought to justice, to which end the army we shall new model when the King arrives, and till that be done it is impossible to make them useful.[59]

The Bandon incident represented a clear turning point in the already delicate relationship between MacCarthy and Tyrconnel. James would later insist that the Bandon insurrectionists be tried for treason. To his credit, Justin successfully resisted both James's and Tyrconnel's insistence on this matter. After all, he had given his word to the Bandonians and this could not be reversed honourably. It is a testament to his own honour that he successfully argued their case. The matter did little to endear him to Tyrconnel and may have been the point at which relations with James would start to become strained.

Bandon and the potential for rebellion that had developed in Munster was but a pale imitation of the protracted fight that would develop in the north. Isolated pockets had sought to converge on Bandon at the start. MacCarthy's quick thinking had stopped this. In Ulster, Protestants from outlying regions flocked to Londonderry and Enniskillen. In the east of Ulster, the centre of resistance lay at Hillsborough in County Down. A 'supreme council' led by the Earl of Mount-Alexander was ineffective and schemes to disarm Catholics at Belfast and Carrickfergus came to naught. By 14 March, Richard Hamilton had routed Mount-Alexander's troops at 'the Break of Dromore'. The mismanaged affair broke all resistance in eastern Ulster and the earl escaped to the Isle of Man. In the far north Coleraine held the Jacobite advance in check for a while, but ultimately the defenders fell back on Londonderry. By the end of March Tyrconnel controlled the country, except for the continuing resistance at the two towns. Again, it was not a perfect situation, but good enough to herald the landing of James from France.

Upon landing in 1689, James was received by the young Donagh MacCarthy, Earl of Clancarty, and his uncle, now Lieutenant General Justin

MacCarthy. James enquired after the state of the country and was informed by Justin that Ireland was secure, albeit for the two centres of resistance in the north. The events at Bandon would come to the fore when James reached Cork. Chief Justice Nugent, having been made aware of the articles of surrender at Bandon, promptly cancelled them. When James was made fully aware of the details he too was dismayed. Dr Brady, who had convinced Justin to be lenient at Bandon, asked the king if the walls, previously condemned to destruction, could be spared. Despite d'Avaux's protests the request was granted.

The leaders of the insurrection also pleaded for the king's mercy, in the main receiving a pardon for their actions during the rebellion, since the intrigue of Nugent had seen them once more indicted for treason. James was by now conscious of the importance of appealing to Protestant sensibilities, as much a political move as an act of reconciliation; he would later say 'let the people of England judge us by our conduct in Ireland what they may expect from us.' The Protestants of Munster would receive much harsher treatment from their new French governor, Boisseleau, who would later be accused of sending 30,000 pounds worth of Protestant goods to France from Cork. Despite a later order to destroy the walls once more, it was only partially obeyed and they remained for the most part untouched.

The pardon had not been universally granted and some of the Bandonians were to be indicted for high treason, a crime that could be punished by hanging, drawing and quartering. James left word that those unpardoned be severely dealt with. Nugent would later attempt to ensure that the Bandon men would be arraigned and face a jury, which would show little mercy. Brady, however, with characteristic aplomb, once more approached MacCarthy, reminding him that his act as a general had been done in the king's name. Justin at once felt bound by his agreement. If he let the matter pass, his honour and reputation would be ruined.

Whether he would lose face amongst the Irish or the French for aiding those accused, he acted, perhaps feeling that he would be an accessory if he let matters pass. To this end he urged Nugent to abide by the articles of surrender that had been agreed to in Bandon and signed by himself on behalf of the king. Nugent refused. MacCarthy, taking matters into his own hands, marched into one of Nugent's court sittings and demanded that he back down. Such bonds could not be broken. There is no record of what was said but MacCarthy's tactics worked. Nugent gave way and the twelve remaining Bandonians were released. MacCarthy had won a victory of sorts, but at a cost to his relationship with his fellow Jacobites. He was no stranger to bullying the bench, of course, having at one stage threatened Sir John Meade in 1685. The Bandon incident was different, however. The concern was not with bringing about the verdict that he desired; MacCarthy would not stand to have his honour questioned, no matter the repercussions to his relationships with the other leading Jacobites.[60]

James left Cork on 20 March en route to Dublin, which he reached by the 24th. The entire journey was accompanied by cheering crowds and the king got his first glimpse of the Irish army. The condition and quality of his troops was exemplified by their appearance, many seeming like bandits, and armed only with the ubiquitous Irish *skeine*, a half-pike.[61] This would be of little use on the contemporary battlefield facing the well-drilled formations and numerous flintlocks of the Williamite forces. Justin MacCarthy had meanwhile been tasked with the transport of all remaining French arms and military supplies to Dublin. The king had awarded honours to the Earls of Clancarty and Tyrconnel, but so far it seemed little notice had been taken of the lieutenant general. In terms of the prospective military future of the numerous Irish nobles, the French had only one man in mind.

*** 

Even before James had departed for Ireland the ever-enterprising Louvois had contemplated the Irish plan. If French troops would follow the expedition to Ireland, then Irish troops would replace them on the continent. Louvois had written to Justin in February, making him aware that French aid would require an exchange of troops and could not be a one-sided affair. He had the end of 1689 in mind for such an exchange, depending on how matters proceeded in Ireland. Justin was also invited to command the Irish troops who would go to France. Louvois had played his card despite the earlier disagreements with Seignelay. There were few experienced officers amongst the Irish but, knowing his military machine, Louvois was fully aware that an Anglo-Irish soldier would not be accepted in the French establishment. A Franco-Irish officer, who had come of age in France, fought in and for France, and yearned to return there, would be required. MacCarthy's reply gives an indication of lack of action regarding the early decisions made at James's arrival. He had always wished to return to France and French service and would endeavour to pick the best officers and men from the Irish troops.[62] That the Irish army could not afford to lose such men seems to have been the last thing on his mind.

It is clear that, even at this stage, he was aware that neither the scheming Tyrconnel, despite his overtly French leanings, nor King James, who was more concerned with regaining his lost kingdoms, was the solution for Ireland. His country could only be saved from William's invasion in one way, co-operation with the French; if that meant that he must fight William's armies on French soil, in the hope that professional French troops could win the day in Ireland, then so be it. Justin had also written to Louvois about the state of Ireland, implying that it was quite secure and that William would not dare to come. However, this depended heavily on James putting the Irish army in order, which could only be brought about through French arms and supplies.[63] It was a gamble upon the hopes that the French might recognise the value of sustaining resistance in Ireland and thereby contribute largely to the cost of it.

MacCarthy and Louvois were fully aware of James's preferred intent to regain his kingdoms of Scotland then England via the loyal Irish army. If this was the case then Ireland's security could only be ensured through close co-operation with France. Who better to champion such a cause than MacCarthy? Louvois did not share Justin's optimism on the Irish situation, and the potential for an invasion of England or Scotland. He wrote to Melfort (James's acting Secretary of State) of his concern that James's attempt to retrieve another kingdom would result in the loss of all three.[64]

Indeed, neither James nor the Irish army was ready for such an undertaking, as events would show. For Louvois this was of little importance. The exchange of French troops would make little difference, although the French would have their preferred commander no matter what the result of the Irish distraction. When Justin's departure was discussed with James, he immediately opposed the idea. He could not afford to lose an experienced general, either from the defence of Ireland or, more seriously for James, from the Irish army that he still hoped would help him in Britain. The wily d'Avaux, in keeping with the spirit of his orders from Louis, persuaded James that disciplined French infantry battalions and officers given in the exchange for well-led Irish, were just what the Irish army needed. In a further letter to Louvois he re-affirmed his intention to choose the best of the Irish to send to France. It was initially envisaged that this would not occur until December when French troops would have finished the campaigning season and be in winter quarters. Louvois once more insisted that only the best officers should be included. Louis would only want men of noble birth while James wanted to send Irish officers of poor quality and experience. This would obviously be in his own best interest. D'Avaux then continued to play a delicate political game with the benefits of the Irish diversion in mind and with one eye on events occurring in the Irish army.

***

Justin MacCarthy would represent County Cork at the proceedings and bring the bill from the Commons to the Lords for the repeal of the Act of Settlement. On the second day of proceedings, a new peer was introduced to the parliament: Justin was elevated to the Irish peerage and made Lord Viscount Mountcashel and Baron of Castleinch.[65]

However, he would spend little time in discussion. After James's landing in Kinsale, he had been responsible for transporting the stores to Dublin. With Count Renaud's successful landing at Bantry, he was called upon once more to supervise the transport of French stores and arms to Dublin. By 20 May he was recognised for his efforts and his interest in this field and promoted to Master General of Artillery in Ireland.[66]

De Rosen was especially contemptuous of the raw material of the Irish Army.

> Nearly all are without arms and quite naked: the greater part of the officers are miserable fellows without courage or honour, a single cannon shot passing at the elevation of a clock tower throws a whole battalion to the ground and the only way to get them to their feet is to send horses over their bellies.[67]

D'Avaux, however, with a keen eye for exploiting the situation to the benefit of the French, saw things quite differently. In contrast to de Rosen, he saw the great potential of some of the military 'raw material' within the rough regiments of the re-modelled army, perhaps recognising the virgin anti-English idealism that still drove some of the Irish in contrast with French troops. D'Avaux and many of the French dignitaries knew that the secret to foreign troops' success was their commander, whose role was as much diplomat and ambassador as that of general and leader. Where a French-trained general who remained popular yet firm with his troops was available, Louis's emissaries would strive to obtain him. D'Avaux commented:

> I can assure you that he [Mountcashel] will be very useful in getting rid of a great many bad officers and in recruiting others to keep the Irish troops dutiful and disciplined.[68]

Sir, If I had not believed that it was important to have a man so liked in his Majesty's service, so loved and influential in Ireland that he could keep dutiful the Irish troops in France. He could draw recruits in this country and even raise as many new troops as we would wish. If the King of England would give permission to all those who wanted to follow him, you would have the best officers in the army ... .[69]

Lord Mountcashel, after Peter de Lily.

Even the implacable de Rosen had to admit that Mountcashel was 'a very good man and the only one that we can rely on, but he is unluckily in the same position as myself, of being looked upon as stating his mind and outlining the disorderly state of things'. If Justin was unpopular with Tyrconnel, James and their followers, it was not only due to his representation of the native Irish faction, but to the fact that he told the truth of the situation that he perceived – that James would leave Ireland and the old-English would return to their lands if they could. Not only would little be settled ultimately, but the very real threat of William's invasion was not being dealt with effectively. In Mountcashel the French recognised the qualities they themselves considered sacred. Outspoken he may have been, but he was loyal and a patriot, and displayed the courage of his convictions, truly noble virtues which would have impressed those pompous French who felt that many of the Irish were little better than savages.

For his own part Mountcashel's concerns were made quite obvious to his Gallic colleagues. In June he wrote to Louvois that 'my simple belief is that without French help then all is lost', pointing out also the dearth of both good officers and money. Justin saw only one solution: 'The only way to finish the affair is to send a good body of regular troops led by a good general … ' who should be:

> a man of character with a patient and diplomatic temperament, for rudeness with an ignorant people who do not have the required skills, repels instead of giving instruction, and to teach them obedience they should admire as well as fear you.[70]

Mountcashel was under no illusion as to the Irish army's requirements, and was ostensibly in agreement with those more positive elements of the French cadre. He would also highlight the importance of d'Avaux in the country, perhaps by now his closest ally.

Mountcashel wrote to Louvois again in July. He complained of idleness and the indecision that existed in Jacobite Ireland. James's schemes, supported by Melfort, were hampering the preparations. Factional infighting was preventing not only co-ordination of the disparate Irish elements but diluting leadership: 'If we are not restored by the King of France or Divine Providence, there is a significant risk, since it is a terrible thing to see the efforts with which we seek our own ruin!'[71]

Different parties had different aims, James even considering the native Irish, including Mountcashel, somewhat inferior. There also appears to have been some distrust of the Irish general, his motives and loyalty perhaps regarded as 'questionable' due to his close dealings with the French. D'Avaux was quick to point out the apparent gulf that was slowly developing between the English and Irish, describing them as 'irreconcilable enemies'.[72] Mountcashel had, for instance, offered his services to James to undertake a mission to France where further requests for arms, money and reinforcements would be made. The weak Lord Dover was sent instead when a man of Mountcashel's French experience and reputation might have made a difference. Despite James's insistence that William's imminent invasion meant that he could not release the general, Mountcashel remained unmoved.[73]

Many of the Irish military were by then more deeply concerned with the prospects for resistance than continued loyalty to the deposed king. Many, including Mountcashel, were more inclined toward French protection and reinforcement rather than that provided by the English Jacobites, a force that was all but spent. For Lord Mountcashel, one of the ablest commanders in the field, and despite the concerns and attention of the French, the Irish war would begin in earnest. Many other matters had been discussed at the parliament, including plans for Derry and Enniskillen. Despite the lack of focus, the disagreement and the time wasted in pertinent though poorly-timed debate, the Jacobites resolved to take action. Mountcashel would take the lead and meet the Enniskillen militia head on in a battle that would see a turning point in the war.

*Chapter 9*

# Patrick Sarsfield, *Deare Notorious*

I t is Patrick Sarsfield who is traditionally remembered as the leader of the Wild Geese, the man who, after the second siege of Limerick, would agree to leave with those troops who remained loyal to him. There are complex reasons for this, of course.[1] Mountcashel is less convenient to remember: he did not earn a victory in Ireland, despite his standing with the French, in contrast to Sarsfield. Mountcashel was undoubtedly the more experienced and arguably the better general. There are two mitigating factors, however: firstly, it would be Sarsfield who would gain a victory over the Williamites when it was most needed by routing the artillery train at Ballyneety, helping not only to bolster morale, but earning him his place in the Jacobite army as a military leader. Secondly, and perhaps stressing the finality of the action, it would be Sarsfield who would lead the last Jacobite troops out of Ireland to French service, an act which, despite his hopes to the contrary, demonstrated the last act of the Irish Jacobite Army on their own soil.

## Sarsfield's Early Years

It is estimated that Patrick Sarsfield was born in 1655, which would make him a mere five years younger than John Churchill, the future Duke of Marlborough[2] and the most notable and influential soldier of his day. He would die in his seventies while Sarsfield would be dead before he was forty. It is arguable that the Irishman, infamous or not, could have achieved so much had he lived to see the eighteenth century. The point is moot, as so many of the Irish rakes and leaders would never see their homeland again, due to the violence of the actions they faced in their respective futures. It is interesting nevertheless to speculate what might have been had he survived the Nine Years' War, bearing in mind what he had achieved, in terms of his influence on the Irish and his reputation amongst his enemies.

He was never allowed to command a wholly Irish army in battle, despite his fiery reputation, and the French would consider MacCarthy, Lord Mountcashel, a more accomplished commander, having chosen him over

Sarsfield to command the first Irish Brigade in France. Yet Sarsfield is keenly remembered as the man who led some of those who remained: from the Boyne, from the first siege of Limerick and from bloody Aughrim, and led them, as the last 'free' Irishmen to France, in the hope that there they might fight for a cause that would lead them back to their country of origin.

The Irish tragedy is that such an event would never happen, and thus Sarsfield is remembered as a somewhat sombre figure who died on the continent, leading men in desperate exile, most of whom would never be welcomed home again. It is this, more than the perfunctory and yet functional leadership of Mountcashel, and his own untimely death, that enabled the legend that Sarsfield became in Ireland, and amongst subsequent generations of Irish soldiers.

His ancestry on his father's side was of Anglo-Norman or Old-English stock, while his mother was of the O'Moores, a family of proud Gaelic ancestry; the family lived in the Pale around Dublin and owned land in the south. His family held allegiance to the English crown, while generating relations with the Gaelic Irish. This lineage would enable him to be representative of both those Irish factions that had re-emerged by the time of his leadership. By the Jacobite wars, and especially so after the Boyne, he was among the most prominent leaders of the Irish faction; even before his victory at Ballyneety he had a fearsome reputation amongst the Williamites. Unlike some of his contemporaries, and having neither the particular biased allegiances required of Gaelic Irish chieftains nor Anglo-Norman settlers, he represented both, and so rapidly became emblematic of the new Irish bid to attain what freedom they could, and consolidate those gains made under the English restoration.

His actions were perhaps lesser in stature when compared with Mountcashel, since, as we have seen, he was not the favourite of the French. He commanded units in raids, yet never an entire army in battle; he would speak for the army and lead them to exile after the second siege of Limerick, yet his influence while in French service would have less impact than he might have hoped. His story is one of extremes, and yet he served at some of the most critical junctures in English and Irish history. He was a rake, a rogue, served and was wounded during Monmouth's rebellion; he was present at the only skirmish to occur during William's invasion in 1688, and at every major battle and siege in the subsequent war, although having a knack of being at the wrong place at the wrong time, as we shall see.

This does not detract from his character as the seminal Irish hero, although it is he who is remembered as a leader of the Wild Geese after the second siege of Limerick; it is he who is remembered with fondness, perhaps more as a folk-hero, having seen victory at Ballyneety against the Williamite siege train, and was seen by the army that remained in Ireland after 1689, until its departure in 1691, as the leader. Indeed, in the factional infighting between Gaelic and Anglo-Norman, or Old-English, factions he represented the common soldier. As stated, his victories were small and local, yet legendary, and certainly enhanced an already fearsome reputation. He was to be a symbol of what Ireland might become, were it to survive the Williamite onslaught.

The name is not Gaelic-Irish and can be traced back to Anglo-Norman incursions onto the island in the twelfth century. Over the succeeding centuries, the family established itself in the Pale around Dublin, with significant commercial interests in the south, and had made considerable commercial gains by the sixteenth century. They also took advantage of belonging to a group of Roman Catholics showing loyalty to a Protestant crown, yet not altogether alienated from the interests of the Gaelic Irish who were seen by others as unpredictable at best and potentially rebellious at worst.

Yet Sarsfield's mother and father became graphically representative of a dichotomy symbolised by the growing powerful interests in Irish society. His mother, Anne O'Moore, gave the young Patrick knowledge of Gaelic-Irish culture and much of the semi-mythical belief and genealogies that accompanied it. Such ancestral records were keen to support the belief that noble families and houses could trace their lineage back to the legendary Milesius who supposedly founded Ireland and defended it from the earliest mythical invaders and belief in such ancestry can only have reinforced a sense of belonging.

Anne herself was a daughter of a 'notorious' (a term which Sarsfield, by the time of Newtownbutler, might find himself being ascribed by Berwick) rebel, Rory O'Moore, who had taken part in the uprisings against Queen Elizabeth and become a key player in the 1641 action.[3] His father, also called Patrick, could be viewed as distinct from the norms of the English and Scottish plantation-era settlers. As with most of the culturally integrated peoples in his position, he simply wanted to get on. Although the Sarsfields would undoubtedly have been able to speak Irish Gaelic, it would have been a language secondary to English in the Pale.

It is within this panorama of changing attitudes, and the birth and growth of the power blocs that would shape Ireland's future, that the young Sarsfield found himself growing up. With the 1641 rebellion and Grandfather O'Moore's early and advantageous support of the march on Dublin, it was inevitable that Patrick Senior was besmirched by the taint of rebellion. In 1642 he was indicted for high treason and expelled from the Irish House of Commons.

In the subsequent civil war allegiances were challenged and alliances broke down, leaving a shattered country. Cromwell's arrival, to finish the complex matter, no matter how simply he might have viewed it, left Patrick Sarsfield senior with more land than he had started with, although cruel fate, and, to some, even more cruel Parliamentarians, ensured that the offer was based upon the principle of 'Hell or Connacht'. Sarsfield senior, a Palesman, whose grouping had little inclination to fight anyone and whose shifting loyalties had ended up guaranteeing them nothing, was forced to leave his estates at Lucan and accept land in Connacht.

The last of five children, William, Frances, Anne and Mary before him, the younger Patrick was born into an environment where the game of power politics and religion defined and ultimately consumed his socio-political generation. With the monarchy's restoration in 1660 the hope was that a more magnanimous Charles II might yet exact a more ennobled redistribution of Irish land. Roman Catholics were however, still viewed as having started a bloody civil war in Ireland. The Sarsfields took action themselves to re-acquire their lands, with attempts that remained unsuccessful for a number of years. Hope was renewed whenever William Sarsfield, the second son, married Mary Walter, second child of Lucy Walter, one of the king's mistresses and sister to James, Duke of Monmouth, the king's 'official' bastard and future contender for the throne of England in the guise of the 'Protestant Duke'. Although Mary would never be officially recognised, King Charles did grant her husband an annual pension.[4] The key was that support from the monarchy was gained in terms of William's father's claim on his old lands, although this was shortlived, due to William's untimely death from smallpox in 1675. Subsequent family disputes meant that the matter was not settled satisfactorily within Patrick's lifetime.

Patrick Sarsfield, the younger, left Ireland in the early 1670s.[5] He lacked land and a title, and it was time for him to find his own way in life. Of course, when we consider the plight of the young Hamiltons, and to a greater extent the young McCarthy, this apparent lot in life was fast becoming a characteristic of the Irish swordsman or rake.

## The Irish Rake

The choice of a future based on soldiering, as with many of his contemporaries, was obvious if not altogether straightforward for the young Sarsfield. He was accepted in Monmouth's Royal Anglais Regiment of Foot. The Test Act meant that, as a Catholic, he could not serve in public office or as a soldier in England. He could have taken the oath of supremacy and allegiance, but few Catholics, especially amongst the potential officer corps, acceded to this demand in the name of progressing in English authority, it being significantly easier, if not actively encouraged in some quarters, for Catholics to serve abroad.[6]

Monmouth's English and Hamilton's Irish regiments had been raised to operate in French service, in concert with the requirements of Louis's and Charles's secret Treaty of Dover. The French would ensure that such service would be to their benefit, and thereby be bloody. The losses to the regiments under Turenne, as we have seen, were considerable, including George Hamilton's untimely death in 1676. Sarsfield served with contemporary notables who would later become allies or opponents, in a struggle which would pit men who had fought together in this early period, against each other in the bitterest struggle of the age: Justin MacCarthy, Richard, Anthony and John Hamilton, John Churchill, who would become the most famous soldier of the age as the Duke of Marlborough, and Monmouth himself. They would fight under the French, see men die in foreign service and forge bonds which would be put under pressure and forced apart in the jockeying for the throne of England, and the crucible of the Irish war to come. Such mercenary-style work was a combination of the only military service available, a method of keeping dangerous standing armies from English soil while granting experience to its military elite, but simultaneously allowing England to remain paranoid and religiously insular by virtue of the fears created by its own decade of civil war, whose memory and devastation was still fresh.

Despite the rigours of life in the English and Irish regiments, and the fact that most of the infantry were ex-prisoners and rogues of every sort, Sarsfield's military apprenticeship was soon over. In 1674 he was a captain under Thomas Dongan in the Irish regiment. By 1678 the regiment had been recalled to England, with an understanding of the potential of loyal, and otherwise, English troops serving under the French. Justin MacCarthy led this regiment by 1678 then moved to Danish service in 1679, after its recall. Louis, characteristically, refused to comply easily, setting in motion a situation whereby most soldiers were discharged and penniless, finding their way home eventually, destitute and in rags, if they were lucky.

## The Irish Captain

Sarsfield had found his way back to London and attracted the attention of the king. He had no intention of wasting talent after all, and there were significant numbers amongst Monmouth's old regiment who could be funnelled into a new concern where, under Thomas Dongan, the regiment would continue in French service with a sum of French gold in return. There was great hope that French service would continue. The matter of religion and nationality would have little bearing on military life perhaps, even if certain provisos regarding service outside Britain were in place, and workarounds with regard to religious toleration, or otherwise, had to be practised? It was not of course, to be.

The 'Popish Plot', as it became known, despite lies, cheating and planned insurrection of sorts, beset London and England as a whole in a vice-like grip of paranoia in the same year. Titus Oates's and Israel Tonge's tales of a Jesuit conspiracy to murder the king were dubious although, being followed by the murder of the magistrate Sir Edmund Godfrey and the somewhat treasonous letters of Edward Coleman, the queen's secretary, became enough to set light to the kindling of public outrage that had been stockpiled for so long. Being Irish, and in the military, suddenly became a decidedly dangerous state of affairs. Sarsfield was arrested and brought before two justices of the peace while riding towards Chester with the intention of reaching Dublin before the flames of suspicion reached their height, while Justin MacCarthy was arrested after being sent from London, then ironically arrested for running. The truth was now out and the House of Commons would not be found wanting, demanding to know why an Irish officer had been arrested while fleeing. Worse was the fact that large groups of Irish officers, in an apparent flouting of both the Test Act and the oath of allegiance, held commissions in the English military establishment, and in an atmosphere where many believed that the tipping point of papist violence to usurp the very throne was just around the corner. It was not an opportune time to be an Irish Catholic in England. Many were falsely accused and hanged over the course of the weeks and months that followed. Secretary Williamson would, with the king's guidance, find a solution, where the men in question :

are such as have his Majesty's leave to return to their own country, being Irishmen and dismissed from his Majesty's service. His Majesty has lately caused to be dismissed out of his service a considerable number more of that contingent, with leave to return to Ireland, a list of whose names he encloses.[7]

In some ways the timing was opportune, as the previous incarnation of the regiment lent to the French had been disbanded, although, of course, had those officers been in France, there might never have been the public outcry that arose. In any event, the game was up.

Commissions from 1678 denoted MacCarthy as lieutenant colonel, with Sarsfield as a lieutenant. Under the later Dongan's Regiment of February 1678, Sarsfield was listed as a captain, along with later notables such as Lord Galmoy and Ulick Burke.[8]

And so Sarsfield, with other Irish officers, despite the great hope of new command and further French service, found himself sailing for Ireland, and out of a job. The situation was made worse by the fact that he was also in debt and faced a dubious future as an Irish 'swordsman'. Despite England still being gripped by the rigours of the Popish plot, Sarsfield petitioned the Lord Lieutenant of Ireland, the Duke of Ormonde, in the hope that he might still recover any monies owed MacCarthy and his Irish officers for their English service in France. The duke was sympathetic, noting that several of the ex-military men were indeed 'in prison for their lodging and diet' and due at least 'some consideration and relief which it is not in my power to give them'.[9]

Under the circumstances, Irish officers' back pay was not a priority for the treasury; there would be no sign of monies until 1680, on the precise condition that the recipients had no intention of returning to London. Sarsfield was still petitioning for monies owed in 1683. All of this left him in a quandary, and a young military swordsman, in need of work, and still adventurous at heart, would inevitably find himself being drawn into troublesome encounters. There would inevitably be a cooling-down period after the plot, although a calming of the waters would not be enough to prevent the arrest and trial and execution of the Archbishop Oliver Plunkett of Armagh in June.

Despite the cooling of the worst excesses of the plot, there was unlikely to be a change in English policy any time soon, Sarsfield's mounting debts led to him becoming embroiled once more in the quagmire that the quest for his lost lands at Lucan had become. This proved fruitless and he returned to London. Nicolas Luttrell recorded in London in 1681 that:

> A tall Irishman to be seen at Bartholemew fair, and the Lord Grey having seen him was pleased to say he would make a swingeing evidence; on which one Captain Sarsfield, an Irishman sent his lordship a challenge, taking it as an affront on his countrymen.[10]

The remark had alluded to recent witness statements by various Irishmen against the Whigs, and even those involved with Plunkett's trial and subsequent execution. Highly-trained young military men full of piss and vinegar were perhaps the most dangerous civilians if there was no war to fight and, worse, if their experience was unused and unwanted. Grey was also no mean swordsmen and had garnered considerable influence at court with the Earl of Shaftesbury, who had been at the centre of anti-Catholic sentiment during the plot, and was an accomplished politician. He would come to prominence as a supporter of Monmouth, who would make his claim for the crown in but a few short years. He was a dangerous and shrewd man with considerable influence in Protestant circles, and Sarsfield's rash action could have proved his undoing.

Duelling had been proscribed and so Grey cunningly alerted the Privy Council and a warrant was issued for Sarsfield's arrest, the sergeant at arms eventually taking him into custody. Some might have learned from the results of impetuous behaviour; indeed, it could be argued that some might have been more careful, aware of the anti-Catholic stance that prevailed in state and society at the time. But 'some' did not describe Patrick Sarsfield. He escaped from custody. A subsequent warrant was issued, but the rogue Irishman could not be found.

We could leave the matter there, as it seems the Privy Council did since the new warrant was not followed up, at least effectively. It seemed that he had indeed got away with it. Most might have rested upon their laurels and made sure they stayed out of trouble. To some extent, Sarsfield did try to find gainful employment through one of the few existing avenues left to Irish Catholic military men, attempting to join the Tangiers garrison, which, by its nature, appealed only to those who had little other choice.[11]

His family estates offered little, and garnering funds for his Tangiers attempt forced him to petition the king once more for monies owed while serving under MacCarthy. His previous reputation, emboldened by the Grey affair and his escape from custody notwithstanding, meant that what happened next appears even more unbelievable. He became involved in yet another duel at the end of 1681 in London.[12]

Two young teenage lords, Newburgh and Kingsale, had resolved to duel on 6 December. Kingsale was a favourite of Ormonde, and therefore most likely the route through which Sarsfield became his second. In line with the customs of the day, and perhaps not entirely unexpectedly, even if completely ill-advised, Sarsfield took to duelling with a Mr Kirk, the second of the young Lord Newburgh, during the fracas. In the process, Kirk ran him through, near the shoulder, before convincing the young Lord Kingsale to surrender.[13] Sarsfield remained in London while recovering, reminded, if not entirely convinced by now, that the dangerous practice of duelling was probably not his forté. This theme of youthful impetuosity is one that we see continued. The wound had also ensured that any hope of joining the Tangiers garrison was hindered by the fact that he was unfit. Once more he faced becoming penniless. In this predicament we see him become involved in ventures which could, in hindsight, be seen as even less honourable than his duelling escapades.

Despite the fact that the politics of the time frowned upon adventurous swordsmen, and in particular upon adventurous Catholic swordsmen, Sarsfield, by his very nature, could not leave well enough alone. He had been seen as a 'popish recusant' by May 1682 when he appeared on an arrest warrant with others in London and had already garnered something of a reputation.[14] He had also, perhaps unsurprisingly, still kept contact with his former colleagues from Monmouth's and Dongan's regiment, the equivalent of what we might call 'networking' today, and this led him to further trouble, when Captain Robert Clifford took a discernible interest in a young widow called Ann Siderfin.[15] His intentions not entirely reciprocated, he resolved to kidnap her, enlisting a certain Irishman in support of the endeavour, together with a number of soldiers with whom the two had previously served.

Despite some setbacks, mainly due to the authorities being rapidly alerted with regard to the escapade, and even the involvement of the king, the two reached Calais with their prize, who was not taking well to Clifford's advances. Despite attempts by the authorities to arrest them, they escaped. Subsequently, any of those who had been indirectly involved were captured; when Clifford decided to return to London he was arrested and spent time in prison.[16]

Sarsfield, on the other hand, got away with his part in the kidnapping, even petitioning once more for monies owed to him for previous service. His part in the affair obviously gave him a taste for such adventures, as he decided to concoct his own endeavour. Perhaps drawing inspiration from his previous escapade, Sarsfield organised a kidnapping of his own. In an attempt to force another widow, Lady Herbert, into marrying him, after a previous relationship of sorts, possibly established when he had served with her son in Monmouth's Regiment and in the hope that she might yet relent to marriage, he kidnapped her in the middle of the night and made off to an unknown location. Unsurprisingly, Lady Herbert had lost interest by then, and did not take kindly to being kidnapped, although she agreed to sign documents to the effect that she would take no legal action against Sarsfield.[17]

Did Sarsfield live for adventure? We can speculate that he had little regard for what others might consider the niceties of English society. However, the matter was far from over. Sir John Parsons, who was acquainted with Sarsfield, had helped him during the kidnapping. Sarsfield had included his name on the signed document and asked him to keep it safe. When Parsons refused to return it, the two argued, and Sarsfield found himself involved in another duel in April 1683 near the Strand. Both were injured, Sarsfield taking the blade through the belly into the lungs. Both recovered, even if their former relationship did not.

Had Sarsfield learned his lesson, or was his behaviour part of his character? Even if his recklessness could not be curbed, he clearly had a long memory, if we try to ascertain who might have been responsible for Captain Clifford's release from prison. Narcissus Luttrell recorded:

> Capt. Clifford sometime since convicted of a great misdemeanour in stealing and carrying away Mrs Siderfin into France, for which he received 1000*l* damages, as also Mrs Siderfin recovered 1500*l* in a special action, and there in the Fleet prison having since layn for some time, some gentlemen came under pretence to see him, but rescued him, and carried him away, notwithstanding the endeavours of the officers.[18]

We can guess that this was Sarsfield's work. If so, this might have been his last escapade in London, but it would certainly not be the end of his adventure.

The exclusion crisis of 1678-81 raised the profile of those parties, including the Whigs, who sought to prevent the Duke of York's accession, on account of his Catholicism. The fear, exaggerated by some yet genuinely felt by others, was absolutism, akin to what the average Englishman might consider as the despotic rule of Louis XIV in France. In the midst of Sarsfield's and other Irish troops' recall from French service, the Whigs, most notably led by the Earl of Shaftesbury, a civil war veteran of both sides no less, created the exclusion crisis in a bold move to achieve a succession which might be deemed as acceptable; indeed, he would be the centre of the propaganda hub driving the popish plot and would promote, and thereby legitimise, Monmouth, the 'Protestant Duke' as a rightful and legitimate heir to Charles II.

Despite the Whigs' machinations, and Charles's attempts to keep a semblance of order, Monmouth bided his time, and began to believe the propaganda that he was hearing. He would be pardoned for his connections to the Rye House Plot, which helped legitimise his belief in his own destiny. His actions would set in motion the most significant upset in the accepted view of monarchy since the civil war.

In February 1685 Charles's death meant that everything would change, yet the accession of James seemed almost reserved when compared with the perpetual storm that had blown in a vain attempt to keep him from the throne.

Despite the rigours and activities of the Whigs, the Test Acts and the Popish Plot, Charles professed his Catholicism at the time of his death, yet he had not been short-sighted and had ensured that James's daughters, and heirs, would both be brought up as Protestants, and that Mary had married the Protestant Stadtholder of the Dutch Provinces; indeed he had made his thoughts clear with regard to the short-term nature of his brother's Catholic succession.

If Charles had been charming, and what we might today call a good 'man manager', his brother lacked tact and empathy (yet had shown the former king's love of womanising, albeit with a bias toward less than stellar beauties).

## Rebellion

Monmouth's rebellion in 1685 presented Sarsfield with arguably his greatest opportunity to make his name, in full view of a Catholic king who was seeking both allies and loyal leadership at a military level. As a gentleman volunteer he served under Theophilus Oglethorpe alongside the young Lord Newburgh whose second he had fought in his earlier duel. As the armies traversed across southern England, destined to define a kingdom, Sarsfield rode with the troops who provided reconnaissance.

It is arguable that Monmouth's actions, buoyed by Dutch, English and even other Protestant European kingdoms' support, was misguided and doomed to failure from the start. Even more controversial is the contention that the move was a 'testing of the waters' by William, in a machination to discover the breadth and depth of support for a supported insurrection in an England that feared, perhaps more than anything, a second English Civil War fought on the basis of religious differences. In the event, the matter was resolved quickly, and quite conversely, proved to those who watched on the European stage that, at least initially, support for the king, be he Catholic or Protestant, was the uppermost priority of most English soldiers and officers. Only after the event did doubt start to seep in.

Monmouth had made the most of his exile in Holland, aware of course of William's interest in his wife's access to the succession, his ultimate aim being one of an English alliance in the inevitable war with the French. The worst-case scenario would be an English crown which fought alongside France against him. That was something he couldn't accept and, if fostering Monmouth's Whiggish aims was a means of furthering his own, then so be it. Charles's death had been the catalyst for action. His favourite bastard was isolated, alone, yet could easily be the lever that upset the delicate balance of the swaying English power bloc. For William to continue to keep Monmouth, disconsolate at his father's death, in the manner to which he was rapidly becoming accustomed, threatened to anger his uncle, now deciding where his future loyalties might lie.

But it was the Whigs who ultimately swayed the ambitious Monmouth. Lord Grey, a passionate backer of exclusion, and the oft accused Earl of Argyle among them, would convince Monmouth that he had a destiny other than serving as a mercenary leader in Europe as his Irish contemporaries had done. He could be King of England instead.

The scheme was ambitious, if not altogether practical. Argyle would raise support in Scotland, while Monmouth would land in the south; but even by the time that Monmouth sailed, Argyle had been captured and put to death. Nevertheless, the die had been cast, and Monmouth arrived at Lyme Regis in June 1685. Word spread through the west country as Monmouth promised to end the supposed tyranny of James's reign. Parliament was quick to act. Sunderland outlined the details of the rebellion against the new king, voting James £400,000 to remove the threat, and placing a price on Monmouth's head. Sarsfield's time to shine had finally come.

The army was led by Louis Duras, the Earl of Feversham, a Frenchman in English service, whose second, John Churchill, whose influence pervades the entire story, was perhaps not yet entirely trusted.

It was an act that would never be entirely forgotten by the future Duke of Marlborough.

Sarsfield knew Monmouth well, and indeed it is arguable that he owed him much, although times were changing, and reason and sentiment could readily be displaced by a Catholic succession and the chance of a hegemony based on religious freedom and a reduced fear of 'popery'. Indeed, he must have felt that a resurgence of anti-Catholic sentiment could not be further away, especially so if this very Protestant rebellion could be undermined quickly. Sarsfield served under Colonel Theophilus Oglethorpe in a fighting patrol, that would be fast-moving and hard hitting if it encountered the enemy unprepared, although its role was mainly one of scouting for Feversham's larger body. Monmouth had assembled a force of 4,000 men, and despite their lack of experience and arms, he hoped to disorder the hurriedly assembled government forces which, by early July, had camped near Bristol to prevent his taking the town.

Oglethorpe clung close to Monmouth's army for days, watching him walk into the small village of Keynsham, five miles from Bristol, at some point committing to a skirmish in amongst the buildings, cutting down several rebels. Characteristically, Sarsfield was wounded in the hand in the process, although his horsemanship and general courage allowed him to disengage. He remained in the fight.

He had been with Oglethorpe's patrol for eight wet days, finally watching the march into Bridgewater, and awaiting further movement from their vantage to the north. That night, Monmouth's force, in the hope of surprising the Royal army as they slept, as his only real chance of defeating James's regulars with his rebel force was to catch them unawares, marched towards the patrol at Knowle Hill. They remained undetected, even as Oglethorpe sent word that he would advance to Bridgewater, which had been vacated. By the time that he learnt of the enemy's movements, he could already hear the distant sound of musketry as the night-time battle commenced. Monmouth's hope of ambushing a sleeping army had come to naught.

Oglethorpe's patrol dashed back down the Bridgwater road, and under Feversham's orders, galloped around the rear of the royal army, gathering reinforcements as they went, and engaged Grey's cavalry farther to the east across the Bussex Rhine river, before forming a flanking force and charging into the frightened infantry, who had already been undermined by flanking movements ordered by Churchill.

Sarsfield, amongst Oglethorpe's charging horse, had plunged into the rebel infantry and pikes, quite in keeping with his characteristic reckless abandon. In the melee, he was clubbed off his horse and left for dead. An hour later, the battle was over; Monmouth had fled, but would be captured within two days of the battle, despite his attempts at disguise and flight. Although he had been wounded again, Sarsfield had been noticed, and even recorded in the king's diary, which included details of how he had been knocked from his horse.

Feversham would send a report to Sunderland, the Secretary of State, that:

> I do not believe that we have lost fifty men killed in that place, and nearly two hundred wounded. There was only one ensign killed, two captains, six lieutenants and six ensigns wounded…
>
> Sarsfield was also wounded in several places but not mortally.
>
> I am assured that the enemy have been killed in thousands and nearly three hundred prisoners taken.[19]

Monmouth had arrived in England in June 1685, proclaiming that he had come to relieve tyranny. For his own misguided endeavour, Monmouth would be on Tower Hill for his treason. The 'Bloody Assizes' followed in the West Country and beyond, their notoriety and long-standing bitter memory echoing down through the years, arguably in a manner similar to what would follow in Ireland. Percy Kirke, who had been a lieutenant in 1675 before Sarsfield in the Royal English Regiment in France, would see history castigate him as the villain of that piece.[20]

## 1686 The New Regime

A year after James's accession to the throne saw the fractures start to appear, more keenly than they had before. In this period we see Sarsfield's significant rise, at least in terms of his military standing. From a mention in James's memoirs regarding his bravery at Sedgemoor, to his promotion to lieutenant colonel of the 4th Troop of Life Guards by mid-1686, his star was finally starting to shine.[21] Gone were the rigorous implications of the Test Act, or so it seemed. Sedgemoor had given James confidence that the army and thus the people would follow a Catholic king, if he remained just. Sedgemoor had also convinced him of the sense of retaining a standing army. He could not foresee how each of his assertions would evetually force an unravelling of his reign.

Sarsfield found himself in the ascendancy. Even the new king remarked upon his having been wounded at Sedgemoor, and his name was being remarked upon in quarters where influence could be managed. The fallout from the Test Acts and the parliamentary-led concerns at their mismanagement was in the past or, at worst, a mere trifle in terms of Sarsfield's progress. If Monmouth's rebellion had indicated anything to King James, it was the clear advantage of having a standing army: it guaranteed the authority of the realm, and his standing within it, although such a course would be anathema to a Protestant parliament in the long term.

Although monarchical authority and fear of its absolutist style rule, with a standing army, had thus far guaranteed parliament's reticence to promote its implementation, memories of how and why a civil war had been fought were still relatively fresh. Royal prerogative, and the backing of the judiciary in parliament, would allow James to make changes, which were progressive, at least in his own eyes, but were in turn damaging incrementally to his continued authority.

Yet Sarsfield must have cared little by 1685, perhaps even daring to believe that the new light shining in London would be of lasting benefit, as he was given a commission with Richard Hamilton's dragoon regiment on the Irish establishment. He didn't have time to take up the position as with the new authority had come new opportunities and he was quickly awarded a commission in a regiment of horse under the Catholic Lord Dover, effectively meaning that he would manage much of the regiment's affairs himself.[22] The troops would also take part in the mass displays of military might on Hounslow Heath. However, he would see some limited action on English soil which, in the grand scale of wars to come, would matter little in terms of numbers involved, but would serve to set light to the touch-paper of the explosive change that was coming to England.

In April 1687 his cavalry were called upon to defend the Catholic chapel at Lime Street, on the occasion of its consecration, from a Protestant mob. It was exactly the style and nature of event which, politically at least, James had wanted to avoid. Seeing the events in context with the re-modelling of the army in Ireland, we can start to imagine the beginning of the end of James's reign. The militia at the gate were overpowered and the crowds set about destroying crucifixes and the trappings of 'popery'.

Sarsfield's men overpowered the mob and sent them packing, but it must have been clear to all that the depth of feeling and its chance of reversal if that was what was required in James's new vision for the kingdom, was a mountain to climb.

Of course, not all of the mania that grew with each passing day could be blamed solely upon James. Louis XIV's revocation of the Edict of Nantes in 1685, and the subsequent anti-Huguenot dragonades had already forced thousands of French Protestants to flee persecution. The tales had grown with the telling as yet another example of how a Catholic hegemony, and perhaps more importantly, absolutist government with its inevitable standing army, could redefine the very nature of government.[23] Adding to the mix was James's remodelling of society with Catholics appointed as local magistrates in lieu of Protestants, Tyrconnel given free rein in Ireland to re-model the army, and taking to the task with gusto, and his insistence that he was shaping a fairer and more religiously equitable society, and the quick-to-anger Protestant majority would predictably seek a solution outside their own realm.

## 1688, Revolution

The history of the 'Glorious Revolution' of 1688 has been unkind to James, but a precedent for the rise and fall of a potential Protestant succession had already been experienced with Monmouth's rebellion. That the population and, more especially, the army had remained loyal was not in question. The pace of change, however, was more than most, at least those influential 'most', could bear.

When James renewed his 'declaration of indulgence' and ordered it to be read across the land's churches, the subsequent outcry from seven bishops saw their prosecution. They were acquitted although, instead of a mere political hiccup, the fire was now lit. By June 1688 civil and military leaders had written to William Prince of Orange, inviting him and his army to England, there to take his father-in-law's throne. Of course, William had his own agenda. A second war with the French was coming and the last thing he needed was to fight a Catholic French ally in the form of English troops. James's queen, Mary Beatrice, was also pregnant. A son would rule William out of the succession and push James into the arms of Louis. By November he had landed at Torbay with an army.

That James had lost his nerve and did not face William is not surprising, considering that he must have realised that, unlike the Monmouth incursion three years earlier, he had lost support. In the event, he had not lost as much as he must have feared but the defection of men like John Churchill, ever open to the benefits of opportunity, to William, along with the growing paranoia born of his realisation that many of the senior officers and Whigs had actively conspired against him, can only have engendered a distinct paranoia.

William landed at Torbay on 5 November. Accompanying him were Whigs, Huguenot generals, the Huguenot Count Schomberg, a former French marshal, now lending his skills to William, and the cream of the Dutch army. It had been a scant few years since Sedgemoor and the subsequent bloody assizes of Judge Jeffreys, where the last 'invasion' of England had threatened the crown. William, however, already had an army and had little intention to recruit from the local population as Monmouth had been forced to do. He had too much work to do, too quickly, without burdening himself still further.

The defections were rapid and open, John Churchill, Lord Cornbury, the Duke of Grafton. With the open removal of key figures from the army, and the inevitable paranoia amongst other officers about the safest way to turn, the English army began to fall apart.

To James, the greatest test was that of loyalty from his troops, although his own assessment of this, and its own subsequent failings, even if minor, were enough to unseat his confidence. The fact that many of those defectors were well aware of James's strategic intentions as he marched his army to Salisbury probably exacerbated his paranoia about how far royal loyalty might stretch and, indeed, whether his military strategy could be planned around by William.

With the army hamstrung through lack of intelligence, Kirke sent for Sarsfield so that a reconnaissance might be carried out. He set out with 120 horse, together with Henry Luttrell, riding thirty miles toward the village of Bruton, although there was soon evidence of enemy forces gathering at nearby Wincanton. Scots from Colonel Mackay's foot regiment, which had formed part of the Scottish Brigade in Holland, had been sent to Wincanton to collect horses until the main body of the army could catch up.

Sergeant Campbell of Mackay's was alerted to the approach of the mounted men, enabling him, outnumbered as he was, to set up an ambush along the lane that allowed entry into the village from Bruton. Upon their approach, and still unsure as to their allegiance, Campbell is reputed to have started a discourse with Sarsfield:

'Stand! For who are ye?'
'I am for King James. Who are you for?'

'I am for the Prince of Orange!'
'God damn you! I'll prince you!'

At the very least, historical precedent and the reliability of source material notwithstanding, the last line is certainly reminiscent of the Sarsfield that we have come to know.

In the subsequent ambush a horse-trooper was shot dead and the cavalry surged forward, trying to catch the infantry in the open fields. A report of approaching Dutch reinforcements convinced him to regroup, although a second attack was made when it was proven that the Dutch attack was but a ruse. The Scots had by now vanished, and he had lost three men killed and six taken prisoner for twelve Scots infantry killed. Sarsfield returned to Salisbury, but it was the only action, if indeed a minor one, that would occur in the short campaign. As William moved east, there was confusion, talk of other protracted skirmishes, and confused rumours about the loyalty, or otherwise, of James's army.[24]

Had Englishman been forced to fight Englishman upon the field of battle, perhaps James might have engendered some loyalty, a sense of national pride, even a reticence to start another civil war in his wake. As it was, his pessimism was his undoing, and he ordered the army to return to London, although plots involving Kirke and many of his contemporaries were later suggested as having been waiting simply for James to make a wrong move before they were put into action. Indeed, Sarsfield would be noted as one of those who might confound such a scheme.[25]

With James's ultimate flight, and the beginnings of William's dominance and eventual accession to the crown, Sarsfield was placed in a very dangerous position. In characteristic style, his impression and opinion was reported to William as a 'man of desperate and daring nature', a succinct if recognisable description, although followed by the advice that 'it might be advisable to secure him for fear he might assassinate his person'. William almost dared him to try, but was convinced that Sarsfield and other officers were unsuitable for service and should be issued passes to travel to their king in exile, in France.[26]

And so the wily, if unlucky, Sarsfield left for Ireland, like so many of his kin, to write the next chapter in the story of the Irish exiles. Although his subsequent story will be told in the chapters that follow, it is pertinent to sum up his character with a note intercepted during the Jacobite wars, written to him by Berwick, who addressed him as *Deare Notorious*. The *Notorious* Sarsfield was far from finished.

*Chapter 10*

# A Siege

The ballad known as 'The Sash' is emblematic of the modern Orange Order sensibilities, present-day loyalism in Northern Ireland and the tragic history that still divides the community there today. It is popular or contentious depending on a political viewpoint which emanates directly from the activities and resultant stain that remains in Ireland from the very stuff of our period. In many ways, this is what makes the century so fascinating, that it can still have such an effect, and a lasting, if bitterly dividing, echo down the years, is surely of historical note. There is one line in the song which refers to an 'Orangeman's sash' which remains pertinent to our story.

## It was worn at Derry, Aughrim, Enniskillen and the Boyne ...

In this vein the song proclaims to remember the deeds wrought and battles fought in the name of Protestantism and it is, of course, popular within Orangeism for its message and tone. Naturally it is viewed as divisive or even extreme by the opposite side, and is still used in Scottish football stadia as a rabble-rousing cry against 'Popery', by youths who ignore its origins, and perhaps understand little of its roots. What we remember, and how history recalls the events, does not take account of the political context, or the participants, who would go on to fight with Irish troops in mainland Europe and, for the most part, never see their native land again.

Yet the line is inaccurate, at least as far as the context of our story is concerned. Although the Williamite, and thereby Protestant, resistance in Fermanagh was centred on the island town of Enniskillen, the battle that decided its fate, and raised MacCarthy's name once more to French attention, took place near the small village of Newtownbutler, twenty miles from Enniskillen (or Newtown as it was called at the time, being renamed several years later, although we will refer to it here as Newtownbutler, the name by which the battle is more popularly known).

Before we look at events in Fermanagh, it is pertinent to examine events at Derry (or Londonderry – even today the echoes of this turbulent episode are felt amongst the divided communities there). Events there in 1689 marked one of the longest episodes of the war, and almost completely undermined Richard Hamilton's reputation, arguably, for all the wrong reasons. As with most seventeenth-century actions, the bulk of the fatalities and suffering were felt amongst the civilian population. The siege exacerbated the worsening relations between Jacobite and Williamite, Catholic and Protestant, in a manner that would echo through the centuries to the present day. There were over 105 days of blockade and siege, although it could scarce be called a siege by European standards. It was accompanied by skirmishes, deadly close-quarter fights, arrogance, blatant incompetence, starvation and treachery: perhaps not the stuff of legends, but certainly a landmark in the Irish Jacobite war as a whole. Richard Hamilton was now poised to become either an Irish Jacobite hero or the greatest failure of the age, dependent upon the result.

That result would also determine whether James could proceed to Scotland, in support of Dundee's Highlanders, and thus return to the English and Scottish throne. Whether a successful siege could have led to a successful Jacobite revolt in mainland Britain is very much open to question, however. James, fully convinced that a secure Ireland could be used as a 'springboard' to English invasion (it is supremely ironic that this very fear had shaped his grandfather's Irish plantation plans), saw the taking of Londonderry as crucial to his perceived destiny, that he would once more be king of England. The province of Ulster represented a very different and dangerous undertaking compared to what had occurred in the rest of Ireland, thanks mainly to the legacy of James I's plantation experiment. In the countryside outside Dublin, in Munster, Leinster and Connaught, Catholicism outnumbered Protestantism by around forty to one. In Ulster, the numbers were matched, a factor that would seriously affect the efforts of the Jacobite army.

Of the numerous Protestant towns and enclaves in Ulster, two would play a significant role in the war; both Londonderry and Enniskillen would resist Tyrconnel's plans, considerably dilute the effectiveness of the Jacobite army and point to the cracks in a convenient yet obviously shaky relationship between the native Irish, the old-English Irish, James and the French. The commencement of rebellion in both towns is based on remarkably similar events. Early events in Enniskillen unfolded in a fashion similar to those at Derry.

The city of Derrie had been destroyed in May 1608 by the O'Dohertys and McDevitts. A new city was built in its place five years later, and named *London-Derrie* to mark the forced investment by the London livery companies.

As James Hamilton, Richard and Anthony's grandfather, had led the Hamilton expedition to Strabane, London businessmen had been granted leave to rebuild the ruined Derry. An early Gaelic uprising had destroyed the original town in the seventeenth century, despite English interests. By way of thanks to the London Guildsmen, the city was renamed in the early seventeenth century.

Even by the 1680s the city remained small; it did, however, possess a wall. Compared to cities on the continent, the defences were less significant. Vauban had designed an exact science for siege warfare, though the Jacobite army would be far from expert in their siege. It covered a circumference around the area of less than a mile, excruciatingly small considering the numbers that would be crammed inside. The defences consisted of seven bastions and a number of demi-bastions. This system, as with other types of fortifications, had been developed from European doctrine. The bastion was normally an outcropping from the town's perimeter that would allow an excellent field of fire against an attacker approaching close to the wall. The concept and system, however, were primarily designed around fortifications operating in conjunction with the bastions, such as ravelins, crownworks and demi-lunes, all designed to guard approaches and prevent the enemy getting close. Londonderry, due to its size and relative strategic value on a European scale, had few such innovations although Lieutenant Colonel Lundy would make significant improvements in the months before the siege.

Would fortifications matter here? Tyrconnel had put garrisons in many towns in the north. At Londonderry matters had proceeded differently; a majority Catholic corporation, resisted as far as possible by the mostly Protestant population, had been put in place. To preserve the peace, the town had been garrisoned only by Mountjoy's Regiment, one of the few left which still had some Protestant officers and men at the time. Mountjoy, the commanding officer, and Lieutenant Colonel Lundy, his second in command, were both Protestants.

All this was to change in November 1688 when Mountjoy's troops were withdrawn to Dublin. Tyrconnel had ordered the seventy-six-year-old Alexander MacDonnell, third Earl of Antrim, to raise a regiment, which was destined for Londonderry. The reaction in the town was one of shock, exacerbated by news of a letter received in Comber in County Down, addressed to Lord Mount-Alexander. This warned of 9 December as a day when a general massacre of Protestants in Ireland would begin, in a style reminiscent of the 1641 rebellion.

> Good My Lord,
>
> I have written to you to let you know that all our Irishmen through Ireland is sworn: that on the ninth day of this month they are to fall on to kill and murder man, wife and child; and I desire your lordship to take care of yourself, and all others that are judged by our men to be heads, for whosoever of them can kill any of you, they are to have a captain's place; so my desire to your honour is, to look to yourself, and give other noblemen warning, and go not out either night or day without a good guard with you, and let no Irishman come near you, whatsoever he be; so this is all from him who was your father's friend, and is your friend, and will be, though I dare not be known, as yet, for fear of my life.[1]

The stories of murder in 1641, combined with worrying changes in recent years, had attuned Protestant fears to the extent that the mere thought of a recurrence became a signal for panic. Antrim, however, would play into the hands of many of the concerned citizens – he was late! A two-week gap between Mountjoy's troops' departure and the arrival of the 'Redshanks', as Antrim's barelegged Scottish Catholic troops were known, allowed Derry's populace to consider, and then to plan. On 7 December, with the Redshanks about to cross the river Foyle, a final decision was still in doubt, at least in the minds of the town's dignitaries. For a group of the city's guild apprentices, however, there was no further decision to make. Taking matters into their own hands, the apprentices closed the Ferry Gate, quickly followed by their closing of the wall's other three gates, an act still commemorated in the city today.[2]

The actions of a few men and boys had defied Antrim's regiment. This meant that they had also defied the authority of the king, an action that still many of the citizens, both Protestant and Catholic, found hard to accept, despite the talk of impending massacre. In the days to follow, the ranks were swollen by Protestants who had previously remained outside the walls, who now not only agreed with the action but saw Londonderry as the last refuge for themselves against a closing Jacobite army.[3]

After hearing of the entire incident and flying into a rage, Tyrconnel ordered Mountjoy and his men to return. The period between the departure of the Redshanks and the arrival of Mountjoy once more worked to the advantage of Derry's citizens. Their attempt at resistance had, it seemed, worked. Why should they now back down at all when they apparently held the initiative? Mountjoy's Regiment returned to the city but was initially refused entry since the citizens knew that it included a significant number of Catholics (it had been the garrison unit for three years). Mountjoy negotiated a compromise with the city fathers whereby two companies of Protestant soldiers under Lieutenant Colonel Lundy would be allowed inside the walls. Lundy's companies entered on 22 December while the other companies were dispersed to Strabane, Newtownstewart and Raphoe.

Tyrconnel's attention was now focused, however, on attempts from London to negotiate a deal and the infamous return to Ireland of Richard Hamilton. Hamilton's subsequent campaign in the north and the Break of Dromore would, by March, concentrate Protestant numbers upon Londonderry and Enniskillen.

James's landing at Kinsale in March occurred around the same time as another landing, on this occasion at Londonderry in the guise of Captain Hamilton's ship, *Deliverance*. Captain James Hamilton, who would later become 6th Earl of Abercorn, son of Richard and Anthony's deceased brother James, and a devout Protestant and Williamite, landed on 20 March with arms, ammunition and other stores for the garrison. Over 7,000 muskets with powder and over £8,000 would help with the defence, although the young Captain Hamilton had other orders. He was to deny the military stores to the garrison until such times as Lieutenant Colonel Lundy had sworn an oath to King William, who had been proclaimed joint monarch with Queen Mary after much deliberation in February. Lundy's loyalties, it seemed, were held in some doubt in London. Despite Hamilton's acceptance of Lundy's oath, there would later be concerns as to his convictions. The loyalty of Captain Hamilton, however, despite the side chosen by three of his uncles, was not in question. With his re-supply, the garrison inside Londonderry had arms and ammunition for over 7,000 men, seven regiments of foot and one of cavalry.

Lundy's knowledge marked him out as the natural leader of the garrison; he had already been appointed military governor by the corporation in December 1688. Indeed, as his experience included the siege of Tangiers, he must have seemed the natural choice for the position of governor and military commander. He recalled many of the garrisons gathered in nearby towns, ordering them back to Londonderry, advice that was ignored at Enniskillen. He did improve the city's defences and fortifications, including the construction of a ravelin – efforts which prevented the early fall of the city.

Richard Hamilton, after pursuing the remnants of Mount-Alexander's force from Coleraine, had to move quickly if he hoped to link up with the main Jacobite army and attack the city, or even take it himself. He had already sent a small vanguard towards it, which had fired on the defenders. With sufficient manpower, however, the garrison could attempt to stop his crossing, or at the very least make Hamilton pay dearly for it by occupying key crossing points to the south.

By 15 April, as Irish cavalry began to cross the swollen river Finn at Cladyford, each horseman with an infantry soldier in tow, and other Jacobite troops setting about repairing bridges, the response of the defenders was negligible. Indeed, the apparent determined nature of the crossing succeeded in breaking the will of Londonderry's garrison after a single un-coordinated musket volley that did little damage. Scattered across a wide area of operation, which even an experienced commander such as Lundy would have found difficult to co-ordinate, they broke and ran. A similarly determined Jacobite pursuit killed hundreds of stragglers as the vanguard of the retreat reached Londonderry's walls once more. At least one regiment was trapped outside the town, taking their chances by night to avoid discovery amidst the confusion surrounding the Jacobite pursuit, before eventually gaining admittance.

The subsequent meeting held in the city, with Lundy and the council of war, made up of senior residents, rapidly became beset with Lundy's concerns and his belief that the situation in Londonderry could not be sustained. Defences were adequate but questionable in terms of a protracted siege, there was some artillery although the Jacobite army outside the walls was growing in strength with each passing day. His determination was infectious as the council agreed that the troops should withdraw and supplies should leave with them. This action was a prelude to Lundy's eventual attempts to seek terms with Hamilton.[4] Richard Hamilton had after all offered significantly generous terms, at least in the eyes of Lieutenant Colonel Lundy who was also keen that such a decision should not reach the town's populace, and provoke a reaction that could have had him lynched. Lundy's own military experience would also have made it obvious, to him and other soldiers, that hopes of successfully holding the city would fade daily, and that an honourable surrender now, could potentially allow troops to march freely from the city and later support a large Williamite landing. The wider strategic picture of allowing James to take a port, and therefore enable travel to Scotland, may in such circumstances have been a moot point.

Upon returning to the city, he had to reassess his ability to hold after the debacle at the fords. He had, after all, seen the indigenous Williamite forces defeated thus far whenever they had faced the Jacobites, and witnessed first-hand the effectiveness of their elite cavalry arm. He also knew that Jacobite artillery could be equally effective if deployed and well commanded, against walls which were not specifically designed for protracted siege. The more immediate prospect of realistic resistance and limited supplies would not sit well with the fervour of a populace under siege, and many were losing confidence in Lundy.

With councils of war and discussion of negotiating terms with Hamilton or James himself, confusion and potential for surrender still existed. James enters the story personally at this stage. There were many rumours around the city with regard to his approach. In reality, despite the protests of d'Avaux, James set off from Dublin for Ulster, reaching Omagh by the 14th. D'Avaux tried again to dissuade him from proceeding; with the information regarding a relief fleet having been spotted at Lough Foyle, and the resistance at the fords, James did indeed change his mind, and prepared to return to Dublin. General de Rosen, and other senior officers were ordered to make their way to Derry. However, James would reconsider once more when he received word from Berwick, in relation to the decision that had been made on the 16th by the city's council of war, to open talks with James, and even that a delegation had subsequently been sent to Hamilton. Berwick informed his father that he believed that the gates would be opened if he were but to appear in front of the city. It was all that James had hoped for, and he must have believed that his personal intervention could end the Irish war before it could really start.[5]

There were indeed talks with Hamilton, who had agreed with the city's leaders that Jacobite forces would not approach within four miles of the city whilst surrender was under consideration. Hamilton too, must have been sure that a speedy resolution was in the air, aided by Lundy's seemingly reduced role in events.

James, with d'Avaux and de Rosen in tow, complete with imposing flag bearers and escort troops, accordingly appeared before the walls on 18 April, confident that Berwick's prediction would be correct, and that the once and future king might see the previously locked gates of Derry opened to him. There had been no discussion with regard to Hamilton's arrangements, however. The defenders, therefore, did not see James's good intentions, nor the hopes that bolstered this apparent act of good faith. Instead they simply saw the most potent symbol of Jacobite deal-breaking and treachery. As James rode toward Bishop's Gate, despite some attempt by commanders to hold fire and understand what was happening, muskets and cannon were fired. Some of James's party were injured or killed, prompting his immediate retreat, with the cry of 'no surrender' shouted from the city walls as he withdrew.

Lundy, in an attempt to save what he could of the situation, tried to send an apology to James, linking himself to accusations of supposed treacherous intent, assuring him that such a welcome had neither been intended nor ordered. James responded by sending his personal guarantee that the garrison would be pardoned if they surrendered, but it was too late. Lundy's council and James's appearance had been the final acts that would unify the people inside the walls, or at the very least take control from those who had wanted a peaceful surrender, and influence over both the situation and the garrison had been lost. James returned to Dublin 'extremely mortified'.[6] Hamilton, now meeting with French advisors de Rosen, Maumont and Pusignan, was faced with a decaying situation.

In such circumstances, and in a fashion similar to which matters had developed at Enniskillen months before, a leader would emerge. In this case the garrison looked to Colonel Adam Murray, a local man who commanded a cavalry regiment. The siege had brought him south from Culmore. Another council meeting saw Murray quickly brought in, perhaps due to his popular appeal and apparent ability to lead. Lundy's surrender proposals were drafted but Murray refused to sign. There would, as far as he was concerned, be no surrender. His subsequent denunciation of the governor's actions to date saw the council evict Lundy from the meeting and place him under arrest, although he was allowed to escape, in the guise of a soldier carrying musket 'match' cord.[7]

A new chapter had opened in the 'siege', and there would be neither further prevarication nor serious attempts to surrender in the foreseeable future. Refusing the post of governor, seeking only military command, Murray deferred to Major Henry Baker to govern with the Reverend Walker asked to assist. D'Avaux, who would develop clear reasons as to the success or otherwise of the affair, blamed both Hamilton and Maumont for letting so many civilians leave. They could, after all, under the proper and rigid conditions of siege and blockade, have become a problem for the garrison's food supply, helping to bring matters to a close. Instead, they were being allowed to leave freely; d'Avaux reported that fifty to one hundred people were leaving daily.[8]

Despite earning the enmity of Jacobite writers after the action,[9] regarding his decisions in permitting the reduction in numbers in the city, Hamilton left little doubt with the defenders as to the serious nature of a siege:

> Your ruin seems inevitable, by withstanding an army so well disciplined and so powerful, which resolves, if you continue obstinate, to give no Quarter to Man, Woman or Child. When once our Cannon and Mortars have rent the Walls in pieces and the Town is taken by storm, then the thousands of your Wives and Children shall fall upon their knees and with repeated Sighs and Groans implore our Pity. We shall doubtless be inexorable and all their Cries will be drown'd in the loud Acclamations of our victorious Army, which will then be deaf and merciless.

James's much vaunted mercy would then be absent from an army 'whose Fury cannot be withheld by his Majesty, much less, Gentlemen, by your most Humble Servant: Richard Hamilton'.[10]

However, Hamilton's threats were difficult to enforce. The strength of his Jacobite force at Derry was around 10,000, although this would fluctuate wildly as the siege wore on. In addition, descriptions such as 'well-disciplined' and 'powerful' could not be used to describe most of the Irish army encamped around the area.

Outlying regiments began to move closer to the city. Men were encamped at Pennyburn mill north of the city, to the east across the river Foyle at Stronge's orchard and on the higher ground to the west. As part of this envelopment, Maumont, whose headquarters were to the north at Culmore Fort, had ordered troops to occupy Pennyburn village, about a mile north of the city on the west bank of the Foyle. Observing the closing in of additional Jacobite forces from the walls, Murray resolved to set matters alight, with a counter-attack against the Jacobite troops attempting to surround him; an action at Pennyburn mill resulted in Maumont being killed, and the loss of eighty Jacobites.[11]

If the skirmish had been a signal to Hamilton's surrounding forces that there was still plenty of fight in the garrison, it had its desired effect. Few could have predicted, however, that, a few days later, Murray would attempt a second attack at Pennyburn. On this occasion, in a pitched battle that lasted most of the day, Irish reinforcements succeeded in holding the village. Another senior French officer, Major General Pusignan, was wounded severely. In other circumstances, on another battlefield, Pusignan might have survived but the lack of a field hospital and medical attention meant that he died within a few days of the action.[12]

D'Avaux was convinced that Hamilton would show little concern over the deaths of the French officers. He informed Louvois that Richard Hamilton and his fellow Irish officers had shown little respect for the Frenchmen. He reasoned that such behaviour was a result of Hamilton's belief that they would 'rob him of glory', reporting that if he 'persists in behaving as he has done, there is little hope of his winning glory'.[13] Tyrconnel, firmly stuck in the Irish camp, had already assured Hamilton of 'all the honour'.[14] Already, it seemed the inevitable friction between the Jacobite allies had affected efficiency, something that neither James nor the Irish needed under the circumstances.

Londonderry had been surrounded. Had the siege occurred in mainland Europe with professional armies trained in the latest doctrine, this form of 'positional warfare' might have unfolded differently.[15] Vauban's work on perfecting the science of this sophisticated and engineered defensive battlefield also gave rise to his methodology as to how it could be circumvented. Intrinsic to such operations was an initial 'investment' by cavalry and mounted troops. This would surround and cut off the fortress or city. The city was then literally surrounded once more by trenches. Lines of circumvallation would face outwards, protecting the besiegers from counter-attack, whilst lines of contravallation would face inwards toward the siege. Matters at Londonderry, however, were markedly different. Indeed, initial investment of the town and effective blockade left much to be desired. The armies' respective methods, training and defences were on a scale radically different to anything on the continent.

Characteristically, d'Avaux bragged that a single French battalion could have taken Derry almost overnight and Coleraine, too, something Hamilton had failed to do. However, French battalions were still very far away and James, as far as d'Avaux was concerned, would not have a Frenchman in charge. The whole affair would reinforce the need for French troops in d'Avaux's mind which, in discussion with Louvois, would have far-reaching repercussions for some of the best Irish troops. As early as May, d'Avaux was convinced that Hamilton was not the man for the job.[16]

Tyrconnel, displaying some of the affection that he still held for the Hamiltons, wrote to Richard:

> I am sensible, you want necessary fitting to take in such places, and what is yet worse, [you have] all sorts of officers … you must do as well as you can.

> As for your brothers Anthony and Jack [John] ... [I will] do
> by them as if they were my own. Anthony has a regiment and is
> Brigadier and will very soon be Major General. Jack has Mountjoy's
> regiment and I hope [will be] brigadier as soon as Anthony is
> [promoted].
>
> Adieu Richard
>
> You know how I love you and them and that I will do all in my
> power for them. [17]

However, Tyrconnel could not open the gates of Derry with kindly
correspondence. For troops behind the walls, news was considerably better.
Although artillery supply had been poor, they were able to place four light
guns at each gate, other guns on the bastions and further light guns within
the town itself to guard approaches should the Jacobite infantry get inside.
Rations, too, were quite generous at this stage, especially for fighting men,
although the thousands of non–combatants also trapped behind the walls
would soon take their toll on supplies.

Murray carried out smaller forays against the Jacobite lines, each
relatively successful, and thereby retained the initiative. Richard Hamilton,
left in sole command at Derry, having lost both his French advisors, was still
expecting heavier artillery from James. Hamilton had only been reacting to
the forays, rather than taking the initiative and attempting to assault the
town; it was time to take more decisive action. The expected siege guns
would need a firing position that could pour shot on the city, or attempt a
breach of the walls. Hamilton, surveying the surrounding terrain, settled on
Windmill Hill as the best high ground from which to get shots inside the
walls. On the night of 5 May Jacobite troops forced Murray's men, who had
been encamped there for some time, off the hill in a rapid attack. Within
hours, they were beginning to dig trenches and artillery positions in the
high ground, close to the walls. Murray and Baker, realising that such a
position afforded considerable advantage, knew that a rapid and effective
counter–attack was essential. [18]

The Irish, too, had their problems with the conditions, camped in the open
as they were. Disease and the effects of exposure, due to the Irish weather,
took their toll on the troops. Despite losses to the elements, Hamilton was
able to complete his blockade by sealing off the river at the start of June.
The Marquis de Pointis designed a heavy timber 'boom' joined with chains
yet buoyant enough to rise and fall with the river tides, to span the Foyle
waterway one–and–three–quarter miles north of Derry. This was preferred

to sinking shipping in the channel, blocking it, as this would, according to Hamilton, and upset Jacobite passage when Derry was taken.[19] With extra ordnance, Hamilton even had enough guns to set emplacements on each bank near the boom, to guard the approach. This did little to help him get behind the walls of the city. The position could have been strengthened still further by an additional boom, which Pointis began to construct. Hamilton stopped the work, convinced that English reinforcements would not use the approach.[20] It would be a fateful decision.

Richard Hamilton needed Windmill Hill if he was to have any chance of denting the town's defences; starvation would take longer than anticipated. On 4 June an attack was launched against the hill with over 5,000 men, including fifteen squadrons of cavalry. However, using co-ordinated musket volleys and firing by ranks, the garrison kept up a sustained hail of musketfire, enough to disrupt much of the advance. The remaining infantry was unable to stand in the face of rank after rank of massed musketfire and broke, leaving hundreds of their comrades dead. Hamilton was rapidly losing control.[21]

By 11 June another victory of sorts could be reported. Thirty English ships, a relief force led by Major General Percy Kirke, ex-governor of Tangiers and the scourge of the Monmouth rebels in 1685, had arrived in Lough Foyle with over 2,000 troops and, more importantly, supplies. However, there was little direct communication between the garrison and the fleet. Over the next few days, attempts to force the blockade and test the boom received a fiery reception from Hamilton's guns on the bank. His men, disheartened by the initial sightings of Kirke's relief force, were encouraged when inaction seemed the order of the day. Kirke had been ordered not to risk the fleet, and was taking the order seriously. Hours turned into days, with little activity as the garrison became unnerved. Attempts were made to send messengers from both directions. One messenger, who drowned and whose body was subsequently found by the Jacobites, had carried written word of the city's desperate predicament. Hamilton thus gained knowledge of the state of the garrison and, in their own words, news that they could only last out for a few more days.

Despite the fact that conditions had been exaggerated to move Kirke to action, matters were desperate enough inside the city. Hamilton knew that he had one last chance with the garrison; to offer terms in such desperate circumstances could be all that was required to open the gates, especially so in light of Kirke's inaction. Matters were taken out of Hamilton's hands once more, however. De Rosen arrived with orders from James to pursue matters more vigorously. In addition, Lord Clancarty nephew to Lord Mountcashel, (whom d'Avaux referred to as a 'young madcap') would be involved in an unsuccessful attack against Butcher's Gate, led by Lieutenant Colonel Skelton. Walker would note an Irish prophecy 'that a Clancarty should knock on the gates of Derry'. It was not to be, despite the best efforts of the Jacobite command. Two days later however, with the death of Governor Baker inside the walls, it must have seemed that the situation could not get much worse.

The unsubtle de Rosen believed that he could end the entire affair at a single stroke, announcing to Louvois that he would 'exterminate the rebels in the entire area'[22] and stating that he 'would demolish the town' and bury the people 'in its ashes'.[23] As Hamilton's latest peace offer was rejected, de Rosen took matters into his own hands and had thousands of Protestants from the surrounding area, man, woman and child, rounded up and paraded beneath the walls of Londonderry. Many had died on the way, but those who survived would be left to starve outside unless admitted by the garrison, an act which de Rosen was convinced would end the siege immediately. The garrison's reaction, by now surely predictable from those who had promised to 'eat' their Irish prisoners rather than starve, was to erect a gallows in plain view of the Jacobites, with the promise that those Irish troops who had been captured would be hanged unless those starving outside the walls were escorted home.[24]

They also wrote to Richard Hamilton asking that he intervene, sensing that he wanted no part of the affair. His reply was probably influenced by the presence of the French general, since, as the refugees had been driven through the Irish camp, Hamilton had arranged for them to be fed, in contradiction of de Rosen's orders.

> Gentlemen,
>   In answer to yours; What these poor people are like to suffer, they may thank themselves for, being their own fault; which they may prevent by accepting the conditions which have been offered them; and if you suffer in this it cannot be help'd but shall be reveng'd on many thousands of those People (as well innocent as others) within or without that City.
>   Yours, R.Hamilton.[25]

However, the pleas of Irish prisoners inside the walls were enough to convince de Rosen to back down.

By the end of June, with such drama occurring outside the walls, Kirke had at last decided to act, but not in the manner expected. Having received no message from the garrison, he sailed around the coast line, entering Lough Swilly. Anchoring off Rathmullan, he disembarked his troops straight into the area where the Jacobite army had been obtaining food and forage. Seeing the arrival, Berwick attempted to dislodge Kirke from his excellent strategic position, but to no avail. By 18 July Kirke was well ensconced in the area and set about fortifying the nearby island of Inch.[26]

James was incensed by de Rosen's action. There would be no repeat of it, although within a few weeks he would once more be communicating with Hamilton in apparent desperation, and rambling anxious fashion:

> Whereas we have through the whole course of our Reign endeavoured to reduce our subjects to their duty by clemency rather than force we are at this time resolved to give an additional instance thereof in regard to our subjects of the Protestant religion now in arms against us. We do therefore authorise and empower you to treat with our said subjects now in arms against us for the rendering up of our City of Londonderry into our hands or that of Inniskillen or any other town or castle of this our kingdom now in their possession upon such terms as you shall think fit for our service which shall be ratified by Us without exception whatever they may be, notwithstanding of any crime fault or treason committed by any of the said persons or their adherents, and notwithstanding of any law or act of parliament made or to be made for all whom we promise hereby to protect and free them in all times .... [27]

James's message regarding the citizens of Londonderry was more earnest now; again to Hamilton:

> You shall let them know that if they do not now yield to such propositions as you shall offer to them we will hereafter exclude them from ever partaking of our Royal mercy. You are to endeavour to give them as little as possibly can be, but rather than not get the town delivered to Us you shall give them their lives, fortunes, our Royal pardon for all that's past and protection as others our subjects have in time to come...[28]

By 12 July (o.s.), under increasing pressure, James was keen to have the matter over and done with, even with the help of de Rosen. To Hamilton again:

The long continuance of the siege of Derry has been of so ill consequence to our affairs that though we believe that you thought best for our service, yet we do think fit hereby to will and require you that if the City of Londonderry shall not yield on the conditions we have offered you may in your station be assisting to the Marquis de Rozen in the pressing of it with all the vigour imaginable that no time may be lost in bringing it into our power...[29]

With the apparent withdrawal of the English fleet, many of the besieged citizens of Londonderry must have felt that all was lost. With all the desperate attempts to reach Kirke, courageous yet ultimately futile, the future seemed bleak. Against the odds, however, a resourceful small boy eventually reached the fleet from the garrison; he would be made an ensign for his work. At last the English relief force was aware fully of how desperate matters had become inside the city. The proximity of the fleet, despite its lack of action so far, had convinced James to push forward with negotiation. He urged Hamilton to offer generous and beneficial terms to the people, terms that would be difficult to decline. The garrison, eventually aware that word had reached Kirke, could now afford to bide their time, and thus waste Hamilton's, by asking for terms which simply could not be granted. This was a dangerous game, with very high stakes. Five thousand starving combatants lay behind Derry's walls, with a hundred people collapsing or dying each week.

However, Kirke's delay had done more than leave the garrison with new-found despair. It had ruffled feathers in London. General Schomberg, the ex-French marshal who had joined William after Louis's persecution of his Huguenot religion, and who would lead the expedition to Ireland, urged Kirke to action. He was immediately ordered to break the boom and relieve Londonderry. Kirke returned to Lough Foyle and prepared for the assault. By 30 July the relief fleet was ready. Captain Micaiah Browning, originally from the city, and captain of the *Mountjoy*, would attempt to break the boom accompanied by an escort ship and the *Phoenix*, following with provisions for the shattered garrison. On the evening of the 30th, the tide remained out, leaving the bank, close to Jacobite guns, as the only passable route along the river.

The escort's guns fired at those Jacobite positions that threatened action as *Mountjoy* crashed against the barricade. Irish battle-cries rang out from the nearby shore as they saw Browning's ship run aground, stuck, and open to attack. The ship's guns however, were still primed and ready to fire, as were those of the escort. The firing of the guns, at such close range, convinced

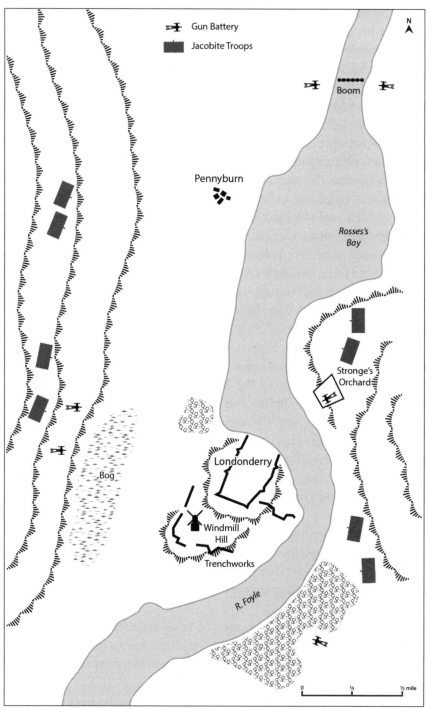

Hamilton's siege positions, 1689.

the advancing Jacobite troops to break. The recoil from firing also righted *Mountjoy* which floated once more. However, Captain Browning had been killed by musket fire. The boom was ultimately broken by men from HMS *Swallow*, who attacked with axes from a longboat. The broken boom and subsequent action had allowed supply ships to get past the barrier and on upriver to Londonderry, reaching the quay by around ten in the evening. On a European scale, it was hardly a momentous event; however, it had not been a conventional siege, with an expectation of victory. In Ireland, however, the day would see an important turning point in the war.

The following day saw the Jacobite army begin withdrawing towards Strabane and Coleraine, exhausted, and destroying much of the provisions and forage that could be used by Kirke's forces.[30] Hamilton had lost perhaps 8,000 men and gained nothing. The circumstances surrounding the army, the protracted siege and indeed the ineffective command of the Jacobites surrounding Derry, saw him take much of the blame for the fiasco. In the city, effective fighting strength had been halved and estimates put civilian dead in the thousands. Hamilton would have reason to regret the entire affair.

There had been severe logistical problems. In many respects these were out of Hamilton's control since it was the French, responsible for getting much of the ammunition to the Jacobite army, who had failed early on through the delay of supplies and Seignelay had been reticent in terms of committing naval ships.[31] However, d'Avaux had doubts over Hamilton from the beginning. His close communication with Louvois, who still disliked Richard, could not have helped matters.[32] The French ambassador had been against Hamilton for most of the siege, even at one stage hinting at his disloyalty on the basis of his incompetence.[33] Louvois was keen to see Hamilton salvage as little as possible from the situation, and preferred rapid departure from the city when news of pending invasion became more pertinent, on the basis that the besieging troops would be required elsewhere. Matters at Londonderry were finished, as, perhaps, was Hamilton's career.[34]

The most savage detractors were the Jacobites themselves:

> And so it was in the present case; for, besides the neglect committed by the Irish Catholic managers of the king's war in Ireland, and by others who had a hand therein, vice reigned amongst them at that very juncture.
>
> However, in the meantime we must promote the beginning of this unlucky war, which is the ridiculous siege of Londonderry.[35]

The siege, as had been predicted, would make or break Hamilton's fortunes in Ireland. As years passed, the garrison's victorious stand would be hailed as the final victory and defining moment of William's Glorious Revolution. There was no question that it had helped reduce Jacobite effectiveness in Ulster as James's dominance in Ireland began slipping still further from his grasp. Londonderry, however, would not see the only reversal of Jacobite fortunes in the summer of 1689. Anthony Hamilton, fighting with Lord Mountcashel to deter the actions of the Enniskillen garrison, had his own difficulties to contend with.

# Chapter 11

# Enniskillen

At Enniskillen events unfolded somewhat differently. There was no protracted siege. The population also saw more active forays against the Jacobite forces when compared with the besieged defenders farther north. The Jacobites' failure to act proved decisive, and a cohesive plan to deal with the Enniskillen troops, the 'Inniskillingers' as they became known, and their cavalry raids would not be formulated for some months. The Inniskillingers became bolder, strengthening the town's and the surrounding area's defences, equipping themselves and raiding Jacobite positions. Londonderry was strategically important since it was a major port and James's goal of returning to the English throne via seaborne invasion of Scotland was still very much in his thoughts, despite the odds against its success. However, the concentration on Londonderry resulted in the tying up of resources which would find the Jacobite forces wanting, and unable to respond cohesively to the threat from Enniskillen where early action might have thwarted all opposition, changing the course of the war. Lord Mountcashel, whose fate was entwined with the activities of the Inniskillingers, was by now an essential part of the new Irish ascendancy, both in military and political terms. Impending events would see the first real battle of the war and stunning examples of how the Jacobite strategy could be un-coordinated and ineffective despite the presence of good, and even exceptional, commanders such as Mountcashel.

In December 1688 a letter from Tyrconnel had been intercepted by the provost of Enniskillen detailing the requirement for quarters for two companies of foot, loyal to James, within the town. At the same time, rumours of an impending massacre of Protestants had spread, a common theme throughout the source material. Of course, with armed bands of Jacobites being raised across the country, led by soldiers loyal to Tyrconnel, a certain amount of concern is not surprising. The slow erosion of Protestant authority in the army and public office must also be considered. The effect of the order was to reinforce resistance within Enniskillen and the surrounding area.[1]

Unlike Londonderry, Enniskillen's only fortification was its castle, built by the Maguires in the sixteenth century, and the town had no walls to speak of. The resulting actions of the garrison were forced upon them to a large extent. Cavalry raiding and support of outlying towns in the region was required to prevent the Jacobites from forming organised forces that could take Enniskillen. The holding and fortification of Ballyshannon, for instance, held open a supply route on the Donegal coast. By the start of 1689 victory was by no means assured, although Jacobite forces in the area were poorly led and lacked cohesion.

Led by Gustavus Hamilton, the new governor of Enniskillen who was part Swede, and Thomas Lloyd, the town began preparing for war. Lloyd would become an excellent leader in the months to come and carve out his reputation as a cavalry raider. Ironically, Hamilton and Lloyd had been sacked from the Irish army during the purges; both had experience and were able to train and lead the Enniskillen populace. There were few firearms to

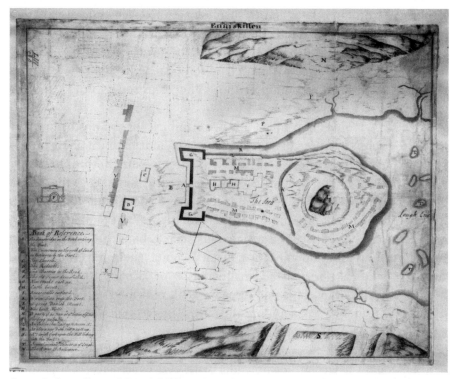

A period outline of Enniskillen, the island town, and MacCarthy's ultimate objective in Ulster. The topography shows just how difficult a siege would have been. (*The British Library*)

speak of but increased efforts were made to fortify the town against attack and siege. By the start of 1689 Enniskillen was also becoming the focus for assembling Protestants in the surrounding area and word was sent to England requesting arms, ammunition and money. Fortification continued into February 1689, while Mountcashel was engaged with subduing resistance in Munster. Lieutenant Colonel Lundy was placed in charge of newly-formed Protestant regiments by virtue of the general council held at Hillsborough. His first act was to request the Enniskillen garrison to join him at Derry, a request which Gustavus Hamilton politely refused. March saw an influx of frightened Protestants into the town as Lundy ordered the evacuation of Cavan due to the presence of Lord Galmoy and a large part of the Irish Army.

Piers Butler, Lord Galmoy of Kilkenny, advanced to Belturbet, twenty miles from Enniskillen. He laid ineffectual siege to Crom Castle, which commanded Lough Erne and was an important base of operations for actions against Enniskillen. Then, by late March, he issued a letter to Gustavus Hamilton asking him to surrender Enniskillen and advising that James had arrived in Ireland. Better conditions, and thus quarter, would be available now rather than later, should the town have to be taken by force. The offer was rejected, and Hamilton instead helped relieve Crom. Galmoy's subsequent execution of Inniskillinger prisoners would do little to endear him to the populace.

By now Tyrconnel controlled all of Ireland except the north. In other parts Protestants had been disarmed and a Catholic army and administration was in control. James had landed and made his entry into Dublin and Richard Hamilton had routed the north-eastern Protestants at the 'Break of Dromore', causing Lord Mount-Alexander to flee. Enniskillen's allies were becoming fewer, prompting the garrison to carry out raiding activities, led by Lloyd, on local Jacobite strongholds such as Omagh and Augher.[2] In April he set out again upon hearing that a Jacobite garrison had re-entered Augher castle. He pursued the small garrison of Jacobite troops through Monaghan and Cavan, cattle raiding as he went, returning to Enniskillen by the end of the month. Such raiding and attacks on Jacobite strongholds were typical of the kind of war being waged.[3]

By May, however, the garrison would face its first real test. So far they had not fought a Jacobite commander with real experience. They would now do battle with Patrick Sarsfield, a man who had fought under George Hamilton and Justin MacCarthy in France. At the start of May, word from

Ballyshannon warned of Sarsfield's approach. Lloyd set out with twelve companies of foot and some horse. [4]

Sarsfield knew that Ballyshannon had refused to surrender because it could expect help from the larger force at Enniskillen. Castle Caldwell also held 400 troops and was only nine miles away. Between the two lay Belleek, and Sarsfield was obliged to split his force, drawing the larger part of it to the town. There, almost completely surrounded by bogland and water, his Jacobite troops held a well-defended rampart, leaving only a narrow causeway through the bog for means of access. Lloyd was preparing to undertake the dangerous task of attack over the swampy ground, when a local informed his scouts of a safe route. He immediately sent his men across that safe passage, out of musket range, and much to the dismay of Sarsfield's men. An orderly retreat turned into a rout as the Jacobites fled. Sarsfield withdrew to Sligo, having lost almost 200 killed and wounded, with sixty men taken prisoner.

Later in the month, amid reports that the Irish had garrisoned Redhill and Ballynacarrig in County Cavan, Lloyd set out with 1,500 men. News of his approach, together with exaggerated rumours of his numbers, convinced both garrisons to flee or surrender. Rumours of the size of Lloyd's force put their number at 15,000 and capable of threatening James at Dublin. In reality his men formed a raiding party and he returned to Enniskillen with firearms and herds of cows and flocks of sheep. Sarsfield would prove to be less honourable than he had at first appeared, rounding up Connaught Protestants and jailing them in Sligo, sending their wives to Enniskillen, to plead for mercy. Gustavus Hamilton relented and released some of his Jacobite prisoners, but the episode did nothing to endear their cause to the Inniskillingers. The situation was improving, however, and the garrison's holding action would reap benefits. Kirke had already disembarked reinforcements and supplies for Londonderry and Enniskillen. However, the situation was far from safe, and waterways had to be kept open to permit such valuable resources to reach the town.

In June Lloyd's troops stole Jacobite cavalry horses, and Enniskillen even contemplated sending relief to Londonderry where mobile cavalry raiders could have a distinct effect on Jacobite moves in the countryside, although the Enniskillen garrison still had little powder and too few firearms for any kind of undertaking against Richard Hamilton's main body on the Foyle. Recognising the importance of the continued siege, however (since without it, all eyes would be turned to Enniskillen), the town felt compelled to do something, hoping to supply Londonderry with much of the sheep and cattle that had been taken and thus avoid further starvation. The expedition that set out on this venture got as far as Omagh before news of Jacobite incursions near Enniskillen persuaded the men to return.

Lloyd was ordered to march against Sutherland at Belturbet with as many troops as he could spare. By the 17th he had reached Maguiresbridge, halfway between Enniskillen and Belturbet. Irish pickets advised Sutherland of the advance, his force consisting of two regiments of foot, one of dragoons and some troops of horse. He also had some artillery, and additional arms and powder with which to equip new recruits. A subsequent skirmish in Belturbet reminded all sides of the increasing urgency of the situation.

The threat from the south had been averted for the time being. By July Enniskillen was in its strongest position since the start of the war, and one of the Navy's ships that had left in May, with supplies and English troops, had reached Ballyshannon. News reached Enniskillen and the officers aboard sought news of the town's condition and its requirement for supplies. The biggest problem was lack of powder and so a party of horse and foot, led by Lloyd, was sent to meet Captain Hobson aboard the *Bonadventure*. On 5 July (o.s.), the Enniskillen representatives boarded the ship, acquainting the English captain with the town's condition. The party received thirty barrels of powder and some muskets. Men would be sent on to Kirke near Londonderry for supplies. Kirke could not supply men but he could provide experienced officers: Colonel William Wolseley was made commander in chief and colonel of horse, while Captain William Berry, who had served in Tangiers with Kirke, was made lieutenant colonel of horse. Additional officers were put in place to lead battalions. These were very capable English soldiers and commissions were also granted for existing Enniskillen officers.[5]

Had the Jacobites at last formulated a strategy around the Enniskillen problem? Jacobite forces were converging on the town for the first time. While the Enniskillen party were at Ballyshannon, scouts warned the town of the approach of forces under the Duke of Berwick. MacCarmick was ordered to defend the straight pass at Enniskillen Mill, through which Berwick's force would have to approach, with two companies of foot and two of horse. Berwick's subsequent victory in the skirmish at Cornegrade castle was indicative of what well-led Jacobite troops could still accomplish.

Was there, however, a Jacobite strategy to address any potential weakness amongst the Enniskillen garrison? The siege of Derry had been immensely important to the Jacobite cause and not simply because of its strategic importance as a port. After the events of April 1689 it was important for

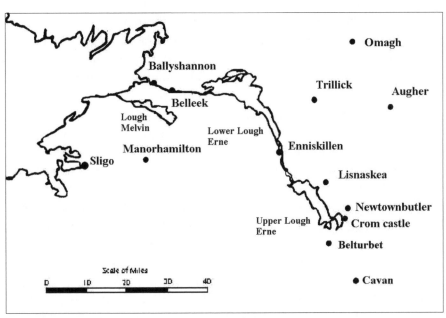

Enniskillen and the surrounding area, the focus of Mountcashel's Enniskillen campaign in 1689.

James to reduce all centres of Protestant resistance, especially in Ulster. William prepared his invasion force in England and thus the blockade and siege of Derry meant that the strategic importance, to Enniskillen at least, of towns such as Ballyshannon and Belleek, near the inlet to Lough Erne, became paramount. The Jacobites also realised this, hence Sarsfield's early action in the area, indicative of a concern with the potential for re-supply and reinforcement from the mainland. It is arguable, however, that even where the will was present amongst seasoned Jacobite officers, the quantity, organisation and quality of the troops was lacking. This situation was exacerbated by the success of Inniskillinger raids and the resultant demoralising effect on inexperienced Jacobite troops, who seemed relatively powerless in Ulster as a whole, most of their strength still bogged down in the north. In real terms, Enniskillen would prove a greater thorn in James's side than Londonderry. This would not become obvious until June 1689, however, by which time it was too late to divert sufficient forces to capture the town. It may have been easier in retrospect to take a town without a defensive wall, whose troops had barely enough powder and matchlocks to fight a pitched battle prior to July 1689.

Although considered very much a secondary objective even by May and June, the matter of Enniskillen was at least discussed; indeed, it was hoped that around 8,000 men could be sent to take the town. As with many of the confused Jacobite strategies, however, the protracted siege and a general crisis with logistics proved decisive. Potential threats from Enniskillen, especially with English officers, supplies and ammunition having been landed by Kirke, were becoming more likely. Jacobite fears over the Inniskillinger counter-thrust toward Londonderry became very real.

By mid-July the matter was discussed openly in the Dublin parliament. Plans were formed for a three-pronged assault: Berwick from the north, positioned between Derry and Enniskillen, Sarsfield from the west and Mountcashel from the south, the three creating a stranglehold around the town. Berwick, frustrated from lack of activity with Richard Hamilton at Derry, even requested additional troops to allow him to move on Enniskillen, receiving two regiments of horse, some dragoons and four battalions of infantry – 3,000–4,000 men in all. Elements of this force appear to have been present at the Cornagrade skirmish, although they remained well away from Enniskillen after that. By July of 1689 Galmoy had joined Anthony Hamilton and Mountcashel in Belturbet, just south of Enniskillen. Maguire also joined this force with some troops from Ulster. Some records speak of a 7,000-strong force, although this number seems high.[6] Anthony Hamilton had been promoted once more, this time to the rank of major general, and commanded part of Mountcashel's force.[7]

The plan to use three small armies, each effectively a combined arms 'taskforce', must have seemed simple in principle, yet, under the conditions, implementation proved impossible. Berwick, seemingly ignoring the plan for the most part, requested that Sarsfield should ensure that English shipping not enter Lough Erne by attacking Ballyshannon again; Berwick would attempt to join him at a later stage. Sarsfield camped near Lough Melvin, five miles from Ballyshannon. Despite his earlier moves against Enniskillen, Berwick was recalled to intensify the blockade against English shipping that had been sighted near Lough Swilly. The link-up never took place.

Sarsfield, with characteristic optimism, urged Mountcashel to move north from Cavan and attempt a link-up with Berwick upon his return. It must have been obvious to both Mountcashel and Anthony Hamilton, however, that the plan was beginning to fall apart. Despite any reservations that the two might have had, orders from James indicated that they should advance on Enniskillen without support from Berwick or Sarsfield. James had considered going to Enniskillen himself but had been dissuaded by d'Avaux, memories of the debacle at Derry in April probably still fresh in his mind.[8] Had Berwick's troops at least been available, subsequent events might have been different; Mountcashel and Anthony Hamilton determined to follow James's order alone and take on the Enniskillen garrison. There would be no attempt to link up with Sarsfield; Enniskillen had held out for long enough and Mountcashel would force them to battle.

At Londonderry events were moving quickly. Kirke's arrival had encouraged the demoralised Protestants. De Rosen now feared a pincer movement with Kirke to the north and the Inniskillingers in the south. Sarsfield moved his force closer to Ballyshannon again, with over 3,000 men. Despite further Enniskillen probes, he remained strong, and the Inniskillingers would not risk facing him while leaving their town unprotected. The defensive situation was becoming critical. By 28 July the new officers had arrived at Enniskillen. The arms and ammunition were to follow soon afterwards.

Logistical difficulties and a lack of equipment, problems that appeared to bedevil the Jacobite cause most of the time, prevented Mountcashel and Hamilton assembling an effective force until 27 July (o.s.); it also proves interesting to speculate on the numbers involved. Enniskillen sources number the Jacobite force at 6,000 by this stage, while at least one Jacobite reference puts their number at 4,000, a 'flying camp' of horse and foot.[9] D'Avaux, in a concise description of the subsequent battle, described Mountcashel's force being composed of three battalions of infantry and sixteen troops of horse and dragoons, together with four small-calibre guns. A sizeable force, although unless supplemented by considerable numbers of untrained levies, it would consist of 3,000–4,000 men, and certainly not 6,000.[10]

The Inniskillingers, on the other hand, had been gaining experience and a degree of daring based on the desperate nature of their situation. Whether the Jacobites could have seriously threatened Enniskillen without following a clearly defined strategy is arguable, although where the garrison of the town was concerned, the perceived threat of the Jacobite army was more than enough. Many of the experienced Enniskillen militia had been troops sacked in Tyrconnel's purges, and they had knowledge of the local area as well as a cause to fight for. Both Gustavus Hamilton and Thomas Lloyd had been soldiers; the majority of armourers in Ireland were Protestants, and the purges had changed little in this respect.[11]

As the 1689 campaign had dragged on, the Inniskillingers became steadily bolder and better equipped, both through raiding and re-supply. In comparison, the Jacobite forces were, for the most part, inexperienced, had only a small professional officer corps, and logistics and supply were frequently found wanting. Many troops had neither pike nor musket, relying on the Irish *skein*, or half-pike.[12] The situation changed little during 1689. Indeed, French supply was limited and Tyrconnel's attempts to reduce the numbers of troops in the army, and thus spread equipment more evenly, did little to reverse the trend.[13] Neither side, composed as they were for the most part of indigenous inhabitants, had the experience or, indeed, competent officers, to fight in the manner of their European cousins, apart from those notable exceptions such as the Hamiltons, Lloyd, MacCarthy and Sarsfield. There were still stark differences between the capability and experience of the two sides. The question would rather be one of command, leadership and the morale of irregular troops.

On the night of the 28th Enniskillen received an urgent message from Crom Castle. For the second time in the year it was under siege. Mountcashel had arrived from Belturbet and Enniskillen faced enemies on two sides. The battle to follow would determine the fate of the town.[14] James had ordered Mountcashel to take Crom Castle prior to an assault on Enniskillen itself. Sixteen miles from Enniskillen, the castle had already withstood Galmoy's siege earlier in the year, and assault would prove difficult as the position was covered on two sides by the waters of Lough Erne. Taking Crom could remove its focus as a rallying point for

Enniskillen reinforcements, however. It was a fortified position in the very heart of Mountcashel's advance. It was vulnerable to artillery fire from the opposite bank, although guns could not carry the position for the Jacobites as Mountcashel's guns were small-calibre weapons. Only a direct assault would take the castle.

Mountcashel took up positions east of the castle upon Ardandillure Hill, within half a mile of the position.[15] The garrison had placed two forward 'encampments' in front of the castle, to impede any general assault, although the earthworks had been hastily assembled and would be of little use against protracted attacks.[16] Knowing the terrain well, it is likely that the works had been constructed when scouts or pickets had picked up the intent of Mountcashel's movements. Indeed, outmanoeuvre and knowledge of Jacobite movements underpins most of the events that follow, the Inniskillingers knowing the countryside and the most likely routes of advance. This is understandable; the garrisons were mostly composed of locals who not only knew the area exceptionally well, but also would stay one step ahead of Mountcashel and Anthony Hamilton in terms of intelligence.

Upon observing the approach of Jacobite troops, Abraham Creighton, the garrison commander at Crom, had sent word to Enniskillen. This arrived in the town on the night of the 28th (o.s.), informing the garrison that Mountcashel had arrived from Belturbet and had artillery. William Wolseley made preparations to move, having been in command for less than a week.

On the same day, Mountcashel's and Clare's Regiments attacked the position at Crom Castle. The fortified positions in front were taken relatively quickly and preparations were made to assault the castle. Mountcashel had ordered his own regiment to reform whilst Bophin's Regiment prepared for an attack on the right. Mountcashel's troops, however, ignored the order to reform and charged on toward the fort, exhibiting their somewhat impetuous nature. The charge was unsuccessful as expected, the regiment being forced to take cover around the castle walls before having to withdraw under cover of artillery fire. By Monday the 29th, Mountcashel had withdrawn to Newtownbutler in apparent anticipation of an Inniskillinger attack, a fact that gives credence to the belief that Crom had either been a feint designed to draw out the Inniskillingers or, alternatively, designed to discover its relative strength. Two armies now advanced towards one another and the battle that would decide Enniskillen's fate.

The rolling and boggy terrain at Newtownbutler favoured the defender. It is also clear that Mountcashel endeavoured to prevent becoming outflanked using mounted troops to determine the nature of his enemy's advance. To this end, he despatched Anthony Hamilton with a significant force of dragoons on a mission to scout, gain intelligence and, if necessary, intercept those scouting elements of Wolseley's force. According to the Enniskillen sources, Wolseley, aware of Jacobite movements, despatched his own troops to meet the Jacobites.[17] For Anthony Hamilton, the week that saw the end of the siege at Derry for his brother Richard would bear witness to another military drama. Although the besiegers were about to pull back even as far as Dublin, in a thoroughly dispirited and exhausted state, a victory near Enniskillen was essential to bolster Jacobite morale and make headway in Ulster; it could change everything.[18]

Mountcashel had withdrawn the main body of Jacobite troops to Newtownbutler, where the terrain favoured static defence and where, theoretically, he would have time to design a deception plan, to pull the Enniskillen force into a prepared ambush. He ordered Hamilton north-west to Lisnaskea with a force of thirteen troops of dragoons, around 500 men.[19] Hamilton most likely set out on Tuesday the 30th, ordered by Mountcashel to occupy a position where he could ambush the scouting elements of Wolseley's force. Writing of the events afterwards, d'Avaux commented to Louvois:

> As Mylord Monkassel after having withdrawn from Crom, wanted to protect himself from those coming from Enniskillen, he said to Antoine Hamilton to go with 13 dragoons companies to chase a group that was appearing, and then to occupy a position where 100 men could stop 10,000.[20]

Mountcashel could have sent scouts forward to reconnoitre the area; indeed d'Avaux implies that he was aware of movements from Enniskillen. There was no shortage of suitable ambush sites in the wild countryside, especially amongst the narrow passes around the nearby Colebrooke river. In a similar vein to the plans made by the Jacobite force, Colonel Wolseley had ordered Berry to make for Lisnaskea with eight troops of horse, three companies of foot and two of dragoons. His orders were to garrison or destroy the castle at Lisnaskea, depending on the proximity of Jacobite troops. Berry was also to determine the size of the enemy force, if possible. Wolseley, perhaps concerned over the apparent Jacobite intent to take local fortifications as the basis of future reinforcement, to gain strength or prepare for a larger more co-ordinated attack, would not allow Fermanagh castles to fall into Jacobite hands. He could not permit a stranglehold to be created around Enniskillen.

To this end, he further assured Berry that reinforcements would be rushed to his aid as he required. Berry and Anthony Hamilton, with similar orders, set out on their respective reconnaissance expeditions.[21] By the evening of the 30th, Berry had moved south-east. His mounted troops scouted ahead of the main body, with orders not to engage enemy troops if spotted, but to retreat to more favourable ground and set up an ambush if possible. He arrived at Lisnaskea the same day and found it deserted. He also discovered that the castle was in a considerable state of disrepair, possibly due to Galmoy's sacking of the area earlier in the year. He endeavoured to press on and find the Jacobite force the following day, the men camping in the surrounding fields that night. Similarities between Hamilton's and Berry's orders are striking. It should be borne in mind, however, that despite some evidence as to Inniskillinger advantages in local knowledge and intelligence of enemy movements, the nature of seventeenth-century warfare, exacerbated by the relatively small numbers involved, meant that even finding the enemy became difficult. Berry and Hamilton would play a game of move and counter-move until an ambush site could be found.

On the morning of the 31st Berry's scouts moved along the old Donagh road, his main body of troops following close behind. Anthony Hamilton had also moved his dragoons along the road to Donagh towards Berry, and was just six miles from the Enniskillen force. As Berry's scouts moved two miles closer to the village, they encountered the forward elements of Hamilton's troops. The men reported a large force of Jacobite dragoons, foot and horse rapidly moving on their position. Berry, not wishing to be caught on the open road, where he could not deploy, nor being sure of the size of the enemy element, retreated towards Lisnaskea. As he moved, he was able to size up Hamilton's force from high ground. He continued to pull back, seeking a more easily defended position, and avoiding a dangerous fight in the open. Hamilton pushed hard, aided by the fact that his men were all mounted, possibly with dragoons on foot, and could pursue rapidly. Berry must have been hampered to a significant degree by the large force of infantry that he had. He could not retreat at will, and must also have been forced to use his mounted elements to fight rearguard actions with Hamilton's dragoons, thus preventing the retreat becoming a rout.

As he moved, Berry sent word to Wolseley in Enniskillen, informing him that he had encountered Jacobite forward elements and needed help. If he could find a solid defensive position or ambush site, he could at least turn the situation to his advantage temporarily. Berry also must have been aware that, although not regular or professional troops, the Inniskillingers knew the lay of the land and were fierce fighters in the right situation. With rapidly moving Jacobites attacking his rear, he had to do something before his men were routed.

Anthony Hamilton followed Berry's retreat closely, placing his rearguard under increasing pressure with fast-moving dragoons, who by now must have sensed victory. Hamilton could not push too hard, however. The threat of Berry's rallying and counter-attacking was all too clear. D'Avaux recorded that Hamilton pushed on for five miles, well out of contact with any elements remaining with Mountcashel, and farther into unknown territory. Whether Berry had retreated in the hope of isolating Hamilton or had believed his force to be much larger is not known. Berry, undoubtedly aided by the advice of his Enniskillen troops, passed once more through Lisnaskea. It was now around nine in the morning.[22] Heading for Enniskillen, Berry had the choice of taking the old or new road. Choosing the newer road, and undoubtedly with the benefit of local knowledge with regard to the availability of ambush sites for the retreating force, he continued to move past the town. Anthony Hamilton, becoming more isolated, continued to follow.

Berry continued through Lisnaskea and moved out of the town for approximately a mile, across a small river to a pass where surrounding bogland turned the road into a narrow causeway, a feature of much of the surrounding bog in County Fermanagh, and a position which could only be approached via the now open road, where an attacker or pursuer would be fully exposed. Berry and his Enniskillen officers immediately took advantage of the position. The troops were deployed along the flanks and at the end of the causeway, where he hoped that he could set up a defensive position until relieved by Wolseley. The approach road to his position was the only passage that avoided bogland and even a flanking move on the part of Hamilton would take far too much time. Berry's troops were for the most part secure.

As Anthony Hamilton's dragoons emerged close to the river, they were met with a hail of musket balls. Immediately recognising the danger, Hamilton knew that to retreat would mean an Inniskillinger charge. To show fear in front of his men, who had moved so far unsupported, would probably encourage a rout. Hamilton also knew that to charge along the unprotected road would be deadly, as all enemy muskets were trained on that spot. Even with the rudimentary restrictions on reloading that bedevilled the matchlock, there were numerous muskets, and volley fire would have been used to heighten the effect of the ambush. Whether to show that bravely moving forward was the only option, or because the horses were beginning to break through fear, Hamilton dismounted and began to move forward with a party of dragoons along the causeway, his men firing as they advanced. The Inniskillingers returned fire, killing several dragoons and wounding Hamilton in the leg; the flank ambush also fired, causing further casualties. Hamilton's efforts had been in vain and he pulled back, sending another officer in his place, who was subsequently shot and killed. Moving forward into the musket fire became increasingly deadly as the advantages of the ambush position became startlingly apparent.[23]

The events that followed seem extraordinary, even under the difficult circumstances, and subtly demonstrate the desperate nature of communication, cohesion and confusion on the seventeenth-century battlefield or, indeed, all battlefields of the horse-and-musket era. Four primary sources recount this action; two are Enniskillen sources, with one Jacobite and one French, d'Avaux, who was mostly scathing about Hamilton's conduct:

> [Hamilton] went on marching until he met 2 battalions of the enemy, well ensconced, and some cavalry to the right and to the left, then he had a group of his dragoons go on foot to attack the rebels who were stronger than he, but on the first fire, all his people escaped and ran pursued by the enemy as far as Mylord Monkassel's camp.[24]

One Enniskillen source recorded:

> [Hamilton] being hurt retreated a little, and mounted his horse, ordering another officer to lead on the men, who very soon was likewise killed, with some more of their men. The enemy seeing their men thus drop by our shot, and their general, Colonel Hamilton, being gone a little way back, and no chief officer there to lead them on, began to retreat from the end of the causeway, which our men seeing, gave a huzza, and called out that the rogues were running.[25]

Both sources give fairly straightforward accounts. Other accounts are more specific regarding the actual detail of the Jacobite rout, an event which, it appears, may have been triggered by more than the Inniskillingers' ambush. The *Jacobite Narrative* recorded:

> But after a short dispute, brigadier Hamilton sent the word by captain Lavallin to his men to wheel to the left, as if it were to

rejoin Mountcashel. Lavallin delivered it 'to the left about,' as he thought it was, though Hamilton maintained it afterwards that it was as aforesaid; whereupon the men marched off the field and flew away as did the brigadier.[26]

This account questions the nature of the rout. Was it occasioned by the misinterpretation of Hamilton's order? Had Hamilton actually given the order as Lavallin interpreted it or, indeed, would the order have mattered in the end? Hamilton's dragoons suffered many casualties in the initial exchanges and, aware of their exposed position, were perhaps keen to break. Of course, this is supposition, although the matter is made all the more interesting by MacCarmick's account. He was an Inniskillinger who was at the battle:

> Hamilton being wounded, went off, sending another officer to command the Dragoons; but Capt. Cathcart plied them so warmly with his Shot, that Officer being killed, the Dragoons were commanded to face to the Right-about, to draw them further out of our Shot: But as soon as they faced, they ran for it … .[27]

Some interesting points are raised with the addition of MacCarmick's account, and his belief that the Jacobites were ordered to face to the 'right about'. Firstly his right would have been Hamilton's left. Additionally, there is no account of 'wheeling' in this instance. Whether Hamilton panicked and issued the order to withdraw, contriving a different story after the fact, cannot be proven. It seems likely that, in the midst of a deadly ambush, receiving fire from front and flank and having just been wounded, any commander would have ordered a withdrawal. There was little option. However, a court martial would decide the matter at a later date.

With the withdrawal of his troops from the fray, the Inniskillingers seized the opportunity that they had been waiting for and their cavalry charged along the causeway to break the fleeing Jacobites. The impetus of the charge caught many still dismounted dragoons off guard and many more were killed. Those who were mounted or had time to find a horse escaped for the most part, although the pursuit by Berry's cavalry was relentless. MacCarmick described the chase lasting for three miles, 'all which way the road was filled with their dead bodies'. The chasing cavalry passed through Lisnaskea and beyond and were only halted when Berry's scouts reported that part of Mountcashel's main force had been spotted moving towards him. Berry had killed or wounded around 200 of Hamilton's men and captured thirty prisoners, who were quickly sent back to Enniskillen. D'Avaux was quite clear on the repercussions of Hamilton's actions, believing that the success of the Enniskillen force at Lisnaskea prompted them to attack Mountcashel that same day.

Hamilton's relentless and unsupported pursuit had proved to be his undoing, despite his escape. Indeed, the misinterpretation of the order at the causeway becomes less significant when it is considered that his men had little possibility of taking the Inniskillinger position. Hamilton's wound was not serious, as he seemed able to rejoin Mountcashel later and there is no further mention of its effects. The skirmish had illustrated two points: the Inniskillingers could use the terrain to their advantage and the nature of the bogland and its approaches could restrict severely the movement of mounted troops. Both factors would affect the larger battle to follow.

The Lisnaskea skirmish had occurred at around nine on the morning of 31 July (o.s.). By eleven o'clock, Berry still held the pass beyond Lisnaskea at which he had fought Hamilton. He then received word from Wolseley, who had marched along the old road from Enniskillen upon hearing of the action. The two met north of Lisnaskea; Wolseley and the Enniskillen troops had moved so quickly, however, that they had only eaten before leaving the town and lacked adequate provision for a protracted engagement. Wolseley's men were made up of militia and volunteers; unsupplied and isolated, he risked putting himself in a dangerous position. Electing with his officers to let the men make the decision to go on or not, he received emphatic agreement that the Jacobites under MacCarthy should be pursued and attacked.[28]

Of course, such a decision was naturally affected by Berry's success that morning, but it should also be remembered that any attempt at preventing Mountcashel from re-grouping and gaining reinforcements, must have been prevalent in the minds of many of the men. If Mountcashel were allowed to stay in County Fermanagh unchecked, he could combine later with Sarsfield or Berwick and threaten Enniskillen. Better then to strike quickly and decisively. Wolseley had little idea of the capabilities or otherwise of his own troops, although they had proven their worth at Lisnaskea. A battle against Mountcashel and Hamilton, if unsuccessful, could have severe repercussions for Enniskillen. He took four men from each cavalry and dragoon troop and thus formed a scouting party that would reconnoitre the road half-a-mile ahead as the column advanced. The force now consisted of sixteen horse troops, three troops of dragoons and twenty-one companies of foot, around

2,000 men. The organisation highlighted the need for combining both foot and mounted elements in the respective commands, as shown by Hamilton's pursuit of Berry, where foot elements could become endangered on the road, whilst mounted troops were sometimes restricted in their movements by bogland, the terrain defining the composition of the taskforce. Tiffin's battalion of foot was supported with dragoons, as was Lloyd's (now Colonel Lloyd). Wolseley's foot in the main body had eleven infantry companies, supported by sixteen troops of cavalry.

The officers were briefed to the extent that should Mountcashel be encountered in force Lloyd would take the left flank, Tiffin the right and Wolseley would command the main body in the centre – in reserve if subsequent attacks were required. The horse would take the flanks while the dragoons would afford closer protection to the infantry.[29] Mountcashel, having been made aware of Hamilton's defeat at Lisnaskea, knew that a larger battle would be unavoidable. Aware that an Inniskillinger advance was underway, he had the advantage in that he could choose his ground, a decision made all the easier by the undulating nature of the countryside. Therefore, he could set ambushes of his own and lead the Enniskillen troops into an trap. Wolseley's troops marched from Lisnaskea through the small village of Donagh towards Newtownbutler.

Mountcashel moved his position to a hill approximately a mile south of Newtownbutler at Sandholes. This position would have been obscured from the town by the Kilgarret hill; the dramatic topography of this area can still be seen today. However, Mountcashel had not been naïve enough to create a single position and had moved troops acting in a skirmishing role, to the hilly ground just north of the town. His guns stayed with him in the southerly position, in anticipation of administering a few well-aimed shots at the Inniskillingers as they advanced.[30] Mountcashel's attempt at defence in depth was further improved by his position at Sandholes. MacCarmick stated that he was 'advantageously' posted between Newtownbutler and Wattlebridge, with guns positioned in a 'lane' facing a narrow pass through a bog.[31] The approach to Mountcashel's position was indeed dominated by a large expanse of bogland, the best access, indeed the only access for cavalry, being via a 'causeway' or raised road, a feature so typical of the surrounding townlands.[32]

Mountcashel had taken advantage of the causeway feature on the high ground north of Newtownbutler where his small delaying force was deployed. Wolseley's Forlorn Hope had marched less than half a mile from Donagh when they encountered forward elements of Mountcashel's troops outside the town. The Jacobites, as ordered, retreated as Wolseley's men advanced until they could gain cover in the high ground half a mile north of the town itself. As with Mountcashel's position south of the town, and indeed Berry's position at Lisnaskea, the approach to the high ground was dominated by a large expanse of bogland, with only a narrow causeway leading to the crest. Jacobite skirmishers hid behind the soft cover of bushes and fences as they prepared to engage the superior numbers of the Inniskillingers. Theirs was, however, a delaying action; they were not expected to become embroiled in a protracted fight.

Once more Wolseley deliberated with his officers. As discussed at Lisnaskea, they would attack with Tiffin on the right flank and Lloyd on the left, dividing the dragoons in support of these two elements. Berry's cavalry would advance along the causeway while Wolseley would await developments with the reserve, hoping to ascertain a weakness in the Jacobite position if the situation turned into a trap. As the Enniskillen troops deployed, the Jacobites opened fire, the volume of fire intensifying as the advance progressed. The Inniskillingers fired a few volleys in response, before resuming the advance. Before they could reach the scattered Jacobite positions, however, Mountcashel's men withdrew in good order, their comrades setting the town alight as they moved.[33]

At this point Mountcashel's plan and its relative subtleties become clear. As the Jacobite skirmishers began to retreat, there were signs that the Inniskillingers were about to break ranks, abandon any form of disciplined fire, and thus give chase, in the hope of pursuing the fleeing enemy through the town and beyond. Was this what Mountcashel had hoped for, an abandonment of order and discipline creating a lack of cohesion in the Enniskillen force that he could exploit? His own troops were by no means professional, and any attempt to upset the delicate balance of order that those experienced officers had engendered in the troops could pay dividends later. Perhaps one or two battalions could be disordered through these means, markedly affecting the battle to follow given the limited numbers present.

The Enniskillen and English officers had considerable difficulty controlling their troops and preventing a disorganised pursuit. Mountcashel had correctly anticipated the potential of the Inniskillingers to break order and trust to their emotions on this day, rather than the orders of their officers. It was a sensible plan. Mountcashel could break up attacking battalions and engage them in a piecemeal fashion with his more professional mounted elements farther south, rather than be forced to fight with the weaker element of his army, his infantry. However, Wolseley was no fool. He had seen the Jacobites retreat in reasonably good order and must have assumed correctly that their flight was a ruse, believing the move either a feint prior to an ambush or designed to gain better ground. He sent orders to Tiffin and Lloyd to have their troops remain in good order.

Mountcashel was receiving reports of a much larger enemy force than actually existed from his retreating troops. His infantry action north of the town, and the proximity of Wolseley's men, meant that he would have to stand and fight. He reinforced his relatively strong position. As the Enniskillen men marched past the burning buildings and around a mile past the village, they encountered Mountcashel's position on the high ground at Sandholes, in the midst of a vast expanse of swampy bogland, at least half a mile wide, which could only be crossed on foot, referred to in the *Jacobite Narrative* as 'on a pass, which was on a causeway, on each side of a morass'.[34]

Mountcashel had positioned his troops on high ground overlooking the northerly approach. Only a narrow causeway led to his centre. His guns sat at the end of the causeway. He had positioned his foot regiments on either side under cover, with most of the horse on the right.[35] This decision would have serious repercussions as most of the foot regiments must have been placed in a skirmish formation to take advantage of cover, meaning that their ability to volley fire when ordered would be diminished. Lack of training amongst some of the men worsened the state of affairs and reduced the effectiveness of that vital first musket volley. There would be little time to reload with the distances involved, and the Jacobites' first volley might prove their best chance of inflicting losses on the Enniskillen troops if they decided to charge. Men spread in such a position would also gain little support from their respective regiments in a close-in fight and would break sooner, with more devastating results.

Wolseley ordered the infantry to advance across the bog as before, Tiffin on the right and Lloyd on the left, with Berry's cavalry left on the causeway. MacCarmick recorded that pikes and colours (one third of the battalions in this case, perhaps due to shortages of firearms) were left behind, and only musketeers advanced. With the nature of the ground, a Jacobite cavalry attack would bog down in the mud; pikes were not required. Berry's attempts to move his horse along the causeway were rapidly met by Jacobite artillery-fire. D'Avaux recorded that three 'ramshackle' battalions attacked, indicating that Wolseley also threw the reserve into the fray, or perhaps that he could control them no longer. Mountcashel's Jacobite troops opened fire.

The Inniskillingers, still apparently in some degree of order, returned fire:

> When our foot advanced through the bog, the enemy fired extream thick upon our men, notwithstanding we could not see a man of them; but when we came close upon them, we fell a firing where we saw the smoke rise.[36]

The Jacobite musket discharge was seemingly ineffective; the attackers neither broke nor received excessive casualties. One volley was returned at the troops on the hill and then all hell broke loose. The Inniskillingers charged.

Covering the remaining distance to the Jacobite position, less than 100 yards, the day would be decided through savage and relentless man-to-man combat. Mountcashel's men had lost the initiative. There was no time to reload the clumsy matchlock muskets, their use now becoming restricted to that of a heavy club. Training and drill would matter little; it was man against man, as swords were drawn and men screamed. The impetus of the charge allowed Wolseley's men quickly to gain the upper hand and seize the guns that had prevented Berry's cavalry charge along the causeway. MacCarmick described the ferocity of the scene:

> our Foot immediately seized their cannon, where one lusty man that formerly had belonged to my Lord Kingston, finding one fellow with a Hatchet, repairing somewhat about the Cannon, snatch'd the Hatchet out of his Hand, and laid so well about him, that in the twinkling of an Eye he killed seven or eight of those that were guarding the Cannon, some with the Edg of the Hatchet, and some with the Head of it... [37]

Seeing the guns seized, Berry's cavalry raced along the causeway. Mountcashel still had hopes that the charge could be broken by his own regiment's musket volleys, and the approaching cavalry could be stopped by his own mounted troops. It was not to be. The charge had created an infectious panic in the Jacobite ranks. To Mountcashel's horror, his dragoons wheeled about and fled south along the road towards Wattlebridge. Amongst them was Anthony Hamilton, fleeing with his horsemen for the second time that day. They had not fired a shot and many discarded weapons and coats in their eagerness to flee.

A Dutch print of the Battle of Newtownbutler, the town in the background being slightly misrepresented. It is thought that this may be a depiction of Enniskillen.

The Jacobite foot stood for a time. Many must have realised that the situation was hopeless without horse and artillery, dispersed as they were. The outlook was bleak, especially so with the arrival of the Enniskillen cavalry. D'Avaux recorded that Mountcashel's regiment performed well, although he was not well supported by Clare's and Bophin's men. He also recorded Mountcashel's capture, although the Enniskillen sources record more colourful events. The general and a number of his officers had escaped to a wooded area near the former Jacobite artillery position, which was then guarded by Inniskillingers. Apparently resigned to his fate, Mountcashel is said to have charged the position and the men holding the guns, opening fire with his pistol. The Enniskillen infantry returned fire, wounding Mountcashel in three places. Being recognised by the Enniskillen troops, thus saving his life, he was captured and taken to Enniskillen.[38]

By now, the Jacobite foot had also been routed and were fleeing. Upon leaving the hill, most of the infantry fled west, towards Lough Erne and the vast steaming bogland 'full of bogs, pools and loughs', dropping weapons and equipment as they stumbled. The pursuers slaughtered many of the retreating Jacobites as they floundered in the marshland. Some of the infantry headed south towards Wattlebridge, but to no avail; the Enniskillen horse who had pursued Anthony Hamilton's dragoons over the narrow road had passed through Wattlebridge and left a rearguard, which now beat back Jacobite attempts to cross the river. Advancing Inniskillingers pursued around 500 infantry to a wooded area near the lough. The Jacobites attempted to swim across the waterway; only one survived.[39] That night the Inniskillingers sought bloody retribution on those men trying to remain hidden, the English officers having apparently lost control. The incident was a bloody one, yet remains representative of the terrible events that occurred on all sides across Europe in this desperate age of religious conflict.

D'Avaux, writing afterwards in a letter to Louvois, claimed that the Inniskillingers had not pursued effectively. After all, Hamilton had escaped. He would add that the dragoons could have turned the tide of battle had they stayed. D'Avaux's version of the battle and his emerging opinions of both Richard and Anthony Hamilton are translated here for clarity. His comments help outline the general state of the Jacobite cause shortly after the battle:

> This deed [Lisnaskea] gave the rebels so much encouragement that they came to attack Mylord Monkassel the same day; as he heard that they were coming after him, he changed position and placed his cannon on the main road, guarded by dragoons; the enemy that came with three ramshackle battalions but very courageously, were received firmly by Mylord Monkassel's regiment, the other two did their duty very poorly, and the very dragoons who had cowardly ran away in the morning fled with the remainder of the cavalry without firing a pistol shot, and fled with such fright that they threw their muskets, pistols and swords, and most of them having exhausted their horses, took off their clothes to move faster on foot. Mylord Monkassel remained at the head of his regiment and having been wounded and his horse killed, the enemy leapt on him and took him; his regiment was decimated and the rest of the army dispersed. Marigny, the captain in Champagne, major for the Claire regiment, distinguished himself in this instant, for after giving orders that were not obeyed, he led the battalion, his colonel having remained in Cork and his lieutenant-colonel having fled; but the regiment did not support him very well and he was taken prisoner and shot in the face three times almost at close range. As the enemy are not soldiers any more than we are, they

did not take advantage of their position and pursued no-one, and if we had come back after them with four or five hundred horse, in no order, we would have defeated them. We abandoned four cannon and the little luggage the army had, which was not much.

This reversal will do more harm to the King of England, because of the courage it has given to the enemy, the terror that has settled amongst the troops, and by the quantity of arms lost, than by the number of men killed or those who have escaped; although the loss of a dragoons regiment and three battalions is no small defeat, and until now only a few soldiers have been found.

I have feared greatly, Sir, that those in Enniskillen might beat the Duke of Berwick and Sarsfield, one after the other. I talked to the King about it, who said that he would let the people on the ground deal with it for fear of giving them inappropriate orders. However, as I could foresee with great displeasure, that we were risking losing a lot of time round Enniskillen and ruining the freshest troops we have here, while waiting for the Marshal of Schomberg, I felt it my duty to insist with the King that the few troops that were in Derry be sent to Dublin at once, without sending any to the Duke of Berwick, and if the Duke of Berwick was not strong enough with Sarsfield to scatter the rebels that are in the country, he should return also.[40]

According to d'Avaux, Hamilton had fled deep into County Cavan with his horsemen, even then galloping miles towards Dublin in his flight.[41] Ever outspoken, and having little allegiance to any Irish or English faction, he showed a degree of faith in Mountcashel, but in few others. Terror had indeed set in amongst many of the Jacobites as the fearsome reputation of the Enniskillen garrison grew. D'Avaux could see the flaws in the Jacobite strategy at Enniskillen and, it seems, had always had doubts over Derry. In fact, his concerns over the Inniskillingers now centred on their ability to attack Berwick and Sarsfield. Worse news followed:

You can see, Sir, through all that I have requested, that we are not capable of holding strong for Marshal de Schomberg. I had great difficulties in making the King of England agree that we should set up a camp. Boisseleau went yesterday to encamp his first battalion; the others will set up camp as they arrive. The camp is two miles from Dublin, where as many battalions as possible will be stationed;

another one will be set up in the Cork area, but we do not think we will have enough people to set up a third one near Charlemont.

But, Sir, not even a quarter will be armed because the King of England has only 3,000 muskets beyond the 17,000 that were sent from France; among those the last 7,000 are not worth much, as you will have seen from the letters sent by M. Roze and M. de Fumeron; and what good muskets we had, have been for the most part lost or damaged through the negligence of the soldiers, and even more so through that of their officers, and unfortunately there are here very few gun makers, at least they are Protestants; thus most of the time they damage the arms more than they repair them. In spite of all that, we issued a proclamation giving permission to all colonels to reform all the regiments that had been broken.

No garrison has twenty shots to fire; and at the time of writing, I have not been able to obtain that an account of the troops position could be brought to the King, with a map to establish an overall plan of the places where a garrison should be left and where to abandon the position, the places where encampment will be set, how big they will be, and the officers that will be in charge.

Concerns were now moving south, and away from the Ulster debacle, but problems with muskets, and even ammunition, did not just affect Mountcashel at Newtownbutler; this problem was army-wide. With the threat of William's invasion, matters were in disarray.

It is very upsetting indeed that we should have so many difficulties in making decisions here, and that it can be executed so badly once it has finally been taken. We thought it advisable to despatch 200 barrels of powder to Athlone, with fuses and bullets. I learnt, Sir, that all this only had a fifty-men escort, and that we were going to pass approx. ten miles from a castle where there were more than 200 armed rebels. I immediately informed the King who told me that he would give orders. A lord who had come across this convoy some twenty miles from here, with only a fifty-men escort, came to warn me about it; I contacted the King again, who told me that it could not be so, and that there were a hundred and fifty cavalry men to escort the powder, but they have not arrived yet. God willing that they should arrive in time.[42]

However, d'Avaux's correspondence would not encourage dramatic French action. French reinforcements would come, but at a significant price. D'Avaux only confirmed Ireland's position as a distraction for William's resources in the eyes of Louis, certainly not worth supporting. The distraction would have far-reaching consequences for the Irish troops. With Mountcashel's subsequent capture and retention in Enniskillen, the Jacobite cause in Ireland became caught between the somewhat questionable nature of the foundation and acts of James's Irish Parliament, and the more serious and debilitating potential of the pending invasion from England.

*Chapter 12*

# The First Flight

Three weeks after the events at Lisnaskea and Newtownbutler, Anthony Hamilton and Captain Lavallin faced a court martial in Dublin over the events at Lisnaskea, and the fateful order. Many blamed this debacle for Mountcashel's subsequent defeat at Newtownbutler, although this clearly ignores many of the important factors related to troop quality and command that doomed the Jacobites in the later action. De Rosen, who, by this stage, had poor relations with both Anthony and Richard Hamilton, presided over the court.[1] Despite the odds stacked against him, Hamilton was acquitted and Lavallin condemned to death. However, he insisted until the end that he had passed the commands as he had received them. Anthony Hamilton remained silent. Despite the protests of Lavallin's friends from his home town of Cork, who spoke of his honour, he was executed and the affair was over.[2] The event, in a similar vein to Richard Hamilton's experience at Derry, did little to endear the Hamiltons to either Irish or French allies. Indeed, murmurings amongst the Irish troops gave notice that many of Lavallin's accusers deserved the death penalty instead, due to their conduct.[3]

In the end, most of the blame for reversals and disaster at both Londonderry and Enniskillen was heaped on the Hamilton brothers. D'Avaux remarked that Anthony had not done his duty, did not deserve his rank, and sought only to please Tyrconnel.[4] Melfort, who had little time for the Hamiltons or their efforts, wrote to Lord Waldegrave:

> For what's past, it is in vain to talk to you about it, nor to tell you the blame thrown on the two Hamiltons, or the diffidence the natives have of them. All we must look to now is what's to come and that depends on what the King of France will do.[5]

In apparent agreement, d'Avaux commented to Louis: 'The Hamiltons are much hated in this country ... .'[6] He also wrote to Louvois of Richard Hamilton: 'Hamilton, who commands the best of the infantry is hated and despised by the troops and they suspect him more than I can guess.'[7]

The problems that had beset Jacobite military activity and its distinct lack of success cannot have helped the Hamiltons' standing amongst Jacobite leaders and the troops who had suffered at Derry and Newtownbutler. Despite the emergence of a scapegoat mentality amongst some of the elite, any further blame or indeed persecution of the Hamiltons would be diluted by friction within the Jacobite camp itself.

Mountcashel, who had been taken as a wounded captive to Enniskillen, faced months of waiting and endless negotiation about his fate. Having been taken to Enniskillen with hundreds of Jacobite prisoners, he was given fair treatment as a member of the Irish nobility and an officer. The battle and Mountcashel's capture had removed any Jacobite threat. There would be no link-up between Berwick and Sarsfield, who began to move south.[8] D'Avaux wrote of Jacobite expectations and the possibility of getting Mountcashel back:

> The troops from the siege of Derry have come back completely destroyed. Those commanded by my Lord Mountcashel were beaten and routed in such a way that bodes ill for such troops. Those from Iniskillen came in total confusion but very bravely attacked my Lord Mountcashel. The cavalry and the dragoons fled without firing a shot and later most of them having exhausted their horses in their flight, dismounted and continued on foot. They threw away arms, swords and even their doublets in order to run faster. My Lord Mountcashel remained at the head of the infantry, who also did very badly. To be fair to his battalion, he was wounded, his horse killed and he was taken prisoner. As he was abandoned by everyone, he was believed dead but he is in Iniskillen and well looked after. The rebels are already asking for my Lord Monjoye in exchange.[9]

Two points are immediately apparent: d'Avaux praised Mountcashel whilst damning Hamilton and was keen to get the former back. If a plan could be drawn together to exchange Mountjoy, who still languished in the Bastille, for Mountcashel, many of the French saw a future for him. They already planned to send Irish troops to France under a trusted commander, in exchange for French regulars.

Mountcashel's wounds had been severe enough that he was permitted to inform James of his plight, who sent one of his personal physicians and a surgeon, together with provisions and wine, to Enniskillen.[10] Mountcashel pleaded for parole in the coming months to go to Dublin but previous experience with Richard Hamilton did little to encourage Schomberg, who had arrived in Ireland with William's forces two weeks after Newtownbutler. He would not give credence to Mountcashel's honour or intent.[11] The possible exchange with Mountjoy also proved unsuccessful.[12]

Instead Mountcashel looked to his own fate and seized his chance to escape the town in November with the aid of an Inniskillinger, who was subsequently shot as a traitor.[13] Schomberg, echoing earlier references to Richard Hamilton's defection, stated that he would know what to expect of Irish honour in the future. However, d'Avaux greeted the news with joy. French plans were proceeding as intended.[14] Mountcashel and Louvois had for some time been discussing the possibility of sending Irish troops to France.[15] For Mountcashel's part, this was seen as a means of helping the Irish plight by opening direct lines of communication to Louis through fighting his enemies on the continent. For the French, foreign and fresh troops were welcome, especially since those French troops sent in exchange would remain relatively uncommitted in the battles in Ireland, unlike their Irish counterparts on the continent.

From the beginning, d'Avaux's comments about Mountcashel indicated his sentiments; Mountcashel had made a very positive impression on d'Avaux and the French:

> If we did not have a man of such authority, we could not do such a thing without upsetting everyone here. What I wanted to say, Sir, is that without the help of Milord Montcassel, I would have had difficulties in setting up things here.[16]
>
> Although he managed to escape to then serve in France. This alone Sir, would not have led me to agree, if I had not believed that it was absolutely necessary for the King to have a man so devoted to his service and so liked and of such reputation in Ireland, as to keep the Irish dutiful in France and to raise recruits in this country, and even as many fresh troops as you wish. If the King of England [James] wished to give permission to all those who want to follow him, you would have all the best officers in the army.[17]

As for the other senior commanders in the Jacobite army, the French, it seemed, had little time for Berwick while Sarsfield, although respected, was described as 'not of noble birth'.[18]

> I have found out Sir, that the King of England intended to have the Irish troops go to France led by the Duke of Berwick. I cannot help telling you that, although he is a respectable man, so they say, he is a bad officer and he lacks common sense. I replied, when I was told that he was not Irish, that I believed the King wished the commanding officer and all the corps to be of the same nationality.[19]

For the Hamiltons, the combined effects of reverses at Londonderry and the rout at Newtownbutler had ended their chances of advancement in the French establishment. Indeed, d'Avaux's correspondence is quite clear on the matter. Louvois, especially, even prior to Newtownbutler and complete disengagement from Derry, was quite clear when corresponding with d'Avaux; he had not forgotten the circumstances surrounding Richard Hamilton's departure from Paris, and it seemed he had little faith in Anthony:

> I must inform you through this letter, that His Majesty does not want Messrs Hamilton who served in France, the last of which was a colonel in an infantry regiment. This last Hamilton has now gone to lead the Irish troops due to come out of service and is not even one of the [regimental] colonels. His Majesty would be grateful if you explained these matters only if absolutely necessary. This would be only to inform the King of England in particular and to ask him not to mention these matters to anyone.[20]

Writing after the battle and the end of the siege, between September and November 1689, Louvois had not changed his mind:

> His Majesty [Louis] is asking you to train the best officers and as far as possible people that the King could trust and whose change of mood, so common in that nation [Ireland], he should not fear, noting also that he does not want any of the Hamiltons.[21]
>
> Above all, His Majesty [Louis] does not want any Hamilton to head these regiments, a fact that you will disclose only when you have no option.[22]

Not only did the French want little to do with the Hamiltons by then, they were also keen to avoid discussing the matter until absolutely necessary. D'Avaux also reported Richard Hamilton's declaration that he had been unjustly treated in France, and that he would have his revenge.[23] In turn, Richard thought little of d'Avaux.[24] Louvois and d'Avaux had discussed Mountcashel's role in the French army as early as April 1689.[25] The French, it appeared, had their man, aided by his timely escape from Enniskillen, yet they still desired as quiet a disengagement from Ireland for Mountcashel as possible, with no interference from the Hamilton brothers. Their time with Louis's army had passed.

Mountcashel's entry into Dublin in December was hailed with processions and celebration, echoing the events surrounding the triumphant return of Richard Hamilton the previous year. His arrival was turned into a public event, with twenty carriages and several hundred horsemen. However, the Irish had regained a general only to lose him to France. The Irish situation had never been intended specifically by the French to put James back on the throne, but to convince William that such a threat existed, thus drawing valuable Williamite resources from England to Ireland, rather than to the continent. The diversion worked to an extent. William's forces would be committed for two more years.

By the summer of 1689 and Newtownbutler, d'Avaux echoed James's thoughts on the urgent requirement for French support to aid the situation – French troops to shore up the ailing Irish army. Louis agreed, but the price would be Irish troops. Louis's regiments in Ireland, arriving in March 1690, supported the Irish without suffering excessive casualties. Ultimately, they would be returned to France. Theirs was but a show of force.

As with most Irish political affairs, friction and the development of internal factions within the government took their toll, both on James's authority and effective resistance to William's invasion, as advisors and generals fought for space, influence and their respective convictions. Tyrconnel complained about Melfort and Melfort about d'Avaux. James, too, fought with his Scottish advisor, yet remained strongly influenced by him. The newly-arrived Lauzun had accompanied the French reinforcements and would succeed de Rosen. He appealed to James's wife, Mary of Modena, about d'Avaux, accusing him of highlighting James's reliance on Berwick's advice and Berwick's dependence in turn on the Hamilton brothers.[26]

As intrigue begat intrigue, a situation that was scarcely credible in the midst of an ever-growing state of war, Melfort became a scapegoat for Irish prejudice, being forced to leave James's service and retire to France by August 1689. He later commented to d'Avaux that he considered the entire affair as having been devised by Lord and Lady Tyrconnel, so that his comments and opinions about the Hamiltons' behaviour at Derry and

Lisnaskea could no longer be heard. Richard Hamilton's experience at the siege, as with many of the Jacobite troops, had a serious effect on his health. Exposure and the effects of the Irish weather throughout the operation had convinced him to seek to spend the winter at Montpellier to recover. His relative unpopularity in Ireland could only have made his decision all the easier. However, with Schomberg's landing in Ulster, and the immediate threat presented by the long-expected intervention of William's regulars, he instead resolved to stay.[27]

Schomberg, who had landed in August, had captured Carrickfergus and moved to Newry. There would be little further activity that year as he consolidated his position in the north, the rigours of an Irish winter reducing his numbers. Anthony and Richard Hamilton spent most of the autumn in Dublin. The Jacobite army was trimmed to make it more effective, yet still suffered supply problems into 1690.[28] The youngest of the brothers, John Hamilton, now an officer in the re-structured army, was given his own regiment. However, his finest hour had yet to come.

D'Avaux and de Rosen returned to France in the spring. Mountcashel sailed to France with 6,000 Irish troops in April 1690, on the very ships that had brought Lauzun and the French regulars. James had lost an experienced officer and thousands of men, although further French aid was promised. Those who remained in Ireland would have a far more significant battle to fight. The legacy of that confrontation would echo through Irish history for hundreds of years.

Twenty carriages and several hundred horsemen, officers and locals had led the procession that had welcomed Mountcashel back into Dublin. James received him at Dublin Castle and, that night, bonfires were lit in celebration all over Dublin. Celebrations were also held in Cork and throughout Justin's home province of Munster when the news was received. His wife, Arabella, who had waited in Dublin for six months, also received the husband whom she must have feared she might never see again. Only Tyrconnel was unhappy to see Mountcashel. The Jacobite rejoicing was shortlived; Mountcashel would help form the Irish Brigade for service in France. D'Avaux, at least, was happy:

> Sir, as you did me the honour from the start, to tell me that the King was asking Sir Makarty to command his troops and you have had the courtesy to write since that His Majesty was no longer thinking of having Makarty because he was convinced that he was the prisoner

of the Prince of Orange under the name of Montcassel, I thought that Makarty having escaped from prison, his Majesty intended me to execute the orders given concerning Makarty. Although he had undertaken to escape in order to serve in France, that alone would not have convinced me, Sir, if I had not believed that it was important to have a man so liked in his Majesty's service, so loved and influential in Ireland that he could keep dutiful the Irish troops in France.

However, James was still seen as somewhat of an impediment.

> If the King of England would give permission to all those who wanted to follow him, you would have the best officers in the army; but his Britannic Majesty is far from consenting to this
>
> ... Makarty has done what he could to remove the bad lieutenant colonels and majors; but he has not been able to succeed. He reckons that in the last resort they should be removed from office on arrival in France and thinks that it will not have any adverse effect in this country. If we did not have a man of such authority, we could not do such a thing without upsetting everyone here. He claims, Sir, that he will be able to replace these discharged officers with a few Irish who are serving at present in France in the German regiments. But I believe that his Majesty thinks that these officers are already his and would want some other sent from Ireland. What I wanted to say, Sir, is that without the help of Milord Montcassel, I would have had difficulties in setting up things here.[29]

And of Mountcashel's Regiment:

> Milord Moncassel did not want to surrender himself or these regiments. He will be happy to do whatever you will judge appropriate. He is working on gathering a good regiment, the King has given him permission to take what is left of the one he commands, and that is the best regiment in the kingdom.[30]

The Irish were regaining an experienced general only to lose him again. Without Mountcashel, however, French hopes of obtaining suitable troops would have been hampered, if not blighted altogether, which would have changed the political landscape for Louis's Irish diversion. For his part, Mountcashel had pinned all his hopes on French service and his loyalty would not be found wanting. He had been keen to command the troops destined for France as early as February 1689 and had written to the French war department in this vein.[31] We can therefore put credence in the fact that it was partly Mountcashel's own insistence that he be the man to command Irish troops in French service that had instigated the scheme. That is not to say that he thought the Irish, or Jacobite, cause was lost. On the contrary, he wrote to Sarsfield of his hopes that his French service would underline the Irish plight to the French, and gain further aid.[32]

At the time of James's landing in Kinsale, Mountcashel had sought assurances from the French that his acceptance of the position of Master of Artillery in the Irish Army would not complicate, or otherwise jeopardise, his wish to lead the Irish Brigade in France, his actions motivated by his desire to appeal directly to the French for their continued assistance in Ireland.[33] Louis's Irish diversion may have been a way of playing for time on the European stage but Mountcashel still believed that the French would support Ireland. For Louis's part, his communication indicated clearly the course of action. Both Louis and Louvois preferred Mountcashel. His future career was secure. D'Avaux also saw him as the only eligible general, with little competition it seemed. James's hope that Berwick was a suitable candidate held little water with d'Avaux.[34]

Then there were the Hamiltons. Both Richard, the commander at Derry, and Anthony, who had fared so poorly at Newtownbutler, were held in barely concealed contempt by the French court. Louvois, the French minister of war, had stated that not only was the command not to be considered for either brother, but neither was to be given a colonelship in any of the regiments, if nothing else creating a negative bias in relation to their military careers. Louvois's letters to d'Avaux are evidence of the degree of contempt with which the brothers were held in France:

> His Majesty [Louis] is asking you to train the best officers and as far as possible people that the King could trust and whose change of mood, so common in that nation, he should not fear, noting also that he does not want any of the Hamiltons.[35]

Patrick Sarsfield, Mountcashel's friend and fellow officer from their days in France and England, fared somewhat better in the eyes of d'Avaux who described him as 'not of such noble birth' as Mountcashel but 'brave, honourable and of a never failing honesty', who had distinguished himself through his own merit in the war so far. Sarsfield had also served in France and, had not Mountcashel escaped, might well have led the brigade to France, being the only alternative in French eyes. D'Avaux, ever enterprising, attempted to get both. James would have none of it. Mountcashel had made a positive impression with all the French observers.

> Although he managed to escape to then serve in France. This alone Sir, would not have led me to agree, if I had not believed that it was absolutely necessary for the King to have a man so devoted to his service and so liked and of such reputation in Ireland, as to keep the Irish dutiful in France and to raise recruits in this country, and even as many fresh troops as you wish. If the King of England [James] wished to give permission to all those who want to follow him, you would have all the best officers in the army.[36]

Mountcashel was seen as a professional in the French mould, his qualities achieved through his early experience and training, yet those same qualities appeared to be lacking amongst his contemporaries. Who else then but this Irish gentleman to organise and lead the apparently undisciplined Irish regiments for Louis? D'Avaux understood and, having had some experience with foreign troops in French service, must have been fully aware of how important it was for such troops not only to be properly led, but also to have a leader who appreciated and embraced the French way of war.

Foreign officers rarely rose to high rank, however. The French system was almost designed to prevent such eventualities. D'Avaux stated that Mountcashel's short-sightedness would prevent his becoming a great general or French marshal. This statement was probably designed to protect him in the early years, and to alleviate fears amongst potential French rivals for higher military office. Of course, events at Enniskillen had left Mountcashel little choice in terms of where his future lay. James was reluctant to lose him but the nature of his escape opened up the question of his honour, despite Mountcashel's attempts to avoid such a prospect. If he was captured again, the Williamites could shoot him out of hand. This must have provided further inducement, should any have been required, to strive for command of the brigade. Tyrconnel, too, seemed content with Mountcashel's leaving for France. The two would never meet again.[37]

## Foreign Troops in French Service

In practical terms the French economy had already suffered greatly in the wake of Louis's wars. This was another major European conflict, and foreign troops were essential to support it. His aggressive defence against the Grand Alliance would cost millions of livres and, although the war would solve little in the short term, France would pay dearly. In light of this, it was felt that Louis's Irish diversion should be extended for as long as possible.[38] That diversion was not designed specifically to put James back on the throne, but simply to convince William that such an event was possible, thus drawing valuable Williamite military resources from mainland Europe. By summer 1689 and Newtownbutler, d'Avaux echoed James's thoughts about the urgent requirement for experienced French troops to shore up the ailing Jacobite army. Louis agreed, but there would be a price to pay; 6,000 French troops would be sent, but 6,000 Irish would return to fight in France.

The exchange was never to be without conditions. Louis was not so naïve as to give away his finest regiments. They were under orders to support the Irish, but not to become involved in battle to the extent that they would suffer excessive casualties. At the Boyne in 1690 the French troops kept the route of escape for the Jacobites open but this was their only part in the battle. The French were more than a show of force, but still less than an effective addition to the ailing Irish army and Louis knew, even if James did not, that once his diversion and Ireland's usefulness had ended the troops would be coming home. However, he would reap greater benefits from Ireland as, by the end of the war, he would receive most of the displaced Irish troops.

This was in the future. For now there were regiments to form. The French requested that 6,000 men be recruited to replace on the continent the men Louis would send to Ireland, in the form of five regiments. Compliance with the French requirement would be a different matter, however. The Irish army was in disarray. The besiegers at Derry had fled from Ulster. Mountcashel's Newtownbutler force had been mostly scattered, captured or killed. The French would arrive in March in preparation for the Williamite assault in the summer and Mountcashel was set an enormous challenge: to establish and organise the fledgling Irish Brigade within a very short time.[39]

Attempting to comply with the French requirements as far as possible, the Irish tried to raise four regiments initially. James, in an effort to gain men of some quality, and also to allow him to keep those experienced officers that he had, appealed to the Irish noble families, who would send a son along with the regiment to command overseas. The O'Neills could not raise any troops, and Lord Clanrickarde had little intention of sending his men anywhere. However, Lord Dillon would have a regiment available and ready, under the command of his son Arthur.

Mountcashel had to re-establish his own regiment which had been destroyed at Newtownbutler. By January he had 400 men under arms, hardly an auspicious start. The following weeks, however, were to see something of resurgence in his popularity and his ranks swelled to 1,200 men. It became easy to see then why the French held him in such regard, if such was his effect on the men. But it would not be so easy to raise the troops for other regiments. D'Avaux commented to Louvois:

> I have nothing further to ask you concerning the state of the troops, but I think it is necessary to tell you again today, what I have had the honour of saying so often: there is little effort made to satisfy the promise made to the King to send Irish troops; there are only eight hundred men ready to embark for France at the time of my writing, except for Moncassel's regiment.
>
> Regarding this regiment, there are twelve hundred good men; there were hardly four hundred when Mylord Moncassel arrived in Dublin after his release from jail, and he increased the regiment to the level I relate within three weeks, although he was give no help, on the contrary many hurdles were put in his way.[40]

We can only speculate about the 'hurdles' that were placed in the way of recruitment, that perhaps Tyrconnel had little inclination to help the newly-escaped general in his task. Nevertheless, Mountcashel used his influence to help his fellow colonels. Colonel Robert Fielding was an Englishman who had joined the Jacobite cause after James's flight, and had also married Mary Ulick, widow of Cormac MacCarthy, Mountcashel's older brother. Justin, came to his aid, helping him raise sufficient numbers to form a regiment. Mountcashel's was not the only regiment re-formed after Newtownbutler. Clare's Regiment had also been recruiting and was able to raise men for France. Again, the popularity of the colonel played a significant part. D'Avaux had scathing comments:

> Concerning  O'Brien's regiment, Mylord Claire's son, we have found only seven hundred and forty eight men in the thirteen old companies of the regiment plus the three new ones, and some

of them will be rejected. Mylord Claire has so little purpose in organising this regiment to go to France that he has not informed any captain to raise his company to one hundred men; moreover, there are only three captains in this regiment with royal commissions, all the other ones are lieutenants or ensigns, most of them insignificant and without presence, whom he picked up to replace those who were killed, left the services or were taken prisoner at Enniskillen. He has not yet decided which one of his children or nephew would lead the regiment; there is no lieutenant colonel or major.[41]

Lord Clare had not intended to send his son to command the regiment but the men declared that they would disband if not led by an O'Brien. Clare relented and named his son Daniel as colonel.

Lord Galmoy, the man who had first besieged Crom, and who is conspicuously absent from the later events at Newtownbutler, despite his presence with the northern Irish a few days before, also raised a regiment. This could not have been difficult since his lack of attendance at the earlier battle would have left the bulk of his troops intact.[42] By March 1690, in preparation for the arrival of French troops from Brest, Mountcashel had formed five regiments – his own, Dillon's, O'Brien's, Butler's (Galmoy) and Fielding's. The brigade as a whole included around 5,800 men.

They would fight for Louis against his enemies, whosoever he would command them to fight, except James II, the only clause in their 'contract'. Soldiers' pay had also been agreed prior to the troops leaving Ireland, the rates being familiar to Mountcashel since they dated back to the arrangements made for George Hamilton's Regiment of Foot in French service in 1671. The rates also corresponded to James's preference for Jacobite troops in Ireland. A captain received five livres (francs) per day, a lieutenant two francs and twenty-five cents and an ensign one franc and eighty cents. Common infantry soldiers received nine francs per month, but deductions were made from the common soldier's pay for the colonel of the regiment, in addition to his pay of around 2,700 francs per year. The Irish troops would certainly not become rich through their service, and differences between the Irish and the French troops were marginal.[43]

French troops arrived at Cork on 20 March. The Comte de Lauzun, who was to succeed de Rosen as the French commander in Ireland, commanded them. If the Irish who remained thought that the change might be for the better, they would be disappointed. Lauzun was unfit for such a high level of command or responsibility but would ensure that, as Louis commanded, the French troops would remain uncommitted and intact.[44]

Irish troops stood ready to embark for Brest in France and would leave on 7 April. The men had been recruited quickly and, although numbers were adequate, Mountcashel was to be plagued once more by the quality. Many had seen no military service, and Mountcashel must have hoped that the French would see undiscovered potential in many of the recruits rather than their inadequacies. Indeed, we can presume that the numbers quoted were inflated through last-minute recruitment in a desperate bid to impress the French. The troops were in bad condition, even prior to embarking, with many clothed in rags; the situation with arms and requisite training was something that Mountcashel hoped that French aid would overcome quickly.

There had been some disagreement between d'Avaux and Louvois over the matter, even prior to the Irish Brigade being formed. D'Avaux had insisted that 6,000 to 7,000 good troops could be recruited in Ireland. Louvois had wanted quality over quantity and would accept 4,000 of the experienced Irish with good officers rather than an untrained rabble. Even by the time the troops had been selected and had sailed, Louvois would have his way.

The Irish reached Brest on 23 April. Mountcashel was summoned before Louis at Versailles, where he was well received, and presented with 4,000 écus (French crowns) to equip the brigade and an annual pension of the same sum, in addition to his colonel's salary. He also submitted himself to a French court martial to clear his name, in French eyes, over his escape from the island town of Enniskillen; predictably, he was pronounced innocent of having breached the terms of his parole. The French military and Louis would certainly not hold these actions against the Irish commander.

The French were still concerned about respect, that being the quality of the troops they had received from Ireland. They had insisted that, as far as possible, each regiment should consist of sixteen companies of one-hundred men each, a challenge, even if there had been a surplus of experienced troops in Ireland at the time. Their immediate decision was to reduce the complement from five regiments to three. The Butler and Fielding Regiments were broken up, and the useable troops dispersed to the other regiments. A surplus of around 700 men was shipped back to Ireland almost immediately. Over the course of the following weeks, additional men were weeded out until the French had obtained their three regiments with 1,600 men each.

Even with the reduction in numbers, Mountcashel's men were in a sorry state. They had brought no arms from Ireland and were clothed mostly in rags. A French record of the time speaks of them being 'shirtless, shoeless, hatless and afflicted with vermin'. This opinion must be taken in context with a number of other factors. The native French were little used to seeing Irishmen, let alone those who had just emerged from an active campaign across the sea. A little intolerance is not unexpected, especially in an age where its use was the rule rather than the exception; at least one source records that French troops were in a similar state upon their return from Ireland in 1691. Irish weather and conditions are nothing if not consistent.[45]

However, Mountcashel's men needed arms and uniforms, and it had never been intended that they should arrive as a fighting force ready for battle. Louvois had already implied that the Irish would be quickly 'fitted out':

> I must also add that His Majesty [James] should not worry about clothing these soldiers, on the contrary, it would be better that whatever little material is left in Ireland, should stay there for the purpose of clothing the king of England's troops, rather than the Irish, who will find far better materials in France than those: this will be more advantageous to the Irish colonels who will come, since the uniforms of their soldiers, dressed with better cloths, will last at least two years.[46]

Despite their initial shock, the French military set to work to outfit the new regiments. It is interesting to note that, despite being initially issued with grey coats (there was a surplus of grey material in this regard as evidenced by the amount supplied to Ireland at this time – known in France as *gris-blanc* or 'off white'), the Irish appealed for the more distinctive red, as previously worn. The Enniskillen records refer to troops of the town taking the red coats from captured Jacobites prior to the battle of Newtownbutler. Clearly then, the Irish had no qualms over wearing the red coat, which may be explained, albeit in a strange manner, by their need to express their identity. Individual regiments within the vast French army generally remained indistinguishable when deployed *en masse*. Only guards' regiments and, perhaps more importantly, some of the foreign regiments such as the Swiss were characterised by unique uniform colours.

The Irish troops had no idea if they would ever see their native land again, even if they survived French service. Standing out from the mass of French infantry gave them an identity and symbolised their nationality. The colour of the uniform was not so important as the fact that it was not distinctly French. In an age where uniforms were so closely tied to regimental identity, morale and esprit de corps, it is not surprising that insistence on wearing French grey would create serious concerns amongst the Irish. Initially, however, there seemed little choice, and the matter was not settled until Mountcashel had gained assurances that the next uniform issue, in the field, would be red. It is not clear when this occured, although the Irish regiments recorded in French service in later years wore red.

The flag of the brigade had a Saint George's cross with a lion in gold under a golden crown. Although seemingly English in style rather than Irish, this was a typical flag of the period. The cross device was used in the majority of French and English flags and typically 'Irish' symbols had not yet appeared. The regiments had been clothed and armed and were ready to march. Encamped at Nantes, Mountcashel had been made a lieutenant general of France and, by the start of June, commissioned as colonel of the Mountcashel Regiment. He had held both positions in England and Ireland, and now in France.

Daniel O'Brien, fourth Viscount Clare, was the young colonel of Clare's Regiment. His father, who had intended not to send his son with the regiment until pressurised, had gone into exile with Charles II and been rewarded with considerable tracts of land in County Clare in 1662, shortly after the restoration. O'Brien had remained loyal to the king upon James's flight and by 1689 sat in the Irish Parliament in Dublin, was Lord Lieutenant of County Clare and had raised a regiment of dragoons and two regiments of infantry for service. Those troops had fared poorly at Newtownbutler, if d'Avaux's report of the plight of Captain Marigny is to be believed, and the flight of Clare's Dragoons had not been forgotten. James had also selected the young Daniel O'Brien and his regiment for French service. Whether the action at Newtownbutler had motivated this decision is unclear, but Clare would have to work hard to remould the regiment's reputation.

Arthur Dillon commanded the third regiment of foot and similarly represented one of the noble Irish houses. During the English Civil War, and the subsequent wars in Ireland, Dillons had fought abroad in Spain and France, commanding Irish regiments. The seventh viscount, Theobald, had inherited the title in 1682. He was a lieutenant colonel in the Earl of Clanricarde's Irish Guards by 1685 and had himself raised two regiments of foot for James. Dillon's two sons, Henry and the younger Arthur, commanded those troops. Arthur's regiment was selected for French service, and he was only twenty years of age when he landed in France.

The original aim had been for the Irish regiments to fight under Noailles on the Catalonian border but the war was not proceeding as Louis had planned, and the situation in the Savoy region of northern Italy meant that reinforcements were needed quickly. By the end of July, the Irish regiments had received their orders to fight under Saint Ruth and Marshal Catinat in Savoy.[47]

At this stage it is useful to set the participation of the Irish troops in context. This was not the first of Louis XIV's wars; neither was it the most successful for France. In fact, it would almost bankrupt the country. Therefore it is important to establish the reasoning behind Louis's employment of the Irish and the massive front that he had to defend. The war had its roots in the earlier part of the century, a time when Louis's lust for power and glory was insatiable. The contemporary French concept of *gloire* meant that manhood was tested in combat and battle and this suited the young Louis's personality and direction.

The French saw *gloire* as essential for any young nobleman. What better way to promote oneself but to bathe in the glory of conquered territories? In this respect, Louis would portray the very essence of French nobility. Despite his position and the popular opinion that we now have of the Sun King, the young Louis was present at most of the major battles and sieges and ensured that he was trained by the best French generals of the time. His need for personal achievement effectively dictated French foreign policy for many years.

## The War of the Grand Alliance

It is not necessary within this work to outline the details of Louis's reign but it is important to determine the nature of the conflict in which Mountcashel had become embroiled. Louis XIV came to the throne in 1643 at the age of four and France was already at war. However, it was as an adult that the king, finally able and keen to make his own decisions, would start five major wars in Europe, ending only with the War of the Spanish Succession (1701-14), in which John Churchill, first Duke of Marlborough, would gain such notoriety. The young king began his conquest in 1661 in an attempt to conquer new territories for France.

For so long in the shadow of Spain, France saw Spanish power diminishing, and eyes were slowly turning to the Spanish Netherlands in northern Europe. The great commander Turenne backed Louis, as did many important French nobles despite the warnings of the young Louvois. As a pretext for war Louis could always fall back on the absence of dowry payment, promised by Spain as part of the Treaty of the Pyrenees earlier in the century. When King Philip IV of Spain died in 1665 the stage was set for Louis to make his move.

Louis had not counted on the Dutch, however. The French and Dutch had allied against Spain in the sixteenth and early-seventeenth centuries, a move that had ensured that limits were placed on Spanish expansionism. The Dutch United Provinces had secured their independence from Spain in 1648, an independence that could easily be threatened by the wrong alliance. History was repeating itself. French moves in the Spanish Netherlands were a little too close to home for the Dutch and, this time concerned over French expansion, they formed an alliance with England and Sweden to deter France. The Dutch had become a sea power and wielded great commercial influence, they and the French now being business rivals. They were understandably concerned over having the French on their doorstep. Louis's moves may not have been motivated by concern over trade, but Dutch resistance to French power was certainly motivated by the possible loss of such bargaining power. Louis had to be satisfied with gaining twelve fortified towns on the French border, but his eyes were still on the Spanish Netherlands. He soon realised that the once friendly Dutch were a problem. For the Dutch came the slow realisation that the French were a much bigger problem than Spain had ever been.

Louis would not be denied. He had been flouted at the beginning of his career by Dutch independence and would use the French army to enforce his will. He had supported the Dutch faithfully and they repaid him with disdain. By 1672 French plotting had ensured that a war with the Dutch was inevitable. Louis's armies under Turenne and Condé crossed the Rhine into Flanders, initially with rapid progress. But Louis was facing the young William of Orange, the new Dutch Stadtholder, who, rather than surrender after substantial French gains in the south, flooded the low-lying countryside, preventing further French gains. It was the first time that Louis and William had faced each other, but the Dutch war had sparked off the enmity that would plunge Europe into war and force kings from their thrones as the two sought to outwit each other.

The Dutch War had also seen the death of Turenne and the retirement of Condé, two of Louis's best marshals. Men such as Louvois, the minister for war, and Vauban advised Louis now. Although not directly responsible for Louis's use of defensive operations in the coming year, the loss of such men and rebuff in Flanders cannot have given Louis the feeling that French might was unstoppable. It clearly could be stopped or, at least, held at bay, and William had gained many allies through his resistance. Spain, the Holy Roman Empire and other German states had rallied behind the young Prince of Orange. The Treaty of Nijmegen ended the Dutch War in 1678. Louis had made some gains, adding some cities and a province to his borders, but had realised that the prize of the Spanish Netherlands would not come easily, nor would it come through the use of brute force alone.

By the late 1670s Louis's attitude towards France and his personal *gloire* had changed from that of a conquering nation under an aggressive king to that of an absolutist monarchy guarding the delicate borders of the nation. France was a greater power geographically but could little afford further costly wars. However, it would still fight if necessary. The alliances against Louis in the late-seventeenth century would take their toll, not helped by the defeat of the Turks by the Habsburgs, allowing the Holy Roman Empire to ally with the smaller European nations against France. Louis regarded these fledgling German states as a real enemy and acted defensively, in his view, by conquering many of the large cities on his eastern frontier in the 1680s. His seizure of Strasbourg in 1681 and Luxembourg, through legal machinations and the language of treaty, allowed him to control many vital crossings on the Rhine. Europe could not ignore the fact that Louis was still acting aggressively, no matter how much the French king felt that he was protecting his own borders. He may well have felt that his attitude to Europe had changed but could not advertise the fact. Louis could not admit that his policy and attitude had altered, and Europe could only believe that the Louis of old had returned. The language of treaties and the political activity of false wars continued long into the 1680s, further opening the gulf between Louis and his neighbours. By 1688 Louis's seizure of Phillipsburg on the Rhine in Alsace was the final straw, not only amongst the Grand Alliance, but amongst the Dutch who then gave support to William's appeals to allow him to take action in England before that kingdom became a strong ally of France.[48] As we have seen, Louis's actions had dire implications for Ireland and Lord Mountcashel.

By June 1690 the Irish regiments were ready for battle. Mountcashel had received a royal commission from Louis allowing him to command the Irish troops in French service. In addition, he had, for the third time, been commissioned as a lieutenant general, a rank he had held previously in Ireland and England under James II. Louis also awarded him the colonelship of his own, Mountcashel's, regiment, perhaps a formality by this stage but important nonetheless, especially for any troops who had been with Mountcashel for a long time, and who would fight and die for him.

# Chapter 13

# The Boyne

William, so soon after his accession to the throne, would still have concerns over English loyalties; was there still an underground body of support for James? To this end, the majority of his troops who would make the journey to Ireland would be trusted allies who had proved their loyalties in the past. On the Jacobite side, despite James's need for continued English acceptance and his very English preferences during the Irish parliament of 1689, his Catholicism convinced the Irish to the extent that he could rally considerable support. Ireland had been gripped by the erstwhile English king's 'cult of personality' and devout religious beliefs, an indicator, it was hoped, of better prospects for the Irish. The Irish nobility, native Lords and old-English, saw Irish estates in the Jacobite future while the landless natives saw potential freedom from the dictates of England.

There were, of course, cracks in the façade of Anglo–Irish unity, exacerbated by events in the Irish Parliament of 1689. James had shown his reluctance to upset his loyal English subjects. Only forceful Irish persuasion had pushed through a repeal of the Cromwellian land settlements. The Parliament, and the slow confirmation of fears that Ireland was but a stepping-stone for James, alienated many Irish while simultaneously confirming many English fears. The last of the Stuart kings with only the Irish throne now, was in a no-win situation. However, he still retained Irish support, albeit suspicious and somewhat estranged; the alternative for the Irish, drawing parallels with the aftermath of the 1641 rebellion and Cromwell's invasion, was too terrible to contemplate.

Nevertheless, James's continued support was to create hesitancy in the attempts of William's allies to force the matter in the Irish war. Since the victories at Newtownbutler and Londonderry, there had been some movement on the part of William's forces; despite early hopes that Marshal Schomberg would reach Derry as part of the relief expedition, he had been delayed until August, arriving with twelve infantry regiments, with the balance of his army to follow. At last, William's moves in Ireland were underway, accelerated by success in the north. Schomberg was a veteran in every sense of the word; in his seventies, he had fought in the Thirty

Years' War and risen to the rank of marshal of France in Louis's forces. His relationship with the French had ended, however, with Louis's revocation of the Edict of Nantes and the subsequent persecution of French Huguenots. His experience and services were now at William's disposal, although their relationship was far from perfect: Schomberg's deliberate, cautious approach to contemporary warfare contrasted with William's sometimes ad hoc approach; their relationship would be tested during the Irish campaign.

Schomberg's crossing and landing had been unopposed. There were Jacobites in eastern Ulster of course, who would remain uncommitted, and a French fleet, which opted not to become entangled with the Royal Navy in the Irish Sea. With additional infantry and cavalry reinforcements, and the addition of indigenous troops – units raised mainly from the Londonerry and Enniskillen garrisons – Schomberg commanded over 20,000 men by the end of September 1689. Carrickfergus was taken swiftly, although Schomberg was forced to intervene to prevent Scots-Irish anger being vented on the Catholic garrison; the propaganda effect of such atrocity so early in the campaign would do little to further William's cause, despite the apparent norms of seventeenth-century warfare.[1]

Melfort's departure for France and James's own doubts over the decaying situation helped make a bad situation worse;[2] there was panic in Dublin as rumour spread of a Protestant uprising.[3] De Rosen had little faith in the Irish army or its generals, citing lack of arms and ammunition as unwelcome disadvantages for an untrained and untested army that could put too few men in the field.[4] The French, perhaps predictably in light of a grander strategic game, wanted to play for time. They advised James to cut his losses in the north and retreat west to Athlone along the more easily defended Shannon river, and wait there for French reinforcements. They felt that James could not hope to defend Dublin without having his Irish army cut to ribbons by Schomberg's regulars. An Irish army defeated early in the campaign was of little use to French efforts to sustain a costly war. James ignored French advice to burn Dublin and move. He would instead stand and fight.[5]

Tyrconnel, in an unprecedented show of support, agreed with James, although he advised that a rapid re-organization of the Irish army was required. On this occasion James's words had been more than simple rhetoric. In an unexpected move, he rapidly headed north to Drogheda with a few hundred of his guards and volunteers while Schomberg remained at Carrickfergus. The move caught the attention of the Irish. Was this a bold counter from the king? Would it be enough to bolster dwindling support across the war-torn glens and bogs? James ordered Berwick north to Newry to help delay Schomberg's advance while Tyrconnel, with growing reinforcements, headed for Drogheda.[6] Was this the James of old, enabled once more in the fight for his throne? More importantly, would James's apparent will to resist instil new vigour in the Irish army where, despite restrictions in equipment and training, a will to fight was urgently required if any attempt at saving the rapidly deteriorating situation was to be made.

Of course, holding Dublin meant little to the French; for the Irish, however, it had become symbolic as the base of the all too recent Irish Parliament, a seat of government and the promise of new beginnings. If Dublin should fall, surely the country would follow. The French knew all too well that this was inevitable. James and the Irish could only hope that some fragment of possibility remained of saving the country and, perhaps, even winning a few battles, thus creating the need for William to make terms and end the destructive conflict that would cost him so much on the grander European scale. If James hoped to save Dublin, he could not afford to squander opportunities.

Schomberg started south in early September, arriving in Newry by the 5th to find that Berwick and his men had burned it down, together with much of the forage in the surrounding countryside. At the Moyry Pass, where the legendary Ulster hero Cuchulain had reputedly stopped the forces of Queen Medb from entering Ulster, an opportunity was missed where a small Jacobite force could have held back Schomberg's approach in the narrow defile between Newry and Dundalk. By then, however, Schomberg's men were under a greater threat than that of Jacobite ambush. They were out of supply, support shipping still being at sea, delayed by the unrelenting storms on the Irish Sea. Schomberg would have to rely on his tenuous supply lines to Carrickfergus and his advance slowed. By September his troops were encamped in soggy marshland north of Dundalk. Under normal circumstances, an army on the move would shrug off such conditions as an everyday occurrence during an aggressive march. However, the army would remain in this rain-soaked locale for two months. Schomberg's caution and pause for planning his next move would debilitate his troops and, more crucially, allow the Jacobites time to gather forces at Drogheda.

The lack of action in Ireland was not universal. The Inniskillingers would see further fighting almost immediately. Thomas Lloyd, now known as 'little Cromwell', who had become a hero around Enniskillen, commanded troops in Sligo, west of County Fermanagh, by the autumn of 1689. As he had done in Fermanagh, he held the initiative, even attacking Jacobite positions in

Roscommon. Patrick Sarsfield, clearly in more aggressive mood than he had been in Fermanagh, was still dangerous and indeed vigorous enough to act decisively against Lloyd's troops with a Jacobite army of 7,000 men. Lloyd was forced back to Sligo, and its defences. Sarsfield's attacks eventually took forts and town; terms of surrender were honoured and he permitted the garrison to leave with arms and goods.[7] The Jacobite army could still be a force to be reckoned with when well led.

Despite the repeated urgings of his officer corps, and of William in England, Schomberg refused to attack. Having easily gained intelligence regarding the apparent lack of movement in the Williamite camp, the gathering of Jacobite troops began to move slowly north to Schomberg's position.[8] Schomberg's reluctance to take any risks could only have one result, that of further galvanising Irish opinion and support in favour of a pitched battle. D'Avaux was confused by the entire affair, convinced that the lack of action was a ruse to lure the Jacobite army from Dublin, perhaps to aid a naval attack, or that a Protestant rising in the capital was to be the trigger for an attack.[9] By the middle of September the Irish army, with James at their head, had moved to Ardee; within a few days they were within five miles of Schomberg's position. By the end of the month the armies were within cannon shot of each other. William's complaints fell on deaf ears as Schomberg complained of poor officers, the quality of local regiments, equipment and logistical issues. He complained that a second landing was required and that James's army was superior. D'Avaux reported that a French deserter blamed Schomberg's hesitancy on his lack of faith in the loyalty of his Huguenot French regiments, which contained some Catholic officers and men.[10]

Such rhetoric played into the hands of James, who, however, suffered criticism from the Irish for not seizing the initiative:

> At last the king resolved to try his fortune. Whereupon he drew out his army on the twenty-first of September, and marched in order of battle near unto the enemy, in hopes he would quit his trenches and accept of the challenge. But the marshal durst not, as finding the royal troops too numerous for his; and the king would not attack him in his trenches, fearing the victory would prove too dear, though general de Rosen, upon good grounds, was altogether for it, since they could not get the enemy to fight otherwise. And he took the king's refusal to attack the foe so ill, that he resolved not to stay in the kingdom. His opinion was confirmed by several officers,

who showed that the attempt was not so dangerous, as it appeared at a distance.[11]

With barely a shot fired, Schomberg's army stayed exactly where it was. The cost was high, even by the standards of the late-seventeenth century; around 7,000 troops died of disease at Dundalk with several thousand more dying after being moved to Belfast or during attempts to ship them back to England. Poor sanitation and a lack of organisation for a protracted stay signed the death warrants of many men before they had made any offensive moves in the Irish war.[12] James's troops also suffered as they stayed close to the Williamites. By the start of October, however, the Jacobites moved back to Ardee which, by November, had been turned into a well-defended position, although disease and poor food continued to undermine their position too.[13] James subsequently left for Dublin while Schomberg left for Lisburn; their respective armies had to survive in their desperate positions, with no offensive action, over an increasingly deadly Irish winter.

William was forced to intervene, despite Schomberg's objections regarding supply and the size of the Irish army; in William's view, Schomberg did not have the tenacity and drive required for the Irish war. To win, and for William's wider European purposes it was important to win quickly, the new King of England and Scotland would have to intervene himself and prevent French plans in Ireland creating more of a diversionary war than was absolutely necessary. James, on the other hand, could be reasonably satisfied with events; indeed, if a victory could be construed as raising an army and having it remain intact, in position and with the potential to further hinder Williamite plans, James had gained much from Schomberg's inaction. Without a shot fired in anger, he had defied the Williamite advance. The key benefit of such defiance was the morale-boosting effect on the Irish army. Even this had to be handled carefully. However, encouragement to attack Schomberg's position took little account of the state of the Irish force, in terms of ability and equipment. John Stevens gave a clear picture:

The army daily increased in numbers and expressed a great alacrity and readiness to march towards the enemy, though most of the men were very raw and undisciplined, and the generality almost naked or at least very ragged and ill shod. The only creditable and hopeful part of the army were the horse, who were for the most part good men, well-armed and mounted, but their number not very great.[14]

The unexpected delay could have been used to great effect. There was an army to train. Equipment and effective officers could have been concentrated within several better regiments. The entire winter could have been devoted to preparing the army for war. Despite the optimism and high morale, the Irish remained difficult to control:

> This too great confidence of the good posture of our affairs produced in all men such a security as proved without doubt very prejudicial to our interest in the end. Every one laying aside the care of the public wholly devoted himself either to his private affairs or to his pleasure and ease. The main business of recruiting and disciplining the army was for a long time laid aside, and instead thereof the forces that were on foot suffered to disperse about the country to live at ease without restraint, without exercise and without order.

As regiments at Dundalk dwindled and dispersed, trenchworks and defences were established around Dublin. James's early confidence and activity quickly lapsed into apathy as he moved to Kilkenny, leaving the army and its officers to their own devices. The French, including d'Avaux, found the situation, which had held so much promise late in 1689, becoming untenable with the onset of winter.[15] Another chance had been missed. Schomberg, too, had retreated and his troops were dispersed through much of war-torn Ulster, to avoid further death at the shambles of the Dundalk camp. Despite the attempt, however, poor conditions and food killed still more troops in the winter of 1689-90.

English anger over the affair was predictably fervent. The government demanded answers, and William had little choice now but to intervene himself.[16] Bentinck, William's closest friend and trusted Dutch counsellor, disagreed with his decision, as did many members of the government, but there was little option. The war on the continent would have to wait; William had to take care of Louis's Irish diversion first. Renewed vigour, not wholly born of panic, marked the Williamite campaign of 1690. William would take no chances as reinforcements headed for Ireland during the spring, including 7,000 Danish troops headed by the German Duke of Württemberg-Neustadt. Dutch and English troops followed and properly-organised means of supplying the growing army were established. Yet again, French naval interdiction was not present and it seemed that, for now, William had control of the Irish Sea; indeed in a sensational attack on Dublin harbour a Jacobite twenty-gun frigate was spirited away by a Williamite task force.[17]

In exchange for a force of handpicked Irish troops, to be led ultimately by Mountcashel after his escape from Enniskillen, James would receive 6,000 French regulars together with additional arms and equipment, a war-winning proposition indeed.[18] Weren't these the feared scourge of Europe, the ultimate extension of Louis's wider European ambition? Their effect on the Irish scene could have been more dramatic had they not been ordered to keep themselves intact at the expense of native Irish troops. Louis could not afford to waste French regulars in what was rapidly becoming a sideshow with each passing day. William's inevitable intervention would complete the plan. Then it was a matter of playing for time. A stray shot could even kill Louis's enemy in one fell stroke.

However, the French force that arrived in March 1690, a year after James had first set foot on Irish soil, was commanded by the unpopular and vain Count de Lauzun, who had been requested by James to replace de Rosen. Lauzun, the supreme courtier, had helped James's young wife and child escape to France during the 1688 revolution and seemed destined for notoriety in the Irish campaign. His military experience was questionable, to say the least; more importantly, perhaps, he was seemingly not on good terms with the powerful Louvois, although the French war minister had advised him to play for time in Ireland, and he remained unpopular with many of the French officers and with Tyrconnel.[19] D'Avaux, too, had little affection for the French dandy, and when notified that he would be returning home to France on the ships that would transport the Irish, expressed some pleasure at being rid of a situation that, with Lauzun's arrival, could only get worse in many ways; indeed it was thought that his presence could encourage many Irish into the arms of Schomberg, rather than encourage continued resistance.[20]

Initial hopes of French salvation proved a little overzealous. Two of the five French regiments that landed in Ireland weren't French at all, but Germans and Walloons, many of whom were captured Protestants who would ultimately defect to the Williamites. Also, the condition of the arms and supplies delivered was questionable at best, poor when compared with the equipment that William was pouring into Ireland. Inevitably perhaps, hostility and disagreement characterised the Franco-Irish relationship.

Lauzun ran into trouble almost upon immediately arriving on Irish soil. He complained that Lord Dover, whom James had sent to Cork to assist the French commander with unloading troops and supplies, was unhelpful. He implied that no effort was made to procure horses for the French officers and that the governor of Cork was 'wretched' and had little love for his allies.

Finally, after much complaining, he set off for Dublin. In his stead he left the Marquis de la Hoguette, who found himself once more confounded by Lord Dover who, in the end, decided that he had had enough of Frenchmen and resolved to return to his king. Things were not going well. French arrogance, although expected, was a little out of place under the circumstances.

William's journey to Ireland was somewhat grander than Lauzun's. Hundreds of ships, artillery and 15,000 troops sailed into Belfast Lough by mid-June, William landing at Carrickfergus on the 14th. Accompanying the new king were several influential allies. These included the young Duke of Ormonde, William's trusted friend Bentinck, and several experienced and influential allied generals and colonels. William met Schomberg halfway between Belfast and Carrickfergus at Whitehouse. Also assembled were many of the experienced notables who would form the core of the Williamite military leadership: Meinhardt Schomberg, the elder Schomberg's son, Württemberg, commander of the Danish division, senior Dutch and English officers and even Gustavus Hamilton, who had seen so much success with his Enniskillen garrison, and whose men were now at William's service and ready to fight vigorously for his cause. There seemed little time for reflection regarding Schomberg's actions at Dundalk. It was a time to rapidly end the frustrations of the Franco-Irish problem.

Schomberg's plans had centred on a two-pronged strategic move, one to Dundalk and the other west then south through Belturbet in Fermanagh. William rejected most of the plan. He would lead the army straight for Dundalk, with Douglas taking a detour through Armagh, protecting William's flank and meeting him at Dundalk. James, too, was in a mood for action, heading for Dundalk himself by 16 June, full of planning and intent to face his son in law, despite Lauzun's pleas for caution. James's intent was to strip the area of William's advance of forage and he was encouraged to try to hold the Moyry Pass. Despite capturing a handful of Williamite prisoners, there was no significant action taken to halt William's advance. Within days, the Williamite and Jacobite armies faced each other once more, this time on either side of the river Boyne, north of Dublin.

***

Later commentaries related to the battle of the Boyne would, depending on affiliations, make light of the defeat or exaggerate the significance of the victory. Whether significant on the grander continental European stage or not, the fact remained that two kings would face each other, one seen by many as a usurper of the English throne, although determined not to be beaten by Louis XIV's machinations, the other viewed as a failed Catholic monarch, although still able to command enough respect to field an army that would drag William from his new English possessions. Neither was a great commander, at least when compared with Turenne or Montecuccoli, although it was clear that the key to this victory would be leadership, and taking the initiative. The battle at this river, the only significant obstacle between Dundalk and Dublin farther south, would decide the fate of kings. James had no intention of burning Dublin despite French advice.[21] Even then, when a decision had been made to stand, there was some indifference about defences, with earthworks being erected in patchwork fashion along the riverbank. Lauzun, predictably, considered the entire position untenable; his reconnaissance of the site uncovered a multitude of fording points with little opportunity to channel an advancing enemy into ambushes at pre-defined choke points. By 29 June James's 25,000 men, including his French regulars, had encamped on the southern side of the river, their impending clash with the Williamite army more certain than ever.

The battlefield was characterised by the river and its local towns and villages. To the east, downstream and nearest the coast, lay Drogheda, which would play no part in the battle but was quickly garrisoned by 1,300 Jacobite troops. Over two miles upstream lay the small village of Oldbridge, at least one point where the river could be forded. Another crossing point was available in the form of a bridge at Slane, four miles to the west. Although a river in theory should have stopped an army, and thus prevented an outflanking move against James, the tactic was fatally flawed due to the presence of numerous and poorly-defended crossing points along the Boyne's length; indeed, the ability to move quickly on William's part would prove to be James's undoing.

For some of the remaining Hamiltons the battle would see still more momentous events. There is evidence that Anthony Hamilton was present and many of the elements that he had previously commanded at Newtownbutler took part.[22] He would play no obvious part, however, and would not see the involvement in key events that his younger brother Richard would. The younger John Hamilton was also present, although, again, his activities during the battle would be limited to a certain flank action.

Had further preparations been considered, there was little time; William's 36,000-strong army appeared on the heights north of the river on 30 June (o.s.). Despite the difference in numbers, there were other marked factors that would affect the tide of battle. The Irish Jacobite infantry was poorly trained and equipped, many regiments having few matchlocks or training in how to use them. The Jacobite cavalry, however, was second to none, composed as it was of Irish nobility mounted on good horses and with excellent morale. William's army was collected from across Europe, yet was for the most part professional. Dutch guards regiments used more reliable flintlock muskets and were drilled in 'platoon fire', which meant that part of the firing line would be loaded and ready at all times, a more efficient battle tactic when troops had been well trained. Williamite artillery consisted of thirty-six field guns compared to a paltry number of Jacobite pieces of variable quality. Although William's cavalry in some cases lacked the edge of the Jacobite mounted element, they were regular troops, well drilled and experienced and used to the sights and sounds of desperate battle. In addition, morale amongst the Williamites was good; there would be no hesitation in engaging the Jacobite army on this occasion.

Williamite guns had started their bombardment on the evening of the 30th. It was a Monday; whether through superstition or due to the need to rest his army after the march south, William was determined that he would not attack yet. He did, however, carry out a reconnaissance close to the river where enterprising Jacobite gunners tried their luck with a shot, echoing the events that had led to the death of Turenne so many years before when George Hamilton had fought under the great master. William was wounded by the shot, as gleeful cheers arose from the opposite side of the river and the Jacobites were convinced that he had been killed. The news eventually got as far as France where it was celebrated with great pomp and ceremony; however, much to the disappointment of Louis, James and the Jacobites, the information was inaccurate. William had been wounded lightly, the glancing shot having lost much of its velocity and been blunted by his bulky leather tunic. The wound was treated quickly and preparations for attack continued; celebrations in France were premature.[23]

Monday evening was spent with deliberations held at William's council of war north of the river. Schomberg favoured a diversionary attack across the river at Oldbridge, directly into the teeth of the Jacobite defence, while the balance of the army, having previously marched upstream and crossed the river, could not only outflank the Jacobite army, but cut off its retreat. Other officers favoured a frontal attack only. William adopted a compromise. Schomberg's son Meinhardt would be sent with a third of the army to attempt a river crossing upstream to the south-west. However, the flanking movement would be a diversion. The main assault would be at Oldbridge, where two thirds of William's army would hit James's troops head on.

The plan was a good one in theory, mainly due to the Jacobite dispositions south of the river. James's Franco-Irish force was centred at Oldbridge, east of the sharp bend in the Boyne. There were troops at Drogheda, although James had taken little action as yet about his apparently weak flank. James had also held a council of war the day before the battle; in at least one account it is suggested that Richard Hamilton proposed that eight regiments should be sent to secure the bridge at Slane, five miles west of Oldbridge. In response James agreed in principle, although stating initially that only fifty dragoons were to be sent to secure the bridge. Hamilton is reputed to have bowed and remained silent, in apparent bewilderment.[24] In the end James detached 800 dragoons under Sir Neil O'Neill as his flank protection – 800 troops who would ultimately face up to a third of William's army in their attempts to cross the river.

The degree of Williamite intelligence is unclear, although it is likely that William received word during the night, rather than the following morning, that the bridge at Slane had been rendered useless. The flank marching element would therefore be forced to plan for another crossing point. Apparently using local knowledge, Gustavus Hamilton suggested that some of his Inniskillingers act as guides to help the troops move to a closer crossing point, the ford at Rosnaree. This was much more accessible than the bridge at Slane and, under the circumstances, made tactical sense, situated as it was closer to Oldbridge, and two miles farther south from Slane as the river ran, thus more easily permitting a rapid flank march that could pin the Jacobite army within the loop of the river.

William's plans, at least in terms of the flank march, were set in motion on the following morning. In the early hours, around 5.00 a.m., with gathering fog obscuring Williamite movements, the riverbank was alive with the sounds of thousands of men and horses making ready to move on their march. Jacobite sentries can only have reported what they heard, the sound of an army on the march. James must have believed that William planned a massive co-ordinated flank attack. It was the natural thing to do under the circumstances. Why should the Dutchman waste men in an expensive frontal assault across the river? James may even have believed in the unassailable value of his river defence. Had he actually managed to foil William by his own positioning? He had, however, only placed 800 dragoons on his flank. He knew that he had to act; James can only have believed that Oldbridge would not see the focus of the battle. His flank and, more importantly, his route of retreat to Dublin was under threat. In a bold move, he determined to lead most of his army toward Rosnaree, leaving 8,000 men under Tyrconnel at Oldbridge, and no French infantry: the best foot troops had gone with James. Although he could not have known it, he had left Tyrconnel and Richard Hamilton to face three times their number on the far bank. If William's flanking plan had been a deliberate ruse, events would transpire to show that it had been truly inspired.

Sir Neil O'Neill with 800 dragoons was under orders to hold the crossing at Rosnaree until James's troops could reach him. With three small field guns and his men in reasonable defensive positions, O'Neill could hold for a time. Morale was good and O'Neill was an inspiration to his men, although the odds would narrow as the hours passed. Just before 8.00 a.m. the Williamite flanking element reached the ford. Dutch dragoons started across the river as O'Neill's scattered troops opened fire. Casualties were heavy but Meinhardt Schomberg had more than enough men and, as time wore on, pressure began to tell on the Irish dragoons. In the heat of battle, O'Neill was shot through the thigh as his men were forced to retreat through a narrow defile; although carried from the fight, he died a week later. His men, demoralised by the size of the attack and the wounding of their leader, promptly fell back. The young Schomberg had gained the ford and began to push south-east to flank James and the main Jacobite army.

The unfavourable terrain had checked James's rapid advance. The decision to move may have been made quickly, but the physical logistics of marching so many troops three miles toward Rosnaree, over terrain dominated by steep hills, had created significant difficulties and lost precious time. As the Jacobite troops arrived on the edge of a boggy ravine known as Roughgrange, which cut in a south-westerly direction straight across their front, they began to see Williamite troops massing on the far side. Had thorough reconnaissance of the surrounding area been carried out then such factors may have been taken into account; as it was most of the Jacobite army faced a 'detachment' of the Williamite force. On this occasion, unlike in the previous year, the inability of one to attack the other was based less on the reticence of individual commanders than on the nature of the terrain.

The boggy ravine at Roughgrange was so steep and so covered with foliage that it would have proved impossible to attack with cavalry and difficult to co-ordinate infantry attacks without having such efforts become an uncontrolled melee where the reserves of one side or the other could sneak around the battling flanks to cause havoc behind the enemy. The situation would have proven worse for the Jacobites since any additional Williamite move to the east could cut off lines of retreat. James, at least initially, must have felt that he had adequately foiled William's flanking plans, as the two armies watched each other from a few hundred yards across an impassable cut in the landscape. He had, however, made a critical mistake in moving so much of his army from Oldbridge. With only one third of his force remaining there, the Oldbridge front lay invitingly open to attack. James, able Irish commanders such as Sarsfield, the entire French contingent and indeed two of the Hamilton brothers sat miles from William's main body, forced into inactivity by terrain and the presence of the enemy. Two thirds of the Jacobite army would remain out of the engagement.[25]

Around 10.00 a.m., with the tide at its lowest ebb, William's elite Dutch Blue Guards began fording the river at Oldbridge. With so many uniform colours and indeed similarly clothed troops on opposing sides (both sides wore red in abundance for instance), William's troops wore a sprig of shillelagh in their hats while Jacobite troops wore a white paper 'cockade' in the French style. Such distinction between troops would not always prove adequate in the midst of battle however. The Dutch Guards crossed in slow columns, reaching the middle of the river before they began to receive musket fire from the far bank. It was hoped that weight of numbers, successively used for shock effect as they crossed the river at different points, would deter and demoralise the defenders. There would be some hard fighting but, if the matter came to numbers, William had them in abundance.

Richard Hamilton, who had been placed in command of the Jacobite infantry at Oldbridge by Tyrconnel, had six battalions of Irish foot at his disposal. Of these, two were Irish guards, loyal to James and almost certainly better equipped than most other Jacobite troops. With the superiority of Williamite artillery and the advantage they had gained from their positioning on high ground, overlooking most of the open battlefield, Hamilton had been forced to hide most of his men behind a small ridgeline behind Oldbridge, with scattered pockets of defenders within the village itself. These would have little chance to do serious damage against the Dutch guards during the river crossing, as their defensive fire could not be co-ordinated in volleys and remained scattered and irregular. Hamilton's only chance of engaging the Williamite troops was in relatively close combat when they had gained the south bank, where the proximity of friend and foe could deter the attentions of William's gunners on the high ground to the north. The balance of the Jacobite force, three elite cavalry regiments led by Tyrconnel, lay on the high ground to the south.

Lack of adequate defence and continuing pressure from Dutch numbers crossing the river meant that Oldbridge was rapidly becoming untenable. After an exchange of musketry, with some Dutch casualties, although not enough to hinder the advance, the position was abandoned. However, Hamilton, sensing that the time to lead the Jacobite infantry in close to the enemy had come, led an infantry charge from the ridge.[26] Of the six Jacobite battalions, it is likely that only the two guards' regiments actually engaged the Dutch, the others perhaps put off by Williamite artillery shots or by poor morale, equipment or even leadership. A brief musketry duel ensued although, predictably, Dutch drill saw the better of the match. Hamilton is recorded as having pushed almost to the riverbank himself in the infantry charge, where he found that so few men had accompanied him that he had to retreat. The Dutch guards had not only secured a foothold but had tested the mettle of the Irish infantry and found it wanting. Hamilton can only have despaired.[27]

As Dutch infantry gained ground on the far bank, the Ulster regiments, three battalions from Enniskillen and Londonderry, began crossing slightly downstream from the Dutch. Shortly after this, three French Huguenot regiments forded a hundred yards farther downstream, with English and Dutch troops following. Pressure on the Jacobite position was mounting rapidly and Hamilton did not have the men to stop the flood. The Jacobite infantry had been given a scare. These were not troops who could face European regulars. That task would fall on the Jacobite cavalry.

As William's Dutch Guards began to rout the enemy infantry, Tyrconnel realised that his cavalry needed to engage. He ordered Berwick to lead two troops of James's Horse Guards while Parker and Sutherland's cavalry regiments acted in support. Hamilton was to rally the infantry as best he could. The Jacobite cavalry charged off the hill at Donore, half a mile south of Oldbridge and straight into the Dutch Guards; it was the first of many charges that day. Although the pike had not yet seen the end of its days on the European battlefield, elite troops such as the Dutch were also adopting the socket bayonet as a foil to cavalry attack, superior to the older 'plug' bayonet through its design, which left the musket free to fire when fitted, rather than turning it into a relatively powerless 'spiked club'. After the Dutch began to fire at the approaching horsemen, as flintlock shots and caustic smoke 'rippled' across the front of the battalions, horses and riders met a storm of lead. The twenty-year-old Berwick, at the head of 1,000 horsemen braved the volleys but a terrible toll was taken on the charging cavalry. Those who continued lost impetus as the Dutch held up their bayonets to counter the attacking horse. Parker was wounded and his regiment badly mauled. As Richard Hamilton could find few infantry to rally by this stage, he rapidly took command of two of the remaining squadrons of Parker's cavalry and reformed them for a second charge.[28] Sutherland's regiment had lost impetus in the attack, but had come off lightly in terms of casualties. In the thick of the action William was heard to lament upon his 'poor guards'. His guards, however, would give good account of themselves.

The cavalrymen reformed for another attack. Were the Dutch too strong to hit head on? The Jacobite cavalry had other, less professional, targets to attack, however. Hamilton, in apparent desperation at having lost his chance to rally the Irish infantry, gathered Parker's men and what other cavalry he could find and attacked. The second charge hurtled toward Hanmer's English regiment, forming up after having crossed the river, and smashed into them and two of the French Huguenot regiments, passing through as far as Oldbridge itself. Caillemotte's Regiment was broken and its commander mortally wounded, urging his men to further *gloire* as he was carried from the field. The eighty-four-year-old Schomberg had also crossed the river, urging the Ulster and Huguenot regiments forward as the Irish cavalry regrouped. Amidst the melee, smoke and confusion he was slashed by sword cuts and shot by a musket ball in the back of the neck, and fell dead.

Aside from the early departure of the Jacobite infantry, the battle remained fluid. The Williamites had lost one of their most senior commanders after all. Despite the momentum of the cavalry charge against infantry, a psychological force of wills, the Irish cavalry had been stifled to some degree by Dutch bravado and morale, although their subsequent attempts were having more success. At some point during the cavalry-infantry clashes, around 11a.m., William ordered his Danish reserves to cross farther downstream, half a mile from Oldbridge. Seven thousand Danish regulars made ready to ford at what proved to be a very deep crossing point.

A third massed cavalry charge followed – into one of the Londonderry regiments as it started to form from column into line on the flank of the Dutch Guards. The Irish had some success against these less professional regiments although they were receiving heavy casualties from musketry with each charge. Horses and men were becoming tired and demoralised, and the Williamite surge of manpower across the river showed no sign of ceasing. Enemy muskets reduced Hamilton's, Tyrconnel's and Berwick's numbers on each charge and time was running out. In a final act against the Williamite right a fourth attack was organised, although the Irish cavalry had lost the initiative and the attack petered out as the horsemen halted to fire carbines and pistols at the enemy battalions before withdrawing into the smoke. Frightful losses in Irish cavalry, presumably running into the hundreds, had been taken with little effect on the Williamite infantry who remained ensconced on the southern bank of the Boyne. Word began to reach the cavalrymen of Danish troops crossing to the east. Messengers were rapidly sent to James; cavalry reinforcements were required urgently.

Although the 7,000-strong Danish contingent crossed practically unimpeded, the river itself was so deep at this point that Württemberg had to be carried on the shoulders of the tallest grenadiers. A few Irish muskets on the far bank made little difference. Some sources indicate that further Danish volleys scared off those troops on the far bank. With Danish infantry gaining ground, shortly followed by their horse, Irish cavalry arrived on the scene. The Danish appear to have carried *chevaux-de-frise*, stave-like barriers, to be used in place of pikes, or more likely in conjunction with bayonets, which ruined any chance of a successful cavalry charge. Danish volleys scattered the Irish horse and those dragoons who remained. The battle for Oldbridge was over.

Having established a foothold on the far bank and, for the most part, blunted what was left of the Irish cavalry, William was determined to make one further crossing. The fight so far had been costly for his army; most of the troops who had successfully defended against the Jacobite cavalry were in no state to push farther south. Isolated infantry movement at this stage would have left open flanks prone to attack from the remaining Jacobite horse.

Whether pre-planned or otherwise, by midday William had resolved to make another crossing east of Oldbridge, having ordered the Dutch veteran Godart de Ginkel, who had arrived in England with the Dutch contingent in 1688, to find another crossing point. The battle had been raging for two hours across the river when Ginkel saw that his time to cross was most opportune – at Mill Ford near Drybridge, a mile downstream from Oldbridge. William also opted to enter the battle himself and take 1,500 Dutch cavalry with him. His infantry had established a foothold despite Hamilton's and Berwick's frantic charges; however, the advance of so many of William's cavalry would enable the infantry to advance south, their flanks protected.

Before the general advance could occur, William had to get across the river. He had made contact with Ginkel as the first troops began to cross. On the far bank they could already see Jacobite dragoons leaving their reserve positions on the hills opposite to charge to the bank and defend against the latest crossing. Musket volleys or Williamite artillery, or a combination of both, quickly scattered the dragoons. At this point, William began to cross himself. He almost faltered, having trouble in crossing the deepest part.

He was forced to dismount and have his horse dragged as he was helped to the far shore, tradition says by an Inniskillinger, where the shock of the effort gave him an asthma attack. Recovering quickly, he remounted and led the massive cavalry force in a flanking move towards Oldbridge and the re-forming Jacobite cavalry.

The only obstacle to that flanking move was a Jacobite dragoon regiment who, although charging bravely, in some sources allegedly drunk on brandy supplied by Richard Hamilton, were only delaying the inevitable. The remnants of the Irish infantry had earlier retreated to the high ground south of the Boyne and, with the crossing of William's cavalry, began to withdraw completely. Their commander was fully engaged with re-forming what remained of the Jacobite cavalry. What preparations for counter-attack Hamilton and Berwick had made were thrown into further confusion by the appearance of hundreds of Dutch cavalry crossing the river on their right. William's squadrons, having dispersed the enemy dragoons, now closed. Irish horsemen, who had charged again and again against the co-ordinated volleys of William's regulars, and suffered for it, responded predictably. With little hope of withstanding a charge at the halt, and for the most part exhausted, the Irish cavalry retreated, making for the hill at Donore, just over a mile south of Oldbridge.

As the Jacobite infantry line collapsed and began to flee south, casting aside muskets and even shoes in their zeal to run faster, around 1,000 men, the scattered remnants of Parker's, Sutherland's, Tyrconnel's and Berwick's cavalry, with some dragoons, were all that remained to defend against at least 10,000 infantry and cavalry of William's encroaching army. The Jacobite cavalry withdrew to the slopes of the hill at Donore to re-form. Tyrconnel, probably witnessing the approach of thousands of enemy troops from his position on the heights, gave Richard Hamilton his final orders. Hamilton was to command the rearguard, who, for the most part, were doomed, and delay William's troops for as long as possible at the hill. Realising the hopelessness of the situation, having received no reinforcement from James at Roughgrange, and certainly wishing to avoid capture by William, Tyrconnel made off toward Duleek with his escort, following the retreating infantry and leaving Hamilton to his fate.

William moved forward to the leading cavalry regiment, that of the Inniskillingers led by William Wolseley, victor of Newtownbutler. Telling them how much he had heard of their reputation William asked what they would now do for him? In the dust and confusion and the colours that confirmed few as friend or foe, William was almost mistaken for a Jacobite

and shot; finally recognising the king the Enniskillen cavalry followed
William's lead up the hill, pushing Hamilton's exhausted Jacobites back and
leaving the dead in their wake. At the top of the hill in a ruined churchyard,
Hamilton had lined the walls of the area with dragoons and whatever musket-
armed troops he could retain. William, whose luck never seemed to run out,
had been struck by two musket-balls on the way up, one hitting the end of
his pistol and the other the heel of his boot. The Jacobites defended as best
they could amidst the confusion of smoke and noise:

> It was about a mile further on the top of the hill where some
> old walls, that the enemy had well lined with firelocks. Here his
> Majesty led some Dutch troops, but before they had gone in, the
> Inniskillingers had made an assault on the other side, and did very
> bravely at first, but espying another great party, whom they took
> for the enemy, just ready to surround them, they began to fly;
> and did actually put in disorder the Dutch horse and all others
> that stood in their way. The place was unfortunately full of holes
> and dung pits, and the passage narrow; but above all the dust and
> smoke quite blinded them. His Majesty was here in the crowd of
> all, drawing his sword and animating those that fled to follow him.
> His danger was great among the enemy's guns that killed thirty of
> his Inniskilleners on the spot. Nay one of the Inniskilleners came
> with a pistol cocked to his majesty till he called out, what, are you
> angry with your friends? The truth is, the clothes of friends and
> foes are all so much alike, that his Majesty had goodness to excuse
> all that passed.[29]

The hill not only represented the last-ditch effort of the Jacobite army, led by
Hamilton, it had a tactical significance in the battle. The farther south that
William pushed, the more delicate James's inflexible position at Roughgrange
became, facing another Williamite army as it was. Hamilton's rearguard
action was the only stopgap against a general Williamite exploitation of the
Jacobite route of retreat. Hamilton had little choice but to hold if James's
army was to leave the field and fight another day. His actions could affect the
immediate fate of the Irish force. Successive cavalry attacks in support of
the defended positions at the hilltop fell against William's advancing troops.
Chaos ensued. At one stage Berwick, still in the melee, was set to order a
group of dragoons to fire upon his own cavalry, until he realised his mistake.
An Inniskillinger was almost skewered on the bayonet of a Huguenot until

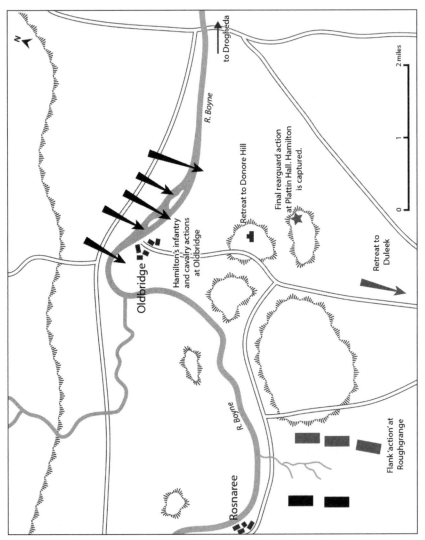

Williamite attack at the Boyne, 1690.

he shouted his identity. There must have been many more unfortunate incidents of mistaken identity in the confusion of men and blood.

Some sources indicate that Hamilton withdrew from the hilltop to regroup at the ruins of Plattin Castle, a half mile to the south,[30] where he would face William Wolseley and his Enniskillen cavalry:

> General Hamilton, in order to favour the retreat of the Irish and French Foot, drew up a Body of Horse very artfully near Plattin Castle, in an enclosed field, into which there was only one entrance, through a gap made by Pioneers. The other eight troops of Inniskilling Horse, commanded by Col Wolseley, not thinking it necessary to wait for help, and being desirous to be sharers of the transactions of that day, went on with a resolution to attack this party though under great disadvantage.[31]

Williamite cavalry and dragoons followed closely as he withdrew and regrouped; there was time for Hamilton to make one more desperate charge. The account also reminds us briefly of Jacobite confusion at Lisnaskea a year before, although it would be Wolseley who suffered casualties on this occasion:

> There was no way of coming to this gap but by marching first by the enemy's front almost within the reach of their shot, in a narrow lane fenced on each side with a dry double ditch; however, they were suffered to pass unmolested. When two troops had gone through the gap and it was time to form them in order to face the enemy, who were drawn up on their right, the colonel by mistake commanded them to wheel to the left, whereby instead of facing they turned their backs to the enemy, which the lieutenant colonel, perceiving, cried aloud to them to wheel to the right on which some wheeling to the left and some to the right, they ran into great disorder and confusion. In this instant, before they could recover themselves, the enemy fell upon, routed and killed about fifty of them on the spot.[32]

Although there are some parallels with events at Donore, a second counter-attack at Plattin is plausible. For Richard Hamilton, however, the attempt would see the end of his battle and the end of his Irish war. In the final charge of the Jacobite cavalry, Hamilton was wounded and captured by

Williamite troops, just a few yards from where William sat astride his horse. Crying out to those of his troops who had rushed to Hamilton to kill him, they instead spared his life. Macaulay's account of the battle is interesting, if a little contrived, referring to memorable earlier events in Hamilton's Irish experience.

> In this encounter Richard Hamilton, who had done all that could be done by valour to retrieve a reputation forfeited by perfidy, was severely wounded, taken prisoner, and instantly brought, through the smoke and over the carnage, before the prince whom he had foully wronged. On no occasion did the character of William show itself in a more striking manner.
>
> 'Is this business over?' he said; 'or will your horse make more fight?'
>
> 'On my honour, Sir,' answered Hamilton, 'I believe that they will.'
>
> 'Your honour!' muttered William; 'your honour!'
>
> That half suppressed exclamation was the only revenge which he condescended to take for an injury for which many sovereigns, far more affable and gracious in their ordinary deportment, would have exacted a terrible retribution. Then, restraining himself, he ordered his own surgeon to look to the hurts of the captive.[33]

In retrospect, Hamilton's tarnished honour, and his 'reputation forfeited by perfidy' was certainly a contentious matter, bearing in mind his escape from England in 1688. He was a prisoner of William once more. His prediction of the continued efforts of the Jacobite troops proved inaccurate. Jacobite resistance to William's advance had rapidly ended. Despite brave yet ultimately futile charges, William's numbers and morale proved decisive as remaining pockets of resistance were quickly silenced or forced to surrender or flee.

James, who had remained idle with the troops at Roughgrange, had been made aware of matters at Oldbridge at about noon as the Danish troops began their crossing. For two hours James sat immobile, perhaps feeling that his flank protection was essential for continued fighting at Oldbridge, perhaps losing his nerve. By 2 p.m., as James was informed of the disaster that had befallen his troops and understood that a full retreat was in effect,

William now led in an effort to finish the battle and the Jacobite army. Anthony and John Hamilton were convinced that their brother had been killed and would not find out the truth until some days later when a French officer informed them that Richard had been spotted riding to Dublin, a prisoner of William.[34]

Having suffered the frustration of listening to the guns at Oldbridge while standing watching the Williamite flanking force, and doing nothing, the news that the army was to retreat south must have been devastating to many of the troops. With the Williamite force opposite beginning to peel off the position and head south in an apparent attempt to cut off his retreat, James listened to Lauzun's advice and hurried south towards Dublin with the remnants of the Jacobite army in tow. The retreat would rapidly become chaotic as troops attempted to squeeze across the Nanny river at Duleek, four miles south of the Boyne. Confusion reigned once more; cavalry collided with infantry in the narrow lanes at Duleek, some even firing their pistols to clear the way. An ordered retreat quickly became a rout. Hats, shoes, muskets and coats were hurled into the road to make better the escape.

William's pursuit was ineffectual and even clumsy and little advantage was taken of the victory. It could even be suggested that the pursuit was deliberately lethargic. William had held James in 1688 for a short time; perhaps holding him again would cause trouble on the international stage and within his alliance. Even after having been crowned King of England, did he want to hold his father-in-law prisoner once more? For the sake of his wife, and the stability of his rule, William must have hoped that James would flee. Had he hoped for a general disbandment of the Jacobite Irish army, however, he would find to his cost that this would not be the case.

The battle had seen around 1,000 Jacobites killed, with 500 Williamites. It had not been a bloody battle by international standards. Neither had it seen bold tactical moves and sweeping tactical genius; indeed it could be argued that the lack of pursuit had undermined a decisive victory. Bloodier battles would be fought in Ireland, although their outcome would not have the same effect on the European stage. William's courageous example of leading from the front could have proven costly and he had been lucky not to have been wounded or killed as Schomberg had been, although it could be argued that much of the professionalism of William's officer corps had been found wanting, and he had been forced to take action. On the Irish stage his generalship had proven superior.

James had not taken part in the battle. Although in 1688 he had remained fatalistic and his leadership had proven ineffective, at the start of the battle he had believed the flank attack to be the main effort. In the end he had been outmanoeuvred by a superior force and a bolder commander. One of the first to reach Dublin, James would blame the Irish for his failures at the Boyne. He would promise never to use Irish troops to fight English again, blaming them for all of his troubles. While addressing the city fathers in Dublin, he stated:

> tho I have been often cautioned, that when it came to the touch, they would never bear the brunt of a Battle, I could never credit [it] till this day, when having a good Army, and all Preparations fit to engage a Foreign Invader, I found the fatal Truth of what I had been so often precautioned; and tho the Army did not desert me, as they did in England, yet when it came to a Tryal, they basely fled the Field, and left it a spoil to my Enemies, nor could they be prevailed upon to Rally, tho the loss in the whole defeat was but inconsiderable; so that henceforth I never more determine to head an Irish Army, and do now resolve to shift for my self, and so, Gentlemen, must you.[35]

A story told at the time would report that Lady Tyrconnel, once the wife of George Hamilton, had been one of the first to meet James in Dublin. James complained that the Irish troops had 'run away'. Lady Tyrconnel replied, 'I see you have preceded them yourself, your majesty.' Within five days, James had reached the south coast and left for France. William did not attempt to stop him.

It is interesting to note that William's victory at the Boyne hinged to a large degree on Meinhardt Schomberg's critical positioning on James's flank, rendering him and most of his army immobile. Had this endeavour not succeeded, and the danger at Roughgrange not been present, the river crossing at Oldbridge would have proven very costly. After the battle, William summoned the young Schomberg, informing him that he owed the day to him, highlighting William's belief in the importance of the holding action that kept both James and his best troops out of the battle.

Richard Hamilton, who had fought bravely under the circumstances, had surely made up for any doubts that the Irish and Jacobite supporters might have harboured regarding his courage, although even then some questions remained. William had ordered his own surgeon to tend to Hamilton's wounds and some days later he was taken to Dublin. He would later be moved to the Tower of London. Berwick, who had escaped with his father, took command of the remaining Jacobite cavalry. Had Richard Hamilton sued for peace with Tyrconnel in 1689, and gone along with William's plans for a treaty of sorts, matters in Ireland, and for James, might have been very different. As it was, although the Jacobite army had largely survived intact and would fight on, it would not last long.

# Chapter 14

# Aughrim, Limerick, and the Second Flight

nglish newsletters had celebrated the capture of Richard Hamilton after the Boyne, a man who had 'run over so basely to King James'.[1] Rumours of Hamilton's death had initially reached his brothers, verified by Boisseleau, who had also been at Oldbridge, only to be confirmed later as untrue. Reports of Hamilton's conduct, in common with the black mark he had received during the Derry debacle, would follow with the inevitable recriminations. It should be noted that a general captured by the enemy had little chance for discourse in answering his many critics on his own side. Hamilton was accused by the French of having made inadequate attempts to resist at Oldbridge. Of course, with French troops four miles away and a degree of arrogance regarding Irish troops and officers, the comments are only to be expected, no matter how inaccurate. More incredulous accusations would follow, the character of which suggest the involvement of the acid-tongued Louvois, who still had a bitter dislike for Richard Hamilton. He was accused, again with little hope of answering the charge, of being involved in some sort of conspiracy with William – having informed him of Jacobite plots and plans, and of those agencies or persons remaining in England who still sought, and would help with, French invasion, so that William might remove their influence. Although Lauzun had written that Richard had been taken prisoner while 'bravely performing his duty', his particular lack of success at the Boyne can only have further impaired his influence with Louvois.[2]

Lauzun also recounted the retreat to Dublin, recording the 'brave conduct' of Anthony Hamilton in helping form the rearguard of the rout. John Hamilton and his infantry battalion were also 'picked up' on the way.[3] Lauzun's position at the 'rear' in the retreat is contradicted to some degree by Zurlauben, commander of a French regiment, who, far to the rear of Lauzun's position, had helped prevent dedicated Williamite pursuit.[4]

The rout and retreat meant that William would enter Dublin quickly, an act that heralded the end of James II's brief time in Ireland. If the battle and lack of co-ordinated pursuit had been designed to force James to leave the country then the plan had worked. If William believed that the Jacobite army was disrupted to the point of breakdown, or that the French ruse was over, he would be sorely mistaken. Like most of the Jacobites in arms, John and Anthony Hamilton would retreat to Limerick, one of the last bastions of defence against William's ever encroaching army and a town where Anthony Hamilton had once been governor during Tyrconnel's purges of the 1680s, all of which must have seemed so distant now.[5] As most of the Jacobite troops and leadership headed for Limerick, the sixty-year-old Tyrconnel, in poor health and no doubt exhausted after helping command the cavalry action at the Boyne, remained despondent regarding the Irish prospects.[6] One Jacobite commentator stated:

> Whereupon the duke [Tyrconnel] made this his mind known to the mixed council of state and war then present at Limerick, and desired their concurrence to make a pacific end of their troubles, leaving to Providence the restoration of their king, since they are not assuredly able to compass it against the powers of England, Holland, Scotland and the Irish Protestants.

Against this opinion of Tyrconnel there arose an opposition which was sustained with vehemence by a few officers of the army, mainly by Major General Sarsfield, Brigadier Henry Luttrell, Colonel Gordon O'Neill and others.

> What these caballing gentlemen can say for continuing the war against the sentiment of the duke, is reduced to these three points, that they have a sufficiency of men, that they have courage enough, and that they will have out of France a consummate general to govern their army ....

The same commentator pointed to the distinct weaknesses in the Jacobite army, factors which undermined everything that the Hamiltons had not only attempted to carry out but for which they would receive much of the blame:

> For their not taking of Derry proceeded from the want of battering pieces, of which if the army had a dozen, they might have well made themselves masters of that town in twelve days after trenches opened. The loss of Croom castle fight [though of course actually Lisnaskea] was caused by mistaking the word that a commanding officer of the Irish gave, by which the strength of the lord

Mountcashel's army was drawn from the field. The losing of the battle at Cavan was occasioned by ordering the Irish to attack the enemies within ditches and hedges. The failure at the Boyne sprang from several defects of military management ... .[7]

Once more, as in 1688, Tyrconnel saw the Williamite threat and felt that negotiation and bargaining might be the only way out of the situation that he, at least, felt had become desperate enough to accept alternatives to war. A major battle had been fought, and terms would be radically different. Even though William was keen to end the conflict and return to mainland Europe, he had an English parliament to placate.

However, Patrick Sarsfield, rapidly becoming the favourite of the native Irish rather than the old-English faction, saw continued resistance as the only way forward. For the native Irish, who had received so little in James's parliament, there was little to gain from negotiation. Although lacking the political skills and experience of the wily Tyrconnel, Sarsfield was a very competent cavalry commander and was gaining support. As the quagmire of dissent and disagreement opened once more in the Irish camp, the French behaved predictably. Lauzun considered Limerick extremely vulnerable, believing that many of the Irish felt the same. They were already asking for officer positions in the belief that their treatment, if captured, would be more favourable. As factional splits grew more pronounced, Lauzun feared reprisals from the Irish who 'hate us so much' but this did not stop him from recommending that the best of the Irish cavalry should be transported back to France to fight for Louis. He complained that he suffered 'the rigours of Purgatory' and would rather 'take the most lowly post in the French army' than serve any longer in Ireland.[8]

Tyrconnel, perhaps for the first time in years, faced massive Irish opposition as Jacobite officers loyal to Sarsfield took control, ensuring that Tyrconnel's influence dwindled and consideration was given to ejecting the French from Limerick.

Stevens commented:

A council being held by the Duke [Tyrconnel] and other leading men to consult what was to be done in this desperate state of our affairs, his grace was of opinion all was lost, and therefore thought convenient to make the best conditions with the enemy and surrender before it was too late. This advice was so far from being approved that it moved much indignation in some of the hearers, and that with just cause, and it was unanimously resolved to suffer the utmost extremities rather than submit to the usurper, and to hold out what was left to the last. Hereupon the duke thinking it impossible to keep the fields, and, running from one dangerous extreme to another no less prejudicial, declared himself for hamstringing all the horses, and bringing the men with what provisions could be gathered into the garrisons, a proposal no less dangerous in the consequences if followed than cruel in the execution. These opinions caused great heats and animosities, all men in general exclaiming against them, and those in particular who were of a contrary faction to the duke laying hold of this opportunity to make him odious to the army, and if possible to remove him from the government ... .[9]

However, William had yet to reach Limerick. If he had hoped that defeat at the Boyne would spell both the end of James in Ireland and the demise of the enemy army, he was to be proven only half-right, despite Tyrconnel's urgings to negotiate. A few days after the Boyne, William's belief in the vulnerability of the Jacobites encouraged him to draw up terms for surrender. Although the poor conscripts in the army and the general populace could expect pardon if they surrendered by August 1690, the 'leaders of the rebellion' would not be so easily excused. With the clear basis of Williamite terms being the continued appropriation of Irish land from the branded 'rebellious' nobility, many of the Irish saw little choice but to fight on. Whether William wanted a quick war or not, there were few in his English parliament who would excuse an Irishman by giving him land or letting him keep his estates. Terms of surrender would follow this pattern closely, and it seemed that William would have little choice but to fight further battles in Ireland.[10] The attempt to divide the common Irish people from the nobility did not work, as not only the survival and continued resistance of the army seemed more likely, but Williamite troops did little to honour terms of surrender as they roved across an Ireland laid waste by war.[11]

It was over a month before William's force began to draw near the Irish army stronghold and, even then, there were attempts at other Irish positions to be made. The Jacobite defence at Athlone under Richard Grace, a veteran of the war in the 1640s, in combination with Sarsfield's attempts to reinforce the position, was enough to convince William's Lieutenant General Douglas to withdraw after a week's siege.[12] Having shown that terms of surrender were unwelcome, and would not necessarily be held by William's troops operating in the countryside anyway, resistance at Limerick stiffened.

William's amendment to the terms in August, for ranking officers and their guaranteed subsistence after surrender, did little to alter the virtually implacable will to resist that had grown amongst Sarsfield and his fellow officers.

William began to doubt whether he would stay for the Irish campaign. In July he was made aware of the French naval victory over the British and Dutch fleets off Beachy Head, a victory which gave rise to the threat not only of French invasion of England in support of James and Louis's continuing plans to exploit William's absence from mainland Europe, but also fears that French ships could enter the Irish sea, thus isolating William in Ireland for the duration. Parliamentary requests for his immediate return began to sound sensible. By mid-July, having reached Waterford, William resolved instead to return some cavalry and infantry regiments to England, while considering whether he should sail back to England within a week. Waterford and Duncannon both surrendered to the Williamites. The Waterford garrison was allowed to march out of the city, while William had turned down their request for guarantees of religious liberty and their estates, but had ensured that they remained unmolested, now more than ever wary of the political ramifications of continued abuse of his surrender terms. Leaving the army, he made his way towards Dublin, intending to leave Ireland. With news of the French fleet's withdrawal from English waters, however, and any apparent plans for invasion thus being nullified, William instead resolved to stay in Ireland and headed for Limerick.

Despite Lauzun's complaints about the defensibility of Limerick, especially its lack of contemporary anti-siege design, it did have some natural advantages. The main town, the 'English' side, was walled and sat astride King's Island in the Shannon, linked to the walled 'Irish' town to the south by a bridge.[13] Having resolved to fight it out, and given an unexpected break due to the lengthy interval before William's arrival, the Irish had made preparations and strengthened what fortifications they had. The Irish town, having no natural protection from the river, was reinforced with a covered ditch dug around its perimeter. Outhouses were cleared and a number of works constructed to deny existing cover to William's troops and provide the defenders with, at least, a chance of bloodying the nose of a direct assault.

Tyrconnel, it seemed, wanted little more to do with the situation:

> The duke of Tyrconnel finding that he could not get a concurrence
> to his design of making a peace with the Prince of Orange, he
> disposed of the army thus: He left almost eight thousand men (of

which some regiments were not armed) for the defence of Limerick, the governor whereof he appointed monsieur Boisseleau, and gave him as assistants the duke of Berwick, major-general Dorrington, who was also colonel of the regiment of guards, major-general Sarsfield, brigadier Henry Luttrell, brigadier Wauchop, and brigadier Maxwell. The rest of the forces he sent into the province of Connaught. The cavalry remained a while hard by in the county of Clare, under the command of the duke of Berwick and major-general Sheldon. This being done, the duke of Tyrconnel departed the town, and went to Galway, thirty miles from Limerick, to provide for the shipping off for France the French brigade, who would not stay any longer in Ireland because the king was gone, and they gave the kingdom for lost after the miscarriage of the Boyne, where they struck not a stroke, but what they did in the retreat.[14]

The French Major General Boisseleau remained in command in Limerick but, with the French infantry's departure to Galway, he had lost his best asset. Lauzun, who would accompany Tyrconnel to Galway with the French contingent, put the army's numbers in Limerick at 14,000, although very poorly armed.[15] Anthony Hamilton is not mentioned as having been at Limerick during the subsequent siege, so there is reason to believe that he accompanied Lauzun and Tyrconnel to Galway. John Hamilton, however, remained in the town and would receive much praise from Boisseleau who recorded his remarkable ability and bravery. The Jacobite army consisted of around twenty-eight infantry regiments with some cavalry and dragoons, although Sarsfield still operated in County Clare with a roving cavalry force, 2,500 strong. William's numbers at Limerick were somewhat reduced from those available at the Boyne by his having returned troops to England and placed garrisons across Ireland. He still commanded 25,000 men, thought to be insufficient for a protracted siege of Limerick, no matter how thin the walls.[16]

By the start of August and William's cautious approach, skirmishes and reconnaissance in force characterised the advance. Capturing the Ireton and Cromwell forts on the outskirts of the town did little to deter the defenders as Boisseleau exclaimed that he would earn William's esteem only through vigorous defence.[17] For their parts, Berwick and Sarsfield had plans to thwart the Williamite siege. Berwick seemed more concerned that he had not been allowed to proceed by Tyrconnel, berating his attitude, and his increasing weight:

I had proposed to the Duke of Tyrconnel, as soon as the enemy sat down before Limerick, to pass the Shannon with our three thousand five hundred horse, and destroy all the magazines they had left behind them, especially at Dublin; which would undoubtedly have reduced them to a necessity of decamping. As all the towns in this country were open and without defence, I was morally certain of succeeding in my enterprise; and as to getting back, which was objected to me as being very difficult, the knowledge I had of the country had already suggested to me by what means it might be effected; for besides that we should have had the start of the enemy, I had no doubt of making my way into the North, and returning to our quarters by Sligo. The Duke of Tyrconnel, who was become heavy and fearful, would not agree to my proposal: perhaps too there might be some degree of jealousy at the bottom on his side; for as it did not suit with the dignity of Viceroy to become a partisan, and that, besides, neither his age nor bulk were accommodated to such an expedition, the whole conduct of it would have devolved upon me.[18]

Although Berwick had little success with his plans to attack the Williamite rear, the Irish army, despite its performance at the Boyne, still had a sting in its tail. Patrick Sarsfield, hearing that William's siege artillery train was on its way from Cashel, had asked for permission to intercept it, and was given leave to do so. With 500 cavalry he attacked the train in its camp at Ballyneety, killed the escorts and disabled the guns by stuffing them with powder and blowing them up. The explosion was heard in Limerick, and encouraged the Jacobites, unlike any other exploit of their armies as 'Sarsfield's ride' passed into Irish legend.[19] The action added massively to his reputation and, for many, resolved what indecision remained regarding Tyrconnel's peace or Sarsfield's urgings to fight on. The effect on William's activities was marked since what siege guns remained would take a further ten days to reach him and the loss in powder was irreplaceable in the short term.

By mid-August, and having retrieved six siege guns, barely adequate for the situation in hand, William's troops began digging trenches and approached the 'Irish town' from their positions at Singland Hill to the south-east. Hard fighting drove the Irish back from their forward positions amongst the redoubts, allowing William's men to push their heavy guns closer and closer to the increasingly vulnerable town walls, to within twenty yards of the defensive ditch.[20] By 25 August, however, the weather turned against William, and the heavens opened, disgorging rain that soaked exposed troops and filled muddy trenches – another delay, although a short-lived one. As the rain cleared, the bombardment began; a breach reported to be twelve-yards wide was opened in the wall.[21]

Military doctrine dictated that an assault should follow. The afternoon saw the attack that William hoped would put an end to matters in Ireland. John Stevens described Boisseleau himself leading the counter-charge:

> on a sudden we commanded to light our matches and that scarce done to march towards St John's Gate and man the walls, but before we could reach it our governor, Major-General Boisseleau, came running and, ordering us to the left, led to the breach.[22]

Confusion reigned in the mass of red coats as the only identifying feature remained the sprig of green of the Williamites and the white cockade of Stevens' comrades. Irish troops who had been driven from the walls were rallied and reinforced by dragoons as desperate minutes passed in savage hand-to-hand fighting. Stevens' line fired into the Williamite mass and began driving the attackers out. In some accounts even local women threw bottles and stones to help staunch the assault.[23] After further hours of hard fighting in the breach, William's troops retreated, having suffered over 2,000 killed and wounded. The following day saw a repeat of the heavy rains. As ammunition and powder began to run out, due mostly to Sarsfield's raid, and the rains threatened to make removal of siege guns difficult, William resolved to end the siege, his time in Ireland having ended without a final victory. There had been mistakes and no shortage of ill luck. However, William's troops would return to Limerick in time.

The siege had been a noteworthy Jacobite success. Anthony Hamilton informed James of the raising of the siege and gave an explanation of why Tyrconnel would soon arrive in France.[24] Boisseleau, who joined him after William's departure from Limerick, would sail with him. John Hamilton remained in Ireland. For Tyrconnel, concerned no doubt with the growing degree of hostility and resentment that faced him, Hamilton reported that he thought it prudent to get the better of those who sought to undermine his position with James.[25] Even with his departure, however, he would insist to Louvois that a further Irish force for France would not be prudent, as surely now, with the success of Limerick, the Irish could hold out until spring 1691.[26] Lauzun, who had held French troops at Galway, postponing their departure to give 'courage' to Limerick's defenders, believed that Sarsfield could keep up a guerrilla war.[27] Perhaps he was now not so 'disgusted' as he had previously implied, far from Limerick and William's troops. Tyrconnel and the French had left Ireland by mid-September with Anthony Hamilton.

Even before the French had left, plans were being made to open up a second front in the Irish war. In August John Churchill, the earl of Marlborough, had submitted plans for a bold attack on the ports of Cork and Kinsale in Munster to the south; strategically important as they were the principal links with France. Although a risky proposition, since most of the remaining regular army would be used and the threat of French invasion of England still loomed in the air, William eventually approved the scheme and the concept of the north–south Williamite pincer move. Marlborough's troops arrived on 21 September. Roger MacElligot, who had commanded troops in England with the Hamiltons during the debacle of 1688, commanded the Jacobite garrison. Sarsfield's and Berwick's attempts to come to his aid failed as Marlborough gained reinforcements from the north – Danish, Dutch and Huguenots – resulting in a dispute over command which was only agreed when he and Württemberg agreed to take charge on alternate days. By the start of October Cork and Kinsale were in Williamite hands; the French had made no attempt to defend or hold either of the critically important ports.[28]

In William's army to the north, the Dutch General Solms had been placed in temporary command. William, his guards and other components of the army had gone. Solms's tenure was also short-lived and Ginkel succeeded him. As winter closed, the Williamite front line shifted east of the Shannon, to the extent that the Jacobites retained control of the river crossings. With such control the Jacobites attempted an attack over the river toward Birr castle but it came to naught, as would attempts to reinforce or even retake the southern ports that had fallen into Marlborough's hands.

In the Jacobite camp, with the inexperienced Berwick becoming slowly overshadowed by the increasingly popular Sarsfield, bolstered by the support of the leading Jacobite officers, John Hamilton, who would assist Berwick, slowly found himself being swallowed by another Irish feud.[29] It soon became clear that peace would be difficult to find within the Jacobite council of war, never mind in Ireland as a whole. The failure of Sarsfield, Tyrconnel or Berwick to hold the position south of Limerick and the south coast against the Williamites had left Cork and Kinsale open to attack. Having lapsed in this decision, the council should have been making plans for the 1691 campaign; instead, they remained divided. John Hamilton naturally fell into Tyrconnel's camp with Berwick. The army was divided in two: one part for Tyrconnel, the other with Sarsfield. Gaelic native Irish, who had little to gain from an accommodation with William, seemed left with little hope but to fight on and appeal for French aid. Common soldiers, the O'Neills, Maguires and O'Ferrals, and the Irish bishops backed Sarsfield, his ancestry, it should be noted, being spilt between old-English, on his father's side, and Gaelic Irish on his mother's. Hamiltons, Talbots, Nugents, Dillons and Burkes supported Tyrconnel's moves for peace, although they were of old-English descent. Division seemed to have become an underlying theme once more, and along longstanding factional lines.[30]

Requests from Sarsfield's party began to centre on sending a delegation to France to appeal to James regarding Tyrconnel's suitability as viceroy, and thus give command to Sarsfield as the army's choice. Having been made aware of the attempt to undermine him, Tyrconnel's departure in September was pre-planned to get to James first. By the time Sarsfield's deputation, including Henry and Simon Luttrell and Nicholas Purcell, had arrived, Tyrconnel had re-established his credibility with James, even asking for help to pursue the war, and he resolved to return to Ireland with the promise of further French aid. Although James would then attempt to give short shrift to Sarsfield's men, he agreed to the proposal that a French general should be sent. Purcell and the Luttrells had also expressed particular dissatisfaction with Anthony and Richard Hamilton, at least one of whom had been firmly in Tyrconnel's camp.[31]

Had James imprisoned the delegation, which included Peter Creagh, the Catholic bishop of Cork, the Irish outcry against him and indeed Tyrconnel could have provoked destructive action in Ireland. Before the Sarsfield delegation's return, two small ships had reached Limerick with goods such as salt and other necessities but without money, equipment or uniforms. The ships brought letters to both John Hamilton and Berwick from James. In both cases, further relief was promised. Limerick had yet to reach the level of depredation known at Derry in the previous year, but conditions for the army were far from perfect; deserters talked of the army being in such a state that two-thirds of them would be glad to surrender![32] The statement is corroborated by John Hamilton, who wrote to James that the men were 'ready to mutiny because of the want of all things necessary'.[33]

With the onset of winter the Shannon defined most of the Jacobite lines; they still held Limerick, Sligo and Athlone. The Williamite line ran from Cork in the south almost through the centre of Ireland. Raiding and looting characterised much of the activity between the lines over the winter, with little attempt to get involved in serious fighting. Further attempts at negotiated settlements foundered on the question of Irish estates and land, and the natural divisions between the Jacobites. The campaign would continue, although forcing the Irish to accede to terms would prove difficult as Williamite moves against Kerry and Sligo floundered. However, there would be no end to internal Jacobite friction. In November Sarsfield was warned that William's forces, aware of the weakened position of the Irish, intended to cross the Shannon and attack Limerick and Galway. The same source, presumably a spy, told Sarsfield how Ginkel's intelligence benefitted to a large degree from assurances made by segments of the Irish army and hierarchy, who had promised the surrender of Jacobite strongholds. Amongst those whom Sarsfield would accuse of having conspired with his enemies was John Hamilton. Others included Judge Daly, Colonel Alexander McDonnell and Lord Riverstown, all of whom were either dismissed from their command or imprisoned.[34] John Hamilton, perhaps still benefitting from the authority of his allegiance to Tyrconnel, escaped persecution together with Berwick, and seems even to have remained unaffected after the initial accusation. That there had been a deliberate pact with William's officers seems unlikely, although arguably it would have been those in Tyrconnel's camp who would have benefitted most from the peace terms being offered, no matter how confused and changeable they had become.

In January 1691 Tyrconnel returned to Ireland, guided to the mouth of the Shannon by French escort ships. Berwick then left for France, leaving in command Sarsfield, who had seen some success in strengthening crossing points on the Shannon. Despite Tyrconnel's granting of an earldom to Sarsfield, James's gift to the victor of Ballyneety, friction remained over command of the army. By March, Sarsfield, now a major general, decided to appear before Tyrconnel at Limerick. He received assurances that French aid would come, despite the bold and somewhat prophetic requests from the French that more Irish troops were required in mainland Europe. Tyrconnel's return did little to build bridges between him and Sarsfield; the French were informed that he was still 'mortally hated' and that his murder was only prevented by Sarsfield himself.[35] Tyrconnel was more concerned with the condition of the army and its potential for further resistance. He complained to Louvois of the insufficient provisions that French shipping had provided, citing his fear that the lack of supplies could mean that the army would die of hunger.[36]

William hoped that the 1691 campaign in Ireland would see Ginkel end the matter. Urging him to move against Athlone, with a reminder that the French watched in anticipation of further delay to his plans, William requested that the Dutch general be more forceful with regard to his allies and his Jacobite enemy, encouraging him with the provision of additional men and equipment, although inevitably perhaps soldiers' pay was delayed. By mid–May, the French general Saint Ruth had arrived at Limerick. Saint Ruth had fought in the wider war on the French borders and had commanded the now well-respected Lord Mountcashel in Catalonia where the Irish troops had attained a solid reputation not seen since the days of George Hamilton. Although hailed as a military boon, the general's arrival did little to heal the rift between the Irish factions, but the addition of such an experienced officer at least created a focus on who should command. Tyrconnel stated that, although he was still viceroy, James had directed that military matters should be left to Saint Ruth.[37] He reported back to Louvois on the poor state of government, inadequate logistics and food shortages, although he remained amazed at the tenacity of the Irish in such a situation. He also remained convinced that Athlone would fall to the Williamites if attacked.[38]

When the attack came in June, 18,000 of Ginkel's troops besieged the town while over 20,000 of Saint Ruth's Irish were posted two miles to the east. These were fed piecemeal into the besieged town; the two armies did not yet face each other. Berwick recorded that Saint Ruth entrusted John Hamilton, now a major general, with two brigades of infantry to reinforce the town. Upon arrival, however, he was forced to retire by Ginkel's troops, who were already in advantageous positions.[39] Williamite pressure and repeated assault, and the rumour of Jacobite treachery, saw the town fall by the end of June. As blame and counter-blame was discussed amongst the Irish, the Williamites had captured a valuable Shannon crossing in a position that threatened the entire Jacobite position. Saint Ruth withdrew.

With the retreat from Athlone, Stevens commented on the fact that 'fear has seized our men'.[40] Once more, the Irish army, with a seasoned French commander whose skill and reputation would grow, found routed troops drifting back to their battalions as the Jacobite force exhibited its remarkable ability to re-form in the face of adversity. French officers reported panic and low morale amongst the troops, although, with the help of regimental chaplains, the battalions were beginning to pull themselves together. Saint Ruth, choosing to ignore Sarsfield's preference for defending Galway and Limerick in significant strength, resolved instead to give battle. After all, he was running out of room, having only the two towns left to hold and perhaps being influenced by French reports of the condition of his army, sensing that, if a battle was not fought now, it would inevitably disintegrate or become ensconced within strongholds to await defeat. He still had considerable numbers with which to fight a well-equipped although equal-sized force and, indeed, the advantage if he could choose the battlefield and establish well-defended positions. Perhaps he could even give the Irish the victory they had been waiting for.[41] What effect this would have had on the ultimate course of the war is arguable, aside from its importance to the French in terms of tying up William's military resources.

Saint Ruth selected his battlefield at Aughrim on the slopes of Kilcommodon Hill. To his left lay a ruined castle, commanding the best approach through a pass. To his right lay a church, two miles from his left flank. Across his front, at the base of the hill, lay a vast expanse of bog, difficult to traverse, aside from two narrow passes on each flank, and advantageous to the defender. Closer to the hill lay the hedges and ditches of the local farmland, ideal for parties of skirmishers who could give harassing fire, and in this case enjoying much better cover than had been available for Mountcashel and Anthony Hamilton's men at Newtownbutler two years before. Some of these were built upon further to create defensive works, increasing still more the difficulty of an attacker's approach. Estimates put the size of Saint Ruth's army at between 15,000 and 25,000, although 20,000 is a more likely figure bearing subsequent casualties in mind.[42] With Ginkel's army of 20,000 approaching the position by 12 July (o.s.), the scene was set for another battle.

The Jacobite army was drawn up in two lines of infantry with cavalry on either wing. There is some dispute over Sarsfield's position, although most likely he was on the Jacobite right wing, defending Tristaun ford. This flank also ostensibly contained cavalry reserves, which could be used to cover a retreat if required. The troops in the centre were commanded by Major Generals Dorrington and John Hamilton, the latter now a very senior figure in the Jacobite officer hierarchy, possibly helped in his position through the influence of Saint Ruth. Within the ruins of Aughrim Castle, 200 infantry held the approach, with Sheldon's cavalry and Luttrell's dragoons nearby. Amongst the hedges and stone walls towards which the Williamite army must advance, Jacobite dragoons and musketeers loitered in ambush, ready to retire, after firing, to a second position, and thus harass the approaching enemy. Sources described how:

> from thence to the bog below was nigh half a mile, and this cut into a great many small enclosures which the enemy had ordered

so as to make a communication from one of them to another, and had lined all these very thick with small shot; this showed a great deal of dexterity in M. Saint Ruth in making choice of such a piece of ground as nature itself could not furnish him with a better, considering all circumstances; for he knew that the Irish naturally loved a breastwork between them and bullets, and here they were fitted to the purpose with hedges and ditches to the very edge of the bog.[43]

Close before the first line of the Irish infantry, there were a few old ditches, which were serviceable to them at the first charge of the enemy. The management of the infantry was assigned to major-general Dorrington and to major-general John Hamilton. Thus was the disposition of the army. No doubt Saint Ruth showed good skill in choosing ground, and in ranging his host for this fight, where his all and the all of the nation lay at stake.[44]

Over half a mile east of the Jacobite position, Ginkel surveyed what he could of the battlefield from Urraghry Hill, an effort made more difficult by the morning fog covering the area. He had been delayed for a week by the need for ammunition to be brought from Dublin. He had more dragoons and certainly more artillery than Saint Ruth, although he had had little success in his attempts to gauge Jacobite numbers and dispositions. The advance was dangerous as attacking infantry were channelled into zones of approach that would quickly be engulfed with Jacobite fire. It was late in the day, 5.00 or 6.00 p.m., by the time Ginkel's troops were positioned. With twenty-eight battalions of infantry and forty-seven cavalry squadrons, Ginkel placed his horse on the flanks, English on his right and Danish, Dutch and Huguenot on the left.

The first attack on the Jacobite right flank towards Tristaun ford followed. Major General Mackay had planned to attack heavily on this flank in the hope of pulling troops from Jacobite positions in the centre and opposite flank, thus weakening these for a major attack to follow from Ginkel towards the castle. The Dutch, Huguenot and Ulster troops concerned with the flank action began to suffer casualties from the well-posted Jacobite skirmishers. Ginkel, in turn, began drawing dragoons from his main force to bolster the attack, which stalled at the ford as the pressure from defending Jacobites hindered further advance. Saint Ruth, who had his headquarters behind his infantry on top of the hill in the centre, moved towards the church to be closer to the action. He ordered Sheldon's cavalry reserve from the castle,

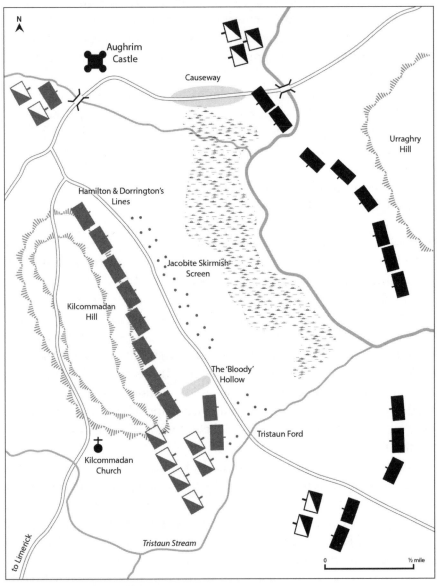

N

Aughrim
Castle

Causeway

Urraghry
Hill

Hamilton & Dorrington's
Lines

Jacobite Skirmish
Screen

Kilcommadan
Hill

The 'Bloody'
Hollow

Tristaun Ford

Kilcommadan
Church

to Limerick

Tristaun Stream

0                    ½ mile

'Bloody' Aughrim, 1691.

with some infantry, to reinforce the position. Fighting continued for over an hour, as artillery on both sides traded shots.

With an apparent stalemate, and seeing the weakening of the Jacobite left flank through Saint Ruth's reinforcement of the right, Ginkel ordered two regiments of infantry across the bog against the Jacobite left, Gustavus Hamilton's Inniskillingers and Percy Kirke's English foot. Struggling through the bog and the stream across their line of march, the Williamite troops reached the base of the hill where they were hit head on by a Jacobite cavalry and infantry attack led by Dorrington and John Hamilton, which forced them back the way they had come. Amongst the English wounded in this instance was Colonel Wolseley, the victor of Newtownbutler. Two other regiments followed, ending up in a defensive position in enclosures and hedges near the hill, and fighting off repeated Jacobite attacks. Once more the pressure of massed counter-attacks led by Dorrington and Hamilton was too much and they were pushed back. The situation was fast becoming critical, repelled on the left and held on the Jacobite right, with few options for cavalry due to the terrain. Ginkel launched another attack in the centre. Huguenot regiments attacked in the southern half, attempting to gain access to a narrow defile, known later as the 'bloody hollow', due to the nature of the desperate fighting. Jacobite artillery fired at close range, devastating the lines of infantry. Lining hedges and walls, skirmishers and dragoons unleashed volley fire against Williamite troops as they battled through the mud and confusion. Irish cavalry charged and counter-charged against the base of the hill. Hamilton and Dorrington ordered volley and assault against approaching enemy infantry and Ginkel could make little headway against Saint Ruth's apparently inspired defensive position.

However, Ginkel still had considerable cavalry available on his right wing, against an Irish flank that had lost some of its strength to the fight at the ford. Two squadrons of cavalry lined up on the only approach to the castle, a narrow causeway. Burke's Irish dragoons, who had been defending the area, had received their ammunition supply, which proved to be the wrong calibre. Luttrell's dragoons began retreating with the approach of the Williamite cavalry and Sheldon's horse had already been pulled away from the position; the entire left flank of Saint Ruth's army was crumbling without a shot having been fired, an event which would result in Luttrell being accused of complicity with William's forces. Saint Ruth, perceiving the deteriorating situation, galloped to the top of Kilcommodon Hill, perhaps to gather his reserve horse or dragoons and plug the gap. As he did so a shot from an enemy artillery piece decapitated him. The timing for the

Jacobites could not have been worse. The flank fell, dragoons either fleeing or surrendering. The poor defence of the causeway would see the end of the battle. Whether aware of Saint Ruth's death or not, Ginkel launched another infantry assault. With the flank open, allowing cavalry to pour through the gap, Jacobite infantry began to realise their predicament and pulled back. With a full cavalry reserve, Sarsfield had been ordered to stay where he was, but soon realised that it was too late to save the situation. His only rational action was to act as a rearguard to allow as many of the infantry as possible to get away and flee to Limerick.

With the end of the battle came the realisation of the terrible death toll; the clash became known as 'bloody Aughrim', estimates putting the numbers killed at 7,000. Less important politically than the Boyne, since no kings were present, the toll in military terms had been heavy for both sides. Amongst the prisoners taken were Dorrington and John Hamilton. Hamilton, gravely wounded, was taken to Dublin where Ginkel is recorded as asking that he be well treated. He died of his wounds in October 1691.[45]

Limerick was the only refuge now left to the dispirited, if not entirely broken, Jacobite army, with most of the host gathering there by August. As with the aftermath of the Boyne, there were still effective numbers of troops, but perhaps only half still had arms and equipment. The strategy was to out-wait Ginkel; if Limerick could be held until the onset of winter, there might yet be hope of a settlement. Of course, it would require French help, and to a greater extent than had so far been forthcoming.

Even Tyrconnel was seen to advocate this path, perhaps all too aware that senior officers might be making their own arrangements with the Williamites in the wake of Aughrim. He proposed that the men should renew their oath to James. It was an obvious calculation to some, who were already thinking that all was lost, and a renewal of the oath would tell their leaders who was still loyal. Luttrell, whose actions at the flank during the battle had already aroused suspicion, was uncovered as having been in conference with the Williamites, much to the dismay of the Jacobite leaders, when a panicking messenger from Ginkel was convinced by Sarsfield to reveal all the messages he carried, including one for Luttrell.[46] The subsequent court martial found him guilty, and only Tyrconnel's insistence that he spend the rest of the war in prison saved him from the French preference for a noose.

D'Usson subsequently arrived from Galway to take charge of the garrison and was appointed governor, prompting a re-organisation, or stocktaking, of the army. Sarsfield was sent to Killaloe and the cavalry was assigned to protect the passes on the Shannon. Soon after this, Tyrconnel was taken ill, and died after five days. Despite the likelihood that he had a heart condition, there were rumours of poison having been administered by the French, or even by Sarsfield, although most would realise that there was little point in Tyrconnel's assassination at this stage. (His wife, the former wife of George Hamilton and sister to Sarah Churchill, Lady Marlborough, survived him by forty years, returning to France, but eventually establishing a convent in Ireland.)

If Tyrconnel's death had meant anything, it was that both sides looked to Sarsfield as the leader and negotiator of the Jacobite cause, most likely due to his being the only notable left with any influence over the army.

It took Ginkel another month to make his move. There was still hope that continued Jacobite infighting might make his job all the easier through fractious loyalties begetting the need for the Jacobite nobles to make their own peace. He had no desire to lay siege to Limerick once more, after the events of the previous year, but started to move in August. By the time he neared the city, he was under orders from William to bring matters to a close. The siege began in earnest by the end of the month with artillery and mortar shelling. By early September, and with some strategic movement of batteries to effect a breach in the 'Englishtown' wall, an assault was made ready.

A pontoon bridge was constructed at Lanahrone, and a party successfully landed on the far side. Brigadier Robert Clifford, whose Jacobite cavalry had been assigned to watch the position, fell under suspicion for lack of action. Sarsfield had been warned of Clifford's loyalties but had done little. Perhaps even he felt that it was too late, but the landing meant that Limerick was surrounded and Ginkel could blockade it.

To save time, and lives, Ginkel issued another request with terms of surrender, giving the garrison eight days to agree. There was no response; it is thought that the Irish still held out for French aid, which would never come. Ten battalions of infantry with supporting guns and dragoons crossed the river and moved towards the Jacobite outer defences near Thomond Gate. They met resistance in the form of 600 Jacobite horse under Colonel Lacy. Ferocious fighting forced the vastly outnumbered Jacobites back, firstly on the works, then towards King John's castle and Thomond Gate, and the sanctuary of Englishtown. The French officer in charge of the drawbridge denied them sanctuary, raising it too soon and creating a trap as the Jacobites were slaughtered in droves, both by the sword and by drowning in the Shannon.

The Irish and the French argued over how and why it had happened. Was this more French treachery? Where was the French relief force? It did not take long for the truth to sink in, even to the normally implacable Sarsfield. There was no option but to capitulate.

Such action has been criticised through the years, even in the light of evidence suggesting that Ginkel had not expected such a relatively short siege. There are questions to consider, however. The fortifications had received a considerable battering for the previous six weeks, the Thomond Gate debacle had reduced numbers and morale even further, and, key, Sarsfield was in no position to fight a pitched battle, or suffer a siege in the manner that Derry had two years previously, against a general with more aptitude and resources than Richard Hamilton. The army, or at least some of the notables, seemed riddled with treachery and sought to make their own deals as quickly as possible. Despite the fact that Sarsfield was ostensibly leader of the disparate factions, he was no long-term politician, and had little to offer all parties regarding hope for the future. But, if he could obtain an advantageous agreement for the survivors, knowing that Ginkel most likely wanted a quick end to the matter, he might still have some cards to play. He must have prayed that history, and Ireland, would remember him with kindness. Many disagreed, smashing muskets and breaking swords, claiming that Ireland had gone forever, but there was little real choice; better a capitulation with some conditions, rather than a complete surrender, when there was nothing left to bargain with.

Sarsfield and Ginkel headed the two parties during the treaty negotiations, together with bishops, lawyers and lords justices. Sarsfield opened by requesting forfeited estates to be restored, freedom of worship and equal footing with Protestants, and Jacobites who wished to transfer allegiance to the Williamite forces being given the same rights. Predictably, Ginkel refused. The talks were destined to collapse, it seemed, and both sides resigned themselves to continuing the siege, until Sarsfield asked for further details on the terms that Ginkel had been authorised to offer. Terms would only be accorded to those in arms and resisting, indicating that civilians would not be included. Sarsfield objected and had his way; the terms were extended to include all those 'under the protection of the Irish army'.

On 3 October the negotiators wrote out the articles on a large stone near the Thomond Bridge, reputedly the 'Treaty Stone', which still sits near the bridge in Limerick today. There were both military and civil articles.

Of these, the most important would be that individual soldiers could elect to leave for France or, if wishing to stay in their homeland, join William's forces. Ginkel made every effort to recruit, but even he must have known that there would be few who would forget all that they had fought for. Sarsfield promised, in a counter argument, that they would be back within a year to fight for their homeland. Ginkel would provide shipping for those wishing to leave.

The thirteen civil articles affected the country at large, and perhaps Sarsfield's own conviction that he would be returning with a victorious army meant that he paid scant heed to the repercussions of these. There were three conditions, affecting religious toleration, security for soldiers remaining in Ireland, and security of the civilian population. The administration of the treaty, however, depended largely on the goodwill of the crown and Irish parliament, the new all-Protestant Irish parliament, the members of which had long memories and were now doubly paranoid about Jacobite and Catholic sympathies. The subsequent Irish penal laws of 1697 managed to turn most of the toleration aspects of the treaty into mere fallacy. Limerick became known to history as 'The City of the Broken Treaty'.[47]

On 5 October the Jacobite army was allowed to make its decision about exile to France or joining William's forces. The regiments would march out and advance towards their chosen flag, an English standard or French *Fleur de Lys*, planted beyond the city walls. Out of almost 14,000 soldiers, just over 1,000 chose service in the Williamite forces.

It only remained for Ginkel to uphold his part of the bargain in what would become one of the most tragic episodes of the whole affair. As the time for departure closed in, much of the bravado shown by some of the Jacobite soldiers disappeared and growing numbers began defecting to the Williamite forces, and offer of service. To stem what might have become a flood, Sarsfield elected to move the force destined for France to King's Island, where he guarded against further defection. He also expedited the mechanics of leaving, setting out with the exiled army on 16 October. The four-day journey was bitter, and the roads were packed with families who wanted to journey to France with their soldiers, husbands, brothers and sons. It was inevitable that, by the time the force reached Cork, its numbers had been thinned. Ironically, and perhaps tragically, as he reached Cork there was word of a French relief force at Limerick. When Sarsfield found out, he is reported to have said, 'Too late. Our hour is pledged.'

Predictably, it was soon discovered that, even with the thinning of numbers, there were not enough ships. As boarding neared an end, it was clear that there would not be enough room for the women and relatives who wished to leave. They had crowded at the water's edge and, as word passed, were on the verge of panic. Many flung themselves into small boats in an attempt to make it to the ships. Even Macaulay, with characteristic drama, and usually misplaced pathos, is not out of place in this instance as he described:

> As the last boats put off, there was a rush into the surf. Some women caught hold of the ropes, were dragged out of their depth, clung till their fingers were cut through, and perished in the waves. The ships began to move. A wild and terrible wail rose from the shore, and excited, unwonted compassion in hearts steeled by hatred of the Irish race and of the Roman faith. Even the stern Cromwellian, now at length, after a desperate struggle of three years, left the undisputed lord of the bloodstained and devastated island, could not hear unmoved that bitter cry, in which was poured forth all the rage and all the sorrow of a conquered nation.[48]

*Chapter 15*

# The End of the Beginning:
# The Nine Years' War in Europe

The fact that the Nine Years' War, 1688-1697,[1] is not well known, and has been given a number of titles, indicates its relative position and effect on the history of Europe, its effects on England, Ireland and Scotland, notwithstanding.[2]

We can therefore see this War of the Grand Alliance, or War of the League of Augsburg as it was named by the Dutch who framed the league, as sharing a number of characteristics with earlier wars in the early modern period. A military escapade for which militaries of Europe were neither large enough nor well managed enough, where logistics could not handle the demands placed upon them and where contemporary tactics and technology was not sufficiently placed to fight serious pitched battles. Sieges would dictate much of the slow pace of change, the relative advantage of ground held being in the form of well stocked fortresses.

By the late 1670s Louis's attitude towards France and his personal *Gloire* had changed from that of a conquering nation under an aggressive king to that of an absolutist monarchy guarding the nation's delicate borders. France was a greater power geographically but could ill afford further costly wars. It would still fight if necessary, however. The alliances against Louis in the late-seventeenth century would take their toll, not helped by the defeat of the Turks by the Habsburgs, allowing the Holy Roman Empire to ally with the smaller European nations against France. Louis regarded these fledgling German states as a real enemy and acted defensively; his seizure of Strasbourg in 1681 and Luxembourg (through legal machinations and the language of treaty) allowed him to control many of the vital crossings over the Rhine. Europe could not ignore the fact that Louis was still acting aggressively, no matter how much the French king felt that he was protecting his own borders. Louis, however could not admit that his policy and attitude had altered, and Europe could only believe that the Louis of old had returned. The language of treaties and the political activity continued long into the 1680s, further opening the gulf between Louis and his European neighbours. By 1688 his seizure of Phillipsburg on the Rhine in Alsace was the final straw, not only amongst the Grand Alliance, but amongst the Dutch who now gave support to William's appeals to allow him to take action in England before that kingdom became a strong ally of France.[3] As we have seen, Louis's actions would have dire implications for Irish troops.

William's effective defence of the Dutch provinces in 1672 had propagated a growing sore between him and Louis. This was not a time of controlled strategy, military domination based upon economic needs, or even a policy designed to bring about greater economic prosperity for the working classes; instead, much of Louis's foreign policy was determined by *la Gloire*, and such glory became a driving concern, ignoring the more subtle aspects of foreign policy and diplomacy; patience, vision, subtlety and international relations were not characteristics that came to the fore, although it is arguable that Louis was simply a man of his time. He saw his destiny as that of defining France. Few would argue that he didn't, defining inviolable orders, perhaps his own subtle version of everlasting *gloire*, despite himself.

By the time of the Nine Years' War, the rivalry between the Bourbons and Spanish Habsburgs was already a symptom of past glories. The new France's destiny was at stake, and it was fast becoming the chief political and military power on the European stage. That meant that martial prowess, through fair means or foul, in pursuit of dynastic power, had to be shown to be real and effective.

The Dutch provinces, on the other hand, had seen a very different emergence and their destiny was less than certain. After the Eighty Years' War with Spain, to define their freedom, which must have been anathema to Louis who saw them as rebels, the Dutch pursued their two primary aims: commercial supremacy through effective trade and a Calvanist Protestantism, whose very concepts flew in the face of France's Catholic underpinnings. There being no natural boundary between France and the Spanish Netherlands, as there was with Spain itself, almost invited trouble to brew in the area, and for their ownership to be a matter hotly contested. Practically, Dutch efforts to seek a buffer state had helped propagate the 1672 war, and the Treaty of Nijmegen had granted the United Provinces some advantages. Louis wouldn't forget, however, and continued to intrigue on the European stage, even having a hand in Turkish incursions into Hungary and Austria. German states looked to the rapidly developing League of Augsburg as a means of uniting split factions against a term that might be scarcely whispered, that of a 'common enemy'. By 1686 William of Orange and the Elector of Brandenburg were already talking of abandoning their hitherto solid neutrality towards France; it would quickly become antipathy, although the Germanic states were not the only thing on William's mind.

Since Charles II's restoration in 1660 English foreign policy had been irresolute, and lacked clear strategy. The king was determined to avoid the parliamentary diatribes that had ultimately sealed his father's fate, and almost all feared the depredations of a second civil war. If Charles were to be pro-French, it had to be delicately balanced with a predatory and very Protestant House of Commons. As we have seen, English and Irish troops in French service were an active part of Charles's policy, and until Test Act lapses and political expediency intervened, the Irish Brigades were seen as an investment in future French aid, as was the secret Treaty of Dover.

But these were mere plays. England, with its watery channel and strong navy, could *afford* to pay little heed to European affairs. Charles's interest in France could be a mere dalliance, as his borders were not threatened in the same manner as William's. Rather than an exercise in French martial glory, political power-plays with England were designed to bring alliances to protect a flank and underline a treaty or alliance. There were familial connections, little threat to trade, and, with the Duke of York's change of religion and possible hold on Charles's throne, potential for an English Catholic monarchy. Charles, although mainly inconsistent in terms of his dealings with foreign governments, was at least committed to the concept of the troops in French service, although little of these political facts mattered, as geography allowed a modicum of detachment when it suited.

Consider the French position then, with war looming: a naval sea power, a staunch ally, and troops who had already fought in his armies. For Louis, the question was not one of if, but when, Charles would ally with him. It is arguable that an alliance against the European coalition that was rapidly growing was essential, lest, economically and militarily, he be left on his own. What better ally than an England with an accomplished navy, and yet no thoughts of expansion into the mainland, versus a landlocked France which lusted after territory and had Dutch and Spanish sea power to contend with.

England's place in Europe had been transitory. It had become embroiled with bloody civil war and flirted with experiments in radicalised government afterwards, only to throw in its lot once more with the concept of hereditary monarchy, albeit sanitised with a parliament quivering with somewhat misplaced fervour and arrogance. Post-civil-war England had developed rapidly; by the mid-1680s it had rich colonies, trade and agricultural prowess, and an economic resurgence through advanced banking mechanisms, all held up by a standing army and significantly more powerful navy. It is no surprise that it would be held as the prize in any alliance. By 1685, and James's accession, everything was 'to play for'. Charles had excelled at neutrality. James, although perhaps believing that his subtleties and influence were lent credence through his lineage and position, suffered from a key weakness: his relationship with his nephew/son-in-law, William, was steadily worsening.

With Huguenots and stories of persecution filling Holland, the return of British regiments from Dutch service and the reality of William's claim to the English throne through marriage were ever-present. James and his Italian princess, Mary of Modena, were childless, and so Mary, child of Anne Hyde, James's first consort, was next in line for the throne. There was a belief amongst the English Whigs, and perhaps even William, that all they had to do was await James's death. In the late 1680s, however, everything changed. Of course James was seen as more likely to side with Louis due to his religion and his European proclivities, and his return of English brigades to England was part of this. There were other, more pertinent, matters, however.

As Tyrconnel's influence in Ireland took hold and the army was effectively re-modelled, questions were inevitable. An Irish model for England was the foremost fear in the minds of the Whigs and the influential notables. Neutrality was a word which was being associated less and less with James's actions. In June 1688 his wife gave birth to a son and everything changed. Despite doubts cast as to whether Mary of Modena was the boy's true mother, there was little that James's enemies could do. Tensions were mounting, and some turned to William for a solution – a solution which of course, was in his own best interests.

The decision as to which side England would choose would prove critical to winning the war. Had neutrality been guaranteed, then perhaps matters might have been different; as it was, each passing day, at least in the eyes of Europe, brought England closer to Louis. France was already in the ascendency in terms of numbers. William's next decision would in large part be forced upon him.

However genuine James's increase in royal authority, his degree of religious toleration, or his extent of disagreement with the established church authority might have been, he had created a domestic crisis which could be interpreted in different measure, especially by those most influential parties who wished to see him fall. The Treason Club, the Tangerines and other influential parties in the English establishment sought action from the Dutch provinces. William's decision to take direct action through a substantial military landing in England was an enormous gamble, which might easily have failed, but he had been convinced that there would be an English revolution of sorts, if not a 'glorious' one, that would support him.

Even without an invasion there was a chance of rebellion against James, even a second civil war and republican settlement, although such events would leave England even more neutral than before, something William could not rely upon, especially when English forces would prove such a boon on the continent. Perhaps more dangerously, his lack of intervention might leave England's course even more indeterminate than before. He could not take chances. Whatever might occur at the end of 1688, he needed to gain the initiative to prevent a disaster. English troops, supplies and money were the prize. In reality, the number who had sought William's direct intervention, at least in the manner that it had occurred, were few, those who thought that he might take the crown, even fewer, but the wheels were in motion, despite Louis's attack on Phillipsburg in September, a move designed to focus Dutch attentions on their homeland's defence rather than gamble upon rash foreign adventures, no matter what the stakes. The French, it seemed, were well aware of the dangers of William's 'descent on England',[4] the attack upon Phillipsburg being very much a diversionary effort aimed at destabilising the Dutch authority's willingness and ability to react to multiple crises. If their intent had been to convince the Stadtholder that becoming involved in foreign interventions, no matter how valid he might perceive them, would not work, on the contrary the threat of further French dominance persuaded William to continue.

The dangerous by-product of the landing would result in even more divisive events in Ireland. Louis would be offered the opportunity to play upon the growing and rich vein of the Irish problem. If he could perpetuate Irish resistance to William, and force him to position troops there for an extended period, he would make greater gains on the continent. Indeed, d'Avaux, his ambassador to Ireland during the crisis, would write as if the thought of bringing Irish troops into the European conflict, rather than even consider a longer-term defence of their own soil, was more pertinent and arguably effectively planned well in advance. To those in Ireland, who would be fighting for their futures, both Irish and English, the threat was very real. To Louis, perpetuating a sideshow to the main event, was the focus of his efforts. It is arguable that plans were in their infancy, in that Louis's immobility across a grand strategic spectrum simply afforded William the time needed to conduct the bloodless British Revolution.

Despite economic advances, British authorities still worried about their coffers and the potential cost of William's proposed war, although events in Ireland entailed greater concerns. William had other means by which English ire, and thus commitment, might yet be stimulated. England was still a Protestant country and the real and perceived effects of James's supposed machinations might yet be played upon. In addition, French Huguenots had streamed across Europe with horror stories related to French persecution; much could be made of French attempts at corruption under Charles, and the point could be stressed that it could only be worse under his brother.

Although Tyrconnel had changed the Irish army and state since the mid-1680s, his patron no longer had immediate influence, and he was ready to negotiate, especially so when faced with the Dutch army and their English and European allies. He sought a settlement that would permit a measure of Irish autonomy, although Richard Hamilton's arrival as negotiator, subsequent defection, and the preponderance of Irish hawks over doves, would mean an active resistance was inevitable. Any alternative measure would dilute support for Tyrconnel.

Louis saw the strength of the Irish diversion, especially if he could convince James to journey there and become a leader. Ireland could re-assert its historical role, at least in English eyes, as a route for foreign invasion of England, either French or a Jacobite army led by James, and thus would need to be pacified. For William, this was a rebellion to be quashed; for Louis, 'delay' was the watchword, a delay of forces being able to return to Europe. In Ireland, as usual, the agenda was different, even amongst the 'Irish'.

For Tyrconnel and the old-English and Anglo-Norman faction, a resolution or even partial resolution to the land question was the main aim, and, indeed, only hope. Amongst the Gaelic Irish, however, whose memories were longer, and sense of perceived injustice deeper, there was a question of righting ancient wrongs. The two factions would never, and could never, wholly agree. There was no question of a deal when Irish blood was up.

The Dutch Republic declared war on France in March 1689. The Grand Alliance, incorporating the Republic and the forces of the Holy Roman Emperor, later to be joined by England, the Duchies of Lorraine and Savoy, Spain, Denmark and with support from the Electors of Brandenburg and Bavaria, sought to re-establish the boundaries that had been in place since the 1678 Treaty of Nijmegen.

The oft mooted invasion of England by James and Irish Jacobite forces with French backing was still a possibility and its potential aided and abetted the House of Commons' support for an English declaration of war. This was the real crux of the matter. Despite the unconventional, or treasonous manner (to Jacobite eyes) in which a new king and queen had been crowned, there was a renewed fear of invasion from a reconstituted and deposed monarch. Without immediate and effective action, events would transpire to create the singular circumstance which England dreaded more than anything else, a second civil war.

Louis's war would become his 'Great Miscalculation'.[5] He could not avoid conflict which had perversely become intrinsic to European politics. However, he expected the war to be short. Hadn't the French army always gained success, becoming invincible under the correct circumstances? The war, in Louis's eyes, was one of consolidation, not conquest, an underlining of French security rather than an undermining of European hegemony. The rest of Europe would never agree with his outlook. The Grand Alliance would suffer; in fact Louis would obtain notable French victories, although it would become a difficult war to win. In terms of battles, France could be seen as the ultimate victor, yet conversely Louis would make large concessions to bring it to a close. France would become drained, and Louis, and his *Gloire*, humbled. If there had been purpose it had been lost; only Louis's enemies could profit from that.

The war that followed would break France, which could not afford to fight it effectively, nor would effective victory really be attainable in any event. The Nine Years' War would deeply affect its ability to fight subsequent conflicts, whilst English fortunes would wax at France's expense. It's therefore arguable that William's alliance of disparate English power blocs, in pushing James into the arms of Louis, reinforced English resistance against the potential response of a deposed monarch. So long as James remained under Louis's protection, there was threat of invasion, civil war and anarchy. French and Jacobite attempts in the 1690s at a return to England were enough to convince most that the right path had been chosen. Of course, by that stage, there was a reduced threat. The succession, or at least what it had developed into, was largely secured, and the Spanish Netherlands (Spanish 'Flanders') would become the crucible of war after the Treaty of Limerick in 1691. The fact that Ireland had made a difference is made clear by the fact that the diversion had allowed the French to win two major victories on the continent during the period of the Irish war.

France's attempts to capture land and expand her dominance had to be opposed. William and the States General had more practical aims: the expansion of trade and commerce could only be supported by opposing French aims, and thus permitting the region's real strengths to flourish. England had similar concerns and aims, although her objectives were underlined by the need to protect the 1688 succession, for better or worse.

An international settlement, a workable English succession and the support of European commerce were simple aims, yet difficult to accomplish in the face of French territorial needs. It was not, therefore, a war of attrition based upon jarring defeats, more a conflict between points of view, and the definition, through martial means, of accepted European frontiers and, thereby, a degree of dominance. Flanders had remained the crucible of European conflict. Elizabeth I had been the last monarch to push English troops into a protracted war there; William would do the same, in addition to utilising British naval capabilities. Both efforts, in an attempt to protect trade and repel the French, would be performed at great cost. Yet Britain had everything to lose through defeat, including the succession. A successful war, on land and sea, was essential.

## Crucible of War – The Spanish Netherlands

Covering an area now commanded by modern Belgium, the Spanish Netherlands was crossed by dykes and rolling plains. Its inevitable crucible as the centrepiece of contemporary warfare was based upon its geography and relative richness in forage and perpetuation of supply in terms of vast, poorly co-ordinated and supplied armies. The period would see the rise of logistics 'contractors' paid to supply and feed the British Army. The armies were far from the well-oiled machines that would herald the war of the Spanish Succession; indeed, the lessons that would lead to the strategic movements of vast numbers of men would find their source here, through understanding the mistakes made.

The theatre of operations encompassed an area moving east from Dunkirk, through Antwerp, to the area north of Maastricht, then south to Liège, and finally sweeping west then north-west, back to Dunkirk. It would include the mountainous Ardennes region which, although scarcely rising above 900 feet, was a major impediment to the movement of seventeenth-century armies.

This 'buffer state', between France's territorial ambitions and the Dutch United Province's trading empire, was threaded with waterways which had to be protected by fortresses that became objectives in the campaign, together with land which provided foraging.

Armies had increased in size dramatically, in comparison to the number of men who had fought in earlier wars in the century. Armies numbering 40,000 men at the start of the conflict had more than doubled by the end, necessitating gentlemanly agreements about dispositions of resources, although the new age of large armies meant that agreements were not always honoured. There was little to prevent the military ravaging an area if desired, and the war opened with a savage reminder of this when the Palatinate and Rhineland were systematically wasted and despoiled, their major towns burned to the ground.

Seizing Phillipsburg, despite its diversionary element, had also been designed to protect the French Alsace region, which had been attacked by the Dutch in the previous war. It barred the door to Imperial/German provocation due to its position, a political move whereby Louis could even decree that he might return the territory, if given certain guarantees by the Germans. By the end of the year French forces had taken German towns from south of Mainz to the Swiss border, even starting to hope that the war might be over. It was not to be, and the Germans resisted. Notables, including the Elector of Brandenburg and the Duke of Hanover, met in late October to strike an alliance. Within a year Louis would face a far greater one.

Louis then devastated the Palatinate, collecting contributions, destroying towns and creating a wasted buffer state to deny the enemy forage and subsistence. Duras commented on the events, remarkable even for the time, highlighting the effect upon the king's *Gloire*.[6] Attempts were even made in 1689 to resurrect the Deynze Confederation agreements, relating to the sensible (read peaceful) and agreed levies upon the population; the French ignored the requests.

As civilian authorities took a greater role as the war progressed, damage was more limited, and essentially managed, and the treatment of the civilian population in the breadbasket of north-west Europe improved.[7]

We tend now to view horse-and-musket warfare very much in a Napoleonic style – massive conscript armies, moving in grand patterns under the orders of great generals, against similarly large, though less well-led armies. This was certainly not the case at the end of the seventeenth century. The logistical management, some might say marvels, that were developed and used with such effect in the early 1700s by the Duke of Marlborough were scarcely even thought about, never mind in their infancy, despite the presence of the duke in the wars in Europe at this time, where, clearly, lessons were learned.

Destruction of the enemy army, although it may have been desired, was simply impossible under the means of making war. Yes, the coming war of the Spanish succession would see considerable differences, although those days were far in the future in terms of how conflicts were being fought. Instead, the aim was to capture towns and areas of land, which could be used as barter at peace conferences and foraged while the army sat in place. Major roads and waterways were protected by networks of fortresses, and these, like satellites orbiting a sun, were essential to holding sway over the area. To bypass a fortress meant leaving the army's rear exposed; to allow an enemy freedom of movement on flanks or rear could mean that supplies or convoys of provisions could be taken and plundered. The slow methodical effort of besieging and taking every fort and major town or city became the focus of war in the area. That armies could outgrow the ability of the parent country to keep them supplied was simply another concern for field commanders.

The British corps for the 1689 campaign was led by John Churchill, aided by Percy Kirke, the Duke of Ormonde, Douglas, Ramsey and George Churchill, John's brother. As we have seen in Ireland, neither army in the field had a distinct technological advantage which would be decisive. The transition of weaponry from pike and matchlock to flintlock and bayonet was at its height, and this would change the way that battles were fought. Most new regiments, allied at least, would be fitted out in the 'new style' after 1689.

Before 1678 one-third of the regiment used pikes; in 1689 a few units still had a ratio of two muskets to one pike although, even two years after this, many regiments were being fitted out with full flintlock and bayonet combination, removing pikes completely. The French did not abolish the pike completely until 1703. The familiar bandolier of dangerous charges of gunpowder evolved into the paper cartridge, while artillery expanded and became more important, although not yet dominant; for instance eight 12-pounders transported by the British contingent in 1692 evolved into twenty 24-pounders by 1694.[8]

The *Abridgement of Military Discipline* with its 1685 revision after Monmouth's rebellion was still in evidence as a training manual for the English forces at least, and tactical flux was the order of the day, with old drills and formations, marching and counter-marching still in evidence. Although Dutch and English regiments were experimenting and flirting with 'platoon fire', cavalry tactics, use of artillery, and its civilian contractors, and the role of dragoons, be they clearly horsed infantry, or substitute cavalry, were seen in different lights by different commanders. The sweeping tactical renaissance would not be complete for ten more years.

Close-range exchanges of fire, with relatively slow-moving battalions, slow reloading rates, 'thick' battalions with many ranks and groups of men trained to advance or give ground slowly, were not battle winners. Contrast this with the fact that sieges were rarely a failure.[9] Battles were important, although for different reasons than they would be in later years. They were, for the most part, avoided, siege warfare becoming the principal military and political means of 'winning', although siege could not occur without the protection of a strong army.

Although naval exploitation by either side was scarcely used to the fullest potential, there were some notable successes. French moves in Catalonia in 1694 and 1695 were thwarted through judicious use of the British and Dutch navies in the Mediterranean and, for a time at least, kept the Duke of Savoy from leaving the Alliance.

As we have seen, the armies on land lacked subtlety, had little operational use other than co-ordinating areas of land in order to propagate siege, and lacked the weapons and technology with which to annihilate one another, at least in terms of removing the opposing army from the field. Despite the enormous numbers involved, field armies could only prove their worth by exploiting a chink in the armour made elsewhere; even then, logistics problems could slow the movement of large bodies of men to a crawl.

In terms of overall strategy and what Louis termed 'war feeding war', however, there was merit in possessing large field armies, simply by virtue of their ability to hold ground and prevent their opponents doing the same. The effects of this would force economies into collapse and kings to the conference table. The key was developing the right combination of strategy, manoeuvre and luck. Louis had considered that the war might be won quickly and cleanly. William had not laboured under the same misapprehension.[10]

As with the strategic aims of the day, William appreciated fully that he could protect the Dutch provinces only through successful siege and acquirement of fortresses and larger towns, denying them to his opponent, while simultaneously protecting his own economy, trade and prosperity at the expense of his enemy. If he kept his nerve, and no ludicrous strategic errors were made, Louis would succumb but there were many factors at play, not least the thorny question of the still open wound of the succession. As the war wound on, England would begin to realise the true cost and implication of fighting it, and the financial workings of international war and politics. In turn, the threat of Louis on her shores through the actions of a resurgent James II, and the general threat were Louis to gain Catholic dominion over all of Europe, were magnified and very real in English eyes, to William's ultimate benefit.

But, even then, France lacked clearly strategic goals. Preservation of the status quo featured highly in the war aims of both parties, whether Louis yet knew it or not. William's yearning for a physical maintenance of the United Provinces as they were, and the preservation of frontiers along the lines of the 1678 Treaty of Nijmegen, established his particular direction.

## 1689

The nine battalions under Marlborough in Flanders at the start of the war were representative of the state of the British Army. One of Louis's early war aims was that there would be no acceptance of William III as King of England, that position being rightfully held for James II in his view. Of course, Louis expected a quick war, a rapid movement, a caving in of the power blocs that would end up being ranged against him. The British element at least was still of dubious loyalty, there being no concrete confirmation of the new king who had, in the view of some, usurped power the year before, thus propagating dubious political and religious affirmation.

That England was a key player on the European stage meant that there was no room for doubt. The fact that Marlborough entered Flanders with a 6,000-man force, half the establishment strength, was testament to the fact that some, at least, had decided to choose the monarchy over religion or, at the very least, were unsettled by the delicate balancing act that still described the succession.

French action in the Palatinate had ignited German ire in a manner in which few other actions could, and the major powers of the League of Augsburg, combined with England to form the Grand Alliance, would prove to be numerically superior to France, although co-ordination of such a force would prove altogether impossible. The Grand Alliance was deployed around the north-eastern and eastern borders of France. In the Spanish Netherlands, the Marquis de Castanaga was more concerned with defending Spanish interests in Flanders than a wholesale invasion of France. Waldeck was positioned in the Brabant region, with an army of 35,000, while the Germans had three field armies to co-ordinate. Waldeck, although a seasoned veteran, found to his cost that only William had the international recognition and authority to get things done. Such was the setting that the British Army under Marlborough and Ormonde entered in 1689.

William's thoughts were focused on the difficult counterpoise between risky decisive action and doing nothing as the campaign season slipped away.

The Battle of Walcourt was relatively small when taken in context. Waldeck's 29,000 men (of which thirty-five were infantry battalions) against d'Humieres' 31,000 men (with twenty-eight infantry battalions), but then Newtownbutler and the Boyne were small, yet proved to be turning points. In this case, however, only a minority of each army would be engaged, in similar fashion to the Boyne, although it would be the major action of the campaign year. In common with many of the European battles, it would be 'innocently' instigated by the foraging actions of courageous parties on either side.

The French commenced an assault against Waldeck's well-chosen position, using the village's stone-wall defences and enclosures. Brigadier Talmash, later at Aughrim, led the Coldstream Regiment of Foot Guards to reinforce Walcourt, with Marlborough and Slangenburg later leading flanking actions, forcing the French to withdraw. Both sides suffered hundreds killed although the action was far from decisive. A search for foraging and suitable camping areas characterised the balance of the year. Louis's hope that the war would be swift and decisive was ill-founded, and there was no clear indication that the Grand Alliance was going to disperse or give up.

## 1690 Fleurus, the Boyne and The Wild Geese in Savoy

By 1690, with the entry of Savoy, under Duke Victor Amadeus II, into the Grand Alliance, due to French interference and moves against him, the alliance was uniquely positioned to approach French lines from three directions:   via the Spanish Netherlands, through the Alsace region, or northern Italy. It would have been remiss of the allies not to expect Louis to respond in some form. The limited advantage was timely as the allies had been hampered by a substantial British withdrawal from the theatre of operations, such that troops could be moved to the Irish campaign; this included five infantry battalions and all available cavalry, leaving just six infantry battalions in Flanders for operations. Thomas Talmash was in overall command of the Irish expeditionary force. Louis had deployed four armies, in Flanders under Marshal Luxembourg, one on the Rhine at Villeroi, in Catalonia under Noailles, and in Savoy and Piedmont under Marshal Catinat.

The Savoy-Piedmont region lay sandwiched between southern France and Milan, a Habsburg dominion. The region had a troubled past and the head of state, Duke Victor-Amadeus, had a reputation for playing politics with the more powerful factions around him. His troubles stemmed partly from Louis's revocation of the Edict of Nantes in 1685 when French religious intolerance of the Huguenot Protestants finally spilt over. The Vaudois also represented a small Protestant community in Piedmont on the border of the French region of Savoy. So that the flight of Huguenots to this region might be stopped, Louis decided that French might would fall hard on the mountain people. Penalties were harsh for Huguenots caught fleeing the country but, in this instance, Louis would send a message to those communities who sought to shelter them.

The Vaudois, or 'Barbets' as the French called them, had lived in the Alpine valleys to the south-west of Turin and had been persecuted by the Inquisition and the Savoyard government, and through their labours had become an implacable foe when necessary. William also knew this and would ply them with English gold in the years to come. Ever the efficient king, Louis delegated and ordered that Victor-Amadeus, Duke of Savoy-Piedmont, do something about the Vaudois. The duke, a young man of twenty married to a French princess, was not easily intimidated, but the presence of the nearby French fortress of Pinerolo in central Piedmont meant that the French garrison could help or force, as Louis decreed. The Marquis d'Arcy, the local ambassador, was ordered to force the duke's hand in the matter, and deny tolerance to the Protestant subjects of his dominion.

The duke preferred more subtle measures but Louis would have none of it, insisting that French troops be used to 'aid' the duke should his actions prove fruitless. Louvois saw Victor-Amadeus as a vassal of France, and little more. The sending of French troops onto his land was a mere formality. In January 1686 the pressure brought to bear by Louis's political ranting and the presence of French troops in the nearby fortress had worked, and the duke gave in. He would convert his subjects to Catholicism, by force if necessary, and with French help if the situation demanded it. Victor-Amadeus decreed intolerance and issued his declaration. His troops marched into the valleys of the Vaudois but it was not enough. By February d'Arcy was petitioning Louis for French troops. Marshal Catinat, a man whose destiny would become entwined with the region, marched to Turin with five infantry regiments and ten squadrons of French cavalry. After some discussion with the duke, the French force moved on to the fortress at Pinerolo. Despite a last-minute attempt by the Swiss to allow the Vaudois to leave peacefully, the mountain people resolved to stay and fight, a brave decision in the face of the implacable will of Louis XIV. Victor-Amadeus gave the Vaudois a final chance in April 1686. If they would lay down their arms and return home, he would grant an amnesty. Their refusal meant that troops were used after a delay of eight days. The Barbets stubbornly refused to negotiate and the combined French-Piedmontese operation, with around 7,000 men, began. Troops moved simultaneously from the French fortress and the Piedmontese town of Bricherásio.

The Vaudois had learned to fight as irregular troops. They ambushed French and Piedmontese troops and columns, using hit-and-run tactics, and became an annoyance to the regular force that pursued them in their mountain strongholds. Those rebels who were caught were executed. The countryside was desolated and the mountain people killed or captured, including those who tried to escape across the Alps. By June Victor-Amadeus held over 8,000 Barbets prisoner; the total would reach 12,000 by the end of the campaign. Louis and Catinat made it clear in their correspondence that they would like to see the end of the mountain people once and for all and, with the echoes of the atrocities of the Thirty Years' War, only a half-century before, the Vaudois could expect little quarter. They were held in Piedmont, in concentration camps, where some died through inadequate food and water, while most died from disease, certainly a despicable chapter in French history, although at least consistent with many of the actions of the time. By December 1686 only 5,000 Vaudois remained. The Swiss, whose offers of assistance had been ignored in preference to resisting the French, now helped re-settle the survivors in Protestant areas of Germany. But this was not the end of the mountain people. In the years to come, many Vaudois would return to their valleys and mountains, this time aided by William. William did not see the region as secondary in terms of its military importance, as did the French. Instead, he saw an opportunity to attack France along its south-eastern borders, also generating rebellion amongst the Huguenot populations of the region. Louis had not eradicated the Vaudois as he had hoped and the stage would be set for a clash with the Irish troops fighting for France.

By 1690 the situation had changed. Not only was there an active war, but Victor-Amadeus II had, perhaps unsurprisingly, changed allegiance and joined the alliance against Louis. Victor was still under political and military pressure, sandwiched as his kingdom was between the Dauphiné region of France and Habsburg Milan. His lands would be hotly contested in any European conflict. Within his territories, encompassing coastal Nice, mountainous Savoy and the Piedmont region, treaty obligations had allowed Louis to hold the vital fortresses of Pinerolo and Casale, both well inside the duke's borders, where Marshal Catinat was governor. The situation gave Louis vital political and military leverage even before the war had started. At the start of the year Victor-Amadeus was still on reasonable terms with Louis. His insistence that the duke hand Turin over to the French, however, was enough to convince Victor-Amadeus that it was time to change sides.

The war began in earnest in the region in June when the duke had French residents of Turin arrested. Louis can only have known of Victor-Amadeus's questionable loyalty, and not-so-secret talks with the Grand Alliance. His response was immediate, ordering troops to the south-east of France. Saint Ruth, who would lead the Irish at Aughrim a year later, was ordered to command in the region, but would be delayed. In the interim Louis needed troops in the area fast. The Marquis de Larré would lead 10,000 militia and 200 cavalry, while Catinat commanded 12,000 French troops. He began by taxing the town of Carmagnola, then demanding over 1,000,000 livres from Turin.

The duke, however, was not out of the fight and had two options. Firstly, and vital to any fighting that he would have to do in the region, he had made amends with the Vaudois, the mountain fighters whom he had once sent to their deaths. Now reconciled with their former oppressor, and eager to have their revenge on the French, many had returned to their valleys and taken up arms. This guaranteed a savage, brutal war, characterised by atrocity and massacre as Vaudois and French indulged in mutual hatred. The duke had also received reinforcements in the form of Spanish troops and with the promise of Germans to follow under the command of Prince Eugene of Savoy, a brilliant young commander who had sought French service and been turned away, a decision which would have dire consequences for Louis.

It was the summer of 1690 and the Irish regiments marched toward the Savoy region of France. The defeat of the Turks had created the situation where numerous Imperial troops were freed for service on the Italian border. Louis's fears had been realised and the French needed reinforcements in Savoy, and quickly. Enter the Irish, arriving in late July, in an attempt to boost the numbers of the French army on the Italian border under Marshal Catinat, who had advanced into the Po valley, leaving his second in command, the Marquis de Larré, to deal with the Vaudois in northern Savoy and keep open the vital lines of supply and communication. Although militarily weak in a conventional sense, the Vaudois/Barbets, were infamous guerrilla fighters, and could close the French army supply routes if necessary. Catinat was also facing increasing numbers of Imperial troops.[11]

It is not clear exactly when news of James's defeat at the Boyne reached Mountcashel – perhaps as he marched, or upon arrival. It was clear, however, that he could do little save protect the honour of his own regiment and show France how the Irish exiles could fight. He still believed that creating a good impression with the French and, more especially, Louis would create the correct conditions for the French to send more direct help to Ireland in the form of troops. His later communication with Sarsfield certainly supported this argument. He was not simply an Irish general fighting for the French; he was still a patriot. After the battle, James once more lost his nerve and returned to Kinsale, and then to France, leaving responsibility for the rapidly deteriorating situation with Tyrconnel, Berwick and Patrick Sarsfield. He never set foot in Ireland again.

More than ever both Mountcashel and the troops under him had to show how disciplined and well-armed Irish soldiers could fight, and die if necessary. Catinat, Mountcashel's new commander, was the son of a French magistrate and had reached his rank through merit rather than wealth or family connections. A good soldier and favoured by Louis, he had a reputation for being cautious in the field. He could also be ruthless and brutal as the situation demanded, ably demonstrated by his treatment of the Vaudois to date. He faced numerically superior Imperial forces, but his plea for reinforcements had at least been answered, in the shape of 5,000 able Irishmen under Lord Mountcashel, enabling him to continue the 1690 campaign in Upper Savoy. Catinat's main adversaries were the Duke of Savoy and the young Prince Eugene, who had greatly distinguished himself against the Turks. (Catinat and Eugene would meet again in the War of the Spanish Succession a decade later when Eugene would get the better of his old adversary.) Imperial troops on the defensive also had the advantage of the countryside and the terrain. Mountains dominated the region and many Imperial strongholds were characterised by inaccessible and thus easily-defended approaches. The area also contained the Vaudois/Barbets, well used to both the mountains and the nature of warfare in the inhospitable terrain.

Catinat and the other French officers had little knowledge of the Irish soldier, and must have had reservations, especially since the task ahead seemed so difficult. These were untested regiments and, although some officers spoke French, few of the men did. They had not been trained in the French school of military discipline, had not been constantly drilled until orders became second nature and movement in battalion fluid. To this end, Catinat appointed a trusted officer to command one of the regiments:

Andrew Lee (or André Lee), Marquis de Lee, had left Ireland and joined Sir George Hamilton's Regiment as an ensign. After the demise of that regiment, Lee remained in France, obtaining a commission as a lieutenant in the Furstenburg Regiment. He had served with much distinction in France thus far, becoming a lieutenant colonel, and so was placed as second in command of the Clare Regiment, joining it at Vienne.

Lee was trusted where the French could not yet place trust in the untried Irish. He was a link between the French staff officers and the new men, and would become a source of information, effectively allowing the Irish to be monitored closely. The French in the field must still have had some doubts. How would these rough Irish exiles fare in a real battle? This campaign, perhaps more than any other, would see the real forging of the reputation of the Wild Geese in French service.

Catinat's task was difficult and the questions surrounding the Irish would be answered soon enough. He had already advanced as far as the Po valley, leaving some troops under de Larray in Upper Savoy to protect lines of communication and supply against the Vaudois. Advancing into Piedmont, however, Catinat was faced with a larger Imperial army, which was also being reinforced. He summoned the troops from Upper Savoy. This left the lines of supply dangerously isolated to attack, and additional reinforcements were required to plug the gap and prevent the threat to his rear. He would have to use the untested Irish. Mountcashel's troops reached their destination by the end of July, and joined the French army near Chambéry, capital of Savoy. Saint Ruth had also arrived with his new command. Although his ultimate fate would be connected with the Irish at Aughrim, Saint Ruth was an experienced soldier, having served Louis since 1667 in Holland, Flanders and Germany. By 1688 he had been promoted to lieutenant general. Catinat's difficulty with lack of troops had prolonged matters, and the late arrival of both Saint Ruth and the Irish meant that a campaign based on long sieges or attrition was out of the question. Saint Ruth had a strategy in mind, however. He ordered the Marquis de Varennes to march against Chambéry via les Echelles (the ladders), an obviously mountainous and rugged patch of the inhospitable terrain, while he with the balance of the force, including the Irish, would approach via Champarluen.

Count de Bernix, the governor of Chambéry, who garrisoned a well-fortified position in a town which could have held out until Imperial forces arrived, decided that the situation was futile and opted to withdraw, citing that he had too few men to man the works. Saint Ruth reached the town by 12 August, and garrisoned it with 800 Irish troops under the Marquis de Thùoy. Imperial troops Annecy also fled but, as French troops reached Rumilly, the duke had decided to make a fight of it. Rumilly was well fortified when compared with other towns in the region and the French assaulted the works, overcoming the defenders. The campaign was going Saint Ruth's way; the duke had attempted to defend too many towns with too few men despite the reinforcements that were available. Aggressive French moves were paying dividends.

Success continued. The passage to the Ruè river was defended by only 2,000 to 3,000 militia and 500 troops. French pressure dispersed most of the troops, the balance surrendering. This action allowed them to roll through the areas of Chablais, Fausilly, Iserentaise and the area around Geneva, moving to the borders of the Republic of Geneva itself. Victor-Amadeus could only now occupy the sparse regions of Montmelian, Moutiers and the higher Alps. The terrain was becoming more difficult to master; indeed the duke must have counted on this, hoping to draw the French into a costly war of attrition in the Vaudois mountains.

O'Conor described this most accurately:

> The Piedmontese troops, commanded by the Count de Bernix and M. de Salles, evacuated the Duchy, retreating by the valley of Maurienne, and afterwards crossing the mountains that separate it from the valley of the Isere. That river, rising at the foot of Mount-Iseran, and collecting the cascades and rivulets that flow from the inexhaustible glaciers of the Graian Alps, turns to the north at the foot of the little St Bernard, and forces its foaming course through a chain of mountains, winding round projecting rocks, that present admirable positions for the defence of this great pass into Italy. The mountains forming its boundaries rear their snowy tops to the skies, and in many places descend almost perpendicularly to the river, narrowing its channel to a few hundred feet, and deepening it so as to be unfordable. No trees or shrubs facilitate the ascent; impending rocks, whose adhesion is often dissolved by the summer sun, threaten destruction, and fragments and loose stones, as slippery as the glaciers, endanger, at every step, the bold adventurer who dares to climb these precipitous steeps; gloom, barrenness, desolation, the thunder of avalanches, the roaring of cataracts, the colour of the waters, as dark as Cocytus, and the solitude of these dreary abodes, unnerve the arm and appal the heart. Wildness and grandeur characterize this defile through an extent of forty miles.[12]

Victor-Amadeus and the Piedmontese knew that the country would hamper French efforts. This, combined with the irregular activity of the Vaudois, would make the rest of the campaign difficult for Catinat and Saint Ruth. The Duke of Savoy was not having an easy war, however. His troops had been pushed back to the borders of Italy. The Imperial troops were divided into two armies, one under the Marquis de Salles and one under Count de Bernix. They would eventually find two easily-defended positions on the Isere river, where the mountain passes led into Italy, at the Little St Bernard and Mont Cenis. On this occasion, well-defended passes and the implacable Vaudois acted in the duke's favour. He did not, however, count on the equally relentless Irish.

Saint Ruth needed results. What better way to test his new Irish troops? The nature of the French marshal's profession was ruthlessness, and he certainly would have had no qualms over using the exiles as 'shock troops' in preference to wasting French lives in what could still prove a fruitless assault against a well-prepared enemy. He would also have calculated on the Irish troops' readiness to prove their ability and their determination in the inhospitable terrain. De Thùoy and the 800 Irish garrisoned at Chambéry were immediately ordered to march towards Saint Ruth's position. Simultaneously, the Marquis de Vins, with the balance of the Irish troops, three regiments of dragoons and some cavalry, was ordered to march from Annecy. The reinforcements, together with some light artillery, would join Saint Ruth with two infantry battalions and a cavalry regiment on the banks of the Isere river. O'Conor recorded the terrain's defensive bias in an excellent description:

> The village of Cintran, on the right bank above Moutiers, retains the name and revives the memory of the *homines intensi et inculti* who opposed, in this very defile, the march of Caesar to the conquest of Gaul. At Moutiers the valley becomes enlarged, less savage, and has an appearance of industry and civilization, but still bounded by barrenness and desolation. Escaping from this spot of momentary tranquillity, the river again rushes into a defile, precipitating its waters over ledges and rocks into deep chasms, through which it foams on in a lengthened and furious rapid, and after another expansion above Aigue Blanche, rushes through the rocks of La Batie, which it nearly surrounds, and forms a natural, and almost impassable moat, rendering the position of that fortress as impregnable as any that military science could devise. Lower

down it enters the Iserentaise – the Davantasia of the ancients. Here it maintains its original impetuosity, and runs rapidly through a defile equally savage, narrow, and tortuous, where a handful of resolute men, by precipitating loosened rocks and avalanches, might arrest the career of armies, however numerous, though guided by the genius of a Hannibal or a Napoleon. In Caesar's time the unarmed and undisciplined barbarians opposed him in vain from the high grounds, not daring to encounter in the valley underneath the disciplined valour of the legions. These same passes, guarded by great bravery, by military science, and all the improved implements of war, were forced by the valour of the Irish, and generalship of Saint Ruth.

Saint Ruth's force now assembled, he entered the Isere valley using a scouting element of 300 picked men to reconnoitre the land ahead, and spring an ambush without allowing full battalions to be destroyed rapidly in close infighting where French drill and musketry could make little difference to the outcome. The scouts were probably dragoons or similar light troops for this very reason.

De Salles and his troops were discovered in the lower part of the valley. He had 1,200 men ensconced on a rocky plateau (O'Conor and his contemporaries described this simply as a 'rock'), fronted by the river and flanked by mountainous terrain, its difficulty for the attacker further enhanced by the presence of defensive works and *abattis*. De Salles was in no hurry to be shifted on this occasion. Saint Ruth was equally determined that the opportunity for victory should not slip away once more. On the night of 11 September 1690 he ordered de Thùoy to the foot of the mountain with the Bretagne dragoons and 100 Irish troops. These troops would prevent de Salles's men easily escaping, should he change his mind about defending the position. De Salles, however, did not attempt to escape and spent the time available reinforcing his position, using felled trees and additional *abattis* to further slow the French forces that would undoubtedly attempt to carry the position by assault. Rugged defiles and easily-defended passes characterised the approach and Saint Ruth can have been in little doubt of the degree of slaughter that would be the inevitable outcome of having to attack.

His reconnaissance, using some of his dragoons and hand-picked infantry, had made him aware of de Salles' defences, no doubt giving an indication of where they were weak and where the most advantageous approaches were located. Saint Ruth chose to assault at three different points. Firstly, the Marquis de Vins would lead a dragoon force along the river, ascending the plateau downstream; Saint Ruth would be with these troops. Then, his cavalry force, presumably dismounted and acting as a feint or diversion, would assault the centre, climbing the 'rock' itself in a bold yet dangerous move. Finally, Mountcashel, at the head of his own regiment with de Thùoy, would march along the mountain through a narrow gorge or defile, gain access to the plateau and assault the position. Saint Ruth was obviously using only a fraction of the troops at his disposal.

This illustrates, perhaps, that he felt that there was little hope of success, at least in the first foray. He must have believed that it would take several assaults and he was saving his troops for a hard fight. Mountcashel, however, would be in the vanguard, with his Irishmen in their first fight since Newtownbutler. The defenders would have had each point of access well defended. The results of the action would indicate that Saint Ruth had found a flaw in the defences. The frontal assault, no doubt planned to draw attention away from the flanking moves, could not have been carried through fully, the cavalry perhaps recognising their role as expendable, since French casualties were relatively light.

The records of the action available speak mainly of Mountcashel's role. Despite their defensive position, it is clear that a determined charge dislodged de Salles's troops. We can speculate that Saint Ruth had found a poorly-defended pass for Mountcashel and his men to move through, giving the Imperial troops with matchlocks little time to defend against a charge – echoes of Newtownbutler. The defenders were rooted out of their works by Mountcashel and his regiment and pursued into the mountains, with around 150 killed. In the mêlée, de Salles's lieutenant colonel was killed beside him. De Salles took cover in the undergrowth but was discovered and taken prisoner. French records speak of Saint Ruth losing only ten to fifteen men in the entire action, three of them Irish, with two Irish wounded. This seems incredibly light. However, Mountcashel had also been hit by musketfire while leading the charge. Some French records state that this was not a serious wound, although this may have been made light of based on his importance. Other sources talk of Mountcashel being badly wounded. Dangeau, for instance, noted that 'Saint Ruth reports that in the late battle of Savoy the Irish troops had performed marvellously'. He also reported that Lord Mountcashel had been 'dangerously wounded' by a musket ball in his chest.

O'Callaghan related the event from both French and Imperial sources.

> Three Irish killed, and two wounded, with Milord Moncassel slightly, by a musket-shot, in the left breast; having been very much distinguished; as well as those of his nation.
>
> The Irish, commanded by Milord Moncassel, who were present at this encounter, fought exceedingly well, and having seen how their chief was wounded, they refused to abandon the pursuit of their enemies, till they should have taken the Comte de Sales, who commanded them. They led him in triumph to Lord Moncassel, in order to console him for the wound which he had received.

A number of points are clear. The Irish had performed well, having carried the position and conducted a pursuit, suggesting that their morale had been high and they had remained a cohesive force. Mountcashel's men had purged the ghost of Newtownbutler, a recent defeat which must still have haunted the survivors. Mountcashel had also proven that he could lead his men in battle and they would fight well for the French and, perhaps more keenly, for him. The suggestion that de Salles had to be brought back to Mountcashel suggests that his wound at the very least prohibited him from continuing the pursuit with his men, and certainly makes it sound more serious than the French suggested at the time. He had been injured at Newtownbutler just over a year before. Combining the relative severity of his wounds with the fact that he was now almost fifty, relatively old for the period, he was lucky to be alive.[13]

After the battle Saint Ruth was reinforced once more with O'Brien's Regiment and some additional cavalry. The force moved higher into the Alps towards the source of the Isere along the Little St Bernard and Mont Cenis river valley. The Count de Bernix was entrenched in another well-defended position with 400 men. Again, the duke's men had used the natural defensive features of the local countryside to their advantage, and Bernix's position lay in a narrow defile flanked by apparently inaccessible mountains and the river. Andrew Lee, then commanding the O'Brien Regiment, was ordered to find a way through the mountain. Perhaps using local knowledge, but certainly relying on the determination of his Irish troops, he found a pass that enabled him to emerge at a position behind the enemy defences. Little expecting an attack from the rear, Bernix's troops fled, leaving their positions, artillery and stores, and escaping across the river bridges towards Italy via the Aosta valley. French forces pursued the retreating troops in order to prevent their rallying, and it seemed that Saint Ruth's late-summer campaign was becoming more successful by the day.

The Irish contribution was fully recognised and Saint Ruth distributed the captured provisions and spoils of the enemy, mainly to the Irish troops, who enjoyed the bread and wine. The French moves and incredible successes had frightened the populace of the surrounding towns and villages to the extent that, on the night of Lee's victory, Saint Ruth received officials from the town of Montiers, receiving its keys from the archbishop and magistrates the following day. Two days later the French troops had marched to Morienne, where a similar surrender was arranged. Brisansonnet also fell, and the army encamped, ready for the onset of the colder months.

Mountcashel and 3,000 Irish troops garrisoned Chambéry through the winter. In Savoy only Montmelian remained defiant against the French and Saint Ruth blockaded the town, bombarding where possible. The amount of captured land in Savoy would yield sizeable revenue for the French. It had been an important and wholly successful campaign for Saint Ruth, but greater still for the Irish exiles who were slowly re-establishing their reputation.

Catinat had not been idle during the period of Saint Ruth's triumphs. The use of Irish reinforcements had allowed him some flexibility. What would these troops be able to accomplish, however? A siege of Turin was beyond the scope of the numbers involved but, with his lines of supply and communication secure, he ordered Antoine de Pas, Marquis de Feuquières, to tax or where necessary burn the enemy-held towns and strongholds. These undertakings were not easy, and at Luserna the marquis suffered heavy casualties, after being forced to abandon the town through counter-attack. Victor Amadeus then seized his opportunity. He had been securely defending Villafranca until the opportunity to attack a weakened Catinat emerged.

Catinat, his forces bolstered with French militia, moved south to Saluzzo. The two armies clashed on 18 August at the Battle of Staffarde. Near Saluzzo the battlefield was characterised by marshland and hedges, making reconnaissance and movement difficult. The duke's army was defeated, suffering 2,800 casualties and losing 1,200 prisoners and eleven of their twelve guns. Catinat's casualties numbered 1,000 killed and wounded. Saluzzo quickly fell and the duke fled once more to Turin. Catinat wasted no time after breaking the enemy and taxed Cerisoles and Autrives amongst others. Towards the end of the campaign, the duke attempted to defend the route to Susa but was outmanoeuvred by Catinat, who captured the town on 13 September.

The French troops wintered in Savoy, Dauphiné and Provence at the end of a well-conducted campaign. A small number of troops, including French regulars and militia and the previously unknown quality of the Irish troops, had combined with outstanding generalship to outclass and outmanoeuvre an implacable foe. For the Irish it was just the beginning.

In Ireland, with the wintering of troops the previous year at Dundalk, with little real aim in sight, William had been forced to act and take command himself, there being a degree of drive, authority and willingness required to get things done. Waldeck, the seventy-year-old veteran, was left in charge on the mainland, facing his French opposite number Luxembourg with 25,000 men, with Boufflers in command of a cavalry element that could provide rapid reinforcement.

For Louis the unexpected victory was another early success in the war. In Flanders both armies had been under pressure to engage, and needed to do more than simply probe each other's defences. Luxembourg instigated a series of night marches near Ligny on 21 June (o.s.) to force Waldeck to give battle on unfavourable ground near Fleurus with 30,000 men against the 40,000 French. The Dutch left flank collapsed against concerted pressure, while the Spanish right held fast. Six hours of Dutch infantry action to defend fragile flanks followed. The result was characteristically inconclusive as the Spanish horse allowed the allied army to escape toward Nivelles and Chareroi, although without much of its artillery and baggage, and discouraged any ordered French pursuit.

Despite the mistakes, Luxembourg's manoeuvring had been superlative; it was ever the nature of slow-moving warfare, without either side having an edge, that would result in anything other than a rough stalemate. News of William's victory at the Boyne, however, would reach the armies by the end of July, the only point of light in the allied campaign, although, again, a characteristic battle where pursuit was limited and/or ineffective.

Rivalry in the Williamite camp did not help matters; senior commanders would consistently have different priorities. Despite news of the Boyne, the naval defeat at Beachy Head had worsened the news of Fleurus, and the wily Catinat at Staffarde had cemented a successful year, although a decisive victory would be impossible.

William was badly needed in the Low Countries, and appeared to be the only notable who might provide unity of purpose despite the fact that Louis and a powerful, hungry France should have generated more than enough impetus to consolidate a united alliance. In Ireland, the effects of the rout after the Boyne spread like wildfire. The surrender of the garrison at Drogheda shortly after the battle precipitated a collapse that rapidly gained momentum. Small Jacobite garrisons fell or fled, at Wexford, Duncannon and Waterford, at the approach of William's forces. Many of the Williamites were convinced that there was little fight left in the Irish army.

When William's troops laid siege to Athlone the Jacobites made a stand, a strategic necessity since the town commanded many of the crossings over the river, one of the few natural defences that acted in the Jacobites' favour. The siege proved difficult for the Williamite forces and was quickly given up in preference to a pursuit towards Limerick and the rest of the Irish army. By the beginning of August William was being forced to waste valuable time on the Irish affair, time that Louis knew he could use to his advantage in mainland Europe.

As he had met with success at the Boyne, the French at the Battle of Fleurus had defeated his allied army in Flanders. Louis's navy had also won a victory at Beachy Head. The news forced William to return to Dublin with the intention of returning to England. However, the French successes, as so often occurred in this deadlocked and indecisive European conflict, were not followed up successfully. William finally made his decision, changed his mind once more, and continued towards Limerick with his army.

His decision and ultimate intention of defeating the Irish remnants, rather than serving to bolster the town's defence, and thus unite the Irish factions through an understanding of what was coming, only served to further divide the leading Irish parties. Berwick, in particular, cited that 'The place had no fortification but a wall without ramparts, and some miserable little towers without ditches'. Tyrconnel also questioned the prospects of holding the town. Only Sarsfield seemed hopeful, being of the opinion that Limerick must be held since otherwise all was lost.

The successful defence of Athlone and Limerick had meant that the lines of the Shannon had held but there was little cause for celebration. The restraining authority of James had, to some extent, held back the squabbles and intrigues of the Jacobites, though his absence meant that the factions were would remain. Many of the native Irish were committed not only to the pursuit of French protection but the creation of a separate Irish state. The old-English, however, saw the developing of agreement with William. To this end, the native Irish saw French security as the only means to end the land question, gain religious freedom and even their remaining in Ireland; their best troops and perhaps their best general were currently in France after all, highlighting and underlining just such a prospect. The

French troops who had served in Ireland waited at Galway for the arrival of the transports to take them home. The Irish would have no such respite. Tyrconnel would travel with the French, in the hope of securing more direct aid in the court of Louis. In the interim, he handed control of affairs over to Berwick.[14]

## The 1691 Campaign

The relative successes of the individual regiments within Mountcashel's Brigade resulted in the regiments being split up for the 1691 campaign. Some of the Irish would fight in Catalonia on the Spanish border while the rest would remain in Savoy. Saint Ruth, the French marshal who had helped secure Savoy for Louis, handed command over to the Marquis de la Hoguette, who had returned from Ireland with Lauzun. Saint Ruth would take his place, leading the Jacobites at the Battle of Aughrim in July 1691 where his career would be savagely cut short as he was decapitated by a cannonball.

As Hoguette took charge in Savoy in autumn 1690, the citadel of Montmelian, although not besieged in strict seventeenth-century terms, was blockaded via trench lines and redoubts in the hope of provoking surrender through starvation. The methods of the French siege expert, Vauban, although tried and tested, were manpower intensive, and numbers were not a luxury that was available. By February 1691 French guns were close enough to bombard the town, causing damage to the grain stores. Surrender seemed far from the mind of the defenders, however, as they continued to make forays against the French lines. The summer eventually saw the opening of more traditional siege trenches. Montmelian surrendered in August, but the citadel within the town held out until the end of the year.

Mountcashel had been in close communication with Sarsfield earlier in the year. He had high hopes of continued success after the Williamite debacle at Limerick. As ever, the request for French aid in terms of arms and equipment was prominent, although for the most part ignored. Sarsfield also requested that Mountcashel encourage Irish interests in the French court; in addition to being best placed for the job, he had the ear of the French. The divisions had not been healed in Ireland and it was clear that Limerick had been a turning point, but for all the wrong reasons. The representatives of the native Irish party, including the Bishop of Cork and the Luttrell brothers, travelled to France to make their case and to denigrate and thus undermine Tyrconnel. Sarsfield wrote to Mountcashel denying that such activity represented a split, citing its purpose as representing the Irish army, their aim to oppose those who would deal with William and thus deliver Ireland to him. Mountcashel wholeheartedly backed the Irish faction, but he must have known that the absence of James, even as a weak focus for unity, could only result in chaos.

In his next move he was not only motivated by patriotism, perhaps tinged with desperation at events in Ireland, but hoped to use some of the goodwill he had generated with Louis. He wrote to the French king in August declaring his support for the Irish faction and, with characteristic frankness, declaring that French aid had been wasted in Ireland to date. James's dismissal of the Irish should not therefore signal that Louis would do the same. Mountcashel was clearly aware of the dangers in ignoring the developing situation, obviously still believing that the French saw more in Ireland than a simple sideshow to prevent Williamite concentration in Europe. With his usual candour, he warned of the imminent defeat that would occur without intervention. It was time for the facts to be made clear, and thus force the French to show their hand.

Tyrconnel had also journeyed to France to set the record straight, from his point of view, about the Irish and the state of French backing. Despite rumour of his growing apathy with the situation and matters of Irish defence, French promises once more inspired his will to resist. However, he made clear his objection to Mountcashel's and others' alleged distortion of the facts. The feuding between the two would continue. Tyrconnel was asked to raise more troops for French service on his return to Ireland. It would have been difficult under the circumstances to give troops away, although Tyrconnel's subsequent procrastination was blamed on other factors. He claimed that few would want to serve under Mountcashel, an excuse which even the French found hard to stomach since the general's popularity did not seem in question. Louvois would have none of the deception, warning Tyrconnel that his quarrel with Mountcashel should not be 'prejudiced against the service of the King who is trying so hard to maintain you, you should therefore overcome your petty grievance against my Lord Mountcashel'.[15] The French would not stand to see their Irish commander rebuked.

Mountcashel was ordered to Catalonia on the Spanish border with Arthur Dillon and 1,000 picked Irish troops, a largely experienced force by now. The 1690 campaign in Italy stood in stark contrast to the events of that year on the French-Spanish border. The Marquis de Noailles led around 12,000 troops in the region, facing 13,000 Spanish troops commanded by

Villahermosa. One aspect of the campaign, however, was similar to that of Italy, in that local irregular troops, familiar with and comfortable in the mountainous regions of the country, were present. In contrast to the Vaudois, these mountain people or 'Miquelets' fought for both sides. In 1690 Noailles had conducted a defensive campaign against the Spanish and there had been little movement. For the 1691 campaign, and under increasing pressure from Versailles, Noailles would go on the offensive. In common with Savoy, the terrain in the area was rocky, mountainous and unforgiving, favouring the defender, and requiring the use of explosives to move artillery in many instances.

By late May Noailles had 10,000 men in fourteen battalions, with eight squadrons of cavalry and some Miquelets. Initially he moved against the town of Urgell. Again, as with the Savoy campaign, lines of communication and supply were dangerously open to attack at the hands of irregular troops who could simply fade away. In addition, the French had to repair the roads ahead of their advance. Noailles established his camp at the town of Bellver and garrisoned it with the 1,000 Irish troops. The heavy artillery had to be brought across the dangerous mountains, the troops literally blasting a path as they advanced. The Marquis de Quinson commanded siege operations at Urgel and digging commenced on 5 June. By the 10th the vital artillery had arrived and was emplaced, the bombardment commencing the following day. Within a few hours the Spanish governor of the town had surrendered with 1,000 troops and 1,200 irregulars. Urgel's fortifications were demolished and Bellver was further strengthened against enemy attack. In order to strengthen his position still further, Noailles moved a detachment under Chaseron toward Barcelona, ostensibly on a foraging expedition. Although the Irish troops remained in garrison, protecting the newly fortified Bellver, Mountcashel accompanied the expedition. Chaseron's troops were also able to capture several fortified towns and castles and put the Spanish to flight wherever they were encountered. The towns of Valence, Boy and Soor were captured quickly. Mountcashel was present at the operations around Valence and Boy.

The Duke of Medina Sidonia then advanced towards Noailles's position at Bellver. Noailles had received some reinforcements in the form of the Roussillon militia to supplement his small force. The fortifications and the reinforcements acted in his favour and Medina Sidonia, arriving on 15 August, moved swiftly west to lay siege to Prats-de-Mollo. Acting upon the opportunity to take decisive action, Noailles assembled his troops and pursued the Spanish force, relieving the town and forcing the withdrawal of the enemy. Both French and Spanish troops went into winter quarters and the campaign ended for the year. There had been little fighting for the Irish; the 1,000 troops had been used as camp guards, although Mountcashel had seen some of the limited action in the theatre. In the two years of fighting, the Savoy campaign had taken the heaviest toll on the 6,000 Irish who had landed at Brest. Louvois's letter to Tyrconnel in spring 1691 requested a further 1,200 men to fill the ranks of the Irish regiments. Many men had been lost toward the end of the campaign at the costly siege of Montmelian. The Irish had re-acquired their reputation as professional troops, but at a terrible cost.[16]

Even at this late stage Mountcashel believed that the Irish cause was not lost. French relief could stop the Williamites. Mountcashel wrote to Louis and the French court once more. He again spoke of French resources having been wasted to date; Saint Ruth's death and the defeat at Aughrim had been outrageously ill fated, but conduct under his guidance had shown how the Irish army could fight. The troops at the very least should be paid and another good general, together with continued French support, could still rescue the situation. He also believed that Limerick could withstand another siege, provided that the French engineers there provided adequately for defence. Although Mountcashel did not wish to leave French service, he would gladly return there to muster more recruits for his regiment if necessary. It was already too late, however. By October 1691 the number of Irish recruits available for service in the French army would no longer be a problem. Limerick had fallen after a second siege and Irish exiles sailed to France to fight for Louis under the conditions of the Treaty of Limerick. Tyrconnel had died prior to the siege, along with many of the Irish hopes.

### The 1692 Campaign – Namur and Steenkirk

Mountcashel spent 1692 on the Catalonian border. The year that followed proved decisive. By the end of it the French king desired peace but was in no way sure how he could achieve it. William had similar thoughts since the war was becoming difficult to pursue both militarily and economically, even at this relatively early stage. With no solution in sight, however, and keen not to show weakness, Louis raised even more troops, increasing the size of the French army to 400,000 men. The war had become an end unto itself, with little dramatic victory and stalemates in most theatres. War was feeding war.

With the Treaty of Limerick, William's troops were almost universally available for service in the Low Countries, as conversely were the Wild Geese led by Sarsfield. However, the French would not use the troops together.

Plans to take Dunkirk and secure a seaward flank on the French frontier were hatched and deliberated upon, although betrayed to Versailles by a sympathiser at the English court. Louis planned to use the 12,000 men of the newly-refreshed Irish Brigade, supported by French troops numbering 12,000 in an attempt to invade Britain. James II was politely requested to lead them by Louis; he remained reluctant and uncertain. Such uncertainty never entered the calculations of the English government who remained convinced that the concentration of French and Jacobite troops on the French coast were destined for one mission only. This secondary diversion, despite at least some serious intent, interfered with the movement of troops to the Low Countries, forcing some British regiments to sail home and thus prevent disaster. Selwyn's, Beveredge's and Lloyd's battalions were directed back, while six further battalions stood by at Willemstadt if needed, with a further 10,000 men around Portsmouth and the Isle of Wight.[17] There were even, by no means baseless, fears of naval betrayal, bearing in mind James II's former rank in earlier years, and the perceived loyalty of the Royal Navy to an admired Lord High Admiral.

The plan collapsed, however. Admiral Edward Russell's victory over Tourville off Cap la Hougue between 19 May (o.s.) and 20 May would deny the French any command of the English Channel. There had been twenty-three battalions in England at the time and it was hoped that these might be used for an action against the European coast in order to draw off French troops. The French had also hoped to create diversion enough to draw off troops to England and thus move towards Namur to lay siege. Seizing the city would hamper allied operations and allow the French to gain another foothold along the Meuse. Louis even believed that capturing Namur and threatening the British succession, even at this hour, would force all parties to the negotiating table.[18]

Louis moved forces from Savoy and Germany, hoping in turn to put the English forces on guard, knowing also that James's potential invasion had hampered allied speed of response.

Castanaga was replaced as governor of the Spanish Netherlands by the Elector of Bavaria, his inefficiencies during 1691 being a factor.[19] Louis ordered twenty infantry battalions, four full regiments of horse and two of dragoons to be recalled from Catinat and re-deployed in the Low Countries, to make ready for Namur. The combined French armies of Luxembourg and Boufflers comprised 115,000 men. With a long planned intent to deflect allied moves and besiege Namur, the French opened their trenches in May, while Luxembourg, with the balance of the army, flouted the statutes of the day and went in search of a battle.

Subsequent rains prevented William's army engaging with Luxembourg across the Mehaigne river, which slowed the Namur 'siege clock' virtually to a standstill by the end of June, threatening to end the siege unsuccessfully and prematurely. The use of French guile and an imaginative taking of the Coehorn and Terra Nova forts, through the aid of a sleeping sentry, contributed to the beginning of the end, however, and Namur was taken after twenty-seven days of siege, with 2,500 French having been killed in the endeavour. The end of the siege meant that Luxembourg was supported rapidly with troops, and there was little that William could do to stop it now.

A force of 80,000 Allied troops would face 115,000 French, now with their flanks secured, and conscious of the fact that William had lost the initiative. He had neither been able to relieve Namur, nor out-manoeuvre Luxembourg. To make matters worse, forage was scarce, or had been blockaded, and time was running out for the allies. William's sole chance of success in the campaign year lay in facing Luxembourg in battle.

The armies were brought together in an area characterised by low hills around the town of Steenkirk, on the north bank of the Senne river. The French position stretched over seven miles, centred on the town of Enghien. The country favoured infantry, rather than the fearsome French cavalry. A spy in the allied camp had been turned and had relayed false intelligence to the French that allied moves would only be on the basis of foraging rather than attack.

Neither general had done enough reconnaissance, and William would suffer for it, being forced to attack. When he did, it was over a very narrow frontage due to the heavily-wooded nature of the region. He still went through with it, despite all advice to the contrary. It began on 23 July (o.s.). Allied artillery could not deploy effectively in time due to poor planning and errors in their route of march. Instead, Wurttemberg led six battalions, four British and two Danish, with pioneers leading the way to the south and west, against the French flank.

Despite having been fooled initially by the foraging ruse, the sight of enemy battalions deploying into battle lines was enough to convince the French that something was amiss. Infantry poured from their tents as orders were issued and rapidly masked Enghien with nine battalions although their deployment and line of battle was disorganised and ad hoc. The French retained the high ground, however, and were protected by woods, enclosures and ditches. The river protected the French right and the unengaged left could still threaten the allied flank.

Poor deployment afflicted the allies too; a choked approach played havoc with dispositions and cavalry had been pushed too far forward on the flank. By midday, Württemberg's force was around thirteen battalions, 8,000 men, and he had used the disorganised cavalry to form units that could provide support, attaching them by midday. Having no real flank support, and facing a strong enemy position exacerbated by enclosures and ditches, as his own linear cohesion became rapidly disrupted, his chances of success were diminished rapidly. But the French were still trying to deploy, even as Württemberg marched almost into their camp, having sustained casualties, but nonetheless still an effective force. Luxembourg himself rallied the French and organised them to repel the attack, and stiffen resolve. But there had been a general repulse, which required further allied reinforcement or a renewed attack. Neither was immediately forthcoming.

Sarsfield and Berwick had both performed particularly well during the defence, being some of the first into the fray, and Sarsfield had been 'exposed to the hottest fire'. Luxembourg removed any doubts that Louis might have had:

> The duke of Berwick was present from the commencement when we proceeded to reconnoitre the enemy and behaved during the entire combat as bravely as in the last campaign, of which I informed your majesty at the time.
>
> With him was the earl of Lucan in whom we have particularly noticed the valour and the fearlessness of which he has given proofs in Ireland. I can assure your majesty that he is a very good and very able officer.[20]

It seemed that Sarsfield and Berwick were 'coming of age', at least in the opinion of the French notables, and had enhanced their reputations considerably, when compared with d'Avaux's comments during the Irish campaign. The word was passed that Sarsfield should receive his own command at the earliest opportunity.

The Dutch General Solms, somewhat indifferent to his allies' concerns, refused twice to accede to Württemberg's request for aid, although his inaction may have been exacerbated by the fact that Württemberg had carried forward so far that his own deployment from column into line was still in progress far behind. The allies were forced back with heavy casualties, and the cavalry could not charge. Despite counter-attack, no ground could be gained and, by nightfall, although only half the army had been engaged, over 5,000 had been killed.[21]

Events such as these would later support Marlborough and Talmash's contention that Dutch oversight of the fledgling British army was intrusive and inefficient. In turn, such accusations would see Marlborough at least, land himself in trouble politically. The battle had been fought almost as an act of desperation and, operationally, had been a disaster.

## The 1693 Campaign – Landen

Despite local gains it was clear by now that the French economy would not stick the pace of the war. With over 250,000 men in arms, rampant taxation and a run of poor harvests, the conflict had almost broken the country and Louis was all too aware that discussion, aimed at a peaceful, if face-saving, settlement would be a necessity rather than a strategic option.

But it would not be a settlement easily made, and Louis would force the issue to the negotiating table through a violent and bloody campaign year. William's previous year had been a disaster and he knew that a change in allied fortunes, and thereby a reassurance of the countries in the Alliance, would be his only hope. With the non-starter that had been the French attempt on the English throne with the by now deflated James, William at least could feel that the succession was secure, but its dissolution still remained a declared war aim of the French.

For the French, all that they could now realistically afford was a land offensive which had been reasonably successful thus far, thus precluding any further thoughts regarding an invasion of England. The Grand Alliance was still capable of decisive military action although Louis's machinations would see Sweden leave under the pretext of becoming a peacemaker. As ever, Louis's refusal to recognise William as King of England was a sticking point, however moot the question had become.

The war continued as Prince Eugene attempted to seize the fortress of Pinerolo, and thereby invade France, but Catinat took advantage of his failed siege and crushed him at Marsaglia in the autumn. More than a simple defeat in battle, the action convinced the perhaps ever doubtful or merely enterprising Victor Amadeus that he was in the wrong camp entirely and he made overtures to rejoin the French.

In the Low Countries, Luxembourg conducted an aggressive campaign to maintain pressure on the allies. Would it become another disastrous year for William and his fracturing alliance? Allied garrisons on the Meuse, with seeming success, were able to dissuade Luxembourg from French plans to lay siege to a major allied fortress, such as Liège or Maastricht. By July the French had taken Huy and William feared that their next target might be Liège. He could not afford to lose it.

By July, with William's main force encamped at Neerwinden and Landen, he decided that the time was right to strike. 50,000 allied troops, comprised of fifty-two battalions and 150 squadrons would face 66,000 French, with eighty-six battalions and 210 squadrons of cavalry.[22] However, French manoeuvring and the benefit of numbers had meant that William was caught unprepared, and had been trapped in a disadvantageous battlefield. The area had been chosen for its forage potential but, two miles behind the position, the Little Geete river, with its bridges and pontoons meant that a retreating army, attempting to disengage from a large enemy force that held the initiative, would be caught and placed in tactically inhibiting bottlenecks.

In a manner similar to Steenkirk the previous year, one general had been trapped by another on a site originally selected for its forage value. Luxembourg was in an optimum position to attack the allies. William was trapped in a bottleneck. Liège had 17,000 allied troops in defence, while Württemberg, now at Hainaut, had a similar number, and another force garrisoned Maastricht. He faced perhaps 50,000 men, and his chance had come. He sent troops both towards Liège and Hainaut in the attempt to goad William into pulling further troops away from his camp. He attacked on 18th July (o.s.), the advance guard of the large army sighting William's camp as they pushed north through Overwinden. With such movements, the allies were not surprised, although their tactics were dictated by their containment. Rather than become embroiled in a panicked retreat he would defend as the French had done at Steenkirk. That evening, the French army occupied Landen, Overwinden and St Gertrude after marching eighteen miles.

Should the allied army be forced back from this position, they were in trouble as the bottleneck effect of the rivers and limited exits would make orderly withdrawal impossible. It could even mean wholesale destruction of a defeated army. The allies spent the night of 18 July (o.s.) fortifying their positions in the village and building breastworks. Their left rested on the hamlet of Neerlanden and the Landen Beek to the east. The area was boggy and was a natural defensive position, although William placed a cavalry reserve there. The line ran south, then west to Rumsdorp, garrisoned by British infantry, to the larger town of Neerwinden, with the village of Laar, key to the defence and occupied by British foot and horse, while Landen would be defended solely by infantry. The breastworks and defences were less than adequate and certainly not meant to withstand concerted French attacks.

Luxembourg's original plan was to force the allied centre between Neerwinden and Rumsdorp and exploit the gap with cavalry, although it was clear that the defences, however hastily put in place, would be effective in disrupting the movement of horse. Instead, he resolved to engage with British positions at Neerwinden and Laar, with the aim of unhinging the allied lines, and gaining access to the flank and rear, effectively disabling and destroying the allied army. In addition he would make exploratory manoeuvres against the allied flanks.

During the hours of darkness, William concentrated his artillery pieces on the centre at Neerwinden, ignoring advice that he should begin moving the army out of its hemmed-in position during the night.

In the early hours of the morning Luxembourg sent 15,000 foot and 2,000 dismounted dragoons toward Rumsdorp and Neerlanden on the allied left. In front of Neerwinden itself, the French formed up in eight linear formations, two with infantry, but with an overwhelming six of cavalry; if the French could break the allied defences, the dominant French cavalry would pour through the gaps like a waterfall, and overpower the defenders. That was the theory at least, although shortage of space meant that he had to form column and attack in the same formation (not an accepted, nor practised, French tactic as it would later become) which allowed some support in the assault and enhanced movement, but would limit those forces that he could bring to battle at any one time, akin to a human battering ram against the allied defences. It would also limit French superiority in numbers somewhat, and permit at least some further benefit to the allied field defences.

The centre division of the left wing was commanded by Berwick, with the division on the right commanded by Lieutenant General Rubantel, with Sarsfield as his Marechal de Camp. The French advance began at 6.00am, with three infantry columns moving toward Neerwinden, supported by six regiments marching towards the English positions at Laar. At least some of the cavalry was used to deny support to the allies by engaging on the allied right.

As leading ranks of the French engaged the defenders behind walls and enclosures at Neerwinden, they carried forward for a time, but the attack quickly slowed and bogged down. For the first time in the war, fighting within a town characterised the battle. Gone were the well-trained ranks of men, taught to fire in platoon volley or by rank, in the French style. Instead, pockets of desperate soldiers fought hand-to-hand to deny the enemy their position. Where musketry was in use, it was close-range and deadly, and it was inevitable that the French, in the attack, would suffer horribly. Tight streets and seventeenth-century town patterns were hardly conducive to the deployment of contemporary troops and, once engaged, most battalions were no longer under control, for better or worse. English and Dutch guards, and the Scots Guards, with Hanoverian battalions, held the defensive line as they clung on desperately to Neerwinden against the assaults led by the Duke of Berwick and other French notables. Berwick led Irish troops in the assault, and we can be sure that their blood was up.

Berwick described:

> I attacked first. I forced the enemy to give way and drove them from hedge to hedge as far as the plain, at the border of which I again formed up in line of battle. The troops which should have attacked to my right and left, instead of doing so judged that they would be less exposed to the enemy's fire by throwing themselves into the village: thus, all of a sudden, they found themselves behind me. The enemy, on perceiving this bad manoeuvre, re-entered the village on the right and the left upon which the firing became terrible. The four brigades under Rubantel and Montchevreuil were thrown into confusion and driven out of the village and in consequence I found myself attacked on all sides. After the loss of a vast number of men, my troops likewise abandoned the front of the village and while I was endeavouring to maintain my ground in the hope that M. de Luxembourg, to whom I had sent for assistance, would advance to relieve me, I found myself at last completely cut off.[23]

Brandenburg troops, who had held between Laar and Neerwinden, were also under severe pressure, while Ramsay's troops at Laar were driven out of the village during the assault, and de Bezon's horse poured in through the gap. The flank was under terrible threat and the allied cavalry, under the Elector of Bavaria, forced the French incursion back in disarray, allowing Ramsay to retake the position and secure the flank. Berwick had been taken prisoner during the attack by John Churchill's brother, Charles. The initial assault had been repelled.

The plan had failed, however. Luxembourg had intended to pin the allies in such a manner that they could not operate freely with reinforcements and thereby plug gaps in the line, but they had been able to do so. The attacks had not been properly co-ordinated. He would learn from his mistakes in the second assault. As the rallied columns moved forward again, French dragoon regiments moved toward Neerlanden in hope of turning the flank, although Neerlanden's four battalions held but had required William himself to intervene and reinforce Brigadier Selwyn with Danish infantry.

On the opposite flank the key village of Rumsdorp fell, and its defenders were pushed from the line; a desperate battle for Neerlanden was also in progress. Luxembourg's plan was working, and it was proving difficult for the allies to move troops to reinforce breaches in the line. Despite contrary advice, Luxembourg persevered, knowing that if he could take another stronghold the allied position would finally fall. He moved the reserve in to renew the attack on Neerwinden. The defenders there, and out towards Laar, had started with 15,000 troops, of whom one third had become casualties. As elite French guards attacked, well supported, the hopes of the English, Hanoverian and Dutch infantry faded rapidly and the allies were forced to withdraw, the French forces finally getting the better of the fortifications and defences.

As allied troops tried in vain to plug the gaps, they had to withdraw from the flanks. The French had been closely observing their movements, and now was the time to strike On the right, Feuquieres had noted the movement of allied infantry towards the centre. He attacked, supported by the French centre. The allied infantry formed a large ad hoc square with nine battalions, but the French cavalry bypassed it and prepared to charge as much of the allied flank as they could.

With a flank about to be turned, and having lost the lynchpin of his defence at Neerwinden, the battle was lost for William. His priority was to save as much of the army as he could. The cavalry was called upon to screen the retreating infantry, although the Bavarian cavalry was outmatched, salvation coming in the form of the cavalry reserve that William had placed on his left flank, now led by himself in the hope of letting as much of the infantry escape across what river access remained open. Some passages were blocked, and many troops drowned trying to swim and save themselves. William came close to being captured, although he was saved by English cavalry.

As with Steenkirk, neither side's entire army had been involved in the battle, and it had come down to a focus on salient points of the battlefield and the timely use of the correct amount of force at the right point in the battle. Cavalry on both sides had stood idle until critical points at the end of the battle, although the nature of the fight had dictated this.

During one of the final charges, Sarsfield rode at the head of a French cavalry regiment. Driving the enemy toward the river, and clearly in the thick of the action, he was struck in the chest by a musket-ball and fell, mortally wounded. He was taken to Huy, but it was too late. He died later of a fever.[24]

Boulger recorded:

> His chief Rubantel was already severely wounded. Montchevreuil was killed, Berwick was a prisoner, and thus Sarsfield had his chance of coming to the front for the direction of the attack passed into his hands. It was just as the French reinforcements had finally made their way into and through the village, and the supporting cavalry following in their track had reached the plain stretching northwards of it that Sarsfield was struck by a bullet in the breast.[25]

His last words were reputedly, 'Would to God that this were for Ireland', in a single statement summing up much of what the members of the Irish Brigade must have felt while fighting a European war for a French King, despite the pretence of its importance toward putting a Jacobite back on the English throne.[26]

An eyewitness stated somewhat poetically:

> As I was walking over the field a message from Sarsfield reached me, he had been wounded to death in one of our last charges; he sent an aide de camp to call me to his side. The noble form of the hero lay on a pallet in a hut; he feebly lifted his nerveless hand and gave me a letter which he had dictated.
>
> It read: I am dying the most glorious of death; we have seen the backs of the tyrants of our race. May you, Gerald, live to behold other such days; but let Ireland always be uppermost in your thoughts.[27]

He would be remembered in Thomas Moore's poem of Aughrim, as the 'Last of the Brave'. Others would say that 'No man was ever more attached to his country, or more devoted to this king, and religion'.[28]

Around sixty guns had been lost, and casualties were in the thousands, with as many as 15,000 lost killed and wounded on the French side, while William had lost around twenty per cent of his army. The excuse for lack of pursuit in this instance is understandable as it so often was in contemporary battles of this nature. The French army was exhausted. Luxembourg would drive his efforts towards a relevant siege of nearby fortresses. In turn, this also meant that the campaign season, at least in terms of important battles, had ended. The French would take Charleroi in October.

It had been another bad year for the Allies. The loss of Charleroi and Huy gave the French control along the Meuse and Sambre rivers, and a base for further advances. The action at Landen was beginning to make it clear to many of the allies that William was no military genius, and yet Luxembourg could not be trifled with. It had been another defeat in the campaign year for the allies, but this was becoming irrelevant as the French ability to continue fighting the war was diminishing rapidly. Luxembourg had won victories, but it was not enough to make the campaign a decisive French win. Unknown to William, the French would not have the resources, or the will, to mount such offensives again in the war.

There had been other suggestions that the French were not strong in Flanders if an attack with impetus could be made against them, even now. There was hope yet left for the allies.

What then had Irish troops come to do? How could they affect their own future, if France was becoming war-weary. Had the promises that the now dead Sarsfield made in Limerick been false? Was there any hope left for the displaced Irish? They had little choice left. They had made their decision to fight and, if necessary, die for the French. They had been not only displaced, but were scarcely allowed to fight together as a single corps, but had been spread thinly throughout the French army. If anything, they had only one course left to pursue. The Hamiltons' involvement in further attempts to restore the English succession, however desperate, could only be applauded by the displaced Irish. They had one transferable skill set, the ability to fight for something in which they still believed, no matter how vain the hope of achieving anything concrete was becoming.

The 1693 campaign would see Mountcashel serve with the Army of Germany on the Rhine, under Lieutenant General Marshal de Lorge. Clare's (O'Brien's) Regiment still served in Piedmont. The fourth Viscount Clare would die at Pignerol that year from wounds received at the Battle of Marsaglia. Andrew Lee would succeed him. Dillon remained with Noailles. Sarsfield's death at Neerwinden must have sat heavily with Mountcashel, perhaps making him consider his own mortality. A new theatre of war loomed for him. The war in Germany had, in a similar fashion to Italy, moved to and fro with little real progress. The war had started when French forces crossed the Rhine in 1688 seizing Phillipsburg and other large towns. Despite early successes, Louis's attempt to create a line of defensive fortresses and his resultant scorched-earth policy created a tide of resentment in Germany, where the atrocities of the Thirty Years' War had not been forgotten.

In 1689 the French had been surprised by the degree of German resistance, led mainly by Charles, Duke of Lorraine. The long siege of Mainz lasted from July until September when the French took the town. This victory was tempered by losses in the theatre. The front stagnated in 1690 with little activity. By 1691 the threat of French offensive action prompted the release of Dutch reinforcements to the allied forces, holding the French in check, and prolonging the stalemate. The French Marshal de Lorge commanded the army of the Rhine and, by 1692, heavily outnumbered by the allied army, complex manoeuvre and decisive battles seemed as distant as ever. By 1693 the theatre would remain in intractable stalemate unless decisive action was taken.

It was to this area that Mountcashel and his regiment were ordered. Mountcashel would serve as a lieutenant general commanding his own regiment, now of three battalions, and the regiments of Charlemont and the Marine, around 6,000 men, many of whom had arrived in 1691 after the Treaty of Limerick. The Irish element of the French army now numbered over 16,000 men.

De Lorges joined the army in early May and immediately attacked Heidelberg. He then crossed the Rhine at Phillipsburg and split his forces, the larger part moving towards the Germans under the Prince of Baden at Heilbronn, while the smaller force attacked Heidelberg, laying siege on 21 May.

The garrison surrendered the following day. Louis, seeing at the very least movement and potential victory on this uneventful front, despatched reinforcements to de Lorges, increasing his strength to twenty-seven infantry battalions and forty-five squadrons of cavalry by mid-July. Baden had withdrawn across the Neckar river. De Lorges joined with additional French troops to form an army of 45,000 men. Baden, however, could not be drawn out of the defensive position that he held, although small actions were fought, including the reduction of Besigheim where Mountcashel's grenadiers joined with the French grenadiers of the Picardy and Auvergne Regiments in the assault. The Irish force and Mountcashel were also present in the reduction of Heidelburg, Wingemburg, Eppenheim and Darmstadt.

There had been a remarkable degree of movement in 1693 in the German theatre, but only in comparison with previous years, and in real terms the stalemate was becoming worse.[29]

At home, if it could still be called home, the year had not been a good one for Mountcashel. The Irish Parliament of 1689, along with its policies, stood redundant, and those senior Jacobites who survived, including Mountcashel, became 'attainted' in a similar manner to those Protestants who had been listed as rebels in 1689. The land that he had accumulated in Munster was confiscated, but worse was to come. The town of Bandon, where Mountcashel had shown mercy, demanded reparation from those lands. These were fairly large and the Bandonians requested that the £1,500 that they had paid as their pardon be paid out of the value of the seized estates. Ironically, William Wolseley, of Newtownbutler fame, had helped endorse the Bandonians' requests. What was left of the estates was granted to the Earl of Romney, later to be sold on.[30]

Mountcashel had also made his will. Trouble with his wounds, and Sarsfield's death, had perhaps made him uneasy. Having lost his estates, however, he only had his name and title to give. As he and Arabella had no children, he gave the title to his third cousin, Florence Callaghan MacCarthy of Carrignavar. He insisted that the young man should attempt to regain the lands taken by the Williamites and give continued service to both the Stuart dynasty and the King of France, his legitimate sovereigns.[31]

Mountcashel's suggestion of loyalty to the Stuarts in 1693 is questionable. James's last act in which Mountcashel was involved unfolded with the erstwhile king's declaration that he would uphold the Act of Settlement in Ireland. His obvious attempt at winning back English support was treated with contempt by the Irish faction, despite James's promise of recompense to those Irish who had remained loyal to him. Events had come full circle since those heady days of the 1689 Irish Parliament. Mountcashel, in particular, protested strongly over James's reversals and was answered by the Earl of Middleton, James's Protestant 'Secretary of State' in June:

> The King was pleased to declare, yesterday, that his declaration had been dispersed, by his order, in England. I suppose none will be surprised to hear, that the people of England should have so

just a value for the Kingdom of Ireland, as never to be induced to resign the interest they had in it. The reasons are too many and too obvious to trouble your lordship with them. I shall only tell you, that the King promises, in the foresaid declaration, to restore the settlement; but at the same time, declare that he will recompense all those who may suffer by it, by giving them equivalents. I mean those who have served him; and not only those here, but all who were included in the capitulation of Limerick, which will be a better security for them, than what they have by the acts of the Dublin parliament, considering the many circumstances. I do not doubt but your lordship is fully convinced of this truth; and it will be of great service to the King to convince others of it, which, I hope, will be no difficult matter. For there is no man of common sense but will think himself engaged by interest as well as duty, to contribute to his Majesty's restoration; which without the concurrence of the greatest part of his subjects, is impractable. This I have laid by the King's command.[32]

Despite James's hopes that French aid would come, there would be no restoration this time.

## 1694

The run of French victories in 1693 had not been sufficient to force the allies to the negotiating table. There had been greater problems which could not be weathered through French triumphs on the battlefield. The famine of 1693 had been one of the worst on record. The harvest failure brought starvation, disease and death, and France lost 10 per cent of its population within months. The impact of the famine was made worse by Louis's war; after all there were troops to feed and a huge logistics effort to make food available for the massive force that was trying to beat, or at least settle with, William and his allies. War and famine disrupted the country and raised prices to the extent that the French people suffered still further. In addition, lower tax revenues reduced the means by which Louis could propagate the war. He therefore remained on the defensive in Flanders; any movement that did take place was slowed through the necessity of finding forage and food.

A German move in the Alsace region which threatened battle came to nothing. In Italy, Louis urged Catinat to action, although with only fifty battalions of infantry, doing anything of consequence would prove difficult.[33]

Victor Amadeus, despite his clandestine contact with the French with a view to changing sides, managed to hold on.

Noailles had 26,000 men. Although a small force in contrast with the mighty, and lumbering, armies in Flanders, he marched into Catalonia in May, with naval assistance from Tourville along the coast, taking Verges, then Palamos by June, then Girona by July. In strategic terms, these were small gains, although the effort had been enough to urge the king of Spain to threaten making a separate peace with France, unless Dutch and English naval assistance was forthcoming.

The move had left the Atlantic coast less than well defended and Louis's concerns over an attack at Brest prompted him to despatch Vauban to resolve the issue. The attack was a disaster, and the allies were repelled with considerable loss, with 600 prisoners taken and 400 killed. The allies sailed away in defeat. In the Mediterranean they had better results. Tourville was forced away from Barcelona and the presence of the allied fleet kept Spain in the alliance until the end of the war.[34] Despite Louis's attempts at subterfuge in the United Provinces itself, there was going to be little alternative to the peace table.

Mountcashel received orders for 1694. As expected, he would again serve in Germany with his men. Before the start of the campaign period, however, he had been having problems with his wounds. In his fifties, he had reached the 'old age' of the time and many of his contemporaries were dead, and he had been wounded twice, at least once seriously. In light of the evidence, therefore, it is not surprising that his first trip of the year was to the curative waters of the Barréges region in the Pyrenees in June. There seems little mystery as to what occurred there, and it is unfortunate that the curative waters did not have their desired effect. Mountcashel died on 1 July, having led his men to France and re-established the Irish army abroad. His death was announced in Paris on 31 July 1694, five years after the Battle of Newtownbutler:

> Mylord Moncassel, Lieutenant-General of the Armies of the King, Commander of three Irish Regiments, died the 1st of this month at Barrege, of the wounds that he has received on several occasions, in which he was always extremely distinguished.[35]

He had requested that he be buried in Ireland. Since this was impossible, he was buried at Barréges. Andrew Lee took command of Mountcashel's Regiment and would go on to become a successful officer in French service.

Despite the fact that Mountcashel was recognised as a more than competent officer and general, and for the most part made the correct political moves, he is sometimes forgotten in popular histories in relation to the 'Wild Geese' with preference given to Sarsfield and those troops who travelled to France after the second siege of Limerick. Perhaps the more youthful, romantic and somewhat reckless figure of Sarsfield appeals to the modern reader. As we have seen, however, he was not the first choice of the French. Mountcashel had not only paved the way for these Irish troops, but had proved to France both his own worth and that of his countrymen after the Newtownbutler debacle.[36]

Like so many of his Irish contemporaries, the negative aspects of Justin's career and personality are frequently highlighted; his defeat in Ireland, his escape from Enniskillen and his shrewdness with regard to his nephew and Catholic Ireland in the 1680s. He was, however, a man of his time and the machinations of many of his contemporaries are rarely questioned in the same way. We could cite Marlborough, for instance, with his strategic genius; yet he was an irrefutable politician. Despite being impulsive and, for the most part, frank with both kings and commoners, both sides in Ireland at times appreciated his efforts and his honour. He also demonstrated the qualities, unlike many officers of the time, that enabled him to understand his men and the nature of disciplined soldiery. Both his own troops and his military peers respected him for this very reason. He understood that the nature of battle, in whatever era, hinged on the reliability of the man who fought and died.

The pioneer of the Irish brigades in France in the 1690s, Mountcashel represented the close links with France that would blossom in the eighteenth century. Despite co-existing with the multifarious factions that had ultimately proved Ireland's undoing, Lord Mountcashel had also remained a patriot, something that the French could recognise and even respect.

## 1695-1697 The End of the Beginning

More deaths would follow. Perhaps the biggest blow to the French war effort was the death of Luxembourg in January 1695. His talent would not be equalled until the next war, although Louis still had his present conflict with which to contend. Louis would choose Neufville, Duke of Villeroi, to lead the army in Flanders, although he was a soldier of less talent than his predecessor.

An extension of the defensive lines was the order of the day since Louis's conviction was that 'if in holding the lines, we lose a great many troops, we can hope that the enemy will lose more …'.[37] The strategy was sound and encouraged the allies to besiege Namur in June in an attempt to take it back after its fall in 1692, under Coehoorn, who had defended it so well against his counterpart Vauban. On this occasion, however, Boufflers would co-ordinate the French defence, although the city would fall by September, despite French diversionary attacks against Brussels.

Taking the city allowed William to retain the line of the Meuse river, but it had rendered the allied army impotent during the campaign year. On the other hand, in Piedmont and Savoy, negotiations between Louis and the worried, or treacherous, Victor Amadeus had moved apace. He, as correctly assessed by Louis, had been the weak link in the alliance. They had been in negotiations for two years, and Victor Amadeus had come to fear Habsburg interference in his future affairs more than that of the French. Although Casale was taken as part of the agreement, it was demolished, and the formal treaty was agreed the following year.

There was limited action in Catalonia too. Noailles became ill and was relieved by Louis-Joseph, Duke of Vendôme, and one of Louis's most competent commanders. The French were able to maintain their army in position, while the only minor Spanish victory was in taking Ostalric. Even the minor victories mattered little now. Louis had been winning; now he was simply limping along, ready for peace or at least an end to the war, although his pride would possess him to insist upon one final all-out endeavour, if not to end the war, then at least to secure the peace, even supporting a further attempt by James II to secure his lost throne. Despite the pressure to prolong, there was equal pressure to bring matters to an end at the table.

When news broke that Victor Amadeus had made an independent peace with Louis, there was a rush to negotiate before the French could profit from the agreement through being able to move troops away from Italy. However, there was a growing sense of urgency based on the fact that King Carlos II faced imminent death, and the throne of Spain would be up for grabs. The importance to continental Europe of who might win that particular battle could not be underestimated.

Movements of troops in Flanders in the year were more concerned with finding forage than with fighting battles and conducting siege operations. The most dangerous action in the campaign year, as far as William was concerned, was another planned descent on England, a landing designed to place James II back on the throne with up to 16,000 troops and the support of the French navy and money. He expected, as ever, strong support in England and, with English commitments scattered across Europe, the timing was highly favourable. The Duke of Berwick had been sent ahead to prepare the way, but William, through his own network of spies, had not only been made aware of the proposed operation, but also of an assassination plot. He received enthusiastic support from Parliament for action, and had James's supporters arrested. Catholics over the age of sixteen were commanded to leave London. Twenty battalions would be shipped back home, and the Royal Navy would make efforts to stop any moves across the Channel. Despite all that had happened, the threat to the succession was still valid. However, James's plans were coming apart at the seams. His Jacobite supporters in England would not rise until he had landed, and the French would not move until the English element had taken up arms at home. The assembled troops never sailed, and were moved to Flanders instead. But the attempt had diverted French naval power to Brest. Despite the timing concerns for the prospective English invasion, this had helped move allied ships away from the Mediterranean and thus permitted more aggressive French moves in Catalonia.

During 1697 the warring parties agreed to meet in Ryswick. As the initial conference appeared to go nowhere, William despatched his friend and confidante Bentinck to carry on secret negotiations with Boufflers in July, where most of the contentious matters were resolved. This would not stop armies undertaking operations, however.

Louis's three armies under Villeroi, Catinat and Boufflers were committed to Flanders, a total of 190,000 men. The siege of Ath proceeded slowly but methodically as with the pattern of the day. Ath fell in June, while Villeroi attempted to cut the allied armies off from Holland, but was outmanoeuvred by William. Vendôme besieged and finally took Barcelona in August, an act which had been delayed in the past through the presence of the allied fleet and yet, with peace talks already in progress, would mean little more than adding a bargaining chip to the talks.

The Treaty of Ryswick had been agreed and signed by all parties by October. It set the Rhine boundary of France, an important aspect but, for the Irish at least, the fact that Louis agreed to recognise William as King of England, and to give no further aid to James II to regain the throne must have come as a hammer blow.

France had won the major battles, and gained ground during the long, almost decade-long war; they had won the war, but lost the peace, and were clearly in no condition to keep fighting a conflict which both sides knew would make them weaker when the next war, for the Spanish succession, came. Louis had retained much of what he had fought for and the aim in 1697 was to 'win' through guaranteeing an end to the exhausting and debilitating conflict; in that sense, there had been small victories on both sides, but only in lieu of what was to come.

The war had been a miscalculation on Louis's part, both on the basis of its length and the staying power of the alliance ranged against him. He had rapidly become used to enduring the conflict rather than gaining decisive victory, although we can argue that this was very much forced upon him by the nature of the time.

The only decisive action, with lasting repercussions, had come in Ireland where James had been crushed and the Wild Geese dispersed. In contrast to the European war, it had been fought without the possibility of real compromise. In contrast to the European mainland, where it seemed that fighting had been carried out with a view to getting to the negotiating table, the Irish war had been fought such that it could be ended quickly, and almost at any cost, so that forces could return to Europe.

For the Irish, the agreement that there would be no descent on England through either plan or design would have repercussions. What could the exiles now do? The land that they had left would change forever and, in their imaginations, would become more fantastical, mythical even, yet even more unobtainable as the years wore on.

*Chapter 16*

# Despair at Saint Germain

John Hamilton was buried in Ireland after his death at Aughrim. Anthony Hamilton had little option but to remain in France. Anthony, Richard and John Hamilton had been declared outlaws in Ireland, alongside most of the Jacobite notables, in 1691. However, their pursuit does not appear to have been dealt with vigorously, certainly after the fall of Limerick. Indeed, Richard had seen his name on the English Attainder Bill since 1689.[1] Elizabeth, *la Madame de Gramont*, enters the story once more at this point. In all ways, and to the best of her ability, she had used her influence in both French and English courts to help her brothers. She had secured an English pension for James Hamilton's widow, had ruthlessly vilified Louvois over the decisions related to Richard Hamilton's military interests, and had taken an interest in matters in Ireland to the extent that Louis himself would send her news as he received it.[2] Madame would, it seemed, not be taking 'no' for an answer.

Her obvious reaction in the aftermath of the Boyne, with Richard Hamilton being held as a Williamite prisoner, had been to urge Louis and those influential members of the English Parliament to consider a prisoner 'exchange' between Hamilton and the Ulster Lord Mountjoy, who had languished in the Bastille through Tyrconnel's machinations since 1689. However, Louis had little inclination to comply with Madame Gramont's wishes; holding onto Mountjoy could prolong events in Ireland and exacerbate the situation where, after the Boyne, an end to the affair was in sight.[3] Elizabeth would then turn her attention to James and the exiled court at Saint Germain, which had seen one of her brothers imprisoned and left another to risk death in Ireland. Her appeals would have little effect on an exiled court whose feelings had for the most part turned sharply against her family, apparent 'disgrace' having befallen them since events at Derry and Newtownbutler, despite Richard's endeavours at the Boyne.

Even Madame Gramont no longer held the favour she once had as 'la Belle Hamilton', despite the attentions of a few members of the French court, although her relationship with Louis appears still to have borne some affection at least. In her position as *Dame du Palais* she commanded favours and pensions for herself and her husband.[4] With increased favouritism from the king through the 1680s she had roused the jealousies of the court, being noted as a particular favourite of Louis, and a constant and dedicated friend of those on whom she could rely.[5] Her scathing wit, influence and apparent inability to suffer the weaknesses of the soft underbelly of French society earned her jealous enemies, not least Madame de Maintenon, formerly the governess of seven of Louis's illegitimate children by his mistress Madame de Montespan, who would become his wife after the death of Queen Marie-Thérèse in 1683.

The later 1680s would also see Elizabeth develop increasingly religious trends, brought about particularly by her close relationship with the convent at Port Royal where she had been educated.[6] Indeed, it would be through her activities at Port Royal that the first cracks in her relationship with Louis would begin to show. One of the most famous French convents, it had exercised considerable influence on the Roman Catholic Church and French society during the seventeenth-century struggles with the Jesuits. However, Port Royal's distinction could only leave it open to opposition. Following the Jansenist teachings of Cornelius Jansen, Bishop of Ypres, with regard to reform and 'new' thinking in the church, Louis had felt, even since the days of Mazarin, that the organisation was not entirely loyal to either him or the French state; indeed members of the sect had been suspected during the Fronde, and they had applauded Spanish victories in the wars of the 1660s. That Port Royal was popular amongst French families for their daughters' education was rarely in doubt and it was this experience that had formed Madame de Gramont's attachment to the place. The Gramonts' own daughter, Marie Elisabeth, would attend the college. Her mother's sincere, almost stubborn, devotion to Port Royal would see her lose favour in the face of Louis's antipathy although it should be remembered that the institution had educated, fed and even clothed the young Elizabeth Hamilton when her family, languishing in exile before the Restoration, had little money or prospects.

With the death in 1679 of the Duchess of Longueville, an influential patron, Louis took steps to suppress the community. The Archbishop of Paris ordered all daughters to be returned to their parents. Questions over the establishment's suitability for the youth of the nobility were raised at Versailles.[7] Madame de Gramont approached King Louis directly. Despite her pleas over the innocence of Port Royal, Louis would report it as a den of 'assemblies and cabals'; court gossip even reported that Madame was one of the chief members of the Jansenist 'cabal'.[8] Elizabeth's rivals for Louis's attention hoped that such talk would put an end to their relationship. Madame de Maintenon, for one, tried in vain to bring about such a conflict, citing Port Royal's importance with Madame de Gramont.[9]

By 1688 Elizabeth's religious beliefs had reached new heights, perhaps in the face of a growing perception of trouble for her brothers in Ireland. Her health declined, possibly made worse by the fate of her brothers and Gramont's deteriorating health in turn.[10] The 1680s also marked the marriage of the two younger Hamilton sisters. Lucia had married Sir Donagh O'Brien of Leminagh while Margaret, the youngest, had married Matthew Ford of Coolgreny in County Wexford in January 1688.[11] Unlike *la Belle Hamilton*, the younger Hamilton sisters had remained in Ireland.

Richard Hamilton's release and exchange for Lord Mountjoy was agreed in March 1692. He was released from the Tower of London. For Lord Mountjoy, freedom was short-lived; he was killed fighting the French, as part of William's army at Steenkirk in August that year.

For the Hamiltons there would be no return to battle in French service, or even an opportunity to fight under a flag. In common with many of the Irish troops who had departed Limerick, there would be exile, although it would remain without the privations of battle and military hardship. Only three of the six brothers remained; James and George were long dead and the grief surrounding John's death at Aughrim was still very recent. There is no record that Thomas, now an important British naval officer, ever saw his brothers again; indeed, the religious and political scene may have prevented this as much as geography. For Anthony and Richard Hamilton, exile amongst the dejected court of James II beckoned, a court the French would describe as led by a king who had 'lost the crowns of three kingdoms for the sake of religion'.[12] Ironically, this exile was shared with the Duchess of Tyrconnel, who had lost two husbands during the wars of France, Ireland and England. She was made one of the 'ladies of the bedchamber' although noble titles would mean little in this expelled and derisory court. Could there be a last chance for James, however? When he reviewed the Irish troops in France in 1692, he hoped that he looked at the force with which he could still recover England. Louis would also lead James to believe that the Irish force was ostensibly *his*, despite the fact that the 20,000 strong corps now formed an integral component of the French army. Since Louvois's death in 1691 Louis had become more open to James and his plight. In February 1692, as Louis co-ordinated the siege of Namur in person, the Irish troops were given a secondary role in the hope that James would need them for an invasion of England.[13]

James's, and indeed Louis's, hopes regarding England were not based entirely on the large army being put at the former's disposal. News had reached James of growing discontent in William's England. There had been intrigues with two admirals who, James felt sure, would come over to his side despite their protests that the French fleet should not come, although there remained no concrete evidence that the British fleet would defect. Indeed, it seemed that James's hopes were based on his own fantastical belief that he could get the throne back. Even the Marlboroughs and Anne, younger sister of Mary, were implicated in the plot, Anne with an apparent design to be re-united with her father.

However, by the end of 1691, the plot fell foul of its own notoriety and conspirators were arrested and executed while those more widely-known adherents distanced themselves rapidly from the entire affair. James, still believing in the principle and guaranteed success of the business, continued into 1692 with his preparations. With the assurance of French naval and military support, James prepared declarations of religious freedom, general pardons to the population, with some notable exceptions, and guarantees that French and Irish invasion troops would be returned to their countries of origin. It is notable that James should remember the circumstances of his previous downfall even if he could not see the truth of the developing situation.[14]

A force of 8,000 French from the Normandy garrisons and 12,000 Irish had been assembled under Marshal Bellefonds at Brest, with de Tessé who had served with John Hamilton at Aughrim. By April 1692 the 20,000 strong invasion force stood ready. Political and military advisors joined James, Melfort and Lieutenant Generals Patrick Sarsfield and Richard Hamilton, another chance for Richard to right the perceived wrongs of his past in Jacobite service perhaps. Once more the Jacobites were optimistic. Once again, the chance for restoration of the monarchy had arrived. Once more the effort was doomed to failure.

The cross-channel invasion would be preceded by a massive French naval attack. At this point the plans began to come apart. There were delays at Brest in assembling the required numbers of ships, ammunition, and even sailors. When some ships sailed in May, those that had not been readied were expected to follow. Reinforcements from Toulon would also be late. Orders were changed, and fleet movements became unco-ordinated. Tourville, in command of the fleet of forty-four ships, was given orders from Louis who believed that he had over seventy ships. By the time that the truth of the situation was realised, it was too late. On the morning of 29 May the British and Dutch fleet was spotted as Tourville lay off Plymouth. Ninety-nine allied vessels significantly outgunned the French and rapidly enveloped them in battle line. Critically outnumbered, Tourville was able to withdraw under cover of fog that quickly engulfed the ships. The respite was costly, however, as the French vessels scattered in the encroaching darkness. The slower ships were forced to weigh anchor due to changing tides at Cape la Hougue at the end of the Cherbourg peninsula. Over the days that followed Tourville was forced to beach the remnants of his fleet in and around la Hogue as the enemy fleet cornered the French. Allied attacks and assaults by long-boats captured most of the vessels and fifteen were put to the torch, the crews for the most part getting away.[15] The disaster quickly removed any hope of an invasion of England and destroyed French sea power in the English Channel, an advantage that, as with their French counterparts in the Irish Sea in 1690, the allies would fail to exploit adequately. The Irish troops were dispersed to the Rhineland and Hamilton returned to Saint Germain with James. A week later, toward the end of June, James's daughter, the Princess Marie Louise, was born. Louis would be her godfather. Despite the disappointment of the past months, Louis, uncharacteristically perhaps, maintained good relations with James.

The exiled court resided at the chateau of Saint Germain en Laye, twelve miles from Paris. It had been Louis's principal residence between 1660 and 1682 before the removal of the court to Versailles. The old palace had been left to fall into decline, requiring rapid renovation prior to the arrival of James's court. Richard Hamilton had at some stage been made Gentleman of the Bedchamber to James and, in the 1690s, would also be made Master of the Wardrobe with a salary of 400 pistoles. Such titles meant little, although monetary reward helped solve the perennial Hamilton poverty problem.

Anthony Hamilton had no royal functions within the court although he would excel in his writing at this time, recording the scandals, plotting and passions of Charles II's household, drawing unflattering comparisons between the indulgence of Restoration England and the reserved atmosphere of Saint Germain, citing its corridors haunted by priests as 'the very worst place in the world'. Anthony's description of the court in exile is recalled by Macaulay, although, in its original French, it was probably written with tongue firmly in cheek:

> It is difficult to conceive a duller place than Saint Germains was when he [James] held his Court there; and yet there was scarcely

in all Europe a residence more enviably situated than that which the generous Lewis [Louis] had assigned to his suppliants. The woods were magnificent, the air clear and salubrious, the prospects extensive and cheerful. No charm of rural life was wanting; and the towers of the most superb city of the Continent were visible in the distance. The royal apartments were richly adorned with tapestry and marquetry, vases of silver and mirrors in gilded frames. A pension of more than forty thousand pounds sterling was annually paid to James from the French Treasury. He had a guard of honour composed of some of the finest soldiers in Europe. If he wished to amuse himself with field sports, he had at his command an establishment far more sumptuous than that which had belonged to him when he was at the head of a great kingdom, an army of huntsmen and fowlers, a vast arsenal of guns, spears, buglehorns and tents, miles of network, staghounds, foxhounds, harriers, packs for the boar and packs for the wolf, gerfalcons for the heron and haggards for the wild duck. His presence chamber and his antechamber were in outward show as splendid as when he was at Whitehall. He was still surrounded by blue ribands and white staves. But over the mansion and the domain brooded a constant gloom, the effect, partly of bitter regrets and of deferred hopes, but chiefly of the abject superstition which had taken complete possession of his own mind, and which was affected by almost all those who aspired to his favour. His palace wore the aspect of a monastery. There were three places of worship within the spacious pile. Thirty or forty ecclesiastics were lodged in the building; and their apartments were eyed with envy by noblemen and gentlemen who had followed the fortunes of their Sovereign, and who thought it hard that, when there was so much room under his roof, they should be forced to sleep in the garrets of the neighbouring town.

Among the murmurers was the brilliant Anthony Hamilton. He has left us a sketch of the life of Saint Germains, a slight sketch indeed, but not unworthy of the artist to whom we owe the most highly finished and vividly coloured picture of the English Court in the days when the English Court was gayest. He complains that existence was one round of religious exercises; that, in order to live in peace, it was necessary to pass half the day in devotion or in the outward show of devotion; that, if he tried to dissipate his melancholy by breathing the fresh air of that noble terrace which looks down on the valley of the Seine, he was driven away by the clamour of a Jesuit who had got hold of some unfortunate Protestant loyalists from England, and was proving to them that no heretic could go to heaven. In general, Hamilton said, men suffering under a common calamity have a strong fellow feeling and are disposed to render good offices to each other. But it was not so at Saint Germains. There all was discord, jealousy, bitterness of spirit. Malignity was concealed under the show of friendship and of piety. All the saints of the royal household were praying for each other and backbiting each other from morning to night. Here and there in the throng of hypocrites might be remarked a man too high-spirited to dissemble. But such a man, however advantageously he might have made himself known elsewhere, was certain to be treated with disdain by the inmates of that sullen abode.[16]

Discord and infighting, while sounding all too familiar, seem not to have been as prominent as Macaulay indicates although, bearing in mind those who had been forced into exile with James, a certain amount of dispute was inevitable. James's first cabinet was headed by the controversial figure of Melfort, until replaced by the Earl of Middleton. Richard Nagle, Attorney General in Ireland during the Irish conflict, headed a 'council of war', a department that, ultimately, would have little to do. As indicated, Anthony Hamilton, with little real function, lived in the small town of Saint Germain with other less prominent members of the court. With the war on the French borders, however, most of those Irish and exiled English noblemen who had accompanied James into exile served with the French army. The Duke of Berwick, together with Lord Galmoy and adherents, Butlers, Dillons, Lees, O'Briens and Nugents, served with the Irish Brigade.[17] The Hamiltons remained at court. They had grown accustomed to a life of displacement, war and tribulation. Now they resided in the pious court of an exiled king who grew more reconciled to his fate with each passing day.

Anthony Hamilton, now in his fifties, had little time for fighting wars; there was little chance of a Catholic succession, and his skills as a soldier were perhaps no longer even recognised. He therefore busied himself with his writing, becoming increasingly exasperated with the presence of priests at court and the pious lethargy that seemed to subdue those around him. During the 1690s he recalled the presence of a 'sad company' and 'ghosts clothed in black' at Saint Germain, perhaps a reference to the presence of so many of James's religious adherents. Others would talk of a multitude of 'Chaplains and Servants below staires'.[18] As the years progressed, Anthony would have less and less time for what he saw as James's excuses and overuse of religion as a foil to the frustration that he must still have felt after so many years, describing his plight as 'spiritual poverty' in a court where his entourage busied themselves with dissension, jealousy and intrigue.[19] Another commentator wrote:

> the bigotry and folly of those at St Germains is unexpressible. Poor King James is hardly thought on or mentioned, an Italian and a Scotch priest govern him and his whole concerns; he is so directly the same man he ever was, persecuting the few Protestants that are about him, though they are ruined and banished for their adhering to him and rewarding and encouraging any sorry creature that he can make a convert of. The child they call the Prince of Wales they breed up with all the abhorrence imaginable to heresy.[20]

The continuing European war was beginning to take its toll, not only on the French economy, but also on those displaced Irish who were helping to fight it. Sarsfield was killed at Neerwinden in July 1693. Mountcashel died of wounds received in his many campaigns in 1694. By the start of 1695 Louis's last old campaigner, Marshal Luxembourg, had also died as the war entered its final phase. By then, with an agricultural crisis in France, Louis was only subsisting militarily rather than defeating the hopes of the Grand Alliance that fought against him. By 1696, with the French state on the threshold of bankruptcy, another vain attempt would be made to place James back on the English throne.

Talk of peace terms had caused alarm at Saint Germain since this would mean France's recognition of William as King of England. James, perhaps believing that such circumstances would create a situation where he would no longer be welcome in France, was therefore keen to propagate a pro–Stuart rising in England and regain the throne. As in 1692, James's government in exile busied itself with preparations and proclamations; James was given full authority over the Irish troops. Berwick was ordered to review the 16,000 Irish in February. Despite orders that they would serve on the Rhine and in Italy, the ruse was designed to fool English spies. The Irish troops marched towards Calais. Berwick was sent to England in disguise to make contact with the Jacobites there and Richard Hamilton was commissioned once more as lieutenant general.[21]

Before Berwick left France Louis had ordered him to tell his father that no French soldiers would depart until the rising had begun in England. James remained on the French coast for three months. William had few troops in England, most serving on the continent, but was well informed by spies not only about movements in France, but of an apparent assassination plot directed at him. Parliament supported his efforts to resist. Not only were troops to fall back on England from Flanders, but the Royal Navy would immediately put to sea to resist French efforts. James's supporters in England were arrested quickly. William's spies were so good that their apparent knowledge of Jacobite movements was enough to convince James's remaining friends in England that the leak lay at Saint Germain and they stopped all communication with their king, leaving him even more isolated. The French invasion fleet never set sail, although the assembly of large French naval forces at Brest had forced the allied fleets to move to counter them thus negating much of the naval actions in the year. Louis removed the troops from the coast, realising that James's restoration was no longer possible and resolving to end the war as rapidly as he could.[22]

By 1696, with the beginnings of internal strife once more emerging within the Jacobite camp at Saint Germain, Madame de Gramont, formerly Elizabeth Hamilton, again sought royal concession for her visits to Port Royal. However, Louis had had enough of such slights, coming as they did with Madame's absence from the court as her time away at her former finishing school increased, and Elizabeth was forced to apologise. Her disgrace was the talk of Paris. Through the medium of Count Gramont, she was informed that it would be impossible for her to ignore the king's dislike of the Jansenist community, a sect which he considered an 'abomination' and a religious 'novelty'. Ultimately, time would heal the rift between the king and his Franco-Irish favourite, much to the consternation of Madame de Maintenon.[23]

Relentless momentum for peace negotiations had continued as the year went on. By 1697, although serious fighting continued in Europe, the parties resolved to meet by the end of the year at Ryswick. With little more to distract their attentions, the divided factions at Saint Germain became even more polarised. The compounders, led by the Protestant Middleton, supported a restoration on the basis of an amnesty and constitutional security while the non-compounders, led by the ubiquitous Melfort, disagreed with any form of conciliation. In drunken quarrels and brawls, rivals would, on occasion, kill each other in their vociferous defence of a principle that had no basis in an actual political movement, merely the death throes of the court of a deposed monarch. A witness wrote, perhaps unfairly, that 'disorders and murders reign wherever this unhappy man lives and his domestic affairs are governed just as his three kingdoms would have been'.[24]

With the unhappy state of Saint Germain and its denizens, and the pious 'awakening' of their hosts, it comes as no surprise that both Hamilton brothers spent little time within its grounds. Having been brought up in France, in another English court in exile, they spoke the language and there was little hindrance to their enjoying the pleasures of courtly life, perhaps in Richard Hamilton's case aided by the death of Louvois. They spoke excellent French, were familiar with protocol and behaviour and, through their sister and her husband, found themselves mixing with the finest nobles of French society once more. For both it must have seemed like a homecoming rather than a painful exile; neither would they have to suffer the rigours of life on campaign as so many of their contemporaries had. Mountcashel and Sarsfield would never see such highlights of French society. The Hamiltons were more French than Irish now. This is unsurprising since in the end the Hamiltons' Irish experience had brought them little success; after all, they had been blamed by the French for much of the misfortune that had befallen the army. No surprise then that, once more, they embraced the French society they had missed for so long.

They spent time with the Gramonts in Paris and at Madame's apartments at Versailles.[25] Richard spent time with Cardinal de Bouillon, a nephew of Turenne, while Anthony grew increasingly close to Berwick's relatives. Both brothers would remain acquainted with the Vendôme family, of which two brothers had served with George Hamilton's regiment during the 1670s and knew the Hamiltons well. The Duke of Vendôme had been wounded in a French regiment during the Altenheim retreat. With other members of the exiled court and French dukes and duchesses, they whiled away the years in apparent good humour. The events at this time in the Hamiltons' life are more akin to the courtly adventures of their older brothers during the English Restoration than the pitiful grind of a court in exile.[26]

By October 1697 all parties involved in the war had signed the Peace of Ryswick. For almost ten years, conflict, economic hardship and suffering had been the lot of a large part of the population of Europe. In terms of vast tracts of territory, there was little difference strategically when compared with the start of the war. Had peace not come at this time, the following year would have seen additional Imperial troops made available, enabling them to be brought into action against the French. France was exhausted, militarily, agriculturally and economically. The French had been victorious in most of the important battles throughout the war, but victories could not feed Louis's troops or help the French economy. The war was proving more and more futile and simply feeding itself. Although undefeated militarily, France had become disadvantaged in terms of European power. Crucially, however, the treaty stipulated Louis's acceptance and recognition of William as King of England. At a stroke Saint Germain ceased to be the strategic headquarters of a deposed monarch striving to regain his crown. James would appreciate his new standing very rapidly as he began to receive indications that his bodyguard would no longer be paid, French horses would be 'repossessed' and, although James's civilian authorities were left largely intact, Louis requested that Middleton not attend Versailles on those days that he received the British ambassador.[27]

For those adherents of James who had done well on their own merits, matters were slightly different. Berwick, who had seen increasing success in the French army and who had married Sarsfield's widow, Honora de Burgh, much to James's initial annoyance, was granted a pension of 12,000 francs in addition to his pay as lieutenant general. However, the Irish troops whose role in the conflict had rapidly disappeared found themselves destitute. Louis's army had depended on foraging to a large extent, which meant that pursuit after victory on land was mostly impractical since an enemy could adopt a 'scorched-earth' policy to deny forage to his pursuer. There was little logistical support at this time to keep a fast-moving army supplied in the field. Belgium, normally viewed as the breadbasket of Europe, was exhausted after the years of war. Louis had had little choice but to disband much of the army at this stage. From 250,000 men in 1697, the force was reduced by almost half in the following year. For the Irish, this meant that 12,000 troops, over two thirds of the Irish brigades, would be thrown out of the army, which no longer had a war to fight.

For the French troops, mustering out of the army was a boon for the French economy as farmers returned to their lands and craftsmen to their trades. The Irish, however, now very much aliens in France, had no culture to return to. With the advent of parliamentary penal laws in Ireland, where those who had served James were now traitors, even returning home would prove problematic. Mountcashel and Sarsfield could never have dreamt that the cream of the Irish Brigade in France would be turned into beggars overnight. For them, the belief that the well-trained Irish troops would one day return to Ireland had still been seen as possible. That James could now never return to his throne was obvious, as was the fact that Irish troops would never see their home again. The consequence of so many cashiered men, ostensibly loyal to James, was a descent on Saint Germain by thousands of starving ex-soldiers, which could not hope to deal with them. For James's part, he gave pensions to many of the officers, as the area became an asylum for the dispossessed. This could not last long and it was only the intervention of the French church that saved many of the rank-and-file soldiers. Thousands more would starve to death, in stark contrast to the decadence that the Hamiltons and their contemporaries enjoyed in the French court. With the reduction in status of Saint Germain and the exiled court, both Hamiltons removed themselves to other locations, at least temporarily. Anthony Hamilton lived with the Gramonts for a period while Richard Hamilton became a constant guest of Cardinal de Bouillon, whose residence became something of a refuge for Irish officers in search of lodgings.[28]

If the Hamiltons, and indeed the Irish, had believed that war against France was a thing of the past, they could not have been more mistaken. Following the Peace of Ryswick in 1697 the question of the succession to the throne of Spain arose again. The invalid king of Spain, Carlos II, was unable to produce an heir. In other circumstances this would have been less critical were it not for the fact that the Spanish inheritance had been prized throughout the seventeenth century. Apart from the Low Countries, its territories included Sicily, Milan, Naples and a large colonial concern, over twenty kingdoms combined. The major powers of Europe would have delighted in such riches but only Louis and the Holy Roman Emperor, Leopold I, were related closely enough to the Spanish ruling family, their wives having been daughters of Philip IV and their mothers having been daughters of King Philip III. In both cases, the French queen had been the eldest daughter.

Most European powers had considerable reservations regarding either outcome since, inevitably, the balance of power in Europe would be affected adversely; in William's case the French threat stood out as particularly dangerous. With French power plays in mind, William suggested another candidate, the Bavarian Prince Joseph Ferdinand. Under the First Partition Treaty, it was agreed that this Bavarian prince would inherit Spain itself while the territories in Italy and the Low Countries would be divided between the Holy Roman Empire and France. King Carlos, however, did not agree to the partition, insisting instead that the glory of Spain could only be maintained by assigning the entire Spanish inheritance to Prince Joseph. The debate was ended quickly in February 1699 when Prince

Joseph died of smallpox, leaving the situation unresolved once more. The Spanish, intent on keeping Spain 'united', agreed that such a goal could only be accomplished through the selection of either French Bourbon or Imperial Habsburg dynasties. Carlos chose Emperor Leopold's youngest son, Archduke Charles. Fearing war, William and Louis rapidly augmented the Treaty of Ryswick with a Second Partition Treaty in June, permitting Archduke Charles to gain the Spanish throne with the Low Countries and colonies, albeit with some concessions to France in the form of the Italian territories going to Louis de France, Dauphin de Viennois, son of Louis XIV.

By 1700, as Carlos lay dying, he interfered once more. To prevent Spain from joining either France or the Empire, all Spanish territory would go to the Dauphin's young son Philip, Duc d'Anjou, Louis's grandson. If he inherited the French crown first, then the Spanish title would go to the Dauphin's next son, the Duc de Berry, and, failing that, to Archduke Charles. Louis had a difficult decision to make. With so much territory and control over trade, the extension of French influence in Europe would be remarkable. In a single stroke Louis would alarm and alienate every Protestant prince in Europe. On the other hand, Louis was advised that accepting only a portion of the inheritance, and remaining within treaty outlines, would cause a war with the Holy Roman Empire anyway. Louis ultimately sided with the Spanish king's wishes, believing that war would result in any event. When Carlos died in November 1700, Philip V became King of Spain. The war that would follow would define the place of the Wild Geese in French service, once more.

# Chapter 17

# Return to the Fight –
# The War of the Spanish Succession

T he War of the Spanish Succession has been suggested as the main reason that France had wanted to wind down the previous war as expeditiously as possible, at least from 1695 onwards. The Treaty of Ryswick had done much to dampen Louis's ardour for the fight, certainly in terms of finally ensuring that he realised the cost, and implications, of that elusive concept known as *Gloire*. He was no longer a young man, and had even started to believe that France's victories meaning so little on a strategic scale during the previous war had been some form of divine justice at work. He had worked towards finding a peaceful way of finding a solution to the Spanish land question that would come with the death of Carlos II.

However, only further war would decide the question when Carlos died, having left his kingdom to Philip of Anjou and a France that had already fought a war over dominance of Europe. In this instance, Marlborough and Eugene would gain years of victories over Louis's less able commanders, after the war in which the once mighty Luxembourg and Boufflers had been so dominant. Yet the Dutch Provinces and England had remained strong in the face of Louis's might, just as France would remain despite the pending string of allied victories. In the end he would win the throne of Spain for his grandson, retain his territory and, despite damage done to French military authority, retain some of his prowess.

Carlos II's childless end was inevitable by the turn of the century, with the French having a strong claim to the Spanish throne. This, and the potential uniting of European power blocs with a Catholic hegemony, was enough to set the rest of Europe, and the remnants of the Grand Alliance, on edge. Both Marie Thérèse, mother to the dauphin, and his grandmother had been Spanish princesses and, being eldest daughters, Spanish tradition allowed them to inherit the throne in the absence of sons. Louis's claim to Spanish lands in the name of his wife could now be made on behalf of his son. Yet Leopold I, the Habsburg Holy Roman Emperor, was also a grandson of

Philip III of Spain, and thus defended the claim of his own son, Archduke Charles, to Spain, although there were also compromises that might prevent war.

A treaty had existed whereby Joseph Ferdinand, electoral Prince of Bavaria, would gain overseas Spanish holdings while the Imperial and French advocates would receive shares, although the death of Ferdinand made the resultant sharing of power untenable. Despite the fact that Louis did not want a war, with resultant deleterious effects on a recovering France, there was no choice. No agreement on dispositions could be made.

The dying Carlos's greatest wish was to keep French lands intact, however, and he had left the lands to Louis's grandson, Philippe of Anjou. A messenger arrived in France first, but, if refused there, was to continue to Vienna to offer the crown to Archduke Charles. Louis had little choice in the matter and Phillippe became Philip V of Spain.

His own dynasty and the securing of lands were his goal. Although not necessarily selfish motives, neither were they wholly dedicated to his own aims, nor the aims of a younger and perhaps power-hungry monarch in search of *Gloire*. He could, in this instance, he reasoned, fight a defensive war on both French and Spanish lands rather than be forced to fight on two, or even three, fronts as in the previous war.

Louis's enemies feared an attempt to unite the thrones of France and Spain. This would have been difficult in practical terms due to the manner in which Carlos had decreed that the succession should work, although it mattered little as, in 1700, Louis's next step was to send French troops to take over the Dutch-held barrier forts on the edge of the Spanish Netherlands, a clear message to the former allies, if they needed one, that Louis's defence of his stated succession 'plan' would be a precursor to being prepared to honour the decision with force of arms if necessary.

The Dutch had occupied the area under agreement with Carlos in 1698. The French surrounded the posts and demanded that the Dutch recognise Philip. They had little choice and the forts were left with French contingents. Louis went further, however, allowing French merchants the right to supply slaves to the Spanish colonies and, most importantly, after James II's death in 1701, he acclaimed his son as the rightful heir to the English throne, denying the principle, if not the wording, of the treaty that had ended the previous war.[1] That meant that, if successful, Louis would not only control large areas and large Catholic empires within Europe, but it would be his stated aim to replace the existing British succession. For the standing British monarchy, there would be little alternative but war. The succession, or more succinctly the further threat to it, and the possibility of civil war, would unite the factions against Louis.

As far as the rest of Europe was concerned, Louis's arrogance was returning, and fear of what else he had in store simply served to re-unite the disparate, and Protestant, factions of Europe. Both sides strove to expand their forces, although, even by 1707, Louis's 250,000–300,000 men in arms would not exceed the totals of his previous war.[2]

An alliance of rivals quickly found its place: France would join with Spain, Bavaria, and Savoy, who had defected from the Grand Alliance at the end of the Nine Years' War. In September 1701 England and the United Provinces, and the emperor signed a second Grand Alliance treaty; by May 1702, despite there having been fighting in Italy well beforehand, England, the United Provinces and Habsburg Austria had declared war on France. When Carlos II died without heirs, he named the Bourbon Philip V, Louis's grandson, as his successor, in a single act creating a Bourbon Catholic monarchy across France and Spain. Once more, a Grand Alliance formed against the potential for a change in the European balance of power. However, it would be Louis's last war and England would play a significantly more important role than it had before. The Irish Brigade, made up not only of Mountcashel's, but also Sarsfield's men, with numbers inflated by additional exiles, would serve with distinction throughout the conflict.

As a new generation began to grow up at Saint Germain, the sons and daughters of the exiles, Europe was once more descending into turmoil. James II, erstwhile King of England, Scotland and Ireland, who had in his final days sought solace in religion and his past, died in September 1701. Despite Louis's opponents' initial acceptance of Philip in Madrid, the French king acted aggressively, cutting off English imports to France and, crucially, ceasing to acknowledge William as King of England once more, opting instead to support the claim of James II's son, James Francis Edward Stuart, known to history as the 'Old Pretender'. The subsequent league between English, Dutch, German and Holy Roman states was not unexpected as a new Grand Alliance was formed. The war that followed continued for most of Louis's remaining reign and, despite some initial successes, with France firmly on a defensive footing after Marlborough's spectacular victory at Blenheim in 1704. Queen Anne would sit on the throne of England after William's death in 1702; his wife, and Anne's sister, Queen Mary II having died in 1694.

***

Eugene of Savoy started as he meant to go on early in the war, outmanoeuvring Catinat and Villeroi in turn, defeating the latter. There was a bizarre turn of events at the end of the campaign year as Eugene attempted to seize Cremona. In the resultant debacle, Villeroi was captured, although the French drove the imperial troops from the town.

> *French gave thanks to Bellona*
> *Your joy is without equal*
> *For you have saved Cremona*
> *But you have lost your general.*[3]

Louis's army, despite numbers and the advantages of acting on the defensive, faced the dual-edged sword of Marlborough and Eugene. Marlborough's conduct had ranged from exemplary to almost traitorous, his imprisonment in the tower related to treason in 1692 being one example, his apparent letter to James warning of the descent on Brest another.

With William's death in 1702, however, Marlborough, based largely upon his own politicking and his talented wife's relationship with the new Queen Anne, was once more in the ascendant, at least for the early part of the war, until a loss of favour and Tory machinations in 1710.

He did not achieve total victory over France: despite his many achievements, and unique talents, the war-winning stratagems were limited by two factors; Marlborough could change certain logistical aspects, but the technological aspects of war remained largely the same, as did the restrictions imposed during the Nine Years' War. While platoon firing supplanted the French firing by ranks, on a strategic scale, the advantage was lessened. Although Marlborough believed in battles, when fought on his terms, siege was still largely prevalent in deciding wars. Secondly, Marlborough faced a complicated command situation with multiple countries and personalities. Despite his damning of the Dutch in this vein, the situation was largely similar to that which had always faced the Grand Alliance, and the unification of disparate elements had been William's 'management' problem before his. Where he could succeed was in his relationship with Eugene of Savoy, staying one step ahead of the apparently deflated French generals, and watching them trying to raise their game as they sought to emulate allied victories.

The French had the advantage of not having to fight a battle on two fronts. Marlborough was faced not only with command of politics in the alliance, but also by English politics, which ultimately sought to deny him the prize, and ensured that the home front was never settled and reliable.

It was noticeable in the early years of the war that French invincibility, which had been so pre-eminent during the Nine Years' War, would start to deteriorate. Losses on the scale of Blenheim had been unheard of in the pre-eminent years of the French military establishment. The war itself was an anachronism, fought as it was over the succession of a king, whether French or allied, although the main power blocs were Catholic and Protestant. It was bigger and wider in scope than the previous war, which had cost Louis so much in blood and treasure, a phrase previously used to describe the Irish war, yet especially relevant in terms of Louis's European obsessions.

It was not apparent that France had not recovered from the effect of the previous conflict; in fact it was bankrupt, or relatively close to being so, the result of taxation, famine from poor harvests, and desperate aims which could never be fully achieved in combination.

\*\*\*

Of course, Louis would have preferred not to have an exhausted France facing another war, although Carlos II's will had left him little choice. At the start of the war Eugene who, with Marlborough, would come to decide who really held the initiative in the early stages of the war, had 38,000 troops in Chiari, including Irish infantry regiments, Dillon's, Berwick's, Bourke's and Galmoy's, and a detachment of Sheldon's horse. Eugene's Austro-German force defended a built-up farm area, and the first French assault was repelled with 2,000 French casualties.

As the campaign year wore on, French forces wintered in the town of Cremona near Milan, on the Po river, an area that would see some of the more memorable events of the war. In addition to 4,000 quartered French troops were 600 Irish, drawn from Dillon's, Bourke's and Galmoy's regiments. If Eugene could seize the town, that could help secure control of Italy, completely undermining French control in the area. Not one to miss strategic opportunities when they presented themselves, Eugene prepared to take Cremona by force. This was made all the easier by the fact that a local Italian priest had granted the allied troops a map and knowledge of how to use the town's sewers to gain access to the streets. Thousands of troops entered the city at night with Eugene, before chaos erupted in the streets, and the French and Irish eventually were roused to the threat.

With what must have been dangerous, close-in street-fighting, where conventional troops and numbers could not be deployed to their full advantage, hand-to-hand fighting with troops awakening to chaotic debacles in the narrow city streets, was the order of the day.

Despite this, a company, fifty strong, led by Captain Stuart, of Dillon's Irish troops held back allied reinforcements at the Po Gate, using the cover of walls and bars to act as a secure position from which to pour musket fire into the attackers. In response, Eugene's German troops started bringing artillery forward to settle the argument.

During the spirited defence, however, Villeroi, the French commander, was knocked to the ground and would have been killed had it not been for the quick actions of an Irish officer, although this time in allied service. Captain Francis McDonnel rescued the French commander and heard appeals that he would be well rewarded if he returned Villeroi to his own lines and subsequently defected to the French. McDonnel was not for turning, however, and brought the French commander to Eugene.

After a lull in the fighting, and respecting McDonnel's actions, Eugene felt that there might be further sense in using the resourceful captain's skills. The Po Gate, the fortress itself and the convent were still held against his troops, the gate and convent by hundreds of Irish. He sent McDonnel forward to speak to them, promising 'higher pay' and 'greater reward' if they would defect to the Allied cause. Their response was to capture McDonnel and remind him that they would show Eugene that they could do their duty, although not 'by cowardice or treachery, unworthy of honour'.[4]

McDonough of Dillon's Regiment helped rally some of the displaced French and sent word that the Irish in holding positions should make ready to counter-attack. The Germans and Austrians had similar ideas, and Baron Freiburg led an assault against the Irish-held positions. In a similar turn of events, Freiburg was captured by Major Daniel O'Mahoney of Kerry who grabbed the reins of his horse, although Freiburg wrenched his mount free and galloped off, only to be shot down as he escaped. The assault had failed and Eugene had little option but to retreat. He would rarely see defeat in subsequent actions during the rest of the war, although he would not always face the Irish. He would later state that Cremona had been 'taken by a miracle and saved by an even greater one.'[5] The action had been an impressive one, perhaps, as O'Callaghan outlined, even saving the French army in Italy.[6]

As with any military endeavour, there was a price to be paid. Despite the fact that half the officers were decorated as a result of Cremona, hundreds had been killed. O'Mahoney carried word of the victory to Louis himself. It is interesting to speculate if Louis remembered his meetings with Mountcashel in previous years while speaking with the Irishman.

O'Mahoney and other Irish officers were promoted for their actions, and even James at Saint Germain would intervene, granting him a knighthood. 'Le fameux Mahoni' would go on to serve with distinction with the Spanish army, finally becoming a lieutenant general.[7] The victory would later become immortalised with an Irish pipe tune, 'The Day we beat the Germans at Cremona.'

\*\*\*

William had again pulled together the disparate elements of a Grand Alliance – England, the United Provinces, and the Emperor. It would his last political act before his death in March 1702. He had proven to be an excellent politician and superlative diplomat, although his generalship had been questionable.

The main thrust of the early part of the war would take place in the well-trodden crucible of Flanders, in the Spanish Netherlands. Louis's strategy had been to hold the area for his grandson, the veritable Spanish state that could foster peace or further conflict. But the fortunes of war, and the partnership of Marlborough and Eugene, would steadily push the French south, until the focus of defence and protracted fighting compelled Louis to position his forces to defend France itself. Defensive lines would dictate French dispositions more so than in any war they had fought previously, so far removed from the young Louis's thoughts of *Gloire*. The lines of Brabant and, later, the *Ne Plus Ultra* lines would change the nature of an already disparate means of achieving outright victory.

The early years of war would go well for Louis. Victor Amadeus would again change sides and (re)join the Grand Alliance, though inevitably the force of French arms over the years that followed would leave him with little left but his capital Turin.

However, the pendulum would inevitably swing in the direction of the allies.

\*\*\*

In 1702 the infantry battalions of Bourke, Berwick, Dillon, Galmoy and, now, Fitzgerald, combined with Sheldon's horse continued the campaign in Italy. Under Vendôme's command, they took part in the attack on the Duchy of Mantua, where Sheldon, despite being wounded, was mentioned in despatches to Louis, while acting as the French general's aide de camp. The Irish Brigade would fight at Luzzara and be forced back, despite having fought 'bravely'.[8]

The same troops took part in routing the Austrians at Bondanello, where Lieutenant Colonel Barnewell of Galmoy's battalion was cited as having led the assault;[9] they defeated an enemy force at Riga, led by Arthur Dillon himself, with 1,500 French troops. Then followed a successful siege of Brescello; O'Mahoney of Cremona fame was installed as governor. Bourke's Regiment was transferred into Spanish service, with Louis's blessing. Already, there were further signs that the Irish Brigade would not be kept together as a formation, and the future would hold further dilution throughout the French Army.

The Irish Brigade was re-deployed to Germany for operations in 1703. Even Sheldon's horse would find glory, routing two regiments of cuirassiers at Speyer, helping attain victory.[10] Sieges, too, were as much part of this war as the last. When the French took the initiative in besieging the Rhine fortresses, engineers from Lee's Regiment were involved. At Kehl an Irish officer called MacSheehy succeeded in getting access via the breach when his French compatriots thought the cause lost, although troops from Clare's Regiment, the first through the breach, suffered terribly, but were victorious, routing German troops into the woods.

\*\*\*

The new generation at Saint Germain appeared to have brought great change to the mood of the place. With James's death, the court of the young 'King' James III and his sister, Princess Marie-Louise, aged thirteen and nine respectively at the time of their father's death, became a different place, perhaps brightened by the needs and peculiarities of such royal youths. Anthony Hamilton, in stark contrast to the dejected records that he left of a doleful Saint Germain, where a disheartened king dwelt, became very much the court poet, celebrating the new joy that appeared to underline his work at this time.[11]

With most of their fathers at war, or having been killed as the war wore on, Anthony Hamilton became a storyteller, poet and even a father figure for many of the children. He would write *L'Enchanteur Faustus* for John Hamilton's daughter Margaret, *La Pyramide et le Cheval d'Or* for Lord

Clare's daughter and would eat supper with James III, writing toasts and songs. His other stories and poems were reserved for his favourites at court, the Duchess of Berwick, Nanette Bulkeley, whom Berwick had married after the death of Honora de Burgh, and the Bulkeley sisters and he became known as a wit at Versailles where he visited his sister.[12] Louis gave Countess de Gramont a small property within the grounds of Versailles in 1703, 'les Moulineaux', which had belonged to the royal surgeon Félix until his death. It was renamed '*la Pontalie*' by the Gramonts. It seemed that Louis had forgiven 'Madame' for any slights, although her husband remarked in jest that he would soon be sending the bills for entertainment to the king, as French notables visited frequently.[13] When Louis, Princess Marie-Louise and foreign dignitaries visited the Gramonts at 'la Pontalie', Hamilton was directed to commemorate the occasion by writing a song. He would recall his sister's property at Versailles in the same manner as Louis would refer to his many stylish palaces.

Although Anthony Hamilton spent considerable time with the young James III, he reserved much of his prose and verses for the young Princess Marie-Louise, sending her poems on her birthday and writing letters and stories during her absence, praising her charm, her dancing and her courteous manners. Hamilton recorded the princess and one of the Bulkeley sisters performing a ballet. Such entertainments were fast becoming the norm in the remnants of the exiled court, with Anthony Hamilton as the gallant resident wit and poet. His later writing of the *Life of Gramont*, demonstrating as it does a cynicism of courtly life in the seventeenth century, stands in stark contrast to his earlier works among the young people of the court, perhaps celebrating their freedom from the dire consequences of the events that concerned their fathers.[14]

Hamilton's correspondence with Berwick in the early 1700s is especially enlightening. Behind the letters describing the daily rituals of the ladies of the court busying themselves with tapestry and games, there is a sense of the sadness and loss for those who were at war. Hamilton and the other elderly members of the small assembly tried to dispel the worries of the many wives, although not altogether successfully.[15] The trivialities of washing and baking only put off the obvious fact that there was another war in progress, and some tactless mention of the latest campaign was enough to trigger tears and anxiety in many of the women. Hamilton did his best in the presence of so much grief.[16]

\*\*\*

1704 was a triumphant year for Marlborough and Eugene. In mid-May, Marlborough started to march thousands of men over 250 miles to reach the Danube in five weeks and, in stark contrast to the vagaries of campaigns dictated by forage that had bedevilled the resource management of armies in the Nine Years' War, he provided logistic support for the army throughout the march.

By August Marlborough and Eugene would attack the French and Bavarian troops on the Danube at Blenheim, each force numbering over 50,000 men. Much has been written of the flanks, the hemming in of French troops into small villages, where their operations were hampered, and Eugene and Marlborough's tactical moves, albeit inadequately foiled through French ineptitude. If anything, it would further disprove the myth of French invincibility. It would be a battle on the scale on the largest, if inconclusive, of the Nine Years' War. This time, however, matters would be settled, after a fashion.

The French had defended stoutly and reinforced the flanks, perhaps wary of likely manoeuvring between Eugene and Marlborough. A strong allied force had brought the French-Bavarian troops to battle. Blenheim and Lutzingen were well fortified on the flanks, although the centre, at Oberglau, was held with fourteen infantry battalions, and massed cavalry. Clare would lead his own, Lee's and Dorrington's Irish battalions.

The French defended the flanks at Blenheim and Lutzingen strongly, where their dispositions would prove untenable and cost them the battle. The Irish deployed in the centre, where the battalions of Clare, Lee and Dorrington defended together with eleven French battalions. Vendôme had considered that the boggy ground in the centre at the river crossing, creating concerns over deploying troops and maintaining line of battle, would prevent Marlborough attacking there. He was proved wrong.

At first the Irish held against a Hanoverian assault, even pushing it back and threatening to destabilise the attack in the centre through their own counter-attack, although such rash action could invite hostile cavalry to nip at the flanks, especially so where Marlborough might lead such troops himself. The Irish were pushed back as they tried to regain the heights at Oberglau, with Clare's troops covering the now dangerously exposed flank from cavalry charge and infantry volley.

Marlborough broke the allied centre after Tallard weakened it by strengthening his flanks, forcing the pride of French infantry into cramped confines of built-up areas that they could scarcely defend with any certainty. The French commander became Marlborough's prisoner.

It had been a disaster, although not enough to end the war, or the actions of the Irish troops in it. Eugene would see defeat again in Italy at Cassano, although he would see victory at the Adda river in an action that cost over 10,000 casualties. The Irish regiments of Dillon, Galmoy and Bourke defended the bridge from attack and pursuit by the victorious allied forces, preventing enemy attempts to cross the river.

Vendôme later commented that 'The Irish had fought in this affair with an exemplary valour and intrepidity, and that they formed a band, whose zeal and devotion might be relied upon, in the most difficult emergencies of war.'[17] This was another compliment from a grateful French general, echoing sentiments that some could remember of Lord Mountcashel, and the first Wild Geese who had come into French service in 1689. For some, it must have made home feel ever more distant.

The year's end saw the allied occupation of Bavaria, and the defeat crushed the myth of French invincibility. As Blenheim stunned Louis's court, the remainder of the war shocked France into the realisation that the young Louis's hopes of a dominant France with centrist Europe bowing to its will was also a myth.

The grinding effect of fighting in Flanders was once more prevalent in 1705, a fact which Louis considered a success, resolved as he was to fight a defensive war.

Ordering Villeroi to action in the following year, Louis had him confront Marlborough at Ramillies in May, again with 60,000 men on each side. As at Blenheim, pressure on the flanks was followed by a coup de grace in the French centre. With the victory so early in the year, and a string of subsequent successes against French fortifications and garrisons, Marlborough won control over most of Flanders. Louis also lost control over northern Italy in 1706. Vendôme had defeated Eugene at Cassano in 1705, laying siege to Turin in 1706, only to be confronted by Eugene's new army, together with the Duke of Savoy's forces at the Battle of Turin in September. French forces were defeated badly, and the subsequent Convention of Milan took Italy out of the conflict for the remainder of the war.

\*\*\*

When Berwick moved to the Spanish theatre with his army, his wife was invited to spend the winter with him. Her sister Henrietta was also invited to Berwick's quarters at Montpellier, which filled Anthony Hamilton with sadness, implying that he held more than a simple regard for her. His poverty, and his age, would not permit him to marry, however.[18] Neither would he be overly concerned with his lack of celebrity in terms of writing. Inevitably, he came to the attention of the French as letters that he penned for Gramont gained notoriety.[19] Nevertheless, he would not allow his works to be published, reserving his prose for his friends and acquaintances although his *Epistle to Gramont* gained him some fame from French critics in 1705, and Hamilton attained a certain amount of celebrity within the French court.[20] At this time he had resolved to leave his work on the *Life of Gramont* to posterity. It would be some years until the manuscript saw print.[21]

1706 saw another memorable victory for Marlborough, and another battle in which Irish troops showed their courage. Their mettle was tested and they were not found wanting. With armies of 120,000 men on each side, these were the biggest battles in which the Irish had fought, and they did so with distinction. Lord Clare's men held the field when French regiments around them had broken, facing down a Scottish regiment in Dutch service. When supported with other Irish regiments, of Lee and Dorrington, they captured not only the Scottish colours, but those of Churchill's Regiment in the process. But such local victories would not win wars, only plaudits. Despite tactical advances on the allied side, where 'platoon firing' became the order of the day while French regiments still 'fired by ranks', Irish triumph against adversity did not stop French defeat at Ghent, Antwerp and Brugge as Louis lost his grip on Flanders, the region he had dominated during the Nine Years' War, even though it had not granted him the war-winning stratagem he required.

There was some success in Italy, at Calcinato where the Danish Count de Reventlau was heavily entrenched, and where Vendôme once more wrote of Irish bravery in relation to Galmoy, Dillon, Fitzgerald and Bourke's regiments, which had performed 'wonders' and had done 'far beyond anything he could say of it, every individual of the battalions engaged, as well as those who commanded them, being entitled to marks of his Majesty's satisfaction'.[22]

After the Battle of Castiglione in September, Arthur Dillon, who had commanded the French left in an engagement where thirty-three colours, with artillery and baggage were captured, routed the enemy's flank. He was recommended for promotion to lieutenant general, the Count de Medavi adding that 'He is a foreigner of merit, and of valour, who, on every occasion, has always served your majesty well.'[23] But the French were losing the war, and drastic action was required if France herself was not to be placed in danger. In 1707, with a defiant Toulon resisting Eugene's attempt at siege, Marshal Villars fought a war based on exhausting the allies rather than with any loftier strategic goal. There was some success along the Rhine and in the defence of Provence against protracted allied assault.

***

Hamilton's seminal work on Gramont would be carried forward by the increasing deterioration of Gramont's health. He had been ill before, although in 1706 his conditioned worsened considerably. His previous recoveries had been miraculous but, on this occasion, his wife and brothers-in-law feared the worst.[24] Witnesses claimed that in his final days Gramont found religion, although he reputedly kept his good humour and high spirits until the end. He died in December 1706, at the age of eighty-five,[25] one of the French adventurers who, in common with the Hamiltons, had witnessed the restoration of kings, enforced exile and the lure of the court and the gaming table. With much of his life story recorded during this period, Anthony Hamilton would see the beginnings of the single work for which he is most remembered. However, Gramont would not always be recorded in favourable terms:

> One cannot speak with much enthusiasm of the hero of the Memoirs. He cheated at cards, and he was a braggart and something of a coward. Yet Hamilton handles the count's shortcomings with such skill that one cannot take them at all seriously. Through his brother-in-law's inimitable felicity of expression Grammont, it has been aptly said, 'has come down through the generations with his grand air unaltered, his impudence unabashed, and his wit in all probability considerably embellished'.[26]

With the various descriptions of Gramont's failings and the requisite excuses, he had also, in common with many of his contemporaries, practised considerable infidelity. Many felt that the Countess de Gramont would, for that reason, feel little loss at his passing. Anthony Hamilton, however, recorded that, by the end of Gramont's *memoirs*, his sister had been the only element of constancy in her husband's life:

> the Chevalier de Grammont, as the reward of a constancy he had never before known, and which he never afterwards practised,

found Hymen and Love united in his favour, and was at last blessed with the possession of Miss Hamilton.[27]

Elizabeth bore everything, including infidelity, with a degree of dignity. The eventual death of her husband, perhaps predictably, had a dramatic effect on her.[28] As time wore on she became more and more downcast despite the best efforts of her brothers to comfort her, falling into ill health herself. Depression and the belief that her friends and acquaintances had abandoned her only made things worse. She contemplated total withdrawal from courtly life, but Louis would not hear of it, despite the best efforts of Madame de Maintenon to see her retire.[29] Her poor health continued. She retired gracefully from public life in 1708 and rapidly became bedridden early in the year. Madame de Maintenon uncharacteristically described her courage and piety in enduring to the end. She died in June.[30] In a ghoulish episode, Louis gave her home, *la Pontalie*, to one of his marshals the day after her death. It appeared that there were many court favourites ready to replace those gracious ladies who danced to Louis's tune. As a final irony, he waited for Elizabeth's death before he carried out his final act in relation to Port Royal. In 1709 he dispersed the remaining nuns to other convents, destroying the buildings and desecrating the graveyard by 1710.[31]

***

In 1706 James III was eighteen. Having accomplished little by remaining at Saint Germain, the Chevalier de Saint George, as he was known, was keen to go to Scotland to foment and lead rebellion and regain the throne his father had lost so many years before. Despite Louis's clear reservations over a repeat of the debacles of the 1690s and James II's repeated and ill-advised attempts to regain the English throne, the French king acceded to public opinion and assigned six thousand men to the young James. With the Act of Union between England and Scotland in 1707, there also emerged considerable discontent. It not only precluded James II's offspring from inheriting the throne, but suggested that Scottish autonomy was at stake; the remaining Jacobites were the first to see the opportunities inherent in rabble-rousing and maximising discontent. Wouldn't a new king, the rightful heir to the English throne, rather than a Hanoverian 'pretender' see the right thing done by his loyal subjects? Their plan was a repeal of the legislation, and 'setting Scotland free' once more by placing James Stuart on the throne. It was a daring strategy, and not without the support of Irish Jacobites, who might finally see history rewritten. Irish Jacobite Nathaniel Hoke reported that 30,000 men stood ready in Scotland if France would only pledge support. Many leading Jacobites had been imprisoned in Ireland, and men there, too, stood ready to resist if called upon. It must have sounded familiar to many, the hope of regaining lost pride and, physically, lost kingdoms and religious freedoms. Again, it was the illusory impact of a diversion that might mitigate against allied actions that appealed to Louis. A French fleet reached Inverness but failed to contact any Jacobite leaders. The plan failed. But it was not the end of the Scottish episode.

***

The campaign season started poorly for Louis in 1708 with the defeat of over 80,000 French by a numerically inferior force at Oudenarde. Vendôme and his grandson, the Duke of Burgundy, were entrusted with the French forces in Flanders. Vendôme had won Ghent and Bruges in July, but Marlborough riposted at Oudenarde. Lieutenant General Lee was wounded at the subsequent siege of Lille, earning the Order of St Louis for his trouble. Thought to be impregnable, the fortress finally fell after four months of siege. The way to France itself lay closer, and invitingly open.

The battle was a meeting engagement, without prepared defences or positions on either side, although the French defeat was maximised more by the unanswered request to the young duke to bring up the reserves on the left than through any lack of planning or position. The defeat cost Louis what was left of Flanders, a distinct reversal when compared with the performances of his generals in the same region only twelve or thirteen years before. An advance upon Lille signalled moves into France itself, although Boufflers's singular defence slowed allied plans and his eventual capitulation at the end of the year allowed the French to buy time.

By March 1708 both Middleton and Richard Hamilton, together with other Jacobite notables, accompanied James to Dunkirk.[32] For Hamilton, now in his late fifties, the oldest of the lieutenant generals, the trip must have seemed familiar. He had made the journey twice before. Indeed, the luck that had bedevilled the earlier ill-fated expeditions was again present. With both logistical difficulties and the poor health of James, the expedition was delayed until the 17th. The small fleet reached the Firth of Forth where British warships were sighted. Despite the insistence of Hamilton and others who preferred a landing in Inverness, Forbin, the French naval commander, decided to withdraw and preserve the French fleet, clearly not wishing to be blamed for a repeat of the la Hougue debacle. Forbin later recorded that returning with the fleet intact had been the best that could have been hoped for, the mission having little chance of success from the start.[33]

Mary of Modena, mother of James III, later wrote to Louis requesting that her son be allowed to join the French army at war. She had been devastated by the failure of his expedition to Scotland and despaired of talk from England regarding her son's lack of military service now that he had come of age. Louis agreed. James would serve under de Bourgogne in the 1708 campaign and was present at the decisive battle of Oudenarde where, in a bloody struggle, the French were again driven from the field in a war where France was increasingly on the defensive.[34] Richard Hamilton, veteran of the Irish campaign, accompanied the young *Chevalier* on his campaigns. Mary, constantly worrying, although seeking to have no further English gossip surrounding her son, wrote to Hamilton:

> My intention was to have writ to you soon after I received your letter and to have told you that the comfortable account you gave me of the king's [James's] behaviour had abundantly recompensed the kindness I had shown the poor Comtesse de Grammont in her sickness, but my unaccountable laziness in point of writing made me put it off so long that I did not know at last how to go about it; but now in the dreadful expectation we are in of a battle, I can not say anything to you but [bid] you to remember your promise to me not to quit the king one step in a day of action and also to tell him frankly and positively what is fit for him to do, for he has promised the king of France and me at parting, that he would upon such occasions, do what you and Mr Sheldon should advise. I rely extremely upon your judgement and am persuaded the affection you have for the king will prompt you to do more than all I can say to you, therefore I will add no more, but pray to God to give you as much strength, and health as I am sure you have willingness, and capacity of serving the king on this important occasion.[35]

Hamilton did as he was ordered and ensured that no harm befell the young *Chevalier*. It was therefore with increasing expectations of *Gloire* that, in 1709, his mother bade him farewell for a further year's campaigning. Accompanied by Hamilton, Sheldon and Middleton, James joined the French army in Flanders under Marshal Villars. The year saw the Malplaquet campaign with Villars commanding an army of over 100,000 men, although he was instructed from Paris to avoid battle if possible. These were no longer the wars of *Gloire* and Louis was more concerned with the defence of his own borders. With the allied capture of Tournai, French positions at Mons were threatened. Villars was ordered to hold the town. Withdrawing 90,000 men to Malplaquet, this was the first occasion where the so far successful Marlborough and Eugene had faced the renowned Villars, who would be wounded badly in the battle. It was recorded that the English officers saw the young *Chevalier* prince before the battle and Marlborough himself drank a toast to his health.[36]

Spain, too, had seen its share of savage fighting. With Berwick's victory at Almanza in 1707, the French had taken the initiative. Valencia, Saragossa and Lerida fell in rapid succession, and the lines were held in 1709.

Famine now stalked France due to the disastrous harvest of 1708 and a freezing winter. Louis insisted that a diplomatic solution be found, although allied conditions were too stringent. Resolved to continue, therefore, he placed Villars in command in Flanders. But the French army was exhausted and dishevelled, facing two of the ablest allied commanders and some of the best troops in Europe. Marlborough laid siege to Tournai, then made plans for Mons, but the French strove to seize the initiative and took up positions against him at Malplaquet.

86,000 Allied troops laid siege to Mons at the end of the campaign season, and a French relief force of 75,000 encamped at Malplaquet to meet it in what would become one of the bloodiest battles of the war. The Irish regiments in Villars's army included those of Lee, O'Brien, Dorrington, Galmoy, and Nugent's cavalry.

French infantry, including newly-raised battalions, deployed in cover in the wooded areas around Malplaquet where they were pounded by allied artillery. Three enemy charges were repelled before the Irish and Swiss counter-attacked with the French. Marlborough himself would comment that the British and Germans 'recoiled a considerable way before the onset of the Irish'.[37]

At this point a curious event took place, one which sets the war, the roots of regimental dispositions in French service, and the plight of the Irish exiles in their full context. A battalion, or detachment, from the Royal Regiment of Ireland under Captain Robert Parker, a Kilkenny Protestant in allied service, was in a position to trade musket-fire with Dorrington's Irish Regiment. At ranges of tens of yards, two red-coated lines exchanged fire, reloaded, and exchanged again as men fell around them.

Of the two sides, the allies fared better. Research related to the advantages of 'platoon fire' over the less deadly and less consistent 'fire by ranks' used by the French would become a point of contention throughout the wars of the period.

The exchange has been analysed in detail, and highlights the differences in allied and French deployments, such that the French lagged behind contemporary military thinking to such a degree that it could make battalions less effective in musketry combat. Platoon firing allowed a rippling continuous fire which would halt, break and rout enemy battalion through loss and wounds. Compared with traditional 'firing by ranks', a single volley of muskets, it was both more effective and more efficient. Parker wrote of an engagement with a French battalion:

> they gave us a fire of one of their ranks: whereupon we halted, and returned them the fire of our six Plattoons at once; and immediately made ready the six Plattoons of our second fire, and advanced upon them again. They then gave us the fire of another rank, and we returned them a second fire, which made them shrink; however they gave us the fire of third rank after a scattering manner, and then retired into the wood in great disorder: On which we sent our third fire after them, and saw them no more.
>
> The advantage on our side will be easily accounted for, first from the weight of our ball; for the French Arms carry bullets of 24 to the pound: Whereas our British Firelocks carry ball of 16 to the pound, which will make a considerable difference in the execution. Again, the manner of our firing was different from theirs; the French at that time fired all by ranks, which can never do equal execution with our Plattoon-firing, especially when six Plattoons are fired together. This is undoubtedly the best method that has yet been discovered for fighting a Battalion; especially when two Battalions only engage each other.[38]

The exchange was all the more remarkable by virtue of the fact that neither side realized until later that they were fighting their own countrymen. Parker wrote:

> We advanced cautiously up to the ground which they had quitted, and found several of them killed and wounded; among the latter was one Lieutenant O'Sullivan, who told us the battalion we had

engaged was the Royal Regiment of Ireland.[39]

James III, the Old Pretender, and the son who so long ago had been known as the 'warming-pan baby' was with Richard Hamilton, and had been leading the French *Maison du Roi* Cavalry in battle, leading charge after charge. He had led the horse in breaking the allied lines, and received a wound from a cavalry sabre to his arm, having behaved with 'all possible bravery and vivacity'.[40]

A weakened French centre was defeated in detail; again, the myth of French invincibility had been shattered, yet the army had remained relatively intact and in good order. Marlborough went on to capture further French fortresses, and crossed the *Ne Plus Ultra* lines successfully.

The French were forced to withdraw after taking heavy casualties although the battle proved costly for both sides and the allies could not give effective pursuit. Over 12,000 French and 20,000 allied casualties were suffered. Ultimately, the engagement had been futile as the allies captured Mons before going into winter quarters.

Over 3,000 Irish had been killed in the battle. It is difficult to trace exactly how many of the troops might have been able to trace their French service, or even their own lineage by then, back to the fateful day when Mountcashel had arrived with Irish troops in 1689. We know of some officers and notables but in terms of those troops who had survived we can be certain that the likelihood of their survival thus far, taking into account the propensity for the French to use Irish troops in assault and as shock troops, would be significantly lessened when compared with run-of-the-mill French regiments.

\*\*\*

With French reverses in Flanders, the initiative shifted to the allies and the war's focus inevitably moved to Spain. By 1709 Irish regiments in the service of Spain were serving with Spanish forces in large battles. Most notable was the Duke of Berwick's victory at Almanza in 1707, the most decisive battle in the peninsula during the long war. Irish troops in Spanish service played a decisive role, charging several English battalions who recoiled in response.

Arthur Dillon was also involved with the siege of Barcelona, which fell after two assaults. Irish troops in Spanish service, supported by their French service counterparts, Dillon's, Lee's, Berwick's and Burke's battalions, took part in the final storming of the city. James Sarsfield, son of Patrick Sarsfield, was wounded during the battle and received the Spanish honour of the Order of the Golden Fleece.

Marlborough would never fight another great battle after 1710. The political climate in England meant that both he and his wife had fallen from favour and, without the political weight of Queen Anne, he had lost influence. By 1712 he had been removed from command entirely. By 1711 the nature of the war had changed. Emperor Joseph I had died, to be succeeded by Archduke Charles. If the allies were to win and place him on the throne, the monarchy would be more dangerous to the European balance of power than Philip V's Spain, and the resolve of the alliance was effectively undermined. When talks began, the French agreed to recognise Anne and the existing Protestant succession, and to ensure that French and Spanish thrones were never united, for a second time. For a second time, too, any faint hope that the Irish troops in French service might have had about Louis's commitment to a Jacobite succession in the British Isles were dashed.

1710 saw the *Ne Plus Ultra* defensive fortifications being built along the French borders and James once more leaving for tutelage under the now recovered Villars. His mother, fearing the worst with the ever increasing and bloody nature of the battles, again urged Hamilton to take care of him and write to her often about his welfare.

> I have been in such a hurry for this week past, that I could hardly find time to write to the king, so that you must not wonder if I have not been able before this to answer your letter of the 2nd by which I had a confirmation of the account Mr Booth and Dr Wood had sent of the king's illness and of the remedies that were given him which I hope in God will have a good effect and that the worst is over; I find you were of the same opinion with the Doctor that he should take a great deal of the rest and not join the army till he was quite recovered which I did beg of him to do.

She received news that:

> the enemies were marching and that if they [the allies] will come to Arras there must be a battle, where I know the king will be, if he be able, and I praise him for it, but at the same time, you can not but believe that my poor heart aches; I put all my confidence in God who has given him to me and I hope in his mercy he will preserve him; after that I put my trust in you that you will be close to him and let him do no more than is fit for him as you promised me,

when you took leave of me; and as the Duke of Berwick told me that
he and you had agreed when he left you, how much or how little was
fit for him in a day of action or at other times, when certainly it is
not necessary to do so much I shall not pretend to enter into that I
being no competent judge of it, but confide in your prudence and
discretion and pray to God to direct you to give the king the best
advice which I am sure he will follow.[41]

Mary put much trust in Hamilton's opinion – significant pressure indeed,
bearing in mind that James was the Jacobite heir apparent. Hamilton,
therefore, hid little from the boy's mother, including the continually
worsening state of his health. Mary's reply was indicative of just how much
news she was receiving. Mary also warned Hamilton that he should not
forget the importance of such information.

I am very sorry to find by yours of the 14th that the king's illness was
grown so troublesome, and uneasy to him, I will hope he was then at
the worst and that I shall soon hear of his being well again, till that is,
    I hope you will not fail writing to me, and let me know exactly
how he is, which is no more than I asked and you promised when
you left St Germain, but you having forgot it once I now put you in
mind of it for fear you should forget it again;
    If you have any news, I hope you will send them to me, as long
as the king does not write, which I would not have him do, by no
means, till he is quite at ease; I conclude you are well, hearing
nothing to the contrary since you left us and I heartily wish you
may continue.[42]

In a matter of weeks, Hamilton had related the true state of James's
worsening condition. He had little option but to obey. If James were to die on
campaign, Mary's grief would be unimaginable. Hamilton therefore agreed
that a doctor should be sent to assess his condition. Mary's reply once more
showed a degree of gratitude, for Hamilton's honesty in the affair at least.

You guessed very right that the account that Dr Baulieu gave me
after having visited the King would set me quite at ease, I thank
God it has done so, and therefore I can not repent my having sent
him nor I hope you don't repent the having written to me the naked
truth of the king's condition, with which I hope he does not find

fault, I am sure I don't for though it gave me some trouble, yet I had rather undergo that and know the truth, than be flattered, and never know what to trust to, but of this last I am sure you are not capable, and therefore it is a satisfaction to me to have from you an account of the king, because I dare count upon it, to be literally true and that is what I would have, and for which and your having done it so constantly in this his last illness, I can never thank you enough, but I am sure I shall never forget it.

I am very glad to find you are of opinion that the king's staying so long at the army may be prejudicial to his health, and of no advantage to him otherways, I am sure I think so but I am afraid of letting myself be judge in these matters.

[if] the king can not ride without venturing to be ill again nor stay in that country without venturing an ache which is but to plan his coming away will soon be decided; the king or you will let me know what he thinks of all this, what else he would have me do; and I shall perform.[43]

It was clear then that the military held little future for James. Hamilton's honesty had seen to that, and the young Chevalier's illness would never be suited to the rigours of campaigning. Richard had seen for himself the worst vagaries of military life at Londonderry. Little wonder that he wished to spare the frail heir to the Jacobite throne such hardships, despite the Chevalier's own preference for military experience.

James spent the summer of 1711 travelling in France and it is likely that Richard Hamilton was his travelling companion. The following year, however, saw his health deteriorate once more as he suffered from an attack of smallpox. He would recover. His sister, Princess Marie-Louise, also suffered ill health that year but she would not recover. She died in 1712 amid much sadness in Saint Germain and certainly to the great distress of her mother and Anthony Hamilton. Peace negotiations for the War of the Spanish Succession began that same year.

By 1712 Ormonde was commanding the British army on the continent and, by July, a suspension of arms had been agreed. Villars would get the better of Eugene for the remainder of the war, but the bolt had been shot. By the treaties at the end, Philip V was recognised as king of Spain by all except the Habsburgs while Louis pledged to keep French and Spanish crowns separated. England gained Hudson Bay, Newfoundland and Gibraltar, Savoy gained Sicily, and Austria the Spanish Netherlands, Milan, Naples and Sardinia. For the French and Dutch, the wars had exhausted their resources and they would never again rise to the heights they had previously seen. For the fledgling British Empire, however, it was only the beginning.

***

Of course, as the years wound on, France's ability to wage war would once more succumb to the vagaries of a lack of major victories and inability to undermine the allies' strategic momentum. In terms of resources, she was fast running out of options but to sue for peace. The final version of the Treaty of Utrecht sought to settle the matter in 1713, with the Treaty of Rastatt almost putting an end to the fighting in 1714, although war in Spain would continue into the following year.

In some respects, the war had settled the old arguments over dominion of Europe, although through economic exhaustion rather than force of arms, and through a reduced willingness to submit to further royal platitudes about *Gloire*, but rather a realisation of the real human and economic cost of a Europe-wide conflict. Spain's decline and fall became inevitable, while French power would be significantly reduced. With the Dutch Provinces' decline, too, came the rise of England and, ultimately, the British Empire, with a powerful Royal Navy supporting lucrative colonies.

The Irish soldiers who remained had become elite troops, certain that their efforts had been courageous but, ultimately, costly. Mountcashel and Sarsfield had died from their wounds during the Nine Years' War. Both had seen Ireland's plight, and future, from different viewpoints, perhaps that very difference between notables sounding the death knell for any cohesive non-factional decision-making about resistance in 1691. Perhaps it is cruel to see both in different lights, although the comparison must be made. The Gaelic Mountcashel has been almost forgotten because he lost a battle, escaped allied captivity and sought French aid as the only means to secure that future, and was welcomed by the French, while the old-English Sarsfield fought few real battles, while remaining at the centre of the factional infighting in 1691, and leading the second batch of troops to Europe. After this second exodus, as years passed, hope of them ever returning waned to nothing.

Had either or both lived a little longer, their influence might have meant that plans for a new 'Descent upon England' with James, or his son, at the head would have been all the easier or, at least, would have gained French support in a more proactive manner than actually occurred. As it was, there were few notables left with significant influence, nor indeed was the brigade kept together as a cohesive whole, factors that were essential if any hope of a return were to be enabled.

Other Irish notables had been killed in the fighting: Daniel O'Brien, 4th Lord Clare, had been killed at Marsaglia, his son killed at Ramillies. Lord Galmoy's son was killed at Malplaquet. Colonel Fitzgerald had been wounded mortally at Luzzara, while Richard Talbot, son of Tyrconnel, died after Oudenarde. The flower of Irish nobility had been judged, exiled and, to a large part, eliminated by the vagaries of European war. But the reasoning behind the flight of the Wild Geese in 1689 and 1691 was not simply to fight Louis's war, at least in Irish eyes: it was to gain favour and reputation such that a return to Ireland was made possible. How far away such thinking must have seemed by 1715. Was there any real chance of a return? Despite the apparently futile attempts during the war, the phantom conflict for the British succession was far from complete.

When Queen Anne died without surviving children in 1714, James III, as he would have been, was precluded from the succession through the Act of Settlement, despite sharing a father with the erstwhile Queen of England. Anne's closest Protestant relative, the Hanoverian Prince George, became King George I of England, Scotland and Ireland. Support had been mounting for further Jacobite moves, and the young James stood waiting in the wings. Again, the Scottish Highlands, where the Stuart line had ruled for centuries before forming the basis of the English monarchy, would be the focal point of rebellion. Feudal belief and semi-formal recognition of the young James III would be enough to unite clans and foster Jacobite opposition in the event of insurrection.

France was close to being broken, however. The war had taxed both physically and spiritually; the same could be said of Louis himself, who could not support the invasion with troops. He died in 1715. It was the end of an era for Europe and, of course, for the Jacobites. The man who had lived through *Gloire*, and had been moved by complex motivations across his years – pride, women, church and state, and a desire, if not a compulsion, to see his country recognised for its greatness – had gone.

Facing his successor, regent Phillippe d'Orleans, was the fact that succession rested upon maintaining the peace with England. It would be calamitous to support another attempt on the English succession. Phillippe would, however, supply volunteers from the famed Irish Brigade, together with French half-pay officers, and James duly requested that the Irish regiments in France and Spain ready themselves for action. Indeed, they had little choice. France would not be fighting a war for some time, and those unique transferable skills of the Irish fighting men were of little use on the continent otherwise. If a renewed attack on the British succession were even partially successful, it could bring benefit to Ireland. There were even plans to draw the Duke of Berwick into the affair, although those would be shelved as a French marshal would be seen as a minor French notable and could possibly collapse Anglo-French treaties in the process.

Plans were hatched. James Butler the younger, Duke of Ormonde, landed in south-east England, with Irish cavalry, but there was no support, and they withdrew. In the north, the Earl of Mar mustered 12,000 clansmen, but his experience was lacking. Nevertheless, the alternative coronation of James VIII of Scotland (James III of England and Ireland) took place in Braemar. A gathering of the clans was called.

The subsequent movement of the Jacobite army took Inverness but was foiled in attempts to take Edinburgh castle. The French fleet, with additional arms and support for the rebellion, remained blockaded in le Havre and Dieppe. If anything, the true victor of the French war was the Royal Navy, which became dominant in the Channel. The Jacobite army was found wanting for supplies, leadership and discipline. The rebellion could not last or even be sustained. The army was defeated at Preston in November, with many notables captured and arrested. A stalemate at Sheriffmuir followed, and the decisive victory and national insurgency that was desired did not materialise. This meant that the Jacobites could be contained in Scotland.

James returned in December when the Jacobites were close to surrender. With him were experienced Irish officers, including Sheldon, Nugent and Bulkeley, although, even bolstered with the support of Wild Geese officers, James lacked the charisma to motivate what remained of the rebellion. Rumours abounded that the Jacobites wanted to hand him over to the authorities in exchange for a pardon, and he departed from Montrose for France, leaving the Jacobites to fend for themselves in an act very reminiscent of his father's actions so many years before in Ireland. The Jacobite force dispersed and broke up, the leaders eventually finding their way back to France. The rebellion had instigated a swelling of Irish troop numbers in the channel ports at Calais and Boulogne, although the failure of the Scottish insurrection did little to encourage anything similar in Ireland. Attacks from disparate bands of *rapparees* did not a rebellion make, so the talk of rebellion fell flat. London had been the intended target of any pretender Stuart, and would continue to be so; the thought of an Irish diversionary attack and uprising was seemingly farthest from Stuart thoughts and strategies, although Louis had proved the value of such a diversion twenty-five years earlier.

The new Spanish regime did not fail to grasp the irony, however, as it, too, sought to encourage further dissent and attempts to change the British succession. By 1719 Philip V of Spain was supporting the Stuart claim in an attempt to regain some modicum of Spanish influence after the war. The Spanish facilitated descents on Ireland, Scotland and England, with Ireland and Scotland very much diversionary. Colonel James Sarsfield commanded Nugent's horse and arrived in Connacht with Spanish and Irish officers in the hope of inciting rebellion, while Ormonde sailed for Bristol with twenty-two ships and troops from Spain's Irish Brigade. Sarsfield's expedition came to naught, and he had to escape because of the large price on his head. Storms once again prevented any landing of the Spanish task force in England.

A Scottish landing was successful, although the small contingent of Spanish troops, despite raising forces amongst highland chiefs, was defeated at Glenshiel and surrendered.

The British government raised a chain of fortresses in response, forming Scottish companies from loyal clans, having learned its lesson about descents upon the British Isles and the apparent ease with which foreign powers could make landings and, perhaps, finally understanding how lucky they had been in the preceding years by virtue of sea power and weather. It would not be the end of matters in Scotland, however.

*Chapter 18*

# The Pretenders and a Victory

By 1713, and the Treaty of Utrecht, most of the contentious questions that had held Europe in the thrall of conflict had been resolved, although it would take a further year for the Holy Roman Emperor to agree. France would, once again, recognise the Protestant succession of Britain. Philip V would be recognised as King of Spain although Louis was forced to pledge that the crowns of France and Spain would remain separated. Amongst other reverses, the Empire received the Spanish Netherlands and most of Spain's possessions in Italy. Louis had made a critical mistake. England had also insisted that James the Younger withdraw from France. His poor health would delay his departure, but it was understood that he would leave as soon as possible. Even those Jacobites who remained were in favour of such a move since a peaceful end to the war was required before any further discussion with supporters still in England could proceed. Even then, hopes of a restoration seemed possible to a few. Richard Hamilton had accompanied James to Châlons in September 1712. By the start of the following year, however, Hamilton had returned to Saint Germain where he was permitted to stay while the king travelled to Bar in Lorraine.

One remaining cruel twist of fate would afflict Hamilton. Secret communications between loyal Jacobites in England and James had been underway for some time. At least some of the discussion had centred upon James being rid of the elderly Middleton, whom many surviving Jacobites considered disloyal, and a belief that he should instead choose Richard Hamilton as his new Secretary of State in exile. Both James and Berwick remained unconvinced, believing that whatever forces were at work were attempting to ruin Middleton. Although he remained agreeable to depart, Mary would have none of it, and James seemed reluctant to be manipulated. Middleton received communication to the effect that:

> the more I think of it the more I am convinced that villainy must
> proceed originally either from the Irish, to remove one they generally
> look upon as none of their friends, and to make way for one of
> their friends, or else that it is a trick of the Whig's intervention to

ruin [the King] by insinuating a correspondence with them to give jealousy to the other party.[1]

James requested confirmation and that an advisor be sent to arbitrate in the matters, insisting that Hamilton could not fill the post. By then Richard was involved to the extent that many were blaming him for instigating the affair. Although ultimately James would believe his innocence, Hamilton was dismissed. Few were convinced of his complicity, among them Berwick who would advise James that a man who had remained loyal for fifty years was unlikely to be suspect now.[2] Ultimately, Jacobite mistrust of Middleton proved to be true and had little to do with Hamilton. By then, however, it was too late.[3] James had been a little rash and clearly presumptuous regarding Richard and it is debatable whether he wanted the position. However, the relationship between the two became more strained in light of these events. Two years later, when Hamilton wished to visit his niece in Lorraine, he had to request permission from James with Berwick acting as a go-between, and promise not to travel through Bar or near James's residence there.[4]

By 1715, and with hopes of a Jacobite resurgence as James, the 'Old Pretender', attempted to provoke a rising in Scotland, Richard Hamilton would play no part. Louis had also died in 1715. By the following year Hamilton had returned to Saint Germain to find his brother Anthony suffering from poor health. The exiles were living in considerably more poverty than they had in the past. Louis's promised pensions were rarely paid and Saint Germain was filled with starving Irish soldiers. Mary had removed herself to live with local nuns, only attending the residence when the public face of what remained of Jacobitism required it.[5] The brothers Hamilton existed in such abject poverty that they had little choice but to find alternative means of living. For Richard, that meant leaving Saint Germain for good and living with his niece, Marie Elizabeth de Gramont, who had been made Abbess of Poussay in 1695 and who had followed the example of her mother in her piety. Although scarcely able to subsist herself, she offered shelter to her uncle in his last days. Richard Hamilton died in December 1717. Maligned by the Jacobites, French and Irish, he had to the end remained loyal to what must, ultimately, have seemed a rather unworthy cause.

Anthony Hamilton was also living his final days. He was considered 'old-fashioned' in a France which had lost a king and was beginning to recover from the rigours of desperate war. His legacy would remain his writing. He was determined to die with the same grace that Gramont had shown, and not become a confused 'old man' in his final days; thus he strived to bear his hardships and failing health with as much dignity as possible. In this he symbolised the life struggle of the family, constantly fighting with hardship brought about by the machinations of the powerful, and it seemed also constantly choosing the losing side. Mary died in 1718 and what remained of the exiles dispersed across Europe, leaving Saint Germain a shell of memories and vain hopes. Anthony died in April 1719, at the age of seventy-four, a man of taste and culture whose writing would convey his pride, levity and to some extent his cynical contempt for the social aspects of seventeenth-century society. His loss would spell the end of a unique family.

An era had passed with the Hamiltons who had, for the most part, remained loyal. Their unique contribution to the history of England, Ireland and France, although ostensibly on the fringes of royal prerogative, and suffering the rigours of political censure, remains their legacy. The requirements of an age where religion and reason at times seemed juxtaposed inevitably forced them to become brothers in arms but, of course, the story would not end with them.

The intervening years between the War of the Spanish Succession and the War of the Austrian Succession were relatively lean times for the Irish Brigades. Berwick had been killed at the siege of Phillipsburg in 1733, after an illustrious career, having led a victorious French army in Spain during the War of the Spanish Succession. Despite the rigours of the Nine Years' War and the War of the Spanish Succession, the Irish had cemented their already fearsome reputation.

The Battle of Fontenoy was fought close to Tournai in 1745, during the War of the Austrian Succession. France had assembled her army there, and the Dutch and Anglo-Hanoverians had responded in kind. George II's favourite son, William Augustus, Duke of Cumberland, was made commander of the contingent. Maurice de Saxe, despite being confined to a wicker sedan chair for the fray, was one of the ablest commanders the French had and would face the allied forces in battle. A teenager during the bloody battle at Malplaquet, he had resolved not to be wasteful of lives, such that the quality of the army would be undermined over time, as had happened in the previous wars. He was fifty now, while his young opponent was still in his twenties. Relatively inexperienced, he would become the villain of the next Jacobite rebellion as the 'butcher' of Culloden.

Saxe had laid siege to Tournai, and Cumberland had sent the army in relief. Responding to his moves, Saxe had marched 45,000 to the small village of Fontenoy, taking the higher ground and making earthwork defences ready, some of which were constructed as artillery redoubts.

For the first time, the Irish served together: all seven infantry regiments, comprising Dillon's, Clare's, Berwick's, Bulkeley's, Lally's and Roths', commanded by the 6th Lord Clare, Charles O'Brien – almost 4,000 men. In addition, the 270 men of Fitzjames's cavalry regiment were also present. It would be the only battle when they were all fielded together, and it is tempting to ponder whether the outcome of other battles, or even wars, might have been very different had the Brigade been allowed to fight together as it did at Fontenoy. What might it have achieved had the best troops and generals been brought together at the tip of the spear to be deployed *en masse* rather than scattered in packets in siege lines and through armies. Certainly such deployment under an able commander would have harnessed the esprit de corps of the exiles to best effect.

At dawn on 11 May 1745 Cumberland's 50,000 troops were positioned in front of Vezon. Saxe deployed in defence, deflecting allied cavalry probes and a Dutch attack through his well-laid guns. Men of the Highland Regiment of Foot, the future Black Watch, led a second assault, but were repelled with heavy casualties. Despite the courage of the Scottish highlanders, the line held.

But Cumberland had seen a potential weakness, an opening in the line, although Saxe, with perhaps a more flexible view of the battlefield, had in turn depended upon it. Cumberland sent his Anglo-Hanoverian force across the open ground between Barri Wood and Fontenoy itself. With 15,000 troops marching in good order across open ground, it was inevitable that fire from the well-placed, enfilading batteries that Saxe had positioned would cut swathes through the advancing lines. The attack was made under the heavy barrage and deadly fire of French artillery. The massive Allied column crowded in upon itself as it stopped within 300 paces of the French first line of defensive battalions. The discipline and experience of British and allied troops stood them in good stead as the battalions in the fore faced six battalions of the French elite, four of the well-trained and highly-experienced *Gardes Francaises*, and two of the veteran Swiss Guards.

Lord Charles Hay, at the head of the British battalions, stepped forward, reputedly commenting 'We are the English guards, and we hope that you will stand until we come to you, and swim the Scheldt River as you swam the Main', referring to an incident earlier in the war where retreating troops had drowned in the river after a boat had capsized. Hays called for three cheers, and the French did the same, before the deadly volleys began.

French ranks fired first, followed by a rippling volley of platoon fire rolling down the British lines, as hundreds of men fell. The co-ordinated fire by platoons, designed and perfected by the allies, had its effect, as the French line began to break and fall back. The British advanced, closing ranks and cutting through the French second line, so much so that French artillery on the flanks was neutralised.

Behind Barri Wood, with the popping of musketry seemingly distant and detached, the Irish regiments stood awaiting orders. Saxe ordered several counter-attacks, to slow the advancing allied column.

There is some confusion in the sources, and therefore allocation of appropriate credit with regard to who 'saved the day'. The allied column retained two-thirds of its original strength and, after rallying, retained the initiative. Dillon's, with the French Normandie and Vasseaux Regiments took part, but were repelled, with significant loss, including Colonel James Dillon himself. Fitzjames's cavalry had men cut down in dozens. Louis XV felt compelled to hand victory to the allies and retreat, although he was convinced by the Duc de Richelieu to remain. This was much to Saxe's agreement: he was in no mood to hand the day to his enemy just yet, so much so that he discarded his sedan chair for his horse, no matter how painful the effort, to join the cavalry in a final, and battle deciding, cavalry charge.

Colonel Thomas Lally queried his design, however. 'On what finer reserves could a general call in a moment of crisis than six battalions of the Wild Geese?'[6] The quotation is spurious, even laden with the romanticism of the day, although it is both fitting and poignant in terms of our story, and sits perfectly in terms of the brigade's lineage and as a measure of just how far it had come in French service, destined to be in the right place at the right time.

Even Cumberland would relate that Saxe came to rely on his reserve in an attempt to save the day: 'a corps on whose courage and behaviour he entirely depended.'[7] Lally had few words to motivate them, but they would be enough: 'Remember Limerick and Saxon perfidy!'

It had been fifty-four years since Limerick. There were no troops left in the brigade who had been there, although their descendants were. They had been brought up on the Jacobite ideal, the vain hopes that the exiles had held out for returning to Ireland and their belief that French service was more than a thin veil, and a pretence in terms of returning a Jacobite to the crown and the English succession.

The head of the British column was hit by French cavalry, while the Swiss Guard attacked the Hanoverian left, leaving the Irish Brigade to charge the

British right, supported by the two substantially weakened French regiments that had supported Dillon earlier. 4,000 Irish troops advanced on rising ground toward the British right, playing 'The White Cockade' on pipes as they advanced, a tune and an instrument which had been banned at home in Ireland to dissuade martial thoughts and gatherings.

So far the British troops had had some success and French lines had recoiled, then broken, but now, as fresh Irish troops clad similarly in red coats, advanced upon the exhausted British, Saxe had renewed hope. Committing fresh troops, with such an esprit de corps, and as much of a point to prove, at the right time, could be a masterstroke, if it paid off, and would blunt both the ferocity and confidence of the victorious allied forces, which had come so far, but yet, as with any eighteenth-century battlefield and formation, could not keep up the momentum of their manoeuvre for long.

'Remember Limerick', some shouted again. It had been decades since the siege of Limerick but the tales of the siege and the flight of the Wild Geese had grown long in the telling, heroic exploits having no doubt been exaggerated to the point where their use in terms of motivation of young recruits, Irish, Irish descendants or otherwise, could not be understated.

In similar fashion to earlier events, and quite in keeping with the lore surrounding the 'Age of Reason', an officer of the Coldstream Guards challenged Captain Anthony McDonough to single combat as the lines converged. McDonough parried the blows of the Englishman and forced him to the ground, exhorting the Irish to greater feats of prowess, as the lines drew closer and deadly musket volleys started to take their toll. The British muskets, predictably perhaps, got the better of the firing, with devastation of the first Irish line. The troops were so close, however, that an Irish charge could settle the day. Fresh troops poured across the gap toward the British who had no chance to reload. They pushed their enemy back, and were ordered to withdraw, lest they might push too far and create disorganisation amongst the brigade. Cohesion in the advance was everything if the battle was to be won. The second line of the Irish Brigade engaged and pushed the 'infernal column' back yet farther, forcing the ordered battalions and column to break and recoil. It was enough to win the initiative and break the allied momentum.

The Irish troops cheered again as they advanced toward the British. The key to linear warfare was knowing when to engage with fresh troops, and the Irish had been kept in reserve, with Saxe committing them against the tired and beleaguered British mass column at just the right moment, having been given an opportunity he could scarcely resist. The allies rallied where they could and retreated through the falling darkness towards Ath, where Cumberland would shed tears at the scale of his defeat, when victory had been so close but had been snatched from him. Saxe would not make the mistake of allowing a capable enemy to rally, and pursued with vigour; the Highland Regiment would hamper the effort, and prevent a retreat becoming a rout.

Louis himself would thank the Irish troops, promoting some of the notables: Colonel Thomas Lally, commanding Berwick's, and Lieutenant Colonel Stapleton, amongst others, were promoted to brigadier generals. 15,000 men had been killed in one of the most murderous battles of the age. The Irish themselves had lost a quarter of their officers and almost 700 men.[8]

When George II heard news of the defeat, he cursed the fact that the Irish penal laws existed and, thereby, the fact that he could not recruit the Irish to serve in his own army, a far cry from the fears of rampant Irish troops fighting for the French and Jacobites, which had been such a concern at the turn of the century, and a fear that had propagated the existence of the Wild Geese.

The British were pushed from Flanders in the months that followed. Fontenoy had been the only real and conclusive French land victory over an English commander since the Hundred Years' War, and would not soon be forgotten.

History, with Jacobite sympathies or otherwise, remembers the battle as the finest hour of the Irish Brigade. It is arguable that, in a larger sense, it was the finest hour of the entire Jacobite cause. A series of ill-judged campaigns, factional leadership, steadfast opposition to changes in the British succession and even the very weather itself, had stood in the face of the Jacobites at every turn. The very notion of French service was a misnomer for the most part, and it must have been clear, even to the Irish, that the principles, at least amongst the ruling classes and the nobility, of French service leading to a descent on England or Ireland at this late stage was a fantastic and misplaced notion. We could argue, therefore, that the Irish had little to fight for, and yet they performed a feat of arms such that they had never been able to do in earlier campaigns and battles. That they had motivation left at all is a tribute to their dedication. That they should have done so well in the face of adversity, even at this stage, when only a notional attempt at the succession might succeed, speaks to their courage. Despite the failed attempts, the pretence at French support as a diversion against wars on the continent, and even though Louis XIV was long gone, all was not yet lost.

More than forty years later, on the eve of the French revolution, veterans gathered in the Luxembourg Gardens in Paris, sharing their memories of the battle and their shared brotherhood. Fifty years afterwards, Thomas Davis's ballad would commemorate the victory:

> *On Fontenoy, on Fontenoy, hark to that fierce huzza*
> *Revenge! Remember Limerick! Dash down the Sassanach!*
> *And Fontenoy, famed Fontenoy, had been a Waterloo*
> *Were not those exiles ready then, fresh, vehement and true.*

Fierce words indeed, laced with a hundred years of bitter truths and despair and even a touch of betrayal. In reality, Louis had done little, and it had been up to the Irish troops to prove their mettle in the face of hardship, although the Ireland that they long yearned for had gone.

Even in the twentieth century, a poem by Emily Lawless was still being taught to schoolchildren in southern Ireland:

> *That brings us on the battle, that summons to their share*
> *The homeless troops, the banished men, the exiled sons of Clare*

In Fontenoy today the battle and the brigade are remembered, as if to forget the nature of such a victory might be a tragedy. A Celtic cross was erected in 1907, with the inscription: 'To the soldiers of the Irish Brigade who on the field of Fontenoy avenged the violation of the Treaty of Limerick'. The tablet on the wall of a churchyard nearby similarly reads: 'In memory of the heroic soldiers who changed defeat into victory at Fonteny, 11 May 1745. God save Ireland.'

Even with such accolade, controversy still surrounds the battle, and the Irish part has been downplayed in favour of French troops and the Normandie Regiment. Much of this can be attributed to the capture of British standards at the battle, the subsequent questions, or lack thereof, of subsequent historians, French concerns over the loss of political favour with the dwindling Jacobite cause, and the fact that foreign troops in French service were rarely venerated for long. That the brigade played a significant part in the battle does not seem in doubt; indeed, despite it all, the Jacobites had one throw of the dice yet to cast.

## The '45

A year before the action at Fontenoy, James II's grandson, Charles Edward Stuart, like his father and grandfather, was planning a renewed invasion of England designed to take back the crown his father had lost in 1688. The '45 rebellion was somewhat different, at least compared with those failed attempts at landing Irish troops in England, in that there was no mass movement of troops although some Irish troops accompanied Bonnie Prince Charlie as he became known.

In March 1744 France had planned an invasion of England; clearly, even after the era of Louis XIV, the French did not give up easily. Again, it would be the apparent divine right of the Jacobite succession that would take centre stage, despite the fact that cruel fate had dictated against it for at least fifty years. Charles was summoned from his home in Rome to help lead the invasion. He would write to his father, the Old Pretender, 'I have taken a strong resolution to conquer or die, and stand my ground as long as I have a man remaining to me.' His will and resolve would be put to the test.

A force of 10,000 troops under Saxe had been assembled on the French coast. It had all happened before, of course, even as the Hamilton brothers had reached old age, accompanying their own young charge on so many adventures which came to naught. Perhaps this time there was even a feeling of triumphalism that at last something might be made of the dwindling Jacobite cause. Charles himself would lead an expedition to Scotland, with 1,500 troops from the Irish Brigade. They must have believed that something felt quite different about this expedition, had even heard of the debacles of the past, and knew that, this time, it could be different, but with a new 'young' pretender, whose fate was far from certain, although in the full knowledge that even God must surely, after all of their past efforts, find favour with their cause?

It was almost inevitable that bad luck bedevilled the expedition from the start. Yet again, and perhaps predictably, severe storms meant that the fighting squadrons and troop transports were dispersed early, with twelve ships lost. Charles urged a further expedition, even despite the withdrawal of French forces and the inevitable loss of interest from the French king, but there was a war to fight, and no strategy would develop, at least until the following year.

The French victory at Fontenoy, however, had brought new focus to the plan. A French victory and the British driven from the field? Perhaps providence shone upon a new effort to finally take back the crown. Charles sought the help of the Irish in France, and ships laden with arms would help incite an uprising in loyal Scotland. Volunteers from the Irish Brigade would help make up some of the troops who would accompany Charles to Scotland. A fight between Charles's escort, the *Elizabeth* and HMS *Lion* resulted in both being damaged, but, aboard the *Doutelle*, Charles was able to land in the Outer Hebrides.

By July, landing again in Scotland, Charles had the support of various notables, but few troops. He argued with the Highland chiefs that the time was ripe for rebellion. After Fontenoy, and the triumph of the Irish Brigades, ostensibly in support of Jacobitism, they agreed. If anything, he had the charisma his grandfather had lacked, and the inspiration that his father could not instil. Perhaps, even now, it was not too late. He promised French support, despite the fact that historical precedent showed that fate had not been kind in this respect.

The Stuart standard was raised at Glenfinnan, and several thousand armed men were raised. With the rising viewed as of little consequence, Edinburgh was easily taken. The coronation of another Jacobite king was serenaded as James's entry into Dublin had been in 1689, with 'The King Shall Enjoy his Own Again'.

Six weeks later, the army marched south. Whether they were a militia, a rag-tag band, or a serious threat to the throne, it was time for action if disaster was to be avoided. Jacobite troops would once more be on English soil. Charles's victory at Prestonpans underlined the threat; his crossing of the border into England made it palpable. There were plans to have his brother Henry lead the Irish Brigade for a landing in England. Although the endeavour remained in the planning stage, many officers of the brigade were landed on the Scottish coast to provide support, together with volunteers, but their numbers never reached the thousands of troops who had taken part in the victory at Fontenoy. Indeed, one-hundred officers and men from Dillon's, Bulkeley's and Lally's Regiments were captured when their ships were taken by the Royal Navy.

The march into England was not well planned. The army had four days' supplies, and the poor weather meant that many deserted Charles's cause. They took Carlisle in November, and had expected support from the north of England, which did not come, their previous popularity in the area having been eroded in recent years by English talk of brutal 'savages'. None of this, in the main, eroded the powerful reputation that Charles had with the men, although it did not stop the fledgling army from arriving at Derby by the end of the year, merely four or five days' march from London. In reality, however, despite Charles's charisma, and obvious support amongst the Jacobites, much about his cause had been dismissed or, at worst, forgotten amongst the populace, who were more fearful of savages from the north than the protestations of a Jacobite cause that had been denied what it saw as its rightful throne. The small force was no match for the English troops who were slowly gathering in force, and Charles was advised to retreat northward again. They had beaten an English force at Prestonpans, and been defeated by winter weather and a lack of local support. An officer was even shot by a local as he passed through Wigan.

The plan had been to send French troops to Scotland in 1746, although Charles's forced retreat had once more placed doubt upon French inclination for a direct attack, and additional Irish troops were despatched instead. Brigadier General Lally attempted to recruit forces in Scotland and Ireland, but the numbers raised were low. By the start of 1746 Cumberland's army retook Carlisle, while the Jacobites withdrew to Glasgow and joined with Irish and Scots troops from France.[9]

The Jacobites faced Hawley's 8,000-strong British army at Falkirk; 350 men from the Irish Brigade took part. Charles said to Lally, 'Those English know you, they were at Fontenoy.' Lally replied: 'Yes, your Royal Highness, but my officers and I would wish to be in the front line of battle in order to renew our acquaintance.'

With tactics honed at Prestonpans, and the ferocity of the Highlander attack, the British centre was broken. In twenty minutes the battle was over, but the Jacobites were not able to pursue. There was no comparison between their serried ferocious ranks and a contemporary army. What they had in terms of the ability to close and engage the enemy and win, they lacked in mobility. A group of Irish and Scots found Falkirk all but abandoned. Underlining the point regarding contemporary armies in the field, much of the Highlander force returned to the mountains with plunder, divesting the Jacobite army of several thousand men just as they were starting to take the initiative.

But Cumberland, the memory of Fontenoy and the disastrous European campaign still fresh in his mind, advanced north with 7,000 men, and linked up with Hawley's battered force. As with so many of the past Jacobite strategies, Cumberland had one advantage: division and argument between factions would become the undoing of the Jacobites. Since the retreat from Derby, Charles had lost faith in the Highland chiefs, while placing his trust in the Irish officers. Indeed, in a bitter twist of irony, the Highlanders were somewhat jealous of the burgeoning relationship that Charles was developing with the Irish, whom they viewed as mere 'adventurers', keen only to secure their own reputations with the French army and court, and who cared little for the cause of Scotland. Ironic indeed that those troops who were descended from Mountcashel's and Sarsfield's Wild Geese should be viewed as anathema to the Scottish, if not Catholic, cause. The chiefs would react with fury when Charles proposed to give command of a regiment to the Irish Captain MacGeoghegan. Despite his anger at their intransigence, there was little he could do. Bad news was coming fast now. The Jacobite force moved to Inverness, even as Charles received news that any hopes for invasion from France had been abandoned.[10]

More Irish would arrive in spring 1746 but, almost predictably, matters would not go according to plan. A squadron of the Fitzjames cavalry regiment reached Scotland, but their horses did not. The Royal Navy, although not intercepting every ship, was powerful enough to render any potential invasion or insurrection which had to be supported by sea, bereft of co-ordinated and predictable supply and reinforcement. They would blockade, capture, chase and destroy any ships that had hopes of landing reinforcements to support the rebellion in Scotland. If anything, years of preserving the British succession had taught the Royal Navy its true role in domestic waters. 400 men of Fitzjames's Regiment were captured aboard the *Bourbon* and *Charité*. Their captors spoke of their being capable of 'a great deal of mischief' had they been able to land successfully.[11] There were a few successful landings, but scarcely with enough Irish troops to make a difference, although rumours of gatherings on the French coast sent 4,000 British troops to Kent.[12]

In April the *Prince Charles*, with money, arms and 150 men of Berwick's men broke through the channel blockade, but was run aground off the Scottish coast. If Charles failed through lack of Irish reinforcement, it was certainly not due to a lack of attempts to succeed. This lack of support meant that Cumberland could move with impunity, forcing a retreating Jacobite force into a smaller and smaller pocket, whilst even receiving foreign, Hessian, reinforcements – 5,000 men to bolster his own 10,000 strong army. He outnumbered the Jacobites by two to one, with 1,200 well-horsed cavalry versus their Irish equivalents mounted on nags, a far cry from the elite riders, the cream of Irish nobility, who had been so active at the Boyne,. The results were predictable.

By 16 April an exhausted and starving Jacobite army had little option but to face Cumberland in battle on Culloden Moor.

The initial Jacobite plan hinged upon a twelve-mile night march with a view to a surprise attack against Cumberland's encampment, but it came to naught as the Jacobites could only make half the distance under darkness and resolved not to attack in daylight; but it left the troops exhausted from the effort. There was no food, and what time there was to discuss a plan for the following day during the inevitable battle that would follow, was used up by sleep or foraging. Charles's decision to make a stand was precipitous, but perhaps also forced by the fact that the army could scarcely stay ahead of a subsequent chase in its condition. Indeed, he had listened to counsel previously which had urged him to retreat – at Derby and at Prestonpans. It was time to make a stand, just as his grandfather had resolved to do at the Boyne. It was either that or lose the army through desertion, starvation, or worse, none of which was an appealing state to be in when cornered by a larger British force.

The night march had taken its toll, with further desertion evident, and the MacDonald clan, normally given the honour of the right of the line, ever since Bannockburn, was placed on the left, an action which would neither go unnoticed nor unanswered. The Jacobite right was anchored on the walls of Culloden House, which remained unsecured and would be taken as a secure flank by Cumberland and used to provide enfilade fire against the Highlanders.

Even from the start, and the artillery duel, Jacobite troops came off worse. The right wing charged and was stopped by musketry and close-range grapeshot, although the charge broke Munro's and Barrel's British regiments. Barrel's colours were captured, albeit temporarily, after his death by broadsword. Cumberland's reinforced line of musketry did its bloody work, mowing down the sweeping charges of the Jacobites while the MacDonalds, disgraced at being on the left of the line, stood by and watched, unwilling to take part.

Charles ultimately ordered a retreat; there was nothing that could save the army in the end and the Irish troops, with Fitzjames's Irish cavalry, covered the manoeuvre. They took cover around the stone walls and fired volley after volley to cover the retreat as best they could. It was Captain O'Shea of Fitzjames's who ultimately had to lead Charles's horse to safety, with an escort of his Horse and Life Guards.

Cumberland subsequently earned his nickname of the 'Butcher of Culloden' as wounded were killed and, in the weeks that followed, locals were driven from their farms to die of cold and hunger. 300 men of the Irish Brigade signed paroles of honour such that they would not attempt escape, and would later be exchanged for British prisoners, although more than one-hundred had been killed. Fourteen Jacobite standards were taken by Cumberland and were burnt in Edinburgh. The heaviest price was paid by the highlanders. An act of 1746 would prohibit highland dress and the carrying of arms but, more succinctly, and in parallel with Irish Jacobitism, their lands were forfeited. Charles spent six months wandering in an attempt to get home, creating a legend in the process, but ultimately got away.

When it is remembered that activity in Ireland was subdued and could not act in parallel with any rising in Scotland due to Penal Laws which left most unarmed and essentially leaderless, it is no surprise that the only real presence of Irish Jacobitism during the campaign had been from the Irish Brigade, even though seaborne superiority had, as perhaps it always had, precluded any dominance in terms of large numbers of experienced troops, and the ever proposed yet rarely tangible factor of French invasion. Those Irish who could have been a deciding factor in terms of local and thereby national support were too few in number and, in light of the Penal Laws, had too much to lose in the end. Indeed, most of the Irish nobility who could have effected any form of local rebellion had already left with Mountcashel and Sarsfield over fifty years before.

There had been numerous rumours about the Irish Brigade whose reputation in light of the recent Fontenoy victory must have been at its height: they would make a landing in Ulster; there had been sightings of Franco-Irish officers across the island; even the French had considered such an undertaking although, with the effectiveness of the naval blockade in terms of the success or otherwise of French activity, we can ascribe a lack of clear direction to French stratagems. The Irish part in the '45 has been somewhat subjugated over the years, although it was important. Simply put, they lacked numbers. Had the campaign been supported with serious French attempts to land the brigade in one form or another, matters might have been very different.

Does the story really end here? It is arguable that the dissolution of the brigades ends the long journey that started with Mountcashel rather than with Sarsfield.

We have links, although not altogether tenuous and still less than clear, between those troops who fought with the Hamilton brothers, who left Ireland with Mountcashel, and then later with Patrick Sarsfield, and the soldiers of post-Fontenoy Europe. Yes, we have Irish battalions in the Seven Years' War and fighting under Napoleon in Europe, but by that stage they were Irish almost in name only. The homeland that their ancestors had left was all but forgotten, and had changed completely. After 1745 there was a greater case to support somewhat disillusioned Irish men in various countries' service, with transferable skills, yet with neither pretender to unite them nor recognisable homeland to return to. They were, perhaps in a truer sense than before, exiles, yet even an exile has a hope of return – to an ideal if not a country altogether, although by the French Revolution, Irish in French service were perhaps more naturalised than even history will acknowledge.

## The End of the Brigade

It was clear that hope of a Stuart restoration was a myth. Some could dream of what might have been but few, if any, could have any real plan to make it happen. Charles retained his charismatic likeability, despite his increasing propensity to turn to alcohol as realisation of reality took hold. That said, his excessive drinking, in part brought on by his penchant for an excess of whiskey drinking during the more stressful, and hungry, moments of the '45, meant that he would argue and alienate some of his erstwhile friends at court. He would blame France for a lack of support during the rebellion in Scotland, and accuse them of having used him in a game of political expediency. It would not be the first time that France could be accused of such activities.

With the peace treaty of Aix-la-Chapelle in 1748, France was required to recognise George II, the Hanoverian who had acceded to the British Crown, as the rightful king, thereby denying, as Louis XIV had once done, albeit temporarily, the rightfulness of the Jacobite succession. Unlike Louis's earlier agreement, however, the French were also required to remove Charles from France. They agreed that they might set him up in Switzerland, and that he could retain his title of Prince of Wales. He refused to leave, and was subsequently imprisoned, then escorted to Savoy. For a man who still believed that he was the rightful King of England, Scotland and Ireland, it was an extreme humiliation, especially so as it had been delivered by the French, for whom there was scant praise for their support beforehand, and even less now.

He eventually moved to the Papal protectorate of Avignon in the south of France with a few hundred of his supporters. The British government tried in vain to have him removed from France entirely; there were even fears that his expulsion might put the continued presence of the Irish Brigades in France at risk, although the fears were not realised. In the 1750s he moved residences quite frequently to confuse those in the British establishment who might retain enough resentment to promote his assassination. In 1750 he ventured to England to establish the roots of a new rising, but the plans came to naught. He secretly converted to Protestantism, as any religious foundation that he had left had failed him. By the 1760s even his right to the throne was no longer recognised by the Pope, a major blow when it is considered that most of the bishops nominated by the Papacy had been approved by the Stuarts from 1687 until 1765. Indeed, such a right had legitimised much of the continued efforts towards supporting the Jacobite cause's divine right to the throne, and helped sustain their position. However, the Pope would continue to support the last of the Stuarts financially, perhaps echoing what the rest of Europe already knew; it was clear that all power blocs were fully aware that there would be no Jacobite succession.

Charles had an illegitimate daughter, Charlotte, by his mistress, Clementina Walkinshaw, much to the anathema of his supporters who preferred a royal match and a legitimate heir. He ultimately married Louise of Stolberg-Gerdern in 1772 but, by then, much of his support had gone. The marriage was childless, and bouts of alcoholism meant that it ended within a few years. He had returned to Rome by 1785, a hundred years after his grandfather had ascended to the throne of England, and died in 1788, a century after William's landing in England.

## The End of the Jacobite Cause

Two years after Fontenoy, with the War of the Austrian Succession having been fought for seven long years, and having embroiled much of Europe, the Irish Brigade was reunited with Saxe once more, having been brought across from garrison duty on the French coast. Saxe, with 120,000 men, had foiled Cumberland once again through preventing his taking Antwerp, and pursued him towards Maastricht. He fought his old British adversary at Lafelt, where thousands of cavalry, in fraught efforts to turn a flank, charged and counter-charged each other. Cumberland recalled that the 'Irish troops' were amongst the best that the French sent in on the assault. Indeed, the turning point of the battle was a result of the Irish troops' combined attack with other regiments, forcing an opening in the Allied lines, compelling the army to give way and retreat.

Cumberland had an opportune escape, with the Irish almost taking him prisoner, when he mistook their distinctive red coats for the colours of his own troops. But there were massive casualties on both sides, with the Irish Brigade suffering 1,400 killed or wounded. Clare's battalion, having been in the vanguard, took the brunt of the casualties. Colonel Edward Dillon had been mortally wounded. Fitzjames's Horse had suffered heavily, too, due to the ferocious cavalry melees which had taken place.

Charles O'Brien, 6th Lord Clare, wrote:

> We lost on this occasion Colonel Dillon, 25 officers, 70 wounded and 1,353 private men killed and wounded. We had to do with the English, Hanoverians and Hessian troops. I wish we had been more particularly employed on your Majesty's service and that this may conduce to your restoration, which is the only and hearty prayer of your faithful subjects but of none more than me.[13]

Thousands were buried in mass graves, with colours taken on both sides, although the French win enabled them to take Maastricht the following year.

By 1748 the Treaty of Aix-le-Chapelle brought matters to a close. It was not long, however, until war broke out again. The Seven Years' War was fought between the old allies of Britain, Prussia and Hanover and their opponents, France, Russia, Sweden and Spain. It was not only fought in Europe; its American and Indian battlefields, and resultant victories, helped seal the fortunes of the British Empire in the eighteenth and nineteenth centuries. Irish troops fought on the continent and in the Americas, an Irish battalion made up chiefly from ex-British prisoners even being present on the French side at the British defeat at Fort William Henry in 1757. But a further two years would see little doubt as to who the victors would be. The British were secured in America, at least until the fires of revolution were sparked twenty years later.

The Irish Brigade continued to find *Gloire* through bravery and destruction in battle in continental Europe as it joined the French army during the German campaign against Frederick the Great's Prussia. Despite the defeat of the French army at Rossbach, the Brigade was complimented by Frederick himself.

By 1759 the Irish Brigade had become part of a French plan to break the war's stalemate, via a perhaps all too familiar plan to invade England, as part of a 17,000-strong task force. Marechal Charles O'Brien was to lead an expedition to south-west Ireland, the Prince de Conti, brother to the king, a force to southern England, while the Duc d'Aiguillon would lead a force to Scotland to instigate another rising there. Charles himself was asked to lead, but was in a poor state due to his drunkenness and insistence upon blaming the French for their lack of support in previous years, and his removal from France. He also disagreed with a French proposal regarding the attack, that the descent had to be on England, and that he should retain the crown if successful. He was written off as a liability by the French, and removed from the planning for the expedition. Predictably, the Royal Navy forced plans to be cancelled when the French covering fleet was intercepted in the channel.

However, the famous French privateer Francois Thurot broke the blockade with six ships, and later made a landing with four of them at Carrickfergus Castle near Belfast in 1759, remaining for a number of weeks, before sailing back to France. He was pursued, being killed in a sea fight near the Isle of Man.

With plans for invasion shelved again, the remnants of the brigade were ordered back to the German campaign. They fought at Marborg, Villinghausen, Soest and Unna. The battered Fitzjames's Horse was almost annihilated at Wilhemstahl, where they were surrounded on three sides and over-run.[14] They had fought in every major battle, in every war in which the brigade had served, even being present at Culloden in 1746. O'Callaghan cites English commentators as stating: 'Is it not a great misfortune, that, through a false principle of policy, we suffer so many gallant men to enlist in our enemy's service?'[15]

Despite talk of another descent on England in 1761, the armies were exhausted. Peace was agreed in 1763 in Paris. The Seven Years' War did not decide the end of the brigade in detail, although the nature of wars in Europe and in the Americas would. With the advent of conflict in 1775 we see a dichotomy with which the Irish Brigades would not see a natural fit, at least not within the context of all that had gone before. Besides the fact that hundreds of thousands of American colonists were Scotch-Irish, or Ulster-Scots, and whose story in early America would form an elegant work in itself, and had an inherent dislike of the monetary controls being put in place by a faraway British authority, we also have the dichotomy of thousands of Irishmen, recruited through a disregard for the penal laws which prevented Irish Catholics joining the military, being sent to America as part of the British force that would attempt to nip the conflict in the bud.

The irony of the situation is palpable. Where the descendants of Anglo-Norman and Gaelic-Irish had once fought on opposite sides for Jacobitism and Anglo-Dutch forces, they now fought for the British army. Where Scots and English plantation settlers had railed against the rebellions of the old-English and native Irish, ultimately seeking English aid, they now fought for independence in the new world, alongside other Irish settlers with the same foundation of having always 'governed ourselves'. Jacobitism was forgotten in the tumult of a 'world turned upside down'.

Over 300,000 had emigrated from Ireland in the period, with most being Scots-Irish Presbyterians, such that at least one in four Continental musketmen were of Irish descent and formed the backbone of Washington's army.

This time, of course, French support would be significant. There was a greater prize at stake, America being of more consequence in terms of trade and exploitation than Ireland could ever have been in terms of its being a diversionary effort. After the short Saratoga campaign in 1777, where a British force under Burgoyne was forced into surrender, the French were reminded of the myth of British invincibility and, at least in this war, it would be worth sending troops in force rather than utilising the clandestine support that had been in place up to that point. A large naval effort, almost 50,000 troops and 100,000 firearms was supplied, a level of support the Jacobite cause might once have hoped for, and which would then have tipped the balance, but yet had never been.

What was left of the brigade was still quite functional, and was led by the descendants of those Irish who had left their homeland almost ninety years previously, although in officer positions mainly, as the rank and file of the battalions were now composed of foreign troops. Dillon's, Walsh's and Berwick's Regiments served in the Americas, with Arthur Dillon, the younger, grandson of Arthur Dillon from the first incarnation of the Brigade, stating that they 'always demanded the privilege of going first into battle against the English, everywhere the French were at war with them'. With the war going against the British by 1778, there was even talk of another invasion, this time of Ireland. But many Catholic landowners, who had become de facto members of the establishment by operating around the rigours of English penal laws, had little appetite for rebellion, and even less inclination to risk losing what gains they had made in spite of the post-Jacobite era.

Several factors were key during this period, at least in terms of the continuance of the brigade or, more succinctly, whether it actually still existed outside of an integrated formation within the French establishment. Firstly, the Irish were sent to the Americas and Africa, rather than assembled for a renewed invasion anywhere in the British Isles. Secondly, the Irish had been away from their home for so long that the descendants of the exiles knew only of a romanticised country, and must have believed many tales and legends which the Catholic gentry who remained knew as patent untruths, despite their continued leanings toward 'what might have been'. Finally, the

Irish Brigade had lost that identity when the wind had been removed from the sails of the Jacobite cause. Integration with the French establishment, for many in the brigade, especially those foreign troops who had never, and would never, set foot in Ireland, became of more importance. Of course, not every Irish officer felt the same but, as the decades passed, the onus was on continued service within the French army. Officers from Dillon's Regiment were present at the Siege of Yorktown in 1781, and Irish troops were present with other French regiments, although their presence as *emigrés* was in sharp contrast to the thousands of their ancestors who, although dispersed, had fought at Blenheim, Oudenarde and Fontenoy. In the wake of Louis XIV's perceived threat to Europe, wars had become different animals, and the failure of the Jacobite cause had simply left the Irish cut off from influencing the politics of the European stage.

The war in the Americas, combined with poorly thought out plans and expansionism in India, had almost bankrupted the French state once more. Poverty was a growing concern, as was discontent amongst the middle-class businessmen and the military, and the divine right of kings that had held the state, 'in check' or otherwise, together for so long was being questioned to the point of revolution. The British establishment of a hundred years before would have sat back and nodded appropriately, claiming that its warnings regarding French absolutism had at last spawned fruit, but even the British government was concerned that similar revolutionary leanings might find their way across the Channel to their own shores. Exposure to dangerous revolutionary fervour in the Americas, the fact that it had won the day, and the societal impetus within martial and government 'unofficial' circles meant that change was in the air.

In Paris, calls for disbandment of foreign regiments were made. The Irish would argue vehemently that they were far from foreign, as events of the past hundred years made plain. But it was too late, and the remnants of the brigade became regiments of the French army. The more aristocratic characters of the brigade did not go untouched as Count Theobald Dillon was attacked by the mob in 1792 for having, in their eyes at least, conspired with the Austrians and tried to lead French cavalry into a trap. He was shot and bayoneted as a 'foreign' officer, although he was later exonerated and his murderers were executed. The Irish in France could not evade the terror of the revolution and the guillotine. For the most part they were considered foreigners since their homeland was still part of the British Isles. The irony of Irish officers facing the guillotine, when the events of Mountcashel's service one hundred years before are considered, is palpable.

Despite the service of Napoleon's Irish Legion in the subsequent Napoleonic Wars, the Brigade, at least in terms of its incarnation and direct descendants, was finished, and it is pertinent for their story to end where it did, rather than dilute its honour with re-establishment under foreign kings and thinning of its original intent.

The Wild Geese in foreign service, as we see them in this context, started with the Hamiltons, became a forced issue under Mountcashel, were enhanced by Sarsfield after the second Siege of Limerick, and saw their way through Louis XIV's European wars, during a period when the Jacobite succession was a very real threat, and their support of it, albeit with the agenda of returning to their homeland under a Catholic king rather than putting James back on the throne, was seen as reason enough to make ready for a descent upon England, although it would never come.

The Irish had fought in most of the major battles since their arrival in France, including Italian and Spanish campaigns with Mountcashel, and the long indecisive battles of the Nine Years' War, in which Sarsfield was killed and Mountcashel died from his wounds. The troops had fought in the War of Spanish Succession, sharing the agony at Blenheim and Ramillies, Oudenarde and Malplaquet, and a myriad smaller battles where it seemed that French invincibility had been lost forever. Yet there had been success at Barcelona, Cremona, Fontenoy and Cassano. Their Spanish counterparts had seen success with the military maturity, if not genius, of Berwick at Almanza and Barcelona.

The Hamiltons, with whom much of our story started, would play their part in terms of guidance at Saint Germain, although their day had passed by the time Irish troops were leaving Limerick. To say that much of Ireland was to be found on the continent has a ring of truth to it. Even the attempts of James's children and grandchildren to take back the throne were well supported by the Irish in exile.

Catholic families provided service to the brigade and resided in France for a century or more. Soldiers who had fought at Newtownbutler, at the Boyne and died at Aughrim would send sons and families into exile. The Dillons were one such family, whose sons saw service throughout the period of Louis XIV's ambition and beyond. They supported James in Ireland, thereby losing their lands in Roscommon and Meath. Arthur Dillon's wife was a maid of honour to James's second wife, Mary of Modena. Dillons were killed at Fontenoy leading the charge; Louis XV said of Richard Dillon that he was an officer 'whom I esteemed and loved'. General Arthur Dillon would still remember the *raison d'etre* of the brigade as late as 1792 when others sought promotion within the French establishment instead. He said that he hoped that 'the time was near when he would give his sword to the service of his own land'.[16] When Louis XV stated that, of all his troops, the Irish gave him most trouble, Dillon responded, 'the enemy make the same complaint, your Majesty'.

Even by the time of involvement of the French in the American Revolution, and when brother faced brother in the crucible of a revolutionary war, Dillons fought under French colours, with seven members of the family fighting for French units outside the brigade. Theirs was a special role within the group of exiles and Marmaduke Coghill stated that 'nobody has been more firmly attached to the pretender's interest than the family of Dillon'.

A descent upon England, despite the hopes of James and his descendants would have been difficult if not impossible as events proved. Ireland, even from the time of Elizabeth I, had been seen as the true way to an invasion of Britain. This very fact had left Ireland open to political and military decision-making, both questionable and strategic, over centuries, those decisions being made by countries outside it. Even returning to the start of our tale, James I's main thrust in instigating the plantation policy was due to security, both to enable a policy whereby 'troublesome' locals, natives and potential insurrection could be removed from the picture.

It was the start of a relationship between the Stuarts and the Irish which would swing sharply, yet never find a balance. Ultimately, and ironically, the Stuarts would represent the best chance that the Catholic Irish might once more find their lands. But if the Irish were pawns, whilst striving to manipulate the Stuarts, the Stuarts themselves were pawns of the French court in a European strategy designed to unseat English policy and divert military resources from where they were most needed. It was the presence of a deposed king and his pretenders, with the backing and enforcement of an Irish Brigade in waiting, ever ready to cross the Channel and support the Jacobite English throne in pursuit of their own 'divine right', that would encourage the new Protestant ascendency in Ireland to cling to the rigours of Penal Laws, and encourage subsequent British policy in Ireland, which would ultimately doom the country to disaster, mismanagement and a loss of national and cross-cultural identity, promoting internal conflict which remains to this day.

Had James died at the Boyne, had Saint Ruth not been killed at Aughrim, would an accommodation between Catholic and Protestant have been arrived at all the sooner? It is tempting, however futile, to play with history. What is certain is that, had the strong military figures in exile been strong political figures at home, an accommodation would undoubtedly have been reached and, without the threat of a Stuart dynasty in waiting supported by a brigade of supposedly vengeful exiles, Irish Penal Laws might have been something of a different nature.

In the event, matters on the national stage and France's inept strategic vision of Ireland and the potential Achilles heel that existed in the British Isles helped to inadvertently forge an empire and, more poignantly, ensured that the Wild Geese would never find their way home.

## The Descendants of the Wild Geese

That is not to say that the Irish and their descendants disappeared from the grand stage of history. On the contrary, despite the fact that the Irish had striven to use the doomed Stuarts just as much as they in turn had tried to use the Irish, both in a manner through which each might achieve their own ends, there was much to herald an Irish awakening on the continent. It is poignant to wonder what might have happened had the MacCarthys, Dillons, O'Briens, Sarsfields and Lallys remained in Ireland, yet, as we have debated, their very presence away from the country reinforced what ultimately would happen in a British Empire poised to be the dominant sea power, and thus trading power, in the world.

Putting this to one side, we must consider the successes of the Irish in Europe. Irishmen would hold office in the courts of Austria and Spain, as well as gaining notoriety in France. Irish wives would be ladies in waiting to Marie Antoinette; Therese-Lucy Dillon, wife of General Arthur Dillon who would see the guillotine, was a great favourite. Of the Irish men, many would see success in the fledgling countries finding their way in South America. William Brown would forge the Argentinian Navy, while Thomas Wright would found that of Ecuador. Alexander O'Reilly from Meath would be the governor of Havana. Napoleon's doctors on St Helena would both be of Irish descent.

In Bordeaux McCarthys, Lynches and Joyces would establish vineyards of distinguished and long repute. Hennessy Cognac comes from the distillery established by Richard Hennessy, from County Cork, who fought with the Wild Geese in 1748, following his forefathers. Irish merchants flourished in Nantes, Cadiz, Ostende and Dunkirk, making their mark and plying their trade in the wake of the boom brought about through the trading focus of the British Empire.

The Irish could count amongst their number in Europe marshals, field marshals, counts, barons, knights and holders of the Spanish Order of the Golden Fleece. In Austria there were over a hundred Irish senior officers or admirals. Marshal Henri Clarke rode beside Napoleon at Waterloo, and the list goes on; even Charles de Gaulle himself could claim a noble lineage stemming from the McCartan clan in County Down in what is today Northern Ireland.

To call such triumphs, and these are scant examples, a legacy berates the scale of the feat. That the Irish Brigade has left a mark, a lasting story in France and across European history is a more applicable legacy, especially since they could so easily have been forgotten.

I recently had occasion to travel in France on business. My French is far from perfect, although passable so long as I don't have to keep up with a naturalised French person in idle conversation. I had remarked to some business colleagues that I was working on this book, believing, innocently, that very few would have heard of the Wild Geese, and even fewer would have been able to understand the importance of their role. How wrong I was.

*Les Oies Sauvages* are remembered in France to this day, and I even generated some excitement that I was not only aware of them, but had been carrying out some related research. I was reminded that not only was Hennessey cognac connected, via Richard Hennessey, but that one of the few remaining seats of the MacCarthy-Reagh Clan was but thirty miles north of the airport where I was picked up. *Les Oies Sauvages* are alive, well and prospering in the very heart of the land where their exile has become tenure.

I make this point to stress that the French have forgotten neither the heritage or lasting impact of the Irish exiles. To this end, neither should we. But what do I mean by 'we' in this quasi-European, early post-Brexit communion in which we live. Amongst the Irish, the story has confirmed one undeniable fact: that, despite the intervening years of violence and conflict in the twentieth century, the Irish themselves, north and south, Protestant and Catholic, are a polyglot Gaelic, Anglo-Norman, Huguenot, Scots, English 'race' who are united more than they are divided, by a shared history, the lessons of which should hold them together rather than split them apart. This is simply by virtue of the fact that the split is neither clean nor clinical, thanks to the melting pot of regional *assemblage*, as the French might refer to their southern *Armagnac*.

Our story has related a tale of disunity, power-grabbing and religious factional dispute across the British Isles. If anything can be learned from it, it is that we are closer than we realise, in terms of a national identity, as well as in terms of an English and Irish one. That the Irish Brigades were denied theirs is a tragedy set within the context of a wider a-historical sea change; that we still struggle to find our own identity, both in an Irish and a wider context, is, perhaps, the greater misfortune.

# Endnotes

## Chapter 1: The Irish Diaspora

1   The title of an excellent work which actually outlines the Dutch, with English backing, invasion of England in 1688, when James lost his crown to William III, who had much to gain and everything to lose, were his father in law to keep the crown. The term 'descent' is used throughout the period to describe an invasion, landing or military intervention in another country.

## Chapter 2: The Plantation of Ulster

1   M. Perceval-Maxwell, *The Scottish Migration to Ulster in the reign of James I*, pp.1-10.
2   Cyril Falls, *The Birth of Ulster*, pp.1-5; Nicholas Canny, *From Reformation to Restoration: Ireland 1534-1660*, pp.143-4.
3   Falls, pp.1-5.
4   *Calendar State Papers Ireland 1606–08*, pp.287-8.
5   P.S. Robinson, *The Plantation of Ulster, British Settlement in an Irish Landscape, 1600-1670*, pp.37-42.
6   For refs on plantation as a whole see; M. Perceval-Maxwell, *The Scottish Migration to Ulster in the Reign of James I*, P.S. Robinson, *The Plantation of Ulster, British Settlement in an Irish Landscape, 1600-1670*, Rev. George Hill, *An Historical Account of the Plantation in Ulster at the Commencement of the Seventeenth Century, 1608-1620*.
7   Maxwell pp.252-3
8   *Calendar of the Carew manuscripts 1603-24*, pp.232-3.
9   Rev. George Hill, *Plantation Papers, containing a summary sketch of The Great Ulster Plantation in the year 1610*, p.60.
10  Hill, *Historical Account*, pp.288-92; Maxwell pp.98-9, 107.
11  *Denmilne Manuscripts III No 45*.
12  Hill, *Plantation Papers*, p.54-7.
13  Maxwell p.104.
14  Maxwell pp.344,346; Hill, *Papers*, pp.60-3, 64.
15  Maxwell pp.333,345; Hill, *Papers*, p.64.

16    Maxwell pp.344-5.

17    *Letters and State Papers of the Reign of James VI*, p.239.

18    Hill, *Papers* pp.58-9.

19    Maxwell pp.88, 119,123, 147, 236, 247; also see *Calendar State Papers Domestic 1611-18*, p.113.

20    Hill *Papers* pp.59-60.

21    *Calendar State Papers Ireland 1611-14*, p.321.

22    Carew Survey Manuscripts – 630, ff102-103, f100; *Calendar State Papers Carew 1603-1624*, p.77; Hill, *Papers* pp.57-8.

23    *Ulster Plantation Papers – Analecta Hibernica VIII*, p.252.

24    *Carew Survey Manuscripts* – 630, ff102-103, f100; *Calendar State Papers Carew 1603-1624*, p.77; Hill *Papers* p.58

25    *Registers of the Privy Council of Scotland*, Vol. X, p.263.

26    Maxwell p.325.

27    Maxwell p.326.

28    Archdall Lodge, *Peerage of Ireland*, Vol. V, pp 110-11.

29    *Registers of the Privy Council of Scotland*, Vols. I-IV; *Complete Peerage*, Vol. I, p.3.

30    Maxwell p.272; *CSPI 1611-14*, p.483

31    *CSPI 1625-32*, pp.512-13.

32    *CSPI 1611-1614*, p.483; *CSPI 1625-1632*, pp.499, 509-13; *CSPI 1625-1660*, Addenda p.173.

33    Archdall Lodge, *Peerage of Ireland*, Vol. V, p.117.

34    Ed. Doubleday and De Walden, *The Complete Peerage or a History of the House of Lords and all its Members from the earliest times*, Vol. VI, p.280; Archdall Lodge, Vol. V p.117; Carte, *Life of Ormonde*, I, pp.209-10; Crawfurd, *History of the Shire of Renfrew*, p.288; *Historical Manuscripts Commission*, 5th Report, Appendix, p.352.

35    *Historical Manuscripts Commission, Calendar of the Manuscripts of the Marquess of Ormonde*, New Series, Volume I, p.43.

## Chapter 3: Rebellion 1641-1651

1    R.Gillespie, *Colonial Ulster: the settlement of east Ulster 1600-1641*, (Cork 1985); Eds C.Brady and R.Gillespie, *Native and Newcomers: the making of Irish colonial society 1534-1641*, pp.191-214.

2    See Kenyon and Ohlmeyer's *The Civil Wars: A Military History of England Ireland and Scotland*, an excellent introduction to this period.

3    Carte T., *History of the Life of James, Duke of Ormond*, Vol. I, p.270.

4    Mary Hickson, *Ireland in the Seventeenth Century*, Vol. I, p.332; Archdall Lodge Vol.V, p.114.

5    Carte Vol.I pp.571, 601, Vol. II, pp.23,38, Vol. III, pp.178-9, 214.

6    *Calendar of the Manuscripts of the Marquess of Ormonde*, New Series, Vol. I, pp.57-8.

7    Carte Vol.I, p.584.

8    Based on Anthony's Acte d'inhumation – from 22 April 1719, where he is recorded as being aged seventy-four.

9    Ormonde Vol.I, p.126.

10   Ibid., p.133.

11   Ibid., p.134.

12   Ibid., pp.146, 161, 162-3.

13   Ibid., p.146.

14   *32nd Report of the Deputy-Keeper of the Public Records*, Appendix I, p.85.

15   This section is based on a number of different sources although the following are best placed: Ed. John Kenyon & Jane Ohlmeyer, *The Civil Wars: A Military History of England, Scotland and Ireland 1638-1660*; Kenyon, *The Civil Wars of England*, *The Stuarts: A Study in English Kingship*, and *The Stuart Constitution*; Sir Charles Petrie, *The Stuarts;* Barry Coward, *The Stuart Age, A History of England 1603-1714*, Ed. Brian MacCuarta, *Ulster 1641, Aspects of the Rising*, Ed. J. Ohlmeyer, *Ireland From Independence to Occupation 1641–1660*, Padraig Lenihan, *Confederate Catholics at War, 1641-49*.

16   Ormonde op. cit., p.187.

17   Ibid., p.195.

18   Ibid., pp.195-6.

19   In the case of Muskerry, Ormonde would strive to find him foreign service when all else failed and saw his troops as 'those I build upon' – see Ormonde Vol.,I pp.210, 221.

20   Ormonde, op. cit., p.201.

21   Ibidl., p.197.

22   See Ed. C.H.Firth, *The Memoirs of Edmund Ludlow, Lieutenant General of the Horse in the Army of the Commonwealth of England 1625-1672*, Vol. I, pp.320-1, 525; P.Beresford Ellis, *Hell or Connaught!, The Cromwellian Colonisation of Ireland 1652-1660*, pp.40-3.

23   *Calendar State Papers Domestic 1660-61*, p.413; Ormonde, Vol.I, pp.57-8.

24   *CSPD 1660-61*, p.413.

25   Ormonde op. cit., pp.161-2, 201.

26   Ibid., pp.299, 304, 311.

## Chapter 4: The Gendarmes Anglais

1  Firth, *Ludlow*, Vol. I, p.341; Hickson Vol. II, pp.192–204, 235; *Complete Peerage* Vol. III, p.215.

2  Carte II, pp.121,138.

3  Ormonde op. cit., p.202.

4  *Calendar State Papers Domestic* 1660–61, p.413.

5  Ormonde op. cit., p.259.

6  *Life of Edward, Earl of Clarendon*, Vol. III, pp.34, 60.

7  Ormonde op. cit., p.301.

8  Amongst her children later with Lord Clandricarde were Ulick Burke, 1st Viscount Galway, who died at the Battle of Aughrim in 1691, and Lady Honora Burke. Honora would marry twice, to Patrick Sarsfield and James FitzJames, Duke of Berwick, a son of James II.

9  Saint Beuve, *Port Royal*, Vol. II, p.167, Vol. V. p.184.

10  M. O'Conor, *Military History of the Irish Nation Comprising a Memoir of the Irish Brigade in the Service of France*, pp.69–70

11  Ibid., pp.70–3; Trans A. Lytton Sells, *The Memoirs of James II, His Campaigns as Duke of York, 1652–1660*, pp.1–8, Marquis de Quincy, *Histoire Militaire du Régne de Louis le Grand*, Vol. I, p.183.

12  Ormonde op. cit., p.302.

13  *Nicholas Papers* Vol. II, p.183, *Calendar Clarendon State Papers*, Vol. II, pp.306, 309,310,314, 378, 457.

14  Ibid., Vol.II, pp.116,129,138,140, 183, 195.

15  Ed. G. Goodwin, Count Anthony Hamilton's *Memoirs of Count Grammont*, Vol. I, p.138; Carte Vol.II, p.180; *Manuscripts of the Marquis of Bath*, Vol.II, p.123.

16  O'Conor, op. cit., pp.76–9.

17  Ibid., pp.80–6.

18  *Calendar State Papers Ireland 1660–62*, pp.246, 431–2; Archdall Lodge, *Peerage of Ireland* Vol. V, p.118.

19  *CSPI Addenda*, 1660–1670, p.671; Ed Jaeglé, *Madame, Duchesse d'Orléans, Correspondance*, Vol. II, p.105.

20  *CSPD 1664–5*, p.455.

21  Gramont, Vol. I, p.94.

22  Cunningham, *The Story of Nell Gwyn*, p.207.

23  *CSPD 1664–65*, p.49.

24  *CSPD 1660–61*, pp.270, 368.

25  *Calendar State Papers Colonial America and West Indies 1661–68*, p.493.

26    Ed. G.A. Ellis, *Ellis Correspondence*, Vol. I, p.79; HMC 12th Report Appendix VII, p.56; HMC 15th Report, Appendix – Part II, p.12; *State Papers Foreign, France*, 130, ff.15,16; *CSPD 1670*, pp.391, 421, 455; see also Affaires Etrangères, *Mémoires et Documents Angleterre*, Vol. 26.

27    Ed. H.B. Wheatley, *Pepys Diary*, Vol. IV, pp.49–50.

28    HMC, *Manuscripts of the Duke of Buccleuch at Montague*, Vol. I, pp.421, 424, 426.

29    Affaires Etrangères, *Mémoires et Documents Angleterre*, Vol. 29, p.234.

30    Ormonde, Vol.III, pp.138-9.

31    Cunningham, *Story of Nell Gwynn*, p.206

32    Carte Papers CCXIV 192, HMC, *Buccleuch*, Vol. I, p.527.

33    Gramont general ref Vol. I, pp.20-80.

34    Affaires Etrangères, *Mémoires et Documents Angleterre*, Vol. 79, pp.214-15.

35    Gramont Vol. I, p.98

36    Ed. J.J. Cartwright, *Memoirs of Sir John Reresby*, pp. 43, 45-7, 50.

37    Archives du Ministère des Affaires Etrangeres, *Correspondance Politique*, Angleterre, No.79, p.215.

38    HMC Reports Vol. VIII, p.65.

39    Affaires Etrangères, *Mémoires et Documents Angleterre*, Vol. 26, No.7

40    Archives du Ministère des Affaires Etrangeres, *Correspondance Politique*, Angleterre, Vol. 80, No.73; Jusserand, *A French Ambassador at the Court of Charles II*, pp.94-5.

41    See Elizabeth Hamilton entry in *Dictionary of National Biography*, also – Affaires Etrangères, *Mémoires et Documents Angleterre*, Vol. 26, No.7; Archives du Ministère des Affaires Etrangeres, *Correspondance Politique*, Angleterre, Vol. 80, No.73.

42    Archives du Ministère des Affaires Etrangeres, *Correspondance Politique*, Angleterre, Vol. 80, No.132, 147; Pepys, Vol. X, p.298.

43    *CSPD 1663-64*, p.438.

44    Pepys Vol. X p.300; *State Papers Foreign, France*, Vol. 132, No.14. The boy would unfortunately die in September 1671. Two daughters would follow, Claude Charlotte and Marie Elizabeth.

45    *CSPD 1664-65*, p.37.

46    Affaires Etrangères, *Mémoires et Documents Angleterre*, Vol. 26, No.23.

47    Cartwright, *Madame*, p.218

48    *State Papers Foreign, France*, Vol. 135, No. 60, Vol. 136, No.124.

49    Ibid., Vol. 136, No.101.

50    Excellent modern works related to both Marlborough's military exploits and his wife are available, see: Ophelia Field, *The Favourite: Sarah, Duchess of Marlborough*.

51    Dalton, *English Army Lists and Commission Registers 1661-1714, Vol. I, 1661-1685*, p.89

52    MacPherson, *Original Papers*, (London 1775), Vol. I, p.32; Carte, Vol. V, p.181; *CSPD 1664-5*, p.407

53    *CSPD 1667*, pp.206-7

54    Ibid., pp.220, 231, 251

55    *CSPD 1667-68*, pp.28,54,82,110; Earl of Arlington, *Letters to Sir William Bennet*, Vol. I, p.185

56    Arlington letters, pp.185-6

57    As an aside, consider that the phrase '*pour la Gloire*' is still used in France today, though it is an ageing expression. I have been told that if someone does something not for money, not for notoriety, but 'for the glory', it is as if they are charging forward across a metaphorical battlefield in the sure sense that the only thing at stake is a sense of personal achievement and courage, which all men must recognise and applaud. Perhaps our closest equivalents are a 'labour of love' or at the worst extreme 'to hell with it!' Set this in context with the young, impetuous and sexually charged Louis, and we begin to understand how '*la Gloire*' might trump all other considerations at the time.

58    Ibid.

59    *State Papers Foreign, France*, Vol. 123, No.199; Michel, *Les Français en Ecosse et Les Ecossais en France*, Vol. II, pp.305-18.

60    Archives du Ministère des Affaires Etrangeres, *Correspondance Politique*, Angleterre, Vol. 89, p.265; Ruvigny to Louis XIV 1667

61    Archives du Ministère des Affaires Etrangeres, *Correspondance Politique*, Angleterre, Vol. 89, pp.343-5 Ruvigny to Louis Oct 1667; Vol. 89, pp.285-6 Ruvigny to Louis Sept/Oct 1667

62    Archives du Ministère des Affaires Etrangeres, *Correspondance Politique*, Angleterre, Vol. 89, p.358, Ruvigny to Louis Oct 1667

63    Archives du Ministère de la Guerre, Vol. 245, No. 241 George Hamilton to Louvois Nov 1667

64    Archives du Ministère de la Guerre, Vol. 245, No. 241 GH to Louvois Nov 1667; Vol. 207, No. 316 Louvois to Hamilton Dec 1667

65    *CSPD 1667-68*, p207; Archives du Ministère de la Guerre, Vol. 202, No.178 Louvois to Hamilton and Louvois to Ruvigny Jan 1668

66    *CSPD 1667-68*, p.167

67    *Diary of John* Evelyn, Vol. II, p.387

68    Certainly later events with regard to his returning to Ireland on a 'recruitment drive' would bear this out; if he did not accompany George at this time, he soon joined the company.

69    Fieffé, *Troupes étrangères au service de la France*, Vol. I, pp.33-5, 169, 175-6
70    Fieffé, Vol. I, p.173
71    Daniel, *Histoire de la Milice Françoise*, Vol. II, pp.247-8
72    Daniel, II, p.257
73    *State Papers Foreign, France*, Vol. 124, No. 48; *CSPD 1667-68*, p.277
74    *State Papers Foreign, France*, Vol. 126, No. 23
75    Archives du Ministère de la Guerre, Vol. 231, No. 129 Louvois to Hamilton Feb 1669 and Hamilton to Louvois 4 Oct 1669
76    HMC *Buccleuch Manuscripts*, Vol. I, p.459; *State Papers Foreign, France*, 138 f 32, 25 Aug 1673
77    *State Papers Foreign, France*, Vol. 129, Nos. 189, 240
78    *CSPD 1670*, pp.296, 391, 421, 455; Magalotti, *Travels of Cosmo the Third, Grand Duke of Tuscany*, p.195; HMC 15th Report Appendix Pt II, p.12; *State Papers Foreign, France*, Vol. 130, Nos. 15, 16
79    Ibid.; Cartwright *Madame*, p.382
80    Archives du Ministère des Affaires Etrangeres, *Correspondance Politique*, Angleterre, Vol. 99, Nos. 231, 245, 220

## Chapter 5: The Irish at War 1671-1685

1    Affaires Etrangères, *Mémoires et Documents Angleterre*, Vol. 99, Nos.310, 332
2    Mignet, *Négociations Relatives à la Succession d'Espagne*, Vol. III, pp.192-3, 198, 259, 264-5, 653
3    *CSPD 1671*, pp.311-12
4    Ibid., p.468
5    Ibid., pp.311-12
6    Ibid., p.256
7    Ibid., p.468
8    *State Papers Foreign, France*, Vol. 131, No 192; Arlington Letters, Vol. II, pp.332-3
9    Bibliothèque Nationale, Cabinet des Titres, Vol. 345, Hamilton 8904 file 39
10    HMC, *Perwich Papers*, p.220
11    Pinard, *Chronologie Historique Militaire*, Vol. VI, p.429
12    *State Papers Foreign, France*, Vol. 134, No. 93
13    J.A. Lynn, *The Wars of Louis XIV 1667-1714*, pp.117-18
14    Archives du Ministère de la Guerre, Vol. 269, p.121 Louvois to Montefranc, Nov 1672
15    Ibid., pp.235, 297, 299, Oct 1672
16    Ibid., Vol. 303, p.94 Louvois to Gaffard, April 1673
17    Ibid., Vol. 333, No.1, 20 March 1673

18   Ibid., Vol. 333, No. 266, GH to Louvois 1673; Vol. 294, No. 387 Gaffard to Louvois, Sept 1672; Vol. 269, p.158, Louvois to Gustavus Hamilton, Nov 1672; Vol. 303, p.104, Louvois to George Hamilton, Apr 1673

19   *State Papers Foreign, France*, Vol. 134, No.181, Godolphin to Arlington, Aug 1672; and No.190, Perwich to Williamson, Aug 1672

20   O'Conor, pp.87-8; Boulger, *The Battle of the Boyne*, pp. 67-8; O'Callaghan, *History of the Irish Brigades in the Service of France*, p.33; Dalton, *English Army Lists and Commission Registers 1661-1714*, Vol. I, p.88

21   Ed Grimoard, *Turenne, Letters et Mémoires*, Vol. II, p.282

22   *State Papers Foreign, France*, Vol. 137, No.127, GH to Williamson, June 1673

23   Earle Edward, *Makers of Modern Strategy*; J.C.R. Childs, *Warfare in the Seventeenth Century*, pp.172-3

24   Childs, *The Nine Years' War and the British Army 1688-1697: The Operations in the Low Countries*, pp.73-6; Lynn, *Giant of the Grand Siécle: The French Army, 1610-1715*, pp.453-7

25   Lynn, *Giant*, pp.457-61; Chandler, *The Art of Warfare in the Age of Marlborough*, pp.76-7

26   Ibid., p.464; Childs, *Nine Years War*, pp.73-80

27   Lynn, *Giant*, pp.464-71, 486

28   Ibid., pp.462-3, 486

29   Ibid., p.483; Childs, *Nine Years' War*, pp.73-4, 79-80; Nosworthy, *The Anatomy of Victory – Battle Tactics 1689-1763*, pp. 15-17; Lynn, *Giant*, pp. 469-72, 476

30   Lynn, *Giant*, pp. 480-4.

31   Childs, *Nine Years' War*, p. 85; Chandler, *The Art of Warfare in the Age of Marlborough*, pp. 50, 177-80; Lynn, *Giant*, pp.506-11,532-7; Nosworthy, pp.100-13

32   Childs, *Nine Years War*, p.272; Lynn, *Giant*, p.121

33   Ibid, p.122.

34   MacPherson, *Original Papers*, Vol. I, p.32; Ormonde, Vol. V, p.181

35   *CSPD 1672*, pp.74,156; *CSPD 1673*, pp.182, 279, 280

36   *CSPD 1673*, p.570

37   Ormonde, Vol. III, p.452

38   *State Papers Foreign, France*, Vol. 137 No. 210, Vol. 138 No. 32

39   *Calendar of Treasury Books 1672-75*, p.163; of the three sons left by George Hamilton James who was later 6th Earl of Abercorn, George – killed in battle at Steenkirk 1692, and William, a captain in an infantry regiment – murdered in Ireland 1686; Ormonde Vol. VII p.439

40   *CSPD 1673-75*, pp.128-134

41   Turenne, *Lettres et Mémoires*, Vol. II, pp.339, 351

42   *State Papers Foreign, France*, Vol. 138 Nos 84,92

43   Sir John Dalrymple, *Memoirs of Great Britain and Ireland*, Vol. II, p.108

44   Lynn, *Wars*, pp.129-30; Childs, *Warfare in the Seventeenth Century*, pp.173-4; O'Conor pp.87-88; Quincy p.396

45   Childs, *Warfare*, pp.172-3; Lynn, *Wars*, pp.128-9

46   *Gazette de France*, 1674, pp.522, 600, 609, 628, 650

47   Lynn, *Wars*, p.131

48   *CSPD 1673-75*, p.479

49   O'Callaghan, p.33; *Gazette de France*, 1674 pp.1066-1067, 1077, 1088-91, 1095

50   *Gazette de France*, 1674, pp.1088-91, 1095

51   Lynn, *Wars*, pp.131-2; Quincy I, p.396, Childs, *Warfare in the Seventeenth Century*, p.174

52   Childs, Ibid.

53   Turenne, *Lettres et Mémoires*, II p.587; *Gazette de France* 1674; HMC 4th Report p.238, 7th Report Appendix p.492a

54   Lynn, *Wars*, p.132, Childs, *Warfare*, p.174

55   *CSPD 1673-75*, pp.479,484

56   Lynn, *Wars*, pp.134-5; Childs, *op. cit.*, p.176

57   Archives du Ministère des Affaires Etrangeres, *Correspondance Politique*, Angleterre, Vol. 115, p.214

58   Ibid., p.390

59   *CSPD 1673-75*, pp.230, 414

60   *Essex Papers*, pp.304-5; *La Guerre*, Vol. 467 No. 4 GH to Louvois Jan 1675, Vol. 422 No. 220 Louvois to GH Feb 1675; *Stowe Manuscripts* Vol. 204 No. 28, Vol. 207 Nos. 70 and 176 GH to Lord Essex Jan and Feb 1675 – also relate to warrant to raise troops in Ireland for French service 1674.

61   *La Guerre*, Vol. 467, No. 92 AH to Ruvigny Apr 1675

62   Ibid., Vol. 103 Ruvigny to Louvois, Apr 1675; Archives du Ministère des Affaires Etrangeres, *Correspondance Politique*, Angleterre, Vol. 15 p.619 Ruvigny to Pomponne Apr 1675; *CSPD 1675-76*, p.56; *Essex Papers*, p.313

63   O'Callaghan p.34; *Chronologie Militaire*, Vol. VI, p.430

64   St Hilaire, *Mémoires*, Vol. I, pp.207-8; O'Conor, pp.89-91

65   Madame de Sévigné, *Lettres*, Vol. IV, pp.97-8

66   Ramsay, *Histoire de Turenne*, Vol. II, p.583

67   O'Conor, pp.91-94; O'Callaghan pp.34; Lynn *Wars*, pp.141-2; De Quincy p.447

68   Pinard, *Chronologie Militaire*, Vol. VI, p.430
69   De Quincy p.448
70   *La Guerre*, Vol. 427 Nos 179, 286 Louvois to Hamilton Aug 1675
71   Ibid., Vol. 429 No. 130 Oct 1675
72   Archives du Ministère des Affaires Etrangeres, *Correspondance Politique*, Angleterre, Vol. 116 Nos 24-5 Ruvigny to Pomponne 1675
73   *Commons Journal*, Vol. IX, p.330
74   Ibid., p.333; *CSPD 1675-76*, p.125
75   Archives du Ministère des Affaires Etrangeres, *Correspondance Politique*, Angleterre, Vol. 116 No 37, Vol. 117 Nos 76, 81; *Commons Journal*, Vol. IX, pp.362-7)
76   *CSPD 1675-76*, p.491
77   *La Guerre* Vol. 473, No. 59 Louvois to Hamilton Apr 1676; *CSPD 1676-77*, p.71; *Essex Papers*, p.41
78   Pinard, Vol. VI, p.430
79   *Gazette* 1676, pp.433,456; *La Guerre*, Vol. 508 No. 114 Luxembourg to Louis, June 1676
80   Lettres Historiques, Vol. III, p.112
81   *La Guerre*, Vol. 375, No72
82   Archives du Ministère des Affaires Etrangeres, *Correspondance Politique*, Angleterre, Vol. 119, No. 48
83   Evelyn, *Diary*, Vol. II, p.387
84   HMC 4th Report p.245; *La Guerre*, Vol. 567 p.143, Lady Hamilton to Louvois Oct 1677
85   Archives du Ministère des Affaires Etrangeres, *Correspondance Politique*, Angleterre, Vol. 119 No. 48
86   Archives du Ministère des Affaires Etrangeres, *Correspondance Politique*, Angleterre, Vol. 115, pp.453, 454
87   *CSPD 1676-77* p.210; *CSPD 1677-78* pp.236-54
88   Carte, Vol. II, p.161; Sergeant, *Little Jennings and Fighting Dick Talbot*, (London 1913), pp.84-86; Petrie, *The Great Tyrconnel: A Chapter in Anglo-Irish Relations*, pp.83-4
89   *La Guerre* Vol. 567, p.143 Lady Hamilton to Louvois
90   HMC 4th Report p.245
91   Archives du Ministère des Affaires Etrangeres, *Correspondance Politique*, Angleterre, Vol. 118 No. 178 and Vol. 119 No. 48
92   Ormonde, Vol. VII, p.85
93   Dalton, *English Army Lists* Vol. I, p.207
94   *CSPD 1676-7*, pp.410-12; Boulger p.69

95   Archives du Ministère des Affaires Etrangeres, *Correspondance Politique,* Angleterre, Vol. 120 Nos 74, 75

96   Archives du Ministère des Affaires Etrangeres, *Correspondance Politique,* Angleterre, Vol. 120 No 85; *La Guerre* Vol. 513 No.114, Dongan to Louvois Oct 1676; *La Guerre* Vol.543 Courtin to Louvois Feb 1677

97   *La Guerre* Vol. 481 No. 41, Vol. 531 Louvois to Hamilton, Dec 1676

98   *Commons Journal,* Vol. IX, pp. 385-7, 400-01, 426; *CSPD 1677-78,* pp.278, 341

99   Lynn, *Wars,* pp.144-159

100  *La Guerre* Vol.534, pp.184, 221, 250, 260,

101  *CSPD 1677-78* p.563, *La Guerre* Vol. 584, p.22 Vol. 585 No. 21

102  *La Guerre* Vol. 534 pp.708-9

103  Ibid., pp.708-9, 671; Vol. 585 No. 58, Vol. 582 No. 223; Vol. 588 pp.49; 118-9; Vol. 582 Nos146, 240, 256; Vol. 588 p.49

104  Ibid., Vol. 534, pp.708-9

105  Ibid., Vol. 534 No.144 Richard Hamilton to Louvois Apr 1678

106  Ibid., Vol. 573 Nos. 88 and 236 Louvois to Hamilton Apr 1678

107  Ibid., Vol. 597 pp.73, Vol. 534 p.738; Vol. 567 p.697, Vol. 587 p.194

108  *Mercure Galant* Jan 1679 p.301

109  Ed. Lalanne, *Bussy Correspondance,* (Paris 1858), Vol. IV, pp.22-4

## Chapter 6: A Return to Ireland

1    S.B. Baxter, *William III,* pp.129-30, 148-50; M. Waller, *Ungrateful Daughters: the Stuart Princesses Who Stole Their Father's Crown,* (2002), pp.27, 64, 93-9

2    For best single treatment see John Kenyon, *The Popish Plot*

3    Ormonde Vol. V, pp.599, 613; Vol. VI, pp.71; Vol. VII, pp.2-3, 12

4    Ibid., Vol. VII, pp.2-3

5    Ibid., p.250

6    Ibid., p.85

7    Dangeau, *Sourches,* Vol. I. pp.188-9, 203; Depping *Correspondance Administrative sous Louis XIV* Vol. II, p.38

8    *Biographia Navalis,* Vol. I, pp.310-12; Ormonde Vol. V, p.326, Vol. VII, p.160

9    Petrie, 35,56,81,96-7,103,120

10   see Luttrell, *Brief Historical Relation of State Affairs*

11   Childs, *The Army, James II, and the Glorious Revolution* (1980), pp.56-62

12   HMC Report on the MSS of the Earl of Egmont Vol. VI, No. 155; Dalton, *English Army Lists and Commission Registers 1685-89,* Vol. II, p.13

13   Ormonde MSS Vol. I, pp.409, 415

14   *Correspondence of Henry Hyde, Earl of Clarendon*, Vol. I, p.218
15   Ibid., p.336
16   *CSPD 1686-7*, pp.195, 576
17   Childs, op. cit., pp.56-62
18   Ormonde Vol. VII, pp.454-5
19   Bagwell, *Ireland Under the Stuarts and During the Interregnum*, Vol. III 1660-1690, pp.149-50
20   Ormonde, Vol. VII, pp.360-3
21   Clarendon, Vol. I, pp.249-50, 255, 343, 360, 400, 479, 491-2, 499-500, 516-18, 537-40, 584-6; Vol. II, pp.32,36,92-4,98-9,103-4, 116, 120-1, 148-9
22   Ibid., Vol. I, p.421
23   Ibid., Vol. I, p.423
24   Ibid., Vol. I, pp.488-9
25   Ibid., Vol. I, p.553
26   Ibid., Vol. II, p.38
27   Ibid., Vol. I, pp.201-2
28   Bagwell, p.149, Ormonde Vol. VIII, p.344
29   See Dalton, Vol. II, p.13 and Chapter IX
30   Clarendon, Vol. I, p.400; D'Alton, *King James' Irish Army List*, Vol. I, p.10
31   Clarendon Vol. I, pp.479, 491-2, 499-500
32   Ibid., p.436
33   Ibid., pp.343, 360, 400
34   HMC, Ormonde MSS Vol. I, p.426
35   Clarendon, Vol. I, pp.248-50, 360
36   Clarendon, Vol. II, pp.34-5, 48, 54, 58, 61-2, 85, 94-101
37   Bishop Cartwright, *Diary*, p.26
38   For best single treatment of this period in the Irish army see Childs, *The Army, James II, and the Glorious Revolution*, pp.65-8, 70-8; also see Clarendon, Vol. I, p.268; Ormonde, Vol. II, pp.378-84; *CSPD July 1686*

## Chapter 7: A Revolution and a King

1   Dalton, Vol. II, p.221
2   Ibid. , pp.13,95
3   Archives du Ministère des Affaires Etrangeres, *Correspondance Politique*, Angleterre, Vol. 165 Nos 382, 383
4   Dalrymple, *Memoirs*, Vol. II, p.185
5   Dangeau Vol. II, p.156
6   Macpherson, *Original Papers*, Vol. I, pp.158-9

7   Dalton, op. cit., p.200

8   Dalrymple, op. cit., p.247

9   For main sources on *Glorious Revolution of 1688*, see: Beddard R., *The Revolutions of 1688 – The Andrew Browning Lectures*, Guy and Smith, *1688, Glorious Revolution, The Fall and Rise of the British Army 1660–1704* Jones J.R.; *The Revolution of 1688 in England*

10  Simms, *Jacobite Ireland 1685-91*, pp.48-51; Ormonde Vol. VIII, p.14

11  Hatton *correspondence*, William King, *The State of the Protestants of Ireland under the late King James Government*, pp.347-52

12  Commons Journals July 1689; Burnet, *History of My Own Time*, Vol. I p.808

13  HMC Report 12 Appendix VI p.141

14  Foxcroft's supplement to Burnet, p.306

15  HMC 14th Report Appendix Part II, p.422

16  HMC 12th Report Appendix Part VI pp.189-90

17  Hatton *Correspondence* Vol. II, pp.132, 133

18  Macaulay, *History of England*, Vol. II, p.330

19  Ed. Hogan, *Négociations de M. Le Comte D'Avaux en Irlande 1689–90*, p.50

20  Clarke, *A Life of James II, Collected Out of Memoirs Writ by his Own Hand*, p.319

21  Ibid.,  p.322

22  Boulger, p.44

23  Tyrconnel to James II, 29 January (o.s.) 1689 with regard to state of the nation. (Recorded in MSS Leeds Papers and Sergeant, Little Jennings, pp.652-5)

24  Simms, op. cit., p.53

25  Ormonde, Vol. VIII, p.359

26  Dangeau Vol. II, pp.324,344

27  Simms, op. cit., pp.58-61

28  Ormonde, op. cit., pp.360-1

29  HMC Montgomery Manuscripts (1895) pp.278-9

30  Ibid.

31  Local tradition is recorded in the nineteenth century notes of Alexander Colvill Walsh who had researched the battle – see Montgomery MSS 1603-1706, Ed Revd George Hill pp.275, 280-1; Mulligan, *A Ramble through Dromore*, 1886

32  D'Avaux, p.91

33  Simms, op. cit., pp.59-60

34  Ibid.

35    Turner, *James II*, p.463

36    *La Guerre* Vol. 963, No 16, May 1689 Pointis to Seigneleay

37    D'Avaux, op. cit., pp.1-6

38    See especially – Powley, *The Naval Side of King William's War – 16/26 November 1688-14 June 1690*

39    D'Avaux, op. cit., pp.85-91

40    Gilbert, *A Jacobite Narrative of the War in Ireland*, pp.46-7; Simms, op. cit., pp.59, 62-3; MacPherson, *Original Papers*, pp.175-6; Bagwell p.206

41    Macpherson, op. cit., pp.175-7; Bagwell, p.207

42    D'Avaux, op. cit., pp.23-4

43    Ibid., pp.49-53, 73, 76

44    MacPherson, op. cit., pp.177-8; Bagwell, op. cit., pp.208-9

45    Ormonde, Vol, VIII, pp.360-1

46    D'Avaux, op. cit., pp.52-58; 85-91

47    Murray, *The Journal of John Stevens, Containing a Brief Account of the War in Ireland, 1689-91*, op. cit., pp.68-70

48    Ibid.

49    For further details see Simms, pp.74-94, Bagwell, pp.224-36; d'Avaux, pp.226, 341-2, 255, 111, 190-2, 89-90

50    Rousset, *Vie de Louvois*, Vol. IV, p.198

51    *La Guerre* Vol. 893 MacCarthy to Louvois, June 1689; Macpherson, pp.319-21

52    *La Guerre* Vol. 896, D'Avaux, pp.298-99, 253-4, 250, 50

## Chapter 8: Justin MacCarthy, Lord Mountcashel

1    For best/older source material, see: J.C. O'Callaghan, *History of the Irish Brigades in the Service of France from the Revolution in Great Britain and Ireland Under James II, to the Revolution in France under Louis XVI*, p.9; also see, Journal of the Cork Historical and Archaeological Society Vol. XIII No.76, *Justin MacCarthy, Lord Mountcashel*, pp.157-62; Dr Sean Pettit, *Blarney Castle, The Story of a Legend*, pp.9-12, Edward Maclysaght, *Irish Families, Their Names, Arms and Origins*, (4th edn), pp.54-5.

2    Firth, *The Memoirs of Edmund Ludlow, Lieutenant General of the Horse in the Army of the Commonwealth of England 1625-1672*, Vol. I, pp. 320-21, 525.

3    Kenyon and Ohlmeyer, *The Civil Wars, A Military History of England, Scotland, and Ireland 1638-1660*, Also see: P.Lenihan, *Confederate Catholics at War, 1641-49*, P. Beresford Ellis, *Hell or Connaught!, The Cromwellian Colonisation of Ireland 1652-1660*, Nunziatra in Irlanda, p.350.

4    Firth, op. cit., p.341.

5    Hickson, *Ireland in the Seventeenth Century*, Vol. II pp.192-204, 235, note on Ormonde's involvement is in Doubleday and De Walden, *The Complete Peerage or a History of the House of Lords and all its Members from the earliest times*, Vol. III, p.215.

6    Firth, op. cit., p.341.

7    *Calendar of Clarendon State Papers* Vol. III, p.210.

8    Smith, *Ancient and Present State of County and City of Cork*, (1749), Vol. II, p.172; Birch, *A Collection of the State Papers of John Thurloe esq (secretary first to the Council of State, and afterwards to the two Protectors, Oliver and Richard Cromwell)*, pp. 94, 406, 693.

9    O'Conor, *Military History*, pp. 76-79.

10   Carte, *Life of James, Duke of Ormond*, Vol. II, p.161; Sergeant; *Little Jennings and Fighting Dick Talbot, A Life of the Duke and Duchess of Tyrconnel*, pp.84-6; Petrie, *The Great Tyrconnel, A Chapter in Anglo-Irish Relations*, pp.83-4.

11   O'Conor, pp.80-6.

12   Macpherson, *Original Papers*, Vol. I, p.32. For excellent modern interpretation of Anglo-Dutch naval wars and battle see Hainsworth and Churches, *The Anglo-Dutch Naval Wars 1652-1674*, pp.103-24; Carte, op. cit., p.181; *Calendar State Papers Domestic 1664-5*, p.407.

13   Carte, op. cit., Vol. V, p.182.

14   *CSPD 1673-75*, p.357, Doubleday and De Walden, op. cit., Vol. III, pp.214-16. *Calendar State Papers Ireland 1667*, pp.388-9; Historical Manuscripts Commission, *Calendar of the Manuscripts of the Marquess of Ormonde K.P. Preserved at Kilkenny Castle, New Series* Vol. III, pp.300-1.

15   O'Conor, op. cit., pp.87-8; Boulger, *The Battle of the Boyne Together with an Account based on French and other Unpublished Records of the War in Ireland (1688-1691) and of the Formation of the Irish Brigade in the Service of France*, pp.67-8; O'Callaghan, *History of the Irish Brigades in the Service of France from the Revolution in Great Britain and Ireland under James II, to the Revolution in France under Louis XVI*, p.33; Dalton, *English Army Lists and Commission Registers, 1661-1714*, Vol. I 1661-1685, p.88.

16   Hogan, *Négociacions de M. le Comte d'Avaux en Irlande, 1689-90*, pp.692-4; Lynn, *The Wars of Louis XIV 1667-1714*, pp.105-6, 113-35, 140-4; O'Conor, pp.87-95; Boulger, pp.67-9; O'Callaghan, pp.33-4.

17   Dalton, op. cit., p.207.

18   *CSPD 1676-7*, p.410.

19   Ibid., pp.411-12; Boulger, p.69.

20   *Historical Manuscripts Commission: Calendar of the MSS of the Marquis of Ormonde*, Vol. IV, p.21.

21    *CSPD 1677-8*, p.504.

22    *CSPD*, 1677-78, p.25.

23    *Complete Peerage*, Vol. III, p.216.

24    *CSPD 1678*, p.444; Dalton, op. cit., p.207; Dalton, *Irish Army Lists of King Charles II 1661-1685*, p.119; Kenyon, *The Popish Plot*, p.117.

25    *CSPD 1678*, p.494, 511-12, 518, 594; *HMC Ormonde* Vol. IV p.469.

26    Historical Manuscripts Commission, *Calendar of the Manuscripts of the Marquess of Ormonde*, New Series Vol. IV, p.261. Also see Earl of Orrery's correspondence with Ormonde on subject, Vol. IV pp.231-6.

27    *CSPD 1679-80*, pp.9,30; Bagwell, op. cit., Vol. III, p.131; HMC Ormonde IV, 230, 236, 238040, 245-6, 261, Vol. V, p.104.

28    Dupuy & Dupuy, *The Collins Encyclopaedia of Military History*, p.621.

29    *CSPD 1682*, p.198.

30    Ibid., pp.325-6, 345-7, 385-6; *1683*; pp.13, 62-4, 98, 116.

31    HMC, *Calendar of the Manuscripts of the Marquess of Ormonde*, New Series Vol. VI, p.498.

32    Ibid., Vol. VI, pp.510-11, 516; *Complete Peerage*, Vol. III, p.216.

33    *CSPD 1684-85*, p.273; Smith, *Ancient and Present State of County and City of Cork*, (1749), Vol. II, p.175.

34    *Complete Peerage*, Vol. 10, p.310.

35    *CSPD 1684-85*, p.287.

36    Burnet, op. cit., Vol. II, pp.449-51; Foxcroft, op. cit., pp.134-5.

37    Kenyon, op. cit., pp.38,305.

38    Bagwell, op. cit., p.149, *Ormonde*, VIII, p.344.

39    *Ormonde*, VII, p.358.

40    Singer, *The Correspondence of Henry Hyde, Earl of Clarendon and Laurence, Earl of Rochester*, Vol. I, pp.215, 219, 227, 229, 247

41    Clarendon I, pp.241, 247, 248

42    Ibid., pp.248-50

43    Ibid., I p.255

44    Ibid., p.343

45    Ibid., p.360

46    Ibid., p.400

47    Ibid p.516-18

48    Ibid. p.584-6, II 1

49    *Clarendon*, Vol. II, pp.14-15

50    Ibid., II 32,36

51    Ibid., II 92-4, 98-9, 103-4, 116.

52   Ibid., II 120-21, 148-9

53   *Ormonde*, Vol. VIII, p.354.

54   *Clarendon* Vol. I, p.584.

55   Bennet, *The History of Bandon*, pp.191, 194-204, Bennet's work is based on local history of the Bandon Insurrection and contains some unique information with regard to the build-up to rebellion in the town. Not all of this can be taken at face value, however. Irish Record Commission Reports p.409 Plate VII, Map of Bandon from the seventeenth century showing town walls and extent of building work and gates; Collins, 'The O'Crowleys of Coill t-Sealbhaigh', appearing in *The Cork Historical and Archeological Journal*, Vol. LVIII, Jan-Jun 1953, p.7; Rowland Davies, *Journal of the Very Reverend Rowland Davies, Dean of Ross, March 8th 1689-Sept 29th* 1690, p.6; O'Donoghue, *Droichead Na Banndan, A History of Bandon*, p.5.

56   Bagwell, Vol. III, p.202; Bennet, p.205.

57   Smith, pp.174-5; O'Callaghan, p.10

58   Bennet, *The History of Bandon*, pp.206-13; For Bandon and surrounding Munster operations of the time see also: Bagwell pp.201-6, O'Callaghan, pp.10-11, Smith, II, pp.192-3, d'Avaux p.138.

59   See note Smith, Vol. II, p.192

60   Bennet, pp.214-15, Simms, p.63, MacPherson, p.178, Bagwell, pp.207-8, *CSPD 1689-90*, p.95, King, *The State of the Protestants of Ireland*, pp.130-1, O'Donoghue, op. cit., p.17. Although the walls were, it appeared, partially destroyed, the job was not completed. At the Cork Assizes in December 1690 it was ordered 'that the inhabitants within four miles of Bandon contribute their labour towards the erecting and securing of the walls of the said town, thrown down by the papists'. This was never completed, however. Boisseleau is also accused of sending £30,000 of Protestant goods to France in notes.

61   MacPherson, pp.177-8, Bagwell, pp.208-9

62   *Archives Nationales, Dépôt de La Guerre*, A1, Vol. 894, No.15, Historical Manuscripts Commission, *Analecta Hibernica*, Vol. XXI, p.27.

63   *La Guerre*, A1, Vol. 895

64   *Analecta Hibernica*, Vol. XXI, p.36.

65   *Complete Peerage*, Vol. X, pp.309-10, Vol. III, pp.216-17.

66   MacPherson, Vol.I, p.176, 190; d'Avaux, p.142; *La Guerre*, Vol. 892, de Rosen to Louvois, 20 May 1689.

67   Rousset, *Histoire de Louvois*, Vol.IV, p.198.

68   D'Avaux p.590.

69   Ibid., p.636.

70    *La Guerre* 892 Mountcashel to Louvois 13 June 1689
71    Ibid., Vol. 893 Mountcashel to Louvois 16 June 1689; also see MacPherson 319-21.
72    Ibid., d'Avaux pp.298-9, 253-4, 250, 50
73    Ibid., Vol. 892, Mountcashel to Louvois 13 June 1689.

## Chapter 9: Patrick Sarsfield, *Deare Notorious*

1    There is a statue of Sarsfield in Limerick today and a bridge and street named after him. Although Mountcashel is mentioned in the writing surrounding the Treaty Stone (moved in the 1990s), he is less well known.
2    Both recent biographies on Sarsfield place his birth date at 1654-55; Wauchope, *Patrick Sarsfield and the Williamite War*; Haddick-Flynn, *Sarsfield and the Jacobites*.
3    *CSPD 1673-75*, p.450, *History of Ireland*; O'Hart, *Irish Pedigrees*, Vol. V, p. 323.
4    *CSPD 1693*, p.483-5.
5    Childs, *Nobles, Gentlemen and the Profession of Arms in Restoration Britain, 1660-1688*, Society for Army Historical Research, No.13, 1987. This work quotes Sarsfield as being a lieutenant in France in 1672, a captain in 1674, then serving under Thomas Dongan in the same year.
6    Lavisse, *Histoire de France*, p.236; Childs, *The Army of Charles II*
7    Wauchope, op. cit., p.16.
8    Dalton, *English Army Lists & Commission Registers*, Vol.I, 1661-1685, pp.206, 209.
9    HMC, *Ormonde*, Vol. V.
10    Luttrell, *A Brief Historical Relation of Affairs*, p.136.
11    *CSPD, Treasury Books*, Vol. VII, p.348; For a general treatment, see also, Childs, *General Percy Kirke and the Later Stuart Army*, pp.31-47.
12    Luttrell, op. cit. , p.160.
13    Ibid., p.150.
14    *CSPD May 1682*.
15    HMC, App *Seventh Report; CSP Treasury Books; London Mercury*, June 1682.
16    *CSPD July 1683*, Luttrell, op. cit., p.210.
17    *CSPD August 1683*.
18    Luttrell, op. cit., p.304.
19    Historical Manuscripts Commision, Stopford-Sackville, p.21.
20    See Childs, 'Nobles, Gentlemen and the Profession of Arms in Restoration Britain, 1660-1688', *Journal of the Society for Army Research*, 1987, p.105; See also Childs' seminal piece on Percy Kirke's life where the ravages of historical

debate are given a more unbiased treatment: *General Percy Kirke and the Later Stuart Army*.

21    Ibid., p.81.

22    Ibid., Dalton, *Army Lists and Commission Registers, 1661-1714*

23    For best recent single treatment of the Huguenots during the period see Matthew Glozier, *The Huguenot Soldiers of William of Orange and the Glorious Revolution of 1688, The Lions of Judah*.

24    The action is most notably recorded in Whittle, *An Exact Diary of the Late Expedition of His Illustrious Highness the Prince of Orange*; Dalrymple, *Memoirs*; HMC Appendix, 7th Report, 12th Report pp.408, 417, 222.

25    MacPherson, *Original Papers*, p.283.

26    Coke, *A Detection of the Court and state of England*, (1719)

## Chapter 10: A Siege

1    Witherow, *Two Diaries of Derry in 1689 – Being Richards' Diary of the Fleet and Ash's Journal of the Siege*, p.29; Ash pp.61-2

2    Witherow, pp.31-4; Ash, p.61

3    Witherow, pp.37-8

4    Ibid., pp.86-8

5    D'Avaux p.102

6    Ibid., p.100

7    Witherow, op. cit., pp.112-17

8    D'Avaux, op. cit., p.159

9    *Jacobite Narrative* p.108

10    Royal Irish Academy, Dublin MS 24 G.1 – much of the spelling is modernised, communication between James and Hamilton.

11    Witherow, op. cit., pp.121-2

12    D'Avaux, op. cit., p.137  Compare this lack of treatment with James's attention of Mountcashel at Enniskillen later

13    Ibid., p.159

14    HMC 8th Report, Appendix Pt 1, p.494, 1 May 1689

15    Lynn, *Wars*, p.71

16    D'Avaux, op. cit., pp.73, 76, 159

17    HMC 8th Report, Appendix Part I, p.496

18    Witherow, op. cit., pp.130-2

19    *Jacobite Narrative* p.66

20    *State Papers Ireland*, Vol. 352, No. 6, Pointis to Louvois 22 June 1689

21    Witherow, op. cit., pp.137-41

22    *La Guerre*, Vol. 895, No. 93

23  Walker, *A True Account of the Siege of London-Derry*, p.32

24  Ibid., p.34

25  Ibid., p.36

26  For details see Ash – excellent ref and map of area

27  Royal Academy MS24 G.1. 5 July 1689

28  Ibid.

29  Royal Academy, MS24 G.1. 12 July 1689

30  For James's agreement as to Hamilton's tactics see Royal Academy MS 24 G.1, James to Hamilton 31 July 1689

31  D'Avaux op. cit., p.114

32  Ibid, pp.186, 221

33  Ibid., pp.258, 259

34  Ibid., p.281

35  *Jacobite Narrative*, pp.65-7

## Chapter 11: Enniskillen

1  Hamilton, *The Actions of the Enniskillen Men: from their first taking up of arms in 1688*, pp.3-6; MacCarmick, *A Farther Impartial Account of the Actions of the Inniskilling Men*, pp.4-6.

2  Hamilton, pp.7-19; MacCarmick, pp.7-23.

3  Hamilton, pp.20-6; MacCarmick, pp.23-30.

4  Hamilton, pp.20-26; MacCarmick, pp.23-30

5  Hamilton, pp.27-49; MacCarmick, pp.31-41

6  D'Avaux, op. cit., pp.257, 311

7  Ibid., p.311

8  *Jacobite Narrative*, op. cit., p.81

9  Hamilton, op. cit., p.63; MacCarmick, op. cit., p.44; Story, op. cit., p.4; *Jacobite Narrative*, op. cit., p.81; cf O'Callaghan, pp.12-13

10  D'Avaux, op. cit., p.384

11  Hamilton, op. cit., p.19; MacCarmick, o[p. cit., p.23

12  Simms, op. cit., pp.53,71

13  Ibid.

14  Hamilton, op. cit., p.50; MacCarmick, op. cit., p.42

15  D'Avaux, op. cit., p.384

16  *Jacobite Narrative*, p.81

17  Hamilton, op. cit., pp.52-3, MacCarmick, op. cit., pp.41-2

18  *La Guerre*, Vol. 893, Aug 1689

19  O'Callaghan, op. cit., pp.14-15; *Jacobite Narrative* records that some cavalry also formed part of the force

20  D'Avaux, op. cit., p.385
21  Hamilton, op. cit., pp.51-2; MacCarmick, op. cit., p.41; d'Avaux, op. cit., p.385
22  Hamilton, op. cit., pp.52-3; MacCarmick, op. cit., p.42; d'Avaux, op. cit., p.385
23  Hamilton, op. cit., p.54; MacCarmick, op. cit., p.42; d'Avaux, op. cit., p.385
24  D'Avaux, op. cit., p.385
25  Hamilton, op. cit., p.54
26  *Jacobite Narrative.*, op. cit., p.82
27  MacCarmick, op. cit., p.42
28  Hamilton, op. cit., p.56; MacCarmick, op. cit., p.43
29  Hamilton, op. cit., pp.55-7; MacCarmick, op. cit., pp.42-3; d'Avaux, op. cit., p.386; *London Gazette* 2481, 1689
30  Hamilton, op. cit., p.57, MacCarmick, op. cit., p.43
31  MacCarmick, op. cit., p.43
32  Known locally as a 'causey' - see Trimble, *A History of Enniskillen*, 3 Vols. Although the raised road at the Newtownbutler site has disappeared due to drainage carried out in the area in the nineteenth century, investigation can uncover its location at Sandholes.
33  Hamilton, op. cit., pp.57-8; MacCarmick, op. cit., p.43
34  *Jacobite Narrative*, op. cit., p.82
35  Hamilton, op. cit., pp.57-9; MacCarmick, op. cit., p.43; *Jacobite Narrative*, op. cit., p.82; d'Avaux, op. cit., p.386
36  MacCarmick, op. cit., p.43
37  Ibid.
38  Hamilton, op. cit., p.62; MacCarmick, op. cit., p.44
39  Hamilton, op. cit., pp.51-2; MacCarmick, op. cit., p.41
40  D'Avaux, op. cit., p.385
41  *La Guerre*, Vol. 893, d'Avaux to Louvois 4/14 August 1689
42  D'Avaux, op. cit., p.385-6

## Chapter 12: The First Flight

1  *La Guerre*, op. cit., Vol. 893 – Rosen to Louvois 15/25 July 1689
2  *Jacobite Narrative*, op. cit., p.82
3  Archbishop King, *Diary*, p.39
4  *La Guerre*, op. cit., Vol. 893, d'Avaux to Louis, 4/14 Aug 1689
5  Macpherson, op. cit., Vol. I, p.313
6  *La Guerre*, op. cit., Vol. 1082 – No.37, d'Avaux to Louvois 20/30 Oct 1689
7  Ibid., No. 6 – d'Avaux to Louvois, 10/20 Sept 1689
8  *Jacobite Narrative*, op. cit., p.83

9    *La Guerre*, op. cit., Vol. 1082 – d'Avaux to Louvois 14 Aug 1689

10   Hamilton,  op. cit., pp.63-4

11   D'Avaux, op. cit., pp.462, 534-5, 538-9, 590, 613, 636

12   Ibid., p.462

13   Ibid., p.590; O'Callaghan pp.23-4

14   D'Avaux, op. cit., p.636

15   *La Guerre*, op. cit., Vol. 960, MacCarthy to Louvois Feb 1689; L to MacCarthy Feb 1899; *Analecta Hibernica*, op. cit., Vol. XXI, p.27

16   D'Avaux, op. cit., p.636

17   Ibid., p.635

18   Ibid., pp. 515, 519-20, 584

19   Ibid., p.531

20   *La Guerre* op. cit., Vol. 893, Louvois to d'Avaux 28 June 1689

21   Ibid., Vol. 1082, Louvois to d'Avaux 15 Sept 1689

22   Ibid., Vol. 1082, Louvois to d'Avaux, Nov 1689

23   Ibid., Vol. 893, d'Avaux to Louvois 30 June, 10 July 1689

24   Bibliothèque Mazarine MS 2298 f.87

25   D'Avaux,  op. cit., p.287 – Louvois to d'Avaux 12 June 1689

26   Ibid., p.250

27   *La Guerre*, op. cit., Vol. 1082, No. 37, d'Avaux to Louvois 20/30 Oct 1689

28   Ibid., No.5, d'Avaux, pp.460, 591

29   D'Avaux, op. cit., p.636

30   Ibid.,  p.636

31   See: *La Guerre*, A1, Vol, 893, Fumeron to Louvois; *La Guerre*, A1, Vol. 894, No.15, Mountcashel to Louvois Feb 1689; *La Guerre* 960, Louvois to MacCarthy, Feb 1689; *Analecta Hibernica*, Vol. XXI, p.27.

32   *La Guerre*, A1, Vol. 1066, Sarsfield to Mountcashel February 1691; *La Guerre*, A1, Vol. 1066, Sarsfield to Mountcashel March 1691; *La Guerre*, A1, Vol. 1109, Mountcashel to Louis August 1691.

33   *La Guerre*, A1, Vol. 892, de Rosen to Louvois May 1689; MacPherson, op. cit., Vol. I, pp.176,190; d'Avaux p.142

34   D'Avaux, op. cit., p.531.

35   Ibid., pp.519, 287, 300, 515, 520, 584

36   Ibid., p.635.

37   Ibid., p.590.

38   Lynn, *Giant of the Grand Siecle*, pp.331, 366; Lynn, *The Wars of Louis XIV*, pp.49,178.

39   O'Conor, op. cit., pp.98-9.

40   D'Avaux, op. cit., p.688.

41    Ibid., p.689.

42    Boulger, op. cit., pp.208-12; O'Conor, op. cit., p.98.

43    Boulger, op. cit., p.215.

44    O'Conor, op. cit., pp.98-9.

45    Boulger, op. cit., p.215.

46    D'Avaux, op. cit., p.658. Letters in *La Guerre* also outline the dispositions of the Irish troops at Brest. See A1, Vol. 961 May 1690, Seignelay to Louvois April 1690 and Vol. 1082 *Etats des Soldats des Regiments Irlandaises*, May 1690.

47    Boulger, op. cit., p.216; Hamilton, op. cit., pp.31-8, MacCarmick, op. cit., pp.35-41, Trimble, op. cit., pp.408-9; Maguire, *Kings in Conflict*, p.62.

48    Lynn, *The Wars of Louis XIV* ; *Giant of the Grand Siècle, The French Army, 1610-1715* ; Childs, *Warfare in the Seventeenth Century*

## Chapter 13: The Boyne

1    Macpherson, Vol. I, op. cit., p.222; Story, op. cit., p.10

2    D'Avaux, op. cit., pp.313, 344, 379, 390, 434, 509

3    Ibid., 472

4    *Analecta Hibernica*, Vol. IV, p.201

5    D'Avaux, op. cit p.443, James II, p.373

6    Macpherson, op. cit., p.222; d'Avaux, op. cit., pp.459-60

7    Story, op. cit., p.34

8    D'Avaux, op. cit., p.476; Macpherson, op. cit., pp.222-3; Story, op. cit., p.22

9    D'Avaux, op. cit., p.474

10   Ibid., p.616; Story, op. cit., pp.24-5

11   *Jacobite Narrative*, op. cit., p.88

12   Story, op. cit., pp.35-9

13   D'Avaux, op. cit., p.547

14   Stevens, op. cit., p.79

15   D'Avaux, op. cit., p.694

16   Story, op. cit., p.38

17   Ormonde, Vol. VIII, p.380

18   D'Avaux, op. cit., p.701. Many of the troops would still be rejected by the French upon landing – those who remained would, however, prove to be fearsome shock troops in Louis's continental campaigns.

19   *La Guerre*, op. cit., Vol. 960, Lauzun to Louvois Jun 1690

20   D'Avaux, op. cit., pp.521, 609, 618

21   *Analecta Hibernica*, Vol. IV, pp.129-30

22   French records speak of Anthony and John Hamilton's presence during the retreat – see *La Guerre* 963 Lauzun to Seignelay 16/26 July 1690

23   Story, p.75
24   Shepard, *Ireland's Fate*, p.106; Mulloy, *Franco Irish Correspondence 1688-92*, Vol. III, p.121
25   See also *La Guerre*,Vol. 961, No.179
26   *Jacobite Narrative*, op. cit., pp.98-103; Clarke, *Life of James II*, pp.399-400
27   Harris, *History of the Life and Reign of William III*,Vol. III, pp.268-9; Clarke, op. cit., pp.399-400; *La Guerre*, Vol. 961 – No. 171, Boisseleau, No. 178, Girandin
28   Story, op. cit., pp.81-2, see also Burnet
29   HMC Finch manuscripts,Vol. II, p.330
30   Macaulay seems quite clear on this point as well as John Richardson outlined below.
31   Richardson in *5th Royal Inniskilling Dragoon Guards' Journal*, 1938, p.148
32   Ibid.
33   Macaulay; also see Story and *La Guerre*, Lauzun to Seignelay, 16/26 July 1690
34   *La Guerre*, op. cit.,Vol. 963, 16/26 Jul, Lauzun to Seignelay
35   *The Life of James II. Late King of England*, p.353

## Chapter 14: Aughrim, Limerick, and the Second Flight

1   HMC 12th Report, App, Pt VII, p.276
2   Ibid., p.279; *La Guerre*,Vol. 961, No. 94, Bouridal to Louvois 14/24 July 1690; No.177 11/21 July 1690
3   Ibid.,Vol. 963, Lauzun to Seignelay 16/26 July 1690
4   Ibid.,Vol. 961, Nos. 179,180, Zurlauben / Desgrigny to Louvois 10/20 and 11/21 July 1690
5   Ibid.,Vol. 961, No.180, Desgrigny to Louvois 11/21 July 1690
6   *Jacobite Narrative*. op. cit., pp.110-11
7   Ibid.
8   *La Guerre*, op. cit.,Vol. 962, Nos. 1155, 162
9   *Stevens*, op. cit., p.144
10   Story, op. cit., p.102
11   Ibid., pp.94, 99; *Jacobite Narrative*, pp.105-6
12   Story, op. cit., p.102
13   Stevens, op. cit., p.193; Story, op. cit., p.117
14   *Jacobite Narrative*, op. cit., p.113
15   *La Guerre*, op. cit.,Vol. 962, Nos. 167,169
16   Story, op. cit., p.111; *CSPD 1690-1*, p.230
17   Story, op. cit., pp.114-18

18  *Mémoires du Maréchal de Berwick*, Vol. I, pp.72-3

19  Story, op. cit., pp.119-21; Berwick, op. cit., Vol. I,  p.96

20  Stevens, op. cit., p.177

21  Story, op. cit., p.128

22  Stevens, op. cit., p.178

23  Stevens, op. cit.,  pp.179-81; Story, op. cit., p.129

24  *La Guerre,* op. cit., Vol. 962, Nos. 62, 172, 174

25  *La Guerre,* op. cit., Vol. 962, Nos. 62, 172, 174; Clarke, op. cit., pp.420-2

26  *Analecta Hibernica,* Vol. XXI, p.203

27  *La Guerre* op. cit., Vol. 962, No.167

28  Story, op. cit., pp.140-1

29  *Macariae Excidium*, p.58

30  O'Conor, op. cit., p.114

31  James II, pp.421-5; *Analecta Hibernica*, Vol. XXI, p.205; O'Conor, op. cit., p.117

32  HMC 12th Report, app, pt VIII, p.303

33  Luttrell, *Relation of State Affairs*, Vol. II, p.149

34  *La Guerre*, op. cit., Vol. 1066, No.187 Sarsfield to Louvois 14/24 Feb 1691

35  Ibid., Vol. 1066, No.211 13/23 March 1691 Sarsfield to Louvois

36  Ibid., Vol. 1066, No.222 19/29 April 1691 Sarsfield to Louvois

37  Ibid., Vol. 1066, No.240 Fumeron to Louvois 11/21 May 1691; *Analecta Hibernica,* Vol. XXI, p.216

38  *La Guerre*, op. cit., Vol. 1080, No.145 Saint Ruth to Louvois 3/13 June 1691

39  Berwick, Vol. I, p.335. It should be remembered that Berwick was no longer in Ireland at this time and his record may be somewhat questionable.

40  Stevens, op. cit., p.211

41  *La Guerre*, op. cit., Vol. 1080, No. 164 Fumeron to Louvois 9/19 July 1691; No.163 d'Usson to Louvois 8/18 July 1691; Story, *Continuation*, p.114

42  *Jacobite Narrative*, op. cit., p.131, Story, op. cit., p.141

43  Story, op. cit., p.122

44  *Jacobite Narrative*, op. cit., p.138

45  *La Guerre*, op. cit., Vol. 1080, No.168 Fumeron to Louvois 19/29 July 1691; *Jacobite Narrative*, op. cit., p.148; HMC 4th Report, App. p.322; John Hamilton's widow was Elizabeth Macan. His daughter would marry le Comte de Marmier in France – *Bibliotheque Nationale*.

46  Boulger, op. cit., p.248.

47  Simms, *Jacobite Ireland*, pp.243-57.

48  Macaulay *History of England*, Vol. II

## Chapter 15: The End of the Beginning: The Nine Years' War in Europe

1   Not, of course, to be confused with the Nine Years' War in the 1500s. This designation is also used, although recent historical retelling has been less than kind in this instance.

2   Childs refers to at least five titles for the conflict in his seminal work *The Nine Years War and the British Army, 1688-97*.

3   For other references to 'War of Grand Alliance' or 'Nine Years War' see Lynn, *The Wars of Louis XIV*; Lynn, *Giant of the Grand Siècle, The French Army, 1610-1715*; *Warfare in the Seventeenth Century*.

4   See the book of the same name for a detailed and thought-provoking outline of the 'Glorious Revolution': Carswell, *The Descent on England*.

5   See Lynn, *The Wars of Louis XIV, 1667-1714*. Lynn sees the Nine Years War as the turning point in Louis's and, thereby, France's fortunes. For a wider context, see also Sturdy, *Fractured Europe 1600-1721*.

6   Lynn, p.197.

7   Childs, *The Nine Years War and the British Army, 1688-97*, pp.43-63.

8   Ibid., pp.76-7.

9   Although we should highlight the lack of progress at Derry and Limerick during the Irish campaign. Experts such as Vauban and Coehorn were not present at either city.

10   Childs, op. cit., pp.133-4.

11   Rousset, Vol. IV, pp.6, 24, 28; Lynn, pp.179-81, O'Conor, p.209, Childs, p.184, Boulger, p.218.

12   This quote is taken from O'Conor, pp.100-1. More detailed information regarding the general history of this period can be obtained in Lynn pp.210-14; O'Callaghan, pp.54-5; Boulger, pp.217-20; Childs, W*arfare in the Seventeenth Century*, p.18; de Quincy, Vol. II, p.292; O'Callaghan, O'Conor and Boulger, their work stemming from the nineteenth century, do not give clear references, although their work seems for the most part to stem from de Quincy and letters from *de la Guerre*.

13   O'Conor, op. cit., pp.102-3; Boulger, op. cit., p.219; O'Callaghan, op. cit., p.55; de Quincy, op. cit., Vol. II, p.304. Although Mountcashel's wound may have been slight, the nature of warfare and medicine, and the campaign environment, need to be taken into account.

14   *La Guerre*, op. cit., Vol. 1066, Sarsfield to Mountcashel Feb & Mar 1691; *La Guerre*, op. cit., Vol. 1080, Mountcashel to Louis Aug 1691; Ibid., Vol. 1080, Mountcashel to Louis Aug 1691;Macpherson, op. cit., p.233; Simms, op. cit., p.158-73; Petrie, *The Great Tyrconnel*, pp.215-29.

15   *La Guerre*, op. cit., Vol. 1065, Louvois to Tyrconnel, Mar 1691.

16  Boulger, op. cit., p.219; O'Callaghan, op. cit., p.55-8; Lynn, op. cit., pp.214, 221; de Quincy, op. cit., Vol. II 437, 444; Also see in *La Guerre*, Louvois's letter to Tyrconnel in spring 1691 re. requirement for 1,200 additional Irish recruits.

17  Childs, op. cit., p.179.

18  Ibid., p.180.

19  Baxter, *William III*, pp.294-5.

20  Berwick, *Memoirs*; Dangeau, *Journal de Marquis de Dangeau*, Vol. IV, p.149.

21  Walton, pp.219-27; Muller, II, pp.238-41.

22  Childs op. cit., p.227.

23  Berwick, *Memoirs*

24  O'Callaghan, op. cit., p. 175.

25  Boulger, op. cit., p.326.

26  Berwick, op. cit., Vol. I, pp.113-14.

27  O'Conor, *Memoirs of Gerald O'Conor*

28  O'Callaghan, op. cit., p.175 (citing O'Conor).

29  Lynn, op. cit., pp.236-8; O'Callaghan, op. cit., pp.32-3, 39; O'Conor, op. cit., pp.221, 224

30  *CSPD 1694-95*, p.464 7 1697, p.354; Irish Record Commissioners Reports, pp.373, 384-9.

31  Taken from *La France Littéraire* and reported in *The Journal of the Cork Historical and Archaeological Society* 1907 in the article 'Justin MacCarthy Lord Mountcashel'.

32  MacPherson, op. cit., pp.445-6.

33  Lynn, op. cit., p.242.

34  Lynn, op. cit., p.246.

35  O'Callaghan, op. cit., p.39; O'Conor, op. cit., p.224.

36  One example of this is cited in Bishop's *The Irish Empire* where Sarsfield is hailed as the leader of the Wild Geese and Mountcashel does not receive a mention. Otherwise this is an excellent work.

37  AG #81 23 June 1695, Louis to Villeroi, Wolf, Louis XIV, p.481.

## Chapter 16: Despair at Saint Germain

1  Dalton, *King James's Irish Army List*, Vol. I, op. cit., p.194; HMC 12th Report, App Part VI, pp.228-33

2  Cartwright, *Madame*, p.218; Ormonde, op. cit., Vol. VII, pp.84-5; Maintenon, *Correspondance Générale*, Vol. III, pp.208-9

3  *CSPD 1690-91*, p.91; Dangeau, op.cit., Vol. III, p.431

4  Chéruel, *Saint Simon Mémoires*, Vol. XIV, pp.563-5

5  Sévigné, *Lettres*, Vol. V, p.363; Vol. VI, pp.97-8

6    Fénelon, *Correspondance Publiée Pour La Première Fois sur les Manuscrits Originaux*, Vol. VI, pp.209-10
7    Saint Beuve, *Port Royal*, Vol. V, pp.182-4
8    Port Royal, loc. Cit., *Mémoires Secrets*, Vol. II, pp.89-90
9    *Saint Simon*, Vol. XI, pp.111-12
10    Dangeau, op. cit., Vol. II, p.53
11    Archdall Lodge, op. cit., p.118n
12    HMC manuscripts of the Marquis of Bath, Vol. III, p.190
13    Boulger, op. cit., p.295
14    Boulger, op. cit., pp.295-7
15    Lynn, *Wars*, op. cit., pp.229-31
16    Macaulay, op. cit., Vol. III, pp.206-7 – based on Anthony Hamilton's *Zeneyde*
17    Boulger, op. cit., pp.308-17
18    HMC Manuscripts of Marquis of Bath, op. cit., Vol. III, p.410-11
19    Anthony Hamilton, *Oeuvres Diverses*, Vol. III, pp.237-9; Dangeau, op. cit., Vol. VI, p.72; HMC manuscripts of the Marquis of Bath, op. cit., Vol. III, p.410
20    HMC manuscripts of the Marquis of Bath, op. cit., Vol. III, pp.296-305, 334
21    Boulger, op. cit., pp.342-3
22    Lynn, *Wars*, pp.255-6; Boulger pp.346-7
23    Maintenon, *Correspondance Générale*, Vol. I, p.81; Vol. IV, p.90; *Saint Simon*, op. cit., Vol. XI, p.112; Vol. XVI pp.217-18; Dangeau, op. cit., Vol. VII, p.104; Port Royal, op. cit., Vol. VI, pp.163-5
24    HMC manuscripts of the Marquis of Bath, Vol. III, p.236; see also p.296, 334
25    *Saint Simon*, op. cit., Vol. XV, p.416
26    Berwick, op. cit., Vol. I, p.466; Hamilton, op. cit., Vol. III, pp.51,188, 192, 171, 242-3, 449-50
27    Lynn, *Wars*, op. cit., pp.262-3; Boulger, op. cit., p.355
28    Boulger, op. cit., pp.358-63

**Chapter 17: Return to the Fight – The War of the Spanish Succession**

1    Lynn, op. cit., p.270
2    Chandler, *Marlborough as Military Commander*, pp.56-7; Lynn, p.271.
3    Wolf, *Louis XIV*, p.519.
4    O'Callaghan, op. cit., p.207; O'Conor, op. cit., p.250. McDonnel would find his way back to his own army and fight the Irish Brigade again at Luzzara later in the year, where he was killed in battle.
5    O'Conor, *Irish Brigades*, p.216.
6    O'Callaghan, op. cit., p.200.
7    Ibid., p.204.

8   Ibid., p.234.

9   Ibid.,  p.240.

10  Ibid., p.221.

11  Hamilton, op. cit., Vol. III, passim

12  Bibliotheque Nationale, ms 32964,  No. 85, Piéces originales, Vol. 1472

13  *Saint Simon*, op. cit., Vol. XI, p.113; Sévigné, *Lettres*, Vol. X, p.499-500; Hamilton, op. cit., Vol. III, p.356

14  Maintenon, *Lettres inédites*, Vol. I, pp.169, 172, 176; Hamilton, op. cit., Vol. III, p.116

15  Hamilton, op. cit., Vol. III, p.77

16  Ibid., pp.83-4

17  O'Callaghan,  op. cit., p.234.

18  Ibid., p.99

19  Ibid., p.192

20  Ibid., p.48

21  Ibid., p.202

22  Ibid., p.240.

23  Ibid., p.240.

24  Ibid., pp.193-7

25  Saint-Evremond, *Oeuvres*, Vol. V, p.192; Madame, *Lettres*, Vol. I, p.128; Maintenon, op. cit., Vol. I pp.69, 75

26  Gramont, Vol. I, intro, p.xv

27  Ibid., Vol. II,  p.165

28  *Saint Simon*, op. cit., Vol. XVI, pp.73,501

29  Ibid., p.73; Maintenon, op. cit., Vol. I, pp.106, 142-3

30  Ibid., p.266

31  Mitford, *The Sun King*, p.222

32  Luttrel, *Brief Historical Relation of State Affairs*, Vol. VI, p.252

33  Forbin, *Mémoires*

34  Maintenon, op. cit., Vol. I, p.240; Affaires Etrangères, *Mémoires et Documents Angleterre*, Vol. XXIV, No.108; Berwick, *Mémoires*, Vol. I, p.405

35  British Museum, Add. Manuscripts 18, 966 No.7 Sept 1708 – although noted as 1710 it seems more likely that this refers to 1708 bearing in mind the mention of Countess Grammont, Hamilton's sister

36  Dangeau, op. cit., Vol. XII, p.434; Maintenon, op. cit., Vol. I, p.465

37  Coxe, *Memoirs of John, Duke of Marlborough*

38  Blackmore, *Destructive and Formidable - British Infantry Firepower 1642-1765*, pp. 88-9; Parker, *Memoirs*, pp.138-9.

39  O'Callaghan, op. cit., pp.267-9.

40  Ibid., p.269.
41  B.M. Add. Manuscripts 18, 966 f.3 12 July 1710
42  B.M. Add. Manuscripts 18, 966 f.3 16 Aug 1710
43  B.M. Add. Manuscripts 18, 966 f.1 30 Aug 1710

**Chapter 18: The Pretenders and a Victory**

1   MacPherson, op. cit., Vol. II, pp.371-2
2   Ibid., p.425
3   Ibid., pp.371-2
4   Ibid.
5   Maintenon, op. cit., Vol. II, p.411
6   White, *Marshal of France*, p.154.
7   Cumberland, *Historical Memoirs of his Late Royal Highness William Augustus, Duke of Cumberland* p.233.
8   Petrie, 'The Irish Brigade at Fontenoy'. *The Irish Sword*, No.3, Vol.1.
9   O'Callaghan, op. cit., p.424
10  Klose, *Memoirs of Prince Charles*, Vol.1, p.409; McLynn, *The Jacobites*, p.86.
11  O'Callaghan, op. cit., pp. 397, 436.
12  Ibid., p.408.
13  Fagan, *Ireland in the Stuart Papers, 1719-42*, Vol. 1, p.86.
14  O'Callaghan, op. cit., p.598
15  Ibid..
16  Murtagh, *Irish Soldiers Abroad*, p.308.

# Bibliography

Bagwell, R., *Ireland Under the Stuarts and During the Interregnum* (Longmans, London, 1916)

Baxter, S.B., *William III*, (Longmans, London, 1966)

Beddard, R., *The Revolutions of 1688 –The Andrew Browning Lectures* (Clarendon Press, London, 1966)

Beresford Ellis, P., *Hell or Connaught!: The Cromwellian Colonisation of Ireland 1652–1660* (Blackstaff Press, Belfast, 1975)

Boulger, D.C., *The Battle of the Boyne: Together with an Account Based on French & Other Unpublished Records of the War in Ireland 1688–1691)* (Wentworth, London, 1911)

Burnet, G., *History of My Own Time*, (Clarendon Press, Oxford, 1833)

Brady, C., & Gillespie, R. (eds), *Native and Newcomers: the making of Irish colonial society 1534–1641* (Irish Academic Press, Dublin, 1986)

Canny, N., *From Reformation to Restoration: Ireland 1534–1660* (Helicon, Dublin, 1987)

Carte T., *History of the Life of James, Duke of Ormond* (Oxford University Press 1851)

Cartwright, J.M., *Madame, a Life of Henrietta, Daughter of Charles I, and Duchess of Orleans*, (Wentworth, London, 1896)

Chandler, D., *Marlborough as Military Commander*, (Batsford, London, 1973)

Chandler, D., *The Art of Warfare in the Age of Marlborough*, (Spellmount, Staplehurst, 1990)

Chéruel. M., *Saint Simon Mémoires: Historien de Louis XIV*, (Hachette, Paris, 1873)

Childs, J.C.R., *The Nine Years' War and the British Army 1688–1697: The Operations in the Low Countries* (Manchester University Press, 1991)

Childs, J.C.R., *The Army, James II, and the Glorious Revolution* (Manchester University Press, 1986)

Childs, J.C.R., *Warfare in the Seventeenth Century* (Orion, London, 1999)

Coward B., *The Stuart Age, A History of England 1603–1714* (Longmans, London, 1980)

Clarke, J.S., *A Life of James II, Collected Out of Memoirs Writ by his Own Hand* (Longmans, London, 1816)

Cunningham P., *The Story of Nell Gwyn* (John Grant, Edinburgh, 1908)

Cartwright, J.J. (ed), *Memoirs of Sir John Reresby*, (Longmans, London, 1875)

Dalton C., *English Army Lists and Commission Registers 1661–1685* (Eyre & Spottiswoode, London, 1960)

Dalton C., *English Army Lists and Commission Registers 1685–1689* (Eyre & Spottiswoode, London 1960)

D'Alton, J., *King James' Irish Army List* (Dublin, 1689)

Dangeau P., Philippe de Corcillon, *Sourches* (Paris, 1854)

Daniel, R.P., *Histoire de la Milice Françoise* (Paris, 1721)

Depping G.B., *Correspondence Administrative sous le Regne de Louis XIV* (Imprimerie Nationale, Paris, 1851)

Doubleday, H., and De Walden, H., (eds), *The Complete Peerage or a History of the House of Lords and all its Members from the earliest times* (St Catherine Press, London, 1916)

Dalrymple, Sir John, *Memoirs of Great Britain and Ireland* (London, 1773)

Edward, E., *Makers of Modern Strategy* (Princeton University Press, Princeton, 1941)

Ellis, G.A. (ed), *Ellis Correspondance*, (Colburn, London, 1829)

Falkner, J., *Great and Glorious Days* (The History Press, Stroud, 2002)

Falls, C., *The Birth of Ulster* (Constable, London, 1936)

Fénelon, F., *Correspondance Publiée Pour La Première Fois sur les Manuscrits Originaux* (Archevêque de Cambrai, Paris, 1827–1829)

Fieffé, E., *Troupes* étrangères *au service de la France* (Dumaine, Paris, 1854)

Field, O., *The Favourite: Sarah, Duchess of Marlborough* (St Martin's Press, London, 2002)

Firth, C.H. (ed), *The Memoirs of Edmund Ludlow, Lieutenant General of the Horse in the Army of the Commonwealth of England 1625–1672* (Clarendon Press, London, 1751)

Forbin Comte de, *Mémoires du comte de Forbin, chef D'Escadre, chevalier de l'Ordre Militaire de Saint Louis*, (chez François Girardi, Paris, 1826)

Gilbert, J. T. (ed), *A Jacobite Narrative of the War in Ireland* (Barnes & Noble, Dublin, 1971 edn)

Gillespie, G., *Colonial Ulster: the settlement of east Ulster 1600–1641* (Cork University Press, Cork, 1985)

Goodwin, G. (ed), Count Anthony Hamilton's *Memoirs of Count Grammont* (John Grant, Edinburgh, 1908)

Guy & Smith, *1688, Glorious Revolution, The Fall and Rise of the British Army 1660–1704* (National Army Museum, London, 1988)

Grimoard, (ed), *Collection Des Lettres Et Memoires Trouves Dans Les Porte-Feuilles Du Marechal de Turenne: 1672 - 1675*, (Renouard, Paris, 1782)

Hamilton, Andrew, *The Actions of the Enniskillen Men From Their First Taking Up Arms in the Defence of the Protestant Religion, Their Lives and Liberties, to the Landing of the Duke of Schomberg in Ireland* (George Berwick, London, 1818)

Hamilton, Anthony, *Oeuvres Diverses* (London, 1776)

————, *Mémoires de la Vie du Comte de Gramont* (La Haye, P. Gosse & J. Neaulme, Edinburgh, 1908)

Hickson, Mary, *Ireland in the Seventeenth Century*, Vol. I (Longmans, London, 1884)

Harris, W., *History of the Life and Reign of William III*, (Bate, Dublin, 1749)

Hill, Revd George, *An Historical Account of the Plantation in Ulster at the Commencement of the Seventeenth Century, 1608–1620* (McGaw, Stevenson & Orr, Belfast, 1877)

————, *Plantation Papers, containing a summary sketch of The Great Ulster Plantation in the year 1610* (Northern Whig, Belfast, 1889)

Hogan, J. (ed), *Négociations de M. Le Comte d'Avaux en Irlande 1689–90* (Irish Manuscripts Commission, Dublin, 1935)

Jaeglé, *Madame, Duchesse d'Orléans, Correspondance*, (Paris 1890)

Jones, D. (ed), *The Life of James II Late King of England* (Knapton, London, 1702)

Jones, J.R., *The Revolution of 1688 in England* (Weidenfeld & Nicolson, London, 1972)

Kenyon, *The Civil Wars of England* (Weidenfeld & Nicolson, London, 1988)

Kenyon, J., and Ohlmeyer, J., *The Civil Wars: A Military History of England Ireland and Scotland* (Oxford University Press, Oxford, 1998)

Kenyon, J., *The Popish Plot* (Phoenix, London, 1972)

King, W., *The State of the Protestants of Ireland under the late King James Government* (Powell, London, 1691)

King, W., *The Diary of William King, Dean of St. Patrick's, afterwards Archbishop of Dublin kept during his imprisonment in Dublin Castle, 1689* (Ponsonby & Gibbs, Dublin, 1903)

King, C., (ed), *Henry's Upper Lough Erne in 1739* (McGee, Dublin, 1892)

Lalanne, M., (ed), *Bussy Correspondence* (Charpentier, Paris, 1858)

Lenihan, P.,, *Confederate Catholics at War, 1641–49* (Cork University Press, Cork, 2001)

Luttrel, N., *Brief Historical Relation of State Affairs* (University Press, Oxford, 1857)

Lynn, J.A., *Giant of the Grand Siécle : The French Army, 1610–1715* (Cambridge University Press, Cambridge, 1997)

————, *The French Wars 1667–1714* (Osprey, Oxford, 2002)

Lytton Sells, A., *The Memoirs of James II, His Campaigns as Duke of York, 1652–1660* (Chatto & Windus, London, 1962)

MacCarmick, W., *A Farther Impartial Account of the Actions of the Inniskilling Men* (Cleeland, Belfast, 1691, & 1896 edn)

Macaulay, Babington, T.,*History of England* (Folio Soc., London, 1902)

MacCuarta, B. (ed), *Ulster 1641, Aspects of the Rising* (Institute of Irish Studies, Belfast, 1993)

MacPherson, W., *Original Papers* (Strahan & Cadell, London, 1775)

Magalotti, L., *Travels of Cosmo the Third, Grand Duke of Tuscany* (Mawman, London, 1821)

Maintenon, Mme de, *Lettres inédites* (Chalon, Paris, 1864)

———, *Correspondance Générale* (Chalon, Paris, 1865)

Maxwell, P., *The Scottish Migration to Ulster in the reign of James I* (Sage, London, 1973)

Michel, F., *Les Français en Ecosse et Les Ecossais en France* (Herold, Paris, 1862)

Mignet, F.,, *Négociations Relatives à la Succession d'Espagne* (Imprimerie Royale, Paris, 1835–42)

Mitford, N., *The Sun King* (Sphere, London, 1966)

Montesquieu, C. (ed), *Mémoires du Maréchal de Berwick, écrits par lui-même* (Moutard, Parise, 1778 & Univ. Toronto scan)

Mulligan, J.F., *A Ramble through Dromore* (Chronicle, Belfast, 1886)

Mulloy, S., *Franco Irish Correspondence 1688–92* (Irish Manuscripts Commission, Dublin, 1983)

Murray, Revd R.H. (ed), *The Journal of John Stevens, Containing a Brief Account of the War in Ireland, 1689–91* (Clarendon Press, Oxford, 1912)

Nosworthy, B., *The Anatomy of Victory-Battle Tactics 1689–1763* (Hippocrene, New York, 1992)

O'Callaghan, J.C., *History of the Irish Brigades in the Service of France* (Cameron & Ferguson, Glasgow, 1886)

O'Conor, M., *Military History of the Irish Nation Comprising a Memoir of the Irish Brigade in the Service of France* (Hodges & Smith, Dublin, 1845)

Ohlmeyer, J. (ed), *Ireland From Independence to Occupation 1641–1660* (Cambridge University Press, Cambridge, 1995)

Petrie, Sir Charles, *The Stuarts* (Eyre & Spottiswoode, London, 1937)

———, *The Great Tyrconnel: A Chapter in Anglo-Irish Relations* (Mercier, Cork, 1972)

Pinard, M., *Chronologie Historique Militaire* (Hachette, Paris, 1764)

Powley, E. B., *The Naval Side of King William's War* (John Baker, London, 1972)

Quincy, Marquis de, *Histoire Militaire du Régne de Louis le Grand* (St Jacques, Paris, 1726)

Robinson, P.S., *The Plantation of Ulster: British Settlement in an Irish Landscape, 1600–1670* (Ulster Historical Foundation, Belfast, 1984)

Ramsay, A., *Histoire de Turenne* (Arkstee & Merkus, Paris, 1834)

Rousset, C., *Vie de Louvois* (Didier, Paris, 1864)

Saint Beuve, C.A., *Port Royal* (Hachette, Paris, 1867–71)

Saint-Evremond, C., *Oeuvres* (Barbin, Amsterdam, 1726)

Saint-Hilaire O., *Mémoires* (Renouard, Paris, 1903–11)

Sergeant, P.W., *Little Jennings and Fighting Dick Talbot* (Hutchinson & Co, London, 1913)

Sévigné, Marquis de, *Lettres* (Hachette, Paris, 1862–66)

Simms, J.G., *Jacobite Ireland 1685–91* (Routledge, London, 1969)

Stephen L., (ed), *Dictionary of National Biography* (Smith Elder, Oxford, 1885)

Story, *A True and Impartial History of the Most Material Occurrences in the Kingdom of Ireland, 1691 & A Continuation of the Impartial History of the Wars of Ireland* (Chiswell, London, 1691)

Tincey, J., (ed), *Monmouth's Drill Book, An Abridgement of the English Military Discipline* (Partizan Press, Leigh-on-Sea, 1986)

Wheatley, H.B. (ed)., *Pepys' Diary* (Bell, London, 1890–99)

Waller, M., *Ungrateful Daughters: the Stuart Princesses Who Stole Their Father's Crown* (Spectre, London, 2002)

Witherow, T., *Two Diaries of Derry in 1689 – Being Richard's Diary of the Fleet and Ash's Journal of the Siege* (William Mullan & Son, Belfast, 1913 & 1792 & 1888 edns)

Walker, G. A., *True Account of the Siege of London-Derry* (London, 1689)

**Various Additional Primary Source Material (including French sources)**

*Calendar State Papers Ireland* (Various) (London 1860–1911)

*Calendar of the Carew manuscripts 1603–24*

*Calendar State Papers Domestic* (Various)

*Calendar Clarendon State Papers* (Oxford 1869–76)

*Calendar State Papers Carew 1603–1624*

*Calendar State Papers Colonial America and West Indies 1661–68*

*Calendar of State Papers Foreign, France* (Various)

*Letters and State Papers of the Reign of James VI*

*Registers of the Privy Council of Scotland* (Edinburgh 1889)

Historical Manuscripts Commission (HMC), *Calendar of the Manuscripts of the Marquess of Ormonde*, (London 1902)

HMC, *Correspondence of Henry Hyde, Earl of Clarendon*, (London, 1828)

————, *Buccleuch*

————, *Manuscripts of the Duke of Buccleuch at Montague*

————, *Manuscripts of the Marquis of Bath*

————, *Buccleuch Manuscripts*

————, *Perwich Papers*

————, *Finch manuscripts*

————, *Report on the MSS of the Earl of Egmont*

Ulster Plantation Papers – *Analecta Hibernica VIII*

Archdall & Lodge, *Peerage of Ireland* (1789)

*Diary of John Evelyn* (London 1906)

*Essex Papers* (Camden Papers 1890)

*Mercure Galant* (1679)

Hatton Correspondence (Camden) Vol II

Montgomery MSS 1603–1706 (Ed. By the Revd George Hill)

Charnock, *Biographica Navalis*

*Analecta Hibernica*, Vols IV, XXI, XXI

Affaires Etrangères, *Mémoires et Documents Angleterre* (Various Vols)

Archives du Ministère des Affaires Etrangeres, *Correspondance Politique,* Angleterre, (Various)

Archives du Ministère de la Guerre (Various)

# Index